BIRNBAUM'S
2017

Walt Disney World®

Expert Advice From the Inside Source

THE
OFFICIAL
GUIDE

Wendy Lefkon   EDITORIAL DIRECTOR

Jill Safro   EDITOR

Pam Brandon   CONTRIBUTING EDITOR

Clark Wakabayashi   DESIGNER

Alexandra Mayes Birnbaum   CONSULTING EDITOR

Stephen Birnbaum   FOUNDING EDITOR

DISNEY
EDITIONS

Contents

What's New?

To spotlight attractions making their debut, listings are marked with the stamp shown below. Look for it throughout the book. Here are a few 2017 highlights:

- ❤ **AbracadaBAR** (page 302)
- ❤ **Ample Hills Creamery** (page 271)
- ❤ **AVATAR Flight of Passage** (page 199)
- ❤ **Colortopia** (page 147)
- ❤ **Disney & Pixar Short Film Festival** (page 151)
- ❤ **Disney Springs Town Center** (page 218)
- ❤ **Frozen Ever After** (page 167)
- ❤ **Jedi Training—Trials of the Temple** (page 182)
- ❤ **Mickey's Royal Friendship Faire** (page 136)
- ❤ **Na'vi River Journey** (page 199)
- ❤ **Rivers of Light** (page 198)
- ❤ **Royal Sommerhus—Meet Anna and Elsa** (page 167)
- ❤ **Star Wars: A Galactic Spectacular** (page 185)
- ❤ **The Tree of Life Awakens** (page 195)
- ❤ **Tiffins** (page 264)

For Steve, who merely made all this possible.

ISBN 978-1-4847-3777-4
FAC-038091-16218

Printed in the United States of America

Other 2017 Birnbaum's Official Disney Guides:

Disneyland
Walt Disney World for Kids

The Official Disney Fan Club
D23.com

SUSTAINABLE FORESTRY INITIATIVE   Certified Sourcing
www.sfiprogram.org
SFI-00993
Logo Applies to Text Stock Only

A Word from the Editor

or some of us, our first Walt Disney World experience dates back to 1971, the year this new "Disneyland in Florida" made its debut. At that time, the Magic Kingdom was the only theme park to explore. Nonetheless, for those who came, it was love at first sight, and we've returned again and again. Fast-forward four-plus decades and Disney World boasts four theme parks, two water parks, dozens of hotels, hundreds of restaurants, and a whole lot more.

Never before has there been so much incentive to visit (and revisit) the memory-making capital of the world. The Magic Kingdom continues to wow guests with its mix of classic and contemporary attractions, from Pirates of the Caribbean to the Seven Dwarfs Mine Train and a new Castle stage show, Mickey's Royal Friendship Faire. Guests get their fix of the Force via Star Wars–themed shows at Disney's Hollywood Studios, where Tower of Terror remains atop most thrill seekers' must-do

Editor Jill Safro consults with Mickey and Minnie, the ultimate Disney insiders.

lists and Toy Story Midway Mania! brings smiles to folks of all ages. At Epcot, *Frozen* fans are in a frenzy for Norway's Frozen Ever After attraction, while the new Soarin' Around the World sends giddy guests to happy heights. Animal Kingdom—now also an after-dark park—has a new nighttime spectacular known as Rivers of Light and magical evening "awakenings" of the Tree of Life. It's set to unveil a brand-new land in 2017: Pandora—the World of AVATAR, too. And the lively lakefront district Disney Springs is bursting with new dining, shopping, and entertainment opportunities. Of course, that's just the tip of the iceberg, as so much of Walt Disney World has grown and evolved since our last edition. We are privileged and proud to provide readers with our extensively researched, insider look at some of the most cherished attractions, resorts, and eateries on Earth.

When Steve Birnbaum launched this guide in 1981, he made it clear what was expected of anyone who worked on it. The book would be meticulously revised each year, leaving no attraction untested, no snack or meal untasted, no hotel untried. First-hand experiences like these, accumulated over the years, make this book the most authoritative guide to the World. Our expertise, however, is not achieved by being escorted through back doors of attractions (although we would enjoy that). Instead, we wait in lines with everyone else, always hoping to have a Disney experience like that of any other guest. This year, in addition to investigating all of the nooks and crannies of Walt's vast World, we bonded with fellow park-goers while navigating the ambitious Fastpass+ attraction reservation system. And we'll continue to keep a close eye on it and other additions to the Walt Disney World vacation-planning universe—homework we're happy to do for readers like you.

After more than 45 fun-filled years, the World has vastly expanded—and so has our knowledge of the most popular vacation destination on the planet. On some occasions we've encountered sweltering weather and swelling crowds—times when even the happiest of travelers can turn into Grumpy for a moment or two. Had we known then what we know now, we could have spared ourselves some trying experiences. In one case, a staffer waited more than an hour to take a tour at the Studios. Standing in line with a notebook, she was asked by another guest if there was a quiz at the end. When she explained what she was doing, he expressed surprise to learn that she was waiting with the masses. But that's always been our strategy. We believe the best way to gather useful advice for a Walt Disney World guest is to be one. Over and over again!

Take Our Advice

We've done our best to keep you from making any tactical mistakes. We realize that even the most meticulous vacation planner needs detailed, accurate, and objective information to prepare a successful itinerary. To achieve that goal, we encourage the sharing of insight and information from Walt Disney World staffers—however the decision of whether or not to include such information is entirely up to the discretion of this book's editor.

To that end, we have packaged handy bits of advice in the form of sample itineraries and "hot tips" throughout the book. This advice comes directly from the copious notes we've taken during our thousands of days spent in Walt Disney World. We've also used our "Birnbaum's Best" stamp of approval wherever we deemed it appropriate, highlighting our favorite attractions and restaurants—the crowd-pleasers we believe stand head, shoulders, and ears above the rest.

You, the reader, benefit from the combination of our many years of experience that, together with our access to current insider information, makes this guide unique. We like to think it's indispensable, but we'll let you be the judge of that a few hundred pages from now.

Credit Where Credit Is Due

Enormous thanks to the teams of dedicated, detail-conscious Walt Disney World cast members from Guest Communications, the Disney Reservation Center, Food & Beverage,
Merchandise, Resort Operations, Sports & Recreation, Attractions Operations, Disney Cruise Line, Disney Vacation Club, Marketing, and Disney Parks Synergy.

Kudos to Michelle Olveira for her skilled fact-checking and to Tracey Randinelli for her meticulous proofreading. Thanks also to copy editor extraordinaire Diane Hodges and to Jerry Gonzalez, Marybeth Tregarthen, Dushawn Ward, Jennifer Eastwood, and Jessica Ward for their editorial support and production panache.

Heartfelt thanks to our photography team: Mike Carroll, Stacey Cook, Ana Rivera, and Lori Loftis—and, of course, Mickey Mouse and Minnie Mouse.

Hats off to those for whom doing Walt Disney World research is truly a labor of love. The "volunteer" class of 2017 includes the Safro family (Irene, Joy, Hayden Fullerton, and Delaney Irene), the Henning family (Amy, Chris, Avery, Elle, and Reid), the Lagano family (Judy, Chris, Jessica, Max, and Kyle), Linda Verdon, Margaret Verdon, Trace Schielzo, Chris Ozard, Emily Franzosa, Heather Pommerencke, Bob Cook, and Christina Fontana.

Of course, no list of acknowledgments would be complete without mentioning our founding editor, Steve Birnbaum, whose spirit, wisdom, and humor still infuse these pages, as well as Alexandra Mayes Birnbaum, who continues to be a guiding light—to say nothing of being a careful reader of every word.

The Last Word

Finally, it's important to remember that every worthwhile travel guide is a living enterprise; the book you hold in your hands is our best effort at explaining how to enjoy Walt Disney World at this moment, but its text is in no way etched in stone. Disney is constantly changing and growing, and in each annual edition we refine and expand our material to serve your needs even better. For this year's edition, though, this must be the final word.

Have a great visit!

— Jill Safro, Editor

DON'T FORGET TO WRITE!

No contribution is of greater value to us in preparing the next edition of this book than your comments on what we have written and on your own experiences at Walt Disney World. Please share your insights with us by writing to:

Jill Safro, Editor
Birnbaum's Walt Disney
World 2017
Disney Editions
125 West End Ave., 3rd Fl.
New York, NY 10023

Getting Ready to Go

The key to a fabulous vacation at Walt Disney World is advance planning. This remarkably varied complex is too vast and diverse to allow a spontaneous visit to be undertaken with much success—especially when you consider the rapid rate at which the World has expanded and the introduction of Fastpass+: a system that allows guests to reserve attraction times *up to 60 days in advance*. It does not mean that even the most casual visitors can't have some significant fun, but they are bound to have regrets about things they missed because of time pressures or a simple lack of information. The purpose of this guide is to eliminate potential frustration while getting the biggest bang for your vacation buck.

What follows, then, is meant to provide a sensible scheme for planning a satisfying visit to Walt Disney World, one that will offer the most fun and the least amount of disappointment. But how do you know which of the countless activities will be the most enjoyable for you and your family? Do your homework. The best strategy is to make sure you have a clear idea of all that is available long before you arrive in the Orlando area.

When to Go

When talk finally turns to the best time to make a trip to Walt Disney World, Christmas and Easter are often mentioned, as well as the traditional summer vacation period—especially if there are children in the family. But there is also good reason to avoid these periods, namely the tremendous crowds they attract. And when Disney World is crowded, it can be very crowded, indeed. On the busiest days, visitors may wait more than two hours to experience the most popular attractions when waiting in lines. That's at least twice as long as during less busy times of the year. Weekends, in general, are quite popular with locals. Sunday night through Wednesday is typically quieter.

Considering seasonal hours, weather, crowd patterns, and Disney resort rates, optimal times to visit Disney are usually mid-January through early February, late April through late May, and September through December (except Martin Luther King Day weekend, Thanksgiving and Christmas weeks).

Note that during some of the less crowded times of the year—particularly during the winter—some attractions are closed for renovations. In addition, water parks are often closed for refurbishment during cooler months. Call 407-824-4321, or check *www.disneyworld.com* for a current schedule, updated each season.

Mid-November through December is a festive time of year the world over, and Disney World is no exception. The theme parks are decorated to the nines for the holiday season. Epcot holds stirring Christmas concerts, and the Magic Kingdom drapes Cinderella Castle in thousands of sparkling lights. Many other special events are held during this period, including Mickey's Very Merry Christmas Party in the Magic Kingdom (a separate admission ticket is required). The party brings a dusting of "snow"

to Main Street from about 7 P.M. to midnight for several days between mid-November and the first three weeks of December. It also features holiday shows around the park, including Mickey's Once Upon a Christmastime Parade, plus a unique fireworks show: Holiday Wishes. Select performances from Mickey's Very Merry Christmas Party are also staged in the park during regular hours on the days leading up to, including, and following Christmas. Note that this event often sells out way ahead of time. Get tickets in advance by calling 407-W-DISNEY (934-7639). Advance purchase prices start at about $90 (same-day purchases are higher). It's usually easier to snag tickets for dates earlier in the season.

Epcot celebrates with Holidays Around the World, including the nightly Candlelight Processional, complete with a mass choir, 50-piece orchestra, and a reading of the story of Christmas by a celebrity narrator. Dinner packages are available for some World Showcase restaurants. (We recommend the dinner package: It guarantees seating for dinner as well as preferred seating at the Candlelight Processional. Without a package, you should arrive at least two hours before showtime or risk being shut out of your preferred performance.) Note that the Osborne Family Spectacle of Dancing Lights, a longtime staple at Disney's Hollywood Studios, will not be presented in 2017. (It was retired in early 2016.) For updates regarding the park's holiday celebrations, visit *www.disneyworld.com*.

Disney Springs gets into the spirit of the season with Christmas trees, twinkling lights, and jolly entertainment—including visits by Saint Nick. There are holiday decorations at each Walt Disney World hotel, too, including a Victorian Christmas at the Grand Floridian, a seaside party at the Yacht and Beach Club, and a Cajun holiday at Port Orleans Riverside.

For reservations, call 407-W-DISNEY (934-7639), a travel agent, or the Walt Disney Travel Company at 407-828-8101. Visit *www.disneyworld.com*, or call 407-939-7630 for additional information. Special-event tickets are sold separately.

HOT TIP!

The period of time between the week after Thanksgiving weekend and the week before Christmas is one of the less crowded and most festive times of the year.

Crowd Patterns

Day-to-Day Trends

Weekends tend to be among the most crowded days at Walt Disney World theme parks, followed by Mondays, Thursdays and Fridays. Morning through early afternoon is a bustling time for the theme parks and their respective "E-ticket" attractions. Days that offer Extra Magic Hours tend to be more crowded at their respective theme parks (see page 22). When the weather's steamy, the water parks tend to pack them in—so be sure to get an early start if you're headed to Blizzard Beach or Typhoon Lagoon.

When the time comes to plot an itinerary, it's helpful to know about crowd patterns beyond the four theme parks as well. As a rule, Disney Springs (formerly known as Downtown Disney) and Disney's water parks host their largest throngs on weekends. Of course, in these circles, a bigger crowd could possibly mean a better time. Golfers should note that weekend tee times are typically in the highest demand, while Monday and Tuesday tee times tend to be the easiest to come by.

Seasonal Shifts

The chart below indicates the density of crowds in the theme parks throughout the year. Though it's tough to generalize about a property as big and ever-changing as Walt Disney World—special events (such as the Disney Marathon and Epcot's Food & Wine Festival) and package deals can swell park attendance during a period typically marked by smaller crowds—the chart highlights historic trends.

Least Crowded means that there will be lines; however most shows and attractions can be visited with a bit less waiting than during busier times of the year.

Average Attendance refers to times when there are lots of people around, but lines are relatively manageable.

Most Crowded reflects times when lines at popular attractions can mean a wait of as much as two to three hours (or more). As a rule, when school is out, the crowds are most definitely in at Walt Disney World.

Least Crowded

- 2nd week of January through 1st week of February (excluding WDW Marathon Week and Martin Luther King Weekend)
- Week before Labor Day until the start of Epcot's Food & Wine Festival
- Week after Thanksgiving until the weekend at the start of Christmas week

Average Attendance

- 1st week of January (excluding New Year's Day), which is "most crowded"
- 2nd week of February until Presidents' week
- End of February through 2nd week of March
- Last week of April through May
- Period after Epcot's Food & Wine Festival ends until the weekend before Thanksgiving

Most Crowded

- All major holidays
- Presidents' week
- WDW Marathon Week
- 3rd week of March through 3rd week of April
- Easter week
- June through the 3rd week of August
- Epcot Food & Wine Festival
- Thanksgiving week
- Christmas through New Year's Day
- Any time school's out

Holidays & Special Events

Special events are staged at Walt Disney World throughout the year, not only to mark holidays but also to celebrate other interests. The dates and details below are subject to change without notice; call 407-824-4321 to confirm, or check out *www.disneyworld.com* for up-to-the-minute information about specific events.

JANUARY

Walt Disney World Marathon Weekend
(January 4–8): Some 20,000 entrants run through theme parks and other areas of the World during this 26.2-mile race (January 8). Characters and cast members are on hand for inspiration. Similar hoopla surrounds the half marathon (January 7). The 2-day Goofy Challenge (January 7 and 8) covers 4 theme parks and 39.3 miles. There is a 10K run (January 6) and a 5K family run on January 5. (It's okay to walk the 5K, but you must maintain a 16-minute mile.) Hard-core runners may take the "Dopey Challenge"—all of the aforementioned events within the pacing requirements—and earn a Dopey Challenge finisher medal. Packages are available. Call 407-939-4786 for package details or to book. For marathon weekend event information and schedules, call 407-938-3398, or visit *www.rundisney.com* for details. Tickets for this event generally go on sale in the April prior to the January races—and sell out within hours. Note that hotel rooms are in high demand for this event. Reserve yours as early as possible. For details on other Walt Disney World running events, visit *www.rundisney.com*.

MARCH–JUNE

Atlanta Braves Spring Training (Late February–March): The Atlanta Braves have called Walt Disney World their spring training home for 20 seasons—and 2017 may be the last. For updates, visit *www.espnwwos.com/atlantabraves*.

Saint Patrick's Day (March 17): Everyone is Irish on Saint Patrick's Day—especially at the Mighty St. Patrick's Festival at Disney Springs. The family-friendly festivities include music, dancing, dining, and more. Of course, every day is St. Patrick's Day at Raglan Road, the neighborhood's Irish pub. Epcot's United Kingdom pavilion marks the day with Irish dining, dancing, and green beer.

Easter (April 16): Most of the Disney parks stay open late during the two weeks straddling the Easter holiday. The Easter Bunny greets guests in the Magic Kingdom. Epcot hosts a park-wide "Egg-stravaganza" hunt—cost is about $5 for a map with stickers (find all the eggs and win a prize). And many of the Disney World resorts offer special Easter-themed fun. Catholic and Protestant services may be offered at the Contemporary resort. Call 407-W-DISNEY for specifics. This is an extremely busy time to visit.

Epcot International Flower & Garden Festival (March 2–May 30): Epcot is blooming with elaborate gardens (including more than 30 million fragrant blossoms) and topiary displays, behind-the-scenes tours, gardening workshops, concerts, and guest speakers. Learn from the experts how to create a gorgeous garden. Pick up a Garden Passport and get it stamped as you explore the Outdoor Kitchens throughout the day. Passports are free and may be found at the Festival Center, all Disney Vacation Club kiosks, all Outdoor Kitchen stations, and many shopping locations. Each Outdoor Kitchen has its own unique stamp.

Another popular element of the Flower and Garden Festival is the Garden Rocks concert series, presented at the America Gardens Theater by the American Adventure pavilion. Past performers have included The Village People, Taylor Dayne, Little River Band, and Herman's Hermits starring Peter Noone. All shows are included with Epcot admission. Some seats may be reserved via Fastpass+ (see page 25)—the rest are available on a first-come, first-served basis.

Mother's Day (May 14): Celebrate Mom by treating her to a special Mother's Day buffet. Several WDW restaurants, such as Animal Kingdom Lodge's Boma—Flavors of Africa, Chef Mickey's and The Wave at the Contemporary, Captain's Grille at Yacht Club (brunch), and the Swan's Garden Grove (dinner), have been known to offer Mother's Day meals. For details on the 2017 options, call 407-WDW-DINE (939-3463). Note that Walt Disney World resorts are very busy on Mother's Day weekend—book early.

HOT TIP!

Star Wars weekends won't be offered at Disney's Hollywood Studios in 2017, but the Force is growing stronger at that theme park every day. For updates, visit *www.disneyworld.com*.

Sounds Like Summer Concert Series

(June–July): An Epcot annual tradition, rock 'n' roll tribute bands have guests dancing to the likes of the Bee Gees, Bon Jovi, the Eagles, U2, and more. Nightly shows are presented at the America Gardens Theater at the American Adventure Pavilion. There are usually three shows a night, weather permitting. Seats are on a first-come, first-served basis.

JULY

Fourth of July Celebration: Double-size fireworks presentations over the Magic Kingdom, Epcot, and Disney's Hollywood Studios make for a very colorful night. Ben Franklin, Betsy Ross, and Disney characters greet guests at Epcot's American Adventure pavilion throughout the day. That pavilion's America Gardens Theater hosts a patriotic show featuring an expanded cast of the Voices of Liberty. The evening's presentation of IllumiNations (Epcot's nightly lagoon show) may feature a patriotic finale. This is an exceptionally busy time to visit Walt Disney World—possibly the busiest.

SEPTEMBER–NOVEMBER

Night of Joy (September): Two nights of celebration highlight contemporary Christian music presented live at ESPN World of Sports Complex. For dates and tickets, call 407-827-7200. This popular event attracts a bit of a rowdy crowd (of mostly teens and young adults).

HOT TIP!

Holidays and special events make for peak crowds at Walt Disney World theme parks. So much so that they often reach capacity. To ensure entry into the WDW park of your choice, plan to arrive at the front gate very early in the day. We recommend sticking with one park on busy days. Once you're in, stay in!

Epcot International Food & Wine Festival (late September–mid-November): Epcot's World Showcase celebrates the flavors of many different countries (even those not usually represented around the lagoon) through tastings (about $2 to $8 per sample), demos from top chefs, and wine and cooking seminars. It's an exceptionally satisfying way in which to wander World Showcase. It's also insanely popular, so expect lots of company—especially in the evening. For details or to make a reservation for a special event (which you should do *far* in advance), visit *www.epcotfoodfestival.com*.

A Tisket, A Tasket . . .

. . . a "Welcome to Walt Disney World Basket." The Disney Florist can deliver this and a striking array of themed surprises to any room on Disney property (and many that aren't). There's no occasion they can't rise to—from a birthday to Earth Day, from engagements to golden wedding anniversaries. A call to the Disney Florist (the only one serving Walt Disney World) can yield custom-tailored bouquets, baskets, and even Christmas trees. (They also have a division dedicated exclusively to Walt Disney World engagements.)

Not satisfied with a simple delivery to a resort room? The Florist folks encourage creativity. Got a favorite Disney character? Into the basket he or she goes! One package known as "Create a Fairy Tale" (complete with slipper and tiara) can actually be delivered to guests enjoying a romantic carriage ride.

For more information or to place an order, call 407-939-4438 (daily from 8 A.M. to 6 P.M.), or visit *www.disneyflorist.com*.

HOT TIP!

On dates when the Magic Kingdom hosts "special-ticket" events, such as Mickey's Not-So-Scary Halloween Party and Mickey's Very Merry Christmas Party, the park closes early to day guests.

Halloween (late September–October): The festivities vary a bit from year to year. What follows is a sampling of what to expect:

Fort Wilderness Resort and Campground usually hosts a pumpkin-carving contest and a kids' costume contest, followed by a screening of a spooky movie. It also offers Halloween-themed wagon rides with storytelling and surprises along the way. Animal Kingdom may also invite guests to trick-or-treat.

The Magic Kingdom will play host to its Halloween spectacular, **Mickey's Not-So-Scary Halloween Party**, September through October. The special-ticket activities include a kids' costume parade, dancing, appearances by Disney villains (including a new Castle Forecourt show called **Hocus Pocus Villain Spelltacular**), trick-or-treating, and fireworks. This is an extremely popular Magic Kingdom event. Purchase tickets as far in advance as possible. And don't forget to wear a costume. (For costume guidelines, visit *www.disneyworld.com*.) Note that guests with tickets to the Halloween Party may be able to enter the park at 4 P.M. (Ask when you buy your ticket.) As a spooky bonus, **Mickey's Boo-to-You Halloween Parade** makes its way through the Kingdom during the Halloween party. Advance purchase prices start at about $75 (same-day purchases are higher). For additional details, call 407-827-7200.

Festival of the Masters (early November): This fine arts show draws many of the world's top artists to Disney Springs. It has featured paintings, photographs, sculpture, jewelry, and more. *Note that the festival may not take place in 2017. For details, visit www.disneyworld.com/art.*

Thanksgiving (November 24): All WDW restaurants are open on Turkey Day, many of them offering Thanksgiving specialties. For details, call 407-WDW-DINE (939-3463).

AdvoCare Classic (November 24–27): This early-season college basketball tournament features 8 NCAA teams and 12 games. Each team competes in one game a day and advances through a bracket-tournament format. Book your hotel early if you want to stay at a WDW resort for this popular weekend. For details, visit *www.http://espnevents.com.*

Disney's Magical Holidays: Decorations and festivities abound in WDW's parks and resorts. The Magic Kingdom park hosts **Mickey's Very Merry Christmas Party** on select nights from early November through the first three weeks of December, complete with snow flurries on Main Street and complimentary hot cocoa. Entertainment for the special-ticket party includes **Mickey's Once Upon a Christmastime Parade** and a special edition of the Wishes fireworks show; select performances are staged during regular hours just before Christmas. (Guests with tickets to the Christmas Party may be able to enter the Magic Kingdom as early as 4 P.M.) Magic Kingdom may offer a holiday version of the Jungle Cruise, aka the Jingle Cruise. Finally, Queen Elsa lights the Castle on a nightly basis (with the help of Anna and Olaf). Details may change in 2017.

Epcot's **Holidays Around the World** (late November–late December) features the Christmas Candlelight Processional, including a choral concert, plus a celebrity narrator who reads the story of Christmas. The event is included with park admission, but seating is limited and it is exceptionally popular. Arrive at least 90 minutes before showtime, or book a dinner package (which combines dinner at a World Showcase eatery with guaranteed Processional seating). For more information, call 407-939-3463.

HOT TIP!

Lights out! The plug has been pulled on The Osborne Family Spectacle of Dancing Lights (the beloved show was retired in early 2016). For alternative holiday festivities, visit *www.disneyworld.com.*

Disney Springs gets into the holiday spirit with a cheery mix of twinkling lights, seasonal music, a towering tree, and visits from the North Pole's most famous resident. Past years have brought carolers, stilt-walkers, and a lively holiday dance party.

New Year's Eve Celebration (December 31): There are extra-large fireworks displays over the Magic Kingdom, Epcot, and Disney's Hollywood Studios (though there are no fireworks at all at Animal Kingdom—imagine the stampede!). These parks stay open until approximately 1 A.M. Many of the resort restaurants, as well as the nightspots at Disney Springs, also welcome the new year Disney style. La Nouba by Cirque du Soleil features a festive finale to ring in the new year (Disney Springs, West Side).

Keeping WDW Hours

Since operating hours fluctuate quite a bit, call 407-824-4321 or visit *www.disneyworld.com* for current schedules.

THEME PARKS: Disney theme park hours vary seasonally. In May, September, October, parts of November and December, and all of January, the Magic Kingdom is usually open from 9 A.M. to 8 P.M.; Epcot is typically open from 9 A.M. to 9 P.M. (some Future World attractions may close at 7 P.M.), later during peak seasons; Disney's Hollywood Studios is open from 9 A.M. until about an hour after sunset; and Animal Kingdom is usually open from 9 A.M. till at about 8 P.M. (or later). The parks take turns offering Extra Magic Hours throughout the week. That is, on any given day, one park may allow Disney resort guests to enter an hour early or stay in the park for two hours after it closes to the public. Participating Walt Disney World resorts have schedules at the front desk. (Note that while Extra Magic Hours are—by far—the best time to visit for guests craving shorter lines, some attractions do not operate during EMH.)

The Magic Kingdom keeps later hours through summer and other busy periods, including Christmas and Easter weeks. The parks may be open until 1 A.M. on New Year's Eve. Disney's Hollywood Studios often stays open until 10 or 11 P.M. in the summer, too.

DISNEY SPRINGS—MARKETPLACE, LANDING, AND TOWN CENTER: Shops are generally open from about 10 A.M. until 11 P.M. Sunday through Thursday; 11:30 P.M. on Friday and Saturday. Restaurant hours vary, with most venues open until 11 P.M. or midnight.

DISNEY SPRINGS, WEST SIDE: At the AMC cineplex, movies begin as early as 10 A.M. Restaurants are open from about 11:30 A.M. to midnight. Shops are open from about 10:30 A.M. to 11 P.M. (midnight on Friday and Saturday).

WATER PARKS: Water parks are open from about 10 A.M. to 5 P.M., but extend hours during summer months. Note that cabanas should be reserved in advance (see Hot Tip on page 221).

WDW PARK TRANSPORTATION: Bus, boat, and monorail transportation service begin one hour prior to park opening time and continue until about one hour after the parks close. Boats and monorails do not operate for Extra Magic Hours. For specifics, check at Guest Relations.

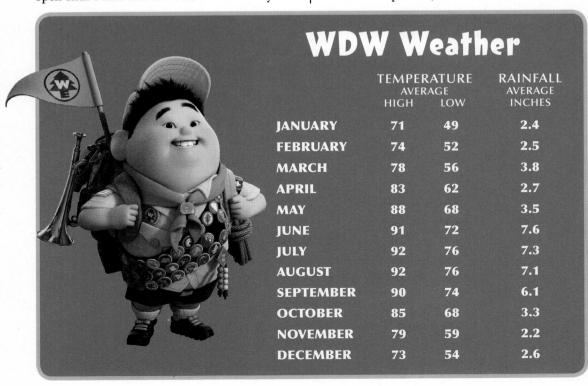

WDW Weather

| | TEMPERATURE AVERAGE | | RAINFALL AVERAGE |
	HIGH	LOW	INCHES
JANUARY	71	49	2.4
FEBRUARY	74	52	2.5
MARCH	78	56	3.8
APRIL	83	62	2.7
MAY	88	68	3.5
JUNE	91	72	7.6
JULY	92	76	7.3
AUGUST	92	76	7.1
SEPTEMBER	90	74	6.1
OCTOBER	85	68	3.3
NOVEMBER	79	59	2.2
DECEMBER	73	54	2.6

How to Get There

By Car

While most visitors to the Orlando area fly in, many prefer to drive. If you opt for a road trip, figure on logging no more than 350 to 400 miles a day—a distance that won't wear you down so much that you can't enjoy your trip.

Contact state tourist boards to inquire about the availability of free maps (yes, they still make maps!); for a Florida map and guide, call 888-735-2872, or pick up a copy of *Rand McNally*

Road Atlas or the *AAA North American Road Atlas*; both are sold in bookstores. If you plan to navigate with GPS, note Walt Disney World's address in the Hot Tip at the top of page 15.

From Orlando International Airport

By car: During rush hour, take the airport's South Exit to the Central Florida Greeneway (Route 417) to Route 536, which leads to Walt Disney World. The tolls run about $4.

For the shortest route, take the North Exit to Route 528, going west toward Tampa. Pick up I-4 west, and go to a WDW exit. Tolls are about $4. The route is usually heavily trafficked, but manageable during non-rush periods of the day. It's busiest on weekday mornings and evenings and any time when a theme park is scheduled to open or close.

By Disney's Magical Express: This tailor-made, complimentary transportation program is available to guests staying at select Disney resorts. For more information, turn to page 16.

By car service: Reliable towncar service is available from Noris Limousines. Friendly drivers take guests directly to their resort. The company offers a special round-trip rate for Birnbaum readers—mention this book and expect to pay about $120 for up to four passengers for a towncar, or about $225 for a limo for up to 8 passengers. Reservations are required and cancellations must be made at least 48 hours ahead. Call 407-240-4533, or visit *www.norislimousines.com*. Prices may increase if there is a significant jump in prices at the pump.

Florida Towncar also offers efficient, direct service to Disney area resorts. And they offer our readers a special rate, too. Simply mention the Birnbaum Guide when you book your ride and expect a round-trip rate (*to and from Orlando International Airport only*) of about $85 for up to five passengers (that's $15 off). Call 407-277-5466 (from Florida) or 800-525-7246 (from out of state) up to 24 hours ahead, or visit *www.floridatowncar.com*. Online reservations should be made at least 24 hours ahead of pickup time.

By shuttle: At Orlando International Airport, Mears Motor Shuttle offers vans and buses 24 hours a day. It serves the Swan and Dolphin, Hotel Plaza Boulevard properties, and other non-Disney area hotels. Shuttles make multiple stops; a trip can take an hour or more. On the return trip, Mears requires guests be picked up at least 3 to 4 hours prior to flight times. Reservations should be made 24 hours ahead. There is often a long wait at the airport (even with a reservation), and employee attitudes fluctuate wildly. This is not our preferred mode of transit.

The shuttle cost to most hotels is $23 one way, $37 round-trip per adult; $18 one way, $28 round-trip per child ages 4 through 11; free for children under 4. Fares to International Drive properties are a little lower. There may be a very long wait to get on a shuttle at the airport, and service is not direct. Call 407-423-5566 for information, or visit *www.mearstransportation.com*.

By taxi: Metered cabs usually cost between $60 and $70 each way, depending on the destination—and the integrity of the driver (prices listed at the Orlando International Airport taxi stand are estimates). Some taxis can accommodate up to 9 people (for the price of one). Bell Services can call for a cab at any WDW resort. Note that many drivers do not have SunPass, so it'll cost you at least 45 cents a minute while waiting to pay each toll. What's more, many drivers do not know the area streets (or pretend not to)—resulting in bigger fares than necessary. Until cabs offer a flat rate to and from the airport, we are sticking with Magical Express or towncars.

Note that gratuities are not included in any of the transfer rates. It is customary to tip for good service.

Reputable automobile clubs offer help with breakdowns; towing; insurance that covers personal injury, accidents, arrest, bail bond, and lawyers' fees for defense of contested traffic cases; and travel-planning services, including free maps and route mapping. Services vary from one club to the next, and membership fees range widely, from about $50 to $120 a year.

By Air

When it comes to airfares, there is no real trick to unearthing the most economical ones: Simply shop around. Call a travel agent, browse the Internet, and keep these tips in mind:

- Take advantage of advance-purchase fares (lower rates that apply if a ticket is bought up to several weeks prior to departure).

- Fly when most people don't: For vacation destinations, that usually means leaving the ground on Tuesday or Wednesday.

Resources for Road Trippers

There are a variety of reputable national automobile associations to choose from. Among the leading clubs:

- **Allstate Motor Club Customer Service Center**
  P.O. Box 3094
  Arlington Heights, IL 60006
  800-255-7828
  www.allstatemotorclub.com

- **American Automobile Association** (AAA)
  1000 AAA Dr. #28
  Heathrow, FL 32746
  407-444-7000 or 800-564-6222
  www.aaa.com

- **Auto Club of America**
  P.O. Box 21443
  Oklahoma City, OK 73156
  800-411-2007
  www.autoclubofamerica.com

- **Ford Customer Relationship Center**
  P.O. Box 6248
  Dearborn, MI 48126
  800-392-3673; *www.ford.com*

- **GeicoNow**
  800-861-8380
  www.geico.com

- **Signature's Nationwide Auto Club**
  Attention: Customer Service
  P.O. Box 968008
  Schaumburg, IL 60196
  800-323-2002
  www.autoclub.com

Travelers may also check with state tourist boards for free maps. Other map sources are the *AAA North American Road Atlas* and the *Rand McNally Road Atlas*; they are sold in many bookstores.

- Keep in mind that the lowest airfares usually carry a penalty if you have to revise or cancel your ticket, and that most discounted tickets are nonrefundable.

- When you call to make a reservation, ask about any fare restrictions, including an obligatory Saturday night stay-over.

- Visit airline websites. They may e-mail details about discounted fares. Most offer a small discount for purchasing tickets online.

By Train

Amtrak serves the Orlando, Florida, area twice daily to and from New York City, with stops made along the way. The trip takes approximately 22 hours and costs from about $220 to $600 round-trip, coach. (Book early for lower fares; discounts are often available, so be sure to ask. Passengers over the age of 18 must present valid government-issued photo ID upon request.) If you're staying at Walt Disney World, plan to take a cab or shuttle to the area hotels. Rental cars are also available. They are not on-site, but are easily reached by shuttle.

For reservations and additional train information, call 800-USA-RAIL (872-7245), visit the Amtrak website at *www.amtrak.com*, or contact a travel agent.

By Bus

Greyhound provides frequent direct service to Orlando and Kissimmee (the latter is closer to Walt Disney World). From either destination, you can take a taxi to your hotel, but first check if your hotel offers shuttle service. For more information, contact Greyhound at 800-231-2222, or visit *www.greyhound.com*.

Disney's Magical Express Service

Disney's Magical Express service is for guests booked at a Walt Disney World-owned-and-operated resort and arriving at Orlando International Airport. Meant as a money-saver as well as a convenience, the service lets guests check luggage at their airport of origin, bypass baggage claim, and board a bus to their WDW resort. The luggage, which guests affix with special tags before leaving home, is usually delivered to the resort room within several hours of arrival. (Note that bags are delivered to rooms for flights landing between 5 A.M. and 10 P.M. If your flight arrives after 10 P.M., you'll need to take your bags with you to the Magical Express bus.) On the final day of a trip, prior to boarding the bus to the airport, guests who fly domestically with participating airlines (at press time, that included Alaska, American, Delta, JetBlue, Southwest, and United) check their luggage at their resort and receive a boarding pass for their airline. (Airline luggage fees apply.) Once at the airport, guests can skip the airline check-in counter and proceed to security. If you'd prefer to schlep your own bags, you can still hitch a free ride on the bus (provided that you are headed to a Disney resort). Here are some specifics:

- Magical Express service is booked when you book your resort and must be done at least 10 days prior to arrival. (Have flight information handy when you make the call.) Be sure to confirm.

- Reservations may be made via *www.disneyworld.com*, 407-W-DISNEY, or a travel agent.

- Tip the driver as you would had you paid for the trip: $1–$2 per bag is appropriate.

- Special luggage tags will be sent to the party that makes the reservation. These tags must be put on all bags that will be checked at the airport.

- Upon landing at Orlando International Airport (MCO), skip baggage claim (only if you tagged your bags) and go to the Disney Welcome Center, located in the Main Terminal Building on the B side, Level 1. Don't forget to have your transfer vouchers, MagicBands (see page 24), and a photo ID handy.

- On the return trip, expect to be picked up at least three hours before your scheduled flight departure time. Consider that when you make your air arrangements.

- Guests who require wheelchair-accessible transportation should make their needs known when making the reservation. Confirm reservations before you leave home.

- Guests flying on "non-participating" airlines are entitled to the free shuttle service, too.

The good news? It is super convenient, and it is a real money-saver. In fact, a family of four can shave at least $130 off their total vacation cost by taking the Magical Express as opposed to other forms of transportation. And it is beyond liberating to leave the lugging of the luggage to someone else. It's also handy to bypass check-in at the airport on the return trip. The downside? Well, to call any service "magical" is to elevate expectations. It's not really express, either—as most buses make multiple stops at Disney resorts. So if time is of the essence, it might not be the best choice. Same goes for the transportation of luggage. While the service truly eases the burden of many a family, it may take one to three hours to arrive at your resort room (occasionally, a bit more). So if you'll need anything right away—swimsuits, pajamas, medication, snacks, etc.—be sure to pack it in a day bag, carry it onto the plane, and transport it to the resort yourself. We could do without the noisy promotional video that's played throughout the journey, but the bus is comfy and the price is right.

Planning Ahead
Logistics

Organizing a trip properly takes time, but most travelers find the increased enjoyment well worth the effort. The fact is, planning can be a pleasant sort of "armchair" exercise, and kids will enjoy their visit to Disney all the more if they, too, are involved in the process. Take it from us, the more information you can gather, the better.

To assist in that effort, we immodestly recommend *Birnbaum's Walt Disney World For Kids*, a colorful look at the World, written for readers ages 7 through 14. For those planning to pair a Disney cruise with a Walt Disney World visit, cruise information beginning on page 309 is a good place to start.

cruise information beginning on page 309

HOT TIP!

So you're using the Birnbaum Guide to plan your trip to Walt Disney World. What are you going to do next? Go to *www.disneyworld.com*! There you can get WDW news and park hours, purchase tickets, make dining reservations, and more.

Information Sources

For additional information about Walt Disney World, call 407-W-DISNEY (407-934-7639) or visit *www.disneyworld.com*. Specifics such as park hours, ticket prices, refurbishment schedules, and directions are available through an automated system 24 hours a day. For information by mail, write to: Walt Disney World, P.O. Box 10000, Lake Buena Vista, FL 32830-1000.

Internet and smartphone users can tap into updates about happenings in the World, get information on trip planning, reserve a room, order tickets, book dining reservations, and get park hours and special-events listings by visiting *www.disneyworld.com* or *mydisneyexperience.com*. Disney Cruise Line vacation packages may be booked at *www.disneycruise.com*.

For info and discounts on (non-Disney) area attractions, restaurants, and hotels, contact the Official Visitor Information Center, 8723 International Drive, Suite 101, Orlando, FL 32819 (it's a satellite office of the Orlando Convention & Visitors Bureau); 407-363-5872, or 800-972-3304; *www.visitorlando.com*.

For details about other Central Florida attractions, contact Visit Florida; 888-735-2872 (to request a complimentary visitors guide and map) or 850-488-5607; *www.visitflorida.com*.

On-site Resources: Those staying at a WDW resort should consider their lobby concierge desk a primary resource. Resort guests also receive information via their room's TV. Fort Wilderness campers are advised to stop at the Pioneer Hall Info and Ticket Window, call extension 2788, or touch 11 on a phone near any restroom. Tablet and smartphone users can access *mydisneyexperience.com* or use the free app.

What to Pack

While there's no formal dress code at Walt Disney World, neat, casual clothing is the rule, with few exceptions. Most notably, jackets are required for men at Victoria & Albert's restaurant in the Grand Floridian resort. Generally speaking, T-shirts and shorts are fine during the day. For evening, slacks, jeans, or Bermuda-length shorts are appropriate. Bathing suits are a must, along with the appropriate attire for any sport you want to pursue.

Light sweaters are necessary even in summer—to wear indoors when air-conditioning gets chilly. From November through March, warmer clothing is a must for evening. Pack for weather extremes so you'll be comfy should it become unseasonably warm or cool. Bring sunscreen and don't forget the bug spray. (Leave selfie sticks at home—they are not allowed in Disney parks. Also forbidden: weapons of any kind, including toys.) If possible, pack lightweight rain gear (a poncho is best). One of the most important items of all? Comfortable walking shoes (two pairs).

Guests at the resorts on Hotel Plaza Boulevard may access a tourist-information television station of their own. Some other area hotels also show a version of the programming, usually aiming to provide an overview of all Central Florida attractions.

For Day Visitors: When purchasing one-day admission to a given theme park, guests receive a complimentary guidemap and entertainment Times Guide for that park. Ticket holders may receive all four park guides upon request. Extra guidemaps are available at City Hall (in the Magic Kingdom) and at Guest Relations (in Epcot, Disney's Hollywood Studios, and Animal Kingdom), as well as in many shops and restaurants throughout the park.

Package Pointers

The sheer number and diversity of packages offering vacations in Central Florida are enough to bewilder even the savviest traveler. Still, such plans are worth exploring. Most offer the convenience of a vacation that's completely organized in advance, and one that will generally cost less than the sum of the same transportation, accommodations, and admission elements purchased separately. In addition, since most package providers purchase blocks of Disney resort rooms, they are an excellent source for securing a room on Walt Disney World property when the hotel of your choice is booked.

Southwest Vacations (800-243-8372), American Airlines Vacations (800-321-2121), *www.expedia.com*, *www.travelocity.com*, and the Walt Disney Travel Company (407-939-6244 or *www.disneyworld.com*) all offer packages that feature Walt Disney World on-site hotels, as well as choice off-property accommodations. Many packages include the added attraction of low-cost air transportation.

Vacations and other travel packages include certain perks and discounts. For possibilities, check the travel section of your local newspaper or consult a travel agent.

Walt Disney Travel Company offers six vacation plans: Magic Your Way base package, Magic Your Way Plus Dining package, Magic Your Way Plus Quick Service Dining package, Magic Your Way Plus Deluxe Dining package, Magic Your Way Premium package, and the Magic Your Way Platinum package. (Visit *www.disneyworld.com/dvd* to order a complimentary vacation planning DVD.) Walt Disney Travel Company packages may include extras such as miniature golf vouchers and savings on participating recreation, dining, and shopping locations throughout WDW.

Travel agents may design packages around a specific type of vacation: say, a golf getaway, honeymoon, or family reunion. They may include extra elements such as unlimited tee times or a carriage ride. Still others are tied to an annual event, such as the Walt Disney World Marathon (see Holidays & Special Events on page 10). Air transportation, rental car, or airport transfers can be added to most packages.

The value of a package depends on your needs. Before considering options, use this book to help determine which of the accommodations, activities, and attractions most appeal to you. There's real value in some package elements, such as airport transfers and meal discounts. Several packages also include meals with the Disney characters, tennis lessons, golf greens fees, spa treatments, boat rentals, and the like.

Never choose a package that includes elements you don't want or won't have time to enjoy. While extras such as welcoming snacks may sound appealing, their cash value is negligible. Also beware of any packages that tout certain services as selling points that are actually available to every Disney guest.

Finally, we highly recommend insuring your trip when purchasing a package, as cancellation fees can be steep and emergencies do happen. Insurance ensures peace of mind (and wallet).

HOT TIP!

When purchasing a Walt Disney World package, pay attention to the type of WDW ticket that's included—and make sure you are able to customize the ticket to meet your needs. See page 21.

"Magic Your Way" Packages

"Magic Your Way" is the name of the game when it comes to Disney World vacation planning. The phrase, meant to reflect each individual's freedom to customize a vacation, covers quite the gamut of options. Most of all, it covers six vacation packages: Magic Your Way, Magic Your Way Plus Dining, Magic Your Way Plus Quick Service Dining, Magic Your Way Plus Deluxe Dining, Magic Your Way Premium, and Magic Your Way Platinum. They can be booked through the Walt Disney Travel Company (407-939-7675), travel agents, and *www.disneyworld.com*.

The packages have some elements in common. They're all intended to be flexible and include a Disney resort stay and a theme park ticket of some kind. They come with "magical extras" such as discounts at select WDW dining, recreational, and shopping locations, as well as admission to one of WDW's mini golf courses and ESPN Wide World of Sports Complex. They must be paid for in full. Packages must be canceled at least 31 days before the trip to avoid a penalty. (For cancellations made 31 days or more prior to arrival, amounts paid minus fees assessed by third-party suppliers will be refunded.) Everyone staying in a room must have the same package and ticket options. Finally, they come with the following perks (also offered to guests with room-only reservations):

- Extra Magic Hours benefit: WDW resort guests may enjoy exclusive access to theme parks on select mornings and evenings. (For details on Extra Magic Hours, see page 22.)
- Disney's Magical Express service: free transportation to and from the Orlando International Airport, plus baggage delivery to your resort room. (See page 16 for details.)
- Complimentary use of the Walt Disney World transportation system (buses, boats, and the ever-popular monorail).

Magic Your Way Base Package: This "package" is, quite simply, a stay at any Walt Disney World-owned-and-operated resort paired with a theme park ticket. The big decisions to be made here are (1) which resort to reserve, and (2) the number of days and add-ons you want on your park ticket. (For more on Walt Disney World theme park ticket structures and pricing, turn to pages 21–24.)

Magic Your Way Plus Dining Package: Take the above description of the Magic Your Way package, throw in a Disney Dining Plan, and you've got a vacation plan with the chance to pre-pay for meals and choose from more than 100 different eateries. The basic package includes one quick-service meal, a snack, plus one meal at a table-service restaurant per person, per night of your vacation. (For more on the Dining Plan, see page 20.) The package also includes a Magic Your Way base ticket and a "Rapid Fill" refillable mug (see page 270).

Magic Your Way Plus Quick Service Dining Package: This plan includes two meals and one snack per day, per guest and all meals are of the quick-service variety. It includes a refillable mug for each member of the party participating in this package.

Magic Your Way Plus Deluxe Dining Package: Similar to the two aforementioned packages, but this plan comes with three meals a

HOT TIP!

All multi-day theme park tickets expire 14 days after the first day is used. The "No Expiration" option was discontinued in February 2015. Tickets purchased prior to then will be honored at the parks.

day, all of which can be cashed in at any eatery that is a Dining Plan participant (regardless of whether it is quick service or table service).

Magic Your Way Premium Package: It's called "premium" because it includes many of the World's most popular features:

- A stay at a Disney-owned-and-operated resort.
- Magic Your Way ticket with "add-ons" (see page 21 for details).
- Premium Dining Plan: breakfast, lunch, two snacks, and dinner per person, per night. For details, see sidebar and call 407-WDW-DINE (939-3463) or visit *www.disneyworld.com*.
- Unlimited access to select recreation opportunities, including golf, guided fishing excursions, water sports, and more. (Restrictions apply, and advance reservations may be required.)
- Admission to Cirque du Soleil's La Nouba show (one admission per person).
- Admission to a Disney Children's Activity Center at a select WDW resort (ages 4–12).
- Admission to select Theme Park tours: Magic Kingdom's Family Magic Tour, The Magic Behind Our Steam Trains, and Keys to the Kingdom; Epcot's Behind the Seeds and The Undiscovered Future World; and Animal Kingdom's Backstage Tales. (See pages 232–234 for details.)

- Special dining experiences, including meals with Disney characters, "Signature" dining experiences, and dinner shows.
- One refillable soft drink mug per person (good at WDW-owned-and operated resorts for the length of your stay).

Magic Your Way Platinum Package: An upgrade from the Premium Package, the Platinum version features a stay at a deluxe Walt Disney World resort, plus options such as spa treatments and high-end dining opportunities.

Disney Dining Plan

The Disney Dining Plan lets guests pre-pay for meals before they arrive at Walt Disney World. While convenient for some, it's not necessarily a money-saver. For Dining Plan options, visit *disneyworld.com.* Consider how much your party can consume before selecting a plan, as some include much more sustenance than others. Here's a summary of the basic table-service plan (details subject to change):

Each day of the plan—which starts at about $64 a day for adults ($23 for kids) and is offered as part of the Magic Your Way Plus Dining package—includes:

- One table-service meal, including entrée, dessert (lunch or dinner), and soft drink.
- One quick-service meal, including entrée, dessert, and non-alcoholic beverage.
- One snack, such as ice cream, popcorn, or a medium soft drink at select quick-service spots or snack carts.
- The option of exchanging two table-service meals for one meal at a high-end "Signature" restaurant or a dinner show, such as the Hoop-Dee-Doo Musical Revue.

To sum up: Say your family of four purchases a five-night package. Together you're entitled to 20 quick-service meals, 20 table-service meals, and 20 snacks. And you are free to use them in any way you want. That is, if you want to skip a meal one day or have five meals in a single day, by all means go for it. (Remember there is a finite number of meals allotted.) Usage can be tracked at Guest Relations in the parks and WDW resorts. Just present a MagicBand (see page 24) or room key card. Taxes are included, gratuities are not. Be sure to tip your servers. Hold on to your receipts, as they show your remaining meal balance.

In addition to traditional table-service meals, certain "character dining" experiences are available to Dining Plan participants, as are some Disney Springs locations. A Quick-Service Only Dining Plan is offered, too. Note that kids ages 3 to 9 must order from the children's menu where available.

To find out which restaurants are participating, turn to our *Good Meals, Great Times* chapter. For updates, call 407-939-3463 or go to *www.disneyworld.com.*

Dining Plans must be purchased at the same time a WDW resort stay is booked. *If you get any Dining Plan (with the exception of the Quick-Service Only option), you must make reservations for table-service restaurants.* Do so as far ahead as possible—180 days.

All About Theme Park Tickets

PHOTO BY JILL SAFRO

Buying a park ticket can be very simple. Do you plan on visiting one park on one day? Just pick up a One-Day Base Ticket. Perhaps you are a frequent visitor and expect to pass through theme park gates dozens of times over the next year. In that case, an Annual Pass is what you're looking for. Now, if your park-going plans lie somewhere in between (and most do), you will have to be a little more strategic.

When it comes to selecting the perfect type of admission ticket, it pays to do some homework. Study the options, evaluate your priorities, and make no hasty decisions. For starters, there are several major factors to consider: (1) total number of days you would like to visit theme parks, (2) to park-hop or not to park-hop, and (3) whether you want to pre-pay (and save some time) for "extras" such as admission to the water parks, the Memory Maker photo package, etc. The following information was correct at press time and is meant to help you make wise choices. Keep in

HOT TIP!

Note that, with the exception of Annual Passes, *all tickets expire within 14 days of first use.* Be sure to keep track of the date activated and remaining days. For help, visit a park guest relations or ticket window or a resort concierge counter.

mind that ticket prices are likely to rise in 2017—they always do. Call 407-824-4321 or visit *www.disneyworld.com* for updates.

Magic Your Way Tickets

Base Tickets: Available for 1 to 10 days. Valid for admission to one park per day—the Magic Kingdom (one-day Magic Kingdom base tickets are priced higher than the other parks), Epcot, Disney's Hollywood Studios, or Disney's Animal Kingdom. (The base ticket does not allow for park-hopping.) Unused days expire 14 days after the ticket is activated, which is the first day a park is visited. (For "peak" pricing, see page 26.) The ticket is called a base ticket because, with the exception of Annual Passes, all other tickets begin as such. Guests may customize base tickets to fit their own vacation needs. Note that you can't use a second day's admission to enter a second park on the same day you visited another park. To do that, you must purchase the Park Hopper Option for the Magic Your Way pass.

DID YOU KNOW?

The phrase "E-ticket ride" is American slang for "the ultimate in thrills." It comes from the early days of Disney parks, back when tickets were used for each attraction. E-tickets were reserved for the most elaborate and exciting rides of all.

Park Hopper Option: This option lets guests visit more than one theme park on a single day. The privilege extends through the length of the ticket. It costs about $40 to add it to a one-day Magic Kingdom base ticket and about $50 to add to a one-day base ticket for all other parks; about $55 for two- and three-day tickets to all parks; and about $69 for all other base tickets (regardless of the number of days on the ticket). We recommend checking operating hours for your planned visit. Hopping is a worthwhile option only if the parks are open late.

HOT TIP!

Want to maximize your theme-park-ticket dollar? Determine how many days you plan to visit the theme parks during your visit and get a multi-day pass for the exact number. It will save on your per-day price—and you won't waste any days. Should you run out of days, you can upgrade your ticket within 14 days of first use.

Water Park Fun & More Option: This option covers entry to Blizzard Beach and Typhoon Lagoon water parks, Disney's sports complex, miniature golf, or a round of golf at Disney's Oak Trail golf course. For about $64, you'll get between two and ten visits to these spots. The number of visits depends on the number of days on your base ticket—the more days, the more visits.

Expiration: Unused days on multi-day base tickets expire 14 days after the first day is used. The No Expire option was discontinued in February 2015; tickets purchased prior to then will be honored at the parks, provided they have the No Expire option. Tickets bought before 2005 are valid, too—they pre-date the No Expire option.

Theme Park Platinum Annual Pass: This pass offers admission to the four theme parks for a year with no block-out dates. It can be used in more than one park on the same day (also known as park-hopping), and includes use of Disney transportation, as well as free parking at the theme parks, and a year's worth of PhotoPass downloads. Annual passes can be purchased at the entrance to any of the theme parks (they can be renewed there or by mail). A valid, government-issued photo ID must be presented for purchase by adults and may be required for future use of the pass. Passes are non-transferable. At press time, the cost was about $649 for adults and kids over age 3.

Annual Pass-bearers qualify for many Disney World discounts and benefits, such as reduced rates at select Disney resorts at certain times of year. A newsletter called the *Mickey Monitor* keeps passholders up to date regarding discount offers. The pass expires one year after it is first used. A discounted renewal rate applies if the pass is renewed before expiration. (The old pass must be presented in order to receive the discounted renewal rate.) A pass may be renewed by mail, online, or at any Disney theme park.

Platinum Plus Annual Pass: This pass has all the Theme Park Annual Pass offers and more—namely, admission to both water parks, ESPN Wide World of Sports complex (non-premium events only), a year's worth of PhotoPass downloads, plus a round of golf at the Oak Trail golf course. Platinum Plus Annual Passholders are eligible for the same discounts and benefits as Theme Park Annual Passholders. Platinum Plus

Extra Magic Hours

How'd you like to visit a Disney theme park before it opens to the public? Or stick around for hours after it's officially closed for the day—at no extra cost? Well, if you're a guest staying at a Walt Disney World-owned-and-operated resort, the Swan, Dolphin, or Shades of Green (a WDW resort for members of the military), you can. It is one of the major perks that comes with staying on Disney property.

Here's how it works: One park opens its doors an hour early or stays open two hours late on any given day. Basically, the park becomes something of a members-only private playground for Walt Disney World resort guests. So, provided that you have a WDW resort ID and valid admission media, you're in! No secret password necessary. Keep in mind that you will need park-hopping privileges if you plan to visit a park other than the one offering extra hours on any given day. If you don't plan to park-hop, you must visit the theme park offering Extra Magic Hours on that particular day. When a park opens early in the morning, guests are admitted starting one hour prior to the official opening time. Transportation to the park starts about 30 minutes before that. Be sure to have your MagicBand or WDW resort ID handy. Flash it and you'll be allowed to visit some (but not all) attractions and mingle with Disney characters.

In our opinion, Extra Magic Hours is the single-most valuable perk available to Walt Disney World Resort hotel guests.

Details about Extra Magic Hours are subject to change. Visit www.disneyworld.com for updates and the schedule for your planned visit.

Annual Passes can be purchased at the entrance to any of the four theme parks (they can be renewed there or by mail). A photo ID must be presented for purchase by adults and may be required for future use. Passes are non-transferable and they expire one year after first use. The cost is about $829 for adults and kids (over age 3).

Premier Annual Pass: This pass provides admission to all Disney theme parks and water parks in the U.S.A. (including Disneyland Park and Disney California Adventure) for one year. It also includes a year's worth of PhotoPass downloads, admission to the ESPN Wide World of Sports complex (non-premium events only) and the Oak Trail golf course. Unlimited park-hopping and parking are included, as are the same discounts offered with Disney's other annual passes (select merchandise, food, and resort discounts).

The Premier Pass costs about $1,439, plus tax. Guests already bearing Walt Disney World or Disneyland Resort Annual Passes may upgrade to the Premier Pass at any time. For details, visit *www.disneyparks.com/Premier*, or call 407-824-4321.

entitles bearers to discounts on everything from dinner shows to room rates.

Note: Only one person per party needs to have an Annual Pass to net a discount on a WDW resort (when available). This option is great for travelers with flexible schedules, as the discounts do vary, and they are often announced shortly before going into effect.

Tickets with Unused Days: Prior to 2005, WDW tickets never expired. That is no longer the case. Any days remaining on a multi-day admission ticket now expire 14 days after the ticket is first activated (with the obvious exception of Annual Passes).

Attractions Outside the Theme Parks: Typhoon Lagoon and Blizzard Beach prices start at about $60 for one day and about $115 for an annual pass for adults; $54 for one day and about $115 for an annual pass for kids (ages 3 to 9). ESPN Wide World of Sports complex runs about $18 for adults, about $13 for kids (general admission). Cirque du Soleil's La Nouba is about $85–$133 for adults, $69–$109 for kids. All prices are apt to rise in 2017.

> **HOT TIP!**
>
> If your child "outgrows" his or her park ticket (by turning 10), you can upgrade the ticket at any of the theme parks.

Deciding Factors

Choosing the Right Ticket: Before you make a decision, it helps to map out your vacation. Remember, all tickets start as Base Tickets. They are a bare-bones, admission-to-one-theme-park-at-a-time deal. That's perfect for many folks—especially those planning a relatively short stay. Still, the first step for every potential guest is to decide just how many days they plan to spend in the theme parks. Keep in mind that as days are added, the average price per day goes down. Unused days expire 14 days after the ticket is activated. Once the length of stay is determined, it's time to customize the ticket. (If the total number of days is undetermined, err on the side of caution—unused days can't be refunded, but you can add extra days up to 14 days after the ticket is first used.) Do you want to park-hop? Add about $69. Want to add the Water Park Fun & More package? That's about $64.

If you are planning a longer visit, or two trips within a year, we recommend a multi-day Park Hopper or an Annual Pass. In addition to unlimited admission to the parks, an Annual Pass

MyMagic+

"MyMagic+" is the all-encompassing moniker attached to all vacation-planning tools managed via the My Disney Experience planning page or smartphone app. It links cards and MagicBands (wristbands that are connected to various vacation features) and includes the Fastpass+ attraction reservation system (see page 25).

My Disney Experience: An app that can be downloaded for free and is compatible with most Android and Apple iOS smartphones and tablets, My Disney Experience is a tool for reserving tables at WDW restaurants and dinner shows; booking, revising, and keeping track of Fastpass+ assignments at theme park shows and

> **HOT TIP!**
>
> To expedite your party's entrance experience, make sure each member is holding his or her own ticket or wearing their MagicBand before getting in line.

attractions; viewing wait times; and more. For those guests without smartphones or tablets, *www.MyDisneyExperience.com* can be accessed by personal computer. It allows for the same advance planning. The service is free and requires guests to create an account (to which all members of the traveling party should be linked). Note that children under age 13 are not permitted to have live, individual accounts. Instead, parents create and manage a profile for each child (kids' profiles are attached to their parents'). There is a bit of a learning curve, so get started as soon as you can.

After linking a WDW resort reservation or vacation package and tickets to your account, guests may link MagicBands, make and monitor WDW dining reservations, book and track Fastpass+ times, and load the Memory Maker Photo Package (see page 27). It is important to link all accounts in your traveling party (parties larger than 10 should call 407-939-5277).

All guests may use this service, whether they stay on WDW property or not, provided they can access the website or utilize the app.

MagicBands: This accessory is something of a technological wonder—it can serve as a resort room key and be loaded with theme park and water park admission tickets. Guests can also use it to make purchases throughout Walt Disney World (provided the MagicBand is backed up with a credit card and a personal PIN code has been selected); use it for Disney's PhotoPass (see page 133), Fastpass+ (in conjunction with *MyDisneyExperience.com* or the associated app); and more. To use it to make a purchase in a shop or restaurant, just tap the not-so-hidden Mickey on the band to the Mickey head on the console.

HOT TIP!
Adults should always carry a government-issued photo ID. You'll need it should you have any issues with your MagicBand and to purchase alcohol while at WDW.

MagicBands are complimentary for guests at Disney owned-and-operated resorts. The standard version comes in gray but may be customized in one of 8 different colors. (We recommend using different colors for each member of a party.) Bands customized 10 or more days ahead of arrival can be sent to your home. Bands ordered within 6 to 9 days will be sent to your Walt Disney World resort. (Bands picked up at a resort may be linked with My Disney Experience accounts at the resort's front desk or by smartphone or tablet.) When your bands arrive in the mail, link them to your party's My Disney Experience accounts. Be sure to link each band to the right account! (If you just need the band as a resort key, there's no need to link.) Note that MagicBands cannot be customized within 5 days of arrival and can't shipped to all countries.

MagicBands are included with Walt Disney

HOT TIP!
We recommend wearing the MagicBand on your dominant hand. That should make it easier to align it with Mickey heads when endeavoring to make a purchase or open a resort room door.

How Do You Book a Room? Let Us Count the Ways

You're ready to reserve a room at a resort on Walt Disney World property. How nice for you! But before you dial 407-W-DISNEY (934-7639) or a travel agent, know this: There are three different ways to book your WDW stay. It's best to know what you want in advance. It will save you time and spare confusion while on the phone. Here's the scoop:

- Room-Only Reservation—What you hear is what you get: a hotel room only. It requires an advance deposit and allows you to cancel up to 5 days prior to the start of the reservation (penalty-free). It comes with a 12-digit confirmation number.

- Walt Disney Travel Company Basic Plan—A package that includes room, luggage tags, and a round of mini-golf for the entire party. Must be paid in full 30 days before check-in and must be canceled at least 31 days prior to check-in to avoid a penalty. (The confirmation number has 8 digits.) We recommend adding trip insurance to the package (at an additional cost), just in case.

- Magic Your Way Base Package—Includes room and theme park tickets. It may be customized in many ways, such as adding the Disney Dining Plan, Water Park admission, and more (see page 21). Must be paid in full 30 days before check-in and must be canceled at least 31 days prior to check-in (any later and there will be hefty penalties). Once reserved, expect to get an 8-digit confirmation number.

Save Time in Line with Fastpass+

Walt Disney World's Fastpass+ is a service that was designed to allow guests to bypass the traditional standby line and enjoy a number of theme park shows and attractions with less of a wait. It's a virtual queue—one you join by visiting "My Disney Experience" via the Internet (with a computer, tablet, or smartphone). Once you've established an account, you can link your ticket (and those in your party) and access Fastpass+ to book times to visit attractions during a pending visit to the park.

To WDW veterans, the term Fastpass conjures happy memories of bypassing lines after securing assignments while visiting the parks. That concept is still the same, but the procedure has changed quite a bit. In fact, we wish they had called the new system something other than Fastpass+, because it really is a bold departure from the original. Think of Fastpass+ as an *advance reservation system*—one that is completely free to all guests bearing a valid park ticket.

The most popular WDW attractions and shows (aka E-Ticket experiences), like the hottest restaurants in town, are often very crowded, with long waits and no guarantee you'll get in. By using Fastpass+, you can reserve a time to enjoy at least one popular ride (and several other attractions) during each day of your WDW visit. In most cases, you won't walk right in, but you will have an expedited wait time and guaranteed admission to some crowd-pleasers such as Toy Story Midway Mania!, Soarin' Around the World, Expedition Everest, or Enchanted Tales with Belle. Ideally, Fastpass+ aims to spread guests throughout the parks, making traditionally congested areas less so. For folks who prefer to do things on the fly or who find the new system a bit daunting or difficult to navigate, traditional standby lines will always be available. That said, tech-savvy, detail-minded guests may relax a bit, knowing each day of their vacation is pre-planned.

Begin by paying a visit to My Disney Experience via the Internet or smartphone app. Set up an account and link it with your park ticket. Then, if it's within 30 days of your visit (60 if you are staying in a WDW–owned-and-operated resort or the Swan or Dolphin), you can start booking Fastpass+ assignments. When the one-hour Fastpass+ window kicks in, go to the attraction and touch your MagicBand or ticket card to the Fastpass+ redemption console, wait for the light, and head inside.

We recommend using Fastpass+ assignments for your must-sees. We've placed our Fastpass+ symbol (FP+) beside the listing for all shows and attractions that were included at press time. However, since experiences may be added or dropped, visit *www.mydisneyexperience.com* for updates. And remember, all WDW attractions continue to offer the option of standing in a traditional queue. Fastpass+ is just a bonus option for folks who like to plan ahead. By using it, we have gleaned the following (specifics may change, as the program was still in a fine-tuning phase as this book went to press):

• To make advance Fastpass+ reservations, you must have access to the Internet.

• It's possible to reserve a same-day Fastpass+ assignment at a park kiosk, but using them can be time-consuming, and the chances of getting convenient, same-day access to the most popular attractions are slim. Get there early!

• Fastpass+ lets you experience at least 3 attractions or shows per day without waiting in the (usually) longer standby line. You may be able to get more same-day assignments via the app and at in-park kiosks once the time for your first one has been used or the time has expired (pending availability).

• Fastpass+ allows for park-hopping after the first Fastpass+ assignment has been used or expired. Although you are able to book 3 Fastpass+ assignments in one park, you can make changes after you use your first Fastpass+ assignment of the day (via *mydisneyexperience.com* or an in-park kiosk) and "hop" to another park to use your remaining 2 Fastpass+ assignments. Additional Fastpasses can be booked at in-park kiosks.

• Fastpass+ times are linked to your MagicBand (see page 24) or park ticket card and can be viewed, modified, or canceled via smartphone, tablet, computer, or in-park Fastpass+ kiosk. To use a Fastpass+ assignment, you'll need to touch a MagicBand or ticket card to a Fastpass+ reader device at the attraction.

• If you want to ride a major attraction twice, we recommend getting a Fastpass+ assignment and going to your attraction as soon as the park opens for your first ride. You can ride again when your Fastpass+ window kicks in.

• Fastpass+ assignments are non-transferable.

• Coordinating Fastpass+ assignments for large groups is possible, but it can be challenging.

• Write the assignment times on paper if you don't have a smartphone or in case your smartphone battery dies. You can check times at a park kiosk, but there is often a wait to do so.

• Parades, fireworks, and select character meet-and-greets may be included in the Fastpass+ system.

• You don't have to use Fastpass+ to have fun in the parks. All shows and attractions continue to offer traditional standby lines.

PEAK TICKET PRICES†

		1-Day	2-Day	3-Day	4-Day	5-Day	6-Day	7-Day	8-Day	9-Day	10-Day
Base Ticket*	**Ages 10 & UP**	$114–$124	$202 ($101.00/ day)	$290 ($96.66/ day)	$325 ($81.25/ day)	$340 ($68.00/ day)	$355 ($59.16/ day)	$370 ($52.85/ day)	$380 ($47.50/ day)	$390 ($43.33/ day)	$400 ($40.00/ day)
	Ages 3–9	$108–$118	$190 ($95.00/ day)	$272 ($90.66/ day)	$305 ($76.25/ day)	$320 ($64.00/ day)	$335 ($55.83/ day)	$350 ($50.00/ day)	$360 ($45.00/ day)	$370 ($41.11/ day)	$380 ($38.00/ day)
ADD: Park Hopper**		$40–$50	$55	$55	$69	$69	$69	$69	$69	$69	$69
ADD: Water Park Fun & More**		$64–$74 2 visits	$64 2 visits	$64 3 visits	$64 4 visits	$64 5 visits	$64 6 visits	$64 7 visits	$64 8 visits	$64 9 visits	$64 10 visits
ADD: Memory Maker****		$149/ $169	$149/ $169	$149/ $169	$149/ $169	$149/ $169	$149/ $169	$149/ $169	$149/ $169	$149/ $169	$149/ $169

† Prices are lower during non-peak times of year. For specifics, visit *www.disneyworld.com.* Note that prices listed here do not include tax.

* Base Ticket admits guest to one theme park each day of use. Park choices are Magic Kingdom, Epcot, Disney's Hollywood Studios, and Disney's Animal Kingdom.

** Park Hopper option entitles guest to visit more than one theme park on each day of use.

*** Water Park Fun & More option entitles guest to a specified number of visits to a choice of entertainment and recreation venues. Choices include Disney's Blizzard Beach water park, Disney's Typhoon Lagoon water park, and ESPN Wide World of Sports complex.

**** Guests who pre-pay for Disney's Memory Maker photo package pay the first price; those who make the purchase within 30 days of their WDW visit pay the second price. The Memory Maker Photo package is available to all guests. For details, see page 27.

World hotel reservation, but specialty versions may be purchased in the parks. Non-WDW-resort guests may also purchase MagicBands at any WDW theme park.

The MagicBand is waterproof (but does not float), hypoallergenic, and can be adjusted to fit most wrists. If a MagicBand is lost it can be disabled via the My Disney Experience app (and the website) or with the help of a cast member. MagicBands are non-transferable. No personal information is stored on the band—it only links to entitlements that were pre-purchased. Remember, you will need to use a PIN code to pay for things with your MagicBand.

Fastpass+: WDW's reservation system for most attractions, shows, and character meet-and-greets at its four theme parks is a free service, available to guests with valid theme park tickets. It may be accessed up to 30 days in advance via the My Disney Experience app or website. Guests with a reservation at a Disney-owned-and-operated resort may book Fastpass+ assignments up to 60 days prior to checking in. It's possible to make same-day Fastpass+ reservations, too—by using the aforementioned ways and by visiting a Fastpass+ kiosk in any of the WDW theme parks. Note that it is not possible to get Fastpass+ assignments at the attractions themselves. For details on Fastpass+, turn to page 25.

Memory Maker Photo Package: Memory Maker includes all photos taken in the parks, including those snapped on select attractions and character meal locations for your length of stay. You can review the photos at sites in the park or when you get home via the Web. It is possible to customize photos with banners and Disney art, too. At press time, the same-day price was about $169; about $149 if pre-ordered. (We think this is one of Walt Disney World's better values.) A one-day package is available for $59. Note that guests can still buy and customize photos via the traditional PhotoPass system (see page 133).

Purchasing Tickets

Admission tickets are sold at park entrances, WDW resorts, Four Seasons, the resorts on Hotel Plaza Boulevard, Orlando International Airport, the Transportation and Ticket Center (TTC), and Disney Springs Guest Relations. Cash, traveler's checks, American Express, Visa, MasterCard, Diner's Club, Discover, JCB Card, Disney gift cards, and Disney Dollars are accepted. Not all tickets are available at each location, so call 407-934-7639 to confirm.

We recommend buying tickets in advance (it can save time when you arrive at the parks) from a travel agent, or in one of these ways:

Tickets by Phone: All tickets can be purchased by phone; call 407-W-DISNEY (934-7639). Allow 15 days for standard delivery; $15 for express delivery (allow 7 days); and $25 for international delivery (allow 12 days). There is no fee for pickup at a WDW Will Call window.

Tickets Online: Tickets can be bought through *www.disneyworld.com*. The fees for delivery are the same as those listed above.

Tickets at a Disney Store: Select multi-day theme park tickets are available for purchase at any local Disney Store.

Tickets by Mail (3- to 7-day Magic Your Way tickets only): Allow at least three to four weeks for processing, and include a return address. Send a money order (for amount due, plus $4 for handling), payable to Walt Disney World Company, to: Walt Disney World, Box 10140, Lake Buena Vista, FL 32830-0030. Attention: Ticket Mail Order.

Ticket Tag System

As a means of enforcing the non-transferability aspect of all Walt Disney World tickets, Disney has devised a system to trace each ticket to its rightful owner. The procedure is as follows: Touch your MagicBand or ticket to the brass orb at any park entrance. While the machine is crunching the data encrypted on your MagicBand or ticket, gently press the tip of your forefinger onto the glowing gizmo perched beside the orb. Remove your finger and presto! Your MagicBand or ticket will link to your forefinger, giving you the bright green light to enter. Grown-ups have to do this every time they use the ticket. Remember to use the same finger every time you enter a park. Kids ages 10 and under are spared the hassle. (It's a good idea to wash your hands after this process.)

Money-Saving Tips

A Walt Disney World vacation can be an exceptionally expensive undertaking, but it is possible to keep costs down a bit. When budgeting for your trip, keep in mind that WDW prices are comparable to those in a big city. Here are a few tips to help you conserve cash.

Lodging

- When it comes to saving money on hotel accommodations, timing is truly the key. While off-season dates tend to vary, depending on the hotel, value season for most Walt Disney World resorts generally means January through mid-February, late August through late September, and early November through late December. Weeknights are generally less expensive than weekend nights year-round.

- The Swan and Dolphin resorts often have rate specials when other WDW resorts have peak rates. Check *www.swandolphin.com*.

- Consider how much time you will actually spend at your hotel, and don't pay for a place with perks you won't have time to enjoy. Hotels often allow kids to stay free in parents' rooms, but the cutoff age varies.

- When considering the cost-effectiveness of off-property lodging, factor in the time, money, and inconvenience of commuting to and from attractions.

- Realize, too, that the advantages of staying on-property (tops among them the Extra Magic Hours perk, Disney's Magical Express, and access to WDW's transportation system) also apply to those staying in the least expensive rooms in Disney's hotels. The most important addresses for budget-watching Disney fans, the All-Star and Pop Century resorts, offer the lowest rates on Disney property. Rooms at Caribbean Beach, Port Orleans French Quarter and Riverside, Disney's Art of Animation, and Coronado Springs are slightly higher priced. Also, note that the only difference between the least and most expensive rooms in a hotel is often the view. Consider how often you'll be looking out that window.

- The resorts on Hotel Plaza Boulevard, located next to Disney Springs, offer rooms starting at about $130 per night. (See page 106.)

Food

- Visit costlier establishments at lunchtime (if you so desire) rather than at dinner; entrées often cost a bit less at the midday meal.

- Club Level accommodations can absorb the cost of some meals, snacks, and cocktails—the more folks in the room, the better the value.

- Carry snacks and sandwich fixings and enjoy them picnic style wherever possible.

- Consider lodging with kitchen facilities. The savings on food may be more than the extra accommodations expense. Note that small refrigerators are available in all guestrooms at Disney-owned-and-operated resorts (no charge).

- Staying on Disney property? We highly recommend purchasing a souvenir RapidFill mug. It's good for unlimited soft-drink refills (including coffee, tea, lemonade, and more) at all WDW-owned-and-operated resorts (see page 270 for details).

- Pack kid-friendly snacks, such as fruit, cereal, or crackers. (Snack stands are plentiful, but not always handy or cost-efficient.)

- Don't plan on eating three big table-service meals a day. It gets expensive—and filling!

- Save money by having groceries delivered to your resort. Items such as bottled water, snacks, fruit, and breakfast bars can be enjoyed in the room or out of a backpack throughout the day. Our go-to for this type of service is *gardengrocer.com*. (This company is authorized to deliver to WDW, but is not affiliated with the Walt Disney Company.)

HOT TIP!

To save money on Walt Disney World golf, merchandise, food, behind-the-scenes tours and more, use the coupons at the back of this book!

Satisfying Substitutes

Fewer frills rarely mean less fun at Walt Disney World. Here are money-saving alternatives to two of Disney's higher-priced treats.

If you'd rather not spring for admission to Disney Springs West Side venues, consider taking a trip to the BoardWalk resort. Among other diversions, you will find Jellyrolls (a sing-along piano bar with a cover of about $12), Atlantic Dance Hall (a nightclub with no cover charge), and ESPN Club (a cover-free sports bar). A short walk will take you to the Swan hotel, home to the karaoke-friendly Kimonos Lounge.

If the Grand Floridian ($574–$1,072 a night) doesn't quite fit into your budget, consider staying in a Mansion room at Port Orleans Riverside ($189–$342 a night). Southern hospitality replaces Victorian splendor, and though the guestrooms aren't quite as spacious, the air of sophistication makes for a most satisfying stay. And for a sweet deal on a suite, consider the vibrant resort known as Disney's Art of Animation.

Discounts

- Theme Park Annual and Premium Annual Passholders receive so many discounts on meals, dinner shows, tours, room rates, and more that it may be worth purchasing an Annual Pass for longer visits or if you plan to take more than one trip within a year.

- WDW resorts that offer Annual Passholder discounts vary from month to month, and discounted rooms aren't always available for booking very far in advance. It's best to be flexible with travel dates. Annual Passholders may net deals on recreational opportunities, too. For details, call 407-W-DISNEY (939-7639). Passholders can save 20 percent at many WDW eateries by joining the Tables in Wonderland program (for a fee). For details, call 407-WDW-DINE (939-3463).

- Discounts on Disney World resort rates and theme park tickets are available to Florida residents, and seasonal promotions occur. Call 407-W-DISNEY (939-7639) for specifics.

- The Swan, as well as some off-property hotels, offers discounts to seniors and the Automobile Association of America (AAA) or AARP members as well. Some AAA branches provide discounts on park passes, as well as discounts on rooms, and more. Check with your local AAA branch for additional information.

HOT TIP!
Bring inexpensive, light rain gear from home. You'll need it—especially in the stormy months of summer.

HOT TIP!
It may be cheaper to get a family suite or spread out over two rooms in a "value" or "moderate" resort than to have everyone stay in one room at "deluxe" Disney digs.

- Web-based *travelocity.com* offers a variety of Disney vacation packages. Vacation Outlet sometimes offers packages at a reduced rate; visit *www.vacationoutlet.com*, or call 800-825-3633 for details.

- To request your free Orlando Magicard, visit *www.orlandoinfo.com/magicard*. Cardholders may net discounts at area hotels, restaurants, shops, and more.

- Disney Visa® Cardmembers who pay with their Disney Visa Card enjoy savings on merchandise, dining, and guided tours. Cardmembers can use the Disney Visa card wherever Visa is accepted. Details are subject to change. For specifics, visit *DisneyRewards.com* or *DisneyDebit.com*.

- Okay, so it's not exactly a discount, but we think that multi-day tickets are worth their weight in gold. The more days you purchase, the lower the cost is per day. (Just don't over-purchase days—unused days expire 14 days after a ticket is activated. Extra days can be added as needed.)

- Visit *disneyworld.disney.go.com/special-offers/* to see if any discounts apply for your WDW visit.

- For discounts on dozens of WDW restaurant, tours, recreational experiences, and more, see the coupons after page 356 of this book.

Making a Budget

A stay at Disney's kingdom need not cost a king's ransom (though it easily can). In fact, with a well-planned budget, money at Disney World can stretch relatively far.

Vacation expenses tend to fall into five major categories: (1) transportation (which may include any combination of costs for airfare, airport transfers, train tickets, car rental, gas, parking, and taxi service); (2) lodging; (3) theme park tickets; (4) meals; and (5) miscellaneous (recreational activities, cover charges, tips, souvenirs, postcards, forgotten items, and home expenses such as pet boarding, etc.).

When planning your budget, first consider what level of service suits your needs. Some people prefer to spend fewer days at Disney but stay at a deluxe hotel or dine at pricier restaurants, while others would rather make their money cover a longer vacation that includes a value-priced resort and less-expensive meals. The choice is up to you. Once you've established your spending priorities, determine your price limit. Then make sure you don't exceed it when approximating your expenses—without a ballpark figure to work around, it's easy to get carried away.

Sample Budget

The following is an example of a low- to moderately priced budget designed for a family of four during "peak" season (two adults and two kids planning to stay at WDW for five nights and six days). Totals do not include tax.

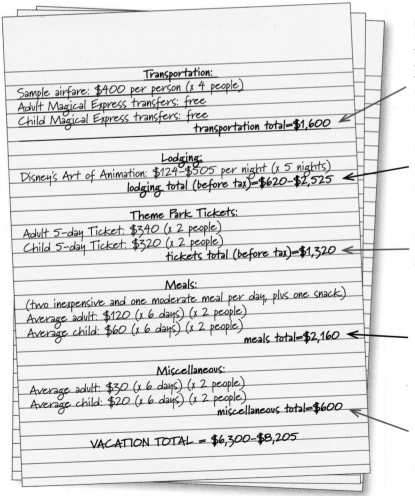

Transportation:
Sample airfare: $400 per person (x 4 people)
Adult Magical Express transfers: free
Child Magical Express transfers: free
transportation total=$1,600

Lodging:
Disney's Art of Animation: $124-$505 per night (x 5 nights)
lodging total (before tax)=$620-$2,525

Theme Park Tickets:
Adult 5-day Ticket: $340 (x 2 people)
Child 5-day Ticket: $320 (x 2 people)
tickets total (before tax)=$1,320

Meals:
(two inexpensive and one moderate meal per day, plus one snack)
Average adult: $120 (x 6 days) (x 2 people)
Average child: $60 (x 6 days) (x 2 people)
meals total=$2,160

Miscellaneous:
Average adult: $30 (x 6 days) (x 2 people)
Average child: $20 (x 6 days) (x 2 people)
miscellaneous total=$600

VACATION TOTAL = $6,300-$8,205

Magical Express service is cost-efficient (hey, it's free!), but it can be time-consuming. If you'd like to get from point A to B quickly (and quietly), take a towncar or taxi.

Extend your vacation by splitting nights between a more and less expensive resort (end with the fancier one).

Unsure of how many days you'll ultimately spend in the parks? Know that extra days may be added to any ticket within 14 days after it is activated.

Even if you stick to fast food, expect to spend at least $45 (adult) and $25 (child) per day.

Careful packing should cut down on miscellaneous expenses, which often include forgotten toiletries like toothpaste or the all-important sunscreen.

Planning Your Itinerary

A TIMELINE

First Things First

• Make hotel and transportation arrangements as far ahead as possible. Note that many WDW hotels fill up more than six months ahead. Call 407-W-DISNEY (934-7639) to book a room; your confirmation should arrive within two weeks. Log it and other pertinent information in your Birnbaum Trip Tracker that starts on page 344.

• Check park hours for your planned visit. (Hours are available up to 7 months ahead; call 407-824-4321, or visit *www.disneyworld.com*.) Closing times will be particularly helpful when making evening plans. Create a day-by-day schedule, deciding which area of WDW to visit on each day of your trip. Use the Trip Tracker at the end of this book.

6 Months

• Choose dining spots from those listed in the *Good Meals, Great Times* chapter. Call 407-WDW-DINE (939-3463), visit *www.disneyworld.com/dine*, or use the My Disney Experience mobile app (which can be downloaded for free) to make restaurant reservations. Guests with a confirmed reservation at a WDW-owned-and-operated resort may call 180 days before scheduled check-in date and book dining reservations for up to 10 days of their planned stay.

• Popular meals such as those at Cinderella's Royal Table, Le Cellier, and Be Our Guest Restaurant (dinner) should be booked 180 days ahead. Call 407-WDW-DINE (939-3463) and have a credit card handy.

• Dinner-show reservations may be secured up to 180 days in advance. Consult page 300 for details, and call 407-WDW-DINE (939-3463) for reservations.

• Unless you have a package that includes park admission, it's time to order tickets. Refer to pages 21–24 for details, and call 407-824-4321; tickets should arrive within four weeks. You may save money by purchasing select tickets in advance.

• Specialty cruises (see page 231) may be booked by calling 407-WDW-PLAY (939-7529).

• If you have purchased a Magic Your Way Premium or Platinum package and plan to play golf, or will be staying at a WDW resort or a resort on Hotel Plaza Boulevard, you may book a tee time on one of WDW's golf courses now (see pages 236–237 for details on the courses). Golf lessons may also be reserved at this time. Call 407-WDW-GOLF (939-4653) for reservations. Those not staying on WDW property may make reservations 60 days ahead.

• Fishing excursions (see page 239) may be booked by calling 407-WDW-BASS (939–2277).

• Tennis lessons may be reserved by calling 321-228-1146. Turn to page 237 for information.

• Parasailing and waterskiing excursions (for details, see pages 238–239) may be booked by calling 407-WDW-PLAY (939-7529) or 407-939-0754 or by visiting *www.sammyduvall.com*.

• Trail-ride reservations may be made up to 180 days in advance. Call 407-WDW-PLAY (939-7529).

• If you'd like to add a behind-the-scenes tour to your vacation, now is the time to make a reservation.

3 Months

• Double-check park hours for your stay, as they may have changed. Take note of Extra Magic Hours (extended park hours for guests registered at a Walt Disney World-owned-and-operated resort).

60 Days

• If you have valid park tickets linked to a reservation at a participating WDW resort, you may book Fastpass+ assignments up to 60 days ahead (for up to 10 days) of your visit to the parks, via the My Disney Experience website or app.

30 Days

• If you have valid park tickets but aren't staying in a WDW resort, you may book Fastpass+ up to 30 days ahead.

10 Days

• Airline confirmation and travel-package vouchers should have arrived by now.

• Will you be staying at a WDW-owned-and-operated resort? If so, check in online! (See page 66.)

• If you haven't already customized your MagicBand color, today is the last day to do it and have it shipped to your home. If customized between 9 and 5 days before arrival, your band will be sent to your WDW resort.

1 Week

• Reconfirm all reservations. Finalize your schedule, including all confirmation numbers and Fastpass+ times.

Step-By-Step

SAMPLE SCHEDULES

Many visitors have a deep desire to cover each and every inch of Walt Disney World in the span of a few short days. While we hesitate to discourage these most ambitious of travelers, we feel the need to enlighten them: Walt Disney World is a staggeringly large place. In fact, it's nearly as big as San Francisco and jam-packed with about as many diversions as you might expect from a city that size. You could spend two full weeks on Walt Disney World property and still not have time to do it all. The theme parks alone require every bit of four days just to see the major attractions.

What's the best strategy for organizing a Walt Disney World visit? Make a list of the parks, attractions, and activities you most want to see and use it to create an itinerary. Don't forget to allow time for swimming, boating, or relaxing on a lakeside swing.

Assuming you've narrowed your "must-do" list to the barely manageable, we recommend a stay of at least four to five days. This allows for a visit to each of the theme parks and some time to enjoy many of the recreational activities at your resort, not to mention relaxing a bit. You are on vacation, after all. Longer stays can include water parks, Disney Springs, a dinner show, and more. When planning your days (which you should do before leaving home), be sure to take into account theme park hours and seasonal temperatures in Central Florida.

The following sample schedules assume that you eat breakfast at your resort (unless otherwise stated) and arrive up to 20 minutes before the official opening time. These schedules, though tirelessly tested and proven successful by Birnbaum's editors, are not carved in stone. Use them as a guide, tailoring the itineraries to suit your family's individual tastes. And use them in conjunction with complimentary theme park Times Guides (available at park entrances).

Note that we have not included specific instructions with regard to Fastpass+ in our sample itineraries. It's not because we don't use the service. In fact, we highly recommend using Fastpass+, even if working it into a daily schedule is an inexact science. Without it, there's always the risk of a long line or missing out on a "must-see." By all means, take advantage of the Fastpass+ opportunity every chance you get—especially first thing in the morning for the ultra popular attractions. Not only might it make you feel like a VIP, but it will free up time in your schedule for things you otherwise might not have gotten to. (If you didn't pre-book Fastpass+, head to an in-park kiosk to see what's available.)

ONE-DAY SCHEDULE

❤ Begin the day with a brisk stroll down Main Street, U.S.A. If you haven't pre-booked Fastpass+ assignments, do so via your smartphone or tablet or stop at an in-park kiosk. Check a park map for kiosk locations. Then head to Splash Mountain and Big Thunder Mountain Railroad. Finish up Adventureland with Pirates of the Caribbean, Jungle Cruise, The Magic Carpets of Aladdin, or Walt Disney's Enchanted Tiki Room.

❤ Access Frontierland via the path near the Enchanted Tiki Room. Be sure to check out the Hall of Presidents in Liberty Square.

❤ Consider lunching at Columbia Harbour House.

❤ If time allows, squeeze in The Haunted Mansion before the Festival of Fantasy parade. Watch the parade and move on to Fantasyland.

❤ See as much of Fantasyland as possible, including Dumbo, It's a Small World, Peter Pan's Flight, Seven Dwarfs Mine Train, and Under the Sea—Journey of The Little Mermaid.

❤ If the timing's right, head to the front of the Castle for a live stage show, or take a relaxing ride on Tomorrowland's PeopleMover.

❤ Haven't seen Tom Sawyer Island, the Haunted Mansion, or the Country Bear Jamboree? Go for it!

❤ If the Main Street Electrical Parade is scheduled to run twice, explore Tomorrowland during the earlier showing. Visit Space Mountain, Buzz Lightyear's Space Ranger Spin, Monsters, Inc. Laugh Floor, and the Tomorrowland Speedway.

❤ View Wishes, an impressive nightly fireworks display, from the middle of Main Street, U.S.A.

❤ Watch the Main Street Electrical Parade from Frontierland. And if there's time, revisit a favorite attraction (guests are usually admitted right up until closing time).

Continued on page 34

Continued on page 34

ONE-DAY SCHEDULE

Continued from page 33

MAGIC KINGDOM MUSTS:

Here's a list of the attractions that put the magic in the Magic Kingdom. Note that these are all Fastpass+ attractions:

- Splash Mountain
- Big Thunder Mountain Railroad
- The Haunted Mansion
- Festival of Fantasy (afternoon parade)
- Pirates of the Caribbean
- Peter Pan's Flight
- It's a Small World
- Space Mountain
- Buzz Lightyear's Space Ranger Spin
- The Many Adventures of Winnie the Pooh
- Seven Dwarfs Mine Train
- Under the Sea—Journey of The Little Mermaid
- The Main Street Electrical Parade
- Wishes (fireworks)

MORE FASTPASS+ ATTRACTIONS:

- *Ariel's Grotto*
- *The Barnstormer*
- *Dumbo the Flying Elephant*
- *Enchanted Tales with Belle*
- *Jungle Cruise*
- *Mad Tea Party*
- *The Magic Carpets of Aladdin*
- *Mickey's PhilharMagic*
- *Monsters, Inc. Laugh Floor*
- *Princess Fairytale Hall*
- *Tomorrowland Speedway*
- *Town Square Theater*

LINE BUSTERS: Even when the park is packed, there

are some attractions with shorter or faster-moving lines. Among them are: Tomorrowland Transit Authority PeopleMover, Walt Disney World Railroad, The Enchanted Tiki Room, Carousel of Progress, Country Bear Jamboree, Mickey's PhilharMagic, It's a Small World, and Tom Sawyer Island.

IF YOU HAVE YOUNG CHILDREN:

- Head directly to Fantasyland (walk right through the Castle if you can) and visit It's a Small World, Peter Pan, The Many Adventures of Winnie the Pooh, Under the Sea—Journey of The Little Mermaid, and Dumbo. Cool off at Casey Jr. Splash 'N' Soak Station.

- Stop for a spin in a teacup or a ride on Prince Charming Carrousel on the way to Frontierland. Sing along with Big Al and the gang at the Country Bear Jamboree.

- Check the schedule for Mickey's Royal Friendship Faire, the Castle stage show.

- Line up for the afternoon parade about 30 minutes early. Or skip the parade, finish up Fantasyland, and take a magic carpet ride in Adventureland. If it's hot (and your tot has swim diapers), head to the tiki statues near Jungle Cruise. They spit water!

- Most little ones enjoy Tom Sawyer Island and the Walt Disney World Railroad, too.

ONE-DAY SCHEDULE

❤ If you haven't booked Fastpass+ assignments, you can do so via your smartphone or tablet and/or a park kiosk. Check a guidemap for locations. Then make a beeline for Future World's Soarin' Around the World and Test Track. Guests with no health issues and no susceptibility to motion sickness *whatsoever* should experience the out-of-this-world adventure known as the "highly intense" Mission: SPACE Orange Team. (Otherwise, ride Mission: SPACE Green Team—the gentler, non-spinning version.) Follow it up with The Seas with Nemo & Friends.

❤ World Showcase generally opens at 11 A.M., but Norway's new Frozen Ever After attraction begins welcoming guests a bit earlier in the morning. Check a Times Guide and arrive as soon as possible. Better yet, book it in advance with Fastpass+.

❤ Stop for lunch at The Land's Sunshine Seasons, The Electric Umbrella, or Coral Reef in The Seas.

❤ After exploring The Land, visit the Imagination pavilion. Be sure to enjoy ImageWorks, a small, high-tech playground. Little kids love it, as well as the "leap frog" fountains outside.

❤ If you're up for some pin trading (or shopping), stop by Pin Central in Innoventions Plaza. (Workers displaying pins are always willing to swap Disney pins.)

❤ Check out Spaceship Earth before heading to Innoventions. If the Universe of Energy is open for business, pay it a visit.

❤ Make your way back to World Showcase by early evening and start your world tour at Canada. Proceed counterclockwise around the lagoon. Don't miss the *Impressions de France* movie in the France pavilion. And take in as much live entertainment as you can—World Showcase has a lot to offer!

❤ After dinner, scope out a spot to watch IllumiNations, the park's nighttime spectacular. (There are excellent viewing locations all around World Showcase Lagoon.) Return to your viewing spot about 30 to 40 minutes before the show.

TIMING TIP: If you have a World Showcase restaurant reservation, allow 30 to 40 minutes to get there from the front gate. Taking a FriendShip water taxi can save some time, but it isn't much faster than brisk walking.

Continued on page 36

Continued from page 35

EPCOT ESSENTIALS:

There is a lot to see and do at Disney's discovery park. Don't leave without investigating these outstanding attractions:

- Soarin' Around the World
- Frozen Ever After
- Test Track
- Spaceship Earth
- Turtle Talk with Crush
- Universe of Energy
- Living with the Land
- IllumiNations—Reflections of Earth
- The Seas with Nemo & Friends
- The American Adventure show
- Mission: SPACE ("non-spinning" version)

FASTPASS+ ATTRACTIONS*:

Group A:
Test Track
Living with the Land
Soarin' Around the World
IllumiNations
Frozen Ever After (in Norway)

Group B:
Mission: SPACE
Spaceship Earth
Turtle Talk
Epcot Character Spot
Journey Into Imagination
The Seas with Nemo & Friends
Disney & Pixar Short Film Festival

LINE BUSTERS:
Tired of long lines? Go to: The Circle of Life movie in The Land, Journey Into Imagination with Figment in Imagination!, Universe of Energy, *Impressions de France* in the France pavilion, or The American Adventure. The Spaceship Earth line thins out in the afternoon, as does the line for the attraction inside The Seas with Nemo & Friends.

IF YOU HAVE YOUNG CHILDREN:

- Begin the day by visiting the Epcot Character Spot and exploring The Seas with Nemo & Friends. Then head over to Imagination! to ride Journey Into Imagination with Figment and experience the ImageWorks interactive playground.

- At World Showcase, head to Norway's new Frozen Ever After attraction. Afterward, hit Mexico's boat ride: Gran Fiesta Tour Starring the Three Caballeros.

- Visit the Kidcot Fun Stop in each country. Don't miss the koi pond in Japan and Germany's tiny village.

- If the weather is warm, let little ones splash in the interactive fountain on the pathway joining Future World with World Showcase or the spray zone in front of Test Track.

* At press time, guests could reserve a Fastpass+ time for 1 attraction from Group A and 2 from Group B. That may change in 2017. Visit *www.MyDisneyExperience.com* for updates.

ONE-DAY SCHEDULE

🐭 Some attractions open later in the morning; consult a park Times Guide for exact times. Also, many shows here run on a schedule (e.g., For the First Time in Forever—A Frozen Sing-Along Celebration, and Beauty and the Beast—Live on Stage). Use a tablet or smartphone or stop at a park kiosk to get Fastpass+ assignments if you haven't booked them in advance. *Note that seismic changes (including a name change) are in store for this park—some attractions may not be operating during your visit.*

🐭 Toy Story Midway Mania! is wildly popular. Arrive as early as possible and pre-book a Fastpass+ assignment if you can. Same for For the First Time in Forever—A Frozen Sing-Along Celebration.

🐭 Daredevils should begin the day with Rock 'n' Roller Coaster, followed by some eye-opening drops at The Twilight Zone™ Tower of Terror.

🐭 If Beauty and the Beast is playing soon, grab a seat. Otherwise, plan to come back later and go to Voyage of The Little Mermaid and Walt Disney: One Man's Dream.

🐭 Pause for lunch at the 50's Prime Time Cafe, Sci-Fi Dine-In Theater, PizzeRizzo, Sunset Ranch Market, or Backlot Express.

🐭 Post-lunch is a great time to visit Voyage of The Little Mermaid or The Great Movie Ride. If live entertainment is offered, be sure to catch it.

🐭 See Muppet★Vision 3-D, followed by Star Tours—The Adventures Continue, and the Indiana Jones Epic Stunt Spectacular. Take tots to see Disney Junior—Live on Stage.

🐭 If you missed Beauty and the Beast—Live on Stage, go now and, if you haven't hit it yet, be sure to experience The Great Movie Ride.

🐭 If Fantasmic is being presented, you want to get a spot in line at least 50 minutes before showtime. Note that if you choose to skip Fantasmic, plan to exit the park before the last performance breaks. If you do stay for the show, know that you can meander through select shops while the throngs exit.

🐭 Is Star Wars: A Galactic Spectacular happening tonight? Make a point of catching this stellar fireworks show.

Continued on page 38

ONE-DAY SCHEDULE

Continued from page 37

STUDIO STANDOUTS*:

If you're short on time, be sure to catch as many of the following four-star attractions at Disney's Hollywood Studios as possible. Note that they are all included in Fastpass+:

Group A:
Toy Story Midway Mania!
Rock 'n' Roller Coaster—Starring Aerosmith
Beauty and the Beast—Live on Stage
The Great Movie Ride
Fantasmic!

Group B:
The Twilight Zone™ Tower of Terror
Muppet★Vision 3-D
Star Tours—The Adventures Continue

More FASTPASS+ ATTRACTIONS*:

In addition to those listed on the left, these attractions are classified by Disney as Group B:

Disney Junior—Live on Stage!

Indiana Jones Epic Stunt Spectacular!

Voyage of The Little Mermaid

For the First Time in Forever: A Frozen Sing-Along Celebration

LINE BUSTERS:

When lines abound at Disney's Hollywood Studios, we suggest the following: Indiana Jones Epic Stunt Spectacular (the theater fits about 2,000 guests at a time); Muppet★Vision 3-D; For the First Time in Forever: A Frozen Sing-Along Celebration (this theater also has a high capacity); and Walt Disney: One Man's Dream.

IF YOU HAVE YOUNG CHILDREN:

• Begin with Toy Story Midway Mania! if your child is old enough to wear 3-D glasses, followed by the Voyage of The Little Mermaid attraction (but warn kids about moments of darkness and a thunderstorm), and Muppet★Vision 3-D. (If kids won't wear 3-D glasses, bypass the Muppets and head directly to Disney Junior—Live on Stage.)

• Have lunch at Sunset Ranch Market, then watch the parade (if it is offered). See Beauty and the Beast—Live on Stage. Skip Fantasmic!—it tends to terrify tots.

• Catch up with Disney characters at Animation Courtyard and on Pixar Place.

* At press time, guests could reserve a Fastpass+ time for 1 attraction from Group A and 2 from Group B. That may change in 2017. Visit *www.MyDisneyExperience.com* for updates.

ONE-DAY SCHEDULE

❤ Guests who arrive at park opening may enjoy a good-morning greeting from Disney characters. Many shows here run on a schedule, so check for times throughout the day. If you want to experience Expedition Everest (and you should), book Fastpass+ or arrive as early as you can. Make a point of perusing the schedules for Festival of the Lion King and Finding Nemo—The Musical. Note that if you haven't pre-booked Fastpass+ assignments, you can make same-day arrangements with your smartphone or tablet and/or at a Fastpass+ kiosk in the park.

❤ As you enter the park, pass through the Oasis and head toward DinoLand. After riding Dinosaur, catch Finding Nemo—The Musical (arrive early). Take young children to the Boneyard before leaving the area.

❤ In Asia, tackle Expedition Everest, ride Kali River Rapids, then visit the tigers at the Maharajah Jungle Trek, and see the delightful Flights of Wonder bird show at the Caravan Stage.

❤ Check a park Times Guide for the Festival of the Lion King schedule. Plan to arrive at the theater at least 45 minutes prior to your preferred showtime (it's a very popular production). If possible, mingle with Mickey and Minnie (at the Adventurers Outpost) before seeing Festival of the Lion King.

❤ Stop at Yak & Yeti, Harambe Market, or Tusker House for lunch. Then jump aboard the Wildlife Express train to Rafiki's Planet Watch. Don't miss the Song of the Rainforest and the Affection Section petting farm.

❤ After experiencing Africa's Kilimanjaro Safaris, take a relaxing hike on the animal-laden Gorilla Falls Exploration Trail.

❤ Take in It's Tough to be a Bug! and revisit favorite attractions. Keep in mind that Kilimanjaro Safaris now operates day and night—it's definitely worth checking out after the sun sets.

❤ If you haven't booked Fastpass+ for The Rivers of Light, Animal Kingdom's nighttime extravaganza, get in line at least an hour before showtime.

Continued on page 40

ONE-DAY SCHEDULE

Continued from page 39

ANIMAL KINGDOM ACES:

An abbreviated visit to Disney's Animal Kingdom is enough to make anybody growl. The following attractions should help soothe the savage beast, er, guest:

- Dinosaur
- Kali River Rapids
- Kilimanjaro Safaris
- Gorilla Falls Exploration Trail
- Expedition Everest
- Finding Nemo—The Musical
- Maharajah Jungle Trek
- Flights of Wonder
- Festival of the Lion King
- It's Tough to be a Bug!
- AVATAR Flight of Passage*
- Na'vi River Journey*

FASTPASS+ ATTRACTIONS:

Dinosaur
Expedition Everest
Festival of the Lion King
Finding Nemo—The Musical
It's Tough to be a Bug!
Kali River Rapids
Primeval Whirl
Kilimanjaro Safaris
Rivers of Light
AVATAR Flight of Passage*
Na'vi River Journey*

LINE BUSTERS:
When herds of guests mob Disney's Animal Kingdom attractions, there are a few places to escape the stampede: The Oasis, Gorilla Falls Exploration Trail, Maharajah Jungle Trek, Discovery Island Trails, The Boneyard playground, and Rafiki's Planet Watch. (You have to take the Wildlife Express train to reach Rafiki's Planet Watch.)

IF YOU HAVE YOUNG CHILDREN:

- Explore the Oasis on your way into the park. As you cross the bridge to Discovery Island, stop at the Wilderness Explorer Headquarters and get started collecting badges. Then go to the Adventurers Outpost to meet Mickey and Minnie.

- Stop by the Tree of Life to notice all of the animal carvings in its trunk. (Note that the show inside the tree, It's Tough to be a Bug!, is very intense and may frighten young children.)

- Eat lunch at Pizzafari or head to DinoLand's Restaurantosaurus. Be sure to see The Boneyard playground, Flights of Wonder, and Chester and Hester's Dino-Rama.

- In Asia, go to the Maharajah Jungle Trek. Ride Africa's bumpy Kilimanjaro Safaris. See the Gorilla Falls Exploration Trail. Then take the train to Rafiki's Planet Watch.

- The Na'vi River Journey, scheduled to open in mid- to late 2017, is super kid-friendly.

- End the day by viewing Rivers of Light. If you don't have a Fastpass+ assignment, arrive as early as possible.

* The attractions within Pandora—The World of AVATAR are expected to open by mid- to late 2017.

HALF-DAY SCHEDULE

Morning/afternoon at the Magic Kingdom*

❤ Where to begin? It's a big decision. Know that the area you postpone may have long lines by the time you get there. We like to start in Adventureland.

❤ Visit Pirates of the Caribbean, then head over to Splash Mountain (if you don't mind getting a little soggy) and Big Thunder Mountain Railroad.

❤ Visit The Haunted Mansion, and then (if you plan on staying through the afternoon) grab a spot for the afternoon parade, Festival of Fantasy.

❤ Watch the Festival of Fantasy parade (and wave hello to Anna and Elsa!) in Frontierland. Or skip the parade and go to Peter Pan's Flight, Winnie the Pooh, It's a Small World, Under the Sea—Journey of The Little Mermaid, and the Seven Dwarfs Mine Train.

❤ Head to Tomorrowland to experience Space Mountain. Follow it up with Buzz Lightyear's Space Ranger Spin. Take youngsters for a relaxing trip on the PeopleMover (but warn them that there will be moments of total darkness).

Afternoon/evening at the Magic Kingdom*

❤ Check a Times Guide and choose a time to take in the Castle stage show. And don't miss the Festival of Fantasy parade. (Warn little ones about the parade's fire-breathing dragon.)

❤ Explore Town Square Theater. If the wait to meet Mickey Mouse is more than 45 minutes, consider coming back in the evening—or get a Fastpass+ assignment.

❤ Start in Adventureland. Ride the Jungle Cruise and Pirates of the Caribbean.

❤ Head to Frontierland. Do Splash Mountain and Big Thunder Mountain Railroad. Then see the Country Bears or Tom Sawyer Island (the latter closes at dusk).

❤ See the highlights of Fantasyland, including It's a Small World, Seven Dwarfs Mine Train, Peter Pan, Under the Sea—Journey of The Little Mermaid, The Many Adventures of Winnie the Pooh, and the Mad Tea Party.

❤ Join the afternoon street party known as Move It, Shake It, Dance & Play It! if it is offered (on Main Street, near Cinderella Castle).

❤ Pop in at The Haunted Mansion and The Hall of Presidents before dinner.

❤ Now it's time for Tomorrowland. (If the Electrical parade is running twice, stay in Tomorrowland during the more crowded early run. But don't miss this spectacular parade.) Go to Space Mountain or Buzz Lightyear's Space Ranger Spin.

❤ Catch the Main Street Electrical Parade. And don't miss the fireworks (presented rain or shine)!

❤ Shop on Main Street, U.S.A., while the exiting masses file out.

* For details on where to meet Disney characters, see page 136.

Half Day with Young Children

Start at Town Square Theater. Meet Mickey inside. If it's close to parade time, grab a spot on the curb. After exploring Fantasyland (do not miss It's a Small World), consider the Country Bear Jamboree. Soar on a magic carpet in Adventureland, then head to Tomorrowland. Cap off the day with Buzz Lightyear, followed by the Main Street Electrical Parade.

HALF-DAY SCHEDULE

Morning/afternoon at Epcot

❦ Head directly to Soarin' Around the World, then Test Track. If you're up for the "intense" Mission: SPACE, go for it. (We prefer the "less intense," non-spinning version of the attraction.) *Frozen* fans should visit Norway's new attraction, Frozen Ever After, as soon as it opens (reserve it with Fastpass+ if possible). Then move on to The Seas with Nemo & Friends pavilion.

❦ See Universe of Energy and check out Innoventions before moving on to World Showcase— most of it opens at 11 A.M. Save Spaceship Earth for later, when the line dies down a bit. When hunger calls, stop for lunch. See the countries that interest you most, making sure to see Norway's Frozen Ever After (if you haven't already!), the show inside The American Adventure, and Mexico's boat ride: Gran Fiesta Tour Starring the Three Caballeros.

Afternoon/evening at Epcot

❦ If you don't have restaurant reservations and would like to try for dinner at a table-service restaurant, stop by Guest Relations to make them. If not, consider dining at the nearby BoardWalk resort (it's a short stroll or FriendShip ride away). Dining reservations may also be made by using the My Disney Experience mobile app. Note that reservations are recommended.

❦ See as much of Future World as possible before heading to World Showcase. (Both sections of the park generally stay open until about 9 P.M., but some Future World attractions close at 7 P.M.)

❦ Spend the evening touring World Showcase. Keep an eye on the clock so you can secure a good spot around the lagoon to watch the evening's presentation of IllumiNations—Reflections of Earth.

❦ Avoid the crush of exiting crowds by browsing the wares in the Mouse Gear shop in Future World or relaxing by the Fountain of Nations.

Half Day with Young Children

Begin with a visit to Frozen Ever After or the Epcot Character Spot, followed by The Seas with Nemo & Friends (take a ride in a clam-mobile, see Turtle Talk with Crush, and romp in Bruce's Shark World). Follow it up with a visit to Spaceship Earth. Check out the Kidcot Fun Stops throughout the park and stop by the miniature village in Germany. If there's time, check out Journey Into Imagination with Figment and ImageWorks in the Imagination pavilion.

WHERE TO MEET THE CHARACTERS*

Epcot Character Spot (Mickey, Minnie, Goofy); **Across from Epcot Character spot** (Baymax, Joy, Sadness); **Legacy Plaza West, near Spaceship Earth** (Daisy Duck); **Mexico** (Donald Duck); **Norway** (Anna and Elsa, in the Royal Sommerhus); **Germany** (Snow White); **France** (Belle and Aurora); **United Kingdom** (Mary Poppins, Alice in Wonderland); **China** (Mulan); **Morocco** (Jasmine and Aladdin); **Showcase Plaza** (Pluto).

Characters subject to change

EPCOT

HALF-DAY SCHEDULE

Morning/afternoon at Disney's Hollywood Studios

❤ Kick-start the day with a visit to Toy Story Midway Mania!, followed by For the First Time in Forever—A Frozen Sing-Along Celebration, and trips to Rock 'n' Roller Coaster and Tower of Terror (just don't do the thrill rides on a full stomach). From there, move on to Muppet★Vision 3-D and Star Tours—The Adventures Continue.

❤ Before lining up for the parade (if one is scheduled), see Beauty and the Beast and The Great Movie Ride (build in time to explore the famous footprints out front).

❤ For a quick bite, stop at The Backlot Express or Sunset Ranch Market.

❤ If time permits, take in Voyage of The Little Mermaid and Walt Disney: One Man's Dream.

Afternoon/Evening at Disney's Hollywood Studios

❤ Begin with Tower of Terror, Rock 'n' Roller Coaster, Beauty and the Beast—Live on Stage, and For the First Time in Forever—A Frozen Sing-Along Celebration.

❤ See Voyage of The Little Mermaid; Star Tours; Muppet★Vision 3-D; The Great Movie Ride; Toy Story Midway Mania! (expect a wait of at least an hour at all times); and the Indiana Jones Epic Stunt Spectacular.

❤ Explore Walt Disney: One Man's Dream before grabbing a spot in line for Fantasmic! (if the nighttime spectacular is being presented today). Or skip Fantasmic! and revisit favorite attractions or shops. Star Wars: A Galactic Spectacular is an impressive fireworks show—catch it if you can.

Half Day with Young Children

Start with For the First Time in Forever, followed by Disney Junior—Live on Stage, Voyage of The Little Mermaid, and Beauty and the Beast—Live on Stage. Youngsters ages 4 to 12 can harness the Force at the Jedi Training Academy. If the weather is warm, take tots to play in the spray from the giant bottle near Pixar Place. Skip Fantasmic! —it's just too intense (and a bit long) for most tykes.

WHERE TO MEET THE CHARACTERS*

Hollywood Boulevard at park opening time (Mickey, Donald, Chip, Dale, and more); **Animation Courtyard** (Disney Junior friends such as Sofia the First and Jake from *Jake and the Never Land Pirates*); **Commissary Lane** (Minnie and Mickey); **Pixar Place** (Woody, Buzz, Green Army Men, or other *Toy Story* characters); **Mickey Avenue** (Mickey Mouse); **Hollywood Blvd.** (Donald Duck, Pluto, Goofy); **Star Wars Launch Bay** (Chewbacca and Kylo Ren).

* Characters subject to change.

HALF-DAY SCHEDULE

Morning/afternoon at Disney's Animal Kingdom

🐾 Go to Asia to ride the thrilling Expedition Everest and the soaking Kali River Rapids, and hike the Maharajah Jungle Trek.

🐾 Experience Flights of Wonder bird show on the way to Kilimanjaro Safaris and the Gorilla Falls Exploration Trail.

🐾 Check a Times Guide to see when the Festival of the Lion King show is playing today. Plan to arrive at least 45 minutes before showtime.

🐾 Finish up with Finding Nemo—The Musical; Dinosaur; and It's Tough to be a Bug!— though the last two are too intense for tots. Take little ones to The Boneyard playground instead.

Disney's Animal Kingdom After Lunch

🐾 Check a Times Guide for Festival of the Lion King and Finding Nemo—The Musical schedules. Arrive 30 to 45 minutes before showtime. Then visit Mickey and Minnie at the Adventurers Outpost on Discovery Island.

🐾 If there is entertainment, such as the Viva Gaia Street Band, stick around Discovery Island to enjoy it. Otherwise, head to the Kilimanjaro Safaris ride. Then do the Gorilla Falls Exploration Trail and take the train to Rafiki's Planet Watch.

🐾 Ride Expedition Everest and Kali River Rapids, and experience the Maharajah Jungle Trek. Try to catch Flights of Wonder, too (the first performance takes place in the late morning).

🐾 Wander the Discovery Island Trails and see It's Tough to be a Bug!

🐾 Before dinner, dodge dastardly dinos on Dinosaur.

Half Day with Young Children

Scope out animal life in The Oasis before stopping at the Wilderness Explorer Headquarters on the bridge to Discovery Island. Then go to the Adventurers Outpost to meet Mickey and Minnie, followed by a visit to DinoLand U.S.A. Explore The Boneyard and ride TriceraTop Spin. If time allows, take the train to Rafiki's Planet Watch, where kids can bond with live animals (mostly goats) in the Affection Section. The Flights of Wonder bird show captivates guests of all ages.

WHERE TO MEET THE CHARACTERS*

Park Entrance at park opening (characters vary); **Cretaceous Trail** (Donald Duck); **Discovery Island** (Tarzan and Flik); **Discovery Island Character Landing** (Daisy Duck and Pocahontas); **Adventurers Outpost on Discovery Island** (Mickey and Minnie); **Rafiki's Planet Watch** (Rafiki, Chip 'n' Dale); **Upcountry Landing** between Asia and Africa (Baloo and Louie); **DinoLand Service Station** (Pluto and Goofy); **It's Tough to be a Bug!** entrance (Russell and Dug).

* Characters subject to change.

Making the Most of Longer Visits

Longer stays allow the chance to sample some of the World's myriad offerings. Spend another day in the one park you most enjoyed. Lounge by the pool, go biking, or play tennis or golf. Go shopping at Disney Springs. Cool off at one of Disney's innovative water parks. Have lunch at a WDW resort, and try a special dinner at Victoria & Albert's in the Grand Floridian or at Flying Fish at the BoardWalk resort. Check out the restaurants at Disney Springs or spend the evening at the BoardWalk. Take golf, tennis, or surf lessons. Go fishing or horseback riding. Visit a relaxing day spa. See a movie. Participate in a behind-the-scenes program. Play a round or two of miniature golf. Catch a game at the ESPN Wide World of Sports complex. For even more ideas, see our *Sports*; *Everything Else in the World*; and *Good Meals, Great Times* chapters.

How to Save a Rainy Day

Florida rain showers come and go with such regularity that you could set your watch by them, especially during summer months. They're usually brief, though torrential. Of course, there are times when gray clouds linger longer. Here are some ways to make the most of a soggy day:

• See a movie on one of AMC Theatres' many screens at Disney Springs.

• Check out Cirque du Soleil's La Nouba.

• Consider taking in an indoor event at the ESPN Wide World of Sports complex. For information, call 407-939-1500.

• Head for an arcade—most Walt Disney World resorts have at least one. Games are appropriate for guests of all ages. (The arcades at Art of Animation and Contemporary are larger than most.)

• Don your rain gear and go to Epcot. The pavilions in Future World house a bounty of sheltered diversions. (Ponchos are sold throughout WDW for about $9 each.)

Customized Travel Tips:
Traveling with Children

Tell kids that a Walt Disney World vacation is in the works and the response is apt to be overwhelming! Our guide *Birnbaum's Walt Disney World For Kids 2017*, written for children ages 7 through 14, can be a useful resource for getting them involved in the planning from the outset. Filled with information about the World from a kid's perspective, it can be used as a reference before and during the trip, a place to collect character autographs, and kept as a post-trip souvenir.

Walt Disney World ranks among the easier spots on Earth for families with children. Keep in mind, however, that kids under 14 must be accompanied by a guest age 14 or older to enter the theme parks; kids under 10 must be accompanied by an adult at the water parks. Note that kids under age 7 must be accompanied by a person age 14 or older in order to board theme park attractions.

Child Care: In-room child-care service can be summoned to all Disney-owned resorts. The service is available 24/7, though it is not run by Disney. For pricing and to make a reservation with Kid's Nite Out, visit *www.kidsniteout.com*, call 407-828-0920 or 800-696-8105, or inquire at your resort's lobby concierge. Another company, Super Sitters, offers this child-care service as well. In addition to resort babysitting, they can accompany a party during theme park visits. This allows parents to take older kids on attractions while the sitter keeps an eye on the younger ones. To reach them, call 407-382-2558, or visit *www.super-sitters.com*.

Children's Activity Centers: The Polynesian Village, Animal Kingdom Lodge, Wilderness Lodge, Yacht and Beach Club, and Dolphin resorts each have an on-site children's activity center. (Note that the Wilderness Lodge center is expected to be closed through summer of 2017.) The cheery centers accept (potty-trained) kids ages 3 through 12. For details and availability, phone 407-939-3463 for all but the Dolphin. "Camp Dolphin" operates daily from 5:30 P.M. to midnight

and accepts children ages 4 through 12. Camp Dolphin costs $10 per hour, per child. For information, call 407-934-4000.

Baby Care Centers: Located in all theme parks, these centers are for parents with young children. They are not meant as day care. All kids must be accompanied by a parent or guardian. There are rooms with rocking chairs and couches in feeding rooms for nursing mothers and screenings of Disney films for kids. Centers have facilities for changing diapers, preparing formula, warming bottles, and washing bottles. Diapers, bottles, formula, pacifiers, and baby food are among the supplies for sale. Baby Care Center locations are listed on theme park guidemaps. There are changing areas in most women's and in many men's restrooms.

Lost Children: Disney employees (also known as "cast members") will know what to do if a child starts to call for his or her parents. If your child wanders off, stop at the Baby Care Center or City Hall in the Magic Kingdom; at Guest Relations or the Baby Care Center in Epcot; at Guest Relations in Disney's Hollywood Studios; or at Guest Relations in Animal Kingdom. A computerized system allows for a detailed description of the child and his or her status, helping to reunite families quickly. It helps if your child has your mobile phone number, too. In emergencies an all-points bulletin can be put out among cast members.

Parental Perk

Families with babies or small children should know about the "rider switch" policy (aka "baby swap") at the theme parks. At attractions with age or height restrictions, a parent who waits nearby with a young child while the other parent rides the attraction can go right on soon after the first parent comes off. Be sure to ask the attendant at the attraction's entrance. They'll tell you how to proceed.

The Guest Relations staff at each Disney park can help, too.

Prepare youngsters for the possibility of an accidental separation. Direct him or her to contact the nearest park worker (someone wearing a costume and a name tag) and ask for help.

Refrigerators: For parents of young children, an in-room fridge is not a mere luxury, it's a necessity. Accommodations at all Walt Disney World–owned-and-operated resorts come equipped with a small fridge, free of charge. Many Disney Vacation Club Villas accommodations are equipped with full-size refrigerators.

Baby Food: Many parents choose to ship a box of food and baby supplies to their resort before they leave home. It is possible to purchase jars of baby food at most Disney resorts, but the selection isn't huge. For a wider variety of foodstuffs to choose from, make a trip to the Winn-Dixie at 11957 Apopka-Vineland Road (just beyond the Crossroads shopping center) or Gooding's at the Crossroads, near Hotel Plaza Boulevard. For addresses for a GPS, inquire at your resort's front desk.

Winn-Dixie and Gooding's, as well as nearby convenience stores, are also within a reasonable cabbing distance. Be sure to hire an authorized cab for the trip. Your resort staff can make the arrangements and give you an estimate of the cost. Another option is to order groceries from *gardengrocer.com*. They are authorized to deliver to most Disney-area hotels and stock a wide variety of items, including many organic, gluten-free, and kosher selections.

If you have a milk (or other food) need after hours, know that these Disney resorts have 24-hour snack bars: Grand Floridian, Polynesian Village, Dolphin, and Buena Vista Palace.

Cribs: Most Walt Disney World resort rooms come with a small, playpen-like crib. (Look for it in the closet. If it's not there, call to request one.) They're free, but somewhat flimsy.

If you'd like something a little bigger or sturdier, consider renting a crib from Orlando Crib Rental (407-433-7770).

Diapers: Each Disney resort has at least one shop in which to pick up diapers. If you're brand loyal, pack your own. (Consider shipping diapers to your resort so you don't have to pack them.) Be sure to throw extra swim diapers into your bag each morning. You never know when you'll run into an interactive fountain on Disney property. They're necessary for pool use, too.

Resort Fun: Most WDW resorts have at least one arcade. Most of the hotels have little playgrounds as well as toddler-friendly pools.

Tips for Tots

PHOTO BY MIKE CARROLL

Walt Disney World is as toddler-friendly as it gets. Here are a few pointers to make it even more so:

• Familiarize your child with Disney characters before your trip. That way they'll be more likely to enjoy meeting them and less likely to be frightened by them.

• Fireworks can scare little ones silly. If your tot is spooked by loud noises, be prepared to make a hasty exit once the booms begin. That said, most babies are enchanted by the Main Street Electrical Parade, the Magic Kingdom's nighttime processional.

• Be sure to bring snacks when you head out for the day. It's tough to find toddler-friendly nibbles once you leave your resort.

• You will be asked to collapse your stroller before boarding a WDW resort bus or boat—but not on the monorail. This makes the monorail resorts even more appealing to the stroller set.

• Don't forget sunscreen that's sensitive to toddler skin. Pack a hat for an infant.

• Pack a small but treasured toy from home and keep it with you at all times.

• Don't underestimate the play value of a good splash. Take time to relax and enjoy the invaluable amenity that is the Walt Disney World resort pool. Of course, swim diapers are a must.

• Remember that your child may enter the parks for free until his or her third birthday.

HOT TIP!

Small children may become a bit anxious when dropped off at one of Disney's child activity centers. If that's the case, plan to stick around until the trepidation passes. And prepare your child ahead of time. Let him or her know they'll be playing with other kids—coloring, playing games, watching movies, and the like. Reassure kids that you'll be nearby, and tell them what time you'll be coming back. That way, little minds can relax and have fun.

Tips for Teens

When it comes to teenagers at Disney World, *The Little Mermaid*'s Ariel has plenty of company. Of course, be they of the fish or human variety, teenage guests have special needs all their own. Here are some tips from our WDW teen experts:

- Bring your own music. It's perfect for the trip to Walt Disney World and for sitting poolside at your resort. But don't wear your earphones for your whole trip.

- Have some of your own money on hand. If it's your hard-earned cash, you probably won't spend it as quickly as you would Mom and Dad's!

- Pack a hat. Why? It's much easier to throw a hat on than waste time doing your hair.

- Try to get along with your brothers and sisters—even if it isn't always easy. Don't bug them to do the things you want to do all the time. Try to do things they want to do, too.

- One of the coolest things for teens to do is an Extra Magic Hours evening at one of the theme parks. They let you stay in a park after hours and ride many of the best rides with shorter waits! Another good thing to do at night is to go shopping, especially at Disney Springs.

- Attention, parents! Try to include your teens in planning the trip. If they get a say during planning, they'll be much happier when they arrive at Disney World. Also, don't make them get up every morning at 6 A.M. Try to give them a day or two to wake up late and lounge around the pool or a water park.

For information on special children's activities at Disney resorts, turn to page 230.

Strollers: Available for $15 for one day and $13 per day of a multi-day rental at stroller rental areas at each of the theme parks. (Strollers are not available for rent at the water parks.) Double strollers cost $31 for one day and $27 per day of a multi-day rental. Note that theme-park strollers are made of hard plastic and are not ideal for babies.

Strollers are not permitted inside attractions (they can be parked near each attraction entrance) and cannot be removed from the park in which they are rented. If a stroller disappears while you're in an attraction, a replacement may be obtained with a receipt. Guests have to pay

HOT TIP!

If you have a baby, you'll need a stroller during your Walt Disney World visit. Although they may be rented at the theme parks, consider bringing one from home. It'll save you money and the hassle of getting one each time you visit a park. Plus, there's the convenience of using it all over WDW property. (Disney rents strollers at the parks and Disney Springs, but they are made of uncomfortable hard plastic and can't leave the place from which they are rented.)

When we do choose to rent a stroller, we call Magic Strollers (866-866-6177). For details, turn to page 67.

only once a day for a stroller. If you rent one in the morning and plan to spend the afternoon at another park, just present your receipt for a replacement there.

If you'll need a stroller for several days, consider purchasing the Length of Stay rental ticket. It'll save you two dollars off the daily price, and it should cut down on time spent in the rental line. Simply buy the ticket on your first visit to a theme park and put your receipt in a safe place—that's what you'll need to show to get a stroller on the remaining days of your stay.

Disney Springs Marketplace and West Side rent single strollers for about $15 a day, plus a $100 refundable deposit (there are no doubles available here). You may also bring your own stroller into the parks.

Note: You will be asked to remove the child and fold your stroller before boarding Disney World buses and boats. There's no folding necessary when boarding the monorail.

Traveling Without Children

Walt Disney World has become an extremely popular destination for adults without children, appealing to singles, couples, and empty nesters alike. Disney has responded to the demand with an entertainment and dining selection for grown-ups without kids in tow.

Couples

There is a place for lovebirds at Walt Disney World. Actually, there are many spots in Walt's World perfectly suited to those with romantic intentions (provided, of course, that privacy is not a prerequisite!).

- Grown-ups love to roam the parks unencumbered by little ones and strollers. The Magic Kingdom's carousel-and-castle combo invokes the enchantment in true fairy-tale tradition. Epcot's World Showcase has the aura of a whirlwind tour (and the inspiration for a future trip?), with countries as exotic and far-reaching as Japan and Morocco. Disney's Hollywood Studios recaptures an era of starry-eyed elegance. And what could be more enjoyable than sharing a safari through Africa at Disney's Animal Kingdom?

  By day, there is romance in the theme parks for couples who are already inclined to hold hands; by night, the parks sparkle with an intensity that inspires sudden mushiness in those who never considered themselves the type, and that's before the fireworks.

- As Disney's themed resorts go about transporting guests to various times and places, they make quite a few passes through settings straight out of everyone's fantasy escape textbook—from the Victorian charms of the Grand Floridian to the exotic island getaway that is the Polynesian Village resort. You won't find a more inspirational backdrop than that at the rustic Wilderness Lodge, marked by geysers, waterfalls, steamy hot springs, and a grand stone fireplace. At the nostalgic

The Most Romantic Places in the World

WDW RESORTS

- Animal Kingdom Lodge
- Coronado Springs
- Grand Floridian
- Polynesian Village
- Port Orleans Riverside
- Wilderness Lodge
- Yacht and Beach Club

WDW RESTAURANTS

- Artist Point
- Cinderella's Royal Table
- Cítricos
- Jiko—The Cooking Place
- Le Cellier Steakhouse
- Monsieur Paul
- Narcoossee's
- Sanaa
- Victoria & Albert's
- Yachtsman Steakhouse

WDW LOUNGES

- Belle Vue Lounge at BoardWalk
- The Boathouse at Disney Springs, The Landing
- Citricos Lounge at Grand Floridian
- Il Mulino New York Trattoria Lounge at the Swan hotel
- The Lounge at The Wave . . . of American Flavors at Contemporary resort
- Portobello at Disney Springs
- Rix Lounge at Coronado Springs

WDW THEME PARK SPOTS

- All of Epcot's World Showcase
- Wishes fireworks presentation at the Magic Kingdom

BoardWalk resort, surrey bikes are available for romantic rides along the waterfront. And a peaceful stroll around Crescent Lake is a lovely way to cap off the day.

- The myriad of recreational activities that couples may enjoy at Walt Disney World includes tennis, golf, water-skiing, sailing, carriage rides, couples treatments at one of four on-property spas, and more.

Older Travelers

Disney World can sometimes be challenging for older travelers. And the heat, particularly in summer, can be hard to take. But with the proper planning and precautions, it's just as delightful for older visitors as for kids.

- For slower times, visit the parks Monday through Wednesday. (Thursdays through Sundays tend to attract lots of locals.)

- The Florida sun tends to be brutal year-round. Always wear sunscreen (don't forget your hands) and a hat.

- Try to eat early or late to avoid the mealtime crowds. In the Magic Kingdom, select restaurants such as Tony's Town Square Restaurant and Columbia Harbour House. Or take the monorail to the peaceful Polynesian Village, Contemporary, or Grand Floridian resorts, where pleasant dining options abound (check ahead to find out which restaurants serve lunch). In Epcot, the Coral Reef restaurant and La Hacienda are pleasant spots. At

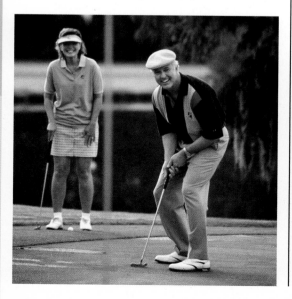

Vacation Insurance

No one books a vacation expecting to cancel it at the last minute—yet sometimes life intervenes and it's simply unavoidable. So it may be worth working travel insurance into your vacation budget (we do). It may include coverage for trip cancellation and interruption, travel delay, loss of baggage, medical expenses, and more. Be sure to ask about travel insurance when you reserve your trip.

Disney's Hollywood Studios, the Hollywood Brown Derby offers a relaxing meal, as does Mama Melrose's Ristorante Italiano.

- If you need to refrigerate medicine, know that small refrigerators are included with the room rate at all Walt Disney World-owned-and-operated resorts. They can be provided at most other resorts for a fee. Park First Aid Stations will store medicine, too.

- Don't underestimate distances at Epcot or Animal Kingdom; you may need to walk more than three miles in a day. Wear comfortable shoes and remember to take breaks.

- Pace yourself. It's smart to head back to your hotel for a swim or a nap in the afternoon and then return to the parks later on. The hotels connected by monorail are particularly convenient for this.

- Many Orlando-area hotels and attractions offer discounts to seniors and AARP members. Contact the Official Visitor Information Center (407-363-5872) for details.

HOT TIP!

Even the fittest of seniors may want to avoid some of Walt Disney World's more physically challenging attractions. Do heed all warning signs at attraction entrances to thrill rides and consider steering clear of high-activity-level experiences such as the Magic Kingdom's Swiss Family Treehouse (seemingly endless stairs!), the Maharajah Jungle Trek, and Gorilla Falls Exploration Trail at Animal Kingdom (lots of walking and few places to rest).

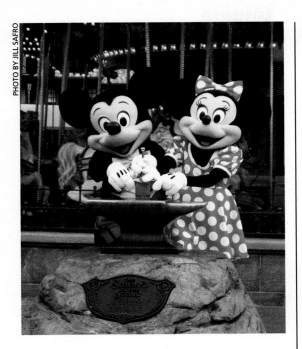

Solo Travelers

Those who travel alone (be it for business or just for fun) can have as memorable a time here as they would anywhere else.

- Solo travelers with extra time should consider taking a behind-the-scenes tour.

- Many of the finer restaurants now have counters at which to eat—perfect for chatting with other diners.

- Sometimes, being a solo traveler can mean shorter wait times at attractions. Test Track is among those with "single rider" lines.

- Other opportunities for unencumbered travelers include parasailing and waterskiing (at the Contemporary), horseback riding (at Fort Wilderness), taking a spin in a motor boat, enjoying bass fishing (407-WDW-BASS; 939-2277) or surfing lessons (407-939-7873), and watching a game (at ESPN Wide World of Sports). Call 407-939-7529.

- Disney Springs's lounges and restaurants can prove to be fertile meeting places. The BoardWalk is another lively destination. Sports fans find its ESPN Club most inviting. And suds fans appreciate the home-brewed libations at Big River Grille & Brewing Works. Sushi lovers fit right in at the California Grill sushi bar (in the lounge section of the eatery).

- The lounges at most Walt Disney World resort hotels are relaxed and welcoming. The same convivial atmosphere prevails at the Tune-In Lounge in the 50's Prime Time Cafe at Disney's Hollywood Studios and at the Rose & Crown Pub (in the United Kingdom pavilion at Epcot's World Showcase).

Important WDW Telephone Numbers

AMC Theatres (Disney Springs):
888-262-4386

Behind-the-Scenes Tours:
407-WDW-TOUR (939-8687)

Central Reservations:
407-W-DISNEY (934-7639)

Dining Reservations:
407-WDW-DINE (939-3463)

Dr. P. Phillips Hospital:
407-351-8500

ESPN Wide World of Sports Complex:
407-939-1500

Florida Hospital Celebration Health:
407-303-4000

Golf Reservations:
407-WDW-GOLF (939-4653)

Recreation:
407-WDW-PLAY (939-7529)

Theme Park Lost and Found:
407-824-4245

Walt Disney Travel Company:
407-828-8101

Walt Disney World Information:
407-824-4321

Weather: 407-824-4104

Tips for International Travelers

Visitors from outside the U.S. need not feel like strangers in a strange land when they arrive at Walt Disney World—even if they speak a language other than English. Information is readily available in many different languages. These tips may also be helpful:

- Free park maps can be found in Spanish, French, German, Portuguese, and Japanese at the entrance to all Disney parks, as well as at Guest Relations.

- Free translation services are available at all four theme parks and include a specially designed translation device called Ears to the World, Disney's Show Translator. The units are lightweight headsets that use wireless technology to provide synchronized narration at several popular theme park attractions. They are available in French, German, Japanese, Portuguese, and Spanish. There is no charge to use the service, but a $25 refundable deposit is required to borrow one.

- Several Disney resorts offer services for their international guests. Ask about them when you inquire about reservations.

- When making your reservations through 407-WDW-DINE or WDW-PLAY, ask to speak with a foreign-language host or hostess.

- Most WDW restaurants offer menus in various languages. Some have picture menus.

- Foreign currency exchange is available at Guest Relations in each of the theme parks. Traveler's checks may be purchased at the SunTrust bank by Disney Springs.

- Disney's MagicBands can act as a charge card (as well as a room key). Purchases made at Walt Disney World will be billed to a credit card that is linked to the band.

- Many Disney employees are fluent in more than one language. Languages spoken are noted on employee name tags.

- Guests traveling long distances and through time zones should conserve their energy. It might be wise to relax by the pool on the day of arrival, instead of trying to fit in a full day at a theme park—it's never beneficial to start a vacation exhausted!

- Phone cards good for international calls can be purchased at several Disney World shops and in many resorts. Inquire at Guest Relations. Resist the urge to direct dial calls from resort rooms (see below).

Telephone Dos and Don'ts

It's a common practice for hotels to assess a surcharge for phone calls, and Disney is no exception. To avoid whopping bills, use your mobile phone, and keep these tips in mind for the hotel phone:

- A direct-dialed, long-distance call will set you back the cost of the call at the AT&T operator-assisted day rate, plus a 65 percent surcharge. The rate applies to both domestic and international long-distance. Applicable taxes are included.

- Prepaid phone cards are available for purchase in most WDW resort lobbies.

- There is no extra fee for guests making credit card, prepaid phone card, or any type of operator-assisted calls from a resort-room telephone.

- There is no charge to call an 800 number from a WDW resort room.

- Landline directory assistance 411 phone calls cost $1.99 each; a 555-1212 call costs $1.40.

- There's no charge to call from room to room within a resort—but there may be a charge to call one Disney resort from another.

- Cell-phone users, check with your carriers to avoid tallying up "roaming" charges. And switch your mobile phone from roaming to Wi-Fi whenever possible.

- All Walt Disney World-owned-and-operated resorts support mobile computing via laptop and tablet. High-speed Wi-Fi service is free.

Travelers with Disabilities

Disney tends to get high marks from travelers with disabilities because of attention paid to special needs. Here is an overview:

GETTING AROUND: Special parking is available for guests at the theme parks; ask for directions at the Auto Plaza upon entering. From the Transportation and Ticket Center (TTC), the Magic Kingdom is accessible by ferry or by monorail. All monorail stations are accessible to wheelchairs. The ramps are lengthy and a bit steep, but manageable.

Wheelchairs: Guests may bring their own wheelchairs. They also have the option of renting them at a theme park, BoardWalk resort, or from a local vendor. Wheelchairs may be rented in theme parks for $12 per day ($10 per day with a Length of Stay rental). In the Magic Kingdom, they are available at the Stroller and Wheelchair Rental. Epcot's rental areas are at the main entrance and at the International Gateway entrance. Oscar's Super Service rents wheelchairs at the Studios. At Animal Kingdom, wheelchairs may be rented at Garden Gate Gifts Stroller Rental area.

If you plan to visit the parks for several days, consider getting a multi-day wheelchair rental. Called a Length of Stay ticket, it comes at a $2-per-day discount. Pay for the entire stay when you first visit a theme park. Simply show your receipt the next time you visit a rental location.

The water parks have a small number of wheelchairs on hand. There's no charge, but the supply is limited. Guests must leave a valid ID as deposit. Disney Springs Marketplace Strollers & Wheelchairs rents wheelchairs for $12 a day, plus a $100 refundable deposit. Electric Conveyance Vehicles (ECVs) are available there for $50 per day with a $100 deposit. Wheelchairs at ESPN Wide World of Sports run $12 per day with a $100 refundable deposit. Walt Disney World Resorts with zero-depth-entry pools may have a small number of wheelchairs available to assist guests entering the pools.

Electric Conveyance Vehicles (ECVs) are available for rent in every theme park. They cost $50 for a day, plus a $20 refundable deposit. They usually sell out early. A word of advice: Practice makes perfect. So before you head into a thicket of park guests, take it for a test drive—and please do not exceed the speed of an average pedestrian.

HOT TIP!

For more information on the various services available to WDW guests with disabilities, call 407-824-4321, or visit *https://disneyworld.disney.go.com/faq/ guests-with-disabilities/attraction-access/*.

Equipment rented at a park cannot leave that park. If you will need to use it for the whole trip, consider calling a company that rents standard and electric wheelchairs, as well as scooters. Keep in mind that you will have to transport the wheelchair or scooter from your resort to your daily destinations. (Monorails and buses are equipped to accommodate, but some boats are not.) Two companies from which to rent are ScootAround (888-441-7575) and Walker Mobility (888-726-6837). Pickup and delivery (often for free or with a small surcharge) are available at all hotels in the WDW area (not just those on Disney property). In our opinion, guests are often better off renting from a local vendor or bringing their own equipment. The quality is generally better, and you don't have to worry about availability. The Walt Disney Company is not affiliated with, nor does it endorse, these companies.

Buena Vista Scooters has an on-property presence at Disney's BoardWalk resort. They have a few first-come, first-served ECVs. The cost is about $30 a day. It's possible to reserve in advance; visit *www.buenavistascooters.com*, or call 407-938-0349 or 866-484-4797. These scooters have a two-day minimum rental period. The company provides free pickup and delivery to all WDW area resorts.

There are designated areas for guests using wheelchairs to view the fireworks at Epcot and to view the parades in each of the theme parks. Check a park guidemap for locations.

HOT TIP!

The theme park disability parking areas can be quite a distance from the wheelchair rental areas. If you require assistance, seek out a courtesy wheelchair to get you to the park's front entrance. The courtesy chairs are easily identified by their blue flags.

Attraction Access

Most park attractions are accessible to guests who are able to get out of their wheelchairs (with or without assistance). And a growing number have queues that can be navigated in a wheelchair. When that's the case, guests are urged to do so. If a wheelchair cannot be accommodated in the queue area, ask an attendant to direct you to an auxiliary entrance. Such entrances are intended for guests using wheelchairs or with service animals. For specifics on this policy, guests should visit a Guest Relations location.

Accessibility: It's relatively easy to get around the parks by wheelchair. Most attractions are accessible to guests who can be lifted from chairs with assistance from a member of their party, and some can accommodate guests who must remain in wheelchairs. Consult each park's *Guide for Guests with Disabilities* (for a free set, write to Walt Disney World Guest Correspondence, P.O. Box 10000, Lake Buena Vista, FL 32830) for details about access, or check with the ride host or hostess. At the water parks, life jackets are available for travelers with disabilities.

All Walt Disney World hotels have accommodations equipped for guests with disabilities, including roll-in showers. Other features—which vary, depending on the resort—include wheelchair-accessible bathrooms, bed accessories, strobe-light smoke detectors, in-room Text Typewriters (TTYs), and more. The following resorts have zero-depth-entry pools: Art of Animation, Animal Kingdom Lodge, Caribbean Beach, the Contemporary's Bay Lake Tower, Grand Floridian, Polynesian Village, and Saratoga Springs. For assistance in choosing a hotel that best fits your requirements, ask for the Special Reservations Department when you call Central Reservations (Voice: 407-939-7807; TTY: 407-939-7670).

RESOURCES: Visual Disabilities: Guests can get a handheld device that verbally describes each park as well as many attractions. Each requires a $25 refundable deposit. Braille guides, Braille menus at most restaurants, and Braille maps are also available.

Hearing Disabilities: Pay phones with Text Typewriters (TTYs) are available throughout Disney World. For more information, call 407-824-4321 or 407-827-5141. Sign language is available for some shows. Call at least two weeks ahead for arrangements.

Assistive-listening devices that amplify attraction audio are available at City Hall in the Magic Kingdom and at Guest Relations in Epcot, Animal Kingdom, and Disney's Hollywood Studios. A $25 refundable deposit is required. Sites with assistive-listening systems are listed on park guidemaps.

Captioning systems, including reflective and handheld devices, are available at theme park Guest Relations windows. The former project show dialogue onto panels; the latter provide captioning on personal devices at certain attractions. A $25 deposit is required.

Note: Trained service animals are permitted in all Disney parks.

Booking the Trip: These organizations specialize in assisting disabled travelers:
- The Society for Accessible Travel & Hospitality (347 Fifth Ave., Suite 605, New York, NY 10016; 212-447-7284; *www.sath.org*)
- Accessible Journeys (35 W. Sellers Ave., Ridley Park, PA 19078; 610-521-0339 or 800-846-4537; *www.accessiblejourneys.com*)
- Flying Wheels Travel (143 W. Bridge St., Owatonna, MN 55060; 507-451-5005 or 877-451-5006; *www.flyingwheelstravel.com*)

Vehicles: Both Wheelchair Getaways (*www.wheelchairgetaways.com*; 800-642-2042) and Wheelchair Vans of America (800-910-8267; *www.wheelchairvansofamerica.com*) rent wheelchair-accessible vans and offer pickup and delivery for most area hotels.

WDW Weddings & Honeymoons

Believe it or not, Walt Disney World is one of the most popular honeymoon destinations in the United States. Why the appeal? The resorts offer romantic stretches of white-sand beaches for evening strolls, fine restaurants, and a host of activities to rival almost any other destination. Add to that the fantasy of the Magic Kingdom, the wonder of Epcot, the glamour of Disney's Hollywood Studios, and the majesty of Animal Kingdom—plus Disney Springs and BoardWalk nightlife, water parks, and the nearby Disney Cruise Line—and it's not hard to see why Disney is tops with newlyweds.

After years of fending for themselves, folks looking to honeymoon here now have help at hand. A variety of packages cater specifically to newly married couples. For information, call toll-free: 877-566-0969.

The folks at Walt Disney World have also received oodles of requests from couples who wanted to actually get married at one of the theme parks. They responded by creating a program known as Disney's Fairy Tale Weddings. Today, couples can tie the knot in evening ceremonies at some parks during seasons when they close early.

The Yacht and Beach Club, BoardWalk, Polynesian Village, and Wilderness Lodge resorts also host their share of weddings. The Wedding Pavilion, on the grounds of the Grand Floridian Resort and Spa, offers a Victorian-style indoor setting with a prime view of Cinderella Castle and the Seven Seas Lagoon. A mix of stained glass, sage green and soft pink florals, and benches with heart-shaped cutouts (seating around 250 guests) creates the romantic ambience. Couples can fill their wedding albums with photos taken at Picture Point, under a trellis of climbing white roses, with the faraway castle in the background.

Weddings range from elegant affairs, without a hint of Disneyana, to ceremonies in which the bride arrives in Cinderella's Crystal Coach and Mickey and Minnie Mouse are among the guests at the reception.

At Franck's Bridal Studio, Walt Disney World specialists work with couples to customize each wedding. Among the services offered are cakes, photography, flower arranging, and musical entertainment. Franck's specialists can help secure accommodations, rehearsal dinners, bachelor parties, and more.

Honeymoon Registry

Launched, appropriately, on Valentine's Day, the gift registry lets happy couples plan their honeymoon. Gifts include theme park tickets, resort accommodations, spa treatments, and more. For more information or to sign up for the free Disney Honeymoon Registry, visit *www.disneyhoneymoonregistry.com*, or call 877-699-5884 during regular business hours.

For details about planning a Walt Disney World wedding and honeymoon packages, call 321-939-4610, or visit *www.disneyweddings.com*.

PHOTO BY JILL SAFRO

My Disney Experience

The folks at Disney have unveiled My Disney Experience—"a whole new way to plan and share your Walt Disney World vacation." All potential guests are invited to visit *MyDisneyExperience.com* or download the free app. After setting up a profile, guests can ostensibly use the site to book most elements of a Disney vacation, including hotel, restaurant reservations, and even Fastpass+ assignments for select theme park attractions. For details, see pages 23–27.

Fingertip Reference Guide

GETTING READY TO GO

BARBERS AND SALONS

One of the most amusing places to get a haircut is the Magic Kingdom's old-fashioned Harmony Barber Shop. It's located beside the Car Barn in the Town Square section of Main Street. Cost is about $19 for adults and $18 for kids. Colored hair gel is $5 (kids love it). Treat tots to a very special "my first haircut" experience for $25. Hours are 9 A.M. to 5 P.M. daily. WDW resort guests may make reservations by calling 407-939-7529. Walk-ins are accommodated on a first-come, first-served basis.

Haircuts, coloring, manicures, and other services are available at Ship Shape at the Yacht and Beach Club (407-934-3260), Ivy Trellis at the Grand Floridian (407-824-3000, ext. 2581), Mandara Spa at the Dolphin (407-934-4772), the Kay Casperson Spa at Buena Vista Palace (407-827-3200), and the Casa de Belleza at Coronado Springs (407-939-7727).

BUSINESS SERVICES

Disney provides a range of services for those who simply must mix business with pleasure. Copiers, fax machines (also found at Guest Relations in the theme parks), and FedEx materials may be available at the lobby concierge or Business Center at many Walt Disney World resorts.

In addition, the Contemporary, Grand Floridian, Animal Kingdom Lodge, Yacht and Beach Club, Swan, Dolphin, and Coronado Springs resorts provide computers, printers, and Internet access for a fee. A video-conferencing center is located near Disney Springs. For more information, call 407-827-2000.

CAMERA NEEDS

Disney's PhotoPass photographers will happily snap shots of you with their camera (see page 133) or with your camera or mobile phone. Note that selfie sticks are not allowed in WDW parks.

Flash photography is not permitted inside any Disney attraction. Note that when capturing moments with Disney characters as video, refrain from using camera lights. (The lights are too bright for the characters' sensitive eyes.)

Camera Supplies: If you need a battery or a memory card, head to the Magic Kingdom's Town Square Theater; the Camera Center near Spaceship Earth or World Traveler at International Gateway in Epcot; The Darkroom on Hollywood Boulevard in Disney's Hollywood Studios; or Garden Gate Gifts in Disney's Animal Kingdom. One-time-use cameras are available at many shops throughout the World. The best selections are available at the aforementioned camera shops.

CAR CARE

There are three gas stations with convenience stores at WDW, all open 24/7. One is on Buena Vista Drive across from Disney Springs; another is on Floridian Way near the Magic Kingdom Auto Plaza. The third, near the BoardWalk resort on Buena Vista Drive, also has a car wash.

Breakdowns happen, but they don't spell disaster. All Disney roads are patrolled by police and security officers who can call for help. If you need a tow or other services, call the WDW Car Care Center (407-824-0976). This service is available to all WDW resort guests. Located in the Magic Kingdom Auto Plaza, the Car Care Center offers full mechanical services and free towing on-property, Monday through Friday, 7 A.M. to 7 P.M.; Saturdays 7 A.M. to 4 P.M.; Sundays 8 A.M. to 3 P.M. After hours, call 407-827-4777. For off-property car care, guests can rely on Riker's Wreckers (407-855-7776) for vehicle towing, Riker's Automotive (407-238-9800) for repairs, or AAA (if you're a member).

DRINKING LAWS

In Florida, the legal drinking age is 21. Minors are permitted to accompany their parents to WDW lounges and bars, but might not be allowed to sit at the bar. In the Magic Kingdom, liquor is served at dinner in the Be Our Guest Restaurant. Alcohol is available throughout the other theme parks and Disney Springs.

Spirits are sold in at least one shop at most Disney resorts. Liquor may be purchased from room service at the Animal Kingdom Lodge, Contemporary, Grand Floridian, Polynesian Village, Yacht and Beach Club, BoardWalk, Swan, and Dolphin resorts; beer and wine are usually available for delivery at other resorts.

LOCKERS

Lockers can be found in the following theme park locations: to the right, just inside the Magic Kingdom entrance; beside Spaceship Earth (to the right, as you enter) in Epcot; near Oscar's

Super Service at the Studios; and just inside the entrance (to the left) at Animal Kingdom. Lockers are also available at the Transportation and Ticket Center (TTC).

Items too big to fit can be checked with the locker attendant at the Magic Kingdom, at Package Pickup in Epcot, and at Guest Relations at Disney's Hollywood Studios and Animal Kingdom. Cost is about $7 per day for small lockers and $9 for large ones (plus a $5 refundable deposit). Items may not be stored overnight. Lockers are cleaned out after the park closes.

Note: Be sure to save your rental receipt; it can be used again that day to secure a locker in any of the four theme parks.

LOST & FOUND

The extensive indexing system maintained by Walt Disney World's Lost and Found department is impressive, especially when a prized possession turns up missing, whether it's false teeth or a camera. (Both have been lost in the past; the dentures were never claimed.)

If you lose (or find) something, report it at any one of these Lost and Found locations: the Transportation and Ticket Center (TTC), City Hall in the Magic Kingdom, the Guest Relations lobby in Innoventions at Epcot, at Guest Relations in Disney's Hollywood Studios, Guest Relations near the Animal Kingdom park entrance, or the lobby concierge at any Walt Disney World resort. At Fort Wilderness, dial 7-2726 from a comfort station telephone; from outside the campground, phone 407-824-2726.

Items lost in a theme park may be claimed on the day of the loss at the park's Lost and Found, and thereafter at the Transportation and Ticket Center (TTC) Lost and Found station. To report lost items after your visit, call 407-824-4245. Hats, strollers, sunglasses, and Walt Disney World merchandise purchases are kept for one month; everything else is kept three months.

HOT TIP!

Nobody starts the day expecting to lose something. But trust us, it pays to plan ahead. Put your name and contact number on your valuables, especially cameras. Disney does a good job of tracking lost items, but it's a whole lot easier to pick a labeled camera out of the heap of look-alikes than it is to find your "little silver" one. (Yes, it happened to us. D'oh!)

We highly recommend attaching contact information to all camera equipment. It makes it a whole lot easier for the folks at Lost and Found to pick your camera out of the giant, silver haystack!

MAIL

Postage stamps are sold at all WDW resorts; World of Disney at Disney Springs; at the Newsstand shop in the Magic Kingdom; at shops near the lockers in Epcot, Disney's Hollywood Studios, and Animal Kingdom.

The old-fashioned mailboxes in the theme parks are not official United States Post Office mailboxes, but postcards and letters (with postage) can be mailed from them. Postmarks read "Lake Buena Vista," not "Walt Disney World." Note: Don't mail anything time-sensitive —it takes much longer for mail to reach its destination when sent from here.

Mail may be addressed to guests in care of their hotel. The address for all WDW resorts is Walt Disney World, P.O. Box 10000, Lake Buena Vista, FL 32830.

MEDICAL MATTERS

Travelers with chronic health problems should carry copies of all prescriptions and get names of local doctors from hometown physicians. However, Disney is equipped to deal with minor medical issues. In the Magic Kingdom, next to the Crystal Palace restaurant, there is a First Aid Center staffed by a registered nurse; there is another such facility at Epcot in the Odyssey Center complex. At Disney's Hollywood Studios, the First Aid Center is inside the Guest Relations building at the main entrance. The Animal Kingdom First Aid Center is located on Discovery Island near the back side of the new Starbucks. **In the case of a medical emergency, call 911 and alert a cast member.** Paramedics will arrive as promptly as possible.

Walt Disney World resort guests and theme park day guests staying at other area hotels have access to services providing medical care. Centra Care Walk-In Urgent Care (*www.centracare.org*), owned and operated by Florida Hospital, has 20 area locations, most near pharmacies and with X-ray facilities. Guests in need of additional care will be transported to the hospital if necessary.

The main facility is at 12500 South Apopka Vineland Road (407-934-2273; close to Disney Springs) and is open 8 A.M. to midnight weekdays and 8 A.M. to 8 P.M. weekends. It is across from the Crossroads shopping center. The facility at 8014 Conroy-Windermere Road (407-291-8975; near the resorts at Universal Studios Orlando) is open 8 A.M. to 8 P.M. weekdays and 8 A.M. to 5 P.M. on weekends. One location in Kissimmee is at 8201 W. Irlo Bronson Highway (407-465-0846). It's open 8 A.M. to 8 P.M. weekdays and 8 A.M. to 5 P.M. weekends. There is also a 24-hour in-room physician service (407-238-2000).

Round-trip courtesy transportation is available from most area hotels to Centra Care clinics, and there is a no-tipping policy. Waits in clinics can be lengthy, but Centra Care drivers can call ahead to learn which has the shortest wait. The most common maladies reported by Disney guests? Sunburn, blisters, colds, fevers, earaches, and injuries from falls. For emergencies alert a cast member and dial 911.

For Diabetics: All Disney parks and resorts can provide refrigeration services for insulin. WDW–owned-and-operated resort accommodations have refrigerators, and small refrigerators may be rented at most other resorts for a small fee. The fee may be waived for folks who need the fridge to store medicine, but a doctor's note may be required.

Prescriptions: Turner Drugs (407-828-8125) delivers medications to many area resorts, including those on Disney property.

MONEY

Cash, traveler's checks, American Express, MasterCard, Visa, Discover Card, Diner's Club, JCB Card, Disney Dollars, and Disney gift cards are accepted as payment for most WDW charges.

A Disney resort guest perk: Swipe a major credit card at check-in and a MagicBand or hotel ID may be used to cover shop purchases, lounge and restaurant charges, and recreational fees incurred inside Walt Disney World. A bill will be sent to your home for all charges made past check-out time. Day guests may use MagicBands to make purchases, too. All it takes is a visit to a MyMagic+ Service Center in any theme park. There they can link a valid MagicBand with a major credit card.

ATMs: Automated teller machines are scattered throughout WDW. Theme park locations include Magic Kingdom (near the locker rental, in City Hall on Main Street, U.S.A., in Frontierland near the Shootin' Arcade, and in the Space Mountain shop in Tomorrowland); Epcot (near the main entrance, on the path between Future World and World Showcase, at the American Adventure, and at International Gateway); Disney's Hollywood Studios (at the entrance and near Keystone Clothiers); and Animal Kingdom (near the entrance and by Chester & Hester's); plus the Transportation & Ticket Center (TTC) near the Magic Kingdom. Most resorts have ATMs; the Fort Wilderness ATM is at Pioneer Hall. There are three at Disney Springs: next to Tren-D in the Marketplace, and near the West Side's House of Blues and Starbucks. Most bank cards and credit cards are accepted; fees range from $2 to $3 (free for Chase customers).

Note: It's always a good idea to notify your bank that you'll be using your debit (or credit) card while on vacation. That should keep fraud protection software from freezing your account when you use it outside your home banking zone.

Banking: SunTrust, across from Disney Springs, offers a variety of services. Guests can get cash advances up to $5,000 on MasterCard, Discover, and Visa credit cards; receive incoming wire transfers up to $3,000 (for a $50 fee); and cash, replace, or purchase American Express traveler's checks (see below). Fees may apply. This branch is open from 9 A.M. to 4 P.M. Monday through Wednesday, and Friday; Thurdays 9 A.M. until 5:30 P.M. The drive-up window is open 8 A.M. to 5 P.M. Monday through Wednesday, and Friday; and until 5:30 P.M. on Thursday; (407-762-4786 or 800-786-8787).

Disney Dollars: While Disney stopped selling Disney Dollars in May 2016, Mickey's money may still be used for purchase at most Walt Disney World shops, eateries, and resorts.

Traveler's Checks: Even the most careful vacationer occasionally loses a wallet. Traveler's checks can take the sting out of that loss. Look for promotions by banks at home in the months preceding a vacation to see if one of the major brands—American Express, MasterCard, Visa, Citibank, and Bank of America—is available free. Stash the receipt bearing the check numbers in a place separate from the checks themselves, along with a piece of identification such as a duplicate driver's license or a spare credit card to speed the refund process should your checks get lost.

To purchase, cash, or replace American Express traveler's checks, guests may go to the SunTrust bank across from the Disney Springs

Marketplace. (If you do not have a record of the check numbers, first contact the place where you purchased the traveler's checks. Then, an American Express referral number is required; call 800-221-7282.)

Foreign Currency Exchange: Up to $50 per person in foreign currency may be exchanged daily at Guest Relations in the theme parks, and up to $500 at the Concierge desk at Disney resorts.

No pets (other than trained service animals) are allowed in the theme parks, Disney Springs, or the resorts, except at certain Fort Wilderness campsites. Of course, that's no reason to leave Fifi or Fido at home—especially when you can treat them to a pampered getaway at the new Best Friends Pet Resort, a sprawling luxury facility (don't call it a kennel!) complete with cat condos, doggy suites, and special accommodations for "pocket pets," including birds and hamsters. Cats or dogs from shared households may share quarters, but cats and dogs are not permitted to cohabitate.

The facility, which is now the only place to board animals at Walt Disney World, provides a full range of hospitality services, including day care (boarding in suites), grooming services, and doggy day camp (group sessions where pups play games and frolic with other dogs under the supervision of a trained animal counselor).

Best Friends Pet Resort is located at 2510 Bonnet Creek Parkway, across from Disney's Port Orleans resort. Its services are available to everyone, but guests staying at Walt Disney World resorts net discounts. Indoor boarding (which includes two walks) costs $44 per day for Walt Disney World resort guests; indoor/outdoor boarding (with one walk) runs $48 a day; vacation villas (one walk, play group, flat-screen TV, and a turndown biscuit) cost $72, and VIP luxury suites (two walks, two play groups, flat-screen TV, webcam, and bedtime story) cost $89 a day (and, with a 3-day minimum, they throw in a "Go Home Fresh Bath").

To prevent separation anxiety, guests are encouraged to visit their pets during regular operating hours. Though hours vary, Best Friends is usually open from about one hour before the earliest theme park opening to about one hour after the latest park closing. The center is not open to the public 24 hours, but it is staffed around the clock (a handy service for guests experiencing travel delays or other emergencies). There are several certified veterinary technicians on staff, and all associates are trained in animal

first aid. For directions, details on services, additional information, or to make reservations, call 877-4-WDW-PETS (493-9738), or visit *www.bestfriendspetcare.com*.

Be sure to bring along your pet's certificate of vaccinations, since Florida law requires proof of immunization for animals involved in biting incidents. Elderly pets must be in good health with bladder and bowel control, and be mobile. Pack your pet's favorite blanket or toy, too. And *never* leave your pet in the car—it is extremely dangerous, and it's against the law.

Outside Walt Disney World: A few hotels in the Orlando area, including the Rosen Inn at Pointe Orlando, let pets stay with guests (there is a $15 pet fee, plus tax, per night; 407-996-8585). Call Visit Orlando (407-363-5872) for more pet-friendly hotels.

Though religious services are occasionally offered on Disney property, regular services are available at local houses of worship.

Protestant: Sundays at 8 A.M., 9:30 A.M., and 11 A.M. at the Community Presbyterian Church, 511 Celebration Ave., Celebration, FL; 407-566-1633.

Muslim: Prayer takes place five times a day at the Islamic Center of Orlando, 11543 Ruby Lake Rd. Call 407-238-2700 for more details.

Catholic: The closest Catholic church is Mary, Queen of the Universe Shrine, 2½ miles southeast of Lake Buena Vista, at 8300 Vineland Ave. This church seats 2,000 people. Call 407-239-6600 for mass times.

Jewish: Reform services are held at the Congregation of Reform Judaism (928 Malone Dr., Orlando; 407-645-0444), near Winter Park, about 20 miles from Walt Disney World. Conservative services are held at Temple Ohalei Rivka, also known as the Southwest Orlando Jewish Congregation (11200 South Apopka Vineland Rd.; 407-239-5444), about two miles from Disney Springs.

At least one shop in every WDW resort stocks a small selection of toiletries. In addition, over-the-counter health aids, plus many other useful items, can be purchased at the Emporium in the Magic Kingdom; they're kept behind the counter, so ask for what you want.

Aspirin, sunscreen, and sundries are also available at the Mickey's Star Traders shop in Tomorrowland. In Epcot, a small selection of sundries is sold in at least one shop in World

Showcase and one shop in Future World. At Disney's Hollywood Studios, stop by the Crossroads of the World souvenir stand. At Animal Kingdom, you can pick up the bare necessities at Island Mercantile.

Local supermarkets include Winn-Dixie (11957 Apopka-Vineland Road) and Gooding's (at Crossroads shopping complex across S.R. 535 near Hotel Plaza Boulevard). Gooding's is slightly closer to WDW, but rather pricey.

Now that all Disney-owned-and-operated resorts rooms come with mini fridges, it's a nice treat to have groceries delivered directly to the hotel. Our go-to source for grocery delivery is *www.gardengrocer.com*. Note that Winn-Dixie, Gooding's, and Garden Grocer are not affiliated with or endorsed by the Walt Disney Company.

SMOKING

Disney's strict nonsmoking policy became even stricter with the adoption of the Florida Clean Air Act. Smoking (including e-cigarettes) is prohibited in all indoor and outdoor spaces, unless specifically designated as "smoking areas." These areas are marked on park guidemaps. All eateries are smoke-free, as are clubs and lounges. Tobacco products are not sold in the theme parks. Guests older than age 18 may purchase tobacco products at some Disney resorts and Disney Springs venues (with government-issued photo ID). Designated outdoor areas are available for those who choose to smoke. Remember, this is a statewide smoking policy, so if you venture off Disney property, the same rules apply. If you have questions about the smoking policy while at WDW, ask a cast member.

TELEPHONE CALLS

Every time a local call is placed from a Central Florida landline, callers must dial the area code and seven-digit number. The rule applies to calls made within the same area code as well as for those that connect with other area codes. For local calls, it is not necessary to dial 1 before the ten-digit number.

Lost Adults

Occasionally, traveling companions get separated in the crush of the crowds, or someone may fail to show up at a meeting spot. When this happens, it's good to know that messages can be left for phone-free or battery-free fellow travelers at Guest Relations in any of the theme parks.

HOT TIP!

The point is to escape the real world, so turn off that mobile phone—or at least stick to texting. That way the magic—for you and those around you—will be uninterrupted. If you have to make a call, do so by the nearest public phone station. And *PLEASE* do not use a phone while experiencing any Walt Disney World attraction. That's just plain rude.

Local calls made from pay phones cost about 50 cents each. Rates charged by non-Disney resorts can vary quite a bit (for all calls). Ask about rates and fees before making calls beyond your resort. See page 52 for more phone tips.

TIPPING

Tips are no less valued at Disney resorts than at any other hotel—$1 to $2 per bag is appropriate for lugging luggage; $2 to $3 per person, per night for housekeeping services (include a note to avoid confusion). Gratuities of 15 to 20 percent (excluding tax) are customary at full-service restaurants. (If service is exceptional or otherwise, adjust accordingly.) Gratuity is included in the room-service bill at WDW resorts and some off-property hotels. Meals that are prepaid with the Disney Dining Plan (except for dinner shows and Cinderella's Royal Table) *do not include gratuity*—please tip your servers.

Give cab drivers at least a 15 percent tip for good service. Baggage handlers at the train station and airport expect about $1 to $2 per bag. The same goes for Magical Express drivers. The ride is free, but it's customary to tip when bags are handled. (See page 16 for details about Disney's Magical Express service to and from Orlando International Airport.)

WEATHER

Call Walt Disney World Weather Information (407-824-4104), or check The Weather Channel website (*www.weather.com*).

WILDLIFE

Florida is home to a vast array of fauna, including alligators, armadillos, snakes, owls, manatees, and more. Never feed wild animals. Doing so alters their natural behavior and is often against the law.

GETTING READY TO GO

Transportation & Accommodations

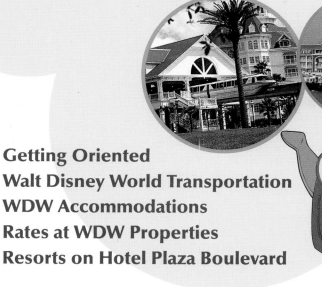

The popularity of Walt Disney World has made the region around Orlando one of the world's major tourism and commercial centers, and transportation sources—from a state-of-the-art airport to an efficient network of highways—bring visitors to the area by the millions.

There's no doubt that getting to and around the Walt Disney World region can be confusing. The only more perplexing dilemma may be choosing the best accommodations for your group from the huge assortment of resort hotels and motels.

The accommodations owned and operated by Disney itself range from futuristic towers to cabins buried deep in piney woods. In between are resorts that evoke striking images of Africa, the South Pacific, historic Florida, the Pacific Northwest, the Caribbean, New England, early Atlantic City, New Orleans, the Southwest, Mexico, and the sports, movie, and music worlds, plus a sprawling, well-maintained campground. And that list doesn't include the many villas or the studios and homes with one, two, and three bedrooms that can be "purchased" through a special vacation-ownership system (aka Disney Vacation Club). What follows should help travelers sort out the broad range of lodging options within the borders of Walt Disney World. Regardless of where you plan to stay, we offer this important piece of advice: Book your room as far in advance as possible. You won't regret it.

Getting Oriented

The Central Florida city of Orlando is the municipality with which Walt Disney World is most closely associated. Disney World, however, is located in a far smaller community called Lake Buena Vista, 15 miles from Orlando's business center. All Walt Disney World hotels and restaurants are located in Lake Buena Vista.

HOT TIP!

Parking lots are cleverly labeled throughout Walt Disney World. Yet many drivers still misplace their vehicles. Avoid being dopey: Always snap a photo or jot down your parking location!

ORLANDO-AREA HIGHWAYS: The most important Orlando traffic artery is I-4, which runs diagonally through the area from southwest to northeast, cutting through the southern half of Walt Disney World. It then angles on toward Orlando and Winter Park, ending near Daytona Beach at I-95, which runs north and south along the Atlantic coast.

All the city's other important highways intersect I-4, and each has a name as well as a number. From south to north, they include U.S. 192 (aka Irlo Bronson Memorial Highway), which takes an east-west course that crosses the Walt Disney World entrance road and leads into downtown Kissimmee on the east; S.R. 528, aka the Beachline Expressway (formerly the Beeline), which shoots eastward from I-4; S.R. 435 (aka Kirkman Road), which runs north and south and intersects International Drive, where many motels catering to WDW visitors are located; U.S. 17-92-441 (aka Orange Blossom Trail), which runs north and south, paralleling Kirkman Road on the east; and S.R. 50 (aka Colonial Drive), which runs east and west.

WALT DISNEY WORLD EXITS: The 40-square-mile tract that is Walt Disney World is roughly rectangular. I-4 runs through its southern half from southwest to northeast. The major Disney destinations are most efficiently reached by taking the I-4 exits suggested in the paragraphs that follow; off the highway, clear signage makes it easy for visitors to get anywhere in the World. This road is congested more often

DID YOU KNOW?

When it comes to fashion, Walt Disney World is the biggest clotheshorse of them all. There are more than 2.5 million garments in its corporate costume closet, making it the largest working wardrobe in the world.

than not. Keep in mind that construction work and special events will often require rerouting of traffic patterns on I-4, so it's best to follow signs as directed:

- **Exit 64A**, marked "192/Magic Kingdom," leads to the Magic Kingdom, Disney's Hollywood Studios, Fort Wilderness, Palm and Magnolia golf courses, as well as the Contemporary, Polynesian Village, Grand Floridian, and Wilderness Lodge resorts.

- **Exit 65** leads to the ESPN Wide World of Sports complex; Disney's Animal Kingdom; Blizzard Beach; Art of Animation; Coronado Springs; All-Star Music, Sports, and Movies; Pop Century; and Disney's Animal Kingdom Lodge. It is also a good alternate route to Disney's Hollywood Studios park.

- **Exit 67**, marked "Epcot/Disney Springs," leads to Epcot, Typhoon Lagoon, Disney Springs, Lake Buena Vista golf course, Disney's Saratoga Springs Resort & Spa, the BoardWalk, Caribbean Beach, Swan, Dolphin, Yacht and Beach Club, Port Orleans Riverside and French Quarter, and Old Key West resorts.

- **Exit 68**, marked "S.R. 535/Lake Buena Vista," is the best route to the resorts on Hotel Plaza Boulevard and the Crossroads of Lake Buena Vista shopping center. It can serve as an alternate route to Epcot.

HOT TIP!

The cost to valet park a vehicle at any Walt Disney World-owned-and-operated resort is $25 per day (not including gratuity). Depending on the resort, there may be a charge for self-parking, too.

WDW Transportation

Walt Disney World transportation is extensive, with boats, buses, and the monorail all doing their part to shuttle guests around. Visitors staying at WDW hotels should receive details about transportation options at check-in. (If you don't, just ask.) For transportation information, call 407-824-4321.

One of the system's hubs is called the Transportation and Ticket Center (TTC), located near the Magic Kingdom. Monorail, bus, and ferry service connect the TTC to points throughout the World. Day visitors must park here before taking a monorail or ferry to the Magic Kingdom. (Most Disney resort guests can bypass the TTC via direct buses.)

The monorail runs along a circular route near the Magic Kingdom, stopping at the TTC, Polynesian Village, Grand Floridian, Magic

Kingdom, and Contemporary resort. A separate extension of the monorail system connects the TTC to Epcot. Bus service is the cornerstone of the WDW transportation system. It is efficient, if a bit confusing. With occasional exceptions, buses arrive every 20 to 25 minutes, from one hour before park opening until about an hour after closing; bus stops are clearly marked. Travel times vary, depending on the route.

Although Disney resort guests are provided with complimentary transportation to all sites on-property, that transportation is not always direct. Build in extra time for travel, especially if you have made reservations at a restaurant. Also, know that traveling between resorts usually requires at least one transfer.

From several Walt Disney World locales, water taxis usher guests to the Magic Kingdom,

Should You Rent a Car?

If you plan to spend all of your time on WDW turf, you can probably spare yourself the expense. Towncar and shuttle service from the airport to all area hotels is available around the clock, and taxis are another option. Within the World, an exhaustive network of transportation brings guests from point to point (if not always immediately or directly). Most area hotels offer their own bus service to and from Disney theme parks (inquire in advance about schedules and costs, if any). Note that strollers must be collapsed before boarding Disney bus and water taxi transportation. (Some folks rent cars to spare themselves this hassle.)

For those planning to resort-hop within WDW or visit Orlando-area restaurants and any attractions outside Walt's world, a rental car is a must. (Just know that area traffic is often rather brutal—always allow extra time, especially if you have a reservation.) It is easy (but pricey) to rent a car at the airport: National (800-227-7368), Alamo (800-327-9633), Avis (800-331-1212), Budget (800-527-0700), or Dollar (800-800-4000)—but note that the rates are much higher than at other locations due to hefty airport fees. For day (or multi-day) trips, consider Alamo or National at the Disney Car Care Center (407-824-3470; free shuttle service is available) or one of the rental agencies that have desks at the resorts on Hotel Plaza Boulevard, or simply inquire about car rental at the front desk of your resort. It is also possible (and convenient) to rent a car from National or Alamo at the WDW Dolphin resort.

Epcot, Disney's Hollywood Studios, Disney Springs, or between resorts. Boats generally depart every 20 to 25 minutes.

TRANSPORTATION ID REQUIREMENTS: Guests who wish to use the Disney transportation system may be asked for proof of riding privileges (especially during busy times of year). Accepted IDs include valid WDW MagicBands, resort IDs and Magic Your Way tickets with Park Hopper options or Water Park Fun & More options, and Annual Passes. WDW resort guests may use all Disney buses, monorails, and boats. Valid one-day theme park tickets permit guests to use monorails and the ferries running between the TTC and the Magic Kingdom, and all buses.

TAXI SERVICE: Taxicabs are available for about $4.20 for the first mile, $2.40 per extra mile. Stick with authorized cabs. Many unauthorized services charge outrageous rates and use surge pricing. When we travel between resorts that aren't joined by boat or monorail and are pressed for time, we splurge for a cab. Inquire at the bell services desk at your resort's front entrance. They'll direct you to the nearest taxi or order one on your behalf. As with all taxi services, keep an eye on the meter and the route the driver takes. (We have been driven in circles on several occasions.)

THE MONORAIL: The Walt Disney World monorail system is usually an easy (and to many, downright exciting) way to travel. There are two main loops, which converge at the Transportation and Ticket Center (TTC) stop. One loop connects the TTC with the Magic Kingdom (and the Polynesian Village, Grand Floridian, and Contemporary resorts). The other loop links Epcot with the TTC. Monorails run from about 7 A.M. until about one hour after park closing. Strollers don't have to be collapsed to ride.

Timing Tip: It can take 5 to 10 minutes to get from stop to stop on the Magic Kingdom's resort monorail loop, making for a grand circle total of about 20 to 30 minutes. The monorail may not run during Extra Magic Hours. Guests

staying at a WDW-owned-and-operated resort can pick up a Times Guide at the front desk—it lists the current monorail schedule.

Transportation Tips

- If you are staying at a Disney resort, you'll find travel info in a folder in your room.

- Most buses are equipped with wheelchair lifts. Such buses have a blue emblem on the windshield and rear door.

- When using the Walt Disney World transportation system to travel between your resort and a theme park, or from one park to another, allow an extra 45 minutes to get to your destination.

- The interval between the arrivals of most Disney buses is about 20 to 25 minutes.

- Be forewarned: It takes a long time to travel by bus from resort to resort. Plan on a trip of up to 90 minutes and at least one transfer (at a park or at Disney Springs).

- Monorails usually run until one hour after the Magic Kingdom closing time (and they don't always run during Extra Magic Hours).

- Note that there is no direct transportation between Disney's BoardWalk and most other resorts. You must first travel to Disney Springs or a park and transfer to the appropriate bus (or take a cab).

- Try to avoid vacating a theme park just as it closes. Instead, plan to linger a bit in a shopping area, or grab a seat and watch the crowds crawl toward their respective buses, boats, cars, and monorails.

- It is not uncommon, especially at park opening and closing times, for guests to be asked to stand on the bus or monorail.

- Keep in mind that the most obvious mode of transportation may not be the quickest. For example, it is often faster to walk to the Magic Kingdom from the Contemporary resort than it is to take the monorail.

- It's possible to rent a car from any Disney resort. For details, inquire at the lobby concierge desk, or contact the front desk.

- Walt Disney World resort guests who arrive with a car receive a complimentary parking permit upon check-in. The permit, good for the length of your stay, allows you to park at all parks and most other places on WDW property for free. Details are subject to change.

DID YOU KNOW?

The Walt Disney World monorail system—a 14.7-mile highway in the sky—has carried more than a billion passengers since 1971.

WDW Accommodations

With hundreds of resorts in the Orlando area to choose from, it's definitely a challenge to select a hotel. Here's our advice.

Weigh the Options: First decide whether to stay on or off Disney property. Many opt for a Disney resort because the conveniences and perks offered to resort guests are appealing (see page 66). Given that, there are still two major factors that tend to lure guests off property: vacation budget and itinerary.

Travelers on a tight budget may find off-property options that are quite reasonable. However, Disney offers rooms as low as about $93–$217 per night (depending on hotel and season), so choose off-property digs only if the price difference is substantial. WDW room rates are based on double occupancy. Additional adult guests will result in an increase in the rate. There is no charge for kids age 17 or younger.

Guests who will spend only part of their trip exploring Disney may also prefer an off-property hotel—one that's closer to the other attractions on their itinerary.

There's also the issue of what one considers deluxe. Disney-owned-and-operated "deluxe" resorts do tend to provide more amenities and services than their "moderate" and "value" counterparts, but do not always rival comparably priced accommodations in the real world.

Deciding Factors: Once the on- or off-property decision has been made, it's time to look at hotels. The big differences among on-property accommodations are in the size of the rooms and bathrooms, level of service, dining options, transportation options, recreational facilities, landscaping, location, and, of course, cost.

Consider how much time you'll spend in the room, whether you'd like to return to the hotel during the day, and if you'll have time to use all the amenities that are included. Parties with five or more members have an additional concern: how best to accommodate their group. It may be less expensive to reserve adjoining, value-priced rooms or a family suite (at All-Star Music or Art of Animation) instead of one luxe room or villa.

Ask the Right Questions: Once a hotel that meets all basic criteria is selected, it's best to do one last round of research, so there will be no surprises at check-in.

For example, ask about any possible hidden costs, like fees for shuttle service to and from Walt Disney World (which run at least $37 per adult [$28 per kid], round-trip) or taxes that may not be included in the quoted price. Though most off-property hotels offer transportation to WDW, the frequency and number of buses vary. Find out the exact schedule and the number of stops made. Ask where the bus picks up and drops off, too. Try to avoid those that stop in busy parking lots.

Some hotels advertise a misleading proximity to Disney. While a hotel may be a short distance from the border, the commute to the parks may be considerable. Get specifics. (Distance from your favorite park is also a factor to consider when staying on-property.)

Last but not least, do not underestimate the value of Extra Magic Hours—a perk offered exclusively to guests staying at all Disney-owned-and-operated resorts, plus the Swan and Dolphin (see page 22 for details).

Reserve a Room: Found the perfect hotel? Book it before someone else does, and don't forget to ask about any special discounts, seasonal promotions, and cancellation policies.

A Room with a View

There's a lot to be said for throwing back the curtains and gazing at a breathtaking view, provided you have the time to appreciate it and your view is within your price range. The following is a breakdown of "views" you may select from at WDW resorts. It will help you choose the best category for your budget.

Although the categories vary, depending on the resort type, the "standard" is always the lowest rate available:

Value Resorts
Standard or Preferred = Location specific. The view can be parking lot, pool, garden, or anything else

Moderate Resorts
Standard View = Parking lot or landscaping
Water View = Pool, marina, lake, river

Deluxe Resorts
Standard View = Parking lot
Garden View = Landscaping
Water View = Pool, lake, or other water
Lagoon View = Seven Seas Lagoon
Savanna View = Animal pastures (at Animal Kingdom Lodge only)
Theme Park View = Magic Kingdom

Walt Disney World Resorts

Walt Disney World hotels fall into two categories: Disney-owned-and-operated and non-Disney-owned resorts. Of all the WDW properties, the Swan and Dolphin, Four Seasons, and the resorts on Hotel Plaza Boulevard don't belong to Disney. Services and benefits in these resorts are slightly modified (see pages 89, 104, and 106).

On-Property Perks: Walt Disney World resorts offer guaranteed admission (with ticket) to the parks in most instances (though there are times when a park hits capacity and no further admissions are allowed); use of the WDW transportation system; the convenience of charging most purchases to the hotel bill; free package delivery to resorts from most WDW shops; and the Extra Magic Hours benefit, which allows extra time in a select park on select days. Guests who stay at a Disney-owned-and-operated resort and arrive via air at Orlando International Airport are entitled to Disney's Magical Express service (see page 16). They also have a 60-day advance window for booking Fastpass+ experiences and attractions (non-resort guests have a 30-day window).

Room Amenities: Disney rooms come with an alarm clock, a small safe, shampoo, phone with voice mail, a flat-panel TV, and free high-speed Wi-Fi. There are hair dryers, irons, small refrigerators (in all Disney-owned-and-operated resorts regardless of their category), and coffeemakers (with coffee, sugar, and sweetened non-dairy creamer) in many rooms. Laundry facilities, dry cleaning, and room service are offered in most resorts (for a fee).

Resort Primer

Payment Methods: Hotel bills and deposits may be paid by credit card, gift cards, traveler's checks, money order, cash, Disney Dollars, or personal check. Checks must bear the guest's name and address, be drawn on a U.S. bank, and be accompanied by proper ID (a valid driver's license or government-issued passport will do the trick).

Room Deposit Requirements: When booked through Central Reservations, a deposit equal to one night's lodging (or campsite rental) is required within 14 days of the time that a reservation is made. Reservations are automatically canceled if deposits are not received by the 14-day deadline. (Reservations booked less than 30 days prior to arrival will receive special instructions for deposits.) Reservations booked through the Walt

Online Check-in

Are you planning a stay at a Disney-owned-and-operated resort? If so, you can take advantage of Disney's online check-in service. Meant to streamline the actual check-in experience, the virtual service is available 60 days in advance of and up through arrival day.

Online check-in expedites the arrival experience by getting the pesky paperwork out of the way prior to arrival. Before you log on, know that you'll be asked to provide the following: the credit card that will be used for room charges, mobile number, address, arrival and departure times, the names of all guests, and room requests (but know that special requests are subject to availability).

With all that info already in the system, guests just need to show up at the resort and present a valid government-issued photo ID. In return, they get a welcome packet including MagicBands (if they didn't have them shipped home) and WDW info. There should be clear signs indicating the spot for packet pickup.

How does one check in via the Internet? Simply visit *www.disneyworld.com* and click on the checking-in section under My Disney Experience. Checking in online does not mean you can check in early. (Unless, of course, there is a room available—a happy surprise that has been known to happen.)

Disney World Travel Company are subject to a substantial cancellation fee. Ask about the cancellation policy when you book your room.

When booking by phone, guests may pay the deposit with a major credit card. Those who wish to use another payment method may do so by mailing it with the payment stub that comes with the reservation confirmation. Call to confirm that your payment was received.

Cancellation Policy: With the exception of Magic Your Way packages, deposits for resort stays will be fully refunded if the reservation is canceled at least five days before the scheduled arrival. Magic Your Way packages must be canceled at least 31 days ahead.

Additional Charges: If you need a crib that is sturdier than the provided Pack 'n' Play, you'll have to rent one from an outside company. For a recommendation, see page 47.

Check-in and Check-out: The relatively early check-out time (11 A.M. at all Walt Disney World-owned-and-operated lodgings) and the late check-in times (1 P.M. at the campsites, 3 P.M. in most hotels, 4 P.M. at Disney Vacation Club accommodations) often come as a bit of a surprise. Guests who arrive before check-in time can pre-register, store luggage at Bell Services (without a fee), and head to the parks or relax by the pool.

Walt Disney World MagicBands: Issued upon check-in at Disney resorts (if not pre-ordered; see page 24), the bands (which double

Magic Strollers

Brought to you by the folks behind Owner's Locker (above, right), this stroller-rental program is truly magical to the parenting populace. For starters, the strollers are all from the popular Baby Jogger City Mini and Summit series; they're delivered directly to any WDW resort (and many

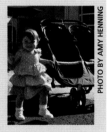

PHOTO BY AMY HENNING

other area hotels) by 7 A.M. on the day guests check in (when the reservation is made at least 24 hours in advance—otherwise delivery is at 10 A.M.) and picked up before 4 P.M. on the day guests head home; and the convenience of using the strollers anywhere and everywhere is a major plus.

Cost is $33 for the first night and $7 or less for each additional night for a single stroller. The rate for doubles is $45 for the first night and $8 or less for each extra night. We recommend getting the insurance, too. For a flat $25, it covers you for any damage or theft that may occur during the time you have the stroller. For additional information or to reserve a Magic Stroller, call 866-866-6177 or visit *www.magicstrollers.com*. To save ten percent off a stroller rental, use the coupon at the back of this book.

Stash Your Stuff

If you count yourself among the merry multitudes who travel to Walt Disney World at least once a year, a system called "Owner's Locker" was devised with you in mind. Simply put, it lets you stash your vacation gear in a private purple locker in the WDW area and have it delivered to you each time you visit the Mouse. That means you'll have less to check at the airport (the locker's great for storing liquids and "must-check" items) and lighten your load overall. Say good-bye to lugging items such as rain gear, sunscreen, baby supplies, cooking items, non-perishable snacks, toys, DVDs, rainy-day activities, first aid supplies, and more.

It's called Owner's Locker because customers actually buy an industrial-strength, secure storage bin when they join the program (extra lockers are an option). After a one-time $75 membership fee, expect to pay about $99 a year for the Standard Annual Plan (including one visit a year; $25 for each additional visit), or about $179 a year for the Premium Plan, which allows for unlimited visits at no additional charge.

How does it work? As soon as you plan a WDW trip, schedule a round-trip delivery via *www.ownerslocker.com*. Your locker will make its way from a climate-controlled storage facility to your resort before check-in time. Call the Bell Services desk and expect the purple chest to arrive in minutes (don't forget to tip accordingly). Owner's Locker service is available at all Disney resorts and many other area hotels (though the business is not owned or operated by the Walt Disney Company). For more details or to join, call 800-431-6588 or visit *www.ownerslocker.com*. The coupon at the end of this book will net you a discount on the initial membership fee.

as room keys) entitle guests to use of all WDW transportation (through the last day of your stay) and charge privileges (if linked to a credit card) to cover most purchases at Walt Disney World. You will be asked to program a personal pin code at check-in. Should you make a purchase on Walt Disney property, you will use that pin code to activate your MagicBand.

Note: Charges that are incurred on a Magic-Band or hotel ID after check-out will be reflected in a revised bill, which may be requested at the resort's front desk or e-mailed upon request. Swan and Dolphin guests may use their resort IDs to charge meals inside the two hotels only.

Walt Disney World Resort Finder

	Name & Location	Setting/Theme	Favored By	Romantic Hideaways
	Animal Kingdom Lodge* Animal Kingdom Area (page 99)	African wildlife preserve	Animal lovers—nearly every room affords a view of wandering wildlife / Art aficionados—authentic African artwork abounds / Disney Vacation Club members	Private balconies by moonlight / Sunset lounge overlooking the savanna
	BoardWalk Inn* Epcot Area (page 91)	Turn-of-the-20th-century Atlantic City	Night owls—the entertainment options are numerous and right in the backyard / Epcot lovers, who will appreciate the short commute / Disney Vacation Club members	Moonlight strolls along the boardwalk / A special fireworks cruise
	Contemporary* Magic Kingdom Area (page 76)	Retro-futuristic exterior, thoroughly modern interior	Families—the monorail whisks through it, and the Magic Kingdom is a short walk away / Professionals, who can take advantage of the hotel's many business services / Disney Vacation Club members	The rooftop lookout (available only to California Grill patrons), which helps make up for the resort's otherwise less-than-romantic atmosphere
	Grand Floridian Resort & Spa* Magic Kingdom Area (page 80)	Victorian seaside resort	Honeymooners—who will love spending much of their vacation basking in the resort's unebbing romantic atmosphere / Magic Kingdom and monorail fans / Disney Vacation Club members	Manicured rose gardens / Honeymoon suites / The Grand Lobby for a cocktail while an orchestra performs on the balcony
	Polynesian Village* Magic Kingdom Area (page 78)	South Pacific	Romantics—fireworks views and lush, tropical setting may make you swoon / Vacationers looking for a hotel with a real resort feel / Magic Kingdom and monorail fans / Disney Vacation Club members	Beach swings for two / Strolls on the beach
	Swan & Dolphin Epcot Area (page 89)	Beachfront whimsy	Guests who want many of the Disney perks but not necessarily the Disney hotel / Bargain hunters—when WDW resorts are "peak," these resorts may offer discounts	A peaceful area beside the grotto pool waterfall
	Wilderness Lodge* Magic Kingdom Area (page 82)	America's grandest national parks	Sweethearts—love is always in the air at this resort / Winter visitors—the warm, cozy atmosphere is even more inviting when the many fireplaces are roaring / Disney Vacation Club members	Steamy, bubbling "hot springs" whirlpools / The cozy alcoves hidden on each floor of the main building
	Yacht & Beach Club* Epcot Area (page 86)	Martha's Vineyard and Nantucket Island	Ambitious guests—those who plan to see and do everything Disney has to offer will like the central location / Everyone—deluxe atmosphere and amenities appeal to all / Disney Vacation Club members	The Yacht Club's peaceful gazebo / Secluded whirlpools / The beach—perfect for strolling hand-in-hand

❤ These resorts host character meals. * Animal Kingdom Lodge, Beach Club, BoardWalk, Contemporary,

Kids Adore	Dining Tip	Resort Category & Amenities	
The kopje, a rocky outcropping from which to spy on critters Story time beside the lobby fireplace Rustic bunk beds (on request)	Sample the exotic eats and atmosphere of Boma while savoring the sights of the savanna.		
The Keister Coaster, a 200-foot waterslide at the main pool The live entertainment on the boardwalk at night	Snack on Ample Hills Creamery's fabulous, freshly-made ice cream while strolling along the boards.		
The "party" held every 45 minutes at Chef Mickey's fabulously fun character meals Watching the monorail whoosh through the resort	Reserve California Grill for a time that's likely to coincide with the Magic Kingdom's Wishes fireworks show—or eat early and come back for the show with your receipt in hand. The view is amazing.	Full-service restaurants, fast-food spots, room service Luggage service	DELUXE
Nightly marshmallow roasts and alfresco Disney films Having dinner with Cinderella and her friends at 1900 Park Fare Zero-depth-entry pool	Have a spot of traditional afternoon tea, accompanied by a scone, at the Garden View Lounge.	Valet parking Swimming pools Beach access ‡	
The hula lessons offered in the Great Ceremonial Hall (on select days) The slide- and waterfall-endowed lava pool	The sushi served at Kona Island is second to none. Enjoy it at the table-service counter, or get it to go and have a poolside picnic.	On-site recreation, such as boat rentals ‡ On-site kids' activities Most rooms sleep five guests	
The swan-shaped pedal boats The giant swan and dolphin statues perched atop their respective resorts	The Swan's Kimonos Lounge serves sushi with a side of karaoke.	Monorail, bus, or boat transport to all parks	
Totem poles, an erupting geyser, and countless Hidden Mickeys—there's even a free tour to help guests find them	Sample Artist Point's signature dishes such as cedar plank Chinook salmon and aged buffalo strip loin, and housemade desserts: warm berry cobbler, or warm donuts. Savor morning coffee from a fireside rocking chair.	‡ Except Disney's Animal Kingdom Lodge	
Stormalong Bay—the sand-bottomed, three-acre pool, with a waterslide and a neat shipwreck to play on	Cape May Cafe's bountiful nighttime clambake has many a surf-and-turf fan lining up for more.		

Grand Floridian, Polynesian, and Wilderness Lodge also have Disney Vacation Club accommodations.

	Name & Location	Setting/ Theme	Favored By	Romantic Hideaways
	Old Key West Disney Springs area (page 97)	Key West	Guests looking for a homey, village atmosphere Disney Vacation Club members Those who appreciate roomy rooms	Private whirlpool tubs— they come with all accommodations but the studios
	Saratoga Springs Resort & Spa Disney Springs area (page 96)	Historic Saratoga Springs, New York	Peace seekers—the atmosphere is meant to soothe Disney Vacation Club members Space seekers. The accommodations are generally more spacious than at other resorts.	Pretty gardens and meandering pathways Private whirlpool tubs— they come with all accommodations but the studios
	Caribbean Beach Epcot area (page 85)	Tropical islands	Families—the colorful design, themed pool, and beach setting make this hotel ideal for families Pirate fans! The main pool and 384 rooms have a buccaneer theme.	Aruba beach—the hotel's longest, most secluded strip of sand
	Coronado Springs Animal Kingdom area (page 101)	Mexico and Southwest USA	Conventioneers—which means more business services (and a health club), higher food prices, and slightly less family entertainment than at the other moderate resorts at WDW	The waterfront in the peaceful Casitas area The gazebo-style boat-rental dock at twilight
	Port Orleans French Quarter & Riverside Disney Springs area (pages 94–96)	New Orleans French Quarter and Antebellum South, respectively	Lovebirds on a budget—the Riverside decor is like many of Disney's deluxe hotels, as is the romance factor, but the price is considerably less The French Quarter, which provides a peaceful, urban alternative	Any room in Magnolia Bend's stately mansions The peaceful gardens scattered about the Riverside quarters
	All-Star Movies, Music, & Sports Animal Kingdom area (page 98)	Larger-than-life fun	Penny savers of all ages—these resorts offer fun, colorful theming, plus all the WDW perks, at a much lower price than at most other Disney resorts Space cravers—who adore the family suites at All-Star Music	All-Star Music's Jazz and Broadway areas (note that Music tends to attract more couples without kids than the other two themes)
	Art of Animation ESPN Wide World of Sports area (page 103)	Classic and colorful Disney animation	Extended families and families with babies—it's great to have the extra sleeping area that comes with the family suites	The Drop Off pool bar is a sweet spot for a (quasi) quiet evening interlude
	Pop Century ESPN Wide World of Sports area (page 102)	American pop culture	Budget watchers and nostalgia buffs—this sprawling resort celebrates pop history with bright colors and big icons Young athletes and their families— ESPN Wide World of Sports is located nearby	Sipping specialty cocktails poolside
	Fort Wilderness Cabins and Campground** Magic Kingdom area (page 83)	Rustic woods	Seasoned RV enthusiasts—Disney's hookups are considered top-notch Families—who appreciate the modern amenities of the cabins, which fit six and fall into Disney's "moderate" category	Horse-drawn carriage rides The Fort Wilderness beach—perfect for viewing the Electrical Water Pageant on Bay Lake

❤ These resorts host character meals. † Known as "Disney Deluxe Villa Resorts" on *www.disneyworld.com*. Animal Kingdom Lodge, Beach

Kids Adore	Dining Tip	Resort Category & Amenities	
Crafts and games offered at Community Hall One super pool slide and poolside activities	Olivia's pleases all palates with a nice mix of pastas and fresh fish. The conch chowder is a yummy way to start a meal.	Kitchens, restaurants, pizza delivery Luggage service Swimming pools On-site recreation, such as boat rentals Front-door parking Villas sleep 4–12 Bus or boat transport to all parks Washers and dryers Boat to Disney Springs	DISNEY VACATION CLUB+
The kids-only water-spray area near the pool Kid-oriented activities offered at Community Hall	Turf Club is a low-key, local dining room. Disney Springs's tempting array of eateries is just across the lake—and conveniently accessed by walking path or water taxi.		
The fortress pool and Caribbean Cay Island The coconut postcards sold at the Calypso shop (real coconuts!) Pirate-themed rooms. Arrrr!	Try a food court kids' meal— it's served in a sand bucket with a shovel.	Restaurant, food court, limited room service Luggage service Swimming pools with slides On-site recreation, such as bikes or boat rentals Rooms sleep four to five guests Bus transport to all parks	MODERATE
The Dig Site—which encompasses the resort's playground and main pool with its Mayan temple waterslide	To start the day in a pleasant way, consider breakfast at Las Ventanas. It's a bit quieter than the Pepper Market, and the sourdough French toast comes with pure maple syrup.		
The pool, fishing hole, and play area at the Riverside's Ol' Man Island. And the "Royal Guest Rooms" rock! The French Quarter's Doubloon Lagoon—a sea-serpent-themed family pool	Sample the fresh beignets from the food court. You'll think you're in the Big Easy.		
Awe-inspiring, super-size icons— the movie and sports themes score the highest points Extra-large arcades	Pick up a pizza at the pickup window in the food court and have a pizza party by the pool.	Food court, pizza delivery Luggage service Swimming pools Bus transport to all parks	VALUE
The Righteous Reef soft-surface squirt zone Super-size icons from *Finding Nemo*, *Cars*, *The Lion King*, and *The Little Mermaid*	Dine in one of the loveliest food courts Disney has ever designed: Landscape of Flavors. Indulge in made-to-order smoothies, hand-scooped gelato, and Mongolian barbecue.		
The state-of-the-art arcade Wildly oversize cell phones, yo-yos, bowling pins, and more The interactive water fountain near the playground	The refillable mug, good for use at all WDW-owned-and-operated resorts throughout your stay, definitely scores points as far as bargains go.		
Pony rides, wagon rides, a blacksmith's shop, and campfire marshmallow roasts with Chip and Dale	Join the nightly campfire circle and roast marshmallows with Disney's famous chipmunk duo. Trail's End Restaurant offers hearty fare at a reasonable price.	Recipient of perfect ratings from *Trailer Life* and *Woodall's* magazines Bus transport to all parks Water transportation to Magic Kingdom	FT. WILDERNESS

Club, BoardWalk, Contemporary, Polynesian, and Wilderness Lodge also have DVC accommodations. **Wilderness Cabins are "moderate."

Rates* at WDW Properties

	Value	Regular	Peak
DELUXE‡			
Animal Kingdom Lodge			
Rooms (sleep 4 to 5)**	$319 – $603	$404 – $650	$414 – $730
Rooms–Club Level (5)	$529 – $644	$582 – $711	$661 – $770
BoardWalk Inn			
Rooms (5)	$408 – $646	$471 – $652	$526 – $728
Rooms–Club Level (5 to 6)	$596 – $882	$669 – $963	$763 – $1,114
Contemporary			
Rooms–Garden Building (5)	$378 – $612	$402 – $634	$436 – $667
Rooms–Tower (5)	$542 – $713	$557 – $731	$638 – $782
Rooms–Club Level (4)	$681 – $943	$710 – $1,045	$835 – $1,049
Grand Floridian Resort & Spa			
Rooms (5)	$574 – $844	$584 – $898	$684 – $1,072
Rooms–Club Level (5)	$688 – $1,214	$762 – $1,317	$917 – $1,513
Villas (4–12)	$746 – $2,996	$791– $2,780	$1,006 – $3,084
Polynesian Village			
Rooms (5)	$452 – $774	$495 – $821	$577 – $976
Rooms–Club Level (5)	$621 – $929	$681 – $1,049	$778 – $1,213
Swan & Dolphin (Rates were accurate at press time but are likely to change. Call 800-227-1500 for updates.)			
Rooms–Standard View (4)	starting at $159	starting at $219	starting at $319
Rooms–Upgraded View (4)	starting at $189	starting at $239	starting at $339
Suites (5 to 10)	starting at $209	starting at $259	starting at $359
Wilderness Lodge			
Rooms (4)	$307 – $619	$367 – $636	$440 – $741
Rooms–Club Level (4)	$515 – $805	$574 – $897	$677 – $1,044
Yacht & Beach Club			
Rooms (5)	$374 – $573	$458 – $642	$507 – $684
Rooms–Club Level (5)	$557 – $1,015	$655 – $970	$722 – $1,145

* Rates for Friday and Saturday night stays are generally higher than other days. Call 407-934-7639 for specifics.

** Room Capacity: Numbers in parentheses reflect maximum occupancy based on existing beds. Playpen-like cribs can be requested for free in most resorts. Rates include up to two adults. There is an additional charge for each extra adult in a room. Details are subject to change.

Rates* at WDW Properties

	Value	Regular	Peak*
DISNEY VACATION CLUB			
Animal Kingdom Villas			
Studios (4)	$318 – $575	$357 – $647	$435 – $702
Villas (4–12)	$513 – $1,997	$544 – $2,389	$684 – $2,547
Bay Lake Tower (at the Contemporary resort)			
Studios (4)	$458 – $666	$528 – $703	$636 – $794
Villas (4–12)	$665 – $2,325	$767 – $2,777	$873 – $2,911
Beach Club Villas			
Studios (4)	$416 – $479	$485 – $509	$543
Villas (4–8)	$566 – $913	$665 – $1,192	$766 – $1,366
BoardWalk Villas			
Studios (5)	$418 – $479	$485 – $509	$543
Villas (4–12)	$566 – $2,281	$665 – $2,436	$766 – $2,569
Old Key West			
Studios (4)	$330 – $370	$373 – $404	$431
Bungalows (4–12)	$452 – $1,474	$507 – $1,629	$586 – $1,756
Polynesian Villas & Bungalows			
Studios (4)	$470 – $689	$539 – $768	$608 – $801
Bungalows (4–12)	$2,272 – $2,996	$2,455 – $2,678	$3,063
Saratoga Springs Resort & Spa			
Studios (4)	$330 – $370	$373 – $404	$431
Villas (4–12)	$452 – $1,474	$507 – $1,629	$586 – $1,756
The Villas & Cabins at Wilderness Lodge			
Studios (4)	$391 – $454	$437 – $510	$540 – $572
Villas (4–8)	$558 – $2,547	$600 – $2,363	$780 – $2,622
Cabins (4–8)	$1,932 – $2,547	$2,145 – $2,363	$2,662

CALL 407-934-7639 FOR RESERVATIONS

‡ For information about suites, call 407-934-7639.

Note: The prices provided here were correct at press time, but rates are likely to rise. Charge is for one day, single or double occupancy. Details are subject to change.

(continued on next page)

TRANSPORTATION & ACCOMMODATIONS

Rates* at WDW Properties

	Value	Regular	Peak*
MODERATE			
Caribbean Beach			
Rooms (4/5)**	$166 – $264	$191 – $331	$211 – $310
Coronado Springs‡			
Rooms (4)	$170 – $297	$199 – $338	$217 – $348
Port Orleans French Quarter and Riverside			
Rooms (4/5)	$189 – $283	$219 – $345	$238 – $342
Fort Wilderness Cabins			
Cabins (5)	$309 – $405	$359 – $419	$406 – $453
VALUE			
All-Star Movies, All-Star Music‡, and All-Star Sports			
Rooms (4)	$93 – $152	$114 – $182	$137 – $199
Family Suites (6)	$225 – $281	$277 – $326	$313 – $384
Art of Animation			
Rooms (4)	$124 – $164	$160 – $196	$181 – $217
Family Suites (6)	$300 – $378	$367 – $460	$393 – $505
Pop Century			
Rooms (4)	$105 – $168	$129 – $197	$150 – $216
FORT WILDERNESS CAMPGROUND			
Fort Wilderness Campsites			
Sites with partial hookup (10)	$53 – $70	$76 – $102	$86 – $113
Sites with full hookup (10)	$74 – $90	$97 – $123	$128 – $140
Preferred/Premium sites (10)	$85 – $106	$117 – $147	$142 – $156

CALL 407-934-7639 FOR RESERVATIONS

* Rates for Friday and Saturday night stays are generally higher than other days. Call 407-934-7639 for specifics.

** Room Capacity: Numbers in parentheses reflect maximum occupancy based on existing beds. A trundle bed (for one) can be rented at some properties for $15 a day. Playpen-like cribs can be requested for free in most resorts. Rates include up to two adults. There is an additional charge for each extra adult in a room.

‡ For information about suites, call 407-934-7639.

Note: The prices provided here were correct at press time, but rates are likely to rise. Charge is for one day, single or double occupancy. Certain holidays and special events (such as WDW Marathon weekend) bring higher resort rates. Call 407-934-7639 for specifics. Details are subject to change.

TRANSPORTATION & ACCOMMODATIONS

2017 Seasonal Dates

VALUE RATES APPLY: January 2 through February 15 for all Value and Moderate resorts; January 2 through February 15 and July 30 through September 30 for Campsites; January 2 through February 15 and July 7 through September 21 for all other WDW properties (except Four Seasons, Swan, and Dolphin).

HOT TIP!

On weekends and when peak rates are in effect at Walt Disney World–owned-and-operated resort hotels, rates at Swan and Dolphin are often much lower. Conversely, Swan and Dolphin tend to have their highest rates on business days and during traditional convention times of year.

REGULAR RATES APPLY: February 26–March 9, April 23–May 28, August 13–August 24, September 17–October 28, and December 10–December 14 for Value and Moderate resorts; April 23–July 29 and December 10–December 14 for Campsites; February 26–March 9, April 23–May 28, September 22–October 14, and December 10–December 14 for Fort Wilderness Cabins; and February 26–March 9, April 23–May 28, September 22–October 14, November 3–November 9, and December 10–December 14 for all other WDW properties (except the Four Seasons, Swan, and Dolphin).

PEAK RATES APPLY: February 16 through April 22 and December 15 through December 21 for Campsites; February 16 through February 25, March 10 through April 22, and December 15 through 21 for all other WDW properties (except Four Seasons, Swan, and Dolphin).

PRE-HOLIDAY RATES APPLY: October 1 through December 9 (applies to Fort Wilderness Campsites only).

HOLIDAY SEASON (HIGHER THAN PEAK) RATES APPLY: December 22 through December 31 for all WDW properties (except Four Seasons, Swan, and Dolphin).

SUMMER RATES APPLY: May 29–August 12 for Value and Moderate properties; May 29–July 6

Category Conundrum

Value vs. Moderate vs. Deluxe—which resort category is best for you? Categories reflect the price of a room, the style of the accommodation, and the level of service.

- Deluxe properties (the most expensive) are defined by their larger, practically appointed rooms, several restaurants, and such amenities as extended room service hours. This category generally includes Disney Vacation Club properties.

- Moderate properties (in the middle range, price-wise) feature comfortably sized rooms, full-service restaurants and food courts, and bellhop luggage service.

- Fort Wilderness Camping covers campsites, but not Wilderness Cabins (which fall into the Moderate resort category).

- Value properties (the least expensive category) offer fewer frills and smaller quarters. Meals are offered at food courts. Recreation and transportation options are limited.

for all other WDW properties (except Campsites, Four Seasons, Swan, and Dolphin).

FALL RATES APPLY: August 25 through September 16 and October 29 through December 9 for Value and Moderate resorts; October 15 through December 9 for Fort Wilderness Cabins; and October 15 through November 2 and November 10 through December 9 for Deluxe resorts. Note that Fort Wilderness Campsites do not have Fall Rates.

NEW YEAR'S RATES APPLY: January 1 through 2 for all WDW resorts (except Four Seasons, Swan, and Dolphin).

HOT TIP!

For rates at the Four Seasons resort at Walt Disney World, call 800-267-3046 or visit *www.fourseasons.com/orlando/*.

Magic Kingdom Area

Contemporary & Bay Lake Tower

PHOTO BY JILL SAFRO

Watching the monorail trains disappear into the Contemporary's 15-story A-frame tower never fails to impress. The sleek trains look like long spaceships docking as they glide inside the resort.

Passengers, for their part, are impressed by the cavernous lobby, with its tiers of balconies and, at its center, the soaring 90-foot-high, floor-to-ceiling tile mural depicting scenes from the Southwest. (Look carefully and you may spot the five-legged goat.)

This imposing structure has 656 rooms in its main tower and garden building, plus those in Bay Lake Tower—occupied exclusively by members of the Disney Vacation Club. There are shops, snack bars, restaurants, lounges, a marina, beach, health club, and more. The pool area incorporates two whirlpools and a waterslide. The convention center offers business services. One of the resort's most notable features is its 15th-floor observation deck. From here, guests dining at the resort's California Grill can enjoy a bird's-eye view of the Magic Kingdom. Another huge bonus: a walking path to the Magic Kingdom (it's a 5- to 10-minute stroll away).

A club-level package is available for guests who stay in the hotel's 14th-floor suites. Amenities include express check-in and check-out, complimentary (light) continental breakfast, evening refreshments, and nightly turndown service. The 12th floor also provides guests with special club-level privileges. To contact the Contemporary, call 407-824-1000.

ROOMS: Boasting a sleek and contemporary design, the standard rooms here are evenly apportioned among the main tower and garden building. All rooms located in the tower have private balconies and (magnificent) views of Bay Lake or the Magic Kingdom. Want to wake up with a view of Cinderella Castle? Request an odd-numbered, park-facing room in the Tower. Most Contemporary rooms can accommodate five guests (plus a child under 3). Typical units have a daybed and two queen-size beds; some rooms have a king-size bed and a daybed. And every room has a flat-screen TV.

Business-minded folks rejoice over the desk space and high-speed Internet connection (free of charge). While the ceiling fans have gone away, room temperature may be set as low as 65 degrees. A heads-up: The bathrooms here, though elegant in design, are far from user-friendly. There's not much shelf or counter space, the flat sinks tend stay wet, the floor can be slippery, and the sliding doors don't lock.

Connecting rooms may be requested, though not guaranteed. Suites, consisting of a living room and one or two bedrooms, can accommodate 4 to 12 people. Weekday newspapers may be picked up in the lobby (free of charge). Other amenities include hair dryers and coffeemakers.

The monorail may be heard from lower rooms in the main tower. For maximum quiet, request a park view on a higher floor or stay in the garden wing. Of course, all rooms get serenaded by the nightly fireworks at the nearby Magic Kingdom park.

The 15-story Bay Lake Tower, a Disney Vacation Club property that sits next to the Contemporary and is connected by a covered walkway, mimics the colors and strong horizontal lines of its neighbor. The tower's crescent shape hugs a lakeside pool.

Studios sleep up to four and offer a kitchenette, queen-size bed, and double sleeper sofa. Sleeping up to five, the one-bedroom villas have full kitchens, two bathrooms, a king-size bed in the master bedroom and queen sleeper sofa, and a sleeper chair in the living room. Two-bedroom villas sleep up to nine, and the two-story grand villas sleep up to 12. All configurations feature a flat-screen TV and free Wi-Fi.

WHERE TO EAT: In addition to the many restaurants and snack spots, 24-hour room service provides a wide range of offerings.

California Grill: On the 15th floor. The specialty is California fare—flatbreads, grilled meats, seafood, and market vegetables. An added treat: the spectacular view of the Magic Kingdom fireworks for dining guests.

Chef Mickey's: Mickey and his pals host daily buffets at this fourth-floor institution. Breakfast and brunch feature Mickey waffles as well as traditional items. Dinner offers carved meats, daily specials, and a variety of entrées, plus a sundae and dessert bar.

Contempo Cafe: A quick-service spot with freshly prepared fare (there's a grab-and-go selection, too), this snack bar is on the fourth floor, next to Chef Mickey's.

The Wave . . . of American Flavors: A splendid spot on the first floor, this eatery offers healthy, creative, locally sourced fare all day.

WHERE TO DRINK: The Contemporary resort is home to several of the World's most inviting lounges.

California Grill Lounge: On the resort's 15th floor, adjoining the California Grill. Picture windows provide a dramatic backdrop for sipping California wines and other drinks, and nibbling on appetizers. Seating is limited. The lounge opens at 4:30 P.M.

Contemporary Grounds: This lobby coffee bar serves cappuccino, espresso, latte, and other gourmet coffees, plus pastries and snacks.

Outer Rim: On the fourth-floor concourse, overlooking Bay Lake, the Outer Rim serves beer, wine, cocktails, and specialty drinks.

Sand Bar and Cove Bar: These poolside spots offer drinks and light snacks.

The Wave . . . of American Flavors Lounge: Inside The Wave restaurant, this bar features wine flights, locally crafted beer, specialty drinks, cocktails, and The Wave's full menu. It's a great destination if you find yourself caught without a dinner reservation.

WHAT TO DO: Volleyball nets may be set up on the beach. Waterskiing, wakeboarding, parasailing, and fishing excursions may be arranged (see *Sports* for details).

Arcade: Game Station, a spacious arcade, can be found on the resort's fourth floor.

Bass Fishing: See page 239.

Boating: Sea Raycer motorboats, Boston Whaler Montauks, and other boats may be rented at the resort's marina.

Health Club: The Olympiad Fitness Center has strength machines, bicycles, sauna, treadmills, lockers, and massage (by appointment). Equipment use is free to Contemporary guests.

Parasailing: Supervised excursions are offered at the marina. Cost is about $95 per person, or $170 for two to ride tandem. Reservations are necessary; call 407-939-0754.

Shopping: The fourth-floor concourse is home to several shops. Fantasia sells plush animals, games, accessories, clothing for kids, and more. Fantasia Market proffers newspapers, magazines, books, snacks, soft drinks, and liquor. Bay View Gifts (BVG) carries character merchandise and apparel for all ages, items with the Contemporary resort logo, jewelry, home decor items, kitchenware, baked goods, and candy.

Swimming: In addition to a round, lakeside pool, the free-form pool features a 17-foot-high curving slide, interactive squirt zone for little ones, and a whirlpool or two. Life jackets may be borrowed at no cost. Cabanas can be rented at Bay Lake pool. Call 407-W-DISNEY for pricing and to make reservations.

PHOTO BY MIKE CARROLL

Tennis: Two tennis courts are available to guests of the Contemporary resort and Bay Lake Tower. No charge.

Watercraft Excursions: Guided excursions on personal Jet Ski-like watercraft are offered for $80 per half hour or $135 per hour. Call 407-939-0754.

Waterskiing, Wakeboarding, Tubing: Ski boats with instructors may be rented for $85 per half hour or $165 per hour at the marina. Call 407-939-0754 for reservations and pricing.

TRANSPORTATION: The Contemporary resort is connected to the Transportation and Ticket Center (TTC) and the Magic Kingdom by monorail. From the TTC, Epcot can be reached by transferring to another monorail. Buses take guests to Disney's Hollywood Studios, Animal Kingdom, Blizzard Beach, Typhoon Lagoon, and Disney Springs. Watercraft travel from the marina to Magic Kingdom, Fort Wilderness, and Wilderness Lodge. Guests may walk to the Magic Kingdom (it takes about 5 to 10 minutes).

PHOTO BY JILL SAFRO

Polynesian Village

The Polynesian Village resort is as close an approximation of the real thing as Walt Disney World's designers could create. The vegetation is lush, and the architecture summons the tropics. The mood is set by a completely renovated lobby that features bright open areas and sweeping vistas of Seven Seas Lagoon. The structure that contains this mass of greenery, the Great Ceremonial House, is the central building in the Polynesian Village. The front desk, shops, and most of the restaurants are located here. Flanking the Ceremonial House on either side are 11 two- and three-story village longhouses named for various Pacific islands. The Bora Bora Bungalows on the Seven Seas Lagoon are part of the Disney Vacation Club accommodations at the resort. The monorail stops at this hotel, making it a convenient place to stay; in fact, it's just a short ride to the Magic Kingdom.

Club-level service offers such amenities as express check-in, continental breakfast, cookies and soft drinks every afternoon, hors d'oeuvres and desserts in the evening, and a lounge with a prime view of the Seven Seas Lagoon and Cinderella Castle (not to mention the nightly fireworks displays in the Magic Kingdom). Club-level rooms and suites are located in the Tonga and Hawaii buildings. The telephone number for the Polynesian is 407-824-2000.

DID YOU KNOW?

The white sand on the beaches near the Polynesian and Grand Floridian resorts and along the Seven Seas Lagoon actually came from the bottom of Bay Lake, located behind the Contemporary resort.

ROOMS: Many of the recently refurbished rooms have balconies, and most have a view of the gardens, Seven Seas Lagoon, or one of the resort's swimming pools. Many rooms have two queen-size beds and a daybed, and can accommodate five guests (plus a child under age 3). Adjoining rooms may be requested (but are not guaranteed). The Polynesian's suites—located in the Tonga building—can accommodate four to nine guests. Some have a king-size bed in the bedroom and one queen-size bed in the parlor. Amenities include a flat-screen TV, free Wi-Fi, coffeemaker (with coffee), hair dryer, and a small refrigerator. This is one of a few WDW resorts to offer snacks and soft drinks via vending machines. Details are subject to change.

WHERE TO EAT: Room service is available between 7 A.M. and midnight. There's also an interesting selection of eateries at which to dine:

Capt. Cook's: On the lobby level of the Great Ceremonial House. This is a good spot for light fare 24 hours a day. In addition to packaged salads and sandwiches, look for items such as sushi and fresh fruit. There is a made-to-order section, too. This is the place to head when you wish to fill your Resort Mug. (For a one-time purchase fee, you're entitled to unlimited soft-drink refills at all "Rapid Fill" locations for the length of your stay.)

Kona Cafe: On the second floor of the Great Ceremonial House. This family restaurant serves lunch and dinner with an Asian flair (including sumptuous sushi), while the breakfast menu is filled with traditional American selections.

Kona Island: A coffee bar by day, this spot delivers one of the best cups of coffee you'll get in all of Walt Disney World. The coffee bar is usually open until about noon. Come 5 P.M., this casual corner morphs into an extension of the Kona Cafe dining room (featuring excellent sushi). Kona coffee is proffered in the evenings, too—as are bags of freshly ground coffee beans.

Oasis Grill: Set beside the new Oasis pool, the Grill serves up items such as cheeseburgers, fish tacos, chicken avocado wraps, and more.

'Ohana: On the second floor of the Great Ceremonial House, 'Ohana serves family-style dinners roasted in a fire pit. Disney characters host a breakfast each morning.

Pineapple Lanai: The Polynesian Village is a happy place for fans of that chilly, tropical treat known as the Dole Whip (a frozen pineapple dessert). It, along with other snacks and beverages, is served at this kiosk near the Lava pool.

WHERE TO DRINK: As might be expected, both the drink offerings and the settings in which they are served are as tropical as they come. In addition to a new bar and grill near the Oasis pool, guests may sip a drink at the following:

Barefoot Bar: Adjacent to the Lava Pool, this watering hole is open seasonally.

Oasis Bar: An alfresco lounge, Oasis offers beer, wine, sangria, specialty cocktails (we dig the Frosty Pineapple), and drinks sans alcohol. Guests may order food from the Oasis Grill menu, too.

Tambu Lounge: There's a tropical air about this lounge near 'Ohana. There's a full bar, but we go straight for the creamy, frozen piña coladas (available with or without alcohol).

Trader Sam's Grog Grotto: The spirited first-floor lounge is next to Captain Cook's snack bar. Sam's is a welcome addition to the Disney bar scene, offering tropical drinks and small plates in a richly themed locale. There is indoor and outdoor seating, with the patio tables much easier to snag than bar stools. FYI: Trader Sam is the "head salesman" in the Magic Kingdom's Jungle Cruise attraction.

WHAT TO DO: A wide range of activities is available at the Polynesian, including a jogging path. Fishing excursions can also be arranged.

Bass Fishing: See page 239 or call 407-WDW-BASS (939-2277).

Boating: Several types of sailboats, Sea Raycer boats, Boston Whaler Montauks, and pontoon boats may be rented at the marina. Specialty cruises are available.

Shopping: BouTiki is the place for resort-wear, souvenirs, and more. Moana Mercantile sells Disney souvenirs, toys, magazines, and fashions. It's also stocked with food, spirits, soft drinks, snacks, and other fixings for an impromptu room party.

Lilo's Playhouse: The supervised activity program for (potty-trained) kids ages 3 through 12 is offered between 4:30 P.M. and midnight. The cost is about $55 (plus tax) per evening. Reservations are recommended; call 407-939-3463. Walk-ins are accepted on a first come, first served basis.

Swimming: There are two pools here: the Oasis, an unguarded "quiet" pool in the shadow of the Tokelau, Hawaii, Tuvalu, Pago Pago, and Moorea buildings; and the larger free-form Lava pool, near the marina. The latter is complete with slide and zero-depth entry. There is also the Kiki Tiki Splash area (an aquatic playground for little ones), a hot tub with views of Cinderella Castle, and an expanded poolside deck. A limited number of wheelchairs are available to borrow for use in the pool. The beaches are strictly for sunbathing, sand-castle-building, afternoon snoozing, and fireworks viewing (no swimming allowed).

HOT TIP!

As signs posted along the beaches indicate, swimming and wading are not permitted in any of Walt Disney World's lakes. The rule is meant to protect guests from unguarded water and from exposure to naturally occurring bacteria and other dangerous wildlife, such as alligators and snakes, common to Florida lakes.

TRANSPORTATION: The Polynesian Village is on the monorail line to the Magic Kingdom and the Transportation and Ticket Center (TTC). It's also possible to get to the TTC via walkway (it takes 5 to 10 minutes). From the TTC, Epcot can be reached by transferring to another monorail. Buses take guests to Disney's Hollywood Studios, Animal Kingdom, Epcot, Blizzard Beach, Typhoon Lagoon, and Disney Springs. Watercraft travel from the marina to Magic Kingdom.

Grand Floridian Resort & Spa and Villas

At the turn of the 20th century, Standard Oil magnate Henry M. Flagler saw the realization of his dream: The railroad he had built to "civilize" Florida had spawned along its right-of-way an empire of grand hotels, lavish estates, prominent families, and opulent lifestyles. High society blossomed in winter, as the likes of John D. Rockefeller and Teddy Roosevelt checked into the Royal Poinciana in Palm Beach, enjoying the sea breezes from the oceanside suites.

Unfortunately, the hotel was lost to a fire, and Florida's golden era faded with the Depression. But nearly a century after Flagler first made Florida a fashionable resort destination, Walt Disney World opened a grand hotel—an 867-room Victorian structure with gabled roofs and carved moldings—on 40 acres of Seven Seas Lagoon shorefront, between the Magic Kingdom and the Polynesian Village.

Like its late-19th-century predecessors, the Grand Floridian resort boasts abundant verandahs, ceiling fans, intricate latticework and balustrades, turrets, towers, and red-shingle roofs. And yet, it offers all the advantages of modern living, including monorail service. With five restaurants, multiple lounges, five shops, an arcade, convention center, two pools, a kids' splash zone, a marina, and full-service health club and spa, the Grand Floridian is not only a grand hotel but also a complete resort.

The main building houses the Grand Lobby, a palatial space soaring five stories to a ceiling of stained-glass domes and glittering chandeliers. Palms and an aviary decorate the sitting area; an open-cage elevator carries guests to the shops and restaurants on the second floor. The turn-of-the-20th-century theme is everywhere,

from the employees' costumes to the shop displays, restaurants, room decor, and music played by the lobby band. The phone number for the Grand Floridian resort is 407-824-3000.

ROOMS: The rooms are filled with charm, decorated as they might have been a century ago—with printed wall coverings, marble-topped sinks, ceiling fans, and Victorian woodwork. Modern amenities include hair dryer, bathrobes, mini fridge, flat-panel TV, clock radio with iPod dock, nightly turndown service, coffeemaker, free weekday newspaper (available in the lobby), and Wi-Fi Internet service (free of charge).

The main building houses club-level rooms and suites; lodge buildings, each four and five stories high, contain standard rooms, slightly smaller "attic" chambers, and suites. Villas are located in a building near the Beach pool.

Most rooms measure more than 400 square feet and include two queen-size beds, plus a daybed, to accommodate up to five people. Many rooms have a terrace. Suites include a parlor, plus one, two, or three bedrooms; there are queen-size beds in the bedrooms. Most of the 15 Deluxe King Rooms, located on the second, third, fourth, and fifth floors, enjoy wonderful views.

On the third floor, the club-level desks offer such services as reservations and information. The fourth floor features a quiet seating area where continental breakfast and evening refreshments are served. Club-level service is also available in the Sugarloaf building.

WHERE TO EAT: Most restaurants and lounges are located on the first two floors of the main building. Room service is available 24/7.

Cítricos: The largest of the hotel's restaurants is also one of the best. It serves market-fresh cuisine from southern Europe. Open for dinner only. All menu items are available in the lounge, too. Ask the bartender for service.

Gasparilla Island Grill: This 24-hour snack bar offers fresh-made selections such as sandwiches, salads, and flatbreads.

Grand Floridian Cafe: Its peaches-and-cream color scheme and verandah-like feel make this a good place for a simple sit-down meal. All meals are served.

Narcoossee's: This sophisticated restaurant and bar has a romantic shoreline location. The seasonal menu includes items such as sustainable seafood paired with award-winning wines. Guests may sip cocktails on the verandah.

1900 Park Fare: A buffet restaurant decorated with carousel horses, plants, and Big Bertha, the carnival organ. Characters host breakfast and dinner daily. This character experience is an excellent alternative to Cinderella's Royal Table in the Magic Kingdom and much easier to reserve.

Victoria & Albert's: The eatery is named after the former queen and prince consort of England. It serves a prix-fixe menu of 7 to 10 courses (to guests ages 10 and up). Jackets are required for men, and reservations are a must.

WHERE TO DRINK: Guests will find the refined lounges here to be lovely escapes. Cítricos and Narcoossee's both have bars, complete with a full menu for dining. Drinks (bought in Mizner's Lounge) may also be enjoyed in the majestic lobby.

Cítricos: Proof that good things come in small packages (eight bar stools and four tables), this lounge has an extensive wine list, specialty coffees, and full menu.

Garden View Tea Room: This pretty spot offers a view of the hotel's lush, landscaped garden and pool area. Afternoon tea is served (as are finger sandwiches and small desserts).

Mizner's Lounge: Named after the eccentric, wildly prolific architect who defined much of the flavor of Florida's Palm Beach County, this bar is on the second floor.

Narcoossee's: Located in the heart of the restaurant, this lounge offers an extensive wine list and craft beer selection, plus a full bar and menu.

Pool Bars: These spots (known as Courtyard and Beaches) both feature a variety of beverages, while Beaches also serves lunch and dinner.

WHAT TO DO: The Grand Floridian offers many of the recreational facilities of a beach resort. Fishing excursions can be arranged (refer to the *Sports* chapter for details).

Arcade: Arcadia Games is adjacent to the Gasparilla Island Grill (near the marina).

Bass Fishing: See page 239.

Boating: Boston Whaler Montauks, pontoon boats, and Sea Raycer speedboats are available for rent (by the hour or half hour) at Captain's

Shipyard Marina. The *Grand 1* yacht (including a captain and first mate) can be rented for about $700 an hour and accommodates up to 18 guests.

Campfire: Resort guests are invited to gather round the campfire (on select nights) and roast marshmallows under the stars. (Guests may bring their own marshmallows or purchase s'mores kits for about $5.) Afterward, everyone is treated to a screening of a Disney film.

Golf: The resort is conveniently close to Disney's Magnolia, Palm, and Oak Trail golf courses. Call 407-WDW-GOLF (939-4653), or visit *www.disneyworldgolf.com* for information or to reserve tee times.

Health Club: The full-service exercise facility, adjacent to the Senses spa, is outfitted with fitness equipment. (Oddly enough, there is no restroom. Health Club patrons may use the facilities at the nearby restroom at the pool.)

Salon: The Ivy Trellis salon offers a full line of hair-care services.

Shopping: On the first floor of the main building is Summer Lace, specializing in women's resort-wear and swimwear, and Sandy Cove, for gifts, sundries, and home decor. One level up is the cheerful M. Mouse Mercantile character shop, Basin for bath supplies, and Commander Porter's, a men's shop.

Spa: The spa at Disney's Grand Floridian resort is a pampering palace called Senses—A Disney Spa. In addition to treatments offered at its sister spa at the Saratoga Springs resort (see page 229), this spot also offers many soothing packages.

Treatment hours are usually 8 A.M. to 8 P.M. daily. Prices start at about $135 for a 50-minute massage and about $150 for a facial. To book an appointment, call 407-WDW-SPAS (939-7727). For info, visit *http://disneyworld.com/spas/*.

Swimming: There are two large pools for guests to cool off in. Both pools have zero-depth-entry and the Beach Pool also has waterfalls and a 181-foot slide. There's an *Alice in Wonderland* splash zone for kids up to 48 inches tall (and their guardians). Kids get absolutely giddy when the Mad Hatter's gigantic hat tips over, dumping massive amounts of water onto bathers below.

TRANSPORTATION: The Grand Floridian is connected to the Transportation and Ticket Center (TTC) and Magic Kingdom by monorail. From the TTC, Epcot can be reached by transferring to another monorail. Buses take guests to Disney's Hollywood Studios, Animal Kingdom, Blizzard Beach, Typhoon Lagoon, and Disney Springs. Watercraft travel from the marina to Magic Kingdom.

Wilderness Lodge & Villas

This resort artfully recalls the spirit of the early American West and the feeling of the National Park Service lodges built during the early 1900s. These grand structures architecturally unified the elements of the unspoiled wilderness parks, kept harmony with nature, and incorporated the culture of Native Americans. The Wilderness Lodge artfully recaptures this rustic charm.

The resort is located between the Contemporary resort and Fort Wilderness on Bay Lake. The lobby, which is shared by the lodge and villas, is in an eight-story, log-structured building. Massive bundled log columns support a series of trusses, while two Pacific Northwest totem poles soar 55 feet into the air. Four levels of corridors surround the lobby, providing access to guestrooms, sitting nooks, and terraces. The monorail does not stop here. Club-level service is available on the top floor. The telephone number for the Wilderness Lodge and Villas is 407-824-3200.

ROOMS: Most of the 725 guestrooms have two queen-size beds and a balcony. Some have a queen-size bed and bunk beds. The bathrooms have separate vanity areas with double sinks. The wallpaper has a Native American–motif border, and the colorful bedspreads and plaid curtains add to the decor. Images of wildlife complete the theme. Rooms include an iron (with board), hair dryer, coffeemaker (with coffee), mini fridge, free Wi-Fi, flat-screen TV, and weekday newspaper (available in the hall or the lobby).

The 114 two-bedroom equivalents (villas) are housed in a five-story building adjoining The Lodge. This tribute to turn-of-the-20th-century design is also one of the Disney Vacation Club properties. The style of the villas building was inspired by the grandeur of Rocky Mountain geyser country. Villas are available to all guests when not occupied by Disney Vacation Club members.

Each studio has a queen-size bed and a double sleeper sofa, plus a kitchenette with microwave, coffeemaker, and mini refrigerator. Larger (one- and two-bedroom) villas sleep four to eight and have dining areas, kitchens, laundry facilities, master baths with whirlpool tubs, and DVD players. They include a king-size bed in the master bedroom, a living room with a queen sleeper sofa, and either two queen-size beds or a queen-size bed and a double sleeper sofa in the extra bedrooms.

Note: Parts of this resort will be under construction in 2017.

WHERE TO EAT: The Northwest theme is carried out with flair in the hotel's eateries. Room service runs from 6:30 A.M. to 11 A.M. and 4 P.M. to midnight.

Artist Point: Decorated with art representing painters who first chronicled the Northwest landscape, this fine-dining spot features salmon, game, steak, and other seafood, as well as wines from the Pacific Northwest.

Roaring Fork: Fast food and light snacks are available at this snack bar. This is also the site of the resort's "refillable mug" station. (For details about the "Rapid Fill" mug program, refer to page 270.) Roaring Fork hours are generally about 6 A.M. until midnight.

Whispering Canyon Cafe: A boisterous, family-style restaurant with all-day dining.

WHERE TO DRINK: Two spots are available for a relaxing break.

Territory Lounge: This lounge honors the survey parties who led the move westward. In addition to specialty drinks, microbrewed beer and snacks are served.

Trout Pass: The poolside bar features a variety of specialty drinks and snacks.

WHAT TO DO: The resort offers many recreational activities. Teton Boat & Bike Rental is in the Colonel's Cabin by the lake. Fishing excursions may be arranged (refer to the *Sports* chapter for details).

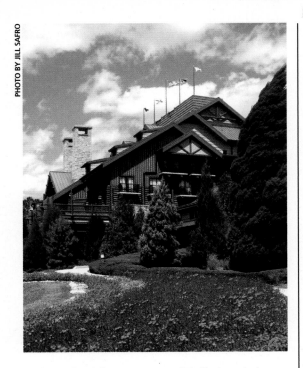

Arcade: The Buttons and Bells Arcade has about 30 different games to keep kids (as well as grown-ups) busy.

Bass Fishing: See page 239.

Biking: Bikes may be rented for scenic rides around the resort. A three-quarter-mile path leads to Fort Wilderness.

Boating: A variety of watercraft may be rented for trips around Bay Lake and the Seven Seas Lagoon.

Carolwood Pacific Room: A fireplace and railroad memorabilia add atmosphere to this relaxing room, equipped with comfy seating, tables, and games. It is located in the Wilderness Lodge Villas building.

Children's Program: The Cub's Den is a supervised dining and entertainment club for (potty-trained) kids ages 3 through 12. Activities, including Disney movies and Western-themed arts and crafts, keep kids entertained from 4:30 P.M. to midnight. The cost is $55 per evening, per child. Dinner and a snack are included. Call 407-939-3463 for reservations. Walk-ins are available on a first-come, first-served basis. *Note that Cub's Den will be closed through mid-2017.*

Health Club: The only thing rustic about the Sturdy Branches health club is the structure it's housed in. Open 24 hours, it features modern equipment, a sauna, and more. Massage and facial services are available. To make an appointment, call 407-939-7727.

Shopping: Wilderness Lodge Mercantile stocks necessities and sundries, as well as a line of clothing with the Wilderness Lodge logo and Disney character merchandise. There is a small selection of grocery items, too. The mercantile is usually open until about 11 P.M. There's also a pin-trading cart in the lobby.

Swimming: The main pool looks as if it were carved from the rockscape. A beach, a kiddie pool, two whirlpool tubs, and a geyser complete the design. Fire Rock Geyser erupts on the hour from early morning until 10 P.M. Kids dig the *Brother Bear*–themed splash zone. A new pool is scheduled to open at this resort in mid- to late 2017.

TRANSPORTATION: Boats go to the Magic Kingdom, Contemporary, and Fort Wilderness. Buses go to Magic Kingdom, Epcot, Disney's Hollywood Studios, Animal Kingdom, Blizzard Beach, Typhoon Lagoon, and Disney Springs. (The Fort Wilderness bus does not stop here.)

Fort Wilderness Resort & Campground

The very existence of this canal-crossed expanse—with more than 750 acres of cypress and pine—always surprises visitors who come to Walt Disney World expecting to find nothing more than theme parks.

Tucked among the campsites are hundreds of Wilderness Cabins for rent, complete with housekeeping service. The cost is comparable to that of some of the more expensive rooms at Disney resorts, but each sleeps up to 6 guests and offers about 500 square feet of space. The phone number for the Fort Wilderness resort and campground is 407-824-2900.

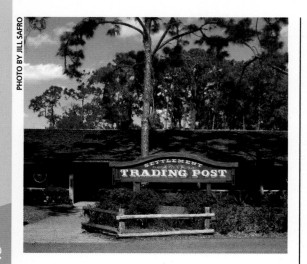

PHOTO BY JILL SAFRO

CAMPSITES: Fort Wilderness has 799 traditional sites. They feature electricity hookups (30/50-amp), water, sanitary disposal, free Wi-Fi, and cable television. Partial-hookup campsites supply electricity and water hookups only. All campsites feature a paved driveway pad, picnic table, and charcoal grill. Most loops have at least one air-conditioned comfort station complete with restrooms, private showers, an ice machine, phones, free Wi-Fi, and a laundry room. A site allows for occupancy by up to ten. Each site has room for one car (in addition to the camping vehicle). Other cars may be parked in the main lot at Fort Wilderness.

The various campground areas are designated by numbers. The 100–500 loops are closest to the beach, the Settlement Trading Post, and Pioneer Hall. The 1500–2000 loops are farthest away from the beach and many other Fort Wilderness activities, but they are quieter and more private. Premium campsites are big-rig friendly and are wider and deeper to accommodate large vehicles. Pets are welcome at certain campsites for a nightly charge of $5. They can frolic at Waggin' Tails Dog Park, the "off leash" pet play area.

WILDERNESS CABINS: These woodland dwellings offer a rustic escape (with all the comforts of home, plus housekeeping). Falling into WDW's "moderate" resort category, the interiors of the six-person, log cabin-like buildings are decorated with wilderness accents. Each one is shaded by a pine canopy. Cabins include air-conditioning, full kitchen, free Wi-Fi, two TVs, full bath, hair dryer, iron, a deck, picnic table, and charcoal grill. DVD players are available upon request.

Note: No extra camping equipment allowed; all guests must be accommodated in a cabin.

WHERE TO EAT: There are a couple of dining options, but many people cook their own meals here. A small selection of supplies is sold at the Meadow Trading Post and the Settlement Trading Post. Ask about nearby grocery stores when you check in.

Trail's End: This log-walled spot in Pioneer Hall serves home-style fare three times a day. Pizza is an option from 4:30 P.M. to 10 P.M. Spirits are available. The breakfast buffet delivers a hefty bang for the buck.

WHERE TO DRINK: Cocktails are served at Crockett's Tavern in Pioneer Hall.

FAMILY ENTERTAINMENT AFTER DARK: The Hoop-Dee-Doo Musical Revue is quite popular. It's offered year-round. Another crowd-pleasing dinner show, Mickey's Backyard Barbecue, is offered seasonally. Reservations are recommended; call 407-939-3463. There's a free nightly campfire program held near the Meadow Trading Post. (For details, see the *Everything Else in the World* and *Good Meals, Great Times* chapters.)

WHAT TO DO: There's a plethora of free activities to choose from, including two pools (the Meadow Swimmin' pool has an aquatic play zone for tots and a slide), tennis courts, and campfire sing-alongs. For a fee, guests can enjoy wagon rides, pony rides, carriage rides, guided fishing trips, Segway tours, archery, boats, bikes, and more. Activities are described in *Everything Else in the World* and *Sports*.

TRANSPORTATION: Buses circulating at 15- to 30-minute intervals provide transportation within the campground, while buses and boats connect Fort Wilderness to the rest of the World. The Magic Kingdom, Contemporary, and Wilderness Lodge are best reached via watercraft that depart from the marina. Buses to Wilderness Lodge depart from the Settlement stop only. Buses to Epcot, Animal Kingdom, Disney's Hollywood Studios, Blizzard Beach, Typhoon Lagoon, and Disney Springs leave from the Outpost stop.

Electric golf carts and bikes may be rented outside the Reception Outpost as an alternative means of getting around within the campground. Call 407-824-2742 for golf cart reservations. Available to Fort Wilderness guests only, golf carts cost about $59 per day, $378 per week. To drive a golf cart, guests must have a valid license and be at least 18 years old.

Epcot Area

Caribbean Beach

This vibrant hotel is set on 200 acres southeast of Epcot and near Disney's Hollywood Studios. It is composed of five brightly colored "villages" surrounding a 45-acre lake called Barefoot Bay. Each village is identified with a different Caribbean island—Martinique, Barbados, Trinidad, Aruba, and Jamaica—and features pastel walls, white railings, and vividly colored metal roofs. There are 2,109 rooms in all, making Caribbean Beach one of the largest hotels in the United States.

The villages consist of a cluster of two-story buildings, a swimming pool, a guest laundry, and a lakefront stretch of white-sand beach. Guests check in at the Custom House, a reception building that projects the feeling of a tropical resort. Decor, furnishings, and staff costumes all reflect the Caribbean theme. Old Port Royale, a complex located near the center of the property, evokes images of an island market. Stone walls, pirates' cannons, and tropical birds and flowers add to the atmosphere. The area houses the resort's food court, restaurant and lounge, arcade, and two shops.

The lakeside recreation area includes a pool with waterfalls and a slide; the main beach; the Barefoot Bay Bike Works, where bicycles may be

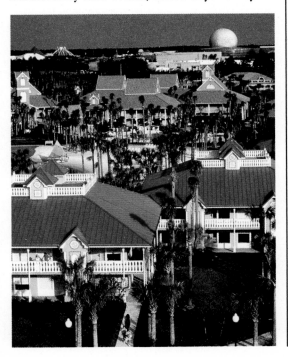

HOT TIP!

Avast, ye hearties! About 400 rooms at Caribbean Beach resort were designed to appeal to the swashbuckler in all of us. The pirate-pleasing parlors are perfect for swapping sea stories. Kids love them.

rented; and a 1.2-mile promenade around the lake that's perfect for biking, walking, or jogging. Kids love it here. The telephone number for the Caribbean Beach resort is 407-934-3400.

ROOMS: Rooms are located in two-story buildings in each island village. A typical 340-square-foot room has two queen beds, and most sleep up to four. Some rooms can sleep up to five (with a fold-down bunk-size bed). The rooms here are a bit larger than standard rooms at Disney's other moderate resorts. Rooms are decorated in tones softer than the colors found on the exterior. Many have a super-kid-friendly pirate motif. Each room has a small fridge, coffeemaker (with coffee), and free Wi-Fi. A note for the budget-conscious: All rooms here are identical in terms of size and comfort, and the only difference between the most and least expensive is the view. To minimize time spent walking, request a room nearest the lobby or bus stop when you check in.

WHERE TO EAT: A full-service eatery called Shutters and the Old Port Royale food court are located in Old Port Royale. Limited room service (predominantly pizza) is available from 4 P.M. to 11:30 P.M.

Bridgetown Broiler: Omelets, biscuits, and French toast are offered for breakfast. Dinner brings rotisserie chicken and other items.

Grab-N-Go Market: Open from early morning until about 11 P.M., this spot sells sandwiches and salads, plus an assortment of pastries, bagels, cheesecake, pies, and more.

Montego's Deli: Breakfast items such as pancakes, sausage, and oatmeal are served in the morning. Salads and deli sandwiches are offered for dinner.

Old Port Royale Hamburger Shop: Sandwiches, cheeseburgers, and fries are served for lunch and dinner. Mickey waffles are offered during breakfast hours.

Royale Pizza & Pasta Shop: Pizza is available in individual portions, along with pasta dishes and salads.

Shutters at Old Port Royale: This full-service Old Port Royale restaurant features items such as N.Y. strip steak and a catch of the day. Cocktails and soft drinks are served, too.

WHERE TO DRINK: The tropical theme is carried out in the specialty drinks found at Banana Cabana. Light snacks are also available at this poolside spot.

WHAT TO DO: There are many recreational opportunities here. The promenade around the lake is ideal for walking, biking, or a jog.

Arcade: Goombay Games at Old Port Royale offers a selection of amusements.

Biking: Bikes may be rented at Barefoot Bay Bike Works. Rides may take guests around the resort's scenic 45-acre Lago Dorado.

Fishing: Guided fishing excursions are offered on Barefoot Bay. Call 407-WDW-BASS (939-2277) for updates.

Playground: A playground is located on the Caribbean Cay Island.

Shopping: Calypso Straw Market carries swimwear and items featuring the resort's logo. Calypso Trading Post has Disney character merchandise and sundries.

PHOTO BY MIKE CARROLL

Swimming: Each village has its own pool, and the main pool—which has a Caribbean-themed setting, conjuring up images of high-seas pirate adventures—has 2 slides, 2 whirlpool spas, and a splash zone for kids under 48 inches tall. Youngsters simply adore it.

TRANSPORTATION: Buses go to the Magic Kingdom, Epcot, Disney's Hollywood Studios, Animal Kingdom, and Blizzard Beach. Other bus routes lead to Disney Springs and Typhoon Lagoon. Getting around within the resort is done via buses bearing an "Internal Resort Shuttle" sign.

Yacht & Beach Club and Beach Club Villas

The New England seaside exists at Walt Disney World in the form of the Yacht and Beach Club, and the Beach Club Villas. Situated beside Epcot, the resorts, designed by noted architect Robert A. M. Stern, are set around a 25-acre lake. The adjacent properties share most facilities—including a convention center offering business services—and transportation options.

The Yacht Club's design evokes images of the New England seashore hotels of the 1880s. Guests enter the five-story beige clapboard building along a wooden-planked bridge. Hardwood floors and brass enhance the nautical theme. A lighthouse on the pier serves as a beacon to welcome guests back to the hotel from WDW attractions. To reach the Yacht Club by telephone, call 407-934-7000.

Distance from the ocean is irrelevant over at the sand-and-surf-focused Beach Club resort, approached along an entrance drive flanked by oak trees. A walkway leads past a croquet court to beachside cabanas on the white-sand shore. Guests are met by hosts and hostesses dressed in colorful beach resort costumes of the 1870s. The telephone number for the Beach Club resort is 407-934-8000.

ROOMS: Yacht Club rooms are decorated in a nautical motif. The Beach Club's rooms are also amply sized and, naturally, reflect a beach motif. In each room, the furniture is white, and (at the Yacht Club) the headboard design on the one king-size bed or two queen-size beds incorporates small ships' wheels. Some rooms have daybeds. Most of the suites have a king-size bed as well as two sleeper sofas. In the bathrooms, there is a separate vanity with double sinks. Each room has a ceiling fan, iron (with board), hair dryer, weekday newspaper (pick up a free copy in the lobby), free Wi-Fi, mini fridge, coffeemaker (with coffee, sugar, and non-dairy creamer), and a small safe. Club-level rooms (with exclusive access to a room with a private concierge, snacks, and drinks) are available.

A five-story building beside the Beach Club is home to 177 two-bedroom equivalents. The villas are available to Disney Vacation Club members. (They are available to all guests when not occupied by Vacation Club members.) Each studio has a queen-size bed and a double sleeper sofa, plus a kitchenette with a microwave, coffeemaker, and mini fridge, as well as a flat-screen TV and DVD player. Larger villas sleep four to eight, and all have a dining area, kitchen, laundry room, and a master bath with whirlpool tub. They include a king-size bed in the master bedroom, living room with queen sleeper sofa, and either two queen-size beds or a queen-size bed and a double sleeper sofa.

WHERE TO EAT: The themes of yachting and the sea play a role in the restaurants that are found at their respective resorts. Room service is available 24 hours a day.

Beach Club Marketplace: Stop here for hot and cold breakfast items such as scrambled eggs, croissants, and pastries, as well as soup, salads, sandwiches, and snack selections. Rapid Fill mugs may be purchased and filled here, too.

Beaches and Cream Soda Shop: A small, classic soda fountain where shakes, malts, and sundaes are the prime lure. Burgers and sandwiches are served as well. The shop is located between the two resorts.

Cape May Cafe: An indoor clambake is held here at the Beach Club each night. The varied and bountiful buffet features several types of clams and mussels, plus beef ribs and chicken. A character breakfast is presented daily.

Captain's Grille: There is a breakfast buffet, as well as an à la carte menu for breakfast, lunch, and dinner. Located at Yacht Club.

Hurricane Hanna's Waterside Bar & Grill: Sandwiches, salads, burgers, and other snacks are served here. A full bar is also located here, and poolside beverage service is available. If you purchase a refillable resort mug, this is a spot to top it off during your stay.

Special Room Requests

Central Reservations accepts requests for rooms with particular views or in certain locations. Agents will do their best to accommodate such requests, but cannot guarantee they will be able to fulfill every wish. Call 407-W-DISNEY (934-7639).

Yachtsman Steakhouse: Select cuts of aged beef are the specialty of the house. Fresh seafood and poultry are also offered.

WHERE TO DRINK: The lounges in both resorts offer a variety of specialty drinks in relaxing seaside settings.

Ale and Compass: This Yacht Club lobby lounge, featuring specialty cocktails and wine, provides a nice respite after a long day. Mornings bring a selection of continental breakfast items.

Crew's Cup: The place to try beer shipped in from the world's seaports before dining at Yachtsman Steakhouse next door.

Martha's Vineyard: This quiet lounge at the Beach Club offers selections from American and international vineyards, served by the glass or bottle, as well as a full bar and appetizers.

WHAT TO DO: There is enough to do here to fill an entire vacation. A sand volleyball court may be found near the Beach Club. Equipment is available at no cost at the Ship Shape health club. Bikes and boats may be rented.

TRANSPORTATION & ACCOMMODATIONS

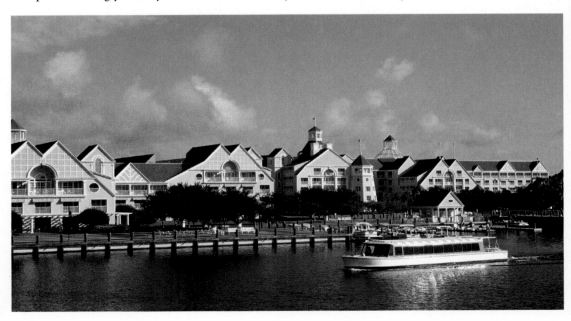

The Fantasia Gardens Miniature Golf complex is close by, and guided fishing excursions may be arranged (see *Sports*). And last but not least, the BoardWalk entertainment district is a short walk around the lake.

Arcade: Lafferty Place Arcade has about 60 video games and pinball machines.

Boating: Pontoons, Boston Whaler Montauks, Sea Raycers, and other boats are available for rent at the Bayside Marina.

Children's Program: The Sandcastle Club, for potty-trained kids ages 3 through 12, is open 4:30 P.M. to midnight. Cost is $55 per evening, per child (including dinner and a snack). Reservations are recommended; call 407-939-3463. Walk-ins are accepted on a first-come, first-served basis. The Club has programming to entertain and educate little ones—with surprise visits from Disney pals.

Health Club: The Ship Shape health club has strength and cardio machines and is open 24/7 to resort guests age 14 and older. (Request an "after hours" keycard during operating hours.) Massage and facial services are available. For an appointment, call 407-939-7727.

Salon: The Ship Shape salon sits between Yacht and Beach Club, poolside. It offers a full line of hair care services; call 407-939-7727.

Shopping: At the Yacht Club, Fittings & Fairings Clothes and Notions is an all-purpose shop stocked with character merchandise and sundries. At the Beach Club, the Beach Club Marketplace has a similar selection of goods.

Swimming: Between the marina and the beach is the centerpiece of the dual resort—Stormalong Bay, a three-acre pool that's like a mini water park. There is a lagoon expressly for relaxed bathing, and another with currents, jets, and sand-bottomed areas. Several whirlpools are scattered throughout the area. Adjacent to the main pool is a shipwreck, where guests can enjoy a waterslide. There is one unguarded pool and whirlpool at the far end of each hotel. There is also an unguarded pool by the Beach Club Villas. Guests may sunbathe on the beach, though swimming is not permitted.

Tennis: There is one lighted tennis court on the Yacht Club side of the property. Rental equipment is available at the Bayside Marina.

TRANSPORTATION: Guests travel to Epcot and Disney's Hollywood Studios via FriendShip water taxis or walkways. Buses go to the Magic Kingdom, Animal Kingdom, Disney Springs, Typhoon Lagoon, and Blizzard Beach.

Meetings & Conventions

Convention centers at Walt Disney World range in size from 20,000 to 200,000 square feet. The Dolphin's center, featuring an exhibit hall and an executive boardroom, is the largest; the Swan provides additional space. The Contemporary has three ballrooms and a spacious pre-function area with lots of natural light. The convention center at the Yacht and Beach Club is reminiscent of a grand turn-of-the-century New England town-meeting hall. The Grand Floridian Resort and Spa has a lavish center with silk brocade walls. The BoardWalk offers a smaller conference area with a lakeside gazebo for outdoor events. And Coronado Springs, the first moderately priced Disney resort to offer convention facilities, boasts one of the largest hotel ballrooms in the U.S.

Among the unique services available to Disney conventioneers is the use of Disney characters and performers for events. Special events can even be held in the parks. Resort business centers have clerical staffs and computers, in addition to faxing and photocopying equipment. (These services are available to all resort guests.)

Those interested in scheduling a convention should call 321-939-7221. Organizers are advised to book their events six months in advance, especially for large groups.

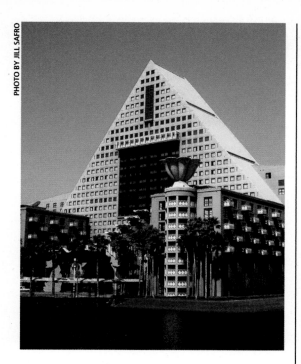

Swan & Dolphin

These sister resorts, situated on the shores of Crescent Lake, can easily be distinguished by the 47-foot swan and 56-foot dolphin statues that top them. The waterfalls, rows of palm trees, and beachfront location all reflect the tropical Florida landscape that was their inspiration. Both hotels were designed by noted architect Michael Graves as examples of "entertainment architecture." The turquoise waves on the colored facade of the Swan's 12-story main building and two 7-story wings are clearly evidence of this design, as is the Dolphin's exterior mural, which features a banana-leaf pattern. The soaring 27-story triangular tower at the center of the Dolphin is flanked by four 9-story guestroom wings.

The resorts share extensive convention facilities, many recreational options, and a host of restaurants. The Swan and Dolphin are operated by Westin and Sheraton, respectively, but are treated as Walt Disney World resorts; guests here enjoy most WDW resort benefits, most notably access to Extra Magic Hours and a 60-day advance window for Fastpass+ assignments. One notable difference: Guests cannot use their room keys to charge purchases on WDW property, with the exception of within the Swan and Dolphin resorts themselves. The direct line for the Swan and Dolphin is 407-934-3000. Reservations for either resort may be made by calling 888-227-1500, visiting *www.swandolphin.com*, or through Facebook at *www.facebook.com/swananddolphin*.

ROOMS: All rooms have gotten a fresh look, reflecting the hotels' water-themed architecture. Amenities include weekday newspaper delivery, safes, mini fridge, irons and boards, two dual-line telephones, and high-speed, wireless Internet access. Rooms equipped for guests with disabilities are available. Valet parking is $26 per day (plus tax); self-parking is $18 a day.

There are 758 rooms and 55 suites at the Swan, each with one king-size or two queen-size "Westin Heavenly Beds." At the Dolphin, the 1,509 rooms and 112 suites feature two double beds or one king-size heavenly bed. Swan rooms also include a separate vanity and dressing area.

WHERE TO EAT: In addition to many restaurant choices, 24-hour room service provides an extensive all-day dining menu. (The room service here is considered among the best at Walt Disney World.)

Cabana Bar & Beach Club: This full-service poolside spot near the Dolphin serves burgers, grilled chicken sandwiches, flatbreads, and more. The full bar serves specialty drinks.

The Fountain: Homemade ice cream is the specialty at this Dolphin eatery. Huge sundaes, shakes, malts, and burgers are also offered.

Fresh: Designed to resemble a cheerful marketplace, this Dolphin spot serves breakfast and lunch only. The menu features "healthy, sustainable, and organic" fare.

Garden Grove Cafe: This Swan eatery, which features a park-like atmosphere, serves three meals daily. A buffet breakfast with Disney characters is held on Saturdays and Sundays, while a character dinner takes place nightly.

Il Mulino New York Trattoria: The highly acclaimed Italian restaurant is located on the first floor of the Swan. The setting, which is reminiscent of an old-world trattoria, is relaxed yet vibrant. Features such as *Piatti per il Tavolo* (family-style dining) and wood-fired pizzas complement Il Mulino New York's family-friendly Walt Disney World locale.

Picabu: A cafeteria with a bit of flair. The 24-hour convenience store here sells snacks and sundries. It has Starbucks coffee, too.

HOT TIP!

The Swan and Dolphin resorts run seasonal promotions throughout the year. For information, call 888-828-8850, or visit *www.swandolphin.com*.

PHOTO BY JILL SAFRO

Shula's: An upscale celebration of two American favorites: steak and pro football. It's a bit pricey, but the steaks are superb and the side orders are big enough to share. There is a children's menu (chicken, cheeseburgers, etc.). The (enforced) dress code is business casual.

Splash Terrace: A poolside cafe near the Swan serving specialty sandwiches, pizza, and snacks. A full-service bar is also located here.

Todd English's bluezoo: This eatery features coastal cuisine, beef, and chicken dishes with international and domestic influences.

WHERE TO DRINK: It's easy to find a nice cocktail spot in this neck of the woods.

Java Bar: This spot at the Swan offers a quick bite for early birds on the go. Enjoy specialty coffees, light breakfast items, and fresh pastries until 6 P.M. most days.

Kimonos: The Asian decor makes this Swan lounge an inviting place for sake, sushi, and other Japanese selections. Karaoke is a house specialty. This place is generally hopping a bit later than most other Walt Disney World resort lounges.

Lobby Lounge: A cozy Dolphin area featuring wine and specialty drinks.

Shula's Steak House Lounge: Settle into a comfy chair and sip a drink in this lounge adjacent to Shula's dining room.

WHAT TO DO: The Swan and Dolphin share many recreation options. Volleyball nets and hammocks are set up on the beach. The Fantasia Gardens Miniature Golf complex and Board-Walk are nearby (the proximity to BoardWalk and Epcot is a big plus). Disney's Hollywood Studios is a FriendShip water taxi ride (or about a 20-minute walk) away.

Arcades: A room full of cutting-edge video games is located near Picabu at the Dolphin. Another game room can be found near the Splash cafe at the Swan.

Boating: Watercraft are available for rent on the beach between the Swan and Dolphin.

Children's Program: Camp Dolphin welcomes children (potty-trained) ages 4 through 12 and has supervised activities from 5 P.M. to midnight. The cost is $12 per child, per hour.

Health Clubs: There is a fitness center near the pool area at the Dolphin. State-of-the-art equipment is available. There's also a smaller health club with basic exercise equipment near Splash Terrace at the Swan.

Playground: A sandy play area with swings and jungle gyms is located on the beach near the grotto pool.

Shopping: Disney Cabanas, located in the lobby of the Swan, features character merchandise and sundries. Four shops may be found at the Dolphin. Sugar3 allows chocolate lovers the chance to sample some tasty concoctions. Lamont's offers resort-wear for men and women. Daisy's Garden is the place to find character goods at the Dolphin. Galleria Sottil is the Dolphin's art gallery. Expect to find paintings, sculptures, and other assorted works of art. The Cabana Beach Hut, by the Dolphin pool, specializes in "pool-fun" essentials, while the 24-hour convenience store within Picabu sells grocery items and sundries.

Spa and Salon: The Mandara Spa features full-service body treatments, plus hairstyling, manicures, pedicures, and more.

Swimming: In addition to a shared kids' wading pool, there are two lap pools, and a themed grotto pool with slides between the Swan and Dolphin. Several whirlpools are scattered around the area.

Tennis: Four hard-surface tennis courts are located behind the pool area closest to the Swan resort. They are open 24 hours a day and are fully lighted. Racquet rentals and lessons may be coordinated at the resort's health club.

TRANSPORTATION: Guests travel to Epcot and Disney's Hollywood Studios via ferryboats or walkway. (It takes about 10 minutes to walk to Epcot's back entrance and about 20 minutes to reach Disney's Hollywood Studios on foot. Water taxis don't move much faster—and they make multiple stops—so allow plenty of time to reach either destination.) Buses go directly to the Magic Kingdom, Animal Kingdom, Disney Springs, Typhoon Lagoon, and Blizzard Beach.

BoardWalk Inn & Villas

The enchantment of a bygone era is recaptured at the BoardWalk. The resort combines a waterside entertainment complex with deluxe hotel accommodations and vacation villas. Dining, recreation, shopping, and entertainment venues line the boardwalk, and twinkling lights trim the buildings. The ambience continues throughout, with detailed architecture featuring colorful facades, flagged turrets, and striped awnings, all reminiscent of the turn of the 20th century. BoardWalk resort is adjacent to Epcot's International Gateway and connected to it via walkway. The phone number for BoardWalk is 407-939-5100.

ROOMS: Accommodations here evoke the charm of early Eastern-seaboard inns. Most have private balconies or patios. The BoardWalk Inn has 372 deluxe hotel rooms decorated with cherrywood furniture, boardwalk postcard-print curtains, and light green accents. Guestrooms at the Inn sleep up to five, and feature two queen-size beds (or one king-size bed) and a child's daybed. Romantic two-story garden suites each have a private garden enclosed by a white picket fence. They sleep four, and have a living room on the first floor and a king-size bed in the unenclosed, bedroom loft. The Inn also has club-level rooms and suites.

The 282 two-bedroom equivalents are collectively called BoardWalk Villas. These are Disney Vacation Club villas, available to everyone when not occupied by members. Each studio has a queen-size bed and double sleeper sofa, plus a kitchenette with microwave, coffeemaker, and small refrigerator. Larger (one-, two-, and three-bedroom) villas sleep 4 to 12 people, and feature dining areas, fully equipped kitchens, laundry facilities, master baths with whirlpool tubs, and flat-screen television with DVD player. They also include a king-size bed in the master bedroom, living room with a queen sleeper sofa, and a queen-size bed, plus a double sleeper sofa in any additional bedrooms.

Rooms at the BoardWalk Inn include weekday newspapers (available near the elevators and in the lobby). All rooms have an iron and board, hair dryer, and free Wi-Fi.

WHERE TO EAT: This resort has a wealth of dining and snacking options. A variety of vendors along the boardwalk tempt with hot dogs, crêpes on a stick, gourmet coffee, and more. For those looking to eat in, room service is available.

Ample Hills Creamery: Enjoy scrumptious hand-crafted ice cream made with hormone-free milk from grass-fed cows and organic cane sugar at this new ice cream shop next to BoardWalk's ESPN Club.

Big River Grille & Brewing Works: This working brewpub features a full menu, complemented by fresh specialty ales. View the on-site brewmaster through floor-to-ceiling glass walls.

BoardWalk Bakery: A popular stop that offers baked goods, sandwiches, soups, and salads. A display area allows customers to watch bakers at work. This is also the place to refill a Rapid Fill resort mug.

Resort Roundup

What's the best place to stay at Walt Disney World? It's a tough question—and one that Birnbaum editors are asked all the time. The answer? Well, it depends. Do you have a favorite park? What's your price range? Will a clown's tongue that doubles as a pool slide make your day? All factors to consider. That said, here are our favorites in each of Disney's price categories:

BIRNBAUM'S ★BEST DELUXE

Yacht Club: In addition to a picturesque setting, this resort is all about location. For starters, you can walk to Epcot (and the Studios if you're feeling ambitious). Of course, you can always take a water taxi. You're a stone's throw from the excitement of the bustling BoardWalk entertainment district, but get to enjoy the relative peace of life on the quieter side of Crescent Lake. Excellent dining options abound. And the Stormalong Bay pool area is tops. We enjoy the Beach Club, too, but Yacht Club is a bit quieter and there are more rooms with full balconies.
Honorable mentions: Contemporary and Polynesian Village

BIRNBAUM'S ★BEST MODERATE

Port Orleans Riverside: One need not be a Southern aristocrat to live like one. Many of the guest buildings at this resort, formerly known as Dixie Landings, were designed to look like historic mansions. Even the food court has a certain Southern ambience. There's a table-service restaurant and a cozy lounge (which may offer entertainment). Kids enjoy dropping their hooks in the fishing hole (strictly catch-and-release) and splashing in the free-form pool on Ol' Man Island. Pretty gardens and a relatively reasonable price add to the appeal.
Honorable mention: Caribbean Beach

BIRNBAUM'S ★BEST VALUE

Art of Animation: This colorful "value" property has some of the boldest and brightest theming around and a top-notch food court—but what sets it apart is the stunning Big Blue Pool and the adjacent splash zone. The family suites are a true value—we're particularly fond of the *Cars*-themed accommodations, but all areas get a thumbs-up.
Honorable mention: Pop Century

BoardWalk Pizza Window: This walk-up window sells pizza by the slice and the pie. It's open for lunch and dinner.

BoardWalk Carts: Stands along the boardwalk offer snacks such as corn dogs, pretzels, hot dogs, and frozen margaritas.

ESPN Club: A serious sports bar for serious sports fans, ESPN provides sports video entertainment and all-day dining. Get there early if there is a big game scheduled.

Flying Fish: This thoroughly refurbished and refreshed restaurant has a show kitchen, and its dinner menu emphasizes seafood, steak, and fresh seasonal items.

Trattoria al Forno: An Italian eatery, Trattoria features old-world favorites for the whole family.

WHERE TO DRINK: Guests have a multitude of options right in their backyard.

Atlantic Dance Hall: This waterfront club is an elegantly designed dance spot. You must be at least 21 to enter. There's usually no charge, but there are exceptions for special events.

Belle Vue Lounge: Listen to old-time tunes on antique radios and play board games in this cocktail lounge near the lobby. The room is open all day, but the bartender doesn't arrive until 5 P.M.

Jellyrolls: Dueling pianos provide entertainment in a casual warehouse atmosphere. The cover charge is about $12 nightly. You must be at least 21 to enter Jellyrolls and able to prove it. Note that this place cranks the A.C. year-round.

Leaping Horse Libations: The carousel-themed pool bar at Luna Park serves a variety of cocktails, as well as sandwiches and snacks.

WHAT TO DO: The three-quarter-mile pathway encircling Crescent Lake provides a ready venue for walkers and joggers. Guests may rent boats from Yacht and Beach Club's Bayside Marina. The Fantasia Gardens Miniature Golf complex is nearby. At the resort itself, Ferris W. Eahlers Community Hall rents equipment for many recreational pursuits, including croquet, table tennis, badminton—even books and DVDs. Fishing excursions can be arranged.

Arcade: Side Show Games Arcade has a selection of video games.

Biking: Ferris W. Eahlers Community Hall offers a variety of bicycles for rental. Surreys (canopied quadra-cycles for four) may also be rented there.

Health Club: Muscles & Bustles health club has steam rooms, modern exercise machines and circuit-training equipment. The health club is open 24 hours a day for BoardWalk guests.

Midway Games: This area on the Board-Walk's WildWood Landing features games of luck and skill similar to those found along traditional boardwalks. There is a charge to play.

Shopping: Dundy's Sundries in the lobby is the source for basic necessities. Character Carnival on the boardwalk has children's apparel as well as character merchandise. Screen Door General Store stocks groceries, dry goods, snacks, and beverages. Thimbles & Threads, also on the boardwalk, carries apparel for men and women. Wyland Galleries features marine and environmental art.

Surrey Bike Ride: A trip around the lake in a pedal-powered surrey is available for a fee.

Swimming: The BoardWalk's swimming area, Luna Park, has a pool with a 200-foot waterslide, "Keister Coaster," patterned after a wooden roller coaster. (The slide, shown at right, is a clown's tongue. Kids get a big kick out of it.) A family of elephants is found posed throughout the area; their trunks act as a shower for adults on the pool deck or children in the wading pool. The resort has two unguarded pools. There are three whirlpools, one in each pool area.

Tennis: Two lighted tennis courts are available for play. Equipment may be rented at Community Hall.

TRANSPORTATION: Guests may travel to Epcot and Disney's Hollywood Studios via ferryboats or walkways. (It takes about 10 minutes to walk to International Gateway, aka

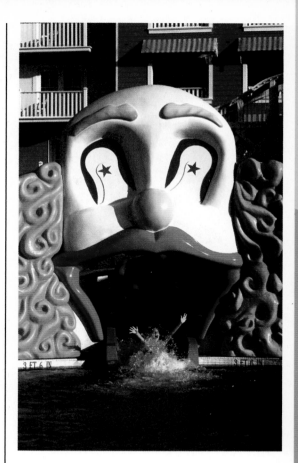

Epcot's back door. The stroll to Disney's Hollywood Studios takes about 20 minutes.) Buses transport guests to the Magic Kingdom, Animal Kingdom, Typhoon Lagoon, Blizzard Beach, and Disney Springs.

Disney Vacation Club

Disney Vacation Club grants members the convenience of flexible vacations from year to year, with the ability to choose when and where to visit, how long to stay, and the type of accommodations. It starts with the purchase of a real estate interest in a Disney Vacation Club property. For a one-time purchase price and annual dues, members can enjoy vacation stays at Aulani Resort & Spa (in Oahu, Hawaii); Bay Lake Tower at Contemporary resort, Animal Kingdom Villas, The Villas at Disney's Grand Floridian Resort & Spa, Old Key West Resort, Beach Club Villas, BoardWalk Villas, the Villas at Disney's Wilderness Lodge, Saratoga Springs Resort & Spa, and the Polynesian Villas & Bungalows at WDW; Disney's Vero Beach Resort in Florida; Disney's Hilton Head Island Resort in South Carolina; and the Villas at Disney's Grand Californian Resort & Spa in Anaheim, California; plus access to additional destinations around the globe. Through Member Getaways, members may also elect to stay at their choice of more than 500 resorts worldwide, including most Disney resorts and the Disney Cruise Line.

Disney's Vero Beach Resort is a two-hour drive from Walt Disney World. It has villa-type accommodations comparable to those at Disney's Old Key West Resort—with lush surroundings, the beach, and local sights. The proximity makes it easy to tack a beach vacation onto a WDW visit.

Disney Vacation Club information centers may be found at each of the Walt Disney World hotels and theme parks. For more information, call 800-800-9100, or visit *www.disneyvacationclub.com*.

Disney Springs Area

PHOTO BY JILL SAFRO

Port Orleans French Quarter

This 1,008-room resort invites comparisons to the historic French Quarter of New Orleans.

Starting at the entrance gate, with its wrought-iron portal and overgrown landscape, the appeal of the Delta City surrounds arriving guests. The entry drive leads to the heart of the "city," which is Port Orleans Square. The central building was based on a turn-of-the-20th-century mint. The Mint houses check-in facilities, a shop, food court, and an arcade. It has a vaulted ceiling, and the check-in desks are designed as bank-teller windows. The musical notes in the mural are the notes to "When the Saints Go Marching In." To reach Port Orleans French Quarter, call 407-934-5000.

ROOMS: The guestrooms are located in seven 3-story buildings (with elevators). Each room has two queen beds; some king-size beds are available. The rooms are a bit smaller than the standard rooms at the more expensive Disney hotels, but they are comfortable for a family of four. (Rooms with a small bunk can fit 5.) Buildings are brightly colored and have wrought-iron railings of varying designs. Connecting rooms may be requested but can't be guaranteed. The least expensive rooms overlook gardens or parking areas, and the most expensive rooms offer water views. All rooms have a coffeemaker (with coffee), mini fridge, and Wi-Fi.

WHERE TO EAT: A counter-service food court has several dining options. Disney Springs, and its plethora of eateries, is accessible by boat or bus.

Sassagoula Floatworks & Food Factory: A variety of specialty foods is available in this food court, including gumbo, chicken with red beans and rice, freshly made beignets, and other traditional Creole dishes. Burgers, pizza, ice cream, and baked goods are also on the menu.

WHERE TO DRINK: A pool bar operates seasonally, and guests on a quest for a cocktail may head to Port Orleans Riverside—it's a short bus ride away. Of course, there's always Disney Springs or any theme park other than the Magic Kingdom. (Epcot has quite a few options.)

WHAT TO DO: A themed pool is the highlight of the recreational opportunities here.

Arcade: South Quarter Games is located at Port Orleans Square. The arcade has a selection of state-of-the art, interactive games.

Biking: Bicycles and surrey bikes are available for rent at Port Orleans Riverside.

Carriage Rides: Refer to page 226 for details on carriage rides.

Fishing: Two-hour guided fishing excursions are available (see *Sports*).

Shopping: Jackson Square Gifts & Desires, located at Port Orleans Square, features Disney character merchandise, clothing bearing the Port Orleans resort logo, and sundries.

Swimming: Doubloon Lagoon is a pool built around a bright blue sea serpent. The waterslide is actually the mythical creature's tongue—kids love it. There is a whirlpool, too. Port Orleans French Quarter guests are also invited to swim in the pool at Ol' Man Island at Port Orleans Riverside.

TRANSPORTATION: Buses go to the Magic Kingdom, Epcot, Disney's Hollywood Studios, Animal Kingdom, Typhoon Lagoon, Blizzard Beach, and Disney Springs. Small water taxis transport guests to Disney Springs, too.

Port Orleans Riverside

Here, the city feel of the French Quarter gives way to the rural South. The resort is divided into "parishes." Closest to the "city," guestrooms are found in Mansion homes; farther upriver are the Bayou guestrooms, with a more rustic feel. The phone number for the Port Orleans Riverside resort is 407-934-6000.

ROOMS: The 2,047 Mansion and Bayou rooms are of the same size, and each has two queen beds (some king-size beds are available); nearly 400 of the Bayou rooms have a bunk-size bed (recommended for kids under age 9) as well. The Magnolia Bend Mansion rooms are situated in elegant manor homes with stately columns and grand staircases. The Bayou rooms are in rustic, weathered-wood buildings that are tucked among flora native to the area. Although all buildings have two to three floors, only the Magnolia Bend Mansions have elevators.

The Bayou rooms surround Ol' Man Island, a 3½-acre recreational area with a pool, playground, and fishing hole. Decorative touches include wood and tin armoires and pedestal sinks with brass fittings. The closet space is not enclosed. The rooms are a bit small, but they can accommodate four guests. Rooms have a coffeemaker (with coffee), fridge, and Wi-Fi (no charge).

More than 500 Riverside rooms invite guests to live like royalty. These "Royal Guest Rooms" feature special touches inspired by Disney's animated classics (all featuring royalty of some sort), ornately decorated beds with fiber-optic special effects, custom bed coverings and drapes, artwork featuring Princess Tiana and other regals, and more. If you want the royal treatment while residing at Port Orleans Riverside, make your wishes known when you book the room. Note that the rates for these rooms run higher than for standard rooms.

WHERE TO EAT: In addition to a restaurant and food court, the hotel offers limited pizza delivery from 4 P.M. until midnight.

Boatwright's Dining Hall: This 200-seat table-service eatery, next to Riverside Mill, serves Cajun specialties and American fare for dinner. Reservations are recommended.

Riverside Mill: This food court resembles an old-fashioned cotton mill with a working waterwheel that powers the cotton press inside. The five counter-service stands offer all sorts of choices. The basic selections are available for breakfast. **Pizza 'n' Pasta** has pasta dishes, pizza, and bread sticks; **Grill Shop** offers fried fish, chicken nuggets, and burgers; **Carving Station** serves freshly sliced turkey; **Specialty Shop** offers soup and sandwiches; and the **Bakery** serves pastries, ice cream, yogurt parfait, and more. If you buy a resort refillable mug, the Riverside Mill is where you fill it.

WHERE TO DRINK: Two lounges possess an enticing degree of charm.

Muddy Rivers: The poolside bar serves beer, wine, cocktails, and soft drinks. Seasonal.

River Roost: Situated in a room designed as a cotton exchange, this lounge features specialty drinks and light hors d'oeuvres.

WHAT TO DO: Many of the resort activities are offered at Ol' Man Island, a recreation center featuring a pool, whirlpool, wading pool, interactive fountains, and a playground.

Arcade: The Medicine Show Arcade features a small selection of games.

Biking: Bicycles for all ages can be rented.

Carriage Rides: Horse-drawn carriages take guests for 25-minute rides throughout the resort grounds. Carriages hold up to 4 adults or 2 adults and 3 small kids. Each trip departs from the marina. Call 407-939-7529 for reservations.

Fishing: Two-hour guided fishing excursions are available (see *Sports*). It is also possible to drop a line at the Fishin' Hole on Ol' Man Island. Catch-and-release only.

Playground: An elaborate play area is located on Ol' Man Island next to the pool.

Shopping: Fulton's General Store in the Riverside building stocks Disney character merchandise, clothing, and sundries.

Swimming: In addition to the main pool and kiddie pool at Ol' Man Island, there are five unguarded pools at the resort. Guests may also swim in the French Quarter pool.

PHOTO BY JILL SAFRO

TRANSPORTATION: Buses go from Port Orleans Riverside to the Magic Kingdom, Epcot, Disney's Hollywood Studios, Animal Kingdom, Typhoon Lagoon, Blizzard Beach, and Disney Springs. Small water taxis also ferry guests to and from Disney Springs.

Disney's Saratoga Springs Resort & Spa

Just across the lake from the happy hustle and bustle of Disney Springs (reachable by bus, boat, or convenient walkway), this Disney Vacation Club resort is a calm complement to its nearest neighbor. Disney's Saratoga Springs Resort & Spa aspires to recapture the heyday of upstate New York country retreats of the late 1800s. The resort covers 65 acres. Some accommodations are nearly a mile from the main building. To contact Saratoga Springs, call 407-827-1100.

ROOMS: There are studios and villas with one, two, and three bedrooms. A studio consists of a room with a queen-size bed and a double sleeper sofa, bathroom, kitchenette, microwave, and coffeemaker. All units have a porch or a balcony, access to complimentary laundry facilities, and Wi-Fi (no charge).

One-bedroom villas have a king-size bed in the master suite and a queen-size sleeper sofa in the living room. The one bathroom has a whirlpool tub. The full kitchen has a fridge, stove, microwave, toaster, coffeemaker, dinnerware, and dishwasher. Each unit has a washer and dryer.

Two-bedroom villas have an additional bath and bedroom, with either one queen-size bed and a double sleeper sofa or two queen-size beds. The three-bedroom Grand Villa has similar features as the two-bedroom models, but is about twice the size and has four bathrooms.

The resort's Treehouse Villas, elevated on pedestals and designed to blend into the woodsy environment, offer serene views of the surrounding treetops. Each "cabin-casual" villa has a full kitchen, flat-panel TVs, three bedrooms, and two bathrooms, and sleeps up to nine.

WHERE TO EAT: There are two eateries here and dozens across the lake. Several barbecue areas are available to resort guests. Note that the only room service is pizza delivery.

The Artist's Palette: Supposedly set in a converted artist's loft, this spot offers all meals. Among the simple selections are salads, sandwiches, flatbreads, and baked goods.

PHOTO BY JILL SAFRO

Turf Club Bar & Grill: Dinner is served in this spot with a horse-racing motif.

Groceries: In these parts, in-room grocery delivery is available from Artist's Palette, and many guests cook their own meals. If you've got a car (and we recommend you do), ask for directions to a grocery store.

WHERE TO DRINK: In addition to local bars, guests imbibe at nearby Disney Springs.

Backstretch Bar: A poolside watering hole.

On the Rocks: A pool bar serving the usual battery of cocktails.

Turf Club Bar & Grill: This spot serves a variety of drinks, plus it has a pool table.

WHAT TO DO: Besides enjoying spa treatments, guests may rent bikes, play basketball, swim, walk, swat tennis balls, and more.

Arcade: Expect to find the usual bells and whistles at "Win, Place, or Show."

Biking: Bicycles may be rented from Horsin' Around Rentals.

Golf: The resort is adjacent to the Lake Buena Vista golf course.

Health Club: This spot features strength and cardio machines and a selection of weight-lifting equipment.

Playground: There is a small kids' play area near an unguarded pool. (Be sure to supervise youngsters at all times.)

Shopping: The Artist's Palette stocks a variety of souvenirs and sundries.

Spa: Senses, the award-winning spa, offers massage therapy, manicures, facials, aromatherapy, and more. Call 407-939-7727 for an appointment.

Swimming: High Rock Spring cascades down rugged rock work and feeds into a free-form, heated zero-depth-entry pool. The splash zone has a waterslide, two whirlpools, and a play area for kids. There are four unguarded pools, too.

Tennis: Two courts are at the ready.

TRANSPORTATION: Buses go from Saratoga Springs to all theme and water parks. Boats ferry guests to Disney Springs (10 to 25 minutes on foot).

Disney's Old Key West Resort

Escape to the spirit of the Florida Keys. Disney's Old Key West Resort is the original Disney Vacation Club property, but villas not occupied by members are available for nightly rental. It has the laid-back feel of a resort community and all the amenities that go with resort life. The homey accommodations have lots of space and the convenience of kitchen facilities, making the resort nice for longer stays. The telephone number for Old Key West is 407-827-7700.

VILLAS: A studio consists of a large room with two queen-size beds, a table and chairs, a small fridge, free Wi-Fi, microwave, and sink. Bathrooms are spacious. Each of the one-bedroom villas has a king-size bed in the master bedroom and a queen-size sleeper sofa and a sleeper chair in the living room; the master bath has a whirlpool tub, sink, and shower.

The two-bedroom villa features a king-size bed in the master bedroom, two queen-size beds in the second bedroom, living room with queen-size sleeper sofa and TV with DVD player, free Wi-Fi, dining room, and a kitchen with a fridge, dishwasher, toaster, and coffeemaker, plus plates, flatware, cooking utensils, and more.

The master bathroom is divided into two rooms with an extra-large whirlpool tub and a sink in one and an oversize shower, sink and vanity, and toilet in the other. There's a porch or balcony off the living room and bedroom, and ceiling fans in each room. The configuration of the two-story, three-bedroom Grand Villas is similar to that of the two-bedroom models, but

adds a third bedroom with two double beds. As for capacity, studios sleep 4 and one-bedroom villas sleep 5 people; two-bedroom villas sleep 9 guests, and the two-story, three-bedroom villas accommodate 12.

WHERE TO EAT: In addition to the restaurant, there are grills and picnic tables. Pizza delivery is available from 4 P.M. to midnight.

Good's Food to Go: The perfect place to pick up fixin's for a continental breakfast, this place also offers burgers, soups, salads, sandwiches, and simple snacks.

Olivia's Cafe: This full-service restaurant serves Key West favorites, plus more traditional items, for breakfast, lunch, and dinner. Menus change seasonally.

WHERE TO DRINK: The watering holes at Old Key West are as laid-back as they come.

Gurgling Suitcase: This tiny bar serves specialty drinks, wine, beer, and soft drinks.

Turtle Shack: This poolside spot serves pizza, salads, sandwiches, and light snacks. Open seasonally.

WHAT TO DO: At Conch Flats Community Hall, table tennis, board games, a large-screen TV, DVD rentals, and planned activities are offered. There are basketball, shuffleboard, and volleyball courts, and equipment is available at Hank's Rent 'N Return.

Arcade: The Electric Eel Game Room is in the Hospitality House; the Flying Fish Game Room is by the Turtle Shack snack bar.

Biking: Bikes and surrey bikes may be rented from Hank's.

Health Club: The Fitness Center, located at R.E.S.T. Beach, offers a nice variety of exercise equipment.

Playground: There are three kids' play areas located throughout the resort.

Shopping: Conch Flats General Store has groceries, books, sundries, and more.

Swimming: The sprawling main pool, with a large whirlpool nearby, is located behind the Hospitality House. The children's pool and play area looks like a big sand castle and features a 125-foot slide. Additional pools are scattered around the resort.

Tennis: There are three courts.

TRANSPORTATION: Buses go to the theme parks, water parks, and Disney Springs. Water taxis also make the trip between the resort and Disney Springs.

Animal Kingdom Area

All-Star Movies, Music, & Sports

The All-Star resorts are among the most brightly and boldly themed at Walt Disney World. Each resort has 1,500 to 1,920 rooms housed in ten buildings devoted to five Disney movies, types of music, and sports.

The All-Star Movies resort celebrates five classic Disney films: *Toy Story*, *The Mighty Ducks*, *Fantasia*, *101 Dalmatians*, and *The Love Bug*. Buildings are adorned with such icons as 40-foot Dalmatians and wildly oversize versions of Buzz Lightyear and Woody.

At the All-Star Music resort, Broadway, country, jazz, rock, and calypso are the themes. A walk-through, neon-lit jukebox; a three-story pair of cowboy boots; and a Broadway theater marquee are among the giant icons.

Sports fans will find themselves in a world of baseball, football, tennis, surfing, or basketball at the All-Star Sports resort. Brightly colored, larger-than-life football helmets, surfboards, tennis balls, basketball hoops, and baseball bats adorn the buildings.

As value resorts, the All-Star properties offer few frills, but the service and whimsical atmosphere are pure Disney.

Guests check in at Cinema Hall for All-Star Movies, Melody Hall for All-Star Music, or Stadium Hall for All-Star Sports. To reach All-Star Movies, call 407-939-7000; to phone All-Star Music, call 407-939-6000; to contact All-Star Sports, call 407-939-5000.

ROOMS: The guestrooms, measuring 260 square feet, are rather small compared with those at Port Orleans, which are 314 square feet. Each

guestroom has two double beds, a vanity area with a sink, a bathroom, free Wi-Fi, a small dresser, and a small table with chairs.

All-Star Music has 215 Family Suites. Each one sleeps up to six and has two bathrooms, a "master" bedroom with its own TV, Wi-Fi (free of charge), and a kitchenette with counter space, mini fridge, sink, microwave, and coffeemaker.

WHERE TO EAT: There are three food courts—World Premiere in Cinema Hall, Intermission in Melody Hall, and End Zone in Stadium Hall. Each features a bakery, convenience store, grab-and-go items, and stations geared to pizza, pasta, salads, and burgers. Each food court has a seating areas with a beverage bar. The All-Star resorts deliver pizza and salads to rooms from 5 P.M. to 1 A.M.

WHERE TO DRINK: There are no traditional lounges at the All-Star resorts; however, the Silver Screen Spirits, Singing Spirits, and Grandstand Spirits pool bars serve drinks throughout the day and evening.

WHAT TO DO: Guests may swim in any of the resort pools. All-Star guests may rent boating equipment at any WDW resort marina.

Arcades: Each of the All-Star resorts has its own arcade.

Playground: A playground is located in each hotel's courtyard area.

Shopping: Maestro Mickey's in Melody Hall, Sport Goofy's Gifts and Sundries in Stadium Hall, and Donald's Double Feature in Cinema Hall all have magazines, books, character merchandise, and sundries.

Swimming: Each hotel has two pools and one kiddie pool. The main pool at All-Star Movies has a *Fantasia* theme (look for Sorcerer Mickey). The smaller Duck Pond Pool is based on *The Mighty Ducks*. At the All-Star Music resort, the Calypso Pool is in the form of a giant guitar, while the Piano Pool bears a striking resemblance to a grand piano. At All-Star Sports, Surfboard Bay has an ocean motif. The smaller Grand Slam Pool pays tribute to our national pastime.

TRANSPORTATION: Buses make pickups at All-Star's Cinema Hall, Melody Hall, and Stadium Hall for trips to each of the theme parks, water parks, and Disney Springs. Each resort has its own bus stops.

A word about All-Star resort transportation: The bus service at these "value" resorts tends to be slightly more efficient than at other locations. The combination of fewer stops and connections is a bonus for guests staying here.

Disney's Animal Kingdom Lodge & Villas

At first glance, Disney's Animal Kingdom Lodge evokes images of a sleepy, little thatched-roof game lodge in the wilds of southern Africa. Upon closer examination, however, it's clear that the only things sleepy or little about this place are the small creatures that live in its shadow. Those animals, along with their more sizable cousins, inhabit acres of meticulously re-created African savanna that practically surround the resort. Birds and all manner of hoofed animals, including giraffes, zebras, and Thomson's gazelles, call the wildlife reserve home. With the freedom to wander within a dozen or so yards of the lodge itself, these critters allow guests to go on safari without leaving their balconies.

The resort is located about one mile from Disney's Animal Kingdom park (which is accessible by bus). The lobby is a huge, high-ceilinged room, richly appointed with colorful African artwork and artifacts. The biggest draw here is the four-story observation window overlooking the savanna. It's one of many portals through which to gaze upon wildlife.

Like the African game lodges on which it is based, Disney's Animal Kingdom Lodge was constructed using a semicircular design. From

overhead, it looks a bit like a horseshoe. This allows for maximum animal-viewing potential. Indeed, many of the resort's guestrooms have direct views of the savanna areas. Be sure to specify your viewing preference when you book a room. The telephone number for Disney's Animal Kingdom Lodge is 407-938-3000.

ROOMS: The 970 rooms, which are noticeably smaller than those at other deluxe Disney resorts, feature dark-wood furniture, sand-colored walls, and earth-tone carpets. Deluxe rooms are a tad more spacious than their standard counterparts. Most rooms have two queen beds (some king beds are available) and sleep up to four people; bunk beds are available in some rooms. All rooms have balconies. Suites include a parlor, plus one or two bedrooms; there are king-size or queen-size beds in the bedrooms. Bathrooms have a separate vanity area with double sink. Rooms have an iron (with board), hair dryer, free Wi-Fi, and small fridge. Free weekday newspapers may be picked up near the elevators. Club-level service is available.

The Villas are located in Jambo House and in the Kidani Village, an area that features thatched-roof, hewn-timber homes. Also included in this village are a pool, fitness center, shop, table-service restaurant, and more. As with all DVC resorts, the homes are available to guests when not being used by members. For information on this member of the Disney Vacation Club family, call 800-800-9100, or visit *www.disneyvacationclub.com*.

WHERE TO EAT: In addition to its restaurants, the hotel offers round-the-clock room service.

Boma—Flavors of Africa: Boma is modeled after a bustling African marketplace. The restaurant boasts many types of cuisine in what chefs describe as a "global fusion" style. Served buffet style, the cuisine is a lovely mix of French, Malaysian, Indian, Chinese, and English.

Jiko—The Cooking Place: The colors of sunset are the backdrop for this reliable restaurant. Wines are from South Africa.

The Mara: A high-quality quick-service spot, The Mara offers above average made-to-order flatbreads, African stew, chicken pita, and salads, plus kid-pleasers as burgers and chicken nuggets.

Sanaa: This Kidani Village star features African- and Indian-inspired cuisine.

WHERE TO DRINK: The lounges here are rustic and inviting. Some even offer the opportunity to sip cocktails while observing wildlife.

HOT TIP!

Balloons are not permitted at Disney's Animal Kingdom Lodge—it's a safety issue for the animals. You can check yours at the Bell Services desk, free of charge.

Cape Town Lounge and Wine Bar: Located inside Jiko—The Cooking Place, this spot features wines from South Africa.

Maji and Uzima Springs: These poolside bars serve specialty and traditional drinks.

Sanaa: A 24-seat lounge located within the restaurant of the same name.

Victoria Falls: Set alongside a soothing waterfall, this mezzanine-level lounge features coffee, tea, domestic and South African wines, and assorted cocktails.

WHAT TO DO: Spying on African wildlife is the main event in these parts. However, if you can manage to pry yourself away from those hoofed exhibitionists for a bit, there are plenty of other diversions available—including tennis, basketball, shuffleboard, and a barbecue pavilion. Note that guests are welcome to partake in activities offered at other Disney resort hotels.

Arcades: Pumbaa's Fun & Games and Safari So Good are both stocked with the latest games.

Children's Program: The Simba's Cubhouse play area, for (potty-trained) kids ages 3 through 12, is open in the evenings, starting at 4 P.M. It costs $55 per evening, per child. Reservations are required; call 407-939-3463. Kids can learn about the wildlife at the resort through nature-themed activities.

Health Club: The Zahanati Massage and (24-hour) Fitness Center has exercise equipment, sauna, and spa services, including massage, facial, and nail services. To make an appointment, call 407-939-7727. Kidani Village's Survival of the Fittest also offers exercise equipment.

Playground: The Hakuna Matata playground is located near the Uzima pool.

Shopping: Zawadi Marketplace stocks Africa-themed gifts, Disney-character merchandise, clothing with the Animal Kingdom Lodge logo, and sundries. Johari Treasures tempts shoppers at Kidani Village.

Swimming: The resort's main pool, Uzima, looks like a natural watering hole. More impressive than the size of the zero-depth-entry pool, however, is the view from the pool deck. In addition to a kiddie pool, there are two whirlpools nearby. Kidani Village is home to another pool (Samawati Springs) and to Uwanja Camp, a watery playground.

Tennis: There are two clay courts available to all Animal Kingdom Lodge guests.

TRANSPORTATION: Buses go to the Magic Kingdom (a 25- to 30-minute ride), Epcot, Disney's Hollywood Studios, Animal Kingdom, Typhoon Lagoon, Blizzard Beach, and Disney Springs.

Coronado Springs

This resort reveals its Southwestern U.S.–Mexican theme in such elements as a tiled and stucco lobby with a fountain and a pyramid with water tumbling down from it that appears to have created the Mayan ruin–themed pool. The 1,912 rooms are found in three guest areas that stretch around Lago Dorado, a 22-acre lake. (It can take five minutes or more to walk to the farthest rooms.) The food court and restaurant are near the lobby. A convention center offers access to business services. The phone number for Coronado Springs is 407-939-1000.

ROOMS: Standard rooms are smaller than those at Disney's deluxe hotels, but adequate for up to four; each has two queen beds (some king-size beds are available). In-room amenities include a coffee-maker, refrigerator, hair dryer, and free Wi-Fi. Decor varies in each section but is characterized by yellow, blue, and scarlet accents. In the Casitas area, where most suites are located, terra-cotta guest buildings occupy a citylike landscape. In the pueblo-style Ranchos, scattered along a dry streambed, rooms have a rustic feel. Cabanas, located along the rocky palm-lined beach, reflect the casual feel of their namesake.

WHERE TO EAT: In addition to two full-service restaurants and food court, limited room service is available for breakfast and dinner.

Cafe Rix: A quick-service eatery, Rix has offerings for breakfast, lunch, and dinner.

Las Ventanas: This quiet, table-service destination serves three meals a day.

Maya Grill: Open for dinner, Maya offers seafood, steak, and authentic Mexican dishes.

Pepper Market: High ceilings make this nontraditional food court feel like an open-air market. The fare includes tacos, empanadas, pizza, pasta, and omelets made to order.

WHERE TO DRINK: There are three places to wet your whistle at Coronado Springs.

Laguna Bar: A lagoonside lounge outside the lobby, this spot serves drinks daily.

Rix Lounge: This lounge provides cocktails and appetizers, and is in the main building.

Siestas Cantina: In the Dig Site area, this pool bar lets swimmers and archaeologists enjoy drinks and light fare (three meals a day).

WHAT TO DO: There is an array of water sports in which to participate, as well as volleyball and a short nature trail.

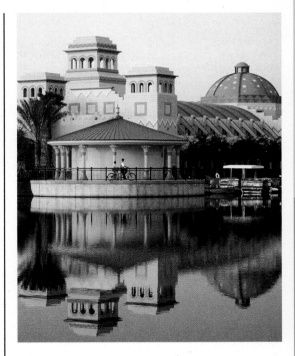

Arcade: Iguana Arcade is in the Dig Site area.

Biking: Bikes and surrey bikes may be rented at La Marina.

Fishing: Two-hour, guided fishing excursions are offered on the 22-acre Lago Dorado. Call 407-WDW-BASS. Fishing excursions are offered seasonally.

Health Club: La Vida fitness center offers a full range of strength and cardio equipment 24/7, plus spa services (by day).

Playground: The Explorer's Playground, part of the Dig Site area, includes a sandbox, complete with Mayan carvings waiting to be excavated.

Salon: The Casa de Belleza Salon is located next to La Vida Health Club. A full-service facility, the salon offers haircuts, sets, coloring, beard and mustache trim, manicures, pedicures, facials, and more. Operating hours are generally from 9 A.M. until 7 P.M. daily. To make an appointment, call 407-939-3965.

Shopping: Panchito's Gifts & Sundries is where to find souvenir items with a Southwestern flavor, Disney merchandise, and necessities.

Swimming: The main pool is in the Dig Site area. It surrounds a Mayan pyramid and features a towering 123-foot waterslide. There is a whirlpool and a kiddie pool. Each guestroom area features an unguarded pool.

TRANSPORTATION: Buses go to the Magic Kingdom, Epcot, Disney's Hollywood Studios, Animal Kingdom, Typhoon Lagoon, Blizzard Beach, and Disney Springs.

ESPN Wide World of Sports Area

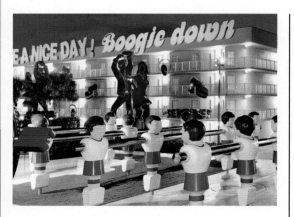

Pop Century

What do you get when you mix decades of American pop culture with a Disney resort? Pop Century! Like the All-Star resorts, Pop Century is a vivid celebration of Americana. The 2,880-room resort represents the second half of the twentieth century. The resort's larger-than-life "time capsules" commemorate the toys, fads, dance crazes, and catchphrases that swept the nation from the 1950s through the 1990s. It's groovy . . . you dig?

As a WDW value resort, the Pop Century property offers few frills, but the service is good, the atmosphere's colorful, and the transportation is efficient. There's even a peaceful lake to stroll around on temperate days. (It's shared by Pop's next-door neighbor, Disney's Art of Animation resort.) Guests check in at Classic Hall, which also features a food and merchandise location, arcade, and guest services desk. To contact Disney's Pop Century resort, call 407-938-4000.

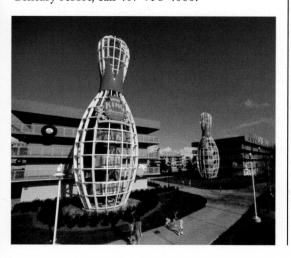

ROOMS: The guestrooms measure 260 square feet (a bit smaller than Port Orleans' rooms, which are 314 square feet). Each room has two double beds, a vanity area with a sink, a bathroom, a small dresser, a table with chairs, a fridge, and free Wi-Fi.

WHERE TO EAT: The food court features a bakery and a convenience market, plus several stands geared to pizza, pasta, and burgers. The Pop Century resort delivers pizza to guestrooms from about 4 P.M. to midnight.

WHERE TO DRINK: Petals is a bar located near the Hippy Dippy pool.

WHAT TO DO: Guests may swim in any of the Pop Century resort pools and enjoy a 1.4 mile walk or run around Hourglass Lake.

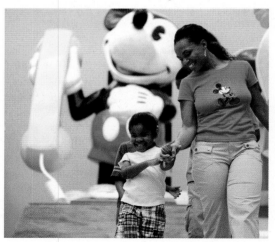

Arcade: Revisit classic video games or discover some new ones at Fast Forward arcade.

Playground: There is one soft-surface playground.

Shopping: The Everything Pop shop has a selection of books, character merchandise, sundries, and snacks.

Swimming: The hotel has three pools (in the shapes of a bowling pin, computer, and a flower), plus a kiddie pool.

TRANSPORTATION: Buses stop at Classic Hall for trips to each of the four theme parks, Blizzard Beach and Typhoon Lagoon water parks, and Disney Springs.

Art of Animation

The Walt Disney World resort landscape has gotten a serious burst of color with the addition of this vivid celebration of Disney animation. A "value" resort, Disney's Art of Animation made its debut in 2012.

Pop Century's next-door neighbor (the resorts share access to Hourglass Lake and the nearly 1.4-mile jogging path that surrounds it), Art of Animation boasts colossal figures from classic animated films. It also has three themed pools, playgrounds, festive courtyards, an arcade, and a splash zone featuring everyone's favorite clownfish, Nemo. The resort also offers free Wi-Fi, laundry, and dry cleaning (fees apply for the last two services).

ROOMS: The 864 standard rooms, which are housed in *The Little Mermaid*–themed buildings, sleep up to 4 and come with the usual amenities afforded to Walt Disney World's "value" resorts (see page 75 for details). Each measures 277 square feet and has two double beds, a vanity area with a sink, a bathroom, a small dresser, a table with chairs, and free Wi-Fi. The 1,120 festive family suites, which are themed to *Cars, Finding Nemo,* and *The Lion King,* feature 3 separate sleeping areas, accommodate up to 6

guests, and come with 2 LCD TVs, a queen-size bed, double-size pull-down bed, and sleeper sofa. Each 565-square-foot suite has a living room, 2 bathrooms, and a kitchenette (with a refrigerator, microwave, and coffeemaker).

WHERE TO EAT: The brilliantly hued Landscape of Flavors food court features four unique cooking stations serving international favorites, Mongolian barbecue, burgers, pizza, pasta, sandwiches, fresh smoothies, and hand-scooped gelato. It's open for breakfast, lunch, and dinner. There is a grab-and-go selection, too. In-room pizza delivery is also an option.

WHERE TO DRINK: The Drop Off is a full-service bar located near the Big Blue Pool.

WHAT TO DO: Guests may swim in any of the Art of Animation resort pools, walk or jog around Hourglass Lake, and more.

Arcade: Pixel Play Arcade is in Animation Hall, across from Landscape of Flavors.

Jogging and Walking: The resort is encircled by a trail that's almost 1.4 miles long.

Playground: The Righteous Reef playground can be found in the middle of the Finding Nemo courtyard.

Shopping: The Ink and Paint Shop has a selection of books, character merchandise, Art of Animation Resort–themed souvenirs, sundries, and snacks.

Swimming: The hotel has three pools: Flippin' Fins, Cozy Cone, and The Big Blue Pool, plus a *Finding Nemo*–themed splash zone known as The Schoolyard Sprayground.

TRANSPORTATION: Buses stop at Animation Hall for trips to each of Walt Disney World's four theme parks, Blizzard Beach and Typhoon Lagoon water parks, and Disney Springs.

Resort on Dream Tree Blvd.

Four Seasons Orlando

Walt Disney World welcomed a Four Seasons resort into its happy hotel fold in 2014. The 443-room luxury property boasts more than 26 lakeside acres of elegant design, as well as a multitude of recreational diversions, and high convenience for Disney guests. Spanish Revival architecture reflects Florida's Golden Age mansions and is surrounded by a vibrant array of 72,000 plants and nearly 1,000 palm trees. Check-in begins at 4 P.M. daily. Check-out time is 12 P.M. There is a 24-hour business center, plus ample meeting space suitable for conferences and social functions. Four Seasons Orlando resort is a AAA Five-Diamond award winner. For additional information or to make reservations for the hotel, call 800-267-3046, or visit *www.fourseasons.com/orlando*.

ROOMS: All rooms have furnished balconies, one king or two double beds, twice-daily housekeeping service, newspaper delivery, 24-hour room service, and high-speed Internet and Wi-Fi. Rooms also come with a safe, coffeemaker (with coffee), DVD player, iPod docking station, flat-screen TV, and minibar. There are terry-cloth bathrobes to use throughout your stay (kids' robes are available upon request). Accommodations feature luxurious marble bathrooms with double sinks and soaking tub, hair dryer, lighted makeup mirrors, and a TV in the mirror (yes, *in* the mirror!). Hypoallergenic bedding is available upon request. Cribs may be requested (no charge), as can high chairs, bottles, and toddler toys. Babysitting services may be arranged for an hourly fee (reservations must be made at least 24 hours in advance).

The resort has many rooms that are accessible for guests with disabilities. Make your needs known when you book the room. Four Seasons is a non-smoking resort.

Room categories include (distant) Park View, Lake View, Golden Oak View, and Four Seasons Rooms. Park View rooms offer a distant view of the Magic Kingdom and Wishes, the park's nightly fireworks presentation. Lake View rooms have views of a lake, golf course, or pool area. Golden Oak rooms offer "residential views" of privately owned homes, while Four Seasons rooms have limited views.

Suites have king beds, two bathrooms, and living area with queen sleeper sofa. To book a room, call 800-267-3046. For suites (including the 9-bedroom Royal Suite or Presidential Suite), call 407-313-6734.

The lobby's Disney Planning Center assists with the purchase of park tickets, making Disney dining reservations, reserving special events, and more. When it comes to Walt Disney World privileges, the resort fits somewhere between Swan and Dolphin and the resorts on Hotel Plaza Boulevard. Among the perks:

• Complimentary transportation to Disney World destinations is provided by a Four Seasons luxury motor coach. (There are on-site vehicles available for rent, too.)

• Guests may use the theme parks Package Express delivery service. Merchandise can be delivered directly to the resort from any WDW theme park and many shops (no charge).

• Fastpass+ assignments may be booked starting 30 days before arrival. (Refer to page 25 for details on this system that allows guests to book advance reservation times for theme park shows and attractions.)

• Disney characters visit the resort's Ravello restaurant for the "Good Morning Breakfast" on Thursdays and Saturdays year-round (and on Tuesdays during school breaks and major holidays). Expect the likes of Goofy and his pals.

WHERE TO EAT: There are four full-service eateries and a coffee bar, plus 24-hour in-room dining. Reservations are recommended for Capa and Ravello (call 407-313-6161).

Capa: This contemporary, Spanish-style steakhouse specializes in prime cuts, tapas (appetizer portions), and local seafood such as freshly shucked oysters. There is indoor and outdoor seating at this rooftop hot spot. Capa is open for dinner only, 6 P.M. to 10 P.M.

Lickety-Split: Located in the lobby, this is the perfect place for gourmet coffees and quick bites. Selections include breakfast pastries, grab-and-go items, gelato, and more. There is indoor and outdoor seating.

PB&G: Think pulled pork, smoked brisket, burgers, and creative salads at this southern-style smokehouse and rotisserie, located poolside (all seating is alfresco). Open 11 A.M. to 6 P.M.

Plancha: A relaxed Cuban-American eatery, Plancha is located at the Tranquilo Golf Club. It offers empanadas, the classic Cubano sandwich, and chorizo burgers. The cocktail menu includes mojitos and Hemingway daiquiris. The hours are 10 A.M. till 6 P.M.

Ravello: Guests are invited to watch the action in this modern Italian eatery's open kitchen. In addition to regionally influenced specialties, Ravello serves fresh bread and pizza, and housemade pasta. Two private dining rooms are also available. Ravello is open for breakfast (6:30 A.M. to 11 A.M.) and dinner (5:30 P.M. to 10 P.M.). The dress code here is "smart casual."

WHERE TO DRINK: Guests may quench their thirst and enjoy creatively prepared nibbles at a duo of lovely lounges.

Lobby Bar: Drinks mix well with the appetizers, entrées, and desserts at this lounge.

Capa Bar: As you sip a beverage on the patio, you may also enjoy the Magic Kingdom's fireworks. Capa Bar is open from 5 P.M. to 11 P.M.

WHAT TO DO: There's no getting bored in these parts. The Explorer Island play province could be enjoyed for days on end. In addition to a swimmer's paradise, the amusing island boasts a rock-climbing wall, volleyball, basketball, pool, Ping-Pong, and more. Outdoor movies are presented on select nights.

Children's Program: The resort's complimentary "Kids for All Seasons" program is open to youngsters ages 4 to 12, daily from 10 A.M. until 6 P.M. Trained staffers supervise and entertain kids throughout the day. Little ones under ages 4 are welcome to participate if accompanied by a guardian.

Fun and Games: The Mansion on the resort's Explorer Island is a family-focused hangout with outdoor activities such as table tennis, bocce ball, and pool (the kind you play with a cue stick). The Hideout has video games, basketball hoops, and beach volleyball.

Golf: Golfers may argue that the resort's crowning glory is the secluded course at the Tranquilo Golf Club. The Tom Fazio–designed, 18-hole, 6,968-yard, par 71 course is a certified Audubon sanctuary with abundant opportunities to view local wildlife between swings. Amenities include a pro shop, instruction, driving range, putting green, club rental, and a restaurant (Plancha). The course is open to both guests of the hotel and daytime visitors (fees apply). To reserve tee times, call 407-313-7777.

Health Club: The 24-hour Fitness Centre has cardiovascular equipment, weights, and yoga, plus a steam room, sauna, and whirlpool spa. Certified trainers are on hand, too (for a fee).

Movies: The resort presents alfresco films on select nights at the Star Struck "dive-in" movie screen (near the pool on Explorer Island).

Spa: The Spa at Four Seasons evokes the peace and natural beauty of Florida's Everglades. The Zen zone features 18 treatment rooms, as well as two bungalows for private retreats. There are also outdoor lounges and a whirlpool. The Salon provides hairstyling, manicures, pedicures, and other services.

Swimming: The resort's swimming areas are part of an enormous playground known as Explorer Island: The Oasis, a lakeside adults-only pool; The Explorer Pool, a zero-depth-entry family pool; Splash Zone, a soft-surface interactive fountain area that sprays water up to 30 feet in the air; a 1,203-foot-long lazy river, complete with a waterfall and bubbling rapids; and two 242-foot water slides.

Tennis: The resort sports three Har-Tru tennis courts for play and instruction (fees apply to both activities).

Weddings: From the rehearsal dinner, to the ceremony, reception, and even the honeymoon, Four Seasons can accommodate the wishes for most fairy-tale occasions, from intimate to grand. Wedding specialists may be reached at *www.fourseasons/Orlandoweddings.com* or 407-313-7777.

TRANSPORTATION: A complimentary bus goes to the Transportation and Ticket Center (TTC) every 30 minutes (from there, guests take a ferry or monorail to the Magic Kingdom); buses go to Epcot, Disney's Hollywood Studios, and Animal Kingdom once every hour. Airport and individual transfers throughout the Walt Disney World area are available for a fee.

Resorts on Hotel Plaza Blvd.

These seven hotels—Best Western Lake Buena Vista, DoubleTree Suites by Hilton, Wyndham Lake Buena Vista, Hilton, B Resort & Spa, Buena Vista Palace Hotel & Spa, and Holiday Inn—though inside Walt Disney World boundaries, are neither owned nor operated by Disney. However, a few have been here since the park opened in 1971 or soon thereafter (sometimes under different names), accommodating Mickey enthusiasts from the beginning. The hotels are not Disney themed, but the three largest (the Hilton, Buena Vista Palace, and Wyndham) do have meals hosted by Disney characters and Disney-themed shops.

Often referred to as Disney Springs Resort Area Hotels, they line the mile-long Hotel Plaza Boulevard. The Hilton, Buena Vista Palace, and Wyndham are across from the Disney Springs Marketplace, with its shops, restaurants, and nightlife. The other four properties are a 10- to 25-minute stroll away. They are also relatively close to the Crossroads at Lake Buena Vista shopping center, home to many eateries and a 24-hour grocery. The privileges of staying in one of these hotels include:

• Car rental desk on the premises (at select Hotel Plaza Boulevard resorts).

• Free bus service to the four theme parks, with limited service to Disney Springs, Typhoon Lagoon, and Blizzard Beach. The buses, which are not part of the Disney transportation network, make stops every 30 minutes, beginning one hour prior to park opening; be sure to allow extra time for bus travel. One bus serves the Hilton, DoubleTree, Holiday Inn, and B Resort & Spa; another serves the other hotels (it takes at least ten minutes to stop at all resorts on the loop). Note that buses load and unload in the middle of the parking lot at some of the parks.

• Flexibility to book tickets for both on- and, in most cases, off-WDW-property attractions.

• Preferred access to Disney golf courses.

• A "Passport to Savings" coupon book with exclusive discounts and specials on dining, shopping, and entertainment.

• Reservations for Disney dinner shows and theme park restaurants.

• Pedestrian bridges connect Hotel Plaza Boulevard with Disney Springs Marketplace.

Note that guests staying in the resorts on Hotel Plaza Boulevard do have to pay for parking at Disney parks and other Walt Disney World attractions, and they cannot charge purchases made at Disney World shops and restaurants with a resort ID.

To book a room at a Hotel Plaza Boulevard resort, call the resort itself or call WDW Central Reservations at 407-W-DISNEY (934-7639). Resorts on Hotel Plaza Boulevard are included in several Walt Disney Travel Company packages.

All of the hotels offer nonsmoking rooms and accommodations for travelers with disabilities. To get to the hotels from the airport, take Exit 68 off I-4.

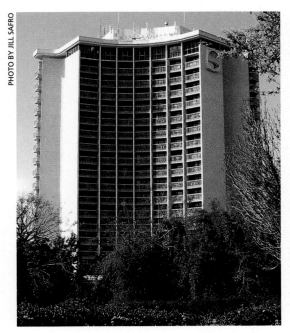

PHOTO BY JILL SAFRO

BEST WESTERN LAKE BUENA VISTA RESORT:

This 18-story hotel is surrounded by pines and has an entry lined with oaks draped in Spanish moss. Each of the 325 spacious, smoke-free rooms and suites features either one king-size bed and a queen sofa bed or two queen-size beds, as well as floor-to-ceiling windows and furnished balcony. Rooms also come with free Wi-Fi, flat-screen TV, coffeemaker, refrigerator, safe, hair dryer, and iron with board. Baths have one sink and plenty of counter space.

Each of the four suites occupies a corner of the 18th floor and features a wet bar, two phones, two TVs, a refrigerator, microwave, whirlpool tub, and an impressive glassed-in porch with skylights and a ceiling fan. Rooms on the seventh floor and higher offer views of Disney Springs or the other resorts on Hotel Plaza Boulevard.

The hotel also has a fitness center, business center, game room, heated pool, small kiddie pool, sundry store, Disney gift shop, and guest laundry facilities (for a fee).

Trader's Island Grill is open for lunch and dinner. The Flamingo Cove offers poolside or inside seating and serves lunch, dinner, drinks, and snacks. For guests on the go, there's Marketplace Café. It offers a variety of grab-and-go items, as well as Pizza Hut Express selections. Room service is also an option.

Rates for this hotel range from about $99 to $239 for rooms; about $299 to $399 for suites. Parking fees apply for both self- and valet parking. There is an additional daily resort fee. Best Western Lake Buena Vista Resort, 2000 Hotel Plaza Blvd., Lake Buena Vista, FL 32830; 407-828-2424 or 800-348-3765; *www.lakebuenavistaresorthotel.com.*

DOUBLETREE SUITES BY HILTON LAKE BUENA VISTA:

This 229-unit property has a stellar staff, homey atmosphere, low-slung facade reminiscent of WDW's Contemporary hotel. Upon check-in, families receive a bag of chocolate chip cookies. The only all-suite hotel in the Disney Springs area, it has roomy (625 square feet) units, each with a living room and sleeper sofa, dressing area, and separate bedroom. The one-bedroom suites sleep up to six; there are five two-bedroom suites. Most of the bedrooms have two queen beds; a few king beds are available.

The renovated decor features cheerful blues and greens offset by contrasting neutrals. Room amenities include two TVs, pay-per-view movies, refrigerator, coffeemaker, microwave, hair dryer, high-speed Internet (for a fee), small dining/work table, and safe.

Recreational facilities include a heated pool, splash pad for kids, and a whirlpool in a landscaped area, plus a fitness room, two lighted tennis courts, jogging trail, and small playground. Evergreen, a full-service restaurant with a pool bar, offers a breakfast buffet, lunch, and dinner as well as snacks and sandwiches

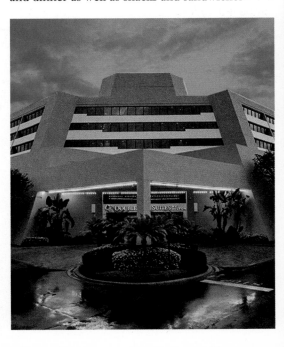

throughout the day. Cocktails are available at the lobby bar. A market/deli provides snacks and groceries, including more of those famous chocolate chip cookies (though you'll have to pay for these). There is a Budget Rental Car desk by the lobby.

Room rates range from about $99 to $399. Parking fees apply for self- and valet parking. DoubleTree Suites by Hilton, 2305 Hotel Plaza Blvd., Lake Buena Vista, FL 32830; 407-934-1000 or 800-222-8733; *www.doubletreeguestsuites.com*.

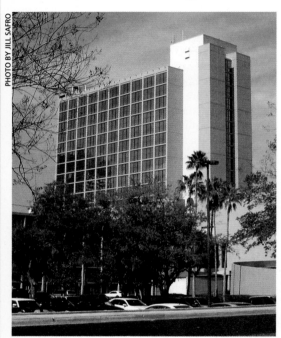

PHOTO BY JILL SAFRO

WYNDHAM LAKE BUENA VISTA

RESORT: The Wyndham sports a spiffy look, obvious upon stepping into the cheerful Bermuda-themed lobby. The 626 refurbished rooms are in a 19-story tower and two wings framing two large courtyards. Most rooms have two double beds, though 77 king-bed rooms are available. There are 7 spacious suites. All accommodations include a refrigerator, coffee-maker, Wi-Fi (free of charge), flat-screen TV, plush bedding, safe, hair dryer, iron, and daily newspaper (by request). Guests receive a discount at many shops and restaurants at nearby Disney Springs—accessible via pedestrian bridge.

Extensive recreational facilities—the hotel's major appeal—include an exercise room, two lighted tennis courts, a sand volleyball court, and a basketball court. The impressive Oasis Aquatic Playground features a heated pool with zero-depth entry, interactive features such as water cannons, and a relaxing hot tub with a lovely

view of the lake. Special, kids-only activities are scheduled throughout the day. There's a health club, arcade, and business center, too.

Lake View Restaurant (on the mezzanine level) serves breakfast and dinner. Breakfast is hosted by Disney characters on Tuesday, Thursday, and Saturday. Sundial (in the lobby), open 24 hours, has snacks and light fare. For cocktails, there's Horizons Bar (next to Lake View), the Eclipse lobby bar, and Oasis pool bar.

A lobby merchandise shop sells assorted sundries and Disney-themed souvenirs. Room rates range from about $119 to $159 year-round; suites range from $150 to $350. There is an additional (daily) resort fee other amenities, as well as an $8-per-day parking fee. Wyndham Lake Buena Vista Resort, 1850 Hotel Plaza Blvd., Lake Buena Vista, FL 32830; 407-828-4444 or 800-624-4109; *www.wyndhamlakebuenavista.com*.

HILTON: This hotel gets high marks for its 23 well-groomed acres, laid-back ambience, pool area, and upscale shops. The 814 rooms, all of which have been extensively refurbished, are outfitted with two queen or one king bed (suites are available for larger parties), have minibars, voice mail, safes, and high-speed Internet access.

Among the resort's restaurants and lounges, Andiamo Italian Bistro & Grille offers American and Italian fare, while Benihana Steakhouse and Sushi serves Japanese favorites and entertainment (both eateries serve dinner only); Covington Mill serves breakfast and lunch (with Disney characters attending Sunday breakfast); Rum Largo Poolside Cafe serves burgers, sandwiches, salads, and tropical drinks alfresco; Mainstreet Market, open 24 hours, is part deli, part country store (serving Starbucks coffee). For light meals, snacks, or drinks, drop by John T's lounge; specialty coffees

PHOTO BY JILL SAFRO

and ice cream are served at Mugs. There is an Avis car rental on the premises. And Disney Springs is a short walk away, across a footbridge.

Recreational facilities include a tropical whirlpool, two heated swimming pools, a kiddie pool, fitness room, and large game room. Rates range from $99 to $299; suites are $149 to $1,500. Parking charges apply for self-parking and valet. Hilton, 1751 Hotel Plaza Blvd., Lake Buena Vista, FL 32830; 407-827-4000 or 800-782-4414; *www.hiltonorlandoresort.com*.

Note: As of January 1, 2016, the Hilton no longer participates in Walt Disney World's Extra Magic Hours program.

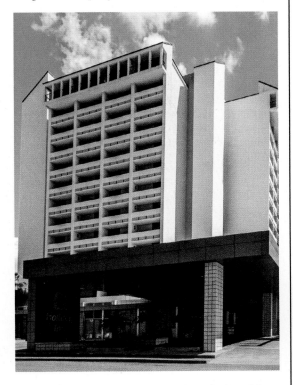

HOLIDAY INN: This family-friendly hotel has reopened after being rebuilt for $35 million. All 323 rooms are nonsmoking and have either one king or two queen beds. Some are available with views of nearby Disney Springs. Guestrooms are decorated in earth tones and include a flat-screen TV with DirecTV, coffeemaker, microwave, mini fridge, safe, and hair dryer. Bathrooms have granite countertops. Free high-speed Wi-Fi is available in all guestrooms and restaurants, as well as in the lobby.

The Palm Breezes Restaurant, located in the atrium, serves three meals a day (kids through age 12 eat free). Palm Breezes has a grab-and-go section, a bar, and provides room service. There is a zero-depth-entry heated pool, a whirlpool,

arcade, Disney store, and 24-hour fitness center. Parking charges apply.

Room rates range from approximately $129–$272. Holiday Inn; 1805 Hotel Plaza Blvd., Lake Buena Vista, FL 32830; 407-828-8888 or 888-465-4329; *www.hiorlando.com*.

B RESORT & SPA: A glitzy addition to Hotel Plaza Boulevard, B pulls out all the modern stops in its 394 guestrooms and suites. Amenities include large HD flat-screen TVs, bunk beds, in-room safe, mini-fridge, and iPad/iPod docking stations. Select rooms have sleeper sofas and kitchenettes. Free wireless Internet service is available to all guests. Complimentary loaner iPads are available upon request.

Resort guests may enjoy the outdoor, heated infinity-edge saltwater pool with interactive water features, the 5,000-square-foot B Indulged full-service spa and wellness center, and the B Active fitness center. American Kitchen Bar & Grill, the resort's signature restaurant, serves classic comfort foods and features a salad bar on the back of a 1950s cherry-red Ford pickup truck that sits in the middle of the restaurant. Stop by the Pick-Up, a casual one-stop shop and ice cream parlor just off the lobby, that serves quick breakfasts, snacks, and various sundries.

B Resort, 1905 Hotel Plaza Boulevard, Lake Buena Vista, FL 32830. For reservations or additional information, visit *www.bresortlbv.com* or call 407-828-2828 or 888-662-4683.

BUENA VISTA PALACE HOTEL & SPA:

The tallest hotel in the Disney Springs area and the largest of the resorts on Hotel Plaza Boulevard (it's actually at the intersection of Hotel Plaza Boulevard and Buena Vista Drive) is a cluster of towers set on 27 acres beside Lake Buena Vista. Each of the 1,014 rooms has a ceiling fan, two phones (one cordless; both with voice mail and speakerphone), high-speed Internet access (wired and wireless), two queen beds or one king, a coffeemaker, 32-inch flat-panel TV, and weekday newspaper in the lobby. Most rooms have a balcony or patio. In addition, there are 122 one- and two-bedroom suites and two-story penthouses with microwaves. Twin/queen sofa beds are in suites and rooms with king beds. All guestrooms have a safe and refrigerator.

The resort's 10,000-square-foot Kay Casperson Lifestyle Spa features myriad treatments and services, a full-service salon, fitness center, and a private lap pool. Recreation Island accommodates two swimming pools, a kiddie pool, whirlpool, lighted tennis court, basketball court, sand volleyball court, children's playground, and arcade.

The hotel also provides room service, a Disney boutique, and a guest laundry room. Dining spots include the lakeside Watercress Cafe, which serves breakfast and lunch only (Disney characters are in attendance Sunday mornings); the Watercress Mini Market, open

PHOTO BY JILL SAFRO

Shades of Green

Shades of Green is a recreational retreat for active and retired military personnel and their families, members of the reserves and the National Guard, and U.S. Department of Defense employees. This 586-room resort is near the Grand Floridian but is not linked with the monorail system.

The resort features two tennis courts, two pools, a small health club, restaurant, bar and lounge, gift shop, arcade, laundry facilities, and free transportation around WDW.

Room rates are based on military or civilian grade. Select multi-day tickets are offered at a discount. The property's three golf courses—the Palm, the Magnolia, and Oak Trail—are open to all WDW guests (see *Sports* for details). All other activities are for hotel guests and their families only.

Disney's Magical Express motor coach service is not available to guests staying at this resort. The number for Shades of Green is 407-824-3400; *www.shadesofgreen.org*.

from 6 A.M. to midnight for house-baked pastries, salads, sandwiches, and snacks; Lobby Lounge (light meals and snacks), and One80 Sportgrill & Bar, featuring 40 TVs broadcasting multiple games and serving lunch and a full dinner menu, including steak, seafood, salads, and sandwiches.

Rates for rooms are generally about $99 and up per night (no charge for kids under 18); suites, which sleep four to eight, are $149 and up. Rollaways cost $30 per night; cribs are free. There is an Alamo/National car rental desk here, too. Buena Vista Palace Hotel & Spa, 1900 Buena Vista Dr., Lake Buena Vista, FL 32830; *www.buenavistapalace.com*; 407-827-2727 or 866-397-6516.

HOT TIP!

The Buena Vista Palace Hotel & Spa is just a 5-minute walk from the Marketplace at Disney Springs. It is directly across the street, safely and easily accessed by an elevated pedestrian walkway.

Magic Kingdom

The Magic Kingdom is the most enchanting part of the World. Few who visit it are disappointed, and even the most blasé travelers manage a smile. The sight of the soaring spires of Cinderella Castle, the gleaming woodwork of the Main Street shops, and the crescendo of music that follows the parades never fail to have an effect. Even when the crowds are large and the weather is hot, a visitor who has toured this wonderland dozens of times can still look around and think how satisfying this place is for the spirit.

What makes the Magic Kingdom timeless is its combination of the classic and the futuristic. Both childhood favorites and space-age creatures have a home here. Every "land" has a theme, carried through from the costumes worn by the hosts and hostesses and the food served in the restaurants to the merchandise sold in the shops, and even the design of the trash cans. Thousands of details contribute to the overall effect, and recognizing these touches makes any visit more enjoyable.

But the delight most guests experience upon first glimpse of the Magic Kingdom can disappear when disorientation sets in. There are so many bends to every pathway, so many sights and sounds clamoring for attention, it's too easy to wander aimlessly and miss the best the Magic Kingdom has to offer. So we earnestly suggest that you study this chapter before your visit.

MAIN STREET, U.S.A.
1 Main Street Vehicles
2 Walt Disney World Railroad
3 Town Square Theater

LIBERTY SQUARE
15 The Hall of Presidents
16 The Haunted Mansion
17 Liberty Belle Riverboat

FANTASYLAND
18 Prince Charming Regal
    Carrousel
19 It's a Small World
20 Mad Tea Party
21 The Many Adventures of
    Winnie the Pooh
22 Peter Pan's Flight
23 Mickey's PhilharMagic
24 Under the Sea—
    Journey of The Little Mermaid
25 Dumbo the Flying Elephant
26 The Barnstormer
27 Walt Disney World Railroad
28 Seven Dwarfs Mine Train
29 Enchanted Tales with Belle
30 Princess Fairytale Hall

TOMORROWLAND
31 Astro Orbiter
32 Buzz Lightyear's Space
    Ranger Spin
33 Stitch's Great Escape!
34 Tomorrowland Speedway
35 Space Mountain
36 Tomorrowland Transit Authority
    PeopleMover
37 Monsters, Inc. Laugh Floor
38 Carousel of Progress
·········· Parade Route

ADVENTURELAND
4 Jungle Cruise
5 Pirates of the Caribbean
6 Swiss Family Treehouse
7 The Enchanted Tiki Room
8 The Magic Carpets
    of Aladdin

FRONTIERLAND
9 Big Thunder Mountain
    Railroad
10 Country Bear Jamboree
11 Frontierland Shootin'
    Arcade
12 Splash Mountain
13 Tom Sawyer Island
14 Walt Disney World
    Railroad

112

Getting Oriented

When you visit Walt Disney World's original theme park, it's vital to know the lay of the "lands." The Magic Kingdom has six lands—Main Street, U.S.A.; Adventureland; Frontierland; Liberty Square; Fantasyland; and Tomorrowland (Mickey's Toontown Fair has left town). Main Street begins at Town Square, located just inside the park gates, and runs directly to Cinderella Castle. The area in front of the castle is known as the Central Plaza or the Hub. Bridges over the waterways here serve as passages to each of the themed lands.

As you enter the Hub, the first bridge on your left goes to Adventureland; the next, to Liberty Square and Frontierland. On your right, the first bridge heads to Tomorrowland; the second, to Fantasyland. The end points of the pathways leading to the lands are linked by a street that is roughly circular, so that the layout of the Magic Kingdom resembles a wheel. All attractions, restaurants, and shops are found along the wheel's rim and spokes.

Guidemaps and Times Guides are available at the park entrance, at City Hall in Town Square, and at many shops. Be sure to pick them up as soon as possible. You'll find them to be valuable navigational and scheduling resources.

HOW TO GET THERE

Take Exit 64B off I-4. Continue about four miles to the Auto Plaza and park; walk or take a tram to the main entrance complex, known as the Transportation and Ticket Center (TTC). Choose a seven-minute ferry ride or a slightly shorter trip by monorail for the last leg of an anticipation-filled journey.

By WDW Transportation: From the Grand Floridian and Polynesian Village: monorail or boat. From the Contemporary: monorail or walkway. (It's roughly a 7- to 15-minute stroll, depending on the pace.) From Epcot: monorail to the Transportation and Ticket Center (TTC), then transfer to the Magic Kingdom monorail or ferry. From Disney's Hollywood Studios and Animal Kingdom: bus. From the resorts on Hotel Plaza Boulevard: bus to the TTC, then transfer to a ferry or monorail. From Fort Wilderness: boat or bus. From Wilderness Lodge: boat or bus. From Disney Springs: bus to any Walt Disney World resort and transfer to the Magic Kingdom bus (or monorail). From all other Walt Disney World resorts: buses.

PARKING

All-day car parking at the Magic Kingdom starts at $20 for day visitors (free to WDW resort guests with a valid resort ID, MagicBand, or an annual pass; trucks, trailers, and RVs cost more). Bear left after passing through the Auto Plaza; attendants will direct you into an available lot. Several lots are within walking distance of the TTC; all others are served by trams.

Note the section and aisle in which you park. (Even better: take a photo with your phone.) The parking ticket allows for re-entry to the parking area throughout the day.

HOURS

The Magic Kingdom is generally open from 9 A.M. to about 8 P.M. However, during busy seasons, it's open later. It's best to reach the park entrance up to a half hour before the opening time. If you prefer to avoid the morning crush, consider postponing your visit until 1 P.M. or later.

Note that on select days, the Magic Kingdom opens early or stays open late for Walt Disney World resort guests only (this is known as Extra Magic Hours). For details and current schedules, visit *www.disneyworld.com*, or call 407-824-4321. The park tends to be more crowded on such days, so consider starting here and "hopping" elsewhere later in the day.

GETTING AROUND

Walt Disney World Railroad steam trains make a 20-minute loop of the park, stopping to pick up and drop off passengers at stations on Main Street, Frontierland, and Fantasyland. (It's an efficient way to travel when parades are being run or there's a lot of foot traffic.) Horseless carriages, a fire engine, and horse-drawn trolleys take turns offering one-way trips down Main Street (during non-peak hours).

Park Primer

BABY FACILITIES

The best place in the Magic Kingdom to take care of little ones' needs is the Baby Care Center. This cheery site, equipped with changing tables and facilities for nursing mothers, is next to the Crystal Palace restaurant. Disposable diapers are for sale at the Baby Care Center (if possible, bring your own—the packages are small and a tad pricey). All park restrooms are equipped with changing facilities.

CAMERA NEEDS

Box Office Gifts in the Town Square Theater has memory cards and batteries, disposable cameras, and more. Note that selfie sticks are not permitted.

DISABILITY INFORMATION

Most Magic Kingdom shops and restaurants, and many attractions, are accessible to guests using wheelchairs. Additional services are available for guests with visual or hearing disabilities. The *Guide for Guests with Disabilities* provides an overview of all services available, including transportation, parking, and attraction access. You can pick one up at the park entrance or at City Hall. For more information, see the "Travelers with Disabilities" section of the *Getting Ready to Go* chapter.

FERRY VERSUS MONORAIL

For guests arriving by car or bus, it's necessary to decide whether to travel to the Magic Kingdom by ferry or monorail. The monorail usually makes the trip from the Transportation and Ticket Center (TTC) in about 6 minutes, while the ferry takes about 7. During busy seasons, the ferry will often get you there faster (long lines can form at the monorail, and most people don't make the short walk to the ferry landing). Guests who use wheelchairs should note that while the monorail platforms are accessible, the ramp

leading to the boarding area is a bit on the steep side, prompting many guests to opt for the ferry.

FIRST AID

A registered nurse tends to minor medical problems at the First Aid Center, located near the Crystal Palace restaurant. For medical emergencies, alert a cast member and call 911.

INFORMATION

City Hall, just inside the park entrance, serves as the Magic Kingdom's information headquarters. Guest Relations reps can answer questions and help with MagicBands. Guidemaps and Times Guides, updated weekly (including details about entertainment and character greeting times and locations), are also available here. Should you have problems with your ticket or a question about the number of unused days remaining on a ticket, City Hall is good place to go.

LOCKERS

Attended lockers are located just inside the park entrance, all the way to the right. Lockers are also available at the Transportation and Ticket Center (TTC). Cost is $8–$10 per day (plus a $5 refundable deposit) for unlimited use. If you "hop" to another park on the same day, you don't have to pay to get another locker. Simply present your receipt to the attendant and you're all set.

LOST & FOUND

On the day of your visit, report lost articles at City Hall or at the TTC. Recovered items can also be claimed at these locations. After your visit, call 407-824-4245.

LOST CHILDREN

Report lost children at City Hall or the Baby Care Center, and alert the nearest Disney employee to the problem.

HOT TIP!

Certain attractions keep shorter hours than the Magic Kingdom itself (e.g., The Hall of Presidents, The Country Bear Jamboree, and Tom Sawyer Island). To make sure you catch all your favorites, check a Times Guide when you enter the park.

MONEY MATTERS

The Magic Kingdom has five Automated Teller Machines (ATMs): near the locker rental site; in City Hall on Main Street, U.S.A.; near the Frontier Shootin' Arcade; near Pinocchio Village Haus; and in the shop next to Space Mountain. Most foreign currency can be exchanged at City Hall.

Credit cards (American Express, Visa, Master-Card, JCB, Discover Card, and Diner's Club) are accepted as payment for admission, merchandise, and at most dining locations. Traveler's checks, Disney gift cards, MagicBands and WDW resort ID cards are also accepted in most places (when backed up with a major credit card). Some food and souvenir carts accept cash only.

While no longer sold, Disney Dollars are still accepted for dining and purchases at most Walt Disney World locations and may be exchanged for U.S. currency. (Production of new Disney Dollars was discontinued in 2016.)

PACKAGE PICKUP

Individual shops can arrange for purchases to be transported to the Package Pickup at the Main Street Chamber of Commerce, next to City Hall, for pickup between noon and park closing time (at least three hours after purchase). Packages may be sent to most Disney resorts, too. The delivery service is free.

PARK RULES

To ensure a comfortable, safe, and enjoyable experience for all guests, visitors are asked to comply with all Park rules, signs, and instructions including:

- All bags are subject to inspection.
- Guests are subject to screening via wand and/or metal detector.
- Proper attire is required.
- Smoking is allowed in designated areas only.
- Selfie sticks are not permitted in Disney parks.
- Weapons (including toys) are prohibited.

For additional details and a complete listing of Disney Park Rules, visit Guest Relations or go to *www.disneyworld.com/ParkRules*.

SAME-DAY RE-ENTRY

Wear your MagicBand if you used it for admission or retain your ticket if you plan to return later the same day.

SECURITY CHECK

All guests entering Disney parks are subject to a thorough security check, including a metal detector screening. Backpacks, parcels, purses, etc., will be searched by security personnel before guests may pass through the entrance.

HOT TIP!

Will you need a stroller during your visit? Consider bringing one from home. It will save you money, and it can be used all over WDW. (Disney rentals may not be removed from the parks.) Chances are your baby buggy is more comfortable than the ones in the parks, too—they are made of hard plastic. If yours is too cumbersome for travel, consider buying an "umbrella" stroller or renting a user-friendly carriage from a company such as Magic Strollers (see page 67).

STROLLERS & WHEELCHAIRS

Wheelchair Rental, located just inside the entrance, all the way to the right, offers wheelchairs (some oversized) and Electric Conveyance Vehicles (ECVs). Strollers are available under the Main Street Train Station. The cost for strollers is $15 per day ($13 per day with a multi-day rental); double strollers cost $31 per day ($27 a day with a multi-day rental); wheelchairs are $12 per day, $10 with multi-day rental; $50 per day for ECVs, with a $20 refundable deposit. Quantities are limited. Hold on to your receipt; it can be used on the same day to get a replacement stroller or wheelchair at any of the theme parks. Multi-day rentals, called Length of Stay tickets, save you two dollars off the daily price. Keep your receipt handy.

Note that during busy times the park may offer "stroller express" service. Guests pre-pay for a stroller before passing through the entrance and bypass the line once inside.

To prevent your stroller from getting lost in a sea of stroller clones, consider personalizing it with an item such as a ribbon or a sign.

Admission Prices

ONE-DAY BASE TICKET
(Restricted to use only in the Magic Kingdom. Prices are presented in the following order: Value, Regular, and Peak. **Prices do not include tax and are likely to rise in 2017.**)

Adult...$105/$110/$124
Child*..$99/$104/$118

*3 through 9 years of age; children under age 3 free

Main Street, U.S.A.

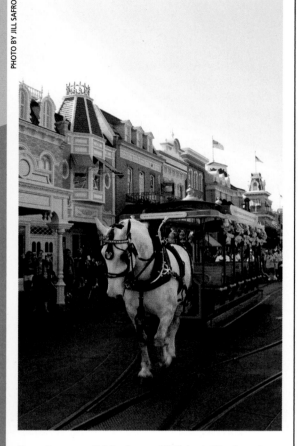

PHOTO BY JILL SAFRO

The street represents an ideal American town. Although such a town never really existed, many claim to have served as the inspiration for it. Chances are Walt Disney got the idea from Marceline, Missouri, the tiny rural town that was his boyhood home.

HOT TIP!

Plan to do your shopping in the early afternoon, rather than at day's end when the Main Street shops are normally jammed.

Most of the structures along the thoroughfare are given over to shops, and each one is different. Some emporiums are big and bustling, others are relatively quiet and orderly; some are spacious and airy, others are cozy and dark. Inside and out, maintenance and housekeeping are superb.

White-suited sanitation workers patrol the street to pick up litter and quickly shovel up any evidence of the horses that pull the trolley cars from Town Square to the Hub. As in the rest of the Magic Kingdom, the pavement here is washed down every night with hoses. There's one crew of maintenance workers whose sole job is to change the little white lights around the roofs; another crew devotes itself to keeping the woodwork painted. As soon as these people have worked their way as far as the Hub, they start all over again at Town Square. The greenish, horse-shaped, cast-iron hitching posts are repainted 20 times a year on average—and totally scraped down each time.

The "attractions" along Main Street, U.S.A., are relatively minor compared to the really big deals such as Tomorrowland's Space Mountain, Frontierland's Splash Mountain, or The Haunted Mansion in Liberty Square. But each and every shop has its own quota of merchandise that is meant as much for show as for sale. It's almost as entertaining to watch the cooks stir up gooey batches of fudge or peanut brittle at the Main Street Confectionery as it is to actually savor a sample. The shop windows, particularly at the Emporium, are also worth a look.

Once you start to meander along Main Street, be sure to notice the names on the second-story windows. Above the Uptown Jewelers store (near the Confectionery) is that of Walt's nephew, Roy E. Disney. And you will see Walt's name above the ice-cream parlor.

Stepping onto Main Street, U.S.A., is like jumping through a time portal. Welcome to turn-of-the-twentieth-century America! Horse-drawn trolleys are the transportation of choice, peppy patriotic music underscores the bustle of merry, moving masses, and the tantalizing aroma of fresh-baked cookies perfumes the air.

A rose-colored retrospective? Maybe. But this is Disney's version of a small-town Main Street—and the charm of this nostalgic land is lost on no one. Anchored by an old-fashioned train station at one end and a fairy-tale castle at the other, Main Street, U.S.A., whisks you from reality to fantasy in a few short blocks.

All of the addresses here feature just-dried coats of paint, curlicued gingerbread moldings, and pretty details. Add to that the baskets of hanging plants and genuine-looking gaslights, and Main Street, U.S.A., becomes a true showplace—both in the bright light of high noon and after nightfall, when the tiny lights edging all of the rooflines are flicked on.

Other names are those of people closely connected with The Walt Disney Company.

Note: Attractions in Main Street, U.S.A., are described in the order in which they are encountered upon entering the park.

WALT DISNEY WORLD RAILROAD:

The best introduction to the Magic Kingdom, the 1½-mile journey on this rail line is as much a must for the first-time visitor as it is for railroad buffs. It offers an excellent orientation as it passes by most of the park's major lands.

Walt Disney himself was a railroad aficionado. During the early years of television, viewers watched films of him circling his own backyard in a one-eighth-scale train, the Lilly Belle (named for his wife). The 1928 steam engine is the same age as Mickey Mouse.

HOT TIP!

Kids under age 14 must be accompanied by someone age 14 or older when visiting any WDW theme park.

The Walt Disney World Railroad also has a Lilly Belle among its quartet of locomotives. The others are named Roy O. Disney, Walter E. Disney, and Roger E. Broggie (a Disney Imagineer who shared Walt Disney's enthusiasm for antique trains). All of them were built in the U.S. around the turn of the century and later taken to Mexico to haul freight and passengers in the Yucatán, where Disney scouts found them in 1969. The United Railways of Yucatán was using them to carry sugarcane. Brought north once again, they were completely overhauled, and even the smallest of parts were reworked or replaced.

PHOTO BY JILL SAFRO

HOT TIP!

Guests staying at the Contemporary resort can walk to and from the Magic Kingdom's front gate. The trip takes about 7 to 15 minutes. It's handy when there's a long line for the monorail.

The train circles the park in about 20 minutes, making stops in Main Street, U.S.A., Frontierland, and Fantasyland. Trains arrive every 5 to 10 minutes. The line is usually shorter in Frontierland, but there's rarely a long wait at any station. The train is the best way to reach the exit when parades take over Main Street, U.S.A.

Note: The Walt Disney World Railroad does not run during fireworks presentations.

MAIN STREET VEHICLES:

A number of these can be seen traveling up and down Main Street—horseless carriages and jitneys patterned after turn-of-the-century vehicles; a spiffy scarlet fire engine; and a troop of trolleys drawn by Belgians and Percherons, two strong breeds of horse that once pulled plows in Europe. These animals—weighing in at about a ton each and shod with plastic (easier on their hooves)—pull the trolley the length of Main Street about two dozen times during each of their working days. Between shifts, they can be seen resting inside Main Street's Car Barn. Feel free to stop by and say hello. At day's end, they go home to their barn at Fort Wilderness.

Note: Main Street Vehicles generally operate during daytime hours on off-peak days.

TOWN SQUARE THEATER: **FP**+

Themed as a Victorian-era theater, this is an ideal spot to meet and mingle with Mickey Mouse. Of course, this being a magic kingdom, Mickey has a few tricks up his sleeve. Yep, in addition to all his other skills, the Mouse is a master magician. Who knew? Note that this is strictly a "backstage" experience, as Mickey's magic show is still in the rehearsal stage. The wait here can be quite long—get a Fastpass+ if you can.

Note: Guests who'd like to meet Minnie Mouse can do so at Pete's Silly Sideshow in the Storybook Circus section of Fantasyland.

HOT TIP!

Tuesday and Wednesday tend to be the least crowded days at the Magic Kingdom.

Adventureland

Adventureland seems to have even more atmosphere than the other lands. That may be due to its neat separation from the rest of the Magic Kingdom by the bridge over Main Street on one end and by a gallery-like structure (where it merges with Frontierland) on the other, or, possibly, it's because of the abundance of landscaping.

The centrally located attraction, The Magic Carpets of Aladdin, sets the tone for this corner of the Kingdom. Still surrounded by tropical splendor, the area has the look and feel of a bustling marketplace—the likes of which one might stumble upon in Agrabah. Shops here offer imports from around the globe.

As guests stroll away from Main Street, U.S.A., they just may hear the sound of beating drums, the squawks of parrots, and the regular boom of a cannon. Paces quicken. And the wonders that are soon to be encountered do not disappoint.

Calling All Pirates!

Captain Jack Sparrow needs your help. He knows there's treasure to be found and enemies to fight in Adventureland (yeah, that means you, Captain Barbossa!), but Jack can't do it alone. So he's recruiting Magic Kingdom guests to join his pirate posse.

The interactive quest, "A Pirate's Adventure —Treasure of the Seven Seas," begins at The Crow's Nest, near the Pirates of the Caribbean attraction. That's where potential pirates use a MagicBand or talisman (which activates magical effects throughout the land) and a mission map. There are five missions in all, some of which involve dodging blow darts and cannon fire. It's free to play (how's that for a little hidden treasure?!), and the maps and talisman are yours to keep. Arrrrr!

SWISS FAMILY TREEHOUSE: This is everybody's idea of the perfect treehouse, with its many levels and comforts—patchwork quilts, mahogany furniture, candles stuck in abalone shells, even running water in every room. (The system is rather ingenious.) Based on the wondrous banyan-tree home in Disney's 1960 rendition of the classic story *Swiss Family Robinson*, it rarely fails to intrigue. It's easy to understand why, when given the chance to leave the island (several adventures later), all but one member of the Robinson family chose to stay on. The only modern convenience the Robinsons could use? An elevator! Expect to burn off a few calories climbing up and down the stairs. Be sure to enjoy the view of the park from the tree-top.

The Spanish moss draping the branches is real; the tree itself—unofficially christened *Disneyodendron eximus*, a genus that is translated roughly as "out-of-the-ordinary Disney tree"— was constructed entirely by the props department. Some statistics: The roots, which are made of concrete, poke 42 feet into the ground, and about 300,000 lifelike polyethylene leaves "grow" on the tree's 1,400 individual branches.

HOT TIP!

During non-peak seasons, the Jungle Cruise may open one hour after the rest of the Magic Kingdom opens for the day.

JUNGLE CRUISE: FP+ Inspired in part by the 1955 documentary *The African Lion* and the classic film *The African Queen*, this ten-minute adventure is one of the crowning achievements of Magic Kingdom landscape artists for the way it takes guests through surroundings as diverse as a Southeast Asian jungle, the Nile Valley, and an Amazon rainforest. Along the way, passengers encounter zebras, giraffes, lions, headhunters, and more (all of the Audio-Animatronics variety); they also see elephants bathing and tour a temple—while listening to an amusing, though corny, spiel delivered by the skipper. (Bet you didn't know that Schweitzer Falls was named after the famous doctor Albert . . . Falls.)

This classic adventure, which is best enjoyed by daylight, is one of the park's slower-moving attractions. It's popular with guests of all ages.

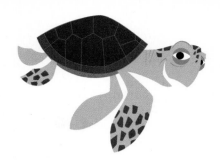

WALT DISNEY'S ENCHANTED TIKI ROOM:

The Tiki Room is back under its original management. That's right, Iago is out and José, Michael, Pierre, and Fritz have once again taken center stage—as they did when the attraction first opened in 1963. Cherished for its historical significance (the Tiki Birds starred in the first Audio-Animatronics attraction ever), the Tiki show has evolved a bit over the years.

The performance features the aforementioned fine-feathered friends, plus some 200 birds, flowers, and tiki statues singing up a tropical storm. Let's all sing like the birdies sing!

THE MAGIC CARPETS OF ALADDIN: FP+

Welcome to Agrabah! Adventureland's high-flying attraction is conveniently situated in the center of the action. It features not one, but 16 carpets that soar through the air in a fashion similar to those airborne elephants over in Fantasyland. Each flying carpet accommodates four guests at a time. Depending on where you sit, you'll have control of the carpet's movement (vertical controls are in the front row; side-to-side are in the back row). Be prepared to dodge the occasional stream of liquid, courtesy of an expectorating camel.

BIRNBAUM'S ★BEST★ PIRATES OF THE CARIBBEAN: FP+

Quite simply, this is one of the very best of the Magic Kingdom's classic adventures. The beloved ten-minute cruise is a Disneyland original, added to Walt Disney World's Magic Kingdom (in slightly revised form) due to popular demand. Here, guests board a small boat and set sail for a series of scenes showing a pirate raid on a Caribbean island town, dodging cannon fire and weathering one small, though legitimate, watery dip along the way. There are singing marauders, plastered pigs, and wily wenches; the observant may note a couple of new rapscallion residents. Yep, that beloved scallywag Captain Jack Sparrow has dropped anchor here, as has his nefarious nemesis, Captain Barbossa.

While it's by no means the most politically correct attraction on-property (far from it, actually), the rendition of "Yo Ho, Yo Ho, a Pirate's Life for Me"—the catchy theme song—makes what is actually a rather brutal scenario into something that comes across as good fun. Note that it is possible to get a little wet on this ride.

And, yes, this is the attraction that inspired the *Pirates of the Caribbean* movies—which, in turn, inspired the attraction.

Frontierland

With the Rivers of America lapping at its borders and Big Thunder Mountain rising up in the rear, this re-creation of the American Frontier encompasses the area from the Mississippi River to the Southwest, from the 1770s to the 1880s. In these parts, shops, restaurants, and attractions have unpainted barn siding or stone or clapboard walls, and there are several wooden sidewalks of the sort Marshal Matt Dillon used to stride along. The Walt Disney World Railroad makes a stop here.

FRONTIERLAND SHOOTIN' ARCADE: This modest arcade is set in an 1850s town in the Southwest Territory. Positions overlook Boothill, a town complete with bank, jail, hotel, and cemetery.

Genuine Hawkins .54-caliber buffalo rifles have been refitted, and when the infrared beam strikes any of the targets, an interesting result is triggered. Struck tombstones rise, sink, spin, or change their epitaphs; hit a cloud and a ghost rider gallops across the sky; a bull's-eye on a grave digger's shovel causes a skull to pop out of the grave.

There is an additional charge to play here (usually about a buck).

COUNTRY BEAR JAMBOREE: The Country Bears may never make it to the Grand Ole Opry, but they don't seem to mind. Disney's brood of banjo-strummin' bruins has been playing to packed houses in Grizzly Hall for more than a quarter century. Judging by all the toe tappin' and hand clappin' that accompany each performance, the show remains a countrified crowd-pleaser. As for the few folks who aren't charmed by the backwoods ballads and down-home humor, well, they just have to grin and bear it.

As guests are settling into their seats (all of which provide a decent view), Buff, Max, and Melvin are beginning to grumble. Despite their status as permanent fixtures in the theater, the mounted animal heads would rather not "hang around all day" waiting for the show to get going. The 11-minute revue opens with a rousing ditty by the Five Bear Rugs. The wheels set in motion, the remaining songs come fast and furious. Together, they capture the spirit of a genre that has a tendency to celebrate and lampoon itself simultaneously.

For example, Bunny, Bubbles, and Beulah bemoan "All the Guys That Turn Me On Turn Me Down"; Henry, the easygoing emcee who sports a coonskin cap (still attached to the 'coon), belts out "The Ballad of Davy Crockett"; and Big Al, the oversize tone-deaf fan favorite, woefully croons "Blood on the Saddle," much to the delight of the giggle-prone audience.

Timing Tip: This attraction typically opens at 10 A.M. each day, even when the rest of the park opens earlier in the morning.

TOM SAWYER ISLAND: This patch of land in the middle of the Rivers of America has hills to scramble up; a working windmill, Harper's Mill, with an owl in the rafters and a perpetually creaky waterwheel; and a few pitch-black caves. To reach the island, guests take a raft across the river. (It's the only way to get there and back.)

Paths wind this way and that, and it's easy to get disoriented. Keep an eye out for mounted maps scattered about the island.

There are two bridges here—a suspension bridge and a barrel bridge, which floats atop some lashed-together wooden barrels. When one person bounces, everybody lurches—and all but the most chickenhearted laugh. Both of the bridges are easy to miss, so be sure to keep your eyes peeled.

Across the suspension bridge is Fort Langhorn. Poke around and you'll discover a twisting and slightly scary escape tunnel. Walk along the pathway on the banks of the Rivers of America and you'll find your way back to the bridges.

The whole island seems as rugged as backwoods Missouri and, probably as a result, it actually feels a lot more remote than it is—enough to be able to provide some welcome respite from the bustle.

One particularly pleasant way to relax here is at a waterside table. It's sometimes possible to buy a snack—and you are always welcome to bring your own. Restrooms are beside the main raft landing and inside Fort Langhorn.

Timing Tip: This attraction closes at dusk.

BIRNBAUM'S ★BEST SPLASH MOUNTAIN: FP+

On the day this attraction made its official 1992 Walt Disney World debut, everyone got soaked—thanks in part to a particularly potent Florida rain cloud. But the rain wasn't entirely responsible for the sea of soggy Magic Kingdom guests. The five-story drop into an aqueous briar patch was. And a steady stream of thrill seekers has been taking the plunge ever since.

HOT TIP!

If you'd like to get soaked on Splash Mountain, sit on the right side of the log.

In this guaranteed smile inducer, guests enjoy a waterborne journey through brightly colored swamps and bayous, and down waterfalls, and are finally hurtled from the peak of the mountain to a briar-laced pond five stories below.

Splash Mountain is based on the animated sequences in Walt Disney's 1946 film *Song of the South*. The scenery entertains as the story line follows Br'er Rabbit as he tries to reach his "laughin' place." It's tough for a first-time rider to take in all the details, since the tension of waiting for the big drop is all-consuming.

It is a bit terrifying at the top, but once back on the ground, it seems most riders can't wait for another trip—even though they may get drenched. (Water-wary guests are sometimes seen wearing rain ponchos on this attraction. On the other hand, if you want to get soaked, try to sit up front or on the right; seats in the back receive a smaller splash.)

By the second or third time around, it's possible to relax a bit, enjoy the interior scenes, and take in the spectacular views of the Magic Kingdom from the top of the mountain. At this point, you may even manage to keep your eyes open for the duration of the final fall—or at least part of it.

Splash Mountain's designers not only borrowed characters and color-saturated settings from *Song of the South*, but also used quite a bit of the film's Academy Award–winning music in this attraction. As a matter of fact, the song in Splash Mountain's final scene, "Zip-a-Dee-Doo-Dah," has become something of a Disney anthem over the years.

Note: You must be at least 40 inches tall to ride Splash Mountain. The final drop may be too scary for some kids (and grown-ups!). There's a small play area for parents to tend to tykes while older kids ride. If you'd like to absorb as little precipitation as possible, sit on the left side of the log—though no seat is splash free.

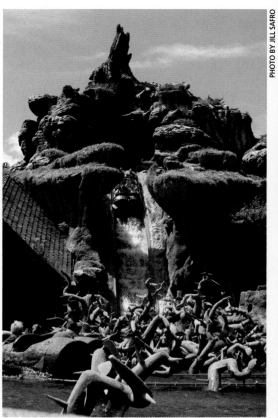

FP+ = **Fastpass+ attraction (see page 25)**

BIRNBAUM'S ★BEST★

BIG THUNDER MOUNTAIN RAILROAD: FP+ It's certainly not hard to spot Big Thunder, the lone red rock formation this side of the Mississippi. Even newcomers to the Magic Kingdom will be able to distinguish the landmark from its famed counterparts—Splash and Space mountains—because it's the only one that actually looks like a real mountain range. The designers took Utah's Monument Valley as inspiration, and the resemblance is actually quite remarkable.

According to Disney legend, the 2.5-acre mountain is chock-full of gold. Unfortunately for the residents of Tumbleweed, the local mining town, a flood has ruined any chance of uncovering the remaining gold. Before the prospectors find drier land, they are having one last party at the saloon to celebrate their riches. Even though in danger of washing away, they don't seem too worried—and guests who decide to take a trip on the Big Thunder Mountain Railroad have nothing to worry about either.

After passing through the new interactive queue area, guests are advised to "hang on to your hats and glasses 'cause this here's the wildest ride in the wilderness." Do heed the warning, but don't despair. The ride, though thrilling, is relatively tame, so relax and enjoy the sights. (Passengers seated nearest the caboose experience more turbulence than those seated closer to the front.)

A bleating billy goat atop a peak, a family of possums hanging overhead, and a dark cavern full of bats, not to mention chickens, donkeys, and washed-up miners, can be spotted along the way. Be sure to keep an eye out for the not-yet-sunken saloon—it's easy to miss the first time around.

A continuous string of curves and dips around Big Thunder's pinnacles and caverns is sure to please thrill seekers of all ages, but the adrenaline surge is caused by more than just the speed of the trip. The added sound of a rickety track, a steam whistle that blows right before the train accelerates into a curve, and an unexpected earthquake all compound the passengers' anticipation, making this attraction one of the Magic Kingdom's most popular.

Note: You must be at least 40 inches tall and immune to motion sickness to experience the Big Thunder Mountain Railroad attraction.

Timing Tip: Plan to visit early in the morning, during a parade, or just before closing time. Of course, you can always plan ahead and get a Fastpass+. If you will be visiting during a parade, consider taking the Walt Disney World Railroad to the Frontierland station. The train circumvents much of the parade congestion.

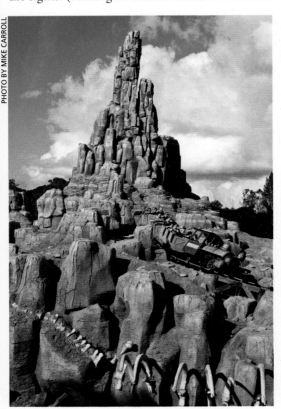

PHOTO BY MIKE CARROLL

Sorcerers of the Magic Kingdom

Uh-oh—Disney villains are trying to take over the Magic Kingdom, and *you* can help defeat them. How? First, Merlin the magician will make you (and everyone with you) an apprentice sorcerer. Then you'll use magic spell cards to beat the bad guys and save the park.

The interactive game starts at the Firehouse on Main Street, U.S.A., or in Liberty Square (behind Ye Olde Christmas Shoppe). Simply present your valid park ticket or MagicBand and you'll receive a special key card, five magic spell cards, and a map. (The folks behind the counter can answer questions, too.) As you follow the clues, you will try to prevent villains from stealing Merlin's crystal ball and keep the Magic Kingdom safe.

There is no extra charge to play, and the magic spell cards are yours to keep. You may get a new set of cards each day you visit the park. Having trouble getting a complete set? Know that other guests are often eager to trade. Many guests—of all ages—enjoy collecting the cards as much as they do playing the game.

Liberty Square

The transition between Frontierland on one side and Fantasyland on the other is so smooth that it's hard to say just when you arrive at Liberty Square, yet ultimately, there's no mistaking the location. The small buildings are clapboard or brick and topped with weather vanes; the decorative moldings are Federal or Georgian in style; the glass is sometimes wavy; and there are flower boxes in shop windows. There's a bounty of shops, plus two of the park's most famous attractions—The Haunted Mansion and The Hall of Presidents—and the Liberty Tree Tavern, one of the few table-service restaurants in the Magic Kingdom park.

THE HALL OF PRESIDENTS: The Hall of Presidents attraction made its debut with the park way back in 1971. Though revered for its status as a classic Magic Kingdom attraction, it was starting to lose some of its luster. It was time for a change. And change it did. The revamped and revitalized show boasts cutting-edge technology and an historically interesting story line.

The 25-minute celebration of U.S. leaders begins with a stirring, original film. It covers the country's origins, the framing of the Constitution, and national triumphs and struggles from the Civil War (which leads Abraham Lincoln to deliver the Gettysburg Address) to the present day. Throughout, it focuses on the role of U.S. presidents in the shaping of American history

and applauds the ordinary people who rose to the nation's highest office and led us through extraordinary circumstances.

Following the film, the curtain rises and all 45 U.S. presidents are represented. (The observant may note that there are only 44 Audio-Animatronics figures on the stage. No, the Disney Imagineers did not misplace a president. Grover Cleveland served two non-consecutive terms, so he is the 22nd and 24th president of the United States.) After all the Commanders in Chief are introduced, both George Washington and Barack Obama deliver patriotic speeches.

Displays in the pre-show area give guests a chance to gaze upon bits of Americana, such as painted eggs from a White House Easter egg hunt and dresses from former first ladies (exhibit items will change from time to time).

Note: This attraction will be closed for a period in early 2017, as the new president is added to the Hall. It marks the eighth time a Commander in Chief has been added since the Hall of Presidents opened in 1971. Show details are subject to change, pending the new addition to the cast.

LIBERTY BELLE RIVERBOAT: Based in Liberty Square and built in dry dock at Walt Disney World, this is a genuine steamboat. Its boiler turns water into steam, which is then piped to the engine, which drives the paddle wheel that propels the boat. It is not the real article in one key respect, however: It moves through the nine-foot-deep Rivers of America on an underwater rail.

The pleasant ride, with narration by an actor playing Mark Twain, is a good way to beat the heat on steamy afternoons. En route, a variety of props create a sort of Wild West effect: moose, deer, a burning cabin, and the like. The tour is completed within 17 minutes. Note that this attraction usually opens an hour or so after the park itself and shuts down before other park attractions do.

BIRNBAUM'S ★BEST★ THE HAUNTED MANSION:

FP+ This eerie, eight-minute experience is among the Magic Kingdom's most enjoyable. However, guests who expect to be scared silly when they enter the big old house, modeled after those built in New York's Hudson River Valley in the eighteenth century, will be just a tad unfulfilled. This haunted house steers clear of anything too terrifying, and a good-spirited voice-over keeps the mood light. Still, some of the scenes, as well as the darkness, may be too much for some tykes.

Once you're inside the portrait hall, entered after passing through the front doors, it's amusing to speculate: Is the ceiling moving up, or is the floor dropping? It's also where you will meet your "Ghost Host" and learn how he met his untimely demise.

The spooky journey through the mansion takes place in a Doom Buggy. The attraction is full of tricks and treats for the eyes; just when you think you've seen it all, there's something new: staircases to nowhere, bats' eyes on the wallpaper, a suit of armor that comes alive, a terrified cemetery watchman and his mangy mutt, and the image of a creepy lady in a floating crystal ball (aka Madame Leota).

One of the biggest jobs of the maintenance crews here is not cleaning up, but keeping things dirty. The mansion is littered with some 200 trunks, chairs, dress forms, harps, rugs, and assorted knickknacks and requires a lot of dust. Cobwebs are bought in liquid form and strung up by a secret process.

When waiting to enter, take time to enjoy the interactive queue area. And on the way out, take a moment to pay your respects at the pet cemetery. Mr. Toad, we hardly knew you. *Sniff, sniff.*

Fantasyland

Walt Disney called this a "timeless land of enchantment," and his successors termed it "the happiest land of all"—and it is, for many. It is also the home of a number of rides that are particularly well liked by children of all ages.

CINDERELLA CASTLE: Just as Mickey stands for all the merriment in Walt Disney World, this storybook castle represents the hopes and dreams of childhood—a time in life when anything is possible and dreams really do come true.

At a height of 189 feet (and sporting 27 turrets), Cinderella Castle is nearly twice the height of Disneyland's Sleeping Beauty Castle. For inspiration, Disney Imagineers looked to the palaces of author Charles Perrault's France, still showplaces of Europe. The design took the form of a romanticized composite of such courts as Fontainebleau, Versailles, and famed chateaux of the Loire Valley. Of course, they also turned to the original designs for the fairy-tale castle in Disney's 1950 classic, *Cinderella*.

Unlike real European castles, this one is made of steel and fiberglass; in lieu of dungeons, it has service tunnels. However, like many fabled castles, it is surrounded by a moat. And from any vantage point, Cinderella Castle looks as if it came straight from the land of make-believe.

Mosaic Murals: The elaborate murals beneath the castle's archway rank among the true wonders of the World. They tell the story of the little cinder girl and one of childhood's happiest happily-ever-afters, using a million bits of glass in some 500 different colors, plus real silver and 14-karat gold.

Cinderella Wishing Well: This pleasant alcove, nestled along a path to Tomorrowland, is a nice spot from which to gaze at the castle. Any coins tossed into the water are donated to children's charities. Don't forget to make a wish as you part with your penny.

PRINCE CHARMING REGAL CARROUSEL: Not everything in the Magic Kingdom is a Disney version of the real article. This carrousel, discovered at the now-defunct Olympic Park in Maplewood, New Jersey, was built back in 1917 (technically making it the oldest attraction in the park). That was the end of the golden century of carrousel building, which began around 1825. During the Disney refurbishment, many of the original horses were replaced with horses made of fiberglass. No two of the 90 horses are exactly alike. Can you spot Cinderella's horse? Hint: It's the only one with a golden ribbon on its tail.

ARIEL'S GROTTO: FP+ The Little Mermaid spends most of each day greeting guests in her Fantasyland grotto. She loves to pose for photos and sign autographs. PhotoPass photographers will happily snap your photo with her, too.

FAIRYTALE GARDEN: This special spot is tucked beside Cinderella Castle. Several times a day, Merida (the heroine from *Brave*) stops by to visit with guests. Check a park Times Guide for appearance schedule. Character subject to change.

MICKEY'S PHILHARMAGIC: FP+ Mickey Mouse and a panoply of his pals (including Donald, Simba, and Ariel) strut their musical stuff in this 3-D production.

The show is an amalgam of music, effects, and animation. Of course, this being Fantasyland, the film is by no means ordinary. It's colorful, crisp, and to the delight of many a goggle-wearing guest, three-dimensional. The lively experience unfolds on a 150-foot-wide canvas. Special effects and surprises take place off-screen, too.

As with many attractions, there are moments of darkness. If you're unsure as to whether your child might find this (or any attraction) unsettling, express your concern to an attendant. They will help you make the right decision. Note that all guests must wear 3-D glasses to enjoy the show.

PHOTO BY JILL SAFRO

BIRNBAUM'S ★BEST

PETER PAN'S FLIGHT: FP+ "Come on, everybody, here we go!" So says Peter Pan at the start of this nonstop flight to Never Land. The 3-minute adventure, which takes you soaring in a pirate ship, fancifully retells the story of Peter Pan—a boy with a knack for flying and an immunity to maturity. The effects in this classic Fantasyland attraction are simple, but enchanting.

The journey starts in the Darling family nursery—which siblings Wendy, Michael, and John quickly abandon to follow Peter Pan on a trip to his homeland. As in Disney's animated feature, one of the most beautiful scenes—and one that makes this attraction a treat for grown-ups as well as smaller folk—is the sight of nighttime London, dark blue and speckled with twinkling lights. Keep your eyes peeled for Big Ben and Tower Bridge.

By the time you spot your first mermaid, you're deep in the heart of Never Land. Alas, something is terribly wrong—Captain Hook and his buccaneer buddies have taken the Darling kids captive. It's all really a trap for Peter (Hook is still peeved at Pan for serving his hand to Tick Tock the crocodile). Does everyone live happily ever after? We'll never tell.

HOT TIP!

Many Fantasyland attractions are dark, and, in some cases, special effects may be too intense for tots and small children. However, they all tend to *love* It's a Small World. Nothing scary about that!

PRINCESS FAIRYTALE HALL: FP+ Practice your curtsey as you approach this hall—once inside you'll meet regals such as Cinderella, Aurora, Rapunzel, Tiana, and Snow White. Characters vary. This royal residence occupies the space formerly occupied by the Snow White's Scary Adventures attraction. The line is always frightening—get a Fastpass+ if you can.

IT'S A SMALL WORLD: FP+ *Hola! Guten Tag!* Hello! No matter what language you speak, what you look like, or where you live, you still have a lot in common with folks the world over (including an especially high tolerance for a singsong melody that repeatedly reminds us that it's a small world, after all). That's the message driving this ten-minute boat ride around the world.

PHOTO BY JILL SAFRO

Originally created for New York's 1964–65 World's Fair, the attraction is an oldie-but-goodie (and is quite popular with young children). The ride moves at slightly swifter than snail's pace, drifting past hundreds of colorfully costumed dolls from around the world—all of whom know all the words to the ride's infectious theme song (written by the Sherman brothers).

A showcase of diversity, the attraction is a simple celebration of human similarities. It's also a relaxing alternative to many of the park's higher-tech, longer-line attractions.

PHOTO BY JILL SAFRO

DUMBO THE FLYING ELEPHANT: FP+ This is purely and simply a kiddie ride, though children of all ages have admitted to loving it.

A beloved symbol of Fantasyland, the ride moved to the Storybook Circus area and doubled in size—but rest assured, the Dumbo experience remains the same. Consider stopping here early in the morning, or during a parade, when the line—which is often prohibitively long—thins a bit. Inspired by the 1941 film classic *Dumbo*, the ride lasts a memorable two minutes.

Note: Guests in Dumbo's standby line receive a pager and are free to frolic in a covered play zone while they wait to ride. The lines for Dumbo tend to dwindle late in the day, especially when the park is open late.

FP+ = Fastpass+ attraction (see page 25)

THE BARNSTORMER: FP+ At this mini roller coaster attraction, guests of most sizes follow the same fluky flight path taken by the daredevil pilot known as the Great Goofini. Don't let the size fool you: This 1-minute ride proves that big thrills do indeed come in small packages. Although guests as young as 3 may ride, they must be at least 35 inches tall. It may be too turbulent for some.

CASEY JR. SPLASH 'N' SOAK STATION: The famous locomotive Casey Jr. invites Magic Kingdom guests to cool off in this colorful, interactive splash zone, conveniently located beside Fantasyland's train station. Be sure to dress tykes in swim diapers.

MAD TEA PARTY: FP+ The theme of this two-minute ride—in a group of oversize teacups that whirl and spin wildly—was inspired by a scene in the Disney Studios' 1951 movie production of *Alice in Wonderland*. During the sequence in question, the Mad Hatter hosts a tea party for his un-birthday.

Unlike many rides in Fantasyland, this is not just for younger kids; the 5-to-20-something crowd seems to like it best. Keep in mind that when the cups stop spinning, your head may continue to do so. Skip this ride if you suffer from motion sickness or if you've recently enjoyed a snack. Don't miss the woozy mouse that pops out of the teapot at the center of the platform—he ignored our advice.

BIRNBAUM'S ★BEST★ THE MANY ADVENTURES OF WINNIE THE POOH: FP+ Everyone's favorite honey-lovin' cub treats Magic Kingdom guests to continuous, wild and whimsical 3½-minute tours of his home turf—the Hundred Acre Wood.

The attraction features a most unlikely form of transportation: honey pots! They whisk (and bounce) guests through the pages of a giant storybook and into the Hundred Acre Wood,

where the weather's most blustery. The wind is really ruffling the feathers of one of the locals. Sight gags abound, from a bubble-blowing Heffalump (hey, this is Fantasyland) to a treacherous flood that threatens to sweep Tigger, Piglet, and the rest of the gang away. When Pooh saves the day, it's time to celebrate—and everyone is invited to the party.

Like other Fantasyland attractions, some parts of this one take place in the dark. Some children may find it a bit unsettling. That said, little ones dig Pooh's interactive queue area. While waiting to ride or for others to do so, youngsters can bang on giant vegetable "drums," play tug-of-war with a gopher, and scrawl their names in a flowing wall of honey.

UNDER THE SEA—JOURNEY OF THE LITTLE MERMAID: FP+ In the Magic Kingdom's first attraction to feature everyone's favorite Disney mermaid, guests are invited to board continuously moving clam-mobiles and embark on a jolly journey above and below sea level. Along the way, they join Ariel, Flounder, and all of their aquatic acquaintances, and enjoy major musical movements and pivotal plot points from the classic animated feature. It's fun for the whole family.

BIRNBAUM'S ★BEST★ SEVEN DWARFS MINE TRAIN: FP+ Heigh-ho, heigh-ho! A roller coaster is whimsically transporting guests on a musical journey through the workplace of the Seven Dwarfs—the mine where a million diamonds shine. The ride vehicles swing back and forth a bit as they zoom along the track, so folks with motion sickness or other health issues should sit this one out. Intensity-wise, the smooth, family-friendly attraction fits between the Barnstormer coaster and Big Thunder Mountain Railroad. The queue has a few interactive surprises, too. This 2½-minute attraction is extremely popular—get a Fastpass+ assignment if you can. Guests must be at least 38 inches tall to ride.

ENCHANTED TALES WITH BELLE: FP+ This clever mix of show and character meet-and-greet is one of those "you have to see it to believe it" experiences. Located in Maurice's exquisitely detailed cottage, the 30-minute experience includes lifelike Audio-Animatronics versions of Lumiere and Madame Wardrobe, plus an audience-participation performance by Belle in Beast's library. There are lots of parts to play—be sure to volunteer!

Tomorrowland

The original Tomorrowland attempted a serious look at the future. But as Disney planners discovered, it isn't easy to portray a future that persists in becoming the present. So the old Tomorrowland has given way to a friendlier, space-age town whose neighborhood atmosphere is more in keeping with the other lands in the Magic Kingdom. This is the future that never was, the fantasy world imagined by the science-fiction writers and moviemakers of the 1920s and '30s. It's a land of sky-piercing beacons and glistening metal, where shiny robots do the work, whisper-quiet cars glide along an elevated highway, and even time travel is possible.

Note: Tomorrowland attractions are described in the order in which they are encountered upon entering the land from the Hub and heading away from Cinderella Castle.

STITCH'S GREAT ESCAPE!: Like its predecessor, The ExtraTERRORestrial Alien Encounter, this attraction features the adventures of a renegade alien. In this case, however, said extraterrestrial is more of a menace than a threat—not so much scary as ill-mannered and mischievous. The 20-minute show is a prequel to *Lilo & Stitch*, but one need not be familiar with the drooling, intergalactic imp to follow the attraction's story line.

HOT TIP!

Parents take note: This attraction is much less scary than The ExtraTERRORestrial Alien Encounter. Still, there are moments of darkness, and Stitch's shenanigans may be daunting to little ones.

The action begins with a short pre-show, followed by the crowd spilling into a circular theater-type room. All chairs face center, where there's a mysterious tube. (Sit up straight when the shoulder harness is lowered—this will enhance the effects and make for a slightly less restraining experience.)

What's the fuss about? Bad-boy Stitch, aka Experiment 626, is being moved to a prison processing center, and you have been recruited to keep an eye on him. Up to the task? Chances are you're not: The blue rascal escapes every time. While amusing to many, this attraction is starting to show its age and the effects aren't quite as special as they used to be.

Note: Some youngsters may be frightened by dark moments and loud noises. Also, the shoulder restraints may spook claustrophobes and/or cause discomfort to sensitive shoulders. You must be at least 40 inches tall to enter.

BUZZ LIGHTYEAR'S SPACE RANGER SPIN: FP+ The Evil Emperor Zurg is up to no good. As soon as he swipes enough batteries to power his ultimate weapon of destruction— KERPLOOEY!—it's curtains for the toy universe as we know it. It's up to that Space Ranger extraordinaire Buzz Lightyear and his Junior Space Rangers (that means you) to save the day.

So goes the story line of Tomorrowland's video-game-inspired spin through toyland. The adventure is experienced from a toy's point of view. Guests begin their 4½-minute tour of duty as Space Rangers at Star Command Action Center. This is where Buzz gives his team a briefing on the mission that lies ahead. Then it's off to the Launch Bay to board the ride vehicles. The ships feature dual laser cannons, glowing lights, and a piloting joystick.

Once Junior Space Rangers blast off, they find themselves surrounded by Zurg's robots, who are mercilessly ripping batteries from toys. As Rangers fire at targets, beams of light fill the air. For every target hit, you will be rewarded with sound effects and points. The points, which are tallied automatically, are accumulated throughout the journey. Although the vehicles follow a rigid "flight" path (they're on a track), the joystick allows riders to maneuver the ships, arcing from side to side or spinning in circles while taking aim at their surroundings.

When the star cruiser arrives at Zurg's spaceship, it's showdown time. Will good prevail over evil? Or has time run out for the toy universe? And will you score enough points to be a Galactic Hero? Most people improve their scores with a little practice. Note that seats on the left side of the ride vehicle have better access to the high-point-yielding targets in the first room.

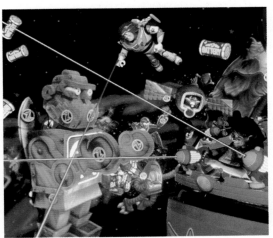

HOT TIP!
To up your score at Buzz Lightyear's Space Ranger Spin, keep the trigger depressed at all times. Also, be sure to aim for moving or distant targets—they provide some of the biggest point payoffs.

INCREDIBLES SUPER DANCE PARTY: Put on your dancing shoes and join Mr. and Mrs. Incredible and Frozone as they celebrate saving the world once again! The party takes place several times a day at the Agency Headquarters' outdoor deck, aka Rockettower Plaza. Check a Times Guide for the schedule.

MONSTERS, INC. LAUGH FLOOR: FP+ That Mike Wazowski is one enterprising eyeball. It seems the fuzzy fellow from *Monsters, Inc.* has opened a comedy club. Why? Well, it turns out his hometown is experiencing a bit of an energy crisis. Mike's clever plan is to tap into a decidedly alternative (not to mention free) fuel source to provide power for Monstropolis . . . laughter. But where can he gather enough giggles to fuel an entire city?

In a 400-seat theater in Tomorrowland, that's where. To accomplish his goal, monster of ceremonies Mike has recruited a couple of cornball comedians. Their job is to make you laugh yourself silly. And they are not too proud to resort to slapstick while doing so. Guests are encouraged to text a joke while waiting in the queue. (Standard text messaging rates apply.)

TOMORROWLAND TRANSIT AUTHORITY PEOPLEMOVER: Boarded near Astro Orbiter, these trains (known to Disney purists as the WEDway) move at a speed of about seven miles per hour along almost a mile of track, beside or through most of the attractions in Tomorrowland. They are operated by a linear induction motor that has no moving parts, uses little power, and emits no pollution.

The peaceful, breezy excursion through Tomorrowland takes about ten minutes. There's rarely much of a wait to board. It's one of our favorites. However, moments of darkness (as the train passes through Space Mountain) may be a bit unsettling for some little ones. Warn them before you board.

ASTRO ORBITER: Here, passengers fly for two minutes in machine-age rockets designed to look more like oversize Buck Rogers toys than twenty-first-century space shuttles. Riders are surrounded by vibrantly colored, whirling planets as they get an astronaut's-eye view of Tomorrowland.

TOMORROWLAND SPEEDWAY: FP+
Little cars that burn up the tracks at this attraction provide quite a bit of the background noise in Tomorrowland. Kids especially enjoy the not-so-speedy, herky-jerky driving experience.

The vehicles have rack-and-pinion steering and disc brakes, but unlike most cars, they run along a track. Yet even expert drivers have trouble keeping them going in a straight line. (Don't panic when you notice the lack of a brake pedal—when you take your foot off the gas, the car comes to a quick, if not screeching, halt.) The one-lap tour of Tomorrowland takes about five minutes.

Note: You must be at least 54 inches tall to drive the car by yourself. Guests must be at least 32 inches tall to ride shotgun. Babies younger than 12 months may not go on the ride.

BIRNBAUM'S ★BEST★ SPACE MOUNTAIN: FP+ This attraction, which blasted onto the Magic Kingdom scene in 1975 (and was completely refurbished in 2009), is a can't-miss crowd-pleaser for throngs of thrill seekers. Rising to a height of more than 180 feet, this gleaming steel-and-concrete cone houses an attraction that most people call a roller coaster. The ride takes place in an outer-space-like darkness that gets inkier and scarier as the journey progresses. The rockets that roar through this blackness attain a maximum speed of just over 28 miles per hour—but somehow it feels a whole lot faster.

The Space Mountain experience is wild enough to send glasses, purses, wallets, and even an occasional set of false teeth plummeting to

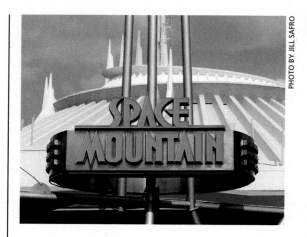

PHOTO BY JILL SAFRO

the bottom of the track, so be sure to find a safe place for your possessions before the ride starts. It's also turbulent enough to upset the stomachs of those so unwise as to ride it immediately after eating. (Those who change their minds at the last minute have access to a "chicken" exit.)

Note: Guests who are under 44 inches are not permitted to ride, and you must be in good health and free from heart conditions, motion sickness, back or neck problems, or other physical limitations to ride. Expectant mothers should skip the trip. Children under age 7 must be accompanied by an adult.

WALT DISNEY'S CAROUSEL OF PROGRESS: First seen at New York's 1964–65 World's Fair and moved here in 1975, this 20-minute experience showcases the evolution of the American family and how life changed—and ostensibly progressed—with the advent of electricity. The hook here is that as a scene ends, the audience moves to the next one—not unlike being on a carousel (hence the name of the attraction). This is a great place to escape the crowds and heat, not to mention take a much-needed load off weary feet.

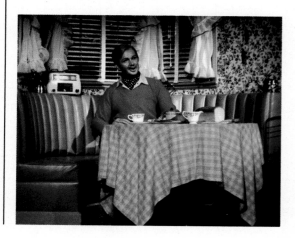

FP+ = Fastpass+ attraction (see page 25)

Shopping

No one travels to the Magic Kingdom just to shop. But as many a visitor has learned, shopping is one of the most enjoyable pastimes here.

The Magic Kingdom's boutiques and stores stock much more than just Disneyana. Along with the more predictable items in Main Street shops, it's possible to find cookbooks and dishes, pirate hats and toy frontier rifles, 14-karat gold charms, and filigreed costume jewelry. In Adventureland, shops boast many items imported from the exotic regions the area represents. Throughout the park, stores generally have merchandise that complements the themes of the various lands.

HOT TIP!

Your WDW shopping spree doesn't have to end when your vacation does. Simply download the free Shop Disney Parks mobile app and shop away. To download, visit *www.DisneyWorld.com/shop*.

In some shops, you can watch people at work: a candy maker hand-dipping caramel apples in the Main Street Confectionery, a glassblower crafting wares in Main Street's Crystal Arts, etc.

We recommend shopping in the early afternoon, rather than at the end of the day, when the shops are more crowded. However, keep in mind that Main Street shops do stay open about a half hour after park closing, in case you need any last-minute gifts on the way out.

Main Street

THE ART OF DISNEY: Nestled inside the Main Street Cinema, the shop showcases Disney-inspired fine art and collectibles, books, Vinylmation, puzzles, and more. This spot also sells collector pins. And, yes, you can still catch classic Mickey cartoons here, too.

BOX OFFICE GIFTS: Found inside Town Square Theater, this shop has camera supplies such as memory cards, batteries, and disposable cameras. It's also the place to view and pick up PhotoPass photos and purchase MagicBands.

THE CHAPEAU: This Town Square shop is the place to buy mouse ears and have them monogrammed, and to shop for straw hats, baseball caps, and assorted other headgear.

CURTAIN CALL COLLECTIBLES: After visiting Mickey Mouse at the Town Square Theater, guests may shop for souvenir items featuring assorted Disney characters, including the Big Cheese himself.

CRYSTAL ARTS: Cut-glass bowls, vases, glasses, and plates glitter in the cases of this crystal-chandeliered emporium. They have a lovely selection of miniature Disney characters meticulously crafted from glass. An engraver or a glassblower is often at work. There's a fireplace, too. Stop here to watch craftspeople mold shields and carve metal—impressive!

Where to Eat in the Magic Kingdom

A complete listing of all Magic Kingdom eateries—full-service restaurants, fast-food emporiums, and snack shops—can be found in the *Good Meals, Great Times* chapter. See the Magic Kingdom section, beginning on page 244.

DISNEY CLOTHIERS: This shop offers clothing for young girls, including shirts and sleepwear, all of which incorporate Disney characters. Look for bags and accessories, too.

EMPORIUM: Framed by a two-story-high portico, the Magic Kingdom's largest gift shop stocks stuffed animals and toys, T-shirts, kitchen items, home decor, hats, and more.

The cash registers always seem to be busy, especially toward the end of the afternoon and before park closing. Nearby lockers make for convenient storage of purchases.

Don't forget to peer into the windows, which usually feature elaborate displays ranging from seasonal themes to character tableaux. Shop early to avoid the crowds, and remember to take advantage of package pickup or delivery to your Walt Disney World resort.

HARMONY BARBER SHOP: Situated next door to the Main Street Car Barn, the quaint, old-fashioned setting for this working shop (with occasional appearances by a harmonizing quartet) merits a peek even if you have no need for a trim. It's open from 9 A.M. to about 5 P.M. daily. This is a popular spot for a child's first haircut, but they serve grown-ups, too (haircuts and beard/mustache trims). Colored gel hair treatments are offered,

Let It Rain

The show doesn't stop just because of a storm. Instead, shops throughout the Magic Kingdom sell plastic Disney Parks–branded ponchos and umbrellas to outfit guests who have left their own rain gear back home, at their hotel, or in the car.

too. For an appointment, call 407-WDW-PLAY (939-7529). Walk-ins are accepted, too (though there may be a wait).

MAIN STREET FASHION AND APPAREL: Character-related gifts and apparel are the hallmarks of this spot. The shop also stocks golf shirts, bags, hats, sweatshirts, and accessories. You'll find it next to Casey's Corner.

MAIN STREET CHAMBER OF COMMERCE: This is the place to go if you have any Magic Kingdom purchases "sent to the front of the park" (aka Package Pickup). Allow at least three hours for the package to get here. It's located near City Hall.

MAIN STREET CONFECTIONERY: Tasty chocolates are sold in this old-fashioned pink-and-white paradise. A delight at any time of day, but more so when the cooks in the shop's glass-walled kitchen dip apples in gooey caramel. Then the candy sends up clouds of aroma that you could swear were being fanned out onto the street. There is a selection of fresh-made fudge, along with jelly beans, marshmallow crispy treats, and dozens of other confections that will satisfy any sweet tooth.

NEWSSTAND: No newspapers are sold in the Magic Kingdom—even at its newsstand, which is near the park entrance. (It's to the left, just inside the entrance.) The stand sells character merchandise and souvenirs.

THE SHADOW BOX: Watching Rubio Artist Co. silhouette cutters snip black paper into the likenesses of children is one of Main Street's more fascinating diversions. The Shadow Box is at the corner of Main and Center streets.

UPTOWN JEWELERS: Designed to resemble a turn-of-the-twentieth-century collectibles shop, this spiffy store specializes in jewelry, watches, handbags, scarves, purses, wallets, shoes, phone cases, and other gift items. This location is also home to the Disney Parks/ PANDORA Jewelry Collection. Other wares include cosmetics, tote bags, luggage, back-packs, and more.

WHEELCHAIR AND ECV RENTAL: Inside the turnstiles and under the Train Station, this rental concession offers a limited number of wheelchairs and Electric Conveyance Vehicles (ECVs). They are available on a first-come,

Disney's PhotoPass

As you wander the theme parks, Disney cast members will be happy to snap your picture—just ask! After mugging for the camera, you'll be asked to scan your MagicBand (see page 24) or a PhotoPass card. It'll link all such photos together for viewing on the Internet. You can ogle and e-mail the low-res images for free for up to 45 days after they are taken. High-quality prints of various sizes are for sale. To purchase or peruse photos, visit *https://mydisneyphotopass. disney.go.com/mymedia/*. Each theme park has a spot for photo viewing. Check a park guidemap for locations. Individual photo downloads cost about $14.95, while the unlimited Memory Maker Package runs about $149 if purchased in advance. (This is a bit of splurge, but a very convenient way to get quality shots of your whole party.) Say cheese!

first-served basis. (Hold on to your receipt—it'll get you a replacement wheelchair should yours mysteriously disappear during the day.) Keep in mind that wheelchairs and ECVs rented here cannot be taken outside the Magic Kingdom. (Save your receipt and you may get a same-day replacement at another theme park.)

Adventureland

AGRABAH BAZAAR: Clothing and accessories with a safari theme are featured at this shop. Also on hand are clothing and accessories with a safari theme, toys, costumes, and items featuring The Orange Bird. They have a nice selection of musical instruments and tropical-wear, too.

BWANA BOB'S: Stop here for tropical-themed jewelry, bags, pins, and hats, plus sunglasses, disposable cameras, and more.

ISLAND SUPPLY: This small tropical shop features a large selection of sunglasses.

THE PIRATES LEAGUE: More than just a crew of plank-walkers, this group of savvy pirates transforms guests into one of their own—in exchange for booty, of course. Once you're swashbuckled up, they'll snap your photo in the

"secret" treasure room. Call 407-WDW-CREW (939-2739) for pricing or to make a reservation. The Pirates League is in the Plaza del Sol Caribe Bazaar, by the Pirates of the Caribbean.

PLAZA DEL SOL CARIBE BAZAAR: Ahoy there, mateys! A swashbuckler's delight, the joint adjoining the Pirates of the Caribbean sells stuff celebrating both the attraction and the feature films of the same name. It also stocks other pirate booty, including Jolly Roger flags, rings, dolls, pirate costumes, themed hats, and eye patches. If that's not enough treasure for you, check out the candy and snacks. The pièce de résistance for pirate fans? Pirate makeovers! (See The Pirates League at the bottom left of this page.) This is one of our favorite shops.

ZANZIBAR TRADING COMPANY: Across from Adventureland's famed Egg Roll Wagon, this corner shop stocks jungle collectibles, including hand-crafted wood items imported from Kenya and letter openers. Also found here are straw and woven items, drums, and animal-print apparel.

Frontierland

BIG AL'S: Named for the most popular (and least talented) member of the Country Bears, this riverfront shop is known for its selection of headwear, including Davy Crockett caps.

BRIAR PATCH: Toys and cuddly character items, plus kids' apparel and hats for the whole family, are featured wares at this shop, located near the Splash Mountain exit. There's also a pair of rocking chairs for those who need to take a load off.

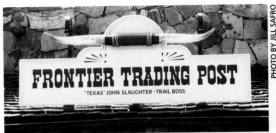

FRONTIER TRADING POST: This is the place to shop for collector pins and the associated accoutrements. Since it's got the largest selection of pins in the park, they might want to rename this the Pin Trading Post. F.T.P. also boasts a selection of Western-themed T-shirts, plus Woody- and Jessie-style hats.

PRAIRIE OUTPOST & SUPPLY: Stop by this turn-of-the-twentieth-century general store for candy (including a wall of jelly beans), coffee, cookies, jams, jellies, and kitchen accessories.

Liberty Square

LIBERTY SQUARE PORTRAIT GALLERY: In the midst of Liberty Square, guests may have their portraits drawn in this open-air studio.

MEMENTO MORI: Welcome, foolish mortals—to a spooky and spectacular shop dedicated to all things Haunted Mansion. Here you'll find everything from gargoyle candle holders and hourglasses to "Ghost Host" gear and hitch-hiking ghost figurines. It's also possible to have your portrait taken, Haunted Mansion-style. Yep, for about twenty bucks, you can be transformed into a spirited version of your future, ghoulish self. So creepy, but so cool!

YE OLDE CHRISTMAS SHOPPE: A wide variety of festive Yuletide items, including decorative Disney-themed gifts and trinkets (many of which can be personalized) and ornaments, is available year-round. Look for items such as stockings, tree-toppers, and more.

Fantasyland

BIBBIDI BOBBIDI BOUTIQUE: Housed inside Cinderella Castle, this shop offers young guests the opportunity to be transformed into princesses and knights. Magical makeovers are available from 8 A.M. to 7 P.M. Prices vary. Magic Kingdom admission is required to enter this location. (There is an additional Bibbidi Bobbidi Boutique shop at Disney Springs. While there is no admission fee, there is a charge for services at both locations.) For pricing information or to book a reservation, call 407-WDW-STYLE (939-7895). Photo packages are offered, too. Reservations are strongly recommended.

BIG TOP SOUVENIRS: Step inside the big tent for Disney-themed merchandise and snacks galore. It's in the Storybook Circus part of Fantasyland, just across from the Dumbo the Flying Elephant attraction.

BONJOUR VILLAGE GIFTS: Visit this charming addition to Fantasyland for items inspired by Disney's *Beauty and the Beast*. Expect to find apparel (we dig the Gaston's Tavern T-shirts), plush toys, royal dinnerware, glowing goblets, tapestries, castle artwork, and more. Also sold: jigsaw puzzles, Mrs. Potts tea sets for kids, and books (Belle would approve).

CASTLE COUTURE: Can't get enough Disney princess merchandise? Stop here for royal toys, costumes, dolls, and kids' "princess apparel," plus jewelry and accessories.

HUNDRED ACRE GOODS: Located at the exit of The Many Adventures of Winnie the Pooh, this shop has wares featuring the folks from the Hundred Acre Wood (among other places). Among the items the Pooh bear proffers are toys, hats, shirts, toddler clothing, and more.

SIR MICKEY'S: Expect to find all sorts of Disney character-themed clothing and souvenir items in this shop with a design based on *The Brave Little Tailor*—the cartoon in which Mickey defeats a giant to win the hand of Princess Minnie. (It was one of the most elaborate and expensive Mickey Mouse cartoons ever made.) Mouse ears may be monogrammed here, too.

Tomorrowland

MERCHANT OF VENUS: The place for anything and everything Stitch to *Star Wars*, including a build-your-own lightsaber station, plush toys, games, and Vinylmation collectibles. It is located near Stitch's Great Escape.

MICKEY'S STAR TRADERS: This is one of the better places to go in the Magic Kingdom for Disney-themed items: plush toys, hats, shirts, candy, etc. Sunglasses and sun-care products are also available. The Tomorrowland Transit Authority passes through here, too. (To catch a glimpse of the TTA, look up!)

TOMORROWLAND LIGHT & POWER COMPANY: After zipping through space, stop here to peruse Space Mountain–themed shirts and merchandise, plus MagicBands with character themes, and accessories for cell phones and tablet computers. It's possible to charge mobile phones here, too.

Entertainment

In this most magical corner of the World, a slate of live performances ranks among the more serendipitous discoveries. The Magic Kingdom's entertainment mix includes dazzling high-tech shows and old-fashioned numbers alike. To keep apprised of the offerings on any given day, pick up a current guidemap and Times Guide.

While details may change in 2017, what follows is a good indication of the park's entertainment repertoire. Visit *www.disneyworld.com* to confirm specifics and schedules.

CAPTAIN JACK SPARROW'S PIRATE TUTORIAL: So you wanna be a pirate? Captain Jack and his mate Mack are looking for new recruits near the Pirates of the Caribbean in Adventureland. They'd like to test your pirate skills (swordplay, menacing looks, etc.) and decide whether you're worthy of the Pirate's Oath and the title of honorary buccaneer.

CASEY'S CORNER PIANO: A peppy pianist tickles the ivories of a snow-white upright, just outside Casey's Corner on Main Street.

CELEBRATE THE MAGIC: A 10-minute animated, musical celebration of Disney storytelling, this takes place on Cinderella Castle. Yes, *on* the castle. (The beloved WDW icon has evolved into a high-tech canvas for Disney artists without losing any of its classic charm.) The action starts with a sprinkling of pixie dust, courtesy of Tinker Bell. Then, a montage of memorable movie moments lights up the night. In addition to the regular show, expect Celebrate the Magic to include seasonal updates throughout the year. The front and sides of the Castle offer slightly different viewing experiences—so if you've already enjoyed it from one vantage point, you might want to try another.

CITIZENS OF MAIN STREET: Performers clad in 19th-century costumes interact with guests throughout the day. They've been known to burst into song from time to time.

DAPPER DANS: You just might encounter a barbershop quartet while strolling down Main Street. Conspicuously clad in straw hats and striped vests, the ever-so-jovial Dapper Dans tap-dance and let one-liners fly during their short, four-part-harmony performances.

FAIRYTALE GARDEN: Merida from *Brave* greets guests in this nook beside Cinderella Castle each day. Check a Times Guide for specifics. Character is subject to change.

BIRNBAUM'S BEST **FIREWORKS:** FP+ Wishes, a dynamite, pyrotechnic extravaganza, is presented most nights when the Magic Kingdom stays open after dark. Narrated by Jiminy Cricket, this is one of the biggest, boldest, and truly eye-popping fireworks shows ever presented in the park. Showtimes vary—check a park Times Guide for specifics. Wishes is ideally viewed from Main Street, U.S.A., but can be seen from many vantage points. It is presented rain or shine.

FLAG RETREAT: At about 5 P.M. each day (check a current Times Guide), patriotic music fills the air as a color guard marches to Town Square, in Main Street, U.S.A., and takes down the American flag that flies from the flagpole.

BIRNBAUM'S BEST **FESTIVAL OF FANTASY PARADE:** FP+ A musical celebration of Disney Animation, this parade wends its way down Main Street once a day. The festival focuses on Disney friends who frequent Fantasyland. Kids love to wave to favorite characters—especially Anna and Elsa.

Festival of Fantasy highlights the stories of *Frozen, The Little Mermaid, Sleeping Beauty, Pinocchio, Tangled, Dumbo,* and more.

FP+ = Fastpass+ attraction (see page 25)

MICKEY'S ROYAL FRIENDSHIP FAIRE: Mickey and his band of merrymakers are hosting a joyous festival in front of Cinderella Castle, and they are welcoming friends old and new—including you! Goofy has invited folks from *The Princess and the Frog*; Donald's guests include friends he met at the Snuggly Duckling; and Daisy introduces her guests Rapunzel and Flynn Ryder. Mickey has a special surprise for *Frozen* fans: He traveled all the way to The Land of Mystic Mountains to invite Olaf, Anna, and Elsa (who brings along a little of her trademark icy magic). The show is presented daily. Check a Times Guide for showtimes.

MOVE IT, SHAKE IT, DANCE & PLAY IT!: Whether you are celebrating a special occasion or just the fact that you are in the Magic Kingdom, this dance party is a treat. A spectacle of music and dance, the 35-minute jubilee invites guests to join in the fun as dancers and Disney characters take over the street by Cinderella Castle.

Holiday Happenings

It's a rare holiday that passes quietly in the Magic Kingdom. During certain holidays, such as Christmas, New Year's Eve, and the Fourth of July, the park breaks curfew, staying open extra late and stepping up its nighttime entertainment. On these occasions, special performances of the Main Street Electrical parade and the fireworks are often in store. Of course, entertainment plans are subject to change, so it's important to call 407-934-7639 for information and schedules.

EASTER: Easter is a delightful, if a bit crowded, time to visit the Magic Kingdom. Mr. and Mrs. Easter Bunny have been known to appear in the park to help guests celebrate the occasion.

FOURTH OF JULY: The busiest day of the summer—and with good reason: There's a double-size fireworks extravaganza that lights up the skies above Cinderella Castle and the Seven Seas Lagoon. It's a thrilling display.

HALLOWEEN: This most spooky of holidays is celebrated on select nights from September through October with a special-ticket event: Mickey's Not-So-Scary Halloween Party. The park closes a bit early on nights when the party takes place. (Guests bearing tickets to the party can stay in the park.) Expect characters in costume, creepy music and fog effects, and trick-or-treating throughout the park. It's a hoot! Mickey's Boo-to-You Halloween Parade takes place, as does a special edition of the fireworks show. Visit *www.disneyworld.com/halloween*, or call 407-824-432 to order tickets to the party.

CHRISTMAS: A towering Christmas tree goes up on Main Street, and the Magic Kingdom is decked out as only Disney can do it. (Cinderella Castle is draped in 250,000 sparkling lights!)

Where to Find the Characters

Mickey and his pals make appearances throughout the day—but you can often find him at Town Square Exposition Hall. Tinker Bell greets guests there, too. Alice and her Wonderland friends may be found near the Mad Tea Party. Pooh and Tigger frequent Fantasyland. Woody and Jessie appear in Frontierland. Disney regals such as Tiana and Aurora greet guests in Princess Fairytale Hall. You'll find Goofy, Donald, Daisy, and Minnie at Pete's Silly Sideshow in Fantasyland. And various characters greet guests in Town Square at park opening time. Ariel greets folks in her Fantasyland grotto. And Anna and Elsa lead the Festival of Fantasy parade. Feel free to wave hello!

Check a Times Guide for updated information. Eateries such as Cinderella's Royal Table and The Crystal Palace offer opportunities to mingle with various characters, too. For details on dining with Disney characters, turn to page 282.

On select nights in November and December, the park hosts a special-admission celebration known as Mickey's Very Merry Christmas Party. The festivities, complete with hot chocolate, cookies, and snow flurries on Main Street, include a running (or two) of Mickey's Once Upon a Christmastime Parade and holiday shows, plus a special Wishes fireworks show. Disney characters are on hand, too.

The Christmas party is a very popular (and enjoyable) event. Purchase tickets way ahead of time. And don't forget to wear red and green; *www.disneyworld.com/christmasparty*.

NEW YEAR'S EVE: It has always been true that on December 31 the throngs here are body to body. Expect a dazzling, super-size fireworks display and oodles of happy holiday decorations. There's plenty of nip in the air as the evening goes on, so dress accordingly.

The Main Street Electrical Parade

BIRNBAUM'S ★BEST★ FP + Whether you are experiencing the Main Street Electrical Parade for the first time or for the first time in 20 years, we guarantee you'll be back for more. This enchanting classic, which made its Walt Disney World debut in 1977, is back after a lengthy hiatus. Cue applause!

A mesmerizing mix of shimmering lights (nearly half a million of them) and merry music, the parade features 23 illuminated floats (some of the originals have been retired and a few new floats have been added), plus 80 performers. As visually stunning as this processional is, it's the infectious score that makes it a truly unforgettable show. The "electro-syntho-magnetic" musical sound of Baroque Hoedown brings a smile to all faces, young and old.

The parade follows the Magic Kingdom's traditional parade route (heading from Main Street, U.S.A., to Frontierland and vice versa).

PHOTO BY JILL SAFRO

PHOTO BY JILL SAFRO

There are excellent viewing locations throughout the route, with many along the curbs of Main Street. It gets quite crowded there, so you must plan to claim your foot of curb about 45 to 90 minutes ahead of time (particularly for the earlier running). We enjoy the view from Frontierland (near the Country Bears).

The parade is presented during peak seasons and select evenings throughout the year.

Timing Tip: When the parade runs twice a night, the earlier presentation is always more crowded than the later one. So, if your party hasn't run out of steam, stick around for the late show. You'll be glad you did.

Note: Some performances may be canceled due to inclement weather.

MAGIC KINGDOM

FP + = Fastpass+ attraction (see page 25)   137

HOT TIPS!

- Start at a Fastpass+ kiosk to book Fast-passes for as many attractions as possible (if you haven't reserved in advance).

- For the best fireworks view, stand on Main Street between Town Square and Casey's Corner. (If you stand too close to the castle, some of the show may be obstructed.)

- If there are two performances of the nighttime parade, the later one tends to draw smaller crowds.

- If you're driving to the park, start out very early. Most people arrive between 9:30 A.M. and 11:30 A.M., and the roads and parking lots are jammed. Plan to be at the gates to the Magic Kingdom before they open, and then be at the end of Main Street when the rest of the park opens.

- Table-service restaurants are in high demand in this park. Book yours as early as possible. And don't forget to confirm.

- Eager to meet Mickey Mouse? Head for the Town Square Theater on Main Street (near the train station). He likes to greet guests there. Get a Fastpass+ if you can.

- You can get in line for an attraction right up until the minute the park closes.

- Avoid the mealtime rush hours by eating early or late: before 11:30 A.M. or after 2 P.M., and before 5 P.M. or after 8 P.M.

- At busy times, take in these less-packed attractions: WDW Railroad, Liberty Belle Riverboat, Hall of Presidents, and Tomorrowland Transit Authority PeopleMover.

- The Main Street plaza gardens are a pleasant place for a picnic.

- Use a smartphone to check all attraction wait times via the MyDisneyExperience app (which may be downloaded for free).

- Break up your day. Consider heading back to your hotel (if it's not too far) for some swimming. Be sure to hold on to your admission pass, stroller and/or wheelchair receipt(s), and your parking stub, so that you can re-enter the Magic Kingdom.

- If your party decides to split up, set a meeting place and time. Avoid meeting in front of Cinderella Castle, since this area can become quite congested.

- The best way to get to the park's exit during parades is to take the Walt Disney Railroad. Board the train in Frontierland or Fantasyland and take it all the way to Main Street, U.S.A.

- For a full-service meal, be sure to make reservations in advance by calling 407-WDW-DINE (939-3463).

- Park guests have the right to chicken out at any time while waiting in line. In other words, should you or a member of your party have second thoughts about soaring on Space Mountain, visiting with the grinning ghosts of the Haunted Mansion, or braving another attraction, simply inform an attendant and you'll be discreetly whisked out a special exit.

- If you have rented a stroller, return it just before the fireworks presentation. That way, after the show, you'll be able to make a beeline for your bed rather than stand in a line to return the stroller.

- Some merchandise found in shops at Walt Disney World may be purchased with the Shop Disney Parks app and through Guest Services. Call 877-560-6477 for info.

- Travel light. The fewer bags you have, the faster you'll pass through security.

- Allow extra time to get through the park entrance—security and the "ticket tag" system can cause delays—especially during peak times and Extra Magic Hours.

den Mickeys

Hid

Disney Imagineers
to track down
Magic Kingd

...rs have hidden Mickey's image all over Walt Disney World. Some are easier ...than others. Here are some of the most popular "Hidden Mickeys" at the ...m. How many can you find? Check the box when you spot each one!

...f the Caribbean: As you enter the
...g and jump on the standby line (the
...left), keep your eyes peeled for four
...ets hanging on both sides of the
...a set of smaller ones on the right
...hese). The locks on the cabinets
...ys. ■

...untain: About halfway through the
...n the room with jumping water, look
...ly to your right and find a turtle floating on
...s back on a small geyser. Now look just above and
behind the turtle for one of the most creative
Hidden Mickeys in the park: It's a bobber attached
to a fishing line. There is a more obvious one in the
clouds beside the riverboat in the "Zip-a-dee-doo-
dah" room, after the big splash. ■

❤ Big Thunder Mountain Railroad: At the very
end of the ride and after the train slows, look to
your right to find two sets of gear shifts laying on
the ground. The second set forms a Hidden Mickey,
although you may notice that the dimensions are
not quite proportional (Mickey's "ears" are
significantly smaller than his "head"). ■

❤ The Haunted Mansion: In the ghostly party
scene, look at the bottom left corner of the
banquet table for a Hidden Mickey made of two
saucers and a plate. ■

❤ Carousel of Progress: In the Christmas scene,
look to the far left for four nutcrackers lined up on
top of the fireplace. The nutcracker farthest to the
left is a Mickey nutcracker. Also in this scene, look
for a Mickey plush toy in a box under the Christmas
tree and a special pepper grinder on the kitchen
counter (it's best seen from seats on the right side
of the theater). ■

❤ Buzz Lightyear's Space Ranger Spin: Once
you enter the interior queue, look for a poster on
the right called "Planets of the Galactic Alliance"

and find the planet "Pollost Prime." One of the
continents forms a Mickey profile. Keep your eyes
open during the attraction's space video scene
(about halfway through) and you'll see this same
planet fly by on the right. ■

❤ The Hall of Presidents: While you're waiting
to enter the theater, take a moment to inspect
the portrait of George Washington—it's hanging
on the right side of the entrance to the show.
There is a gilded Mickey on the tip of the first
President's sword. ■

❤ It's a Small World: Don't rush into the queue,
because the wait time sign forms a Hidden Mickey
if you tilt your head to the left. Once on the ride,
pay close attention to the Africa room and search
for purple leaves hanging from the ceiling that
form several Hidden Mickeys. (Hint: They're by
the giraffes.) ■

❤ The Magic Carpets of Aladdin: You'll feel
a pro once you find this small but very cool Hic
Mickey. First find the Agrabah Bazaar shop (a
from the Magic Carpets of Aladdin exit) and
the pole with a thick blue stripe at the bott
Take three steps toward the attraction and
down to find a charm in the cement with a
Mickey in the center. ■

**❤ Tomorrowland Transit Authority P
Mover:** Toward the end of the ride, yo
past a futuristic lady getting her hair d
lady has a Hidden Mickey on her belt
(Hint: She's on the right side of the ri
forward motion.) ■

❤ Swiss Family Treehouse: As y
trek up (and down) the treehouse
a good look at the giant tree tru
camouflaged by moss and bark?
familiar silhouette. ■

Specifics m

All of the photos on this page were taken at the Magic [Kingdom...]
where? We challenge you to find all the spots where the[se images were shot]
and snap a photo for yourself as you discover each one. H[appy hunting!]

(For locations, turn to page 356.)

1

2

MAGIC KINGDOM

...like
...den
...cross
...find
...m.
...ook

...eople-
...u will glid...
...one. Tha...
...uckle...
de veh...

...u m...
...stai...
...k. C...
A su...

4

6

...ay Cha...

Hidden Mickeys

Disney Imagineers have hidden Mickey's image all over Walt Disney World. Some are easier to track down than others. Here are some of the most popular "Hidden Mickeys" at the Magic Kingdom. How many can you find? Check the box when you spot each one!

❤ **Pirates of the Caribbean:** As you enter the main building and jump on the standby line (the queue on the left), keep your eyes peeled for four large gun cabinets hanging on both sides of the wall (you'll pass a set of smaller ones on the right before reaching these). The locks on the cabinets form Hidden Mickeys. ■

❤ **Splash Mountain:** About halfway through the ride and in the room with jumping water, look quickly to your right and find a turtle floating on its back on a small geyser. Now look just above and behind the turtle for one of the most creative Hidden Mickeys in the park: It's a bobber attached to a fishing line. There is a more obvious one in the clouds beside the riverboat in the "Zip-a-dee-doo-dah" room, after the big splash. ■

❤ **Big Thunder Mountain Railroad:** At the very end of the ride and after the train slows, look to your right to find two sets of gear shifts laying on the ground. The second set forms a Hidden Mickey, although you may notice that the dimensions are not quite proportional (Mickey's "ears" are significantly smaller than his "head"). ■

❤ **The Haunted Mansion:** In the ghostly party scene, look at the bottom left corner of the banquet table for a Hidden Mickey made of two saucers and a plate. ■

❤ **Carousel of Progress:** In the Christmas scene, look to the far left for four nutcrackers lined up on top of the fireplace. The nutcracker farthest to the left is a Mickey nutcracker. Also in this scene, look for a Mickey plush toy in a box under the Christmas tree and a special pepper grinder on the kitchen counter (it's best seen from seats on the right side of the theater). ■

❤ **Buzz Lightyear's Space Ranger Spin:** Once you enter the interior queue, look for a poster on the right called "Planets of the Galactic Alliance" and find the planet "Pollost Prime." One of the continents forms a Mickey profile. Keep your eyes open during the attraction's space video scene (about halfway through) and you'll see this same planet fly by on the right. ■

❤ **The Hall of Presidents:** While you're waiting to enter the theater, take a moment to inspect the portrait of George Washington—it's hanging on the right side of the entrance to the show. There is a gilded Mickey on the tip of the first President's sword. ■

❤ **It's a Small World:** Don't rush into the queue, because the wait time sign forms a Hidden Mickey if you tilt your head to the left. Once on the ride, pay close attention to the Africa room and search for purple leaves hanging from the ceiling that form several Hidden Mickeys. (Hint: They're by the giraffes.) ■

❤ **The Magic Carpets of Aladdin:** You'll feel like a pro once you find this small but very cool Hidden Mickey. First find the Agrabah Bazaar shop (across from the Magic Carpets of Aladdin exit) and find the pole with a thick blue stripe at the bottom. Take three steps toward the attraction and look down to find a charm in the cement with a Mickey in the center. ■

❤ **Tomorrowland Transit Authority People-Mover:** Toward the end of the ride, you will glide past a futuristic lady getting her hair done. That lady has a Hidden Mickey on her belt buckle! (Hint: She's on the right side of the ride vehicle's forward motion.) ■

❤ **Swiss Family Treehouse:** As you make the trek up (and down) the treehouse stairs, take a good look at the giant tree trunk. Cleverly camouflaged by moss and bark? A subtle-but-familiar silhouette. ■

Specifics may change during 2017.

Where in the World?

All of the photos on this page were taken at the Magic Kingdom. Do you know where? We challenge you to find all the spots where these images were shot and snap a photo for yourself as you discover each one. Happy hunting! (For locations, turn to page 356.)

MAGIC KINGDOM

1

2

3

4

5

6

Epcot

I magine a place with an entertainment inventory that includes both a rich sampling of world cultures and a fun, enlightening journey to the technological frontier. You now have an inkling of the eye-opening and mind-broadening potential of Epcot—a place that's evolved most imaginatively in each of the 35 years it's been open.

Walt Disney suggested the idea back in 1966: "Epcot will be an experimental prototype community of tomorrow that will take its cue from the new ideas and technologies that are emerging from the creative center of American industry." It would never be completed, he said, but would "always be introducing and testing and demonstrating new materials and systems." On October 1, 1982, Walt Disney's dream became a reality. Test Track puts guests on the thrilling inside track of the fast-paced world of automobile design. A re-imagined Soarin'—now known as Soarin' Around the World—delivers the breathtaking sensation of flight. And old favorites like The Seas with Nemo & Friends and Imagination! continue to ignite the creative forces within us all.

The park consists of two distinct areas of exploration: Future World and World Showcase. The former examines ideas in science and technology in ways that make them seem not only comprehensible but downright irresistible. The latter celebrates the diversity of the world's peoples, portraying a stunning array of nations, with extraordinary devotion to detail.

Think of Epcot as Disney's playground for curious and thoughtful guests of all ages. The experiences it delivers—all of them wonders of the real world—continue to amaze, educate, inspire, and (of course) entertain.

WORLD SHOWCASE

FUTURE WORLD

N

WORLD SHOWCASE

MOROCCO

FRANCE

INTERNATIONAL GATEWAY

JAPAN

THE AMERICAN ADVENTURE

UNITED KINGDOM

CANADA

IMAGINATION!

ITALY

WORLD SHOWCASE LAGOON

THE LAND

GERMANY

SHOWCASE PLAZA

EPCOT CHARACTER SPOT

CHINA

NORWAY

THE SEAS WITH NEMO & FRIENDS

MEXICO

INNOVENTIONS

TEST TRACK

SPACESHIP EARTH

To Buses

MISSION: SPACE

UNIVERSE OF ENERGY

Entrance Plaza

Getting Oriented

Triple the Magic Kingdom park and you have an idea of the size of Epcot. As for layout, the park is shaped something like a giant hourglass. The pavilions of Future World fill the northern bulb, while the international potpourri called World Showcase occupies the southern bulb. Future World is anchored on the north by the imposing silver "geosphere," dubbed Spaceship Earth.

As you pass through Epcot's main Entrance Plaza, Spaceship Earth looms straight ahead. Pathways curve around the 180-foot-tall geosphere, winding up at Innoventions Plaza. Here, in addition to a show fountain, you'll see signs for Innoventions and Epcot Character Spot, housed in buildings that cradle the plaza. Beyond this central area, there are two roughly symmetrical north-south avenues; these are dotted with the seven pavilions that form the outer perimeter of Future World. Mission: SPACE, Test Track, and Universe of Energy flank Spaceship Earth on the east, while Imagination!, The Land, and The Seas with Nemo & Friends lie to the west.

In World Showcase, the international pavilions are arranged around the edge of sparkling World Showcase Lagoon, with The American Adventure directly south of Spaceship Earth on the lake's southernmost shore. A walkway from Future World leads to World Showcase Promenade, a 1.2-mile thoroughfare that wraps around the lagoon, winding past each World Showcase pavilion in the process.

HOW TO GET THERE

Take Exit 67 off I-4. Continue along to the Epcot Auto Plaza; if you park in a distant lot, take a tram to the park's main entrance.

By WDW Transportation: From the Grand Floridian, Contemporary, and Polynesian Village: hotel monorail to the Transportation and Ticket Center (TTC), then switch to the TTC-Epcot monorail. From Magic Kingdom: express monorail to the TTC, then switch to the TTC-Epcot monorail. From Disney Springs: bus to any resort, then transfer to an Epcot bus or boat. From Disney's Hollywood Studios, Disney's Animal Kingdom, all other Walt Disney World resorts, Four Seasons resort, and the resorts on Hotel Plaza Boulevard: buses.

Note: A second Epcot park entrance, called International Gateway, provides entry directly to World Showcase. It may be reached via walkways and the FriendShip water launches from Disney's

Hollywood Studios, plus the Swan, Dolphin, Yacht and Beach Club, and BoardWalk resorts. The boat drops guests between the France and U.K. pavilions. It is possible to purchase theme park admission here, at Epcot's "back door."

PARKING

All-day parking at Epcot starts at $20 for day visitors (free to Disney resort guests with a resort ID or MagicBand, as well as annual passholders). Attendants will direct you to park in one of several lots named for steps in the creative process, such as Discover and Imagine. Trams circulate regularly, providing transportation between the distant lots and the main entrance. Be sure to note the section and aisle in which you park. Parking tickets allow for re-entry to the area (and other theme parks) throughout the day.

HOURS

Future World is usually open from about 9 A.M. to 9 P.M. (though some attractions may close at 7 P.M.). World Showcase hours are about 11 A.M. to 9 P.M. (though some attractions may open earlier). During certain holiday periods and summer months, hours are extended. It's best to arrive a bit before the posted opening time. On select days, the park opens one hour early or stays open two hours late for Disney resort guests only. Call 407-824-4321 for current schedules, or visit *www.disneyworld.com*.

GETTING AROUND

Water taxis, called FriendShip launches, ferry guests across the World Showcase Lagoon. Docks are located near Mexico, Canada, Germany, and Morocco. (The only other way to traverse the vast area is on foot.) Boats typically close a few hours before the park does.

Admission Prices

ONE-DAY BASE TICKET
(Restricted to use only in Epcot. Prices represent Walt Disney World's Value, Regular, and Peak rates; they do not include tax; and they are expected to rise in 2017.)

Adult ....$97/$102/$114
Child* ....$91/$96/$108
*3 through 9 years of age; children under age 3 free

Park Primer

BABY FACILITIES

There are changing tables and facilities for nursing mothers at the Baby Care Center in the Odyssey Center, between Test Track and Mexico. Disposable diapers may be kept behind the counter at some Epcot shops; just ask.

CAMERA NEEDS

The Camera Center in Entrance Plaza and World Traveler at International Gateway stock memory cards, batteries, and disposable cameras, and other accessories. Note that selfie sticks are not permitted in the park.

DISABILITY INFORMATION

Nearly all attractions, shops, and restaurants are accessible to guests using wheelchairs. Parking for guests with disabilities is available. Additional services are available for guests with visual and hearing disabilities. The complimentary *Guide for Guests with Disabilities* is available at the park entrances and at Guest Relations. It provides a detailed overview of all services. For more information, turn to the *Getting Ready to Go* chapter of this book.

FIRST AID

Minor medical problems can be handled at the First Aid Center, in the Odyssey Center, between Test Track and Mexico. Keep in mind that many guests could avoid a trip to First Aid simply by staying well hydrated. If you have an emergency, notify an employee and call 911.

INFORMATION

Guest Relations, which has one location to the right of the main entrance plaza and another next to Spaceship Earth, is equipped with guidemaps, Times Guides, and a helpful staff. Same goes for International Gateway (Epcot's back entrance).

LOCKERS

Lockers are found immediately west of Spaceship Earth. Cost is $8–$10, plus a $5 refundable deposit for unlimited use all day.

LOST & FOUND

Lost and Found is located at Guest Relations near Innoventions. To inquire about lost items after your visit, call 407-824-4245. If you find an item, give it to a cast member (aka employee).

LOST CHILDREN

Alert an employee and report lost children at Guest Relations or the Baby Care Center.

MONEY MATTERS

There are Automated Teller Machines (ATMs) at the main entrance, on the path between Future World and World Showcase, at International Gateway (near United Kingdom), and at The American Adventure. Some foreign currency may be exchanged at Guest Relations. Major credit cards (American Express, JCB, Discover, Diner's Club, Visa, and MasterCard), traveler's checks, Disney Dollars, and Disney gift cards are accepted throughout WDW. MagicBands and Walt Disney World resort IDs are accepted at most park locations (if backed up with a major credit card).

PACKAGE PICKUP

Epcot shops can arrange for most purchases to be transported (for free) to the Gift Stop in Entrance Plaza or International Gateway in World Showcase for later pickup.

SAME-DAY RE-ENTRY

Be sure to wear your MagicBand (if you used it for admission) or retain your ticket if you plan to return later the same day.

SECURITY CHECK

Guests entering Disney theme parks are subject to a thorough security check. All bags will be searched by security personnel before guests may enter the park. A metal detector screens park guests. Weapons (including toys) are prohibited. For details and a complete listing of Walt Disney World Park Rules, visit Guest Relations or go to *www.disneyworld.com/ParkRules*.

STROLLERS & WHEELCHAIRS

Strollers, wheelchairs, and Electric Conveyance Vehicles (ECVs) may be rented from venues at both park entrances. Wheelchairs are also available at the Gift Stop. Cost is $15 for single strollers, $31 for double strollers, and $12 for wheelchairs. A Length-of-Stay rental yields a $2-per-day discount. It's $50 a day for an ECV, plus a $20 refundable deposit. Quantities are limited. ECVs tend to sell out early. Keep your rental receipt; it can be used that same day to get a replacement at Epcot or another theme park.

Future World

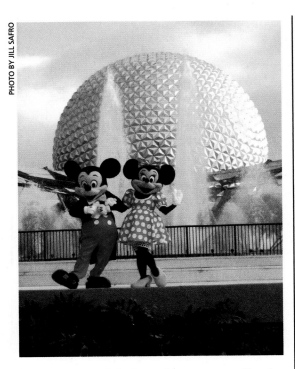

PHOTO BY JILL SAFRO

A mere listing of the basic themes covered by the pavilions at Future World—agriculture, communication, car design, the ocean, the land, energy, imagination, technology, and space—tends to sound a tad academic. But when these serious topics are presented with a special flair, they become part of an experience that ranks among Disney's most entertaining.

Some of these subjects are explored in the course of lively and unusual "adventures," involving a whole arsenal of motion pictures, special effects, and Audio-Animatronics figures so lifelike that it is hard to remain unmoved. The basic elements are also appealing in their own right, from the palm-tree-dotted Entrance Plaza to the dramatic fountain just past Spaceship Earth, the many-faceted "geosphere" that has become the universal symbol of Epcot.

The park is so vast that it's hard to know what to do first. Many guests stop at Spaceship Earth on their way into Future World. As a result, they end up spending more time waiting in line than they need to. A wise alternative is to save Spaceship Earth for later in the day (when the lines inevitably thin out), and head for Soarin', the "less intense, non-spinning" Mission: SPACE, The Seas with Nemo & Friends, and Test Track (if motion sickness isn't an issue for

you) as soon as the park opens (the lines tend to stay long throughout the day). Take in as many Future World attractions as time allows, making sure to see the ImageWorks playground in the Imagination! pavilion, and save World Showcase for the evening hours. This strategy works well for families. (Refer to page 35 for a detailed version of this plan of attack.)

Another alternative—one that requires quite a bit of extra walking, but can help skirt a long line or two—is to explore Future World until World Showcase opens at 11 A.M. Then, in the afternoon, when many guests have shifted over to World Showcase, return to Future World. Innoventions is not only an interesting spot to pass the busy hours after lunch, but also a cool refuge when high temperatures prevail outdoors. And although queues can be found during peak seasons at Soarin' Around the World, Mission: SPACE, Test Track, Imagination!, The Seas with Nemo & Friends, and Living with the Land throughout most of the late morning and afternoon, from late afternoon until park closing is usually less hectic. But don't forget to make it back to World Showcase in time to see the nighttime spectacular, IllumiNations—Reflections of Earth.

Left a Legacy?

Epcot has invited guests to "Leave a Legacy" near its front gate since its big Millennium Celebration. And? More than 550,000 have done so! They left their mark, in the form of a one-inch-square tile affixed on massive stone walls. While the program has officially come to a close, the cluster of monoliths continues to stand near the base of Spaceship Earth.

To locate a tile, inquire at the Leave a Legacy locating station inside the Camera Center by Spaceship Earth.

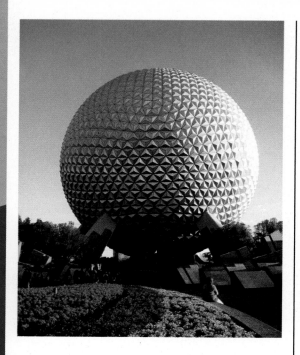

SPACESHIP EARTH FP+

As it looms impressively just above the Earth, this great, faceted silver structure looks a little bit like a spaceship ready to blast off. It appears large from a distance, and it seems even more immense when viewed from directly underneath. It's no surprise that some visitors simply stop beneath it and gawk.

The show inside, which explores the continuing quest by human beings to create the future, remains one of Epcot's compelling—if slower moving—attractions. It's an intriguing, narrated journey through time. It also has an interactive element that's a real hoot.

A common misconception about Spaceship Earth is that it is a geodesic dome. Not so. It is a geosphere. A geodesic dome is only half a sphere, while Spaceship Earth is almost completely round. Affectionately known to many simply as "the Ball," Spaceship Earth is a sight to behold.

Noted science-fiction writer Ray Bradbury, together with consultants from the Smithsonian Institution, the Los Angeles area's prestigious Huntington Library, the University of Southern California, and (among others) the University of Chicago, collaborated with Disney in developing this memorable 14-minute journey. It begins in an inky-black time tunnel, complete with a musty smell that suggests the dust of ages, and continues through history from the days of Cro-Magnon man (30,000 or 40,000 years ago) to the future.

Every scene is executed in exquisite detail. The symbols on the wall of that Egyptian temple really are hieroglyphics, and the content of the letter being dictated by the pharaoh was excerpted from a missive actually received by an agent of a ruler of the period.

Epcot veterans will notice two cool new scenes: a 1970s mainframe computer room and a garage scene depicting the creation of the personal computer.

All of these sights are enough to keep heads turning as the "time machines" wend their way upward. The most dazzling scene is saved for the ride's finale, when the audience is placed in outer space—with a prime view of our beautiful, blue planet, also known as Spaceship Earth. The journey winds down with a clever, custom look at your own future, courtesy of a touch screen in the ride vehicle.

HOT TIP!

Many of Walt Disney World's moving attractions— such as Spaceship Earth— can be slowed down to make the boarding process safer for guests with physical limitations. Just ask a cast member as you and your party enter the attraction.

The post-show area—Project Tomorrow— features several interactive areas, all emphasizing technology and its influence on daily life. Themes include medicine, power, and accident avoidance. You can also take a peek at a photo of yourself (snapped while you were experiencing the Spaceship Earth attraction). Expect to spend up to an hour in this high-tech playground.

INNOVENTIONS

Creativity abounds at Innoventions as guests celebrate the ingenuity and wonders of modern life. This imaginative zone is filled with interactive, hands-on exhibits. A highlight for daredevils is the Sum of All Thrills—an exhibit that explains the importance of science and math in roller

HOT TIP!

The line for Spaceship Earth is usually quite long during the early morning hours and relatively short in the late afternoon and evening.

coaster design. Oh, yeah—it also lets guests design and ride their own roller coaster! This experience is one of the most popular additions to Epcot in recent years.

Across from Sum of All Thrills is a vibrant exhibit that informs and inspires guests about the power of color: Colortopia. Three interactive areas really bring color to life. Kids (and kids at heart) love to paint the walls with electronic paintbrushes. Expect to spend about 30 minutes exploring this wonderful world of color.

One of Walt Disney's dreams for Epcot was for the exhibits to change periodically. And indeed they do. So keep in mind that some of the exhibits mentioned here may close in 2017, and new ones may be added.

> ## HOT TIP!
>
> Innoventions Plaza is home to Pin Central. This area, between Innoventions and the Epcot Character Spot, is the pin-trading headquarters for Epcot. (Of course, there are many other pin-trading locations throughout Walt Disney World.)

Above all, count on spending time exploring Innoventions (at least an hour). There's so much to see and do that curiosity will often get the better of any schedule. And be sure to check out the area between the pavilions—the sidewalks glistening with fiber-optic lighting effects.

MOUSE GEAR: This enormous shop continues to offer a selection of Disney merchandise. Mouse Gear stocks character memorabilia, key chains, T-shirts, hats, candy (including a wall of jelly beans and various gummy treats), Magic-Bands and associated paraphernalia, mugs, photo albums, jewelry, towels, footwear, toys, and more—making this the best source for character merchandise in Epcot. There are also items related to the park itself, along with Disney-themed apparel and children's clothing. Mouse Gear stays open about a half hour longer than the park does.

THE ART OF DISNEY: This is Epcot's spot for a special assortment of Disney collectibles. The store showcases a wide variety of art inspired by Disney animation and theme parks. There is a collection of unique pieces by acclaimed artists, including prints, sculptures, figurines, and more.

THE SEAS WITH NEMO & FRIENDS

Welcome to one of the largest facilities ever dedicated to humanity's relationship with the ocean. It was designed by Disney Imagineers, in cooperation with distinguished oceanographic experts and scientists.

Though it enjoys the distinction of being one of Future World's original pavilions, what used to be known as The Living Seas is as fresh as ever—thanks to a little clownfish called Nemo and some of his fishy friends.

Once inside, guests can find the animated critters' real-life counterparts, including clown-fish, blue tangs, sharks, and puffer fish.

The pavilion also features a Nemo-themed ride, an interactive encounter with an animated turtle, and an engaging post-show area. Little ones enjoy frolicking in Bruce's Shark World—a hands-on play area that celebrates the ocean's toothiest residents. From there, take a look at a simulated Caribbean coral reef environment. For the record, the crowning jewel of the pavilion is the simple-but-spectacular Turtle Talk with Crush.

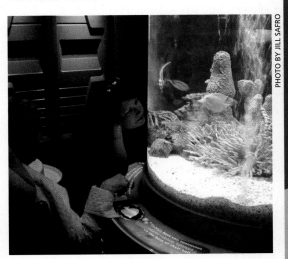

PHOTO BY JILL SAFRO

BIRNBAUM'S BEST ★ **TURTLE TALK WITH CRUSH:** FP+ If ever there was an attraction that left guests smiling and asking, "How do they do that?!"—this is it. The concept is simple enough—a 10-minute, animated show featuring the surfer-dude sea turtle from *Finding Nemo*. The amazing part?

Under the Sea

Three behind-the-scenes tours offer guests a closer look at life in The Seas with Nemo & Friends underwater environs: DiveQuest gives certified scuba divers the opportunity to explore one of the world's largest aquariums. Epcot Seas Aqua Tour lets guests snorkel The Seas. And Dolphins in Depth offers guests the chance to learn about dolphin behavior as they closely observe researchers and trainers interacting with dolphins. Reservations for any tour can be made by calling 407-WDW-TOUR (939-8687). Save money by using the coupons at the end of this book. For details on all of these programs, turn to pages 232–234 of the *Everything Else in the World* chapter.

PHOTO BY JILL SAFRO

The cartoon critter interacts with the audience. In doing so, he imparts turtle-y wisdom, answers questions, and cracks more than a few jokes. You have to see it to believe it. To do that, you'll have to wait in line—it's extremely popular with guests of all ages. It's totally awesome, dude.

THE SEAS WITH NEMO & FRIENDS
ATTRACTION: FP+ Imagineered in the style of classic family attractions, this undersea adventure is fun for everyone. In it, guests climb aboard a clam-mobile and enter a colorful coral reef. It seems Nemo has wandered off again, and his teacher, Mr. Ray, needs help finding him. So keep your eyes peeled! There's a bit of suspense

involved—including moments of darkness and a stressful jellyfish encounter—but rest assured, it all ends happily.

CARIBBEAN CORAL REEF: The man-made reef exists in an enormous tank that holds about six million gallons of salt water and more than 60 species of sea life. Among the 2,000 or so inhabitants are turtles, angelfish, sharks, dolphins, and diamond rays. It's worth it to stop by as the park opens—that's usually when breakfast is served to the fish.

Guests sometimes get to see scuba divers testing and demonstrating diving gear and underwater monitoring equipment as they carry on training programs with dolphins.

THE LAND

Occupying six acres, this enormous skylighted pavilion examines the nature of one of everybody's favorite topics—food. It also gives guests a chance to soar above the clouds in a celebration

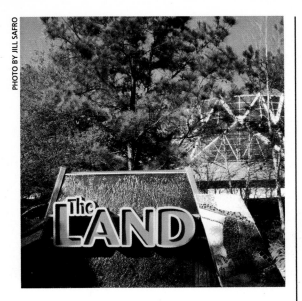

of flight. A film, *The Circle of Life*, uses characters from *The Lion King* to deliver an entertaining yet inspirational message about humanity and the environment. A boat ride explores farming in the past and future. Narration gives visitors the chance to learn about the experimental agricultural techniques practiced in the pavilion.

Timing Tip: The Land pavilion's Soarin' Around the World is an exceptionally popular attraction. So much so that Fastpass+ assignments may all be gone early. It's best to visit first thing in the morning or get a Fastpass+ far in advance!

HOT TIP!

Got a rumbly in your tumbly? Head for Sunshine Seasons in The Land pavilion. There's a variety of counter-service choices—apt to please even the pickiest of eaters.

LIVING WITH THE LAND: FP+ This pavilion's 13½-minute boat ride through meticulously re-created natural locales opens with a dramatic storm scene. Guests sail through tropical rainforests, prairie grain fields, and a family farm. As the boat passes through each realistic setting, recorded narration offers commentary on humanity's ongoing struggle to cultivate and live in harmony with the land. Note the details that make each setting so convincing, such as sand blowing over the desert and light flickering from the television in the farmhouse window.

In the next segment, guests enter a plant research laboratory and solarium. Here, our planet's major food crops are being grown in research projects, along with rare new crops that may someday help meet Earth's ever-growing dietary needs.

Also of interest are the experiments being conducted to explore the practice of farming fish, and a desert farm area, where plants get nutrients through a drip irrigation system that delivers just the right amount of water—important in a dry climate.

As unreal as they appear, all the plants on view in the experimental greenhouses are living. In contrast, those in the biomes (the ecological communities viewed from the boat ride) were made in Disney studios out of lightweight plastic that simulates the cellulose found in real trees. The trunks and branches were molded from live specimens; the sycamore in the farmhouse's front yard, for example, duplicates one that stands outside a Burbank, California, car wash. Thousands of polyethylene leaves were snapped on.

Note that all of the greenhouse flora is quite real—please resist the urge to touch plants or the sand in which they live.

Club Cool

Future World's Club Cool is a great place to beat the heat. Located near the Fountain View coffee shop, it is Coca-Cola's complimentary International Tasting Station. Here, you can sample eight different soft drinks from around the world, some tastier than others.

After you've quenched your thirst, courtesy of the Coca-Cola Company, you may have a desire to do some shopping. Not coincidentally, there's plenty of Coke merchandise to choose from (at this point, you will have to open your wallet or wave that MagicBand if you'd like a souvenir).

At press time, Club Cool was open for business during Future World's regular operating hours.

FP+ = Fastpass+ attraction (see page 25)

SOARIN'

BIRNBAUM'S ★BEST★

SOARIN' AROUND THE WORLD: FP+ Up, up, and away! On this high-flying Epcot attraction (it's one of the most popular attractions at Walt Disney World), you'll be suspended in a hang glider up to 45 feet in the air, above a giant IMAX projection dome, and treated to an aerial tour of

NEW NEW NEW NEW

Mad About the Mouse?

Can't get enough of all things Disney? Then D23 is the place to be. It's the official community for Disney super fans. To join, you'll need nothing more than a computer or smartphone and an unebbing enthusiasm for the House that Walt built. Upgrade to Gold Membership ($80 annual dues) to net access to special events, an official membership card and certificate, a subscription to the D23 magazine, a collectible gift (plus the chance to purchase exclusive merchandise), and more. For additional details or to join the club, visit *www.d23.com*. FYI: Walt Disney founded what would become the Disney Studios in 1923. Hence, the name D23.

some of the most awe-inspiring landscapes the world has to offer. Wait—Soarin' has been here since 2005. Why the "new" stamp? Well, the beloved Soarin' experience is still here in all of its wraparound glory—but instead of hovering over one state (California), the new version offers a broader tour.

Soarin' Around the World showcases some of the world's most glorious sights: The Great Wall of China, the plains of Africa, the oceans of Fiji, the Grand Canyon, Egyptian pyramids, and much more. With the wind in your hair and your legs dangling in the breeze, the hang glider feels so real that you may even be tempted to pull up your feet for fear of tapping the rooftops and landscapes below.

The flight takes about 10 minutes and employs synchronized wind currents, scent machines, and a (new) musical score set to a film that wraps 180 degrees around you. The re-imagined version of this attraction touched down in 2016. It features an all-new digital screen and projection system and is a hit with all ages—get a Fastpass+ assignment if you can.

Character Connection

Where do Disney characters hang out when they aren't marching in parades or dancing in shows? The Epcot Character Spot! FP+ This brilliantly hued, Zip-a-Dee-Doo-Dah zone is the place to go to meet Disney faves such as Mickey Mouse, Minnie Mouse, and Goofy. The gang visits here throughout the day, but it's best to arrive early in the morning—as the line gets downright beastly in the afternoon. The entrance to the Character Spot is next to Fountain View. Check a park Times Guide for the character appearance schedule during your visit to Epcot. Get a Fastpass+ assignment if you can. Just across the way from the Epcot Character spot, there's another opportunity to meet Disney favorites. Stop here to mingle with Baymax from *Big Hero 6* and *Inside Out*'s Joy and Sadness (note that this spot does not offer Fastpass+).

HOT TIP!

Epcot is much bigger than it seems, so allow lots of time to get from place to place. (It can take more than a half hour to walk from Spaceship Earth to The American Adventure in World Showcase.) Keep this in mind if you have restaurant reservations or hope to snag a nice IllumiNations viewing location on the World Showcase promenade.

EPCOT

Note: You must be 40 inches tall and free of back problems, heart conditions, motion sickness, and other physical limitations to ride. It's calmer than traditional "thrill" rides, but the sensation of flight is quite realistic. If you're afraid of heights, sit this one out.

THE CIRCLE OF LIFE: This 20-minute, newly refreshed film uses animation and live action to illustrate some of the dangers to our environment, as well as potential solutions. Presented as a fable featuring *The Lion King*'s Simba, Timon, and Pumbaa, the film takes an optimistic approach to a serious subject. It is shown in the Harvest Theater, just inside the entrance to The Land. Soon after the film begins, Simba's startled by the exuberant shout of "Timber!" and is drenched by the splash of a fallen tree in the water. The culprits are none other than his friends Timon and Pumbaa, who are clearing the savanna for the development of the Hakuna Matata Lakeside Village. Young Simba seizes the opportunity to tell them a tale about creatures who sometimes forget that everything on Earth is connected in the circle of life: humans.

Simba demonstrates to Timon and Pumbaa the consequences of progress, as his lessons are driven home by visual evidence of humans' mistreatment of the air, water, and land. (Timon: "And everybody was *okay* with this?") The effect is a mix of entertainment and a message about responsibility.

IMAGINATION!

The oddly shaped pyramids that house the Imagination! pavilion are quite a striking sight to behold. They certainly set the stage for the atypical experiences inside. One of the main attractions is Journey Into Imagination with Figment, a slow-moving behind-the-scenes tour of the Imagination Institute. Also located here is the Disney & Pixar Short Film Festival.

Another pavilion highlight is the pair of quirky fountains outside—the Jellyfish Fountains, which spurt streams of water that spread out at the top, looking for an instant like their namesake sea creature, and the Leap Frog Fountains, which send out smooth streams of water that arc from one garden plot to another in the most astonishing fashion. Kids just can't get enough of them.

DISNEY & PIXAR SHORT FILM FESTIVAL: FP+ Head to the Magic Eye Theater to enter the imaginative worlds of three animated shorts: *Get a Horse* stars everyone's favorite mouse as he, Minnie, and their friends Horace Horsecollar and Clarabelle Cow delight in a musical wagon ride; *For the Bird*s features a flock of small feathered friends in an adventure on a telephone wire; and, finally, *La Luna* is a timeless fable of a

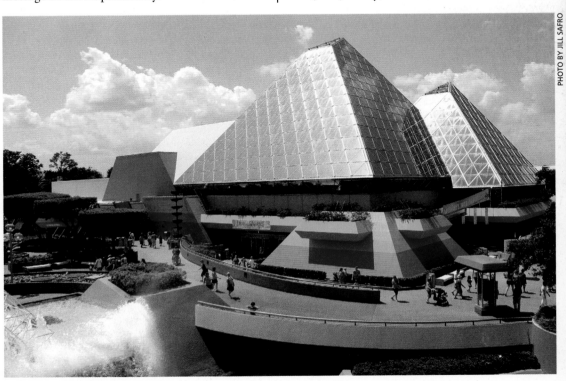

young boy coming of age in most peculiar circumstances. The set of shorts is presented in 3-D (pick up your glasses on the way into the theater) and features entertaining "4-D" effects.

This unexpectedly delightful attraction has appeal for guests of all ages, provided they are old enough to wear 3-D glasses.

JOURNEY INTO IMAGINATION WITH

FIGMENT: FP+ He's back! Figment, the tiny purple dragon with the orange wings and yellow eyes, is on hand to guide guests on an imaginative quest. The goal? To figure out, once and for all, the best way to capture your imagination.

The journey takes place at Imagination Institute, where guests are invited to tour the institute's various labs, such as the Sight Lab, the Sound Lab, and Smell Lab. All in all, it's a tame experience, save for the occasional blast of air or flashing lights.

Nostalgia buffs, take note: The classic song "One Little Spark," which made its debut with the original incarnation of this attraction, underscores the show once more.

IMAGEWORKS LABS: It's a rare tot-aged ImageWorks visitor who doesn't experience at least some of the emotion felt by the little one who cried when her parents tried to tear her away. Plan to spend up to 20 minutes exploring these entertaining labs—especially if you have very young children.

TEST TRACK FP+

BIRNBAUM'S ★BEST★ Fasten your safety belt! This high-octane pavilion puts guests through the creative and frenetic motions of automobile design and testing. The experience starts with guests designing a vehicle in the attraction's high-tech pre-show area. What is important to you in a car: efficiency, power, responsiveness, or capability? Use a touch screen to design your car with your priorities in mind, then take your virtual "SimCar" over to the Sim Track and give her a test drive. (Yes, they easily

PHOTO BY MIKE CARROLL

could have dubbed this attraction Sim Track— a Test Track by any other name would be just as cool.)

The 4-minute ride is similar to the old version of Test Track—there's lots of zigging and zagging on the front end followed by a dramatic near-miss with a big noisy truck. Along the way, you'll learn how well your car did in each of the categories featured in the design stage. Finally, a long straightaway feeds into a series of banked

HOT TIP!

If you don't mind splitting up your party, head for the "single rider" line at Test Track. It generally moves faster than the standby line.

turns and another straight shot that sends vehicles rocketing around the pavilion at top speed (up to 65 mph!). The computer-controlled, six-seater vehicles are equipped with video and audio, but no steering wheels or brake pedals. After all is said and done, guests may create a 15-second commercial for their new car and send the video to a friend via e-mail.

Note: Kids under 7 must be accompanied by an adult; guests under 40 inches cannot ride; passengers must be free of back problems, heart conditions, motion sickness, and other physical limitations. Pregnant women are advised to sit this one out.

MISSION: SPACE FP+

Think you've got "the right stuff"? Well, this is your chance to prove it. Epcot's out-of-this-world attraction has a bold mission—to give you a chance to feel the excitement and extreme intensity of space travel without ever leaving the planet.

There are actually two ways to travel to Mars at this attraction: the "highly intense" way (aka Orange Team) and the "less intense" experience (Green Team). The original Mission: SPACE attraction provides a galaxy of thrills for many brave and sturdy theme park guests. The adventure begins with a white-knuckle blast-off of a spacecraft (which has snug seating for four) on an important mission to Mars. The sustained G-force during the launch is intended to be most realistic. Once en route, expect a rather strange, spectacular sensation. It's not quite weightlessness, but according to astronauts who've felt the real thing, it's pretty darn close. (So much so that it also tends to duplicate the not-so-spectacular sensation of space sickness. In fact, Mission: SPACE has the dubious distinction of being the first attraction in theme park history to be equipped with motion-sickness bags.)

Throughout the journey, you're expected to work with your fellow crew members (assuming the roles of navigator, captain, engineer, and pilot) to accomplish the mission. For the "highly intense" version, we recommend ignoring this call to duty and keeping your eyes glued directly to the screen. This will allow you to sit back and enjoy the ride and decidedly downsize the dizziness factor.

The original attraction can wreak havoc on the equilibrium. To cut the chances of losing your lunch, keep your eyes open at all times and fixed on the screen in front of you. You may be tempted to tilt your head or shut your eyes. Don't. (We promise you will arrive on Mars whether you fulfill your astronaut duty or not.)

Bottom line? Most guests who don't get queasy on the "highly intense" Orange Team version tend to rave about Mission: SPACE. For us, well, we admit we prefer the ride's gentler version—aka the Green Team. It's intended for those who would rather not spin. The experience is a bit different on "Mission: SPACE-lite," but it gives everyone a chance to ride without getting queasy. The effects may be toned down, but they are quite extraordinary. We completely enjoy the "less intense," non-spinning mission to Mars.

Note: All guests must be at least 44 inches tall and free of back and heart problems, motion sickness, and other physical limitations. Pregnant women should skip the trip, as should anyone with claustrophobic tendencies. In fact, if you have any health issues whatsoever, sit this out. And don't eat before riding!

PHOTO BY JILL SAFRO

UNIVERSE OF ENERGY

BIRNBAUM'S ★BEST★ In the mood for a chuckle? Set a course for this attraction. You'll get a few giggles and maybe even learn something to boot.

Although it's easy to spot this pavilion's mirrored pyramid, the facade does not provide any clue at all to the 45 minutes of surprises in store. One of the most technologically complex experiences at Epcot, a show called Ellen's Energy Adventure consists of several movies and a ride-through segment. None of these is exactly what Epcot guests might expect.

The show begins with a film (featuring a few familiar faces). In it, Ellen DeGeneres is watching *Jeopardy!* One of the contestants is Ellen's annoying college roommate, Judy.

Ellen plays along but keeps striking out, particularly in the energy category. As she watches, her neighbor Bill Nye the Science Guy pops in and is aghast at Ellen's ignorance. Shortly thereafter, Ellen dozes off.

Ellen dreams she is a contestant on the show, competing against Albert Einstein and her nemesis Judy. This time, all of the questions are about energy. As Einstein ponders and Ellen fumbles, Judy is racking up points. Ellen, who has a negative score ("this nightmare game is a lot harder than the home version"), decides to freeze her dream and ask Bill Nye the Science Guy for some help.

The second segment leads guests into a theater, where Bill vows to educate Ellen about the importance of energy. He persuades her to

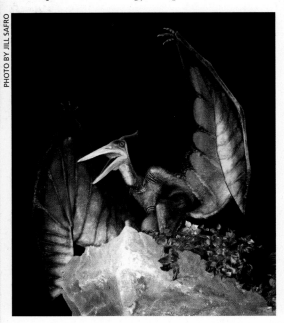

HOT TIP!

As home to a 45-minute attraction, the Universe of Energy is a great place to take a load off your feet and give your body a chance to cool off. Just be sure to take a bathroom break first. There is a 38-minute stretch in a ride vehicle and no opportunities for a pit stop.

travel back in time to see where some of our energy sources came from. Suddenly (but very slowly), the whole seating area rotates, then breaks up into six sections that inch forward. The vehicles embark with Ellen upon an odyssey through the primeval world. Gigantic prehistoric trees crowd the forest. Apatosauruses wallow in the lagoon out front. A lofty allosaurus battles with an armored stegosaurus, and an elasmosaurus bursts out of a tide pool with frightening suddenness—all under the watchful gaze of winged pteranodons. (This zone spooks tots.)

DID YOU KNOW?

There are two acres of solar panels on the rooftop of Future World's Universe of Energy pavilion. Together, they generate 15 percent of the energy it takes to power the attraction housed inside. (It's enough energy to run six average homes.)

Next, guests move out of the forest and view a montage of pictures capturing the history of civilization, from cave dwellers to the present. The issue of alternative-energy sources is raised, and the message is that there is no save-all source, but rather there are many possibilities with promise.

The attraction winds up with Ellen returning to the game show of her dreams. This time, she's beating Judy, who is not at all happy about how much Ellen has learned during the commercial break. To win, she must name the one energy source that will never be depleted. (We won't reveal the answer, but we got it right!)

Almost as intriguing as the attraction is the technology behind it. The vehicles weigh about 30,000 pounds when fully loaded with passengers, yet are guided along the floor by a wire that is only one-eighth inch thick.

World Showcase

Noble sentiments about humanity and the fellowship of nations, which have motivated so many World's Fairs in the past, also inhabit World Showcase. But make no mistake about it: This area of Epcot is unlike any previous international exposition.

The group of pavilions that encircles World Showcase Lagoon (a body of water that is the size of several football fields, with a perimeter of about 1.2 miles) demonstrates Disney conceptions about participating countries in remarkably realistic, consistently entertaining styles. You won't find the real Germany here—rather, the country's essence, much as a traveler returning from a visit might remember what he or she saw.

Shops, restaurants, and attractions are housed in a group of structures that is an artful pastiche of all the elements that give that nation's countryside and towns their distinctive flavor. Although occasional liberties have been taken when scale and proportion required them, careful research governed the design of every nook and cranny.

Equally impressive is the cuisine. With no fewer than 14 upscale eateries to choose from, it's no wonder some guests here do nothing but nosh. (That is especially true during Epcot's popular International Food & Wine Festival, a

time when dozens more nations contribute to an already fortified international menu. See page 11 for additional information.)

In the shops, many of the wares represent the country in whose pavilion they are sold. Craftspeople are occasionally on hand to demonstrate their arts. Thanks to special cultural-exchange programs and recruiting efforts, many World Showcase staffers hail from the countries the pavilions represent.

A diverse lineup of entertainment ensures that all visitors experience more than a little culture, foreign or otherwise. The entertainment is as authentic as the Disney casting directors can make it, with native performers commonly featured and new festivities always in the works.

Pavilions are described in the order in which

HOT TIP!

World Showcase pavilions generally open at 11 A.M. However, guests may use the International Gateway entrance as much as a half hour prior to Future World's official opening time.

155

Phineas and Ferb: Agent P's World Showcase Adventure

Calling all secret agent wannabes! How would you like to help Perry the Platypus save the world from the evil Dr. Heinz Doofenshmirtz? Here's your chance. The interactive game is based on the Disney Channel show *Phineas and Ferb*. Of course, one need not be familiar with the show to get a kick out of the Epcot version. Once you borrow a F.O.N.E. (Field Operative Notification Equipment) or have a smartphone programmed at a special kiosk (near Italy, Norway, or the United Kingdom), you are ready to start the scavenger hunt.

If you and your team follow instructions and find the clues, you will complete your mission: to save the world! There's no extra charge to play, but guests do have to return the F.O.N.E.'s after they declare "mission accomplished."

they are encountered while moving counter-clockwise around the World Showcase Lagoon after crossing the bridge from Future World.

CANADA

Celebrating the many beauties of the U.S.A.'s neighbor to the north, the area devoted to the Western Hemisphere's largest nation is complete with its own mountain, waterfall, rushing stream, rocky canyon, mine, and splendid garden massed

PHOTO BY JILL SAFRO

with flowers. There's even a totem pole, a trading post, and an elaborate, mansard-roofed hotel similar to ones built by Canadian railroad companies as they pushed west around the turn of the twentieth century. All this is imaginatively arranged somewhat like a split-level house, with the section representing French Canada on top, and another devoted to the mountains alongside it and below. From a distance, the Hôtel du Canada, the main building here, looks like little more than a bump on the landscape—as does Epcot's single Canadian Rocky Mountain. But up close, they both seem to tower as high as the genuine article.

The gardens were inspired by the Butchart Gardens, on Vancouver Island, British Columbia, a famous park created on the site of a limestone quarry. The hotel is modeled, in part, after Ottawa's Victorian-style Château Laurier. Entertainment is provided by a group called TradNation. They perform on a stage facing the promenade.

O CANADA!: Step into the Circle-Vision 360 film, *O Canada!*, and find yourself surrounded by the breathtaking sights and sounds of this northern nation. Of course, you won't be alone—Canadian actor Martin Short stars as your guide, taking guests through prairies, plains, snowfields, rivers, rocky mountainsides, and beyond. Humor and hockey are included. The motion picture provides a you-are-there feeling that makes all of this spectacular scenery still more memorable. Know that you'll have to stand for the show, as there are no seats in this theater.

NORTHWEST MERCANTILE: Found to the left upon entering the pavilion's plaza, this spot features NHL T-shirts (Canadian teams, of course), plush toys (moose, owls, otters, etc.), and maple-flavored snacks, tiny totem poles, plus other Canada-themed collectibles. Skeins of rope, tin scoops, lanterns, and antique ice skates hanging from the long beams overhead set the mood, together with the structure itself.

PHOTO BY JILL SAFRO

UNITED KINGDOM

In the space of only a few hundred feet, visitors to this pavilion stroll from an elegant London square to the edge of a canal in the rural country-side—via a bustling urban English street framed by buildings that constitute a veritable rhapsody of historic architectural styles. But one scene leads to the next so smoothly that nothing ever seems amiss. Here again, note the attention to detail: the half-timbered High Street structure that leans a bit, and the hand-painted "smoke" stains that make the chimneys look as if they have been there for centuries. When a thatched roof is required, it's right where it should be—though the roof may be made of plastic broom bristles because fire regulations prohibit the real thing. Off to the side is a pair of scarlet phone booths identical to those that used to be found around the U.K. And there are eight architectural styles characteristic of the streetscapes, from English Tudor to Georgian and Victorian.

There is no major attraction in this pavilion; instead, it features half a dozen shops and a pub that serves a selection of beers and ales that would be the toast of any "local" in London itself. The Rose & Crown serves snacks, too. There's lots of entertainment, including an acoustical group called Quickstep. Every Wednesday through Sunday, the four-member band can be heard playing songs which draw from Scottish, English, and Irish traditions. In the pub, a lively pianist has been known to play late into the evening. A band known as British Revolution plays classic rock favorites in the garden courtyard. They're a true crowd-pleaser. (Entertainment is subject to change.)

THE CROWN & CREST: This shop looks like a backdrop for a child's fantasy of the days of King Arthur, with its high rafters decked out with bright banners, a fireplace (and crossed swords above), and wrought-iron chandelier. Souvenirs featuring the Union Jack flag are the stock-in-trade at this emporium adjoining the Sportsman's Shoppe. Name histories and family crests are also available, as are swords, shields,

HOT TIP!

A great place to watch IllumiNations is from the Rose & Crown Pub in the United Kingdom pavilion. Try to snag a lagoon-side table—whether within the pub's boundaries or in the self-serve sitting area nearby—about 30 minutes before the show is set to begin. (Note that on nights when the wind is blowing directly toward the Rose & Crown, it might be better to grab a bite and watch the show from Mexico's Cantina, on the other side of the lagoon.)

and knights in shining armor. There's also a line of Guinness Stout merchandise (think glasses, shirts, bottle openers, etc.).

SPORTSMAN'S SHOPPE: Head here for clothing and accessories centered on uniquely British locales and sports. You can expect to find a large selection of football (soccer) team gear. Don't miss the tartan map on the wall opposite The Crown & Crest; it identifies plaids from Glen Burn and Gordon to Langtree and St. Lawrence. There's a nice selection of shirts and souvenirs featuring the Rose & Crown Pub (the U.K. pavilion's watering hole), too. Outside, the shop resembles a stone manor built during the last half of the sixteenth century.

PHOTO BY JILL SAFRO

THE TEA CADDY: Fitted out with heavy wooden beams and a broad fireplace to resemble the Stratford-upon-Avon cottage of William Shakespeare's wife, Anne Hathaway, this shop stocks English teas, both loose and in bags, in a wide variety of flavors. Other items include teapots, china, biscuits, and assorted candies.

THE TOY SOLDIER: There's a nice selection of rock-'n'-roll-themed items here, highlighting well-known British bands, as well as merchandise featuring the gang from the Hundred Acre Wood: Pooh, Piglet, Eeyore, and Tigger, too. TV fans will appreciate the selection of items featuring favorite British programs such as *Dr. Who*, *Monty Python*, etc.

THE QUEEN'S TABLE: This shop (opposite the Sportsman's Shoppe) is one of the loveliest in all of Epcot. That is particularly true of the store's elegant Adams Room, embellished with elaborate moldings and a crystal chandelier. The setting is a lovely background for the handbags, jewelry, soaps, and other fragrant items that are available.

Don't neglect to inspect small, serene Britannia Square outside the shop farthest from the promenade. But for its small size and the Florida climate, it feels like London itself.

INTERNATIONAL GATEWAY

Informally known as Epcot's back door, the International Gateway is between the United Kingdom and France pavilions. There's a ticket window just outside the gate. (Yes, it's possible to enter and exit the park here.) In addition to restrooms and an ATM, you'll also find:

FRIENDSHIP LANDING: Disney's water taxis, known as FriendShip boats, ferry guests to the Yacht and Beach Club, BoardWalk, and the Swan and Dolphin resorts, and finally to Disney's Hollywood Studios (the last stop before the boat returns to the resorts and back to Epcot). The dock is located just outside the International

---

Where to Eat in Epcot

A complete listing of all Epcot eateries—full-service restaurants, fast-food emporiums, and snack shops—can be found in the *Good Meals, Great Times* chapter. See the Epcot section, beginning on page 251.

Gateway entrance. It's possible to walk to all of the aforementioned destinations, too. (It takes about 30 minutes to reach the Studios on foot.)

STROLLER AND WHEELCHAIR RENTAL: Strollers and wheelchairs are available for rent at this location. Hold on to your rental receipt; it can be used on the same day in all WDW theme parks, should you leave and return later on. It's possible to get a replacement stroller here.

WORLD TRAVELER: Candy, soft drinks, books, kitchen items, strollers (for purchase), and a package pickup depot are located at this spot near the United Kingdom pavilion. Disney fashions, home items, character merchandise, and Epcot souvenirs are also for sale here.

FRANCE

The buildings here have mansard roofs and casement windows so Gallic in appearance that you may expect to see a Bohemian poet looking down from above. A canal-like offshoot of the lagoon seems like the Seine itself; the footbridge that spans it recalls the old Pont des Arts. There's a kiosk like those that punctuate the streets of Paris and a bakery whose heavenly rich aromas announce its presence long before it's visible.

Shops sell perfumes and other items. Their roofs are of real copper or slate, and the cabinetry is finely crafted. Galerie des Halles—the iron-and-glass-ceilinged market that Paris once counted as one of its most beloved institutions—lives again. But perhaps most special of all are the people. Hosts and hostesses who hail from Paris and the French provinces answer questions in French-accented English. Keep an eye out for Serveur Amusant, the comedic waiter who does one heck of a balancing act.

An interesting background note: The main entrance to the pavilion recalls the architecture of Paris, most of which was built during the Belle Epoque ("beautiful age"), the last decades of the nineteenth century.

Don't miss the garden on the opposite side of this pavilion. It is one of the most peaceful spots in World Showcase.

IMPRESSIONS DE FRANCE: Shown in the Palais du Cinéma, a little theater that's not unlike the one at Fontainebleau, this enchanting 18-minute film takes viewers on a trip through France.

The film shows off a beautiful tree-dotted estate, fields and vineyards at harvest time, a flower market and a pastry shop, a glacier, and a harbor full of squawking gulls. Viewers visit the Eiffel Tower; Versailles and its gilt Hall of Mirrors (just outside Paris); Mont Saint Michel; the French Alps; and Cannes, the star-studded resort city on the Mediterranean coast. All this is even more appealing thanks to a superb soundtrack, consisting almost entirely of the music of French classical composers.

The exceptionally wide screen adds yet another dimension. This is not a Circle-Vision 360 film like the movies shown at China and Canada. The France film used only five cameras, and it is shown on five large projection surfaces —200 degrees around. It's a beautiful film, one of the park's best. We recommend stopping for a French pastry break after the show.

PLUME ET PALETTE: One of the loveliest shops in World Showcase, this Art Nouveau–inspired location is home to the Givenchy Shop—the only location in the world that carries the complete line of Givenchy fragrances, skin care products, and cosmetics.

LA SIGNATURE: Another beautiful spot, this boutique features a nice selection of Guerlain cosmetics and fragrances.

L'ESPRIT DE LA PROVENCE: This little shop stocks a selection of textiles, ceramics, and kitchen accessories from the Provence region of Southern France. They offer loose chocolates and children's books, too.

LES HALLES BOUTIQUE DE CADEUX: Everything from Eiffel Tower statuettes to Impressionist-style prints is offered at this location near the exit of the cinema. Mugs, tote bags, T-shirts, berets, flags, and picture frames are among the offerings available. The area is based on Paris's now-demolished Les Halles, the city's

PHOTO BY JILL SAFRO

old fruit and vegetable market. This space is also the location of the ever-popular bakeshop known as Les Halles Boulangerie & Patisserie.

LES VINS DE FRANCE: Selections in this wine shop range from the inexpensive to the pricey, from *vin ordinaire* going for several dollars to upward of $99 for a rare vintage. Wine tastings are held here to sample the offerings (for a price). Other wares include wine glasses with a World Showcase theme, books about wine, bottle openers and toppers, aprons, candy, kitchenware, and soaps. There's a big barrel of ice cold beer, too. Dig in for a sudsy treat.

HOT TIP!

Don't try to fit all of the World Showcase movies into one day, especially if you are traveling with kids.

MOROCCO

Nine tons of tile were handmade, hand cut, and shipped from Morocco to Epcot to create this World Showcase pavilion. To capture the unique quality of this North African nation's architecture, Moroccan artisans came to Epcot to practice the mosaic art that has been a part of their homeland for thousands of years. Koutoubia Minaret, a meticulously detailed replica of the famous prayer tower in Marrakesh, stands guard at the entrance. A courtyard with a fountain at the center leads to the medina (Old City). Between the traditional alleyways and the more modern sections are the pointed arches and swirling patterns of the Bab Boujeloud gate, a replica of the one that stands in the city of Fez. An ancient working waterwheel irrigates the gardens, and the motifs repeated throughout the buildings include carved plaster and wood, tile, and brass. Live enertainment may be presented at the Morocco Pavilion, on World Showcase Promenade. Check a Times Guide for specifics.

THE BRASS BAZAAR: Interspersed among the decorative brass plates in this store are ceramic pitchers, planters, pots, ornate bottles of rosewater, serving sets, colorful maps, wooden collectibles, books, framed prints, baskets, tiles, couscous, hummus, and tabbouleh mixes, lamps, spices, and other Moroccan selections.

THE ART OF HENNA: In the market for a temporary henna body decoration? Look no farther than this cozy corner of the Morocco pavilion. Henna "tattoos" are available—for a fee—in various sizes and designs between 1 P.M. and 9 P.M. daily (hours may vary).

CASABLANCA CARPETS: In addition to handmade carpets, this store features an intriguing and eclectic selection of merchandise. Look for lamps, fez hats, jewelry, books, and more.

MARKETPLACE IN THE MEDINA: Hand-woven baskets, sheepskin wallets and bags, assorted straw hats, drums, sandals, postcards, scarves, jewelry, clothing, and small carpets are among the available wares.

SOUK AL MAGREB: This waterside enclave located on the World Showcase promenade spills over with hand-crafted keepsakes. Look for Moroccan lamps, baskets, and leather goods. One can also find rosewater and coffee products.

TANGIER TRADERS: This is the place to shop if you're in the market for a fez, woven belts, leather sandals and purses, and other traditional Moroccan clothing and accessories.

JAPAN

Serenity rules in Japan. Except, of course, when the pavilion resounds with traditional music performed by a drum-playing duo or group.

The landscaping, designed in accordance with traditional symbolic and aesthetic values, contributes to the pavilion's peaceful mood. Rocks, which in Japan represent the enduring nature of the Earth, were brought from North Carolina and Georgia (since boulders are scarce in the Sunshine State). Water, symbolizing the sea (which the Japanese consider a life source), is abundant; the Japan pavilion garden has a stream and pools inhabited by koi (fish). Evergreen trees, which in Japan are symbols of eternal life, are here in force.

Disney horticulturists created this very Japanese landscape using few plants native to that country because the climate there is so

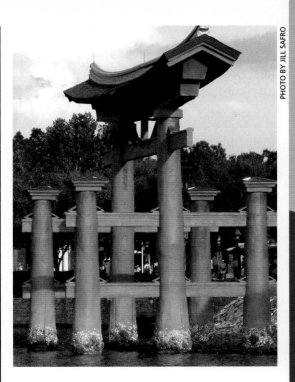

PHOTO BY JILL SAFRO

different from that of Florida. Among the few trees here native to Japan are the sago, near the courtyard entrance to the Katsura Grill; the two Japanese maple trees, identifiable by their small leaves, not far away (near the first stairway from the promenade on the left side of the courtyard as you face it); and the prickly monkey-puzzle trees, near the walkway to the promenade, on The American Adventure side of the pagoda. Needle-sharp thorns make the latter the only species of tree that monkeys cannot climb.

The pagoda was modeled after an eighth-century structure located in the Horyuji Temple, in Nara, Japan. The striking torii gate on the shore of World Showcase Lagoon derives from the design of the one at the Itsukushima shrine in Hiroshima Bay.

BIJUTSU-KAN GALLERY: Housing an ever-changing cultural display, this small museum has offered, among other exhibitions, the Kitahara Collection of Tin Toys, featuring toys produced between 1880 and 1970. Most recently, the exhibit "Kawaii—Japan's Cute Culture" was featured here.

MITSUKOSHI MERCHANDISE STORE: There are kimonos, T-shirts bearing Japanese characters, fine jewelry, and a selection of bowls and vases meant for flower arranging for sale at this spacious store set up by Mitsukoshi—a four-centuries-old retail firm.

DID YOU KNOW?

The five stories of the Japanese pagoda symbolize earth, water, fire, wind, and sky.

The shop features a wall of sake selections (and a small sake bar), plus chopsticks, bonsai, jewelry, china, paper fans, and origami products. There is also a bounty of snacks, candies, and teas. You can even get an oyster and hope to find a pearl! The pleasant atmosphere and variety of merchandise make this establishment a most rewarding experience for both the casual browser and the serious shopper. The building's design was inspired by the Gosho Imperial Palace, which was constructed in Kyoto in 794 A.D.

THE AMERICAN ADVENTURE

BIRNBAUM'S BEST When it came to creating The American Adventure, the centerpiece of World Showcase, Disney Imagineers were given relatively free rein. So the 110,000 bricks of the imposing Colonial-style structure that houses a stirring show, fast-food restaurant, and shop are the real thing—patiently crafted by hand from soft Georgia clay.

The show inside stands out because of its wonderfully evocative settings, its detailed sets, and the 35 superb Audio-Animatronics players, some of the most lifelike ever created by the Disney organization. A stellar a cappella vocal group called Voices of Liberty periodically serenades guests in the building's foyer. By all means, catch a performance.

THE AMERICAN ADVENTURE SHOW: One of the most ambitious Epcot attractions, this 26-minute presentation celebrates the American spirit from the nation's birth. Beginning with the arrival of the pilgrims at Plymouth Rock and their harsh first winter on the western shore of the Atlantic, the Audio-Animatronics narrators— a lifelike Ben Franklin and a thoroughly convincing Mark Twain—recall key people and events in American history: the Boston Tea Party, George Washington and the grueling winter at Valley Forge, the influential abolitionist Frederick Douglass, the celebrated nineteenth-century Nez Perce chief Joseph, and many more. The Philadelphia Centennial Exposition is remembered, along with women's rights campaigner Susan B. Anthony, telephone inventor Alexander Graham Bell, and the steel giant and philanthropist Andrew Carnegie. Naturalist John Muir converses onstage with Teddy Roosevelt. Charles Lindbergh, Rosie the Riveter, Jackie Robinson, and Walt Disney are represented. So are John Wayne, Lucille Ball, Margaret Mead, John F. Kennedy, Martin Luther King Jr., and Billie Jean King.

The idea is to recall episodes in history, both negative and positive, that contributed to the growth of the spirit of America, by engendering "a new burst of creativity" (in the designers' words) "or a better understanding of ourselves as partners in the American experience."

For information about how each of the many featured historical figures spoke during his or her lifetime, researchers contacted historians and cultural institutions—the Philadelphia Historical Commission, the State Historical Society of Missouri, the Department of the Navy's Ships Historical Branch, and others. When recordings were not available, educated guesses were made: Alexander Graham Bell's voice was created on the basis of contemporary comments about his voice's clarity, expressiveness, and crisp articulation, combined with the fact that his father taught elocution. A highlight of the show is the majestic music played by the Philadelphia Symphony Orchestra.

Seats toward the front of the house afford the best view of the Audio-Animatronics figures. If you have some extra time before the show, be sure to read the inspirational quotes that line the walls—Jane Addams, Charles Lindbergh, Herman Melville, and Ayn Rand are among the prominent Americans who are quoted.

AMERICAN HERITAGE GALLERY: Inside the pavilion (on the right side of the grand lobby), the addition of this art gallery brought Epcot's grand total to six. Its current exhibition is from the The Kinsey Collection. The exhibit features more than 40 pieces of art, artifacts, books, and sculptures that, together, tell an inspirational story of African-American history.

HOT TIP!

While all of the seats in The American Adventure theater provide good views, the sound quality is best in the middle and toward the front.

HERITAGE MANOR GIFTS: Visit this shop to find Americana in all of its red-white-and-blue glory. Gifts include T-shirts, tote bags, pillows, tri-corner hats, flags, and books about U.S. history. "Made in America" merchandise includes wine, moonshine, candy, beer biscuits, soaps, candles, and items celebrating U.S. cities.

THE AMERICA GARDENS THEATRE: An ever-changing slate of live entertainment is presented throughout the year in this lakeside amphitheater in front of The American Adventure pavilion. American Music Machine, a popular a cappella group, performs contemporary music throughout the day. Concert Series such as Eat to the Beat and Sounds Like Summer take place on this stage, too—as does the popular Candlelight Processional, which is offered up during the holiday season (see page 12).

Showtimes are posted at the theatre and in the park Times Guide. For details, visit *www.disneyworld.com*.

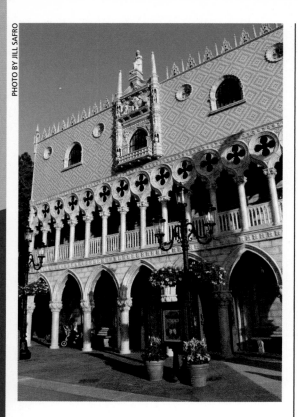

ITALY

The arches and cutout motifs that adorn the World Showcase reproduction of the Doge's Palace in Venice are just the more obvious examples of the attention to detail lavished on the individual structures in this relatively small pavilion. The angel perched atop the scaled-down campanile was sculpted on the model of the original, right down to the curls on the back of its head. It was then covered with real gold leaf, despite the fact that it was destined to be set almost 100 feet in the air.

The other statues in the complex, including the sea god Neptune presiding over the fountain in the rear of the piazza, are similarly exact. And the pavilion even has an island like Venice's own, its seawall appropriately stained with age, plus moorings that look like barber poles, with several distinctively Venetian gondolas tied to them. St. Mark the Evangelist is also remembered, together with the lion that is the saint's companion and Venice's guardian. These can be seen atop the two massive columns that flank the small arched footbridge that connects the island to the mainland. The only deviation from Venetian reality is the alteration of the site of the Doge's Palace in reference to the real St. Mark's Square.

The quaint pavilion is equally interesting from a horticultural point of view. The island boasts kumquat trees, citrus plants typical of the Mediterranean, and a couple of olive trees that can be seen on the sidewalls of a shop. Originally located in a Sacramento, California, grove, the olive trees arrived in Florida via flatbed truck a bit slimmer than when they started out. (Arizona border inspectors decreed that the trees be trimmed to the ten-foot width required by state law; therefore, the ancient olives were shorn en route. The hardy trees survived, leaving only their scars to remind visitors of the ordeal; the darker bark is what remains of the original, while the lighter areas are new growth.) The tall, narrow trees that stand like dark columns are Italian cypresses, which are common in their native country.

LA BOTTEGA ITALIANA: This shop on the edge of the piazza features a selection of red and white Italian wines. (If it's early in the day, take advantage of Epcot's Package Express service and have bottles sent to the park exit—so you don't have to carry them all day.) Items such as cappuccino makers, wine glasses, olive oil, spices, chocolate, cookies, espresso, cookbooks, and decorative bottle toppers are also on hand. It's also possible to purchase an ice cold Italian beer.

IL BEL CRISTALLO: There is an abundance of Italian fragrances, shirts, and accessories, plus purses, wallets, and bags, inside this shop (just off the promenade on the Germany side of the piazza). Other featured wares include scarves, ties, fragrances, and jewelry. This shop also boasts a large assortment of exquisite, hand-crafted Venetian masks (which range in price from about $30 to $500).

GERMANY

There are no villages in Germany quite like this one. Inspired by various towns in the Rhine region, Bavaria, and the German north, it boasts structures reminiscent of those found in urban enclaves as diverse as Frankfurt, Freiburg, and Rothenburg. There are stair-stepped rooflines and towers, balconies and arcaded walkways, and so much overall charm that the scene seems to come straight out of a fairy tale. The beer hall to the rear is almost as lively as the one at Munich's famed Oktoberfest, especially late in the evening. The shops, which offer a range of merchandise from wine and sweets to ceramics and cuckoo clocks, toys, and books (and even art), are so tempting that it's difficult to leave the area empty-handed.

The elements that constitute the Germany pavilion are described here as they would be encountered while walking counterclockwise around the cobblestone-paved central plaza. (The plaza is known as the St. Georgsplatz, after the statue at its center.) St. George, the patron saint of soldiers, is depicted with a dragon that legend says he slew during a pilgrimage to the Middle East.

Try to time your World Showcase peregrinations to take you to the Germany pavilion on the hour, when the handsome, specially designed glockenspiel at the plaza's rear can be heard chiming in a melody composed specifically for the pavilion.

DAS KAUFHAUS: This two-story structure, whose exterior is patterned after a merchants' hall known as the Kaufhaus (located in the German town of Freiburg im Breisgau), stocks athletic apparel and footwear.

DER TEDDYBAR: Located adjacent to the Volkskunst clock shop, this is a toy store with a bit of flair. It's home to one of Walt Disney World's best selections of toys, including an assortment of stuffed keepsakes. Duffy the Disney Bear is among the plush items sold here. They also stock bears of the gummy variety.

KARAMELL-KÜCHE: This caramel display kitchen tempts with housemade sweet treats made from buttery caramel. Many items are made fresh in the on-stage kitchen. Favorites include fresh strawberries hand-dipped in chocolate and drizzled with gooey caramel, caramel-filled chocolate chip cookies, crunchy apples enveloped in caramel, chocolate or vanilla

cupcakes topped with rich vanilla icing with a dab of caramel on top, packaged Werther's candies, and much more. Don't come here on an empty stomach—you could go bankrupt!

KUNSTARBEIT IN KRISTALL: This shop to the left of the Biergarten features Austrian and crystal jewelry (including tiaras), beer mugs, wine glasses in traditional German tints of green and amber, and crystal decanters. Glassware may be etched on the spot.

STEIN HAUS: The "house" is really a tiny shop that celebrates *bier*, featuring steins, mugs, shirts, and collectibles.

VOLKSKUNST: Small and appealing, this establishment is filled with a burgher's bounty of German timepieces, plus a smattering of other items made by hand in the rural corners of the nation. As for cuckoo clocks, some are small and unobtrusive, while others are so immense that they'd look appropriate only in some cathedral-ceilinged hunting lodge. This is also one place to pick up a traditional German beer stein, wine accessories, bells, books, crafts, and music.

WEINKELLER: Germany's wine shop, situated between the cookie shop and the crystal shop toward the rear of St. Georgsplatz, offers about 50 varieties of German wine. Wine tastings are held here daily (for a fee). The selection includes vintages meant for everyday consumption, plus a few fine estate wines. These are white (with a few exceptions), because white wine constitutes the bulk of Germany's vinicultural output. (Only 20 percent of German bottlings are red.) The setting itself is quite attractive—low-ceilinged and cozy.

DIE WEIHNACHTS ECKE: A shop like this can set a visitor's mind to thoughts of Christmas —even on the steamiest dog days of summer. Ornaments, decorations, and gifts manufactured by various German companies line the shelves.

One item of note is the pickle ornament. Pickle ornaments are considered a special Christmas tree decoration by many families in Germany. Historically, it is always the last ornament hung on the tree, with a parent hiding it among the other ornaments. Kids gleefully search for it—and the one who finds it gets a special little present from St. Nicholas, left for the most observant child. Can you find the pickle ornament on each tree in the shop? It's not easy!

CHINA

Dominated by the Disney equivalent of Beijing's Temple of Heaven and announced by a pair of banners that proclaim good wishes to passersby (the Chinese characters translate to: "May good fortune follow you on your path through life" and "May virtue be your neighbor"), this pavilion conveys a level of serenity that offers an appealing contrast to the hearty merriment of the bordering Germany and the gaiety of nearby Mexico. Part of this quiet environment is the by-product of the soothing, traditional Chinese music. The gardens also make a major contribution. They are full of rosebushes native to China, and there is a century-old mulberry tree (to the left of the main walkway into the pavilion), with a pomegranate tree and a wiggly-looking Florida native known as a water oak nearby.

The number of stones in the floor of the pavilion's main structure is not random; the center stone is surrounded by nine stones

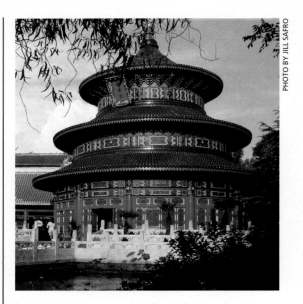

PHOTO BY JILL SAFRO

because nine is considered a lucky number in China. Around the edge of the outer room rise 12 columns—because 12 is the number of months in the year and the number of years in a full cycle of the Chinese calendar. Be sure to stand on the round stone in the center: Every whisper is amplified.

A spacious emporium is devoted to Chinese wares, and two restaurants add to the overall atmosphere. However, all this is secondary to the motion picture shown inside the Temple of Heaven—a Circle-Vision 360 film that is one of the most diverting World Showcase attractions. Keep in mind that this is a standing-room-only viewing experience.

REFLECTIONS OF CHINA: This cinematic presentation shows the beauties of a land that few Epcot visitors have seen firsthand—and does it so vividly that it's possible to see the film twice and still not fully absorb all the wonderful sights.

The film replaced *Wonders of China*, the Circle-Vision 360 movie that played at Epcot's China pavilion since 1982. Just as with the original, filmmakers used nine cameras to capture cultural and scenic images that wrap completely around viewers. The majestic tour includes some rural stops, plus visits to cities such as Hong Kong, Macau, Beijing, and Shanghai.

The film includes footage of many landmarks, such as the 2,400-year-old Great Wall and Tiananmen Square, as well as some newer cultural developments. Overall, it showcases the majesty of this ancient country and highlights some of the more dramatic changes that have taken place over the past 20 or so years. Note that the theater has no seats.

Village Traders

Located between the Germany and China pavilions, this open-air shop sports a selection of hand-crafted gift items from Africa, India, Spain, and Australia. Browse through such souvenirs as wind chimes, handbags, hats, and, of course, T-shirts.

HOUSE OF WHISPERING WILLOWS:
When exiting, pass by the House of Whispering Willows, an exhibit of ancient Chinese art and artifacts. Changed periodically, it invariably includes fine pieces from well-known collections.

HOUSE OF GOOD FORTUNE: This vast emporium, located off the narrow, charming Street of Good Fortune, offers a huge assortment of merchandise—lanterns, hats, wine, beer, fine jewelry, silk robes, shoes (including a variety of sandals and flip-flops), prints, porcelain items, tea sets, candles, neckties, Buddah statues, chess sets, reading glasses, and much more. Kids adore the huge variety of panda-themed plush toys. Handheld fans may be personalized on the spot.

NORWAY

Set between Mexico and China is Norway, a pavilion added to the World Showcase mix in 1988. Built in conjunction with Norwegian companies, the pavilion celebrates the rich history, folklore, and culture of one of the Western world's oldest countries.

The cobblestone town square is an architectural showcase of the styles of such Norwegian towns as Bergen, Alesund, and Oslo. There's also a Norwegian castle fashioned after Akershus, a 14th-century fortress still standing in Oslo's harbor; the castle here houses the Akershus restaurant. Few can resist walking into the bakery for a taste of its treats. In a show of modernity, a statue of Norway's legendary marathoner Grete Waitz stands behind the bakery. Shops stock handicrafts and folk items: hand-knit woolens, wood carvings, and glass and metal artwork.

Frozen fans can also visit Arendelle, in the new attraction Frozen Ever After. And for those guests who would like to meet Anna and Elsa of *Frozen* fame—great news: They're here!

ROYAL SOMMERHUS—MEET ANNA & ELSA: FP+ Attention, *Frozen* fans! Princess Anna and Queen Elsa greet guests throughout the day in this pavilion's new Royal Sommerhus. FYI: Arendelle, the fictional kingdom in which the ladies live, is said to be in Norway.

FROZEN EVER AFTER: FP+
Be prepared to let it go as you're swept off to Arendelle in this enchanting new boat ride. The adventure celebrates the story from

the film *Frozen* and the characters that have become near and dear to just about everybody's heart: Anna, Elsa, Olaf, Kristoff, and Sven—plus the Snowgies from the *Frozen Fever* animated short. The attraction, which replaced Maelstrom, immerses guests in favorite moments and music from the film. This happy addition to World Showcase can have daunting waits—we highly recommend reserving a Fastpass+ assignment well in advance.

THE PUFFIN'S ROOST: Here you'll find a nice variety of Norwegian gifts. Sweaters, activewear, Viking helmets, trolls, toys, fragrances, jewelry, and candy are among the wares for sale at the Roost. Want to pose for a photo with a giant troll? You've come to the right place!

STAVE CHURCH GALLERY: Inside the wooden stave church, there is a small exhibit that explores Norwegian culture. It's interesting (and sad) to note that only about 30 stave churches remain in Norway today.

MEXICO

The tangle of tropical vegetation surrounding the great pyramid that encloses this pavilion and the Mexican restaurant at the lagoon's edge on the promenade provides only the barest suggestion of the charming area inside.

Dominated by a re-creation of a quaint plaza at dusk, the pyramid's interior is rimmed by balconied, tile-roofed, colonial-style structures. Crowding a fountain area is a quartet of stands selling Mexican handicrafts, and to the left is a shop stocked with other handsome wares. A Mariachi Cobre band keeps things lively—as does the tequila bar. To the rear, the San Angel Inn serves authentic fare. Behind it, a waterborne attraction features a whirlwind Mexican tour.

Take a look at the cultural exhibit inside the pyramid entrance on the way in. Note that the building was inspired by Meso-American structures dating from the third century A.D. Epcot's Mexico is a great place to wait out a Florida shower.

GRAN FIESTA TOUR STARRING THE THREE CABALLEROS:

Big news: The Three Caballeros (that would be Donald Duck, Panchito, and José Carioca) are reuniting for a big show in Mexico City! Unfortunately, the ever mischievous Donald has gone missing in Mexico—and guests join Panchito and José in the quest to find him. In doing so, you will be treated to a whirlwind (if slow-moving) boat tour of the country. The cheery montage of film, props, and Audio-Animatronics figures is reminiscent of It's a Small World, though on a smaller scale.

Disney buffs should note that the Audio-Animatronics versions of the Three Caballeros that appear in the finale made their original Disney World debut in 1971. They were a part of the Magic Kingdom's original Mickey Mouse Revue in the Fantasyland Theatre—and remained there until 1980 (when the show left WDW for Tokyo Disneyland).

LA PRINCESSA DE CRISTAL: Presented by Arribas Brothers and located next to the entrance to the Gran Fiesta Tour Starring the Three Caballeros attraction, this alcove offers crystal tiaras, character figurines, rings, bracelets, necklaces, and glass slippers. If you're lucky, you'll get to watch glass blown by an in-house artisan.

PLAZA DE LOS AMIGOS: Brightly colored artwork, sombreros, malachite, baskets, decorative parrots, mariachi music (available on CD), musical instruments, and pottery make this mercado (market) at the plaza's center as bright and almost as lively as one in Mexico itself. Brilliantly hued papier-mâché piñatas figure strongly in the scenery here. Authentic pre-Columbian figures are on display. Also available for purchase are spices, hot sauce, salsa, liquors, cocktail accessories, and candy.

EL RANCHITO DEL NORTE: Located on the lagoon side of World Showcase Promenade, this spot features gifts and souvenirs.

LA TIENDA ENCANTATA: Visit this store inside the pyramid and you'll discover fine jewelry, bags, scarves, accessories, and assorted women's fashions.

SHOWCASE PLAZA

DISNEY TRADERS: Merchandise combining the charm of classic Disney characters and Epcot themes is the primary stock-in-trade. Sundries are also sold.

PORT OF ENTRY: A shop carrying fashions for the whole family, accessories, plush dolls, and toys. It has food and wine-related items, too.

Entertainment

Epcot presents an intriguing array of live performances each day, making it very important to consult a park Times Guide when you arrive. For updates, call 407-824-4321.

AMERICA GARDENS THEATRE: The lagoonside venue at The American Adventure pavilion hosts an ever-changing program of live entertainment, such as the popular Garden Rocks concert series presented during the annual Flower and Garden Festival. Check an Epcot Times Guide for specifics.

ILLUMINATIONS—REFLECTIONS OF EARTH: FP+ This nighttime spectacular presents the entire history of our planet in 13 minutes—from its creation to the present and a look toward the future. A dazzling mix of lasers, fireworks, fountains, and music, this show is a highlight of any Epcot visit.

The extravaganza, visible from anywhere on the World Showcase promenade, takes place nightly at closing time. There are excellent viewing locations all around the World Showcase Lagoon. Note that additional viewing areas have been added to the stretch between the Germany and China pavilions.

KIDCOT FUN STOPS: There is an activity area in each of the countries of World Showcase. These spots invite kids to play games and make colorful cut-outs of Duffy the Disney Bear.

WORLD SHOWCASE PERFORMERS: It's all but impossible to complete a circuit of World Showcase without catching performances en route. Keep an eye on the schedule and be sure to take in entertainment at each pavilion, often performed by natives of the country represented. Among the possibilities: worldly acrobats, a Mexican mariachi band, an American a cappella group, an Italian flag troop, Moroccan belly dancers, Japanese drummers, and more.

Holiday Happenings

During certain holidays, such as Easter week, the Fourth of July, Thanksgiving, Christmas week, and New Year's Eve, Epcot usually offers extended hours and presents additional entertainment to celebrate the respective occasion.

Call 407-824-4321, or visit *www.disneyworld.com*, for schedules and details.

CHRISTMAS: Epcot is exceptionally festive throughout the holiday season. The park celebrates Christmas with a gigantic tree and its popular candlelight choral processional.

The Candlelight Processional, a stirring presentation of traditional holiday songs, features a reading of the Christmas story by a celebrity narrator. This is a very popular event—and one of our favorites. See page 12 of the *Getting Ready to Go* chapter for details.

FP+ = Fastpass+ attraction (see page 25)

EPCOT

- Use a smartphone or stop at a Fastpass+ kiosk to book Fastpasses for as many attractions as possible (if you haven't reserved in advance).

- On your way into the park, pick up a free guidemap and a Times Guide. Consult the entertainment schedule first thing.

- Lines throughout Epcot are longest at midday and shortest in the early evening.

- During peak seasons, preferred reservation times at Epcot's table-service restaurants book quickly—make reservations as far in advance as possible. However, some tables may be available on a first-come, first-served basis (with a bit of a wait). Arrive a few minutes ahead of your reservation time.

- Most World Showcase restaurants seat guests until park closing. To make advance plans, call 407-WDW-DINE (939-3463).

- Kids can get autograph books or World Showcase passports (sold for about $10 inside the park) stamped in each of the 11 countries represented in the park. It's a nice added layer to an Epcot "world tour."

- Interactive fountain areas at Epcot provide guests of all ages with an opportunity to cool off. Be sure to pack swimsuits (and waterproof diapers) for little ones who'll undoubtedly spend time splashing in the water.

- If you plan to play at ImageWorks, the interactive play area inside Imagination, take along the e-mail address of a friend. It may come in handy.

- Allow plenty of time to explore the hands-on exhibits at Innoventions and the post-shows at Spaceship Earth and Mission: SPACE.

- When it comes to park-hopping, Epcot is an ideal park to hop to. It's usually open late.

- FriendShip water taxis are unlikely to transport you across World Showcase Lagoon any faster than a brisk walk, but they are a peaceful, foot-friendly way to make the half-mile-plus journey.

Where to Find the Characters

Epcot Character Spot is a good place to meet Disney characters, including Mickey, Minnie, Donald, and Goofy. (It's next to the Fountain View coffee shop in Future World.) Baymax, Joy, and Sadness greet guests just across from Epcot Character Spot. Characters such as Mickey, Chip, and Dale host dinner at the Garden Grill in The Land pavilion in Future World. Princesses invite you to join them for a meal at Norway's Akershus Royal Banquet Hall. Anna and Elsa meet folks in Norway, too. Snow White mingles at the Germany pavilion. Belle visits France. Aladdin and Jasmine (Morocco), Mulan (China), Daisy Duck, and others have been known to greet guests at World Showcase. Check a Times Guide for schedules and greeting locations.

Hidden Mickeys

These are some of the most popular "Hidden Mickeys" at Epcot. How many can you find? Check the box when you spot each one!

❤ **Mission: SPACE:** When your ship lands on Mars, you may spy a Mickey on a rooftop to the right of the landing strip. (It's made of satellite dishes.) ■
　After you exit the ride and enter the gift shop, look up in the center of the room to find a side profile of Mickey painted on the ceiling. ■

❤ **Mexico:** Toward the end of the Gran Fiesta Tour boat ride, you'll see a barge on your left. On that barge is a Hidden Mickey made of strategically arranged bongo drums. ■

❤ **Living with the Land:** As you walk through the queue, try to find the three bubbles on the large mural that come together to form a Hidden Mickey. (Hint: It's near the middle of the mural.) ■
　About halfway through the ride, you may notice a water hose coiled into the shape of Mickey Mouse's noggin'. ■

❤ **American Adventure pavilion:** Look for a painting of early American settlers crossing a river with covered wagons. One of the wagon-pulling oxen has a Mickey near its left front leg. ■
　Another painting features workers constructing a building. Check out the tops of the beams behind the construction team. They form a classic Hidden Mickey! (The painting is on the first floor, on the right, and toward the back of the rotunda.) ■

❤ **France:** Check out the meticulously pruned bushes on the canal side of the France pavilion—one of them is shaped like a classic Mickey. ■
　Be sure to eyeball the grates surrounding the trees near the entrance to Les Chefs de France. There are several H.M.s in the intricate grillwork. ■
　While in France, pay close attention to the wedding party scene in the *Impressions de France* movie—there is a Hidden Mickey on a second-floor window! ■

❤ **Canada:** It's easy to find the totem poles in this pavilion—but it's a bit more challenging to find the Hidden Mickey on the left one. ■

❤ **The Seas with Nemo & Friends:** In Bruce's Shark World, look for two large posters—one titled "Did You Know?" and the other titled "Bruce's Shark World" (they are on opposite sides of the room). Each has an oyster in the lower right-hand corner that contains Mickey-shaped pearls. If you pay attention at the shark tank you'll be rewarded with a Hidden Mickey sighting (or two). The Mouse's head appears on the bottom of the tank, shaped by strategically placed rocks. ■

❤ **Journey Into Imagination with Figment:** About halfway through the ride and as you move through Figment's house, look up in the bathroom. Figment's commode forms a Hidden Mickey with two red circles on the ground next to it. ■

❤ **Spaceship Earth:** In the Renaissance scene, look quickly to your left to find the first painter standing in front of a table (his back is to you). On the top left of the table, three white-paint circles form a Hidden Mickey. ■
　Later in the ride, keep your eyes open for a Hidden "WDI" (the abbreviation for Walt Disney Imagineering) on the microphone of the radio broadcaster (on your left). ■

❤ **Germany:** Look up to spot three armor-wearing fellows festooning a facade to the right of the clock in St. Georgsplatz. The suit closest to the glockenspiel sports an H.M. ■

❤ **Japan:** Finding the koi pond here is easy—but can you find the Hidden Mickey in the pond? And no, it's not a Mickey fish! ■

Specifics may change during 2017.

Where in the World?

All of the photos on this page were taken at Epcot. Do you know where? We challenge you to find all the spots where these images were shot and snap a photo for yourself as you discover each one. Happy hunting! (For locations, turn to page 356.)

EPCOT

Disney's Hollywood Studios

D isney's Hollywood Studios—formerly (and famously) known as Disney-MGM Studios—has been described as "the Hollywood that never was and always will be." A bit hokey, perhaps—but also true. Enter the gates and the mosaic of flashy neon, chromed Art Deco, streamlined architecture, and star-gazing street characters immediately plunges you into the Hollywood of the 1940s. A nostalgic view of the movie-making capital has been combined with a variety of current TV- and movie-themed attractions and a delightful selection of eateries to create this Walt Disney World enclave. The combined result is an entertainment lineup worthy of a rave review.

Since opening in 1989, the park has continued to grow and evolve. At press time, major changes—including a new name—were in the works. Imagineers are hard at work building Toy Story Land and Star Wars Land. While those new play zones have yet to be unveiled, guests may enjoy a slew of new experiences right now—many of which celebrate the awakening of the Force. New favorites include Star Tours—The Adventures Continue and Star Wars: A Galactic Spectacular, a rousing fireworks extravaganza that thrills guests of all ages. The park's current lineup of attractions boasts such crowd-pleasers as the Twilight Zone™ Tower of Terror, the rollicking Rock 'n' Roller Coaster, and an explosive struggle between good and evil in Fantasmic! Each adds a new dimension to the Hollywood term "action."

A Beauty and the Beast—Live on Stage

B Fantasmic!

C The Twilight Zone™ Tower of Terror

D Rock 'n' Roller Coaster

E Animation Courtyard

F Disney Jr.—Live on Stage!

G Walt Disney—One Man's Dream

H Voyage of The Little Mermaid

I Star Wars Launch Bay

J Toy Story Midway Mania!

K Muppet★Vision 3-D

L Star Tours—The Adventures Continue

M Indiana Jones™ Epic Stunt Spectacular

N The Great Movie Ride

O For the First Time in Forever: A Frozen Sing-Along Celebration

Sunset Blvd.

Pixar Place

Hollywood Blvd.

Streets of America

Walt Disney World Resort Guest Boat Transportation ▶

▶ Bus Transportation

Getting Oriented

PHOTO BY JILL SAFRO

The Disney's Hollywood Studios park, though festive, has a layout with no distinctive shape or main thoroughfare. As such, the Studios can be a bit of a challenge to navigate. Be sure to study a guidemap as you enter.

The park entrance is at Hollywood Boulevard. This shop-lined avenue leads straight to Hollywood Plaza, address of the Studios' Chinese Theater, a replica of Grauman's Theatre that doubles as the site of The Great Movie Ride. Walking along Hollywood Boulevard, toward the plaza, you will come to Hollywood Junction. Here, a wide, palm-fringed street known as Sunset Boulevard branches off to the right.

Stroll down Sunset Boulevard and you'll come across The Hollywood Hills Amphitheater, home of Fantasmic!, and Rock 'n' Roller Coaster. At the street's far end is The Hollywood Tower Hotel, home of The Twilight Zone™ Tower of Terror. The strip is also graced with shops, the Sunset Ranch Market, and the Theater of the Stars amphitheater, where Beauty and the Beast —Live on Stage is performed daily.

Stand in Hollywood Plaza, facing the Great Movie Ride, and you'll notice an archway just off to your right. This leads to Animation Courtyard, home to Disney Junior—Live on Stage and Star Wars Launch Bay. Pixar Place, the area on the street veering off to the left of Animation Courtyard, leads to Toy Story Midway Mania! If you turn left off Hollywood Boulevard and go past Echo Lake, you're on course for such attractions as Indiana Jones Epic Stunt Spectacular and Star Tours—The Adventures Continue. Just beyond Star Tours there is another entertainment zone. The biggie to see there: Muppet★Vision 3-D.

Note: Big changes for Disney's Hollywood Studios park—including a possible name change—were in the works as this book went to press. For updates, visit *www.disneyworld.com*.

HOW TO GET THERE

Take Exit 64B off I-4. Continue about half a mile to reach the parking area. Take a tram to the park entrance.

By WDW Transportation: From the Swan, Dolphin, Yacht & Beach Club, and BoardWalk: boat, or walkway. From Fort Wilderness: bus from the Outpost stop. From Epcot: boat or bus. (Fitness-minded folks may hoof it from Epcot's International Gateway exit to the Studios. The walk takes about 20 to 30 minutes.) From Magic Kingdom, Animal Kingdom, all other Walt Disney World resorts and the resorts on Hotel Plaza Boulevard: bus only. From Disney Springs: bus to any Walt Disney World resort and transfer to a Studios bus or boat.

PARKING

All-day parking at the Studios starts at $20 for day visitors (free to WDW resort guests and annual passholders). Trams circulate regularly, providing transportation from the parking area to the park entrance. Be sure to note the section and the aisle in which you park. The parking ticket you receive allows for re-entry to the parking area throughout the day.

HOURS

Disney's Hollywood Studios is usually open from about 9 A.M. until about one hour after sunset. During certain holiday periods and summer months, hours are extended. It's best to arrive about 20 minutes before the posted opening time—guests are often let in early. Depending on the season, some stage shows do not open until late in the morning.

Admission Prices

ONE-DAY BASE TICKET
(Restricted to use in Disney's Hollywood Studios. Prices represent Walt Disney World's Value, Regular, and Peak rates; they do not include tax; and they are expected to rise in 2017.)

Adult ....$97/$102/$114
Child*..$91/$96/$108
*3 through 9 years of age; children under age 3 free

Park Primer

BABY FACILITIES

Changing tables and facilities for nursing mothers can be found at the Baby Care Center at Guest Relations near the park entrance.

CAMERA NEEDS

The Darkroom on Hollywood Boulevard stocks a variety of camera supplies, including memory cards, batteries, disposable cameras, and more. Note that selfie sticks are not permitted in the park.

DISABILITY INFORMATION

Most Walt Disney World attractions, restaurants, shops, and shows are accessible to guests using wheelchairs. Additional services are available for guests with visual or hearing disabilities. Stop by the park's Guest Relations window when you arrive. For a detailed overview of the services offered, including transportation, parking, attraction access, and more, pick up a free copy of the *Guide for Guests with Disabilities*. For more information, refer to the *Getting Ready to Go* chapter of this book.

FIRST AID

Minor medical problems can be handled at the First Aid Center, located next to Guest Relations at the park entrance. For medical emergencies, alert a cast member and call 911.

INFORMATION

Guest Relations, located just inside the park entrance, has free guidemaps, Times Guides, and an ever-resourceful staff. To make dining arrangements for certain Studios eateries, visit *www.disneyworld.com* or call 407-939-3463.

LOCKERS

Lockers, found by Oscar's Super Service, just inside the park entrance, cost $10 per day for large lockers, $8 a day for small ones (plus a $5 refundable deposit) for unlimited use. They may be rented from the Crossroads of the World kiosk, directly across from Oscar's classic pickup truck. Your receipt entitles you to a locker at any other WDW theme park on the same day (not including the deposit).

LOST CHILDREN

Report lost children at Guest Relations and alert a Disney employee to the problem.

LOST & FOUND

Located at Guest Relations, near the park entrance. To report lost items after your visit, call 407-824-4245.

MONEY MATTERS

There is an Automated Teller Machine (ATM) just outside the park entrance and by the Sunset Club Couture shop. In addition to U.S. currency, credit cards (American Express, Visa, JCB, MasterCard, and Diner's Club), traveler's checks, Disney gift cards, Disney Dollars, MagicBands, and WDW resort key cards are accepted at most park locations. (MagicBands and resort key cards must be backed up with a major credit card.)

PACKAGE PICKUP

Shops can arrange for purchases to be transported to Package Pickup, next to Oscar's Super Service (by the park entrance), where they can be picked up later in the day. Note that packages may take several hours to get to Package Pickup—plan accordingly. The service is free.

SAME-DAY RE-ENTRY

Be sure to wear your MagicBand (if you used it for admission) or retain your ticket if you plan to return later the same day.

SECURITY CHECK

Guests entering Disney theme parks are subject to a thorough security check. All bags will be searched by security personnel before guests may enter the park. A metal detector screens guests. Weapons (including toys) are prohibited. For details and a complete listing of Walt Disney World Park Rules, visit Guest Relations or go to *www.disneyworld.com/ParkRules*.

STROLLERS & WHEELCHAIRS

Strollers, wheelchairs, and Electric Conveyance Vehicles (ECVs) may be rented from Oscar's Super Service, inside the park entrance on the right. Cost for strollers is about $15; about $12 for wheelchairs. A double stroller costs $31. A Length of Stay rental ticket saves wheelchair and stroller renters $2 a day. Cost for ECVs is $50, plus a $20 refundable deposit. Keep the receipt—it can be used on the same day for a replacement at any WDW theme park. Quantities are limited (especially for ECVs).

The Main Attractions

Disney's Hollywood Studios has a brand of attractions altogether unique. Some offer guests behind-the-scenes looks at the creative and technical processes that generate television shows and movies. Others go so far as to allow guests to gain a bit of showbiz experience along with the insight. Still others present popular characters and stories in new forms—from stage shows to thrill rides.

Many shows and attractions are presented at scheduled times, or keep shorter hours than the park itself—consult a Times Guide for the day's starting times.

The Twilight Zone™ Tower of Terror FP+

BIRNBAUM'S BEST The Hollywood Tower Hotel is the creepy home of a spectacular thrill ride. On the facade of the 199-foot-tall building hangs a sparking electric sign. As the legend goes, lightning struck the building on Halloween night in 1939. An entire guest wing disappeared, along with an elevator carrying five people.

The line for the ride runs through the lobby, where dusty furniture, cobwebs, and old newspapers add to the eerie atmosphere. As guests enter the library, they see a TV brought to life by a bolt of lightning. Rod Serling invites them to enter The Twilight Zone.

Guests are led toward the boiler room to enter the ride elevator. (This is your chance to change your mind about riding—ask an attendant to point you toward the "chicken exit.") Once you take a seat in the elevator, the doors close and the room begins its ascent. At the first stop, the doors open and guests peek down a corridor. Among the effects is a ghostly visit by the hotel guests who vanished. The doors close and you continue the trip skyward.

At the next stop, you enter another dimension, a combination of sights and sounds reminiscent of *The Twilight Zone* TV series. In fact, Disney Imagineers watched each of the 156 original *Twilight Zone* episodes at least twice for inspiration. This part of the ride is a somewhat disorienting experience, in part because the elevator moves horizontally.

What happens next depends upon the whim of Disney Imagineers, who have programmed the ride so that the drop sequence is chillingly random. At the top (about 157 feet up), passengers can look out at the Studios below. Once the doors shut, you plummet 13 stories. The drop lasts about two seconds, but it seems a whole lot longer.

Just when you think it's over, the elevator launches skyward, barely stopping before it plunges again. And again. As you exit, Rod Serling claims this is the kind of thing "they don't tell you about in any guidebook." It's been our privilege to prove him wrong.

From the time you are seated, the trip takes about five minutes. Note that you must be at least 40 inches tall to ride. It is not recommended for pregnant women, people with heart conditions, or with back or neck problems. Though thrilling (and scary), the drops are surprisingly smooth. Still, if you'd rather not experience the sensation of being a human yo-yo, sit this one out.

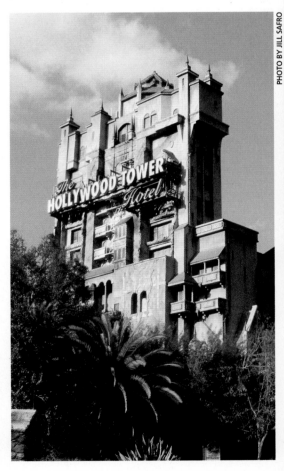

PHOTO BY JILL SAFRO

Rock 'n' Roller Coaster Starring Aerosmith FP+

BIRNBAUM'S BEST The fastest roller coaster in Walt Disney World history is guaranteed to rock your world. Rock 'n' Roller Coaster is ideally suited for those who consider the Tower of Terror just a little on the tame side.

The indoor attraction reaches a speed of nearly 60 miles per hour—in 2.8 seconds flat. Other twists include two loops and a corkscrew —marking the first time Disney has turned guests upside down on American soil.

The ride's premise is this: The rock band Aerosmith has invited you to a backstage party. The only thing standing between you and the big bash is a classically chaotic Los Angeles freeway.

To get to the party on time, you'll have to zip through the nighttime L.A. streets in a stretch limo. The ride vehicles (designed to resemble limousines) are equipped with a high-tech sound system (five speakers per seat make for a mega-decibel ride), and the remainder of the journey features rockin' synchronized sound—adding a very dramatic dimension to the roller coaster experience most daredevils have come to expect.

You must be free of back, neck, and heart problems to experience this topsy-turvy tour. Expectant mothers should sit this one out. Guests must be at least 48 inches tall to ride.

HOT TIP!

This park will have major areas under construction for the foreseeable future, as Imagineers build Toy Story Land, Star Wars Land, and other new play zones. Until the dust settles, consider this a good park to "hop" to or from, using a multiday ticket with park-hopping privileges.

Beauty and the Beast– Live on Stage FP+

BIRNBAUM'S BEST Here's the show that inspired the Broadway musical. Several times each day, Belle, Gaston, Mrs. Potts, and the rest of the cast of the Disney film *Beauty and the Beast* come to life at the 1,500-seat Theater of the Stars, near the Tower of Terror, on Sunset Boulevard.

PHOTO BY JILL SAFRO

The 30-minute show is as entertaining as they come. The staging is just right and the music's simply addictive as it traces the classic tale—from Belle's dissatisfaction with her life in a small French town to the climactic battle between the staff of the Beast's castle and Gaston and the townspeople. Lumiere and friends perform the song "Be Our Guest" with a delightful display of dancing flatware. Check a park Times Guide for the performance schedule.

Voyage of The Little Mermaid FP+

One of Disney's Hollywood Studios' most popular attractions, this is a 17-minute live musical production, adapted from the Disney animated classic. The show is presented in a theater with an underwater feel. In it, many of the film's beloved animated characters, such as Flounder, Scuttle, and Sebastian, are brought to life by puppeteers. The show opens with a lively rendition of "Under the Sea," then animated clips from the movie are shown as performers join the puppets on stage.

Ariel is the star and performs songs from the film. Prince Eric makes an appearance, and an enormous Ursula glides across the stage to steal Ariel's voice. Of course, as in the movie, the happy ending prevails. The story line is a little bit disjointed, hopping from scene to scene, and some of the signature songs are missing. However, most viewers are familiar with the film, so this choppiness doesn't detract much from the show.

PHOTO BY JILL SAFRO

There are a number of special effects, including cascading water, lasers, and a lightning storm that may be a bit frightening for very young children. Note that many of the effects are best enjoyed from the middle to the rear of the theater. Keep in mind that, although this is a Fastpass+ attraction, performances are still presented at scheduled times throughout the day. Current showtimes are always listed on the Times Guide (available at many locations throughout the park). Plan to arrive at least 15 to 30 minutes before showtime.

Disney Junior– Live on Stage! FP+

Fans of Disney Junior shows should enjoy this live, audience-participation production. It features several kid favorites—*Mickey Mouse Clubhouse*, *Doc McStuffins*, *Sofia the First*, and *Jake and the Never Land Pirates* (all from popular Disney Junior TV shows). Familiar characters engage guests with stories, song, and dance as they visit each of the aforementioned Disney Junior realms. The fun culminates with a birthday party for Minnie Mouse. Very young guests tend to be the most enthusiastic members of the audience.

The performance space holds large crowds (of mostly tiny people) at a time. There are a few seats, but there's plenty of room to sprawl out on the carpeted floor. This show is presented in the Animation Courtyard area of the theme park. The park Times Guide lists performance times.

Toy Story Midway Mania! FP+

BIRNBAUM'S BEST This engaging experience is an energetic, interactive toy box tour with a twist: Guests wear 3-D glasses as they take aim at animated targets with toy cannons. The adventure is about as high-tech as they come, yet rooted in classic midway games of skill. As points are scored, expect effusive encouragement from a cast of cheerleaders—*Toy Story*'s Woody, Buzz, Hamm, Rex, Trixie, and, of course, the Green Army Men.

Fans of the Magic Kingdom's Buzz Lightyear's Space Ranger Spin will no doubt delight in this adventure, which takes the experience of the interactive attraction into a whole new dimension. As far as skill level goes, there's something for everyone at Toy Story Mania!—from beginners to seasoned gamers alike.

Note: This is a wildly popular attraction with guests of all ages. Get there as early in the morning as you can, and try to snag a Fastpass+ assignment as far in advance as possible. The herky-jerky motion of this ride (as the vehicles move from scene to scene) may be too much for folks with sensitive backs or other health issues.

HOT TIP!

Don't sweat the accuracy number in Toy Story Midway Mania!—it's meaningless. Fire as fast and furiously as possible. That way, you'll hit more targets in less time!

The Great Movie Ride FP+

Housed in a full-scale reproduction of historic Grauman's Chinese Theatre, this 19-minute attraction grabs guests' imaginations from the get-go. The queue area winds through a lobby and into the heart of filmmaking, where movie scenes are shown on a big screen. The pre-show and post-show, both featuring classic clips, were recently updated by The Great Movie Ride's apt partner: Turner Classic Movies (TCM).

The guided tour begins in an area reminiscent of the hills of Hollywood (which, as the famous, now abbreviated, sign indicates, was once known as Hollywoodland) in its heyday. As a ride vehicle whisks guests under a vibrant marquee, they are transported to the celluloid world of yesteryear. About 60 dancing mannequins atop a cake greet guests in a replay of the

PHOTO BY JILL SAFRO

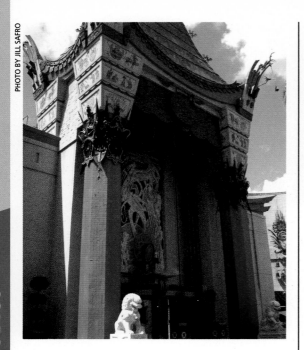

"By a Waterfall" scene from the Busby Berkeley musical *Footlight Parade*.

Gene Kelly's memorable performance from *Singin' in the Rain* is the next scene, in which rain seems to drench the soundstage but does not dampen the spirits of the Audio-Animatronics representation of Mr. Kelly. (Gene Kelly personally inspected his likeness.) Then Mary Poppins and Bert the chimney sweep entertain (Julie Andrews and Dick Van Dyke, respectively), as Mary floats from above via her magical umbrella and Bert sings "Chim Chim Cher-ee" from a rooftop.

Toy Story Land

To infinity and beyond! The re-imagining of Disney's Hollywood Studios will transport park guests to the adventurous outdoors of Andy's backyard. The new 11-acre land will be scaled to make people feel like they've been shrunk to the size of Woody, Buzz, and the gang. Using toys like building blocks, game board pieces, and plastic buckets, Andy is designing the perfect setting for this land. In addition to a higher capacity Toy Story Midway Mania! attraction, the new land will feature a family-friendly Slinky Dog roller coaster and an Alien Saucers attraction in which guests take a spin in a flying saucer and try to elude the legendary Claw. For updates on this playful new zone, visit *www.disneyworld.com*.

HOT TIP!

As new blockbusters are planned for this star-struck theme park, these attractions have ended their run: The Magic of Disney Animation; Studio Backlot Tour; Lights, Motors, Action! Extreme Stunt Show; Honey, I Shrunk the Kids Play Set Adventure; and the American Film Institute Showcase. For updates on replacement attractions, visit *www.disneyworld.com*.

From the world of musical entertainment, guests segue to adventure. James Cagney re-creates his role from *Public Enemy* as the ride proceeds along Gangster Alley. A mob shoot-out begins and puts guests in the midst of an ambush. An alternate route leads to a Western town, where John Wayne can be seen on horseback eyeing some would-be bank robbers. When the thieves blow up the safe and flames pour from the building, heat can be felt from the trams.

As the ride vehicle glides into the spaceship from *Alien*, Officer Ripley guards the corridor while a slimy monster threatens riders from overhead. Note that this and other scenes may be unsettling for young children.

The legendary farewell from *Casablanca* is also depicted, complete with a lifelike Rick and Ilsa. (Ingrid Bergman's daughter Isabella Rossellini once brought her kids here to "see Grandma.") Guests are moved from the airfield to the swirling winds of Munchkinland, where a house has just fallen on the Wicked Witch of the East. Her sister, as portrayed by Margaret Hamilton, appears in a burst of smoke. This Audio-Animatronics figure is realistic—and scary. But happy endings prevail, and guests follow Dorothy and company along the Yellow Brick Road to the Emerald City of Oz. As the ride draws to an end, guests view a revitalized montage of classic movie moments.

Walt Disney— One Man's Dream

Follow Walt Disney from "Mickey Mouse to the Magic Kingdoms" in this multi-media exhibit next to the Voyage of The Little Mermaid attraction. Among the treasures included in this tribute to the man behind the mouse are Walt's second-grade school desk, the original Audio-Animatronics Abraham Lincoln from the 1964 New York World's Fair, *Mickey Mouse Club* props, Jungle Cruise and Spaceship Earth models, costumes from *Mary Poppins*, and more.

Cap off your trip down memory lane with a screening of *In Walt's Words*. The 15-minute film, presented in a theater in the back of the gallery, is hosted by Julie Andrews. Seating is on a first-come, first-served basis.

Note: This attraction may not be operating in all of 2017.

Indiana Jones™ Epic Stunt Spectacular FP+

Earthquakes, fiery explosions, and other dramatic events give guests insight into the science of movie stunts and effects at this 2,000-seat amphitheater. Stunt people re-create scenes from Indiana Jones films and demonstrate the skills required to keep audiences on the edge of their seats. But the 30-minute show isn't all flying leaps. Guests also see how the elaborate stunts are pulled off—safely—while the crew and an assistant director explain what goes on both in front of and behind the camera.

In one segment, a dramatic scene from *Raiders of the Lost Ark* is staged. A 12-foot-tall rolling ball chases a Harrison Ford look-alike out of the temple. The steam and flames are so intense that the audience can feel the heat. The crew then dismantles the set, revealing the remarkable lightness of movie props, as assistants roll the ball uphill for the next show.

In a scene at a busy "Cairo" street market, "extras" chosen from the audience play the scene in which Indy pulls a gun while others are fighting with swords. The explosive action continues and leads to a desert finale in which the hero and his sweetheart make a death-defying escape.

There are moments during this show when audience members might wonder if something has actually gone wrong. But by revealing tricks of the trade, the directors and stars show that what appears to be dangerous is actually a safe, controlled bit of movie magic.

Star Tours—The Adventures Continue FP+

BIRNBAUM'S ★BEST Inspired by George Lucas's blockbuster series of Star Wars films, this beloved attraction— which originally opened in 1989—is better than ever. A new Star Tours experience touched down in 2011, complete with a new story line and eye-popping technology. The 3-D experience offers guests the opportunity to ride on StarSpeeders, the exact same type of flight simulator used by military and commercial airlines to train pilots.

A galaxy of trouble awaits Jedi wannabes, but fear not—the Force will be with you. The best part? There are more than 50 different adventures, so multiple visits yield multiple surprises—and several of those surprises involve scenes from the recent blockbuster and instant classic *Star Wars: The Force Awakens*.

This is a turbulent trip—seat belts are definitely required. Passengers must be free of back problems, heart conditions, motion sickness, and other physical limitations to ride. Guests under 40 inches tall and kids younger than 3 may not ride. Pregnant women must skip this one. To all who ride: Fasten your seat belt and may the Force be with you!

HOT TIP!

Beware of Stormtroopers! Captain Phasma leads a battery of the baddies from Star Wars Launch Bay to a stage by The Great Movie Ride several times a day. Check a park Times Guide for the schedule of Captain Phasma's First Order Stormtrooper March.

Star Wars Launch Bay

Guests don't have to wait for Star Wars Land to be completed to get a fix of the Force—Star Wars Launch Bay offers an immersive atmosphere in which to experience both the Light and Dark sides. Housed in the space formerly occupied by Art of Animation, Launch Bay features props and movie memorabilia (some genuine, some replicas) celebrating Star Wars and the recently reawakened Force. In addition to Light and Dark galleries, guests may meet characters such as Chewbacca and Kylo Ren. The Launch Bay may not be open in all of 2017— check *www.disneyworld.com* for updates.

Jedi Training— Trials of the Temple

Jedi Padawans can learn to harness the Force and properly wield a lightsaber right here in Disney's Hollywood Studios. The 30-minute training program is offered several times a day. To participate, potential participants (ages 4 to 12) should sign up at the Indiana Jones Adventurers Outpost (between Indiana Jones Epic Stunt Spectacular and the 50s Prime Time Cafe) as early as possible (during regular park hours). Kids who make the cut (determined on a first-come, first-served basis) receive a receipt complete with a time to return.

Arrive about 30 minutes before showtime to receive a loaner cloak. When the Jedi master arrives, kids receive lightsabers (strictly for the show) and start the training session. Instruct kids to pay attention to the lesson—they'll need their new skill set to search for a hidden temple and face their fears, not to mention simulate a lightsaber battle against Kylo Ren and other representatives of the dark side. Check a Times Guide for the schedule.

Muppet★Vision 3-D FP+

BIRNBAUM'S ★BEST★ One of the most entertaining attractions at the Studios, this 3-D movie is quite remarkable. A funny 12-minute pre-show gives clues about what's to come. Once inside the theater, many will notice that it looks just like the one from Jim Henson's classic TV series *The Muppet Show*. Even the two curmudgeonly fellows, Statler and Waldorf, are sitting in the balcony, bantering with each other and offering their typically critical commentary on the show.

The production comes directly from Muppet Labs, presided over by Dr. Bunsen Honeydew—

and his long-suffering assistant, Beaker—and introduces Waldo, the "Spirit of 3-D." Among the highlights is Miss Piggy's solo, which Bean Bunny turns into quite a fiasco. Sam Eagle's grand finale leads to trouble as a veritable war breaks out, culminating with a cannon blast to the screen, courtesy of everyone's favorite Swedish Chef.

Including the pre-show, expect to spend about 29 minutes with Kermit and company. Shows run continuously throughout the day. Note that guests must wear 3-D glasses to enjoy this show. If your child is too young to keep the glasses on, skip this Muppet encounter.

Note: The Muppet★Vision 3-D attraction may not be operating in all of 2017.

For the First Time in Forever: A Frozen Sing-Along Celebration FP+

Have you ever heard of a song called "Let It Go"? Yep, we thought so. But have you ever had the privilege of singing it with Queen Elsa herself? Now's your chance! In fact, the whole *Frozen* gang is on hand for a spirited audience-participation sing-along.

Presented in the Hyperion Theater (the building that formerly housed The American Idol Experience), the 30-minute show features a retelling of the *Frozen* story, courtesy of a duo of Arendelle storytellers. It includes clips from the beloved film (presented on a ginormous screen) and live appearances by Anna, Elsa, and Kristoff. Guests of all ages are encouraged to sing along with a few *Frozen* ditties. Don't know all the words? Just follow the bouncing snowflake.

This celebration is very popular with *Frozen* fans of all ages—book a Fastpass+ assignment as far in advance as possible. You won't regret it.

Toy Story Camera Department

Hey, howdy, hey! How'd you like to meet Woody and Buzz? Just follow the letter tiles across the way from Toy Story Midway Mania!, and you will be deposited at Woody's Picture Shootin' Corral. That's where guests have the opportunity to meet the aforementioned character friends, pose for photos, and share a toy story or two. "Meetin' Times" are listed on the sign out front.

FP+ = Fastpass+ attraction (see page 25)

Shopping

Hollywood Boulevard

CELEBRITY 5 & 10: Modeled after a 1940s Woolworth's, this large shop carries housewares such as pillows, towels, teapots, aprons, and Mickey ice-cube trays, plus items that can be personalized—including Mouse ears.

COVER STORY: A small area located just through The Darkroom, this is the place to pick up your picture if you've had it taken by any of the park photographers.

CROSSROADS OF THE WORLD: In the middle of the entrance plaza, Mickey Mouse keeps watch from atop this Hollywood Boulevard landmark. The kiosk deals mostly in pins, but has souvenirs, sundries, hats, and sunglasses, plus park guidemaps and Times Guides. This is also the place to stop if you'd like to rent a locker.

THE DARKROOM: The Art Deco facade of this shop features a giant camera, so it's easy to find. Cameras (including the disposable kind) and photography accessories are sold here.

KEYSTONE CLOTHIERS: Women's and men's fashions and accessories are Keystone Clothiers' specialties of the house.

MICKEY'S OF HOLLYWOOD: The place to find character shirts, hats, plush toys, watches, socks, bags, books, and sunglasses, plus items emblazoned with the Studios park logo. It has a penny-press machine, too.

MOVIELAND MEMORABILIA: This kiosk, located just to the left of the Studios' main entrance, stocks shoes, bags, stuffed toys, hats, sunglasses, key chains, and other souvenirs.

Movieland Memorabilia is accessible from both inside and outside the park entrance

OSCAR'S SUPER SERVICE: In addition to renting strollers and wheelchairs, Oscar stocks diapers, strollers (to buy), snacks, sundries, soft drinks, and souvenirs.

Sunset Boulevard

LEGENDS OF HOLLYWOOD: Modeled after the Academy Theater, which was built in Inglewood, California, in 1939, this store offers items featuring Disney characters and films—with an emphasis on the gang from *Frozen*.

MOUSE ABOUT TOWN: An excellent source for clothing featuring the Mouse. Expect hats, ties, shirts, jackets, pajamas, accessories, and more. There's a line of clothing with a golf theme, and another featuring ESPN.

ONCE UPON A TIME: This shop's exterior replicates the Carthay Circle Theatre in Hollywood, where *Snow White and the Seven Dwarfs* premiered in 1937. The cheery store specializes in children's apparel, plush toys, and souvenirs with Disney touches.

PLANET HOLLYWOOD SUPERSTORE: This shop sells items branded with the P.H. logo. Look for T-shirts, hats, mugs, bottle openers, rain gear, and more. P.H.S. also displays authentic movie memorabilia (some of it is a tad unsettling for tykes). Details may change in 2017.

ROCK AROUND THE SHOP: Survive Rock 'n' Roller Coaster and earn the right to shop here. Look for music-related items, plus shirts, hats, and photos featuring the band Aerosmith.

SUNSET CLUB COUTURE: A sophisticated selection of fashion accessories (watches, bracelets, purses, hats, etc.), plus family apparel with a Mickey or Minnie theme is sold here.

SUNSET RANCH PINS AND SOUVENIRS: This open-air shop carries Disney collector pins, plus plush character toys, souvenirs, memory cards, and assorted sundries.

SWEET SPELLS: This shop within the Beverly Sunset building has a selection of candy, cookies, and other ooey, gooey snack items—and spirits.

TOWER GIFTS: Inside the Hollywood Tower Hotel, near the Tower of Terror exit, this spot specializes in Hollywood Tower Hotel merchandise—shirts, towels, robes, front desk bells, glasses, plates, bellhop hats, handbags, and Tower of Terror Jenga. They also stock a nice selection of collector pins. The shop is a good spot to meet your party should you decide to skip the trip to The Twilight Zone via the Tower of Terror.

REEL VOGUE: Spin your big-screen dreams from reel to real in this elegant emporium of Tinseltown treasure: toys, gifts, games, snacks.

Beyond the Boulevards

LAUNCH BAY CARGO: Located inside the Star Wars Launch Bay, Cargo offers Star Wars–themed collectibles for fans of all ages. It features a nice variety of autographed memorabilia, replica costumes and props, plus books and toys, and more. Guests may customize mobile phone cases, too.

THE DISNEY STUDIO STORE: Expect to find T-shirts, hats, and accessories inspired by Disney films at this Animation Courtyard shop.

IN CHARACTER: In front of the Voyage of The Little Mermaid attraction, this costume shop has everything a child needs to dress like a Disney princess—plus dolls and plush toys.

INDIANA JONES ADVENTURE OUTPOST: Next to the Indiana Jones attraction, you'll discover adventure clothing, as well as memorabilia emblazoned with the Indy insignia.

IT'S A WONDERFUL SHOP: Spot the snowman out front and you've found this perpetual celebration of Christmas. Tree ornaments, stockings, and nutcrackers line the shelves all year long. Ho ho ho!

SPECIAL FX MAKE-UP: Wanna get your face painted like a cat, puppy, princess, superhero or something equally festive? Head here. Most paint jobs cost about $15.

STAGE 1 COMPANY STORE: Situated near the exit of Muppet★Vision 3-D, guests can find toys, shirts, and other merchandise with the likenesses of Kermit the Frog, Miss Piggy, Fozzie Bear, and other Muppet characters, as well as items featuring Mickey and his pals.

TATOOINE TRADERS: A shop near the Star Tours exit, Tatooine Traders has souvenirs themed to *Star Wars*, as well as the Star Tours attraction. This is also the place to "build your own lightsaber." Wanna brag about being selected as the Star Tours Rebel Spy? Pick up a T-shirt here!

Where to Eat in the Studios

A complete listing of eateries at the Studios—full-service restaurants, quick-service emporiums, and snack shops—can be found in the *Good Meals, Great Times* chapter. See the Disney's Hollywood Studios section, beginning on page 260.

Entertainment

In these parts, it's almost always showtime. The following list is a good indication of the Studios' stage presence. As always, we advise that you check a park Times Guide for schedules.

CITIZENS OF HOLLYWOOD: This troupe of enthusiastic performers infuses Hollywood Boulevard with old-time, Tinseltown ambience. Would-be starlets searching for their big break, fans seeking guests' autographs, and gossip columnists chasing leads entertain daily.

JEDI TRAINING: TRIALS OF THE TEMPLE: Star Wars fans and Jedi-wannabes can learn the ways of the Force right here in Walt Disney World. A Jedi Master is on hand to teach young Padawans how to harness the power of the Force and wield a lightsaber, as well as help them fend off a duo of Stormtroopers. Expect an appearance by a notorious villian who will attempt to turn them to the Dark Side. "Younglings" ages 4 through 12 may participate. For additional information, see page 182.

BIRNBAUM'S ★BEST★ STAR WARS: A GALACTIC SPECTACULAR: An aptly named extravaganza, this fireworks show is indeed spectacular. The Star Wars saga plays out in vibrant pyrotechnic bursts, colorful projections, and synchronized sound. It is presented during peak times of year—be sure to catch it if you can. The best vantage point is from Hollywood Boulevard, facing The Great Movie Ride.

STAR WARS: A GALAXY FAR, FAR AWAY: A stage show presented in front of the Great Movie Ride, this intergalactic celebration features iconic moments from the Star Wars saga. Live vignettes shine the spotlight on favorites such as Chewbacca, BB-8, Darth Vader, and others. Check a park Times Guide for the performance schedule.

Trip the Light Fantasmic!

BIRNBAUM'S ★BEST★ FP+ Fantasmic!, a lavish musical production, plays on select nights at The Hollywood Hills Amphitheater on Sunset Boulevard. A dramatic mix of fireworks, fountains, lasers, and Disney characters, it invites guests to take a peek into the dream world of Mickey Mouse.

Though similar to its Disneyland counterpart, half of this 26-minute production is original. The action follows Mickey through a series of dreams. In the first dream, he appears on a mountain, shoots fireworks from his fingertips, and conducts an orchestra of colorful fountains. (Guests seated up front get spritzed.) Soon, Mickey is plagued by nightmares as Disney villains take over his dreams. (This has been known to scare small children.) In the end, the Mouse and his pals prevail (of course!).

Seating begins about 90 minutes before showtime—though some guests line up even earlier. Check a Times Guide for the schedule. We recommend sitting toward the back—the view is good and it's easier to get out after the show. There is standing room, too. After the finale, plan to sit for a bit. It can take 20 minutes for the crowd to exit the theater.

Timing Tip: The show is presented on select nights. Check a Times Guide for the schedule during your visit. On nights when Fantasmic! is presented twice, see the later show. Afterward, as the masses exit the park, take some time to browse the shops that keep their doors open after hours.

HOT TIPS!

DISNEY'S HOLLYWOOD STUDIOS

- Unless you actually enjoy waiting in line, get Fastpass+ assignments whenever you can.

- The line for The Great Movie Ride is generally the longest early in the morning. It thins a bit later in the day.

- Some attractions keep shorter hours than the park itself. Check a Times Guide when you arrive. It lists current hours and schedules.

- Check the My Disney Experience app or website to get an idea of showtimes and crowds.

- Visit Rock 'n' Roller Coaster, Tower of Terror, and Toy Story Midway Mania! very early in the day, before crowds build up.

- Hoping to meet Doc McStuffins and Sofia the First? Know that this is the only WDW park in which they appear. (Refer to the box below.)

- For a table-service meal, make a reservation before you arrive at the park for these eateries: 50's Prime Time Cafe, Mama Melrose's Ristorante Italiano, Hollywood Brown Derby, Sci-Fi Dine-In Theater, or Hollywood & Vine. For reservations, call 407-WDW-DINE (939-3463), visit *disneyworld.com*, or use the My Disney Experience app up to 180 days ahead of your preferred dining date.

- The shops on Hollywood Boulevard are open about half an hour past park closing.

- Tower of Terror is a popular attraction with long lines. Use Fastpass+ whenever possible. And never ride immediately after a meal.

- Your tot may love the Muppets, but if he or she won't wear the glasses necessary to enjoy Muppet★Vision 3-D, skip the attraction.

- Park hoppers, take note: There is a water taxi link between Disney's Hollywood Studios and Epcot. The boat docks to the left as you exit the Studios. You may also reach Epcot, as well as all other parks, by bus. Ambitious athletes may choose to walk. (It'll take you about 25 to 30 minutes to make the trip on foot.)

- Fantasmic! is now offered on most nights. Check a Times Guide to see when it will be offered during your visit. Know that it may be canceled due to inclement weather.

- Many attractions and shows stop admitting guests prior to the park's closing time (and some don't open until a few hours after the park does). Check a Times Guide for schedules. Attractions that you may enter up until the last minute include The Twilight Zone™ Tower of Terror, The Great Movie Ride, Rock 'n' Roller Coaster, Muppet★Vision 3-D, and Star Tours—The Adventures Continue.

- If you choose to skip Fantasmic!, plan to exit the park before the show ends. This way, you'll avoid the inevitable bottleneck at the exit. If you're watching the show, consider making your exit before the big finale.

- Toy Story Midway Mania! is a tremendously popular attraction. If you hope to experience it without sacrificing precious time waiting in the standby line, get a Fastpass+ assignment as soon as possible. Good luck!

Where to Find the Characters

You'll find Disney Channel characters—including Sofia the First, Doc McStuffins, and Jake, the Neverland Pirate—in Animation Courtyard. Woody, Buzz, and other *Toy Story* friends may be found on Pixar Place. Mickey mingles with park-goers in several locations, including Mickey Avenue and in a festive spot dubbed "Mickey and Minnie starring in Red Carpet Dreams." Of course, Minnie appears at that location, too (get a Fastpass+ if you can). Mickey may appear at the park entrance opening time. Goofy, Pluto, Chip, Dale, Daisy, and Donald greet guests in the Center Courtyard. Olaf may be found at the Celebratory Spotlight meet-and-greet location. Disney characters interact with diners at the Hollywood & Vine restaurant, too.

Hidden Mickeys

These are some of the most popular "Hidden Mickeys" at Disney's Hollywood Studios. How many can you find? Check the box when you spot each one.

❤ **Front Entrance Gates:** This is an easy one. Simply look for Mr. Mouse in the grillwork of the gates at the entrance. ■

❤ **Rock 'n' Roller Coaster:** In the pre-show room, look on the floor on the right side of the room just in front of the guitar stand to see some wire coiled into a Hidden Mickey. ■

❤ **Star Tours—the Adventures Continue:** Keep an eye on the folks walking past the "window" in the second room you enter while waiting for the attraction. One of the droids sports mouse ears. ■

There's a Hidden Mickey in the shop at the ride's exit, too—on the front panel of a counter. ■

❤ **Twilight Zone™ Tower of Terror:** Take a peek at the balcony in the lobby, and you may spot a row of Mickeys. ■

Then, as you watch the pre-show, pay close attention to the "disappearing guests." The little girl is clutching a plush Mickey Mouse. ■

❤ **Mama Melrose's Ristorante Italiano:** As you enter, look for the Dalmatian in the waiting area. One of its spots is Mickey-shaped. ■

❤ **Stage 1 Company Store:** Inside the store, locate a tall bureau with paint cans on the top (the shelves are covered with Disney hats for sale). On the desk area, you'll find a green Hidden Mickey. ■

❤ **The Hollywood Brown Derby:** Look for two Hidden Mickeys in the cloud mural outside the restaurant. One is on the left side, above the red Stage 5 sign. ■

The other H.M. can be found on the far upper right-hand side. ■

❤ **Cover Story:** There is a sign in the window of this Hollywood Boulevard shop that says "Melrose." Find it, then look below it for a pattern that creates many Hidden Mickeys in the store's structure. ■

❤ **The Great Movie Ride:** Before you enter the building, find Carol Burnett's footprints out front. When you do, you'll find a Hidden Mickey, too. ■

There is a huge mural in the loading area. If you look at it closely, you will find a Hidden Minnie! (She is toward the center of the mural.) ■

Pay attention to the posters on the left as you enter the gangster area of the ride. When you see a poster for *The Public Enemy*, look in the lower left corner to find Mickey's shoes (they're brown) and his tail poking out from under the poster. ■

You can also spot Mickey Mouse in the Indiana Jones room (aka The Well of Souls). He's hiding in the hieroglyphics on the wall to the left of the ride vehicle. ■

❤ **Muppet★Vision 3-D:** Mickey first appears in a test pattern in the lobby. ■

Next you'll notice him in balloon form during the show's finale. ■

As you exit, you'll see a poster detailing Five Reasons to Return Your 3-D Glasses. Take a close look at the artwork beside number 2. It has a Hidden Mickey! ■

Outside of the attraction, "Director" Gonzo is balancing on a Hidden Mickey raft in the Miss Piggy fountain. Can you spot him? ■

❤ **Toy Story Midway Mania!:** Keep your eyes peeled for a sign that says "Circus Fun!"—the dot in the exclamation point is a pink Hidden Mickey. (The sign is on the wall as the ride vehicle rotates into position for the last game of the ride.) ■

Specifics may change during 2017.

Where in the World?

All of the photos on this page were taken at Disney's Hollywood Studios. Do you know where? We challenge you to find all the spots where these images were shot and snap a photo for yourself as you discover each one. Happy hunting! (For locations, turn to page 356.)

Disney's Animal Kingdom

With a mix of lush landscapes, thrilling attractions, and close encounters with exotic animals, this is clearly a theme park raised to a different level of excitement. Here, guests do more than just watch the action—they live it. They become paleontologists, explorers, and students of nature. And if, by doing so, they leave with nothing more than a great big smile, Disney will have accomplished one of its major goals. But many guests come away with a little bit more: a renewed sense of respect for our planet and for the life-forms we share it with (not to mention a few boffo souvenirs).

The shows and attractions at Disney's Animal Kingdom are meant to engage, entertain, and inspire. They immerse guests in a tropical landscape and introduce them to creatures from the past and present—as well as a few that exist only in our collective imagination.

The park, which is accredited by the Association of Zoos and Aquariums, is home to more than 1,800 animals representing 300 different species. Most of the creatures are of the animate variety, as opposed to the Audio-Animatronics kind. Despite that, you won't see many beasts behind bars here. Instead, you'll go on safari and see a menagerie of wild critters living in spacious habitats, with remarkably few separations visible to the naked eye.

The following pages will help you get the most out of your visit to Disney's Animal Kingdom. It is, after all, a jungle out there.

AFRICA

A Kilimanjaro Safaris
B Gorilla Falls
  Exploration Trail
C Wildlife Express
  to Rafiki's Planet Watch
D Rafiki's Planet Watch
E Festival of the Lion King

DISCOVERY ISLAND

F The Tree of Life
G Discovery Island Trail
H It's Tough to be a Bug!

ASIA

I Flights of Wonder
J Maharajah Jungle Trek
K Kali River Rapids
L Expedition Everest

DINOLAND U.S.A.

M Dinosaur
N The Boneyard playground
O Finding Nemo—The Musical
P Chester & Hester's Dino—Rama!

PANDORA—THE WORLD
OF AVATAR

Q AVATAR Flight of Passage
R Na'vi River Journey

Getting Oriented

Though Disney's Animal Kingdom encompasses about five times the area of its Magic Kingdom counterpart, one need not be in training for the Olympics to tackle it. Most of the land is reserved for non-homo-sapien critters. By all estimates, pedestrians rack up about the same amount of mileage in one day here as they do in a day over at Epcot.

The park's layout is relatively simple: a series of sections, or "lands," connected to a central hub. In this case, the hub is Discovery Island, an island surrounded by a river and home to the Tree of Life, the park's icon. Discovery Island is connected by bridges and paths with all other lands: the Oasis, DinoLand U.S.A., Asia, Africa, and Pandora—The World of AVATAR.

As you pass through A.K.'s entrance plaza, you approach the Oasis. Feel free to meander at a leisurely pace, absorbing the soothing ambience of a thick, elaborate jungle, or you can proceed more quickly and plan to revisit this relaxing region later on. Each of several pathways deposits you at the foot of a bridge leading to Discovery Island. As you emerge from the Oasis, you'll see the awe-inspiring Tree of Life, a 14-story Disney-made tree, looming ahead. The massive tree, which stands near the middle of the island, is surrounded by the Discovery Island Trail.

To the southeast lies DinoLand U.S.A., home of countless prehistoric animals, a fossil dig, a high-spirited stage show called Finding Nemo—The Musical, and an attraction that's sure to induce a mammoth adrenaline surge: Dinosaur. Behind Discovery Island and to the northwest is Africa, where guests may go on an African safari, explore a nature trail, and hop aboard the Wildlife Express train to Rafiki's Planet Watch, the park's research and education center. To the southwest is the park's newest land: Pandora—The World of AVATAR. Its major draws are the thrilling AVATAR Flight of Passage and family-friendly Na'vi River Journey. Asia lies northeast of Discovery Island. Here, guests come face-to-face with the Yeti (aka the Abominable Snowman) on the Expedition Everest thrill ride, encounter real tigers on the exotic Maharajah Jungle Trek, and take a daring journey through the rainforest on a raft at the splashy Kali River Rapids.

HOW TO GET THERE

Take Exit 65 off I-4. Then follow the signs to Disney's Animal Kingdom. Trams run between the parking lot and the main entrance.

By WDW Transportation: From all Walt Disney World resorts: buses. From Disney Springs: bus to any resort or the TTC, then transfer to an Animal Kingdom bus. From the Magic Kingdom: ferry or monorail to the TTC, then bus to Animal Kingdom. From Epcot, Disney's Hollywood Studios, and the resorts on Hotel Plaza Boulevard: buses.

PARKING

All-day parking at Animal Kingdom starts at $20 for day visitors (premium parking costs $35); it's free to guests staying in Walt Disney World-owned-and-operated resorts. Trams circulate lots regularly, providing transportation from the parking area to the park entrance. Be sure to note the section and aisle in which you park. The parking ticket allows for re-entry to the parking area throughout the day.

HOURS

Although hours are subject to change, the gates are generally open daily from about 9 A.M. until about 9 or 10 P.M. During the summer months and other periods, hours may change. It's best to arrive up to a half hour before the official opening time. For current park schedules, call 407-824-4321, or visit *www.disneyworld.com*.

Admission Prices

ONE-DAY BASE TICKET
(Restricted to use only in Animal Kingdom. Prices represent Walt Disney World's Value, Regular, and Peak rates; they do not include tax; and they are likely to rise in 2017.)

Adult ....$97/$102/$114
Child*...$91/$96/$108
*3 through 9 years of age; children under age 3 free

Park Primer

BABY FACILITIES

Changing tables and facilities for nursing mothers can be found at the Baby Care Center on Discovery Island, near Creature Comforts. It's also possible to buy certain necessities, such as formula and diapers, at this facility.

CAMERA NEEDS

Basic supplies such as memory cards, batteries, and disposable cameras are sold at shops such as Garden Gate Gifts, Disney Outfitters, Duka La Filimu, Mombasa Marketplace, and Chester and Hester's Dinosaur Treasures. Note that selfie sticks are not permitted in the park.

DISABILITY INFORMATION

Nearly all of the Animal Kingdom attractions, shops, and restaurants are accessible to guests using wheelchairs. Additional services are available for guests with visual or hearing disabilities. The *Guide for Guests with Disabilities* provides a detailed overview of the services available, including transportation, parking, and attraction access. (For more information, refer to the *Getting Ready to Go* chapter of this book.)

FIRST AID

Minor medical problems can be handled at the First Aid Center, located on Discovery Island on the northwest side of the Tree of Life, near the local Starbucks (aka Creature Comforts).

INFORMATION

Guest Relations, located just inside the park entrance, is equipped with guidemaps, Times Guides, and a helpful staff. Free guidemaps are also available in many shops.

LOCKERS

Lockers are located just inside the main entrance area, near Guest Relations. Cost is $10 for large lockers, $8 for small ones (plus a $5 refundable deposit) for unlimited use all day.

LOST & FOUND

Lost & Found is at Guest Relations, just inside the park entrance. To report lost items after your visit, call 407-824-4245. We recommend affixing contact information to valuables. That'll make them easier to track.

LOST CHILDREN

Report lost children at the park's Baby Care Center, on Discovery Island, and alert the closest Disney employee to the matter.

MONEY MATTERS

There is an ATM at the park entrance and another in DinoLand. Currency exchange is done at Guest Relations. In addition to cash, credit cards (American Express, Diner's Club, Discover Card, JCB, MasterCard, and Visa), Disney gift cards, traveler's checks, and Disney resort IDs and MagicBands (backed up with a credit card) are accepted for admission and merchandise, and meals at most restaurants. Note that Disney Dollars are no longer sold, but they are accepted as cash at most WDW venues.

PACKAGE PICKUP

Shops can arrange for purchases to be sent to Garden Gate Gifts for later pickup or directly to a Walt Disney World resort (packages should be ready for pickup about three hours after purchase). The service is free.

SAME-DAY RE-ENTRY

Be sure to wear your MagicBand or retain your ticket if you plan to return later the same day. A hand-stamp is no longer required.

SECURITY CHECK

Guests entering all Disney parks are subject to a thorough security check. All bags will be searched by security personnel before guests may enter the park. A metal detector screens guests. Weapons (including those of the toy variety) are prohibited. For details and a complete listing of Disney Park Rules, visit a Guest Relations location or go to *www.disneyworld.com/ParkRules*.

STROLLERS & WHEELCHAIRS

Strollers, wheelchairs, and Electric Conveyance Vehicles (ECVs) may be rented at Garden Gate Gifts. The cost is $15 for strollers and $12 for wheelchairs (double strollers cost $31 a day). Length of Stay rentals yield a $2-per-day discount. It's $50 for ECVs, plus a $20 refundable deposit. Quantities are limited (and they run out early in the day). Keep your receipt; it may be used the same day to get a replacement here or at the other theme parks.

The Oasis

Traditionally, one has to travel across a long, sunbaked stretch of desert in order to experience the soothing atmosphere of a tropical oasis. With that in mind, think of the Animal Kingdom parking lot as a concrete version of the Sahara. Once you've trekked across it, your journey takes you through the park's front gate and entrance plaza. What's that up ahead? Could it be a towering African tree? Here in Central Florida? It must be a mirage.

But, no. Within seconds you arrive at the Oasis, a thriving tropical garden filled with waterfalls, running streams, and lush vegetation. The transition is by no means a subtle one. Guests are immediately enveloped in a world of nature. The peaceful setting is most idyllic.

Though not a full-fledged "land" per se, this small jungle simply oozes atmosphere. It is thick and elaborate, and comes complete with critters. (Some are more difficult to spot than others. When searching for the naturally camouflaged creatures, remember to look up occasionally.) As park visitors walk along the pathways, they may catch glimpses of different kinds of animals, from babirusas and iguanas to anteaters and birds. As in the rest of Disney's Animal Kingdom park, there is the illusion that guests are walking among the wildlife.

The Oasis is at once an exciting and calming experience. It sets the stage for what's to come. Guests have several options once they've entered the Oasis. They can continue on a northerly path, making tracks toward the Tree of Life and across a bridge to Discovery Island. They can proceed at a more snail-friendly pace, keeping a tally of the various life-forms that they spot. Or they can simply take time to stop and smell the flowers.

> "I have learned from the animal world. And what everyone will learn who studies it is a renewed sense of kinship with the Earth and all of its inhabitants."
>
> — WALT DISNEY

Timing Tip: Making a trip through the Oasis is the only way to get in (and out of) Animal Kingdom. Some paths can become congested during the hours closest to opening and closing times. To beat the crowds, use a path to the left when you enter and exit the park.

Discovery Island

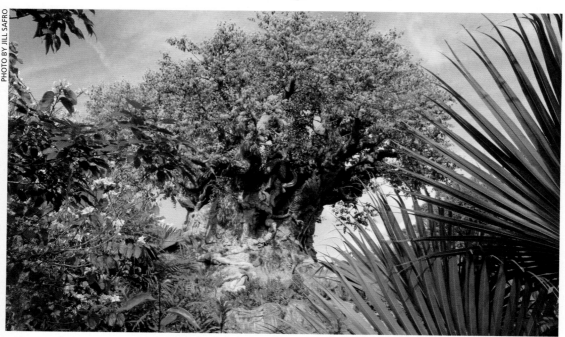

Once you've passed through the Oasis, you will come to a bridge spanning a peaceful river. The bridge leads to Discovery Island, an area at the center of Disney's Animal Kingdom and the hub from which all other realms of the park may be reached.

Discovery Island is defined by the brilliant colors, tropical surroundings, and equatorial architecture of Africa and the South Pacific. The facades of the buildings are all carved and painted based on the art of nations from around the world. Don't fail to notice all the bright, whimsical folk-art images representing various members of the animal kingdom.

This island is the shopping and dining center of Animal Kingdom. Many of the theme park's fast-food restaurants can be found here, including Pizzafari and Flame Tree Barbecue.

HOT TIP!

Take a minute to study a guidemap as you enter Animal Kingdom. It will give you a sense of the layout. The park Times Guide provides information about showtimes for Festival of the Lion King, Finding Nemo— The Musical, and other attractions.

By far the most striking element standing on Discovery Island is the Tree of Life. It is on the map, but chances are you'll have no trouble finding it. Rising from the middle of the island and as tall as a 14-story building, the Tree of Life is hard to miss.

The Tree of Life

The Tree of Life is the dramatic 145-foot icon of Disney's Animal Kingdom. The imposing tree, with its swaying limbs and gnarled trunk, looks an awful lot like the real thing—from a distance. Up close, it's apparent that this is a most unusual bit of greenery. Covered with more than 325 animal images, it is a swirling tapestry of carved figures, painstakingly assembled by a team of artisans. The tree, though inorganic, stands as a symbol of the connected nature of life on Earth. We think Joyce Kilmer would have approved.

DISCOVERY ISLAND TRAIL: The Walkway that wraps around the Tree of Life allow guests to get a close-up view of the trunk and even play a game of "spot the animals." (The spiraling animal images go all the way to the top of the tree. You'll need binoculars if you hope to see them all.) Scattered about the tree's base is a variety of animal habitats. Animals can be seen

Wilderness Explorers

In the movie *Up*, Russell is a very dedicated—and decorated—Wilderness Explorer. He is on a constant quest to add to his merit badge collection. Now Animal Kingdom guests can be Wilderness Explorers, too. Start by heading to the W.E. Headquarters at the Oasis bridge. After taking the official pledge, guests receive field guides describing a variety of challenges. Complete a challenge and earn a badge! There are about 30 different badges to collect. There is no extra charge to become a Wilderness Explorer, and the badges are free. While targeted to the 7- to 10-year-old set, the challenges are fun for the whole family.

in a very open, somewhat traditional park-like setting, with lush grass, trees, and other vegetation. Others to which you may be introduced for the very first time as you meander through the exhibits include ring-tailed lemurs (not quite monkeys' uncles, more like cousins).

THE TREE OF LIFE AWAKENS: The park icon "awakens" each night with a lively projection and music show that features stunning visuals, animal spirits, and enchanted fireflies that combine to reveal stories of wonder and showcase the magic of nature.

BIRNBAUM'S BEST **IT'S TOUGH TO BE A BUG!:** FP+ Inside the trunk of the Tree of Life is a 430-seat auditorium featuring an eight-minute, animated 3-D film augmented by some surprising "4-D" effects. The stars of the show are the world's most abundant inhabitants—insects. They creep, crawl, and demonstrate why, someday, they just might inherit the Earth. It's a bug's-eye view of the trials and tribulations of their multi-legged world.

As guests enter The Tree of Life Repertory Theater, the orchestra can be heard warming up amid the sounds of chirping crickets. When Flik, the emcee (and star of *A Bug's Life*), appears, he dubs audience members honorary bugs and instructs them to don their bug eyes (3-D glasses). Then the mild-mannered ant introduces some of his not-so-mild-mannered cronies, including a Chilean tarantula, dung beetles, and "the silent but deadly member of the bug world"—the stink bug. What follows is a manic, often humorous, revue.

Note: The combination of intense effects and frequent darkness tends to terrify tots and young kids. And anyone at all leery of spiders, roaches, and their ilk is advised to skip the performance, or risk being seriously bugged.

WINGED ENCOUNTERS—THE KINGDOM TAKES FLIGHT: This show features flocks of colorful macaws. Because of their claws? No, because they're macaws! (Sorry, we just couldn't resist a quote from the Enchanted Tiki Room.) Six types of the beautiful bird, some with wingspans of up to 60 inches, are included: hyacinth, green-winged, blue and gold, scarlet, blue-throated, and military. Expect them to swoop and soar overhead and over Discovery Island. Check a park Times Guide for showtimes.

DISCOVERY ISLAND CARNIVALE: As the daylight hours come to an end, Discovery Island comes to life with its nightly cavalcade of dancers, stilt walkers, musicians, and more. The jubilant jamboree was inspired by Carnivale celebrations from around the globe.

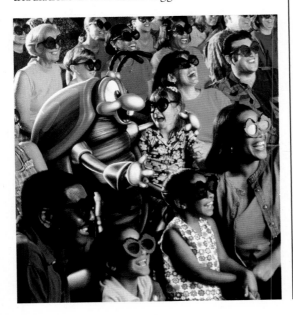

Africa

The largest section of Disney's Animal Kingdom, Africa, is bigger than the whole Magic Kingdom park. This 110-acre, truer-than-life replica of an African savanna is packed with pachyderms, giraffes, hippos, and other wild beasts. All guests enter Africa through Harambe, a village based on a modern East African coastal town. It is the dining and shopping center of Animal Kingdom's version of Africa.

The instant you walk across the bridge to Harambe, you are transported to Africa. Everything here is authentic, from the architecture to the landscaping to the merchandise in the marketplace. The result was achieved after Disney Imagineers made countless trips to the continent. After seven years of observing, filming, and photographing the real thing, they re-created it here in North America. It even feels a bit warmer here than it does at the other theme parks!

The animals that live here, however, are not re-creations. They are quite real, most varied, and extremely abundant. In fact, this chunk of land puts the animal in Animal Kingdom.

Kilimanjaro Safaris FP+

BIRNBAUM'S ★BEST★ The Kilimanjaro Safaris have something for everyone: lovely landscapes, majestic, free-roaming animals, and a thrilling adventure. It is everything you may expect from an actual trip to Africa, and (hopefully) more.

The 20-minute safari begins with a brief introduction from a guide who does double duty as your driver.

HOT TIP!

There's no need to stampede toward the Kilimanjaro Safaris ride first thing in the morning—the animals are out and active throughout the day. That said, if you do ride early, consider coming back later in the day. The beauty of this attraction is that you tend to see something new each time you ride.

Once you climb aboard the ride vehicle, look at the plates above the seat in front of you. They will help you identify the animals you see. And have those cameras ready.

As the vehicle travels along dirt roads, you'll spot free-roaming wild animals: zebras, antelope, hippos, elephants, warthogs, rhinos, lions, and more. Some animals wander near your vehicle, and others cross its path. (Don't worry—only the harmless critters can approach. Others, such as lions and cheetahs, are unable to invade your safe, personal space.)

The majesty of the Serengeti may lull you into a state of serenity, but it's merely the calm before the storm. You'll soon be jostled and jolted as the vehicle crosses pothole-filled terrain, rickety bridges, and flooded dirt roads.

Good news, safari fans—nighttime safaris have become a reality. While the Kilimanjaro Safaris attraction is enjoyable at any time of day, it's nice to ride before *and* after the sun sets. Day or night, try to get a Fastpass+ assignment—the lines can be lengthy at this popular destination. It can be challenging to spot distant animals in low light, but the overall experience is pretty cool—and some animals are more active at night.

If you're prone to motion sickness, back trouble, or have other physical limitations, sit this one out. The ride is a rather bumpy one.

PHOTO BY JILL SAFRO

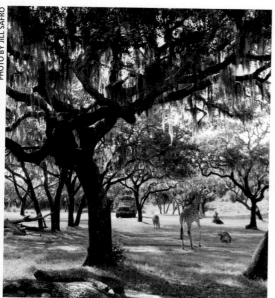

PHOTO BY JILL SAFRO

Festival of the Lion King FP+

BIRNBAUM'S ★BEST★ In addition to rustling up grubs in their new neighborhood, the talented cast of *The Lion King* performs a 30-minute stage show in the new Harambe Theater.

Presented in the round, this lavish musical revue is as bright and boisterous as they come. The dramatic opening features a parade of performers in colorful costumes. What follows is an intriguing, energetic interpretation of the film, including songs, dances, and acrobatics. With the exception of Timon, who plays himself, lead characters are portrayed by humans draped in bold African costumes.

Songs include Scar's nasty version of "Be Prepared," as well as "The Circle of Life," and a rousing rendition of "The Lion Sleeps Tonight."

Timing Tip: Although this theater accommodates nearly 1,400 guests at a time, plan to arrive at least 45 minutes before a performance time.

> "How could this earth of ours, which is only a speck in the heavens, have so much variety of life, so many curious and exciting creatures?"
>
> — WALT DISNEY

Gorilla Falls Exploration Trail

This self-guided walking trail winds past communities of gorillas and other rare African animals. Access it at the end of the Kilimanjaro Safaris or by the entrance in Harambe.

The first major stop on the trail (previously known as Pangani, which translates to "place of enchantment" in Swahili) is the Research Station.

Just outside are a free-flight aviary and an aquarium teeming with fish. Not far away is the hippo exhibit, which provides close-up views of hippopotamuses both in and out of water.

Farther along the trail there is a scenic overlook point, where you can get an unobstructed view of the African savanna. This is also known as the "Timon" exhibit, featuring a family of perky meerkats. Afterward, you may catch an up-close glimpse (through a glass wall) of a cavorting gorilla or two.

As you come to the end of the suspension bridge, you'll find yourself in a beautiful green valley. Congratulations! You've finally reached the gorilla area—an experience well worth the wait. (Note that you may have to wait a little bit longer for that first gorilla sighting. Our evolutionary cousins have been known to play hide-and-seek in the lush vegetation.)

Rafiki's Planet Watch

On the east side of the village of Harambe is the Harambe Train Station. That's where you board the Wildlife Express and experience a behind-the-scenes look at a Disney park while en route to Rafiki's Planet Watch.

As part of the 5½-minute, narrated trip, you'll glide past the buildings where animals sleep. All guests disembark at the Rafiki's Planet Watch station and cover the remaining distance on foot. (It's about a 5-minute walk—and you may encounter Disney characters and/or animal experts en route.) Note that you will have to reboard the Wildlife Express train to return to Harambe Village.

While Animal Kingdom's stories often carry a conservation theme, this part really brings the message home. This is the park's conservation headquarters and veterinary lab, as well as the research and education hub. Exhibits are geared to spark curiosity about wildlife and conservation efforts around the world. Here are a few highlights:

Habitat Habit!: An outdoor discovery trail that yields glimpses of cotton-top tamarins, and helpful hints on how to share our world with all members of the animal kingdom.

Affection Section: An animal encounter area with critters (mostly goats) to see and touch. This is an enjoyable experience for young guests. Be sure to stop at the hand-washing station before leaving this area.

Conservation Station: The center of Disney's effort to promote wildlife conservation awareness. Be sure to take note of the huge animal murals—they are beautiful and chock-full of Hidden Mickeys. Inside, you'll also find:

Animal Cams: Use these guest-operated video cameras to spy on gorillas, hippos, bats, and other critters throughout the park.

Rafiki's Planet Watch Video: This show provides information about endangered animals.

Song of the Rainforest: A thoroughly entertaining "3-D" audio show that surrounds guests with sounds of the rainforest.

Note that Rafiki's Planet Watch is an excellent place to meet Rafiki himself, as well as other Disney character friends.

DID YOU KNOW?

There are 27 million gallons of water in Animal Kingdom's Discovery River. That's enough water to fill about 1,800 average-sized swimming pools!

HARAMBE WILDLIFE PARTI: Party animals, aka uninhibited theme park guests, are invited to dance and frolic with special entertainers and local street musicians and enjoy the rousing rhythms of live African music. It's also possible to sample some exotic food and drink (note that fees apply). Check a park Times Guide for the day's Harambe Wildlife Parti performance schedule.

Let There Be … Night Light!

BIRNBAUM'S ★BEST★ FP+ After the sun sets on the savannah, Animal Kingdom guests gather along the Discovery River for the park's new nighttime spectacular known as Rivers of Light. The illuminating musical experience celebrates the magic of animals (including humans) and the natural world. It features a blend of lively performers, glowing lanterns that float in the air, and theatrical animal imagery.

The ceremony begins with the arrival of a pair of mystical hosts, two complimentary forces who come to the river bearing gifts of light. They set out from shore on lantern vessels, engaging in a dramatic dance of water and light to summon the animal spirits. With these storytellers as guides, the wonders of the show unfold, building to a dramatic finale, complete with bursts of light as animal images soar to the sky—signifying the ancient belief that when animals passed from one world to another, they danced in the sky and became beautiful rivers of light.

Timing Tip: The show is presented on most nights—and it is wildly popular. Do your best to secure a Fastpass+ assignment well in advance. If not, plan to arrive at least an hour before the show starts. Check a Times Guide for the schedule during your visit. Afterward, as the masses exit the park, take some time to browse the shops that may keep their doors open a bit after hours.

Pandora— The World of AVATAR

According to the blockbuster film *Avatar*, Earthlings have a distant, idyllic destination to look forward to in the 22nd century: Pandora, a magnificent moon orbiting the planet Polyphemus about 4.4 light-years from Earth. Pandora, with its lush, bioluminescent rainforest environment, is home to floating mountains and incredible life forms, including trees that stand a thousand feet tall and a myriad of infinitely diverse creatures—such as native people known as the Na'vi. These blue humanoids travel via flying Mountain Banshees and have a sophisticated culture based on a deep connection to each other and all life on Pandora. That connection is made possible via the majestic and sacred Tree of Souls.

If Pandora sounds like a place you'd like to visit, you're not alone—*Avatar* was one of the biggest movie sensations of all time. The good news is humans don't have to wait until the 22nd century to visit the wondrous world of Pandora. Thanks to a bit of Disney Imagineering magic, Pandora has come to Animal Kingdom. At press time, this new land—and its two major attractions —was expected to open by mid- to late 2017.

AVATAR Flight of Passage FP+

BIRNBAUM'S BEST The crowning jewel of Animal Kingdom's newest neighborhood, AVATAR Flight of Passage invites daredevils to take a scenic trip to Pandora on the back of a flying Mountain Banshee. The intense 3-D journey takes place in a cutting-edge, simulator-like environment and offers much more than a thrill a minute. Guests are treated to a bird's-eye view of all the sights, sounds, and smells of the majestic moon that the Na'vi call home.

A high-flying "E-Ticket" attraction, Flight of Passage is a most realistic, immersive experience. It is not recommended for guests with motion sensitivity, heart conditions, fear of heights, or any other physical issues. This attraction is quite popular—book a Fastpass+ assignment if you can. For height requirements, visit *www.disneyworld.com*.

HOT TIP!

As this book went to press, Animal Kingdom's newest land, Pandora—The World of AVATAR, was on course to open by mid- to late 2017. As with all projects of this magnitude, construction may go faster or take longer than anticipated. For updates on the progress of this new theme park play zone, visit *www.disneyworld.com*.

Na'vi River Journey FP+

A musical voyage into Pandora's bioluminescent forest, this trip is as calm and family-friendly as they come. The adventure begins as guests board canoes and venture down a mysterious, sacred river hidden within the rainforest. The grandeur of Pandora is revealed as canoes float past exotic glowing plants and an array of amazing creatures, including native humanoids known as Na'vi. The journey culminates in an encounter with a Na'vi shaman, who has a deep connection to the life force of Pandora and sends positive energy into the forest with her music.

Na'vi River Journey is generally appreciated by guests of all ages (though timid tykes who are spooked by darkness may find parts of this expedition a tad unsettling).

DID YOU KNOW?

The common spirit of Pandora—where all life forms are constantly connected to each other, the environment, and their host planet—is based on the concept of Gaia, proposed by chemist James Lovelock in 1970 and described in Isaac Asimov's novel *Foundation's Edge* in 1982.

DISNEY'S ANIMAL KINGDOM

Asia

PHOTO BY JILL SAFRO

HOT TIP!

Everyone and everything gets wet on Kali River Rapids. Items that simply must stay dry should be stored in a locker (across the pathway at the attraction's entrance) or with a non-riding member of your party.

On the far side of a Himalayan-style bridge, beyond an ancient temple, lies the tranquil village of Anandapur (Sanskrit for "place of delight"). The buildings' design was inspired by structures in Thailand, Indonesia, and other Asian countries known for their rich architectural history.

A product of Disney Imagineering, the village epitomizes the complex, enduring relationship between the animals and ecosystems of the Asian continent. The tiny village borders an elaborate re-creation of a Southeast Asian rainforest. As such, Disney's Asia is an ideal location for trekking through the lush jungle, shooting the rapids on a raging river, and gazing upon the multi-hued inhabitants of this treasured terrain.

Kali River Rapids FP+

Before guests board rafts at Kali (pronounced KAH-lee) River Rapids, a wise voice admonishes that "the river is like life itself, full of mysterious twists and turns." What the voice doesn't say is that this particular river is also full of splashing water and a blazing inferno. This may be business as usual for some daring souls, but for most of us, these elements make for one dramatic, drenching adventure.

All guests begin the journey in the offices of Kali River Rapids Expeditions, a river rafting company. A slide show offers a look at the sometimes unscrupulous business of logging—how it has ravaged the rainforest and deprived animals of habitats. But, thanks to ecotourism

(among other things), there is hope. Peaceful voyages give people a new appreciation and sense of responsibility for this endangered land.

A 12-seater raft whisks "ecotourists" up a watery ramp and through an arching tunnel of bamboo. It proceeds onward, through a hazy mist and past remnants of an ancient shrine. As the raft moves along curves of the river, guests enjoy views of undisturbed rainforest.

The tranquility is shattered by a startling sight. A huge chunk of forest has been gutted by loggers. On both sides of the river, the forest has vanished. As guests absorb the image, they are besieged by more disturbing sights and sounds. Straight ahead, the river is choked with a tangled arch of burning logs—and the raft is headed straight for it. Suddenly, the rainforest isn't the only thing endangered.

Kali River Rapids is an especially soggy experience. It is the rare guest who leaves the ride without a thorough soaking. Should you wish to repel as much precipitation as possible, pack a plastic poncho. Stash valuables in a nearby locker while you ride (no charge).

Note: This is a very bumpy adventure. In order to experience it, you must be at least 38 inches tall. It is not recommended for pregnant women, guests with heart conditions, people with back or neck problems, or anyone who wishes to stay dry.

Maharajah Jungle Trek

BIRNBAUM'S BEST Welcome to the jungle! The Maharajah Jungle Trek is a self-guided walking tour of a tropical paradise, complete with roaming tigers and dense greenery. Throughout the expedition, trekkers encounter a deluge of flora and fauna typically found in the rainforests of Southeast Asia. Komodo dragons, fruit bats, and a conglomeration of colorful birds call this corner of Animal Kingdom home. Majestic Asian tigers can be spotted stalking ancient ruins, strategically separated from would-be prey. Deer and antelope graze and frolic nearby, blissfully oblivious of their fearsome neighbors' proximity.

Approximately midway through the thicket stands a rustic, tin-roofed assembly hall. Step inside to witness the breathtaking sight of giant fruit bats showing off their six-foot wingspans. As you look through the windows, thinking that the crystal clear glass was cleaned by a super-

diligent window washer, think again. There is no glass in some of the windows—and, therefore, nothing separating you from the giant creatures fluttering about on the other side. What keeps the big bats from getting up close and personal with guests? They're a lot less interested in humans than humans are in them. (Can't say that we blame them.) Note that some viewing areas are adorned with wire or glass—for guests who are more comfortable with a bat buffer.

Flights of Wonder

A 1,000-seat, open-air theater, the Caravan Stage features performances by actors wearing nothing but feathers and the occasional crown. Members of more than 20 different bird species have starring roles in Flights of Wonder, a high-flying celebration of the winged wonders of the world. Hawks, owls, falcons, and even chickens have been known to awe spectators as they swoop, soar, and strut their stuff in each 20-minute performance. Some demonstrate how they hunt. Others display their grape-grabbing or money-grubbing talents. Check a park Times Guide for the schedule. This show has morphed quite a bit from its original incarnation. It's a hoot!

Expedition Everest FP+

BIRNBAUM'S ★BEST Walt Disney World's mountain range is a bit more intense these days, as the world's tallest mountain—Everest—has risen from the peaceful village of Serka Zong in Animal Kingdom's Asia. Like its sister peaks, Space, Splash, and Big Thunder, this E-ticket precipice promises to deliver "coaster thrills, spills, and chills." Does it deliver on that promise? Boy, does it ever.

The attraction features an old tea train chugging and churning as it climbs up and around snowcapped peaks. Suddenly, the track comes to an end in a gnarled mess of twisted metal. Lurching forward and backward, the train hurtles through caverns and icy canyons before depositing guests in the presence of the legendary Yeti (aka the Abominable Snowman)—who's not too happy that you've scaled the mountain he so fiercely protects.

Feeling up to the challenge of a dramatic, high-speed train ride? If you are free of heart, back, and neck problems, are not pregnant, have no fear of heights (or abominable snowpeople), and are at least 44 inches tall, go for it. As always, never eat right before experiencing a ride as topsy-turvy as this one.

HOT TIP!

Fastpass+ assignments for Expedition Everest tend to be gone quickly. Get yours as early as possible.

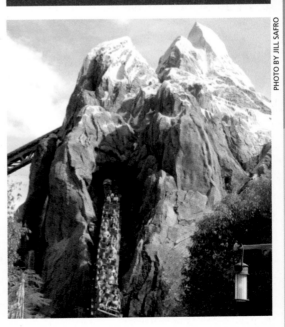

PHOTO BY JILL SAFRO

FP+ = Fastpass+ attraction (see page 25)

DinoLand U.S.A.

If the look and feel of DinoLand U.S.A. seems familiar, there's a reason: It was designed to capture the flavor of roadside America. It is a mixture of culture and kitsch—the likes of which you might stumble upon during a cross-country road trip. Here, you may ride a flying Triceratop, jump into gigantic footprints, and browse through a typically tacky roadside souvenir stand, where you can pick up some dinosaur mementos for the folks back home.

This corner of Animal Kingdom comes complete with its own dramatic entrance: a 50-foot skeleton of a brachiosaurus. As guests stroll beneath the bones, they find themselves smack in the middle of a paleontological dig. Here, guests of all ages (especially little ones) have the chance to play paleontologist as they dig through a fossil-packed pocket of dino discovery.

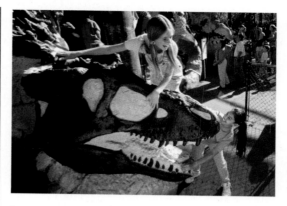

bang out a primitive tune on a bony xylophone (it's located near the car; to make a sound, firmly press on a rib), zip down prehistoric slides, and work their way through a fossil-filled maze. While exploring, watch your step: If you happen to wander into a giant dinosaur footprint, you might be greeted with a somewhat ominous roar.

While in DinoLand, be sure to check out the OldenGate Bridge. It's a gateway structure made from a dinosaur skeleton. The bridge links one end of The Boneyard with the other. This is a good place to take young children while other members of your party ride Dinosaur.

DID YOU KNOW?

Many of the benches in Disney's Animal Kingdom are made of recycled plastic milk jugs. It takes roughly 1,350 jugs to make a single bench.

The dinosaurs that dwell here, though often quite animated, are all of the inanimate variety. But do keep your eyes peeled for the prehistoric life-forms that actually live in this land—that is, for real creatures that exist in the here and now, but whose ancestors kept company with the likes of the carnotaurus and its cousins from the Cretaceous era.

The Boneyard

The Boneyard gives guests—especially the very young ones—an opportunity to dig for fossils in a discovery-oriented playground. They will excavate the ancient bones of a mammoth in this re-creation of a paleontological dig (think huge sandbox). They will also unearth clues that may help them solve the mystery of how and when the creature met its untimely demise.

For serious "boneheads" who just aren't satisfied with simple digging, there are plenty of other bone-related activities here. Youngsters can

Chester & Hester's Dino-Rama!

A colorful land-within-a-land, Chester & Hester's is an area ideally suited for roadside carnival fans. Located just beyond The Boneyard playground, this wild-and-woolly zone features old-fashioned midway games and two rides: Primeval Whirl and TriceraTop Spin.

PRIMEVAL WHIRL: FP+ A small roller coaster (with spinning cars) that seems to have been plucked from a traveling fair, this ride may have a familiar feel to it. By all means, give it a whirl—it's a truly wild ride. You must be at least 48 inches tall to spin. Skip it if you are pregnant or susceptible to motion sickness or think the jarring bumps will cause you discomfort.

PHOTO BY JILL SAFRO

TRICERATOP SPIN: The ride is apt to please fans of the Magic Kingdom's Dumbo the Flying Elephant and the Magic Carpets of Aladdin. Guests ride in one of the 16 flying dinos, each of which resembles an oversize tin toy. It's rather tame when compared to its Dinosaur attraction neighbor, but certainly worth checking out—especially for young dinosaur groupies.

FOSSIL FUN GAMES: Chester & Hester's Dino-Rama is home to several silly games of skill, including Whac-A-Packycephalosaur

Get Involved

When it comes to conservation efforts, the folks at the Walt Disney Company want you to do as they say—and as they do: The Disney Conservation Fund helps nonprofit groups protect and study endangered and threatened animals and habitats. The fund has supported projects from more than 330 non-profit organizations, protecting more than 400 different animal species. And guests who contribute money while making purchases at Animal Kingdom shops and restaurants help make a difference, too.

Of course, as a trip to Animal Kingdom makes clear, there are many ways to help our planet's wild inhabitants. Stop by Rafiki's Planet Watch during your visit. There, you can get information about conservation efforts in your neck of the woods. Don't leave your enthusiasm behind when you leave the park.

(smack mischievous dinos with a mallet), Mammoth Marathon (roll balls into holes to move your woolly mammoth in a race to the finish line), Bronto-Score (basketball toss), Comet Crasher (toss "comets" into moving cups), and Fossil Fueler (a gas-station-themed squirt game). Just like the midway games after which they are modeled, these games come with a fee. Game coupons may be purchased at the souvenir stand in the games area and at Chester & Hester's Dinosaur Treasures. Each game costs about $3 per person. Dino-themed prizes are awarded to winners.

If you'd rather stick to included-with-the-price-of-admission diversions, we highly recommend checking out the fun-house mirror for some simple, silly fun.

HOT TIP!

For a slightly less turbulent experience on the Dinosaur attraction, request an inside seat near the front of the ride vehicle.

Dinosaur FP+

BIRNBAUM'S ★BEST★ This dizzying adventure begins with guests being strapped into vehicles and catapulted back in time to complete a dangerous, albeit noble, mission: to rescue the last iguanodon—a 16-foot plant-eating dinosaur—and bring him back to the present. The iguanodon, which lived more than 65 million years ago (during the Cretaceous period), just might hold the answer to the mysterious disappearance of his dino brethren.

Throughout the frenetic quest to locate the elusive iguanodon, you cling to an out-of-control vehicle while dodging blazing meteors and a mix of friendly and ferocious dinosaurs. Soon you encounter the carnotaurus—a fearsome, carnivorous dinosaur. The carnotaurus, which has horns like a bull and a face like a toad, is a remarkably unsightly specimen. In fact, all of the dinos move as though they were alive. Even their nostrils move as they "breathe."

This 3½-minute attraction offers more than a thrill a minute. You rocket through time, are practically pelted by meteors, and narrowly escape becoming a dino dinner as the carnotaurus suddenly turns the tables and chases you!

Guests reach the attraction through the Dino Institute, a museum-like building deep in the heart of DinoLand. Here, you'll be treated to a pre-show by Bill Nye the Science Guy (audio only) and see a dinosaur skeleton and an assortment of fossils and other artifacts.

This is an extremely rough (and dark) attraction. You must be at least 40 inches tall to experience it. It should be skipped by pregnant women, or people with heart conditions, back or neck problems, or any other physical limitations. Small kids will most definitely be frightened.

Finding Nemo—The Musical FP+

DinoLand is just about as far off Broadway as one could be. Yet, this show's got the ingredients of a Broadway smash: beloved characters (e.g., Marlin, the overprotective clownfish dad; Nemo, his curious son; and Dory, the endearing royal blue tang with the short-term memory loss); original songs by a Tony-winning composer (Robert Lopez); and dancers, acrobats, and the theatrical puppetry of Michael Curry (who designed the richly detailed puppets seen in the Broadway version of Disney's *The Lion King*). You can catch this 40-minute performance at the enclosed and air-conditioned Theater in the Wild. Check a Times Guide for showtimes—and get there early.

This show has appeal for guests of all ages, but the 40-minute run time is a tad too long for some kids (especially the wee ones).

HOT TIP!

Animal Kingdom veterans may note that Camp Minnie-Mickey is no more. What's happening in the space it once occupied? Disney Imagineers are hard at work, building attractions themed to the film *Avatar*. The dust is expected to settle at Pandora—The World of AVATAR by the end of 2017.

Where to Find the Characters

You'll discover Mickey and Minnie at the Adventurers Outpost on Discovery Island. Pluto and Goofy mingle with guests in DinoLand, by the entrance to Chester & Hester's Dino-Rama. Donald can usually be found nearby, on the Cretaceous Trail. Russell and Dug have a clubhouse on Discovery Island, near It's Tough to be a Bug! Rafiki, Chip, and Dale hang out at Rafiki's Planet Watch. Baloo and King Louie greet folks at Asia's Upcountry Landing (near the Flights of Wonder bird show). Look for Tarzan and Pocahontas on the Discovery Island Trail. Characters such as Daisy, Goofy, and Mickey join Donald for meals at Tusker House in Harambe (near the Kilimanjaro Safaris). Reservations are required for all Tusker House meals.

Shopping

Entrance Area

GARDEN GATE GIFTS: Stop here for souvenirs, snacks, sundries, and camera supplies. ECVs may be rented. (Wheelchairs and strollers are available to rent nearby.) This is also the park's package pickup and PhotoPass viewing location.

OUTPOST: A small shop located just outside the park's entrance, Outpost offers character merchandise, snacks, and more.

Discovery Island

DISCOVERY TRADING COMPANY: This sprawling shop is themed as a shipping company that celebrates working animals— camels, elephants, and others. Here, you'll find character merchandise, clothing, candy, and Disney paraphernalia. The Trading Company stays open about a half hour after the park closes for the day. It's connected to the Riverside Depot, which sells character-themed items.

ISLAND MERCANTILE: Nature-themed gifts and apparel are the stock-in-trade here. There's an abundance of clothing (for the whole family), plus various items with an animal theme and Disney souvenirs. Be sure to check out the authentic carved animal totem poles in the center room—they are rather impressive. Note that this shop stays open about 30 minutes after the park closes for the day.

Africa

DUKA LA FILIMU: Situated near the entrance to Kilimanjaro Safaris, this is an ideal place to load up on photo supplies for your trip.

MOMBASA MARKETPLACE & ZIWANI TRADERS: An African marketplace and trading company, these connected shops feature animal toys, safari clothing, T-shirts, books, and Africa-themed gifts such as pottery, masks, and musical instruments. A woodcarver makes unique crafts onsite.

OUT OF THE WILD: Located just outside the exit of Rafiki's Planet Watch, this open-air shop stocks a variety of souvenirs, including shirts, hats, notebooks, and toys.

ZURI'S SWEETS SHOP: Guests visiting Harambe Market will discover Zuri's, a treat-lover's paradise. In addition to sweets with a *Lion King* theme, Zuri sells items such as wine, African-inspired dinnerware, African-spice popcorn and spice rubs, plus barbecue sauce from Animal Kingdom's Flame Tree Barbecue.

Asia

BHAKTAPUR MARKET: A small shop with a big Asian influence, Bhaktapur sells summer shoes, bags, robes, shirts, teapots and teas, toy dragons and plush animals, chopsticks, and items with a Yak & Yeti theme.

MANDALA GIFTS: A stone's throw from Royal Anandapur Tea Company, this spot offers Asian-inspired clothing, scarves, and handbags, plus souvenirs with the Animal Kingdom park logo.

SERKA ZONG BAZAAR: Located at the exit of Expedition Everest (it can be accessed from the outside for those who skip the ride), this bustling bazaar sells souvenirs with a Yeti theme, plus a slew of shirts, hats, books, frames, etc., that celebrate the Expedition Everest attraction.

DinoLand U.S.A.

CHESTER & HESTER'S DINOSAUR TREASURES: Themed as an American roadside souvenir stand, this shop pays homage to all reptiles and prehistoric animals. There is a small selection of dino-themed merch, but Chester and Hester are more focused on Disney stuff.

THE DINO INSTITUTE SHOP: It should come as no surprise that you'll find dino-themed items and other souvenirs here. It's also the spot to view (and buy) that photo of you looking terrified while riding Dinosaur.

Entertainment

HARAMBE WILDLIFE PARTI: A lively street festival, Harambe Wildlife Parti kicks off daily in the late afternoon. Exotic entertainment includes acts such as Muziki, a musical, stilt-walking shaman; the elegant, dancing Karubi Sisters; the interactive (and comical) skilled soccer antics of the Harambe Soccer Meerkats; and the colorfully costumed Harambe Village Acrobats. The Parti offers the excitement of an African village bursting with entertainment and surprises for all.

DISCOVERY ISLAND CARNIVALE: This exuberant new dance party ends the day and welcomes the night with musicians, stilt walkers, and more. The nightly jubilee winds its way from one end of Discovery Island to the other, eventually arriving at the Discovery Island Stage. Check a park Times Guide for the schedule.

DI-VINE: So convincing is Di-Vine, that many a guest fails to notice she is actually a graceful entertainer and not, well, an actual vine.

HOT TIPS!

- Disney's Animal Kingdom recently extended its hours—it now operates well into the evening.

- Most of Animal Kingdom's attractions take place outdoors. Don't become overheated! Make a point of slipping into air-conditioned shops and restaurants from time to time to cool off.

- Narrow, winding paths, grooved pavement, and hilly terrain make this the most challenging Disney theme park in which to navigate a wheelchair or heavy stroller.

- Check the My Disney Experience mobile app or website to get an idea of attraction wait times.

- When the weather gets steamy, keep a reusable water bottle with you at all times.

- Rainforest Cafe generally keeps longer hours than the park does. (Buses run until one hour after park closing time.)

- The line for Kilimanjaro Safaris tends to dwindle a bit by midday. See it then (the experience is enjoyable at any time of day).

- Get a Fastpass+ for Expedition Everest as soon as you possibly can—they run out quickly. It is a wildly popular ride!

- Bumpy rides aren't for everyone—or for every camera. When it comes to thrill (or wet) rides, it's smart to stash your camera in a locker or with a non-riding member of your party.

- Island Mercantile on Discovery Island stays open a half hour after the park closes.

Where to Eat in Animal Kingdom

A complete listing of eateries at Disney's Animal Kingdom—table-service restaurants, fast-food spots, and snack stands—can be found in the *Good Meals, Great Times* chapter. See the Animal Kingdom section, beginning on page 264.

Hidden Mickeys

These are some of the most popular "Hidden Mickeys" at Animal Kingdom. How many can you find? Check the box when you spot each one!

❤ **Tree of Life:** A Hidden Mickey made of moss is on the front of the Tree of Life just to the right of the tiger and to the left of the buffalo. Although you may be able to spot it from several vantage points, the best place is right when you enter Discovery Island and before the path splits to Africa and DinoLand. ■

❤ **Kilimanjaro Safaris:** Pay close attention to the flamingo pond on your left just after you enter elephant country. The center island is shaped like a Hidden Mickey (sit toward the left side of the ride vehicle for the best view). ■

❤ **Maharajah Jungle Trek:** There are more than 10 Hidden Mickeys throughout this jungle trek, but we suggest hunting for these two to start: Inside the first archway near the tiger exhibit, pay attention to the mural on the left and look for three leaves that form a Hidden Mickey underneath the extended arm of a king ■. Now walk to the second arch and look at the mural on the right to find a Hidden Mickey in the clouds. ■

❤ **Gorilla Falls Exploration Trail:** Okay, while not a Hidden Mickey, the Hidden Jafar found in this trail is well worth searching for. Just past the gorilla viewing area, you'll reach a suspension bridge. Look directly to your right and you'll see a huge 3-D head of Jafar carved out of the rock that's covered in moss. ■

❤ **Rafiki's Planet Watch:** Conservation Station is a Hidden Mickey paradise with more than 20 Mickeys in the entrance mural alone. Two favorites: Just inside the building on the right, find a possum with a Hidden Mickey in its eye ■. Then look above it to find a butterfly with two Hidden Mickeys (one on each wing) ■. For good measure, here's a third: Find a frog just to the right of an alligator on the left wall, then find Mickey's smiling face under the frog's right eye. ■

❤ **Expedition Everest:** To find this Hidden Mickey, you'll need a Fastpass+ assignment for Expedition Everest. As you travel through the Fastpass+ queue, pay close attention to the Yeti Museum room. In the second display of expedition artifacts and supplies, look for a lantern on a shelf—three dents in the metal form a sideways Hidden Mickey. ■

❤ **It's Tough to be a Bug!:** This is one of the more challenging Hidden Mickeys to locate at Disney's Animal Kingdom, but cast members are happy to help you spot it if you need them to. After you enter the "underground" room with all the silly musical posters (but before entering the main theater), find the other entrance to the far side of the room. Now look at the far left wall. This well-concealed (but very cool) Hidden Mickey is hiding in the shadows. ■

❤ **DinoLand U.S.A.:** First, find the two large dinosaurs holding up a "Chester & Hester's Dino-Rama" sign near the TriceraTop Spin ride. Stand directly underneath the sign and close to the blue dinosaur. Check out the dino's wrist—there's a Hidden Mickey on it! ■ Then head to the dig site area of The Boneyard playground. Can you spot where two hard hats and a fan combine to form another H.M.? ■

❤ **Dinosaur:** Before you travel back in time, your ride vehicle passes a laboratory scene on the left (the vehicle actually stops here for a second to give you plenty of time to look). Search carefully to find a blue Hidden Mickey drawn on the lower left corner of a whiteboard. ■

❤ **Cretaceous Trail:** At the end of this short DinoLand trail sits a proud dino. We think he's proud of the Hidden Mickey on his back! ■

Specifics may change during 2017.

207

Where in the World?

All of the photos on this page were taken at Disney's Animal Kingdom. Do you know where? We challenge you to find all the spots where these images were shot and snap a photo for yourself as you discover each one. Happy hunting! (For locations, turn to page 356.)

1

2

3

4

5

6

Everything Else in the World

While the total turf of the World encompasses about 40 square miles, the theme parks cover a mere fraction of the property. Much of the remaining Walt Disney World terrain is crammed with irresistible activities of a variety and quality seldom found anywhere else.

There's superb golf and tennis, beaches for strolling and sunbathing, lakes for motorboating and fishing, canoes to rent and winding streams to paddle along, bicycles for hire, campfire sites, horseback riding, hot-air ballooning, nature trails, and picnic grounds. The recreation options continue with Typhoon Lagoon, a lushly landscaped, state-of-the-art water park complete with surfing lagoon; and Blizzard Beach, a thrilling, watery wonderland that translates the hallmarks of a ski resort to the realm of swimming.

A lineup of lavish spas provide guests with ample opportunity to pamper themselves silly. Intriguing "backstage" programs invite the curious to slip behind the scenes and learn about the workings of Walt Disney World. Add to all that, Disney Springs—a dining, shopping, and entertainment district including a colorful assortment of shops, shows, and restaurants. The expansive play zone, formerly known as Downtown Disney, has a brand-new neighborhood: Town Center. It seems this really is a World without end.

Disney Springs

Sprinkled across 120 acres are the shops, lounges, restaurants, and entertainment sites that collectively make up Disney Springs. This timeless place, previously known as Downtown Disney, consists of four neighborhoods interconnected by a flowing spring and vibrant lakefront: Marketplace, Town Center, The Landing, and the West Side. The re-imagined enclave, which has completed a major metamorphosis and massive expansion, is a definite hotspot. The spirited waterfront zone boasts more than 150 establishments—all there for your dining, shopping, and playing pleasure.

Guests staying at most Disney-owned-and-operated resorts can reach Disney Springs via bus. Water taxis ferry guests from Saratoga Springs, Port Orleans French Quarter, Port Orleans Riverside, and Old Key West. Convenient pedestrian bridges connect the area with the resorts on Hotel Plaza Boulevard.

There is a $20 charge for valet parking. (It's available near the entrance to the Orange parking garage from 10 A.M. till 2 A.M. and on the West Side, near the Cirque du Soleil theater from 4 P.M. till 2 A.M.) Self-parking is free. For additional details, visit *www.disneyworld.com*, or call 407-934-7639.

Disney Springs Essentials

GUEST RELATIONS: Inside Town Center and near the House of Blues on the West Side, these information centers are also the places to go for help making dining reservations, Lost and Found, tickets, and more. Note that stroller and wheelchair rentals are available at a location between Tren-D and Once Upon a Toy. There are several ATMs scattered throughout the Disney Springs district. Details are subject to change.

HOW TO GET THERE: Disney Springs is accessible from exits 67 off I-4.

By WDW Transportation: From Old Key West, Port Orleans French Quarter and Riverside, and Saratoga Springs: boats or buses. From all other WDW resorts: bus. There is no direct transportation from Disney theme parks to Disney Springs. The Marketplace is within walking distance of Saratoga Springs and some resorts on Hotel Plaza Boulevard. For more details, see *Transportation & Accommodations*.

By Taxi: Authorized cabs service the Disney Springs area. The cost to most WDW resorts is usually $15 to $25.

Note: Stick with authorized taxis such as Mears Taxi and avoid independent drivers. Their fees aren't regulated and are often outrageous. And pay attention to the route the driver takes to be sure it is as direct as possible.

WEST SIDE

THE LANDING

Marketplace

Located on the shores of Lake Buena Vista, the Marketplace is a relaxing setting for shopping, dining, and much more. The waterside district is sprinkled with gardens featuring whimsical topiaries. Little kids are fond of the Disney Springs carousel (see Marketplace Rides, page 213). While many guests opt to eat in a table-service restaurant, others grab a bite from the Earl of Sandwich and sit at outdoor tables. (Refer to *Good Meals, Great Times* for restaurant details.) Afterward, some gravitate toward Dockside Margaritas for live music and a nightcap.

Shopping

The descriptions that follow suggest the types of wares each store offers. Most shops in the Disney Springs Marketplace are typically open daily from about 10 A.M. to 12 A.M.

ARRIBAS BROS.: This shop sells hand-crafted items from Spanish artisans and designers. Large, cut-glass bowls and vases are available, along with mugs, sculptures, and other wares, many of which can be personalized. Aspiring Cinderellas will appreciate the selection of tiaras and glass slippers. It is located between Basin and Marketplace Co-op.

THE ART OF DISNEY: Original Disney art, porcelain figures, ceramics, posters, and other collectibles are available at this engaging gallery.

BASIN: Products designed to clean you up and calm you down are the stock-in-trade at this soothing establishment. Candles, soaps, and bath crystals are some of the wares on hand. A sampling area allows shoppers to try before they buy. The bath bombs are the best!

TOWN CENTER

MARKETPLACE

BIBBIDI BOBBIDI BOUTIQUE: This country parlor-inspired location gives guests ages 3 through 12 the royal treatment with the help of Fairy Godmothers-in-Training. Kids can get their faces painted with glitter makeup, do their nails and hair, and even don tiaras. The boutique is open daily. Youngsters are transformed into princesses and princely royal knights. Reservations are encouraged; call 407-939-7895 for reservations and pricing (cheap it is not). Note that this shop recently moved from its previous location inside the World of Disney Shop.

DESIGN-A-TEE: Aspiring fashion designer? Step into T-shirt central, visit one of 8 computer kiosks, and design away. First, select a size and color for the shirt (there are sample shirts to help you gauge size). Next, choose art from a set of categories such as Characters, Pirates, Princesses (which includes Princes), or Celebrations. Finally, personalize your creation with text of your own choosing. When you're finished, a ticket will be printed for you. Present it to the cashier to pay for your shirt and plan to come back in a half hour or so to pick it up. Peruse the wares in Disney's Days of Christmas while you wait.

DISNEY'S DAYS OF CHRISTMAS: Here is the best place to deck the halls Disney style— it's the largest Christmas shop on WDW property. In addition to character items, the shop boasts a large assortment of hand-crafted ornaments. Other items to look for: Mickey Mouse nutcrackers, Santa hats with mouse ears, stockings, and books. Some ornaments can be personalized. This store is so thoroughly themed, it actually smells like a candy cane.

PHOTO BY JILL SAFRO

DISNEY'S PIN TRADERS: This shop boasts a tremendous assortment of collector pins and various pin-collecting accessories.

DISNEY'S WONDERFUL WORLD OF MEMORIES: Preserve the memories of your Disney adventure with the scrapbooking supplies, journals, frames, photo albums for sale at this shop across from Disney's Days of Christmas. Camera supplies (memory cards, batteries, straps, cases, and chargers) are available, too. There's a make-your-own-Disney- charm-bracelet station and a wall of mouse ear hats just waiting to be personalized.

GOOFY'S CANDY COMPANY: One-stop shopping to satisfy sugary cravings, this shop has a sumptuous selection of chocolates, a dipping kitchen, and much more.

On warm days, we gravitate to the corner of this shop known as Goofy's Glaciers for a frozen slushie treat, available in flavors with goofy names such as Rootin' Tootin' Red, Orange You Happy, and Pucker Purple. They also serve coffee, cookies, pastries, and ice cream.

PHOTO BY JILL SAFRO

LEGO IMAGINATION CENTER: World of Disney's neighbor, this newly renovated emporium is a showcase for larger-than-life LEGO models. It also invites guests to flaunt their creativity in an interactive outdoor play area. A new computer hub lets guests design LEGO structures and play games. The store sells a vast selection of LEGO products.

LEFTY'S: Step up to southpaw central for scissors, can openers, writing implements, notebooks, and more—all made especially for the differently handed. The open-air stand also sells shirts and hats lauding left-handedness.

LITTLE MISSMATCHED™: Mismatched sock syndrome has finally been solved: Nothing here matches. In addition to socks (which are sold in packs of three), the store sells colorful pajamas, pencil pouches, backpacks, and other miscellany.

MARKETPLACE FUN FINDS: Here's the place to find Disney merchandise at low prices. In fact, most items in the store are under $25. Hey, that *is* fun!

MICKEY'S PANTRY: Stop here for Disney-themed glasses, cookbooks, mugs, and cooking utensils, plus spices, teas, and coffees. Many of the designs are subtle, others not so much: Mickey pasta, anyone? Note that the Spice & Tea Exchange is located inside Mickey's Pantry (see below right for details).

MARKETPLACE CO-OP: A cavernous retail zone, the Co-op is home to specialty shops: **Wonder-Ground Gallery** is a contemporary art space showcasing unusual collections and emerging artists; **Cherry Tree Lane** appeals to "the sophisticated woman with a passion for scarves, shoes, bags, and jewelry"; **D-Tech on Demand** is a place to personalize and customize electronic accessories;

Marketplace Rides

Disney Springs Marketplace has two honest-to-goodness kiddie rides for tykes to enjoy: a carousel and a tiny train. The cost for each is $2 per child. Be sure to purchase a token before boarding (payment can be made with MasterCard, Visa, or cash). Parents can accompany small children on the train (no charge, provided they ride in the same car). The train can only accommodate two adults per trip (hey, we said it was tiny), and grown-ups are not allowed to ride in the engine car. For the carousel, kids under 42 inches tall must be accompanied by an adult (who rides for free). The rides are situated between Marketplace Fun Finds and The Earl of Sandwich.

The Centerpiece showcases home products for folks who dig a dash of Disney in their furnishings, textiles, and everyday ware; and names are represented. **Twenty Eight & Main** specializes in apparel and accessories for distinguished gentlemen who happen to love Disney parks. The vast variety of merchandise at the Marketplace Co-op puts this area on top of many a Disney treasure-hunter's must-do list.

ONCE UPON A TOY: A sprawling toy box of a store, this site features plush toys, action figures, Duffy merchandise, a Mr. Potato Head play zone, and a Build Your Own Lightsaber station. Oodles of brand names are represented. Be sure to look up—there's a model train set suspended from the ceiling.

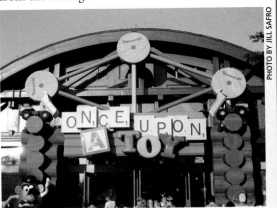
PHOTO BY JILL SAFRO

THE PEARL FACTORY: Pick an oyster, any oyster. Then pry it open (with some assistance), and *voila*—a pearl! The cost is about $16 per oyster and you are guaranteed at least one genuine pearl. The open-air shop, "Hawaii's Original Pearl-in-the-Oyster," proffers pearl earrings and necklaces, too.

SILHOUETTE PORTRAITS: A classic Disney "lasting memory," single silhouettes cost $12, doubles $20, triples $24, and quads $27 (plus tax). You will receive three copies. Black oval frames go for about $9 apiece. It takes the artist about a minute per silhouette—which is pretty amazing when you think about it.

THE SPICE & TEA EXCHANGE: Neatly nestled into a corner of Mickey's Pantry, this fragrant destination offers the opportunity to purchase gourmet spices, salts, peppers, sugars, teas, and more. It's a rather unique shopping experience thanks, in part, to a large selection of sample jars in which you are encouraged to stick your nose.

Where to Eat at Disney Springs

A complete listing of restaurants, bars, and snack spots can be found in the *Good Meals, Great Times* chapter. See the Disney Springs restaurant listings, beginning on page 266. Most of the restaurants here are open from about 11 A.M. to about 10 P.M. or later. Planet Hollywood serves until about midnight. West Side spots may serve as late as 2 A.M.

TREN-D: The Mouse is quite a trendsetter. Need proof? Swing by this boutique. It is bursting with quirky Disney merchandise, from loungewear to jeweled sunglasses and other trendy accessories.

WORLD OF DISNEY: A gigantic space stuffed with a huge selection of Disney merchandise, this is the place for one-stop shopping. Colorful rooms provide the backdrop for the array of goods. Characters are available on everything from watches to luggage. (If you're an annual passholder, you may receive a discount when you present it at the register. It depends on the type of pass, and the discount is subject to change.)

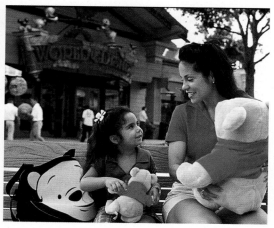

The Landing

Shopping

APEX BY SUNGLASS HUT: Specializing in sporty shades, this eyeglass emporium is located across the street from Paradiso 37.

THE ART OF SHAVING: A premium shave shop, Art of Shaving offers high-end men's grooming supplies—razors, brushes and shaving sets, and aromatherapy-based products—plus the Barber Spa: a place for guests to relax and get a shave and/or a haircut from a master barber.

CHAPEL HATS: Fashion-forward headwear for men and women is the stock-in-trade at this sleek spot. With shelving made of reclaimed wood, decorative tables made from old shipping container hatch doors, and Arts and Crafts–style mirrors, Chapel Hats has classic appeal.

ERIN MCKENNA'S BAKERY NYC: Folks with dietary restrictions (and those just looking for a sweet treat) will be in the pink at this bustling bakeshop. According to founder Erin McKenna, the place "focuses on the underserved people with gluten, dairy, eggs, and soy sensitivities, the health-minded, and, most importantly, allergic kids who are often unable to indulge. The goal is to make eating vegan and gluten-free fun and delicious." Mission accomplished.

THE GANACHERY: A fresh take on an old apothecary, the star of this show is housemade ganache—Disney's own recipe for a luxurious mixture of melted chocolate and cream. The decadent treats aren't cheap, but many a chocolate fanatic finds them worthy of a splurge.

HAVAIANAS: Head here for vibrant flip-flops with a Brazilian flair. Some styles incorporate Disney princesses and *Frozen*, too.

SANUK: Retire those pinchy old shoes and replace them with cool and comfy footwear at Sanuk. (If we could wear our Sanuks every day, we would.) FYI: *Sanuk* is the Thai word for fun.

SOUND LION: Guests here peruse the latest technology in headphones, earbuds, speakers, and more. All items may be tested at the "sound bar" before purchase.

West Side

PHOTO BY JILL SAFRO

AMC DISNEY SPRINGS 24: The most popular multi-screen movie theater complex in Florida is also one of the largest. The many screens show a wide selection of current movie releases. The seats are roomy and comfortable—and some of the theaters offer seat-side food and beverage service (see page 266 for details). For current movie schedules, call 407-298-4488.

BONGOS CUBAN CAFE: Situated across from the AMC Theatres on the edge of Village Lake, Bongos echoes the style of clubs in Miami's South Beach. Created in part by Gloria Estefan, it features the flavors and rhythms of Cuba and other Latin American countries. The bold design is dramatic yet whimsical. Guests dine and, if the mood strikes, even dance amid the colorful, tropical decor (and one remarkably oversized pineapple, which houses a multi-level cocktail lounge). Live entertainment is often presented on Friday and Saturday nights.

PHOTO BY JILL SAFRO

CIRQUE DU SOLEIL: The big, white building that towers over all the others at Disney Springs West Side closely resembles a tent—a circus tent. It's the home of a most extraordinary entertainment experience: Cirque du Soleil. This original show, titled La Nouba, is a Walt Disney World exclusive.

Known for its high energy and artistic performances, Cirque du Soleil performances of La Nouba feature a mix of acrobatics and modern dance combined with colorful costumes and dramatic original music. A cast of more than 60 international performers showcase their physical talents twice a day, five days a week (Tuesday through Saturday).

PHOTO BY JILL SAFRO

Tickets for the show may be purchased up to six months in advance. Call 407-939-7328, or visit *www.disneyworld.com/lanouba* for information or to order tickets. If you have not already purchased tickets to La Nouba, consider stopping by the Cirque du Soleil box office at Disney Springs West Side—some seats may be available at the last minute. Note that the show is quite popular. Book as early as you can.

HOUSE OF BLUES: A combination restaurant-music hall with standing room for 2,000, House of Blues was inspired by one of America's most celebrated musical traditions. There is a lively dose of jazz and country, plus a little bit of R&B and some rock 'n' roll thrown into the music mix. The

Southern-inspired cooking lures diners here—especially on Sunday mornings, when the chefs prepare an all-you-care-to-eat buffet feast, complemented by live gospel music. Tickets can be purchased in advance through Ticketmaster (call 407-839-3900, or visit *www.ticketmaster.com*) or the House of Blues box office (407-934-2583).

The H.O.B. restaurant features a mélange of cuisine, including jambalaya, slow-smoked pulled pork, shrimp with grits, and bread pudding.

WOLFGANG PUCK CAFE: There are three dining areas in this two-story restaurant—an express counter, a cafe, and a formal dining room on the second floor—plus a sushi bar. All feature the celebrated chef's signature pizzas, rotisserie chicken, and other specialties. The sushi bar is a good go-to should you find yourself famished and without reservations.

Shopping

CANDY CAULDRON: Stop here for some homemade sweets in an open candy kitchen. Among the biggest crowd-pleasers here are the made-to-order specialty apples—fresh, crunchy apples slathered in the candy coating of your choice. Yum! Kids love to peek through the windows and watch the candy-makers at work.

Characters in Flight

Up, up, and away! You can float up to 400 feet above Disney Springs while beneath one behemoth of a balloon. Touted as the "world's largest tethered helium balloon," it carries up to 29 guests at a time in a gondola that measures 19 feet in diameter. Flights last 8 to 10 minutes. Guests board from a platform on the West Side (near Starbucks Coffee). Tickets are sold at a nearby window. The cost is about $18 (plus tax) for adults (ages 10 and up) and $12 for kids ages 3 to 9. Babies fly free. Flights begin at 8:30 A.M. daily (weather-permitting) and operate on a first-come, first-served basis. The last flight of the day is usually around midnight. (For a discount on the Characters in Flight experience, use the coupon at the back of this book.)

CURL BY SAMMY DUVALL: You have to figure that anybody who spent not one but 17 years as a champion water-skier has to know quite a bit about trends in beachwear and water-sport equipment. See for yourself at this high-end surf shop. Among the wares you will find sunglasses, watches, jewelry, activewear, earphones, and shoes. The shop can be found next door to Splitsville. It's usually open from 10:30 A.M. until 11 P.M. Save ten percent off your purchase with the coupon at the back of this book.

FIT2RUN—THE RUNNER'S SUPERSTORE: A super stop for guests on the run, this shop sells footwear, apparel, performance sunglasses, jogger strollers, and more. Need help selecting the perfect shoe for you? Take advantage of this shop's high-tech video gait analysis. Ready, set, run! You'll find it next to Splitsville.

ORLANDO HARLEY-DAVIDSON: No motorcycles for sale here (though any employee will happily tell you how to buy one), but the custom Harleys on display are definitely ogle-worthy. Hog fans can browse Harley-Davidson T-shirts, gifts, and other collectibles. Save 15% off your purchase of $75 or more by using the coupon at the back of this book.

POP GALLERY: This gallery features artist-signed limited-edition sculptures and paintings, as well as high-end gift items. There's a champagne bar, too. Hence the "pop." The shop is located next to the AMC Theatres and across from Splitsville.

SOMETHING SILVER: The AMC Theatres next-door neighbor, Something Silver sells fashionable jewelry (rings, earrings, bracelets, and charms) and a collection of timeless classics for men, women, and children.

SOSA FAMILY CIGAR COMPANY: For adults only, this shop specializes in premium cigars. Feel free to puff away here—the shop is a rare smoking zone. In addition to the art of hand-rolling, Sosa Family Cigars features an authentic solid cedar humidor room to keep the wares as fresh as possible. Note that guests must be at least 18 years old with state-issued photo ID in order to smoke tobacco products in the state of Florida.

SPLITSVILLE LUXURY LANES™: Come for some casual bowling, stay for some fab food and live entertainment. This West Side venue features 30 bowling lanes, two high-end kitchens, a full bar, live music—and billiards, to boot.

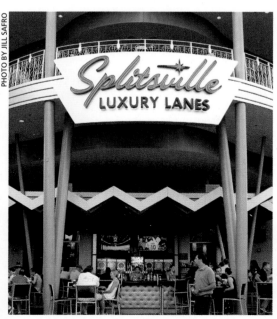

Housed in what was once the Virgin Megastore, this massive 'ville (50,000 square feet) is fun for all ages. However, some areas are restricted to guests over the age of 21 (with legal ID to prove it). It's generally open until about 2 A.M. daily; the restricted "ages 21 and up" area is open on Fridays and Saturdays after 10:30 P.M. Shoppers can peruse merchandise at Memory Lanes, a shop tucked into a corner on the first floor of Splitsville. Expect to find items such as shirts, pants, hats, glasses, jewelry, and more. For more information, visit *www.splitsvillelanes.com* and refer to page 268.

STARBUCKS: That ubiquitous mermaid icon can be spotted on the shore of Lake Buena Vista. Expect to find all of Starbucks' specialties—from fresh-brewed, free-trade cups of joe to sweet and chilly Frappuccinos. Treats include cupcakes, muffins, and cake pops. Smoothies, teas, fresh fruit, crunchy veggies, juice, milk, soda, and water are also offered. (There are several Disney Dining Plan snack options to choose from.)

STAR WARS GALACTIC OUTPOST: The Force is strong with this store. So is its pull on folks strolling the promenade at Disney Springs, West Side. It boasts an impressive bounty of toys, clothes, and accessories inspired by the epic space saga: hats, shirts, handbags, dresses (yes, we actually spotted a BB-8 dress) Stormtrooper helmet banks, talking Finn action figures, Rey, Han Solo, and Kylo Ren shirts, lightsaber key chains, *Millenium Falcon* models, artwork, Boba Fett bowling shirts, plus jammies, jackets, and many more items featuring characters from the Star Wars films.

SUNGLASS ICON: Looking for some super-cool shades? This snazzy shop is full of high-end brands to protect your peepers.

SUPER HERO HEADQUARTERS: Calling all would-be agents of S.H.I.E.L.D.: You can gear up at this shop, plus snag super-hero-themed shirts, hats, mugs, and other items—all featuring characters from the Marvel Universe.

UNITED WORLD SOCCER: Fútbol fans, rejoice! Gather garb to support your favorite club and load up on gear to tackle the game yourself—right here at the well-stocked United World Soccer shop. The *goal* is to meet all your soccer needs. Score!

Town Center

The fourth and newest neighborhood in Disney Springs, the architectural design of Town Square is "Spanish Revival," drawing from a rich history of explorers that landed in Florida centuries ago. It was ostensibly founded in the 1850s, on the banks of one of the Sunshine State's freshwater springs—where its original homestead still stands, having been restored and converted to a family restaurant (D-Luxe Burger). The commercial district of Town Center was designed in the Mediterranean revival style that was popular in Florida in the 1920s, whereas the Welcome Center area features the wooden American revival architecture that was prevalent in the 1930s. Overall, this sophisticated area has a focus on shopping, but also brings several inventive dining opportunities and other pleasant diversions. For more information on dining locations, refer to the *Good Meals, Great Times* chapter.

Dining

AMORETTE'S PATISSERIE: Classic and contemporary cakes and pastries are the stars in this high-end (expensive) pastry shop where guests can watch the chefs decorate signature cakes in the on-stage finishing kitchen. Amorette lovingly packages sweet treats in old-fashioned hatboxes. Champagne, sparkling wine, hot chocolate ganache, and other beverages are served. FYI: Amorette means "little love" in French.

BLAZE FAST FIRE'D PIZZA: This massive eatery allows guests to "build their own artisanal pizzas." Custom-made pizzas are prepared in about three minutes—they don't call it "fast fire'd" for nothing! The 5,000-square-foot restaurant also serves freshly prepared salads and desserts.

D-LUXE BURGER: Come for the burgers, stay for the shakes. D-Luxe Burger is a comfy spot for a casual bite. The creatively prepared burgers are served on fresh-baked buns. Pair yours with freshly cut fries (which come with a variety of dipping sauces) and artisanal gelato shakes (with rotating flavors such as vanilla, chocolate, raspberry, strawberry, salted caramel, and s'mores). There's indoor and outdoor seating (the latter overlooks the water, aka the springs).

HOMECOMING—FLORIDA KITCHEN AND SHINE BAR: Brought to us from celebrity chef Art Smith, Homecoming is a "farm-to-fork" restaurant, showcasing the flavorful bounty of the Sunshine State. The menu features Southern favorites such as Low Country shrimp and grits, deviled eggs, and a grilled blackstrap pork chop with sawmill gravy. Desserts are made daily and shipped from a bakery in Florida's Hamilton county.

SPRINKLES CUPCAKES: "The world's first cupcake bakery," as dubbed by Food Network, the Beverly Hills–based Sprinkles now serves said signature cakes, slow-churned ice cream, and cookies, here at Town Center. The handy cupcake ATM dispenses treats 24/7.

FRONTERA COCINA: Six-time James Beard winner Chef Rick Bayless has brought his signature gourmet Mexican cuisine to Frontera Cocina. The eatery features Mexican specialties such as hand-crafted tortas, tacos, salads, and classic Mexican braised meat entrées, all prepared with locally sourced ingredients. Margaritas, cocktails and craft beers, and wine are also served.

Retail Roundup

Disney Springs, Town Center may look retro-elegant, but the shopping opportunities here are markedly *au courant*. Treasure seekers may peruse wares at these new retail locations:

ALEX AND ANI • American Threads • Anthropologie • Coca-Cola Store • Columbia Sportswear • Edward Beiner • Everything But Water • francesca's • Free People • JOHNNY WAS • Johnston & Murphy • kate spade new york • Kipling • LACOSTE • Lilly Pulitzer • L'Occitane En Provence • Lucky Brand • Luxury of Time by Diamonds International • M·A·C Cosmetics • Melissa Shoes • Na Hoku • Oakley • PANDORA • Sephora • Shore • Sperry • Tommy Bahama • TROPHY ROOM • UGG • Under Armour • UNIQLO • UNOde50 • Vince Camuto • Vera Bradley • Volcom • Zara

For additional information about these and other new Town Center shopping destinations, visit *https://disneyworld.disney.go.com/shops/*.

BoardWalk

A stroll at Disney's BoardWalk is a journey back in time. Inspired by the Middle Atlantic seaside attractions of the early 1900s, BoardWalk recaptures the carefree atmosphere of that bygone era. The resort is surrounded by restaurants, clubs, and amusements similar to those enjoyed by beachgoers of yesteryear. It's bordered by a wood-planked walkway that hugs the shore of Crescent Lake. By day, BoardWalk is a peaceful place to soak up sun, enjoy lunch, or simply walk the boards. After dark, the place turns into a twinkling center of nighttime activity—some of it elegant, some of it downright raucous.

Midway games of the BoardWalk challenge onlookers to test their luck and skill at a collection of classic carnival games, while strolling performers enchant passersby of all ages with magic shows, balloon tricks, or other antics.

BoardWalk is open to everyone. Although there is no admission price, individual venues may charge a cover. There is a $25 charge for valet parking (even for guests staying at a WDW resort). Self-parking is free. For dining details, refer to this book's *Good Meals, Great Times* chapter.

Clubs

ATLANTIC DANCE HALL: This is a lovely atmosphere in which to dance the night away. A deejay cranks up tunes, tempting guests to twist and shout on the spacious dance floor. Request your favorite music videos and bust a move while they play on the big screen.

In addition to traditional cocktails, the club serves specialty drinks. Sample one in the "big room" or on the waterfront balcony.

Guests must be 21 or older, with a legal photo ID, to enter. There was a $5 cover charge at press time, but that could change. Hours are generally 9 P.M. until 2 A.M., Tuesday through Saturday.

This club is known for reinventing itself; specifics may be different during your visit.

ESPN CLUB: A casual sports bar/restaurant, ESPN aims to please sports enthusiasts of all kinds. It has a broadcast facility, table-service eatery, and a bar.

Nearly 100 TVs broadcast sports events, so guests always know the score. (Need to make a pit stop at a crucial moment of the game? Don't sweat it . . . there are even TVs in the bathrooms.)

As you enter the club, you're at The Sidelines area. You can catch a game on a TV above the "penalty box" bar or sit at a nearby table. Beer, wine, and soft drinks are available, as is the usual (and some unusual) pub fare.

Sports Central, the main dining area, has a big screen showing—what else?—the big game. The kitchen is open until 11:30 P.M. for meals, 12 A.M. for appetizers and desserts.

Though the restaurant doesn't typically take reservations, there is a "VIP Seating" option for select sporting events. Call 407-939-3463 to reserve a banquette-style seat on the second tier of the Sports Central dining room. Note that there is a minimum of $75 per adult and $30 per kid when in VIP Seating. Prices do not include tax or gratuity and are subject to change.

JELLYROLLS: You might want to warm up your vocal cords before crossing the threshold. They don't call it a sing-along bar for nothing: Guests are expected to sing, clap, and join in the fun at this warehouse home of dueling pianos. You'll hear everything from Gershwin to *Grease*. The piano players take requests, so plan ahead. Write the request—a cocktail napkin will do—and slip it onto the piano. (Although it's not required, we recommend slipping a tip along, too. It will increase the odds of you hearing the request and help the musicians pay their rent.)

Jellyrolls is open from 7 P.M. until 2 A.M. nightly. There is usually a $12 cover charge to enter. (Note that the cover charge may vary.) To get in, you must be at least 21 years old and willing to prove it. It's often quite chilly in this venue (year-round). Bring a sweater.

Water Parks
Typhoon Lagoon

PHOTO BY JILL SAFRO

This splashy playground was inspired by an imagined legend: A typhoon hit a resort village many years ago, and the storm—plus an ensuing earthquake and volcanic eruption—left the village in ruins. The locals, however, were resourceful and rebuilt their town as this "wateropolis."

The centerpiece of Typhoon Lagoon is a huge watershed mountain known as Mount Mayday. Perched atop its peak is the *Miss Tilly*, a marooned shrimp boat originally from Safen Sound, Florida. *Miss Tilly*'s smokestack erupts every half hour, shooting a 50-foot flume of water into the air.

The surf lagoon is huge: giant slides snake through caves, tamer ones offer twisting journeys, and tiny slides delight small kids. Guests under age 14 must be accompanied by someone over age 14.

SURF POOL: The main swimming area holds nearly three million gallons of water, making it one of the world's largest wave pools. The blue lagoon is surrounded by a white-sand beach, and its main attraction is the waves that come crashing to the shore every 90 seconds. Less adventurous swimmers can loll about in two relatively calm tide pools, Whitecap Cove and Blustery Bay.

HOT TIP!

Guests entering Typhoon Lagoon are subject to a thorough security check. All bags will be checked and a metal detector will be used. Weapons—including toys— are strictly prohibited.

CASTAWAY CREEK: The "creek" is really a 2,100-foot circular river that winds through the park and offers a lazy, relaxing orientation to Typhoon Lagoon. Tubes may be borrowed and are the best way to make the trip along the three-foot-deep waterway. The ride takes guests through a rainforest, where they are cooled by mists and spray; through caves and grottoes that provide welcome shade on hot summer days; and through an area where "broken" pipes from a water tower unleash showers on helpless passersby. There are several exits along the way. It takes 20 to 35 minutes to ride around the whole park.

CRUSH 'N' GUSHER: This "water coaster" thrill ride is one of a kind. In it, daredevils are whisked along a series of flumes and tossed and turned as they weave through an abandoned tropical fruit factory. There are three spillways to choose from: Banana Blaster, Coconut Crusher, and Pineapple Plunger.

GANGPLANK FALLS, KEELHAUL FALLS, AND MAYDAY FALLS: These white-water rides offer guests a variety of slippery trips, two of them in inner tubes. All of the slides course through caves and waterfalls and past rock work, making the scenery an attraction in itself. Gangplank Falls gives families a chance to ride together in a three- to five-passenger craft.

HUMUNGA KOWABUNGA: These three speed slides, reported to have been carved into the landscape by the historic earthquake, will send guests zooming through caverns at speeds of 30 miles per hour. The 214-foot slides each offer a 51-foot drop, and the view from the top is a little scary. But it's over before you know it, and once-wary guests hurry back for another try. Guests must be at least 4 feet tall and free of back trouble, heart conditions, and other physical limitations to take the trip. Pregnant women are not permitted to ride.

KETCHAKIDDEE CREEK: Open only to those children 48 inches tall or under (and their adult guardians), this area has small rides for pint-size visitors. All children must be accompanied by an adult. There are slides, fountains, waterfalls, squirting sea life, a mini-rapids ride, an interactive tugboat, and a grotto with an inviting veil of water.

SHARK REEF: Guests borrow snorkel equipment for a swim through a coral reef, where they come face-to-face with sharks and fish. The reef is built around a sunken tanker. The sharks, by the way, leopard and bonnethead, are passive members of the species. Everyone must shower before entering. Guests must be older than age 5 to experience Shark Reef. Kids under 10 must be accompanied by an adult.

STORM SLIDES: The Jib Jammer, Rudder Buster, and Stern Burner body slides send guests off at about 20 miles per hour down winding fiberglass slides, in and out of rock formations and caves, and through waterfalls. It's a somewhat tamer ride than Humunga Kowabunga, but still offers a speedy descent. The slides run about 300 feet, and each offers a different view and experience.

SURFING: Surf clinics are offered on select mornings before the park opens. For information, call 407-WDW-SURF (939-7873).

Essentials

WHEN TO GO: Typhoon Lagoon gets very crowded early in the day. Hours vary seasonally, but the park is generally open from 10 A.M. to 5 P.M., with extended hours in the summer months. All of the pools are heated in the winter. Note that this park is usually closed for refurbishment during certain winter months. The park may also close due to bad weather. Note that selfie sticks are not permitted. Call 407-824-4321 for updates.

HOW TO GET THERE: Bus service begins from all resorts about one hour before Typhoon Lagoon opens for the day. The buses stop at the water park and then at the Disney Springs Marketplace before 10 A.M. After 10 A.M., resort buses stop at the Marketplace and then Typhoon Lagoon. Buses stop running from the water park about one hour after it closes. Parking is free.

LOCKER ROOMS: Restrooms with showers and lockers are located close to the entrance. Other restrooms are available farther into the park. Small lockers cost $8 (plus a $5 deposit) to rent for the day, while large lockers cost $10, plus a $5 deposit. Towels rent for $2; life jackets and tubes are available free of charge.

WHERE TO EAT: Both of Typhoon Lagoon's eateries offer similar fare and outdoor seating. Leaning Palms has burgers, pizza, salads, and snacks. Typhoon Tilly's (open seasonally) serves fish & chips, wraps, BBQ pork sandwiches, and ice cream. Let's Go Slurpin' has frozen drinks and spirits. Guests may bring their own food to enjoy in designated picnic areas. Alcoholic beverages and glass containers may not be brought into the park. Coolers are allowed.

FIRST AID: A first aid station capable of handling minor medical problems is located just to the left of Leaning Palms.

BEACH SHOP: Singapore Sal's, located near the park's main entrance, is set in a ramshackle building left a bit battered by the typhoon. Swimsuits, sunglasses, hats, towels, sunscreen, souvenirs, water shoes, and Typhoon Lagoon logo products are available.

Admission Prices

Prices do not include sales tax and are subject to change. **Note:** Admission is an option with a Magic Your Way ticket that includes a Water Park Fun & More add-on, and is also included with a Premium Annual Pass.

	ADULTS	CHILDREN*
One-Day Ticket	$60	$54
Annual Pass	$115	$115

* 3 through 9 years of age; kids under age 3 free. Tickets allow for park-hopping, provided both water parks are open on day of admission.

Blizzard Beach

A wintry, watery wonderland, Blizzard Beach is said to be the result of a freak storm that dropped a mountain of snow onto Walt Disney World, prompting the construction of Florida's first ski resort. When temperatures soared and the snow began to melt, designers prepared to close the resort. But when they spotted an animal sliding down the slopes, they realized that they had created an exciting water adventure park! The slalom and bobsled runs became downhill waterslides. The ski jump is one of the world's tallest (120 feet) and fastest (60 miles per hour) free-fall speed slides.

HOT TIP!

Guests entering Blizzard Beach are subject to a thorough security check. All bags will be checked and a metal detector will be used. Weapons—including toys—are strictly prohibited.

The centerpiece of Blizzard Beach is the snowcapped Mount Gushmore and its Summit Plummet. Most of the runs are on the slopes of this mountain, which tops out at 90 feet. At the summit, swimmers have a choice of speed slides, flumes, a white-water raft ride, and an inner-tube run. Most guests reach the top of Mount Gushmore via chairlift. The lift has a gondola for guests with disabilities. There are stairs, too. Kids under 14 must be accompanied by a guest over age 14. One-piece bathing suits are best.

CROSS COUNTRY CREEK: This meandering 3,000-foot waterway circles the entire park. A slow current keeps visitors moving merrily along. Inner tubes, which are free, are the most pleasant way to travel. The ride includes a trip through a bone-chilling ice cave, where guests are splashed with the "melting ice" from overhead.

HOT TIP!

Early birds get the lounge chairs around these parts. If you want to snag a chair at either of Disney's water parks, arrive as close to park opening as possible.

DOWNHILL DOUBLE DIPPER: Guests travel down these two parallel 230-foot-long racing slides at speeds of up to 25 miles per hour. The partially enclosed water runs feature ski-racing graphics, flags, and time clocks. You must be 48 inches tall to ride.

MELT-AWAY BAY: A one-acre pool at the base of Mount Gushmore, the "bay" has its own wave machine. There are no tsunamis here, however—just a pleasant, bobbing wave.

RUNOFF RAPIDS: On this inner-tube run, guests careen down three twisting, turning flumes in a single or double tube.

SKI PATROL TRAINING CAMP: An area designed for preteens, Frozen Pipe Springs looks like an old pipe and drops sliders into eight feet of water. The Thin Ice Training Course tests agility as kids try to walk along broken "icebergs." At the Ski Patrol Shelter, guests under 60 inches grab on to a T-bar for an airborne trip. At any point in the ride they can drop into the water below. Ski patrol participants also experience Cool Runners, where riders can count on hurtling and whirling over lots of moguls on twin inner-tube slides. No bunny slopes for these brave daredevils.

SLUSH GUSHER: This double-humped water-slide offers a brisk journey through a snow-banked mountain gully. Topping out at 90 feet, Slush Gusher is the tallest slide of its kind. You will find it on Mount Gushmore, next to Summit Plummet. Guests must be at least 48 inches tall to take the plunge.

SNOW STORMERS: A trio of flumes descends from the top of the mountain. Guests race down, (headfirst while lying on a mat) on a switchback course that includes ski-type slalom gates.

SUMMIT PLUMMET: This thrilling ride begins 120 feet in the air on a platform 30 feet above the top of Mount Gushmore. Brave souls (who are at least 48 inches tall) travel about 60 miles per hour down a 350-foot slide.

TEAMBOAT SPRINGS: The longest family white-water raft ride in the world takes six-passenger rafts down a twisting, 1,400-foot series of rushing waterfalls.

HOT TIP!

Premium cabana-like spaces known as Polar Patios are available for rental. They include an attendant, beverages, towels, and more. Patios accommodate up to six guests and cost about $250 per day. Premium umbrella spaces are available, too. For details or to make reservations, call 939-7529. Prices vary seasonally.

TIKE'S PEAK: A kid-size variation of Blizzard Beach, this attraction features mini versions of Mount Gushmore's slides and a snow-castle fountain play area. Adults must be accompanied by a child to enter this zone. Kids must be under 48 inches to enjoy most attractions in this area.

TOBOGGAN RACERS: An eight-lane water-slide sends guests racing over a number of dips. They lie on their stomachs on a mat and travel headfirst down the 250-foot route.

Essentials

WHEN TO GO: As a guest favorite, Blizzard Beach gets very crowded early in the day. Hours vary seasonally, but the park is generally open from 10 A.M. to 5 P.M., with extended hours in summer.

All pools are heated in winter. The park is often closed for refurbishment during certain winter months. Know that it may also close due to inclement weather. For schedules, call 407-WDW-PLAY (939-7529).

HOW TO GET THERE: Blizzard Beach may be served by the buses that go to and from Animal Kingdom park, Epcot, and/or Disney's Hollywood Studios. Parking is free.

LOCKER ROOMS: There are restrooms with showers near the main entrance. Other restrooms and dressing rooms are located around the park. Small lockers cost $8, plus a $5 deposit for the day, while large lockers cost $10, plus a $5 deposit. Towels rent for $2, and life jackets and tubes may be used for free.

WHERE TO EAT: Burgers, hot dogs, pizza, salads, and drinks are sold at Lottawatta Lodge in the main village area. Two snack stands are located in more remote areas: Avalunch and The Warming Hut (both open seasonally). Polar Pub offers soft drinks and spirits. Those in need of a java fix can get one at Frosty the Joe Man Coffee Shack, while those looking for frozen lemonade or fresh fruit can find it at Frostbite Freddy's. There are picnic areas for those who prefer to pack their own food. Alcoholic beverages and glass containers may not be brought into the park. Coolers (smaller than 24 inches long, 18 inches high, and 15 inches wide) are allowed.

FIRST AID: Minor medical problems are handled at this station near the main entrance.

BEACH SHOP: The Beach Haus shop stocks bathing suits, T-shirts, shorts, sunglasses, hats, sunscreen, beach towels, and more.

Admission Prices

Prices do not include sales tax and are likely to rise in 2017. **Note:** Admission is an option with a Magic Your Way ticket that includes a Water Park Fun & More add-on, and is also included with a Premium Annual Pass.

	ADULTS	CHILDREN*
One-Day Ticket	$60	$54
Annual Pass	$115	$115

* 3 through 9 years of age; children under age 3 free; Tickets allow for water-park hopping, provided both water parks are operating on the day of admission.

Daredevil Disney

You've catapulted through the galaxy on Space Mountain, braved an encounter with an angry Yeti at Expedition Everest, and become something of a human yo-yo on the Tower of Terror. Now what? Believe it or not, there are plenty of thrills awaiting you outside the theme park gates. Some of them, such as the wedgie-inducing slides at the water parks, are well known. Others may be lower key, but they're definitely high octane. Here's a rundown of our favorite theme-park-alternative thrill rides.

BALLOONING: Going up! A huge, tethered, helium balloon known as "Characters in Flight" lifts guests 400 feet high into the sky. Moored to a landing at Disney Springs West Side, the balloon can accommodate up to 29 guests at a time—treating all to sweeping panoramic views of Walt Disney World and beyond. It operates on a first-come, first-served basis Sunday through Thursday from 8:30 A.M. until 11 P.M. and from 10:30 A.M. until midnight on Friday and Saturday. Adults pay about $18 per flight, while kids (ages 3 through 9) pay about $12. Expect to be airborne for about 8 to 10 minutes. This attraction does not operate during windy or inclement weather.

For a discount on the Characters in Flight experience, use the money-saving coupon at the end of this book.

MOTORBOATING: If you've been to Walt Disney World before, you've no doubt seen folks tooling about in zippy little motorboats. But have you ever actually given one a try? It's an experience we highly recommend.

For starters, the watercraft known as Sea Raycers are indeed speedy. And it's an experience everyone can enjoy (though guests need to be at least 12 years old and at least 5 feet tall to drive). Expect to pay about $35 for a half hour. Be sure to wear a watch, as you're apt to lose track of time. For more info, turn to page 238.

PARASAILING: Even if you've never had the urge to be a human kite, consider giving this a whirl. After a simple liftoff from the back of a boat, you and your parachute gradually climb skyward. Before you know it, you're eye level with the roof of the Contemporary resort hotel. A few peaceful minutes later, the hotel and the nearby Magic Kingdom appear to have shrunk considerably. It's not unlike the illusion of flying over London in Peter Pan's Flight. Only this flight's no illusion: You're really 450 to 600 feet above it all. And don't worry about the landing. It's generally as smooth as the trip itself. The attendants simply reel you in for a soft touchdown on the back of the boat.

For information on prices and reservations, turn to page 238.

PERSONAL WATERCRAFT EXCURSIONS: Strap on a life vest and hang on! Sammy Duvall Watersports Centre (located at the Contemporary resort marina) offers Jet Ski–like adventures on WDW's Bay Lake. All participants must be at least 16 years old. For additional information, see page 239.

SURFING: When the sun comes up, so does the surf at Disney's Typhoon Lagoon. On select days, guests can take part in a surf clinic taught by competitive surfers. Instructors control the height of the waves—and they give Mother Nature a run for her money.

If you've never hung ten before, know this: It ain't easy. But once you've managed to get up on a board, it's a blast. Lessons are offered before the park opens for the day. Set the alarm!

For more information, call 407-939-7873.

WAKEBOARDING: Walt Disney World wakeboarding in a word? Intense! Hang on tight as you are pulled at high speeds and tear back and forth across Bay Lake. The high-octane adventure is open to all ages and skill levels. Inner tubes may be used, too. Sammy Duvall instructors offer private lessons to kids and beginners. Up to five friends or family members may ride in the boat for free (if space allows). For details, see page 239.

WATERSKIING: Florida weather being what it is (hot!), waterskiing (as well as wakeboarding and tubing) never really goes out of season. It's a refreshing way to see the sights of Bay Lake—and a serious workout to boot. Sammy Duvall instructors are on hand to assist. Up to five friends or family members may ride in the boat for free (if space allows). For additional information, see page 239.

Fort Wilderness

In a part of the state where campgrounds tend to look like dried pastures—barren and very hot—the Fort Wilderness Resort and Campground, located almost due east of the Contemporary resort, is an anomaly—a forested, 750-acre wonder of tall slash pines, white-flowering bay trees, and ancient cypresses hung with Spanish moss. Native Americans from the Seminole tribe once hunted and fished here.

There are nearly 800 campsites arranged in several campground loops (including sites that are big-rig ready). There are more than 400 Wilderness Cabins (which fall into Disney's "moderate" resort category) available for rent, completely furnished and fitted with all the comforts of home. For additional information, refer to the *Transportation & Accommodations* chapter of this book.

Scattered throughout the campground loops are sporting facilities, including two tennis courts and many small playgrounds, basketball, tetherball, and volleyball courts. Fort Wilderness has riding stables (with rather mellow horses), two swimming pools, a marina full of boats, a canoe livery, bikes and golf carts for rent, and a nature trail. Some facilities are available to Fort Wilderness guests only; some are open to all.

There's a pony farm (which offers rides to young guests for a fee) and a barn that's home to the horses that pull the Magic Kingdom's Main Street trolleys. The barn houses a small museum that celebrates horses and the cherished role they've played in Disney history.

Two stores—the Settlement Trading Post and the Meadow Trading Post—stock campers' necessities, a limited supply of groceries, and souvenirs. And then there's Pioneer Hall, the home of the Hoop-Dee-Doo Musical Revue dinner show (described in the *Good Meals, Great Times* chapter). This rustic structure (made of white pine shipped from Montana) also houses a popular (and reasonably priced) buffet restaurant and a small lounge area. Mickey's Backyard Barbecue is offered here during busy times of the year (when the weather's nice).

ARCHERY: It takes a steady hand to hit the bull's-eye at the Fort Wilderness Archery Experience. After a brief training session led by a skilled guide, participants (age 7 and up) get to shoot for that coveted bull's-eye. Cost is about $45. To book the Fort Wilderness Archery Experience, call 407-WDW-PLAY (939-7529).

SWIMMING: There two pools for campers' use. The Meadows Pool complex has a twisting slide and water play area. Note that the pools are open to Fort Wilderness guests only. Swimming and wading are not allowed at the beach (due to a naturally occurring bacteria found in many Florida lakes, and the presence of native wildlife such as alligators and snakes).

BIKE RENTALS: Bicycles may be rented at the Bike Barn for trips along the paths of Fort Wilderness—or just for getting around. Bikes cost about $9 per hour or $18 per day. Helmets are included at no extra charge. Florida law mandates that all guests ages 16 and under wear helmets when biking.

BLACKSMITH SHOP: The pleasant fellow who shoes the draft horses that pull trolleys in the Magic Kingdom park is on hand most mornings to answer questions and talk about his job; occasionally, guests may even watch him at work, fitting the big, friendly animals with the special polyurethane-covered, steel-cored horseshoes that are used to protect the animals' hooves. This shop is located at the Tri-Circle-D Ranch.

BOATING: Fort Wilderness is ribboned with tranquil canals that make for delightful canoe trips of one to three hours. Canoe rentals are available at the Bike Barn for about $8 per half hour or $12 per hour. For a trip around Bay Lake, zippy little Sea Raycer motorboats, Boston Whaler Montauks, and pontoon boats are available for rent at the marina, at the north end of the campground. They may be used to cruise on Bay Lake and the adjacent Seven Seas Lagoon. (Refer to the *Sports* chapter for details.)

CAMPFIRE SING-ALONG: Held nightly (weather permitting) near the Meadow Trading Post at the center of the campground, this evening program features Disney movies, a sing-along, and a marshmallow roast. Chip and Dale often put in an appearance. It's open to WDW resort guests only. There is no charge to attend, but s'mores kits come with a small fee. You may roast your own marshmallows for free.

CARRIAGE RIDES: Guests may enjoy a relaxing carriage ride through the picturesque grounds of Fort Wilderness or Port Orleans Riverside resort. The rate for each 25-minute ride is $45.

Carriages can hold up to 4 adults, or 2 adults and up to 3 small kids. Reservations are a must. Rides are offered nightly. Call 407-WDW-PLAY (939-7529) for information or to make a reservation. Walk-up reservations are sometimes possible. (Ask the driver about buying tickets. If they're available, expect to pay with cash, Magic-Band, or Disney Resort ID. Credit cards are not accepted.) Rides may be canceled due to inclement weather. Cancellations must be made at least 24 hours ahead to avoid paying full price.

Guests are picked up in front of Crockett's Tavern at Pioneer Hall or by the marina at Port Orleans Riverside. Feel free to bring your own liquid refreshments.

ELECTRIC CART RENTALS: Available at Reception Outpost (about $60 per day) for sight-seeing or transportation. Renters must be at least 18 years old and have a valid driver's license. Reservations are necessary; call 407-824-2742 for reservations and information.

FISHING EXCURSIONS ON BAY LAKE: Walt Disney World's restrictive fishing policy means plenty of angling action—largemouth bass weighing two to eight pounds, mainly—for those who sign up for fishing excursions.

The price ranges from approximately $235 to $270 for up to five people for a two-hour excursion (one additional hour is about $100) and includes gear, a guide, and soft drinks; no license is required. The price varies based on time of day, with the early morning trips commanding the highest rate.

Know that all fishing is strictly catch-and-release. Call 407-WDW-BASS (939-2277) for exact times and to make reservations. To stretch your WDW fishing dollar, use the coupon at the back of this book.

FISHING IN THE CANALS: In addition to largemouth bass, catfish and panfish can be caught here as well. Those without their own fishing gear will find rods and reels for rent at the Bike Barn. No license is required. Fort Wilderness resort guests may toss their lines in right from the shore (canals only). All WDW fishing is strictly catch-and-release. For pricing and more info, visit *www.disneyworld.com*. Fort Wilderness is the only place on Walt Disney World property where canal fishing is allowed.

PLAYGROUNDS, VOLLEYBALL, TETHER-BALL, AND BASKETBALL COURTS: These are scattered throughout the camping loops. There is no charge to use the courts.

ELECTRICAL WATER PAGEANT: Originally presented for the dedication of the Polynesian Luau dinner show in 1971, this cavalcade of lights is presented nightly on the waters of Bay Lake and the Seven Seas Lagoon. The simple pageant consists of two strings of seven barges, each carrying a 25-foot-tall screen of lights featuring King Neptune and creatures of the sea. And it's all set to music. The show can be seen from the beach at Fort Wilderness, as well as from the Contemporary, Polynesian Village, and Grand Floridian resorts. (We've caught it while waiting for the monorail at the Magic Kingdom, too.) Ask for the schedule at your resort's lobby concierge desk.

PONY RIDES: This enclave behind Pioneer Hall is home to some friendly ponies. Pony rides, offered seasonally, are available between 10 A.M. and 5 P.M. for $8 (cash only). Riders must be at least 2 years old and under 48 inches tall. The weight limit is 80 pounds. Kids must be able to hold on by themselves. A parent or guardian leads the pony. The farm is a good place to visit before the Hoop-Dee-Doo Musical Revue.

TENNIS: Two tennis courts are available; play is on a first-come, first-served basis.

TRAIL RIDES: Guided horseback trips depart five times daily from the Trail Blaze Corral and take riders on a leisurely, meandering ride through the Florida wilderness, where it is not uncommon to see birds, deer, and even an occasional armadillo. Galloping is not part of the experience, so you don't need riding know-how to sign up. Cost is about $46 per person. Kids under age 9 are not allowed to ride. Parents must sign consent forms for kids under age 18. There is a weight limit of 250 pounds. Sturdy shoes with defined heels are recommended; open-toed shoes are not permitted. Reservations are necessary; call 407-WDW-PLAY (939-7529) up to 180 days in advance.

TRI-CIRCLE-D RANCH: This corner of Fort Wilderness is the place that the world champion Percherons and the draft horses that pull trolleys down Main Street in the *Magic Kingdom* call home. WDW guests are welcome to stop in and say hello. The Tri-Circle-D insignia above the barn door—two small circles atop a large one with the letter D inside—is the WDW brand. The barn is also the site of a museum that pays tribute to horses and their role in Disney history. The ranch is also home to the Dragon Calliope—the horse-drawn musical instrument that Walt Disney purchased for the Mickey Mouse Club Circus Parade at Disneyland Park in the 1950s. It's quite impressive.

WAGON RIDES: The wagon departs from Pioneer Hall at 6 P.M. and 8:30 P.M. and carries guests on a trip through wooded areas near Bay Lake. Each ride lasts about 25 minutes and concludes at Pioneer Hall. Purchase tickets from the wagon ride host: $8 for adults, $5 for kids ages 3 through 9. Children under age 12 must be accompanied by an adult.

Group wagon rides are available by calling 407-824-2734 (at least 24 hours in advance). The price is about $300 per hour. Note that wagon rides may be canceled due to inclement weather.

WILDERNESS BACK TRAIL ADVENTURE: A 2-hour "off-road" Segway tour of Fort Wilderness, this experience costs about $95 per person. For details, refer to page 234 or call 407-WDW-TOUR (939-8687).

Essentials

HOW TO GET THERE: From outside the World, take Magic Kingdom Exit 64B off I-4 onto U.S. 192, go through the Magic Kingdom Auto Plaza, and, bearing to your right, follow the Fort Wilderness signs. This is the most expeditious way to go, even for Walt Disney World resort guests.

By WDW Transportation: Buses or boats. Buses can get you just about anywhere, but allow yourself plenty of time—the transportation system, while efficient, is time-consuming.

Boats are also available from Magic Kingdom marinas (about a 30-minute ride) and from the Contemporary and Wilderness Lodge resorts (about a 25-minute ride).

WHERE TO EAT: For a description of the Trail's End restaurant at Fort Wilderness, refer to the *Good Meals, Great Times* chapter.

The Settlement Trading Post, located not far from the beach at the north end of the campground, and the Meadow Trading Post, located near the center of Fort Wilderness, offer a very limited supply of food staples. For serious grocery shopping, head to a nearby supermarket or order from *www.gardengrocer.com*. Ask the lobby concierge for directions.

> **HOT TIP!**
>
> Festive, horse-drawn "sleigh rides" may be offered at Ft. Wilderness from Thanksgiving week through December. For details or reservations, call 407-WDW-PLAY.

WDW Spas

For many guests, a day at the theme parks is an exciting test of physical endurance—complete with sprinting (say, from Dumbo to Splash Mountain before that Fastpass+ time expires), weight lifting (toting tired toddlers), and long-distance hiking (covering more than a mile to reach the American Adventure pavilion from Epcot's front gate—and back again!). Fortunately, there are many ways to rest and rejuvenate weary bones, throbbing feet, and noise-addled noggins. Chief among them is a visit to a soothing spa (aah). There are four such spots on Disney property, open to WDW resort guests and day visitors alike.

SENSES, A SPA AT DISNEY'S GRAND FLORIDIAN RESORT: You don't need a magic wand to make your stress disappear—not if you can pay a visit to the Grand Floridian pampering palace, Senses. In addition to the treatments offered at its sister spa at the Saratoga Springs resort (see page 229), this spot offers a selection of packages. Among them: the Me Time (de-stress bath, massage, organic facial, and pedicure), Head to Toe (featuring an organic facial, manicure, and pedicure), and the Spa for Two package (custom firm massage for two and pedicure for two).

Services include facials for women, men, and teens, including a Berry Bliss facial and a Tropical Coconut Cream facial; revitalizing aromatherapy baths, and an herbal body-toning wrap. Massage options: Swedish, warm stones, warm bamboo, foot and leg, and one specially designed for expectant mothers. Manicures, pedicures, and other hand and foot treatments are also available. There are manicures for kids, too.

Treatment hours are usually 8 A.M. to 8 P.M. daily. Prices start at about $145 for a 50-minute massage and $140 for a facial, plus gratuity.

Spa Tips

- Reserve treatments far in advance and be sure to confirm all appointments.
- If you'll feel more comfortable with either a male or a female spa therapist, let your preferences be known when you make your reservation. The spas will accommodate such requests whenever possible.
- Plan to arrive 30 minutes prior to your appointment. That'll give you time to change and relax. (Arriving late will reduce your treatment time.)
- Guests under age 18 must be accompanied by an adult to enjoy a spa treatment.
- If you're scheduled for a body treatment, leave all clothes in a locker. Robes (and slippers) are provided.
- Leave valuables in your resort-room safe.
- Guests are required to keep cell phones and electronic devices turned off at all times.
- It's always smart to take a shower before a treatment—especially if you've been at the beach or running around theme parks.
- Drink plenty of water after your spa visit. It will counter any dehydrating effects you may experience as the result of a treatment.
- Build time into your schedule to enjoy post-treatment relaxation time at the spa. You'll want to hold on to that glow as long as possible! Bathing suits are required for whirlpools, steamrooms, and other areas.
- Most spas add a 20 percent gratuity with each spa service. Additional gratuities may be added at your discretion.
- Cancellations must be made more than 4 hours in advance to avoid paying full price.

To book an appointment at the Grand Floridian spa, call 407-WDW-SPAS (939-7727). For details, visit *https://disneyworld.disney.go.com/spas/*.

BIRNBAUM'S ★BEST★ **MANDARA SPA AT THE DOLPHIN:** As exotic as it is peaceful, Mandara is on the must-do list for all guests looking to swap their stress for a big, relaxed smile.

Mandara specializes in treatments meant to reflect the "beauty, spirit, and traditions of both Eastern and Western cultures." The spa menu showcases Balinese massage, a variation of Swedish massage. It incorporates stretching, "vigorous yet relaxing" movements, and elements of acupressure. Of course, that's just one of many services offered here—all of which emphasize physical wellness and spiritual well-being. Other treatments include the Mandara Four Hand massage, Elemis Aroma Stone Therapy, and Elemis Deep Tissue Muscle massage. The Elemis Visible Brilliance Facial ($160) targets dark circles under the eyes while smoothing wrinkles. And the exotic Frangipani Body Nourish Wrap ($220, plus gratuity, for 75 minutes) includes 50 minutes of massage and incorporates a special oil from the rare and fragrant Balinese Frangipani flower.

In addition to Balinese-inspired architecture, two interior gardens provide retreats before guests begin the spa ritual. The goal here is to provide a place for guests to rejuvenate their minds as well as those aching "I can't believe I covered four theme parks in two days!" muscles. For more information, call 800-227-1500 or 407-934-4772, or visit *www.swandolphin.com*.

SENSES, A SPA AT DISNEY'S SARATOGA SPRINGS RESORT: Just as Saratoga Springs in New York was developed around the healing mineral waters of the springs, this spa incorporates the healing powers of nature into its design and theming. Services include the ultimate facial to hydrate and revitalize skin (105 minutes) and a warm bamboo massage (75 minutes), the 4-hour Senses Signature package (massage, facial, and pedicure), and the "Berry Bliss Facial" (50 or 80 minutes). Also on tap: Swedish massage, warm-stone massage, rejuvenation treatments focused on the hands and feet, plus body wraps and scrubs. Manicures, pedicures, and organic facials are options, too. Prince and princess pedicures are offered to kids ages 4 through 12 (when accompanied by an adult).

Located on the shore of Lake Buena Vista, the spa is near the Fitness Center at the Saratoga Springs resort. The hours are generally from 8 A.M. to 8 P.M. A 50-minute massage starts at about $145, with facials going for about $140 (plus gratuity). A variety of packages is available. For more information and to make reservations, call 407-WDW-SPAS (939-7727).

THE SPA AT BUENA VISTA PALACE: A plush, peaceful place, this spa is as well equipped as they come. High-tech chairs with whirlpool footbaths make getting a pedicure a real event. And a cool-mud Theme Park Leg Relief Wrap can put the spring back in the step of even the most labored lower limbs. Landscaped, outdoor whirlpools, plus locker room saunas and steam rooms, are there to aid the relaxation process.

Among the more than 75 soothing treatments from which to choose are aromatherapy and massage, including shiatsu, Swedish, deep-tissue, and reflexology. A variety of special facials (including one for sun-stressed skin), scrubs, and wraps are available. The spa also offers massages for kids, as well as Little Princess facials, manicures, and pedicures. A salon offers the usual lineup of services.

The Spa at the Buena Vista Palace hotel is across from the Disney Springs Marketplace, on Buena Vista Drive. Hours are usually 8 A.M. to 8 P.M. but vary seasonally. A 25-minute massage costs about $70, and facials are about $70. Full- and half-day packages are available, as are custom packages. For information, call 407-827-3200. Reservations are recommended and are accepted up to one year in advance.

Internet Access at WDW

We'll resist the urge to chastise you for insisting on checking your office e-mail while on vacation (since we're similarly obsessed) and instead happily report that all Walt Disney World resorts offer free in-room, high-speed Internet access. Of course, you'll need to supply the hardware. Complimentary Wi-Fi (wireless fidelity) is offered at all Walt Disney World-owned-and-operated resorts, plus the four theme parks and Disney Springs. Naturally, your computer, tablet, or phone must be Wi-Fi ready. Note that in-room, high-speed Internet service (Wi-Fi or with a connection cable) is also available at the Four Seasons and the Swan and Dolphin resorts.

If you'd like to access a computer but didn't pack your own, ask your lobby concierge to direct you to the nearest resort business center. There you can email, upload, download, and print to your heart's content. Fees vary—be sure to inquire before you start using business center services.

Just for Kids

Walt Disney World may appeal to the kid in all of us, but some activities are meant for the actual young—not just the young at heart. With the exception of the Princess Tea Party, the following programs are specifically for guests who can't remember life before smartphones. (Grown-ups can relax while their kids are entertained.) The programs are quite popular and accommodate a limited number of guests—so book early: 407-WDW-PLAY (939-7529). Note that the adventures listed are not offered every day. Reservations are required and are available up to 180 days in advance.

ALBATROSS TREASURE CRUISE: Thar be treasure in Crescent Lake! Kids are invited to follow clues and join in the hunt. The 2-hour quest takes young adventurers to several stops and includes a reading of "The Legend of the Albatross." The ship weighs anchor at the Yacht Club marina on select mornings at about 9:30 A.M. Cost per child is about $39. It's open to potty-trained guests ages 4–12. Participants should wear socks and sneakers.

BAYOU PIRATE ADVENTURE: Young adventurers sporting bandannas board a pirate vessel at Port Orleans Riverside and learn all about Captain John Lafitte as they follow his map on a quest for booty. Cost per child is about $39. It's open to potty-trained guests ages 4–12 on select mornings. Participants should wear socks and sneakers.

ISLANDS OF THE CARIBBEAN PIRATE CRUISE: Young buccaneers board a battered pirate ship at Caribbean Beach resort and set sail with a seasoned scallywag at the helm. The captain tells tall tales and leads his crew through treacherous waters (okay, they're actually quite calm) on a hunt for treasure. The cost per child is about $39. It's open to potty-trained guests ages 4–12. Cruise participants must wear socks and sneakers.

PERFECTLY PRINCESS TEA PARTY: Young regals (and their grown-up guardians) are encouraged to dress like their favorite princess for this festive tea party, offered daily from 10:30 A.M. to noon (except Tuesdays and Thursdays) in the Garden View Tea Room at Walt Disney World's Grand Floridian resort. The tea party is hosted by Miss Rose Petal, a magical rose from Aurora's garden that has come to life to lead storytelling, sing-alongs, and a princess parade. Guests may take a break from sipping tea and eating cake to visit with Princess Aurora, aka Sleeping Beauty.

All guests between the ages of 3 and 9 get a My Disney Girl doll, dressed as Princess Aurora, plus accessories. The cost for one adult and child (ages 3–9) is $334, including gratuity (tax is extra). Each extra child is about $182 (plus tax), while an extra adult pays about $99 (plus tax). If you'd like a child under age 3 to receive the merchandise, they should be listed as a 3-year-old. Reservations are required and may be made up to 180 days ahead.

PIRATE ADVENTURE: Ahoy there, mateys! In this adventure, young pirates don bandannas and hit the high seas in search of treasure. The ship shoves off at the Grand Floridian marina on select mornings. From there, it visits exotic ports of call (other resort marinas), where guests collect valuable treasures and enjoy a light snack. It's available to potty-trained kids ages 4–12 on select mornings. Cost per child is about $39. Reservations are required and are available up to 180 days ahead. Note that participants should wear socks and sneakers.

WONDERLAND TEA PARTY: Fans of Alice and her Wonderland friends will have a blast at this party presented at 1900 Park Fare at Disney's Grand Floridian resort. During the event, kids decorate and eat cupcakes. They'll also be treated to a story and have tea with the characters. The cost is about $50 per child, ages 4–12 (potty-trained). The tea party is offered Monday through Friday at 2 P.M.

Specialty Cruises

At Walt Disney World, every evening ends with a bang—which comes in the form of pyrotechnic spectaculars. Two such presentations, the Magic Kingdom's Wishes fireworks and Epcot's Illumi-Nations: Reflections of Earth, are seen by scores of park-goers on a nightly basis. However, these displays are also enjoyed by a privileged few, far removed from the hubbub of theme park crowds yet close enough to marvel at the subtleties of each brilliant burst. These are the guests who chose to book a specialty cruise. This vintage vantage point is available to everyone, provided that the rates don't break the budget and that reservations are made in advance. Of course, there is the other extreme: a peaceful, moonlit cruise on the quiet waterways of the World. This option is also available to guests who book a specialty cruise.

Reservations are accepted up to 24 hours ahead; advance reservations, accepted up to 180 days ahead, are strongly recommended. While specifics may change, the following is an indication of what was available at press time.

THE GRAND I: This striking 52-foot Sea Ray Sedan Bridge yacht escorts up to 18 guests at a time. A 3-hour tour of the Seven Seas Lagoon and Bay Lake culminates with a front-row seat for the Magic Kingdom's fireworks whenever

possible. (The vessel has an audio feed that allows guests to hear the show's soundtrack.)

The *Grand I* yacht departs from the Grand Floridian, but can stop at the Polynesian Village, Contemporary, Wilderness Lodge, or Fort Wilderness on request. It starts at about $700 (plus tax) per hour to rent, with the per-boatload fee covering up to 17 guests, plus a driver and a deckhand. Butler and private dining service are available (for an additional fee). This is the most luxurious watercraft experience at Walt Disney World. Call 407-824-2682 for more *Grand I* yacht pricing details or to make a reservation.

PONTOON BOATS: More practical than luxurious, Disney's fleet of pontoon boats still deliver a crowd-pleasing cruise experience. The boats, which accommodate up to 10, take guests on tours of the Seven Seas Lagoon and Bay Lake, near the Magic Kingdom, as well as Crescent Lake, near Epcot's World Showcase. Those in the Magic Kingdom area are treated to VIP viewing of the Wishes fireworks show (as well as the audio), while Epcot-area cruisers take in IllumiNations: Reflections of Earth, when available. All pontoon boats offer the Wishes soundtrack—a special treat.

Pontoon cruises last about one hour. Magic Kingdom fireworks excursions depart from the Grand Floridian, Polynesian Village, Contemporary, Wilderness Lodge, and Fort Wilderness marinas. IllumiNations cruises leave from the Yacht Club marina. The cost for cruises (which includes a driver) starts at about $299 to $349, plus tax, per boatload (higher for fireworks cruises). Call 407-WDW-PLAY (939-7529) for additional details or to make reservations.

VIP Tour? Sure!

You may have seen them in the theme parks—those cheery folks in the plaid vests. They are VIP guides, leading guests on customized trips through Walt Disney World.

The point is to minimize the hassle factor, while maximizing the overall magic component. Though participating in a VIP tour won't necessarily let you cut the line, it may yield some special seating for stage shows and parades. One tour guide can host up to 10 guests at a cost of about $175–$315 per hour. There is a 6-hour minimum per trip. Parties larger than 10 will require a second guide. Make your needs known when you book the tour. Cancellations must be made at least 48 hours in advance to avoid a fee. Call 407-560-4033 for additional VIP tour information or to make a reservation.

Tours and Programs

Here's your chance to experience Walt Disney World from the inside out. Adult guests may be required to carry a photo ID when attending backstage programs. Tours and prices are subject to change in 2017; for information or to make reservations, call 407-WDW-TOUR (939-8687) between 8 A.M. and 8 P.M. (daily) and have your credit card handy. Photography is not permitted while in "backstage" areas of Walt Disney World. **Note:** Tours marked with an asterisk (*) may be included with the Magic Your Way Premium Package, though restrictions may apply. Prices quoted do not include tax.

BACKSTAGE MAGIC (Monday through Friday; 9 A.M.): This is one of Disney World's best programs. Highlighting the nearly 8-hour exploration of the Magic Kingdom, Disney's Hollywood Studios, and Epcot may be an underground tour of the Magic Kingdom's Utilidors—Disney's tunnel system. Lunch is included, as are a few surprises. Cost is $255, plus tax. Park admission is not required or included. Guests must be at least 12 years old. This is one of the most popular WDW experiences—book early.

BACKSTAGE TALES* (Daily; 7:30 A.M.): This tour offers guests a look at conservation, animal care, behavioral studies, and the Animal Nutrition Center and Veterinary Hospital. The cost is about $90, and theme park admission is required, but not included. Guests must be at least 12 years old to participate in the tour.

BEHIND THE SEEDS* (daily; every hour between 10:30 A.M. and 4:30 P.M.): An opportunity for guests of all ages to get a closer look at the greenhouses and fish farm that are part of The Land pavilion at Epcot. During the tour, guests will have close encounters with insects and plants. A guide shares knowledge of hydroponics growing systems and crops from around the globe. Expect to be on your feet for the full hour of this experience. Cost is $20 per adult, $16 per child (ages 3–9). This tour is best enjoyed by sturdy adults and older kids. Reservations may be made in advance or at the tour desk on the lower level of The Land (to the left of the entrance the Soarin' Around the World attraction).

DISNEY'S FAMILY MAGIC TOUR* (daily; 10 A.M.): Families and friends may join in this 2-hour "scavenger-hunt-style" quest to save the Magic Kingdom. Cost is $34 (it's available to everyone, but recommended for parties with kids between the ages of 4 and 12). Magic Kingdom admission is required but is not included.

DIVEQUEST (Tuesday–Saturday; 4:30 and 5:30 P.M.): The highlight of the 2½-hour program is a 40-minute underwater adventure—complete with sharks, turtles, rays, and other fish—in The Seas with Nemo & Friends aquarium. Participants must show proof of current scuba certification. Cost is about $180. Guests ages 10–12 must dive with a parent or guardian. Gear is provided. Epcot park admission is not required or included in the tour price.

DOLPHINS IN DEPTH (Tuesday–Saturday; 9:45 A.M.): This 3-hour Epcot program (about 30 minutes takes place in the water) teaches guests about dolphin behavior as they interact with the animals and observe researchers and trainers working with them. Cost is about $199. Minimum age is 13. Guests ages 13–17 must be accompanied by a paying adult. Park admission is not required or included. Wet suits are provided; wear your own swimsuit.

EPCOT SEAS AQUA TOUR (Tuesday–Saturday; 12:30 P.M.): A 2½-hour program (about 30 minutes of which is in the water) that lets guests learn about and interact with ocean life in The Seas with Nemo & Friends pavilion. First, guests watch a video about sea creatures, then they join them in their habitat using a Supplied-Air Snorkel system. Cost is about $145. Gear is included, as are light refreshments, a souvenir gift, and a group photo. Guests must wear swim suits. The tour is open to guests age 8 and up. Epcot admission is not required or included.

KEYS TO THE KINGDOM*

(daily; 8:30, 9, and 9:30 A.M.): A 5-hour tour that offers an on-site orientation to the history and workings of Walt Disney World's original theme park, the Magic Kingdom. Guests visit an attraction (waiting in the regular attraction line) and take a peek at the Utilidors (the legendary tunnels underneath the park). Cost is about $80, plus theme park admission. Lunch is included. Guests must be at least 16 years old to participate.

THE MAGIC BEHIND OUR STEAM TRAINS*

(daily; 7:30 A.M.): A 3-hour tour that gives guests an inside look at the Walt Disney World Railroad. In addition to an exploration of Walt Disney's passion for steam trains, guests visit the backstage "roundhouse" where the steam trains are stored and join the opening crew as they prepare for the daily railroad operation in the Magic Kingdom. Guests must be at least 10 to take the tour. Cost is about $54 per person. Theme park admission is required but not included in the tour price.

PHOTO BY JILL SAFRO

WALT DISNEY: MARCELINE TO MAGIC KINGDOM

(Daily; 8:15 A.M.): Explore how events in Walt Disney's life helped shape the Walt Disney World Resort and the attractions within it in this 2½- to 3-hour walking tour. As one of Walt's final visions, the Magic Kingdom shares many similarities with the story of his life. By using the park as a walking timeline, guests discover how Walt's life inspired him to create some of the most cherished stories and attractions the parks have to offer. Guests also get an insider look at several of those aforementioned attractions. Tours cost $35 per person (plus park admission). Guests should arrive 15 minutes

early and wear their most comfortable walking shoes (expect to cover a lot of ground). It's available to guests age 12 and up.

SAVOR THE SAVANNA: EVENING SAFARI EXPERIENCE

(daily, 4:30, 5:30, and 6:30 P.M.): A private, guided journey, this experience is limited to 12 guests per excursion. The evening safari adventure begins with a journey deep in the heart of Harambe Wildlife Preserve. It offers secluded viewing areas of the savanna, plus a sampling of African-inspired, tapas-style nibbles and regional wines, beer, and soft drinks.

Cost is about $169 per person, plus tax. (The price includes food, drinks, and a keepsake.) Guests must be at least 8 years old to participate in this walking program. Park admission is required but is not included in the tour price.

THE UNDISCOVERED FUTURE WORLD*

(Monday—Saturday; 9 A.M.): Walt Disney dreamed about making the world a better place. In this 4-hour tour, guests are taken back to the creation of Epcot and learn about Walt's lofty ambitions and his legacy.

Guests walk to Future World pavilions and learn how each area celebrates humanity's accomplishments and challenges. The goal is to share the vision behind the park.

Cost is about $69 per person, plus tax. Guests must be at least 16 years old to participate in this walking program. Park admission is required but is not included in the tour price.

WANYAMA SAFARI

(daily; 3:30 P.M.): A 3-hour experience that includes a private tour of the animal savannas surrounding Disney's Animal Kingdom Lodge. Following the tour, guests have dinner at Jiko—The Cooking Place. (It's a family-style meal.) Guests must be at least 8 years old and staying at Animal Kingdom

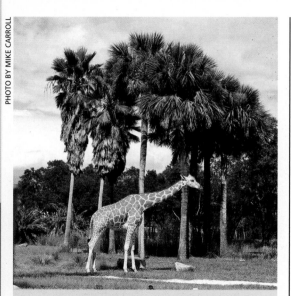

PHOTO BY MIKE CARROLL

Wild Africa Trek

A thrilling, 3-hour adventure, the Wild Africa Trek is not for the faint of heart or those with any trepidation about teetering high in the air on a rickety rope bridge.

The guided tour, which is offered daily at Disney's Animal Kingdom park, is a VIP safari adventure for groups of 12 or less. It includes hiking through jungle, near the edge of a cliff, and over the savanna—plus many up-close encounters of the animal kind.

Available to guests age 8 and above, the rain-or-shine trek costs vary, depending on the season, and includes snacks (you can't bring your own) and an access code to view and download digital photos. Park admission is required but not included. This is an active experience—be sure to wear comfortable shoes and attire. Note that there are no "chicken exits" here. For pricing and information, visit *www.disneyworld.com*. To make a reservation, call 407-939-8687.

Guests who wish to participate in a less physical journey or a wheelchair accessible trek may call 407-938-1373 to request an alternative offering.

park's international pavilions. Lunch is included, as is a traditional tea service in the Morocco pavilion. Cost is about $109 per person. Theme park admission is required, but not included. For pricing, schedules, and additional details, call 407-939-8687, or visit *www.disneyworld.com*.

WILDERNESS BACK TRAIL ADVENTURE (Tuesday through Saturday): A 2-hour experience, this adventure lets guests explore the Fort Wilderness area while aboard a Segway personal transporter. (It's a special model with off-road-type tires.) The first hour is devoted to training (it's not as easy as it looks!), with the second spent exploring with an experienced storytelling guide. Guests must be at least 16 and in good health. (You'll be on your feet the whole time, and operating the Segway requires more muscle than one might expect.) The cost is approximately $95, plus tax.

YULETIDE FANTASY (seasonal): A festive 3½-hour experience, this program showcases the way Disney weaves stories and folklore into decorations found in the theme parks and resorts. It offers a unique perspective on how colors, textures, architecture, and illusions help all of Walt Disney World deck the halls for the holidays.

The cost is about $95, plus tax, per person. Theme park admission is not included or required for this experience. Guests must be at least 16 years old to participate. All guests must present a photo ID.

Lodge. Cost is about $191 per person. (Price includes tax and gratuity.) The Wanyama Safari may be booked up to 180 days in advance. Call 407-938-4755 for details or to make a reservation.

WORLD SHOWCASE: DESTINATIONS DISCOVERED* (daily; 9:30 A.M.): A 4- to 4.5-hour walking tour of World Showcase, DestiNations Discovered covers the culture, architecture, and design details of several of the

Sports

First-time visitors don't always realize that Disney provides a plethora of sporting opportunities. Within WDW's 40 or so square miles, there are more tennis courts than at most tennis resorts and more holes of championship-caliber golf than at most golf centers, plus so many other diversions—from fishing and biking to boating, parasailing, and horseback riding—that the quantity and variety are matched by few other vacation destinations.

So while the family golfers are pursuing a perfect swing on one of several first-rate, 18-hole courses, tennis buffs can be wearing themselves out on the courts, parasailors can soar up to 600 feet above the area near the Magic Kingdom, and anglers can be casting away in hopes of hooking a big bass. Those who prefer to spectate rather than participate can visit a virtual sports mecca at the ESPN Wide World of Sports Complex, an enormous, state-of-the-art facility that hosts an array of sporting events, both amateur and professional. And those who prefer the sedate can treat themselves to a soothing spa treatment.

Instruction, as well as guides, drivers, and assorted supervisors, makes every sport as much fun for beginners as for hard-core aficionados. Moreover, the ready accessibility of WDW sporting activities—via an extensive system of public transportation (see *Transportation & Accommodations*)—means that no family member need curtail playtime to chauffeur others around.

WDW Golf

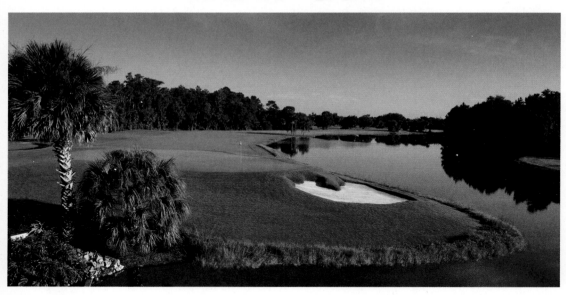

Most people don't immediately think of Disney World for a golf outing. Yet there are superb 18-hole courses here: The Magnolia and the Palm are across from the Polynesian Village resort. Nearby is the Lake Buena Vista course. Its fairways are framed by Saratoga Springs and Old Key West resorts. And the Four Seasons resort boasts a stellar course, too. While the WDW courses won't set anyone's knees to knocking, they're demanding enough to have merited the status of a stop on the PGA Tour tournament trail.

PALM & MAGNOLIA: The wide-open, tree-dotted Magnolia measures 5,127 yards from the front tees, 6,558 from the middle, and 7,516 from the back. The Palm (which was recently redesigned by Arnold Palmer Course Design) is tighter, with more wooded fairways and nine water hazards; it measures 5,213 yards from the front, 6,339 from the middle, and 7,010 from the back. Both courses have received a four-star ("outstanding") rating from *Golf Digest* magazine. The Magnolia and Palm share two driving ranges and putting greens.

Oak Trail: This walking nine-hole, 2,913-yard layout, a walking course tucked into a corner within the Magnolia, was designed for beginners and junior golfers, but it has some tough holes, including two par 5s. Many moderate and accomplished golfers enjoy the opportunity to tune up or play a quick 9.

LAKE BUENA VISTA COURSE: Joe Lee's design measures 5,194 yards from the front tees, 6,264 from the middle, and 6,749 from the rearmost markers. Among the shortest of the 18-hole, par-72 courses, it has a fair amount of water, and its tree-lined fairways are Walt Disney World's narrowest. The course is well suited for beginners but challenges experienced players. A driving range and putting green are also available.

Essentials

WHEN TO GO: January through April is peak golfing season. To beat the crowds, play on a Monday or Tuesday, and tee off in the late afternoons (mornings are very busy when the mercury rises). Summer discounts may apply. From June through late September, guests pay as little as $62 after 10 A.M. After 3 P.M., the price drops to $49. Florida resident, Theme Park Annual Passholder, Military, and Disney Vacation Club member specials may be offered. Annual golf memberships are also a possibility. Call 407-939-4653 for details.

SPORTS

236

RESERVATIONS: Call 407-WDW-GOLF (939-4653) or visit *www.golfwdw.com* to confirm rates and to secure tee times. From January through April, morning and early afternoon tee times should be reserved well in advance; starting times after 3 P.M. are often available at the last minute. Reservations must be made with a major credit card. Cancellations must be made at least 24 hours ahead to avoid penalties.

FEES: At the 18-hole courses, greens fees (including a required cart) vary with the course and season. Rates range from about $85 to $125 for day visitors (not staying at a Walt Disney World resort). Rates are usually discounted for guests staying at any resort on WDW property (including Swan, Dolphin, and the resorts on Hotel Plaza Boulevard).

Midafternoon rates, known as "twilight rates," may yield discounts. Available throughout the year, twilight rates run about $39 to $69.

Cost for adults to play Oak Trail is $40 for 9 holes; juniors (17 and under) pay $22 for 9 holes. Prices don't include tax and are subject to change.

INSTRUCTION: At the WDW Golf Studio at the Palm and Magnolia courses, private 45-minute lessons cost $75 for adults and $50 for juniors (up to age 17). Lessons are customized to all levels of experience. Video analysis may be used. Prices are subject to change. Walt Disney World resort guests may make reservations up to 120 days in advance; call 407-WDW-GOLF (939-4653).

DRESS: Proper golf attire is required. Collared shirts or golf-style collarless shirts are necessary, and any shorts must be Bermuda length.

EQUIPMENT RENTAL: Equipment can be rented at all courses; club rentals start at about

HOT TIP!
The Four Seasons resort on Walt Disney World's Dream Tree Boulevard boasts an 18-hole, par-71, Tom Fazio–designed golf course. Tranquilo Golf Club is available to everyone. For pricing and additional information, call 800-267-3046 or visit *www.fourseasons.com/orlando/*.

$50, plus tax. Photo ID is required for rentals. Range balls (about $7 per basket) are among available items. Guests staying at most Walt Disney World resorts receive $20 club rental when they purchase a non-discounted round of golf at Disney's Palm, Magnolia, or Lake Buena Vista courses. Also included is transportation to and from the Walt Disney World resort via taxi (paid with vouchers). Swan, Dolphin, Four Seasons, and resorts on Hotel Plaza Boulevard are not included in transportation.

Tennis

Saratoga Springs Resort & Spa has two clay courts. All other Walt Disney World tennis is played on hard courts. Yacht and Beach Club share one court; Fort Wilderness, Saratoga Springs, Contemporary's Bay Lake Tower, Animal Kingdom's Kidani Village, and BoardWalk each have two; Old Key West has three; and the Swan and Dolphin share a four-court facility. Courts are free to guests staying at a WDW resort. For details or to make lesson reservations, call 321-228-1146.

Essentials

WHEN TO GO: Courts are often open from about 8 A.M. to 7 P.M. daily; courts at the Swan and Dolphin are open 24 hours a day (lighted courts are available). Weather-wise, January, October, and November are prime months for playing tennis. All courts are available on a first-come, first-served basis. During very busy periods, the length of time a single group of players can occupy a court is restricted to two hours on any morning, afternoon, or evening.

Equipment rental is limited at Walt Disney World (Swan and Dolphin only). Guests should bring their own tennis racquets and balls.

DRESS: Tennis whites are appropriate, but not required, for play on Disney's courts. Tennis shoes are a must.

Waters of the World

Boating

Disney World is the home of the country's largest fleet of pleasure boats. Cruising on Bay Lake and the Seven Seas Lagoon can be excellent sport, and a variety of boats are available for rent at WDW resort marinas. Bay Lake excursions originate from the Contemporary, Wilderness Lodge, and Fort Wilderness. The Polynesian Village and Grand Floridian send boaters out from their marinas on the shore of Seven Seas Lagoon. The Yacht and Beach Club, BoardWalk, Swan, and Dolphin share a boating haven in 25-acre Crescent Lake.

To rent, guests must show a valid driver's license or passport. Rental of certain craft may carry other requirements. No privately owned boats are permitted on WDW waters. All prices and times are subject to change.

AMPHICARS: It's a car! It's a boat! It's a blast from America's motoring past (the 1960s to be precise). Yep, the amphibious Amphicar is back. Disney has brought nine of these classic vehicles out of retirement and put them back to work at Disney Springs. Doing double duty as artwork/water taxi, Amphicars are next to The Boathouse eatery. Up to three guests may enjoy a 20-minute tour of Disney Springs waterways for about $125 (captain included). Tours are offered from 10 A.M. until 10 P.M. daily, weather permitting.

BOSTON WHALER MONTAUK BOATS: These 17-foot motorboats are a good choice for relaxing cruises. They accommodate up to six passengers, and may be rented for about $45 per half hour at the Polynesian Village, Contemporary, Grand Floridian, Wilderness Lodge, Yacht and Beach Club, and Fort Wilderness marinas.

CANOEING: A long paddle down the Fort Wilderness canals is such a tranquil way to pass a misty morning that it's hard to remember that the bustle of the Magic Kingdom is not far away. Canoes may be rented at the Bike Barn at Fort Wilderness (about $8 per half hour, $13 per hour). Ocean kayaks (open-top kayaks) may be rented here, too (expect to pay about $7 per half hour, $11 per hour). Note that these watercraft are for use on Fort Wilderness canals only, not for Bay Lake or the Seven Seas Lagoon.

MOTORBOATING: It seems there are always dozens of boats zipping back and forth across Bay Lake, Seven Seas Lagoon, and Crescent Lake. These are called Sea Raycers, and they're just as much fun as they look. The boats are quick enough so that a lot of watery terrain can be covered in a half hour (for about $35), though it's quite tempting to splurge on a full hour.

Sea Raycers can be rented year-round at the Grand Floridian, Polynesian Village, Wilderness Lodge, Contemporary, Yacht & Beach Club, and Fort Wilderness marinas. Guests must be at least 12 years old and 5 feet tall to rent Sea Raycer boats. Kids under the minimum age and height may ride as passengers, but they're not allowed to drive. We suggest that drivers wear a water-proof watch—it's amazing how the time flies!

PARASAILING: Excursions are offered at the Contemporary resort marina. Each 8- to 10-minute flight costs about $95 for one person to soar to 450 feet and $130 to rise to 600 feet, $170 for two to ride tandem at 450 feet and $195 for two to hit a height of 600 feet. Flights are offered 7 days a week, weather-permitting. (They will be canceled due to lightning, high wind, or other inclement weather—in which case a full refund will be issued.) Reservations must be made at least 24 hours in advance (and made up to a year ahead); visit *www.sammyduvall.com*, or call 407-939-0754. Walk-ups are accepted on a first-come, first-served basis. Wear loose-fitting clothing, but don't bother with a swimsuit—guests take off from and land on the back of the boat without getting wet.

The minimum age to parasail is 6. Guests younger than 18 must have an adult present. The minimum weight requirement is 130 pounds (guests under 130 pounds may fly tandem with another guest in order to reach the minimum weight allowance). The maximum weight per parasailing flight is 330 pounds.

PEDAL BOATS: These Swan-shaped watercraft rent for about $7 per half hour or $11 per hour at the Swan and Dolphin marina.

PERSONAL WATERCRAFT AND GUIDED EXCURSIONS: Three-seat personal Jet Ski-style watercraft are available for rent at Sammy Duvall's Watersports Centre at the Contemporary resort. Hours to rent are usually 9 A.M. to 5 P.M. (They open at 10 A.M. during the winter.) The cost is about $135 (plus tax) for an hour for up to three passengers (of any age). The maximum weight per vehicle is 400 pounds. Participants must be at least 16 years old to drive. Guests under age 18 must have an adult sign a waiver prior to the trip.

It's also possible to start the day with a guided excursion aboard a 3-seat personal watercraft. Starting daily at 9 A.M. from the Contemporary resort marina (departures start at 10 A.M. in the winter), a guide calls attention to points of interest on and around Bay Lake and the Seven Seas Lagoon. After the tour, guests have time to ride on their own, under the guide's supervision. A maximum of 4 rental units operate during each excursion. Cost is about $135 (plus tax) for up to 3 people. For information or to make reservations, visit *www.sammyduvall.com*; 407-939-0754.

PONTOON BOATS: Motorized, canopied platforms on pontoons are perfect for families, inexperienced boaters, and visitors more interested in serenity than in thrills. Available at select resort marinas, the 21-foot craft hold up to ten passengers and cost about $45, plus tax, per half hour. Guests must be at least 18 years old (with a valid driver's license) to drive a pontoon boat.

WATERSKIING, WAKEBOARDING, AND TUBING: Ski boats with Sammy Duvall instructors and equipment are available at the Contemporary resort marina. Watercraft may be reserved here, too. Reservations must be made at least 24 hours in advance and may be made up to a year ahead. Same-day walk-ups are accepted on a first-come, first-served basis; call 407-939-0754, or visit *www.sammyduvall.com* for pricing and to make reservations. Minors under 18 must have a legal guardian sign a waiver prior to departure. Note that activities may be canceled due to inclement weather (such as lightning, wind, etc.). Sammy Duvall's Watersports Centre operates seasonally: 9 A.M. to 5 P.M. in summer; 10 A.M. to 5 P.M. in winter.

Fishing

The 70,000 bass with which Bay Lake was stocked in the mid-1960s have grown and multiplied as a result of WDW's restrictive fishing policy. (It's strictly catch-and-release.) No angling is permitted on Bay Lake or the Seven Seas Lagoon, except on the guided fishing expeditions. Largemouth bass weighing two to eight pounds are the most common catch.

Fishing excursions are presented by BASS, the world's largest fishing organization. Guests who participate in a Walt Disney World excursion receive a one-year BASS membership, which includes 11 issues of *Bassmaster* magazine, a membership pack, decal, handbook, eligibility to compete in national events, discounts, and other benefits.

Bay Lake excursions depart daily (call 407-939-2277 for details). Trips last two or four hours and includes guide, gear, and refreshments (soft drinks). Guides will pick up guests at the Contemporary, Grand Floridian, Polynesian Village, Fort Wilderness, and Wilderness Lodge. Guides will pick up guests at Old Key West, Saratoga Springs, and Port Orleans Riverside and French Quarter, too. Two- and four-hour excursions accommodate up to five anglers and include guide, gear, and drinks. Kids under 16 must be accompanied by an adult.

Anglers might also consider two-hour tours that depart from the Yacht and Beach Club at 7 A.M., 10 A.M., and 1:30 P.M. All trips accommodate up to five people. A guide, gear, and soft drinks are included.

The Magic Kingdom resorts and Coronado Springs resorts also offer two-hour excursions on pontoon boats that accommodate one or two guests. They depart from the resort marinas at 7 A.M., 10 A.M., and 1:30 P.M. daily. The $235 to $455 price includes equipment and a guide.

Reservations must be made at least 24 hours in advance and may be made up to 180 days ahead; call 407-WDW-BASS (939-2277). Note that excursions may be canceled or cut short if the weather is stormy or there is lightning in the WDW vicinity.

Fishing on your own—again, strictly catch-and-release—is permitted in the canals at Fort Wilderness. Fort Wilderness guests may toss in lines from any campground canal shore. Fishing licenses are not required. Rods and reels and cane poles are available for rent at the Fort Wilderness Bike Barn. Bait may be purchased (worms and night crawlers are both about $4).

ESPN Wide World of Sports Complex

Variety is the name of the game at the ESPN Wide World of Sports Complex. The multi-million-dollar complex invites athletes and spectators alike to dive into more than 70 types of sporting experiences. It's a grand slam for die-hard sports fans.

The 220-acre facility—which is teamed up with ESPN—hosts events in everything from jump rope to wrestling. The home of the Pop Warner Super Bowl and National Cheer & Dance championships is also the spring training site for Major League Baseball's Atlanta Braves. (At press time, it was possible that the team would move elsewhere after the 2017 season. For updates visit *www. atlanabraves.mlb.com*.)

Designed as a modern vision of old-time Floridian building styles, the architecture harks back to days when sports facilities were extensions of their neighborhoods; there is even a town commons (which serves as a welcome center).

The complex includes a baseball stadium; a field house that accommodates basketball, wrestling, and volleyball; a track-and-field complex; tennis courts; and multipurpose fields fit for football, soccer, and more.

A general-admission ticket costs about $18 for adults and $13 for kids ages 3 through 9. Tickets may be purchased at the front gate and allow guests to watch all "nonpremium" events. Guests are only admitted on days when events are scheduled. Tickets to premium events may be purchased through Ticketmaster (800-745-3000; or *www.ticketmaster.com*) and include general admission to the complex.

Premium-event tickets may also be purchased at the Wide World of Sports complex box office on the day of an event, depending on availability.

Prices vary from event to event. Note that in addition to traditional seats, the baseball stadium has lawn seating. If you purchase lawn tickets, bring something to sit on and get there as early as possible. Prime locations go fast!

Essentials

HOW TO GET THERE: Direct bus transportation is available at All-Star, Pop Century, and Caribbean Beach resorts (based on the events scheduled). Other WDW resort guests must take a bus (plan to transfer at a park or Disney Springs) to one of these resorts. Allow at least an hour for the commute (more if you're attending a premium event). Buses run Thursday through Monday from 5 P.M. until about 11 P.M. Disney resort buses also run when events are taking place, starting one hour prior to complex opening time, until 11 P.M. or the time the complex closes (whichever is later).

If you are driving, take Exit 65 off I-4 to Victory Way. The complex is between U.S. 192 and Osceola Parkway. Parking is free but limited. If you plan to attend a premium event, arrive as early as possible—or risk scrambling for a spot in an unpaved, auxiliary lot.

WHERE TO EAT: The big-ticket eatery here is ESPN Wide World of Sports Grill. (This venue operates on event days only.)

There are more than 30 concessions for those seeking a somewhat lighter bite. They offer hot dogs, popcorn, soft drinks, and beer, as well as a few more substantial, yet just as portable, snacks.

It is also possible to pre-order boxed meals, pizza, and beverages meals via *www.espnwwos.com*. There is a minimum of $50 and all orders must be placed at least two days prior to the event. For hot buffet options, call 407-566-6698.

Touch Base

Get the scoop on all the scheduled action at the ESPN Wide World of Sports Complex by calling 407-541-5600 or visiting the website *www.espnwwos.com*.

More Sporting Fun

ARCHERY: Channel your inner Robin Hood at a Fort Wilderness program known as the Archery Experience. The 90-minute experience includes a quick but thorough lesson and lots of shooting time. It takes place every Thursday through Saturday at 2:45 P.M. Available to guests age 7 and older, the Archery Experience costs about $45 per person (plus tax). Book it up to 180 days in advance by calling 407-WDW-7529.

BIKING: Pedaling along the rustic pathways and lightly trafficked roads at Fort Wilderness can be a pleasant way to spend a couple of hours. Both areas are spread out, so bicycles are a practical way to get around. Bikes are also available for rent year-round at Old Key West, Wilderness Lodge, Port Orleans, Caribbean Beach, BoardWalk, Yacht and Beach Club, and Saratoga Springs. The cost is about $10 an hour or $20 per day. Bikes with training wheels or baby seats are available. Helmets are mandatory for guests up to the age of 16 and may be borrowed for free.

RUNNING: Except from late fall to early spring, the weather is usually much too steamy in Central Florida for jogging. If you run very early in the morning in warm seasons, the heat is somewhat less daunting. The 1.2-mile promenade around the lake at the Caribbean Beach resort is ideal for running, as is the three-quarter-mile promenade that surrounds Crescent Lake (a waterway that's bordered by the Swan and Dolphin, Yacht and Beach Club, and BoardWalk resorts), and the nearly mile-long path circling Coronado Springs' Lago Dorado. Fort Wilderness and the Wilderness Lodge are connected by a jogging trail that is about 2.5 miles long and features exercise stations. Old Key West also has scenic routes, averaging about a mile in length. There are also trails at All-Stars, Grand Floridian, Contemporary, Art of Animation, Port Orleans, and Pop Century.

MINIATURE GOLF: The Fantasia Gardens Miniature Golf complex, located near the Swan, Dolphin, and BoardWalk resorts, offers players two 18-hole courses themed to the Disney film *Fantasia*. The Fantasia Fairways course offers a difficult layout sure to tantalize serious golfers. It features traditional golf obstacles, such as water hazards, doglegs, and roughs. Don't be fooled by the small size of the Fantasia Fairways course—the challenges are big. (The record for the par-61 course is 47.)

Fantasia Gardens, on the other hand, is all in fun, with clever things (a dancing hippo, xylophone stairs, brooms dumping buckets of water) at every hole. The degree of difficulty varies from hole to hole, but this is an easy course to conquer. There are some challenges out there, however. Hole 15, for example, is one of the trickier ones. Here, golfers aim through mini-geysers that randomly squirt water into the air.

Disney's Winter Summerland miniature golf course is a mere stone's throw from the Blizzard Beach water park (they share a bus stop during Blizzard Beach hours). Designed as a vacation retreat for Santa and his elves, the two 18-hole courses boast a festive atmosphere, complete with Christmas carol soundtracks. The sandy-surface course is a bit more challenging than its snowy-surface counterpart.

A round on any course costs about $14 for adults, $12 for kids ages 3 through 9. The second round is 25 percent off. Typical playing time is about an hour. Hours are generally 10 A.M. to 11 P.M., but vary seasonally. For information, call 407-WDW-PLAY (939-7529).

SPAS AND HEALTH CLUBS: Health clubs include the Contemporary's Olympiad Fitness Center, Sturdy Branches at Wilderness Lodge, Zahanati at Animal Kingdom Lodge, La Vida at Coronado Springs, Health Club at Saratoga Springs, Muscles and Bustles at BoardWalk, the Health Club at the Grand Floridian, Resort Fitness Center at Old Key West, Ship Shape at the Yacht and Beach Club, and the fitness center at the Swan. Registered guests may use their respective resort's facility for free. Guests not registered in a resort with a health club can use the facilities for a fee.

In addition to fitness centers, full-service spas are located at the Grand Floridian, Saratoga Springs, the Dolphin, and Buena Vista Palace. There are special spa packages available at each of these resorts. (See pages 228–229 for details on WDW resort spas.)

SWIMMING: Although the beachfronts are strictly for strolling, sunbathing, and sand castle construction, swimmers may splash in one of the many elaborately themed pools that come in every shape and size imaginable. Typhoon Lagoon and Blizzard Beach water parks only add to the fun (see *Everything Else in the World* for water park specifics).

HOT TIP!

As signs posted along the beaches indicate, swimming and wading are not permitted in any of Walt Disney World's lakes. The rule is meant to protect guests from unguarded water and from exposure to naturally occurring bacteria and other dangerous wildlife, such as snakes and alligators, common to Florida lakes.

POOLS: Walt Disney World resorts have at least one pool apiece. With the exception of sister resorts (Yacht and Beach Club; Port Orleans French Quarter and Riverside; All-Star Movies, All-Star Music, and All-Star Sports; and Swan and Dolphin), which share some of their recreational facilities, WDW hotel pools are open to guests staying at the respective resort. This policy was initiated to prevent overcrowding. All pools are heated in winter. Resort guests may borrow life jackets at no cost. Guests who cannot swim should wear life jackets at all times while in or near a pool.

Featuring one pool each are Animal Kingdom Lodge and Port Orleans French Quarter. The Grand Floridian, Contemporary, Polynesian, Fort Wilderness, the Wilderness Lodge, and All-Stars have two pools each. BoardWalk, Pop Century, and Art of Animation have three pools; Coronado Springs, Old Key West, and Saratoga Springs all feature four swimming holes; Port Orleans Riverside has six, and Caribbean Beach has seven. The Yacht and Beach Club resorts share three unguarded pools, plus a small water park known as Stormalong Bay. It features slides, a sand-bottomed wading area, and a lazy river. Saratoga Springs resort has four pools. The Swan and Dolphin share a lovely, themed grotto pool with a slide, one lap pool, and a third smaller pool. In addition, each of the resorts on Hotel Plaza Boulevard has its own pool.

There are no diving boards; swimmers in search of a big splash should head to Blizzard Beach or Typhoon Lagoon. Each park features a ginormous wave pool. Lifeguards are on duty during most daylight hours at each WDW resort's main pool.

TRAIL RIDES: Guided horseback rides into pine woods and palmetto country set off from the front of Fort Wilderness four times daily. This trip is not meant for seasoned gallopers—you can't wander off on your own. The horses have been culled for gentleness, so trips are suitable for novices. Cost is about $46 per person for a 45-minute tour. Kids under the age of 9 are not allowed to ride, and there's a weight limit of 250 pounds. (Younger kids can saddle up on ponies at the TriCircle D Pony Farm for about $8.) Reservations are necessary and may be made up to 180 days in advance by calling 407-WDW-PLAY (939-7529).

VOLLEYBALL & BASKETBALL: Resort volleyball courts are reserved for Walt Disney World resort guests. Caribbean Beach Resort, the Grand Floridian, Yacht and Beach Club, Fort Wilderness, Swan and Dolphin, Coronado Springs, and Old Key West have volleyball courts. Fort Wilderness, Saratoga Springs, Animal Kingdom Lodge (Kidani Village), and Old Key West have basketball hoops.

Good Meals, Great Times

Although fast food is in great supply, it is hardly the entire Walt Disney World dining story. Epcot adds international flavors to the WDW menu. Tempting options at the other theme parks, BoardWalk, and Disney Springs—not to mention new dining frontiers in the ever-growing brood of WDW resorts—make deciding where to eat a mouth-watering dilemma. Disney's ongoing effort to expand its culinary horizons has certainly been successful, producing prominent palate-pleasers such as Le Cellier Steakhouse, The Boathouse, Morimoto Asia, and Flying Fish, plus family favorites such as The Crystal Palace and 50's Prime Time Cafe.

Because there's such a large number and variety of eateries around the World, this chapter presents dining information in two formats. First, we've included an area-by-area rundown—a comprehensive section with descriptions of food purveyors, including sample menu options, that will prove most helpful when you get hungry in a particular part of the World. Second, we've compiled a collection of what we consider to be the best restaurants in a particular category. To select these standouts, we looked at the menu, theme, and overall enjoyability of each restaurant. And, of course, we sampled the food.

Finally, in the chapter's last section, we offer a guide to the varied lounges of the World, along with a briefing on Disney's reservations system and dinner show options—and assurance that great times are destined to follow.

The Restaurants of WDW In the Magic Kingdom

A lot has changed since Walt Disney World's original theme park opened in 1971. Back then, when it came to quelling hunger pangs, it was pretty much burger or bust. Nowadays, the options are a lot more diverse—with everything from egg rolls to cinnamon rolls, smoked turkey legs to lamb stew, and clam chowder to cannelloni. And yes, you can still sink your teeth into a juicy burger. Regardless of your tastes or budget, the six "lands" in the Magic Kingdom boast a bounty of palate-pleasers for the whole family.

First Things First

The letters at the end of each entry refer to the meals served there: breakfast (B), lunch (L), dinner (D), or snacks (S).

• When you see a not-so-hidden Mickey (♥) at the end of an entry, it means that eatery was a Basic Disney Dining Plan* participant at press time (see page 20).

• Eateries in this chapter have been designated inexpensive (under $15), moderate ($15 to $36), expensive ($36 to $60), and very expensive ($60 and up). Prices are based on an adult-sized meal consisting of a beverage, an entrée, and either one appetizer, side order, or dessert (not including tax and tip). These classifications are reflected by dollar symbols at the end of each entry (all symbols are defined by the key at the bottom of each page). Note that breakfast and lunch generally cost less.

• All Walt Disney World restaurants and fast-food spots (except some with outside seating or at the Swan and Dolphin resorts) are nonsmoking only. Some restaurants at BoardWalk and Disney Springs may set aside outdoor sections for smokers.

• Reservations for table-service restaurants (and dinner shows) should be made 180 days in advance; call 407-WDW-DINE (939-3463) or visit www.disneyworld.com/dining/.

We recommend calling 407-WDW-DINE to confirm all WDW restaurant information.

*Disney Dining Plan locations are subject to change without notice.

Adventureland

TABLE SERVICE

JUNGLE NAVIGATION CO. LTD. SKIPPER CANTEEN: Known to many locals simply as "The Jungle Cruise Restaurant," this jovial joint is run by off-duty Jungle Cruise skippers—and the spirit of the attraction permeates the place in a most amusing manner. The menu, infused with Asian, African, and South American influences, features appetizers such as Ginger's "Croc" of hot and sour soup, Falls Family Falafel, and shumai. Entrées at the Skipper Canteen include sustainable fish, curried vegetable stew, rice noodle bowls, and Trader Sam's Head-on shrimp. The eatery opens daily at 11 A.M. L D • $$ • ♥

FAST FOOD & SNACKS

ALOHA ISLE: After you sing with the birdies in the Enchanted Tiki Room, stop here for all things pineapple—juice, spears, floats, and the ever-popular Dole Whip frozen pineapple soft-serve dessert. This spot has been around forever—they are definitely doing something right. Note that Aloha Isle and Sunshine Tree Terrace have swapped locations. S • $ • ♥

SUNSHINE TREE TERRACE: The snack stand, across from the Swiss Family Treehouse, lets you take a break with a refreshing Citrus Swirl (vanilla soft-serve swirled with orange slush, served in a cup). Piña colada and raspberry lemonade slushies are also served. It's possible to get vanilla soft-serve ice cream in a cup, plus lemonade, hot chocolate, iced coffee, and other soft drinks. Sunshine Tree has been dishing out treats for as long as we can remember. S • $ • ♥

TORTUGA TAVERN: The shady spot across from the Pirates of the Caribbean offers BBQ pork and BBQ chicken sandwiches, beef brisket sandwiches, and roasted corn & veggie salad. Kids choices include mac & cheese and PB&J sandwiches. This venue operates seasonally, so it may not be open during your visit to the park. L S • $ • $$ • ♥

B breakfast   **L** lunch   **D** dinner   **S** snacks   /   **$** under $15   **$$** $15–$36   **$$$** $36–$60   **$$$$** $60 and up

Fantasyland

TABLE SERVICE

BE OUR GUEST: Nestled under Beast's Castle, this eatery transports guests into the realm of Disney's *Beauty and the Beast*. Guests sit in one of three dining rooms—the cavernous Ballroom, West Wing, or Rose Gallery—and enjoy a quick-service breakfast or lunch or a table-service dinner. (Reservations are required for all meals.)

Breakfast and lunch guests enter the Beast's parlor to place their orders at touch terminals. Quick-service meals are delivered via a clever bit of technology involving an "enchanted" rose. Breakfast selections include vegetable quiche, eggs Florentine, open-faced bacon and egg sandwiches, scrambled egg whites, and more. The lunch menu includes items such as *croque monsieur* (ham and Gruyère cheese sandwich), carved turkey on a baguette, tuna niçoise salad, and vegetable quiche. The portions here are a bit smaller and the prices a bit steeper here than at other M.K. quick-service eateries. The kids' lunch menu includes whole-grain macaroni, carved-turkey sandwiches, and Mickey meatloaf. While many lunch guests gravitate toward the stately Ballroom, we head right for the West Wing—just don't tell the Beast!

Dinner is a more upscale affair, with starters such as mussels Provinçal with Pernod, French onion soup, and salad with a champagne vinaigrette. Entrées pay homage to a castle feast from the 1400s with pan-seared chicken breast, spice-rubbed pork chop, and seasonal sustainable catch with vegetables. Cupcakes and mousse-filled cream puffs are served tableside. Beer and wine are offered with the evening meal. Book as early as possible. BLD·$–$$$·❤

CINDERELLA'S ROYAL TABLE: You don't have to be a royal to eat like one. At least, not in the Magic Kingdom. This regal eatery, tucked inside Cinderella Castle, is a high-ceilinged, majestic mead hall. It's tiny as Disney spots go, but there's no feeling cramped—thanks to a small number of tables and towering windows. Hosts and hostesses wear Renaissance-inspired garb and address guests as "my lady," or "my lord." Cinderella welcomes "Fairytale Dining" guests into her home all day and greets them in the Castle lobby, while her princess friends mingle in the dining room. Breakfast favorites include shrimp and grits, baked quiche, and caramel apple-stuffed French toast, along with traditional fare. Lunch and dinner showcase seasonal ingredients, featuring items such as pork loin, chicken, and fish of the day.

The all-inclusive cost for breakfast starts at about $63 for adults and $38 for kids (ages 3–9); lunch starts at about $60 for adults, $36 for kids; dinner starts at about $75 for adults, $44 for kids. Prices include tax and gratuity and may be higher during peak times of the year. (The photo package is no longer included. Guests may pose with Cinderella and purchase a PhotoPass photo for $15 or use their own cameras free of charge.) Reservations are an absolute must. **A 180-day advance booking is necessary for all meals. Full payment is required at time of booking.**

One Tough Ticket

Cinderella's Royal Table is consistently one of the most difficult restaurant reservation to secure at Walt Disney World. Why? For starters, Cinderella is one popular princess. And there's the allure of dining in the castle—the most famous landmark in the world's most popular theme park.

Potential guests may make a reservation by visiting *disneyworld.com/dining* or by calling 407-WDW-DINE (939-3463) at *exactly* 7 A.M. Eastern Standard Time, 180 days in advance. (It can't hurt to start dialing a few seconds early.) The meal must be paid for when the reservation is made. There's no charge for infants, but they must be included in the reservation.

Expect your credit card to be charged immediately upon making the reservation. Cancellations or changes to the reservation must be made at least 24 hours ahead to receive a full refund. The only one who can change or cancel a reservation is the one whose name is on the credit card. Reservations cannot be transferred. Guests using the Disney Dining Plan must also book the table with a credit card, but it will not be charged. However, two table-service credits are required for all meals here, as it is a "Signature" restaurant.

Whew! That's a lot of work for one dining experience. Is it worth it? Judging by the smiles we see day in and day out, we have to say yes.

Guests staying at a Disney-owned-and-operated resort should note our Hot Tip on page 248.

Cancellations must be made at least 24 hours in advance to avoid the $10-per-person surcharge. Cinderella recommends that you arrive a few minutes early. This is an extremely difficult table to reserve (see page 245)—so don't get little ones' hopes up until you actually book it. **B L D · $ $ $ · ❤**

FAST FOOD & SNACKS

BIG TOP TREATS: Inside the Big Top Souvenirs tent, this confectionery-counter serves character apples, caramel apples, cake pops, caramel corn, brownies, cookies, and Goofy's Glaciers (sweet, frosty slush treats). **S · $ · ❤**

CHESHIRE CAFE: This small stand is a good spot to cool off with a lemonade, raspberry and lemonade slush, orange juice, or iced coffee. The cafe also serves muffins, assorted cereals with milk, and whole fruit, plus hot coffee, cocoa, and tea. The French vanilla iced coffee makes us smile like the Cheshire Cat. **S · $ · ❤**

THE FRIAR'S NOOK: A walk-up window next to Storybook Treats, this place sells hot dogs, three types of mac and cheese—plain, pot roast, and barbecue chicken, plus carrot cake, and apple and caramel dippers. They serve soy milk, too. Open seasonally. **L S · $ · ❤**

GASTON'S TAVERN: A cozy little lodge nestled in Fantasyland's Enchanted Forest, Gaston's serves beef stew, hummus and chips, mixed vegetables with dip, fruit cups, sliced apples with caramel sauce, chocolate croissants, warm cinnamon rolls, and soft drinks. The specialty of this teetotaling tavern? LeFou's Brew—a not-too-sweet concoction made from frozen apple juice with a hint of toasted marshmallow and topped with all-natural passion fruit-mango foam. It tends to please palates of all ages. And, yes, Gaston really does use antlers in all of his decorating. **L D S · $ · ❤**

PINOCCHIO VILLAGE HAUS: One of the better spots to target with kids in tow, Pinocchio Village Haus is also a good place to take picky adult eaters. It may seem small from the outside, but there are many dining rooms through that door. One room boasts picture windows that overlook the It's a Small World loading area. It's fun to watch the boats bob by as you munch on lunch. Pinocchio offers pizza (aka flatbread), pasta, chicken Parmesan sandwiches, tomato basil soup, chicken nuggets, Caesar salads, fries, garlic knots, and soft drinks. For dessert there's chocolate cake and gelato. Kids' picks include mac and cheese, PB&J, and pizza, all served with apple slices and yogurt. This is a popular place—try to go before or after a mealtime rush. **L D S · $ – $ $ · ❤**

PRINCE ERIC'S VILLAGE MARKET: Appropriately anchored across from The Little Mermaid attraction, this alfresco snack spot specializes in healthier-than-usual snack fare. Fresh fruit, crunchy veggies, hummus, pickles, trail mix, and Mickey pretzels are served along with all-natural lemonade, iced tea, strawberry lemonade, and vegetable juice. Turkey legs and frozen lemonade are also available. **S · $ · ❤**

STORYBOOK TREATS: Ice cream fans enjoy this window next to the Many Adventures of Winnie the Pooh. It offers soft-serve cones and cups; hot fudge and strawberry sundaes; plus ice cream floats. Soft drinks are also served. **S · $ · ❤**

Frontierland
FAST FOOD & SNACKS

GOLDEN OAK OUTPOST: In the mood for fries? Head here. This little wagon offers specialty waffle fries: BLT or BBQ pork. Also on the menu: chicken breast nuggets, chocolate chip cookies, coffee, tea, hot cocoa, and soft drinks. The Outpost operates seasonally. **L D S · $ · ❤**

Healthier Options

Health-conscious folks need not abandon all restraint for want of suitable sustenance. Walt Disney World recently phased out added trans fats and partially hydrogenated oils from food served in parks and resorts. Most restaurants offer low-fat, low-cholesterol, low-salt, low-carb, and vegetarian entrées. Even fast-food stands feature healthier fare such as salads, grilled chicken sandwiches, fresh fruit, and turkey burgers. The WDW trend toward healthier dining extends to kids' meals, too. They come with a beverage choice of low-fat milk, 100 percent fruit juice, or water, and a side dish such as unsweetened applesauce, baby carrots, or fresh fruit. These healthy selections are easy to find on menus throughout Walt Disney World—keep an eye out for the Mickey Check symbol.

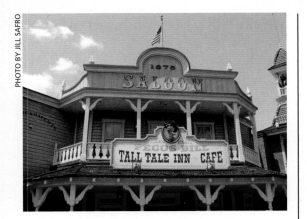

PECOS BILL TALL TALE INN & CAFE:

Pecos Bill has been feeding hungry cowpokes for more than 40 years. The look has changed over time, as have the offerings (the prices have gone up quite a bit, too). These days Pecos Bill is serving up chicken or spicy beef burritos, steak or chicken fajitas, Southwest chicken or spicy beef salad, beef nachos, and Southwest burgers (topped with pepper jack cheese and served with tortilla chips). Churros and yogurt are available, too. Kids can choose from PB&J sandwiches or mac and cheese. (Kids' meals come with grapes and carrot sticks and a choice of low-fat milk or bottled water.) Pecos Bill has a variety of soft drinks, too—including raspberry lemonade slush served in a Country Bears jug. **L D S · $ $ ·** 🐭

WESTWARD HO!: Mosey on over to Westward Ho! for chips, frozen lemonade, and other soft drinks. Corn dogs are offered seasonally. It's across from Prairie Outpost & Supply. **S · $ ·** 🐭

Liberty Square
TABLE SERVICE

LIBERTY TREE TAVERN: Step back in time at this Early American tavern where the decor has a tendency to outdazzle the fare. Here, wallpaper looks as if it might have come from Colonial Williamsburg, the curtains hang from cloth loops, and the rooms are filled with mementos that might have been found in the homes of Thomas Jefferson, George Washington, and Ben Franklin. The restaurant is aptly located across from the Hall of Presidents attraction.

The à la carte lunch menu includes crab and lobster dip for two, pot roast, turkey, fish & chips, pasta with shrimp, and New England clam chowder. Dinner is an all-you-can-eat feast—salad, roast turkey breast, ham, pot roast, mashed potatoes, and more—all served family style. Dinner costs about $35 for adults and $19 for children ages 3 through 9. Note that some beverages cost extra and no alcohol is served. Reservations are recommended (arrive about 20 minutes early). Disney characters do not visit here. **L D · $ $ – $ $ $ ·** 🐭

Magic Kingdom Mealtime Tips

- The hours from 11 A.M. to 2 P.M., and again from about 5 P.M. to 7 P.M., are the mealtime rush hours in Magic Kingdom restaurants. Try to eat earlier or later whenever possible.

- When a fast-food restaurant has more than one service window, don't just amble into the nearest queue. Instead, inspect them all, because occasionally, the one farthest from an entrance will be wait-free (or nearly so).

- Table-service restaurants offering full-scale meals are usually less crowded at lunchtime than they are during traditional dinner hours.

- To avoid queues, eat at a restaurant that offers reservations—Tony's Town Square, Crystal Palace, or the Plaza Restaurant on Main Street; Liberty Tree Tavern in Liberty Square; Fantasyland's Be Our Guest or Cinderella's Royal Table. Reservations may be made in advance by calling 407-WDW-DINE (939-3463), via www.disneyworld.com, or by using the My Disney Experience app. Check for same-day seating at the individual restaurant or City Hall (as early in the day as possible).

- Consider taking the monorail to the Contemporary, Polynesian, or Grand Floridian to have lunch or dinner in a resort restaurant, and then return to the Magic Kingdom after you eat. (Remember to keep your ticket or MagicBand handy for re-entry to the park.)

FAST FOOD & SNACKS

COLUMBIA HARBOUR HOUSE: This lively spot adds some interesting (and healthy!) options to the quick-service lineup, including broccoli peppercorn salad served with chicken, grilled salmon with couscous and steamed broccoli, tuna on toasted multigrain bread (aka the Anchors Away sandwich), and the Lighthouse sandwich (with hummus, tomato, and broccoli slaw). You can still find fried shrimp, chicken nuggets, vegetarian chili, and clam chowder, too. After 4 P.M., seafood mac and cheese and chicken pot pie join the menu. For dessert there's seasonal cobbler. Yogurt is also available. Kids' selections include chicken nuggets, mac and cheese, salad with chicken, and tuna sandwiches.

Disney has done up this fast-food emporium with style—complete with antiques, model ships, harpoons, nautical instruments, and even lace tieback curtains. In addition to the chowder, we savor the salmon and love the Lighthouse sandwich. The upstairs dining rooms are charming (and often less crowded than those on the first floor). L D S · $–$$ · ❤

SLEEPY HOLLOW: Often missed by guests rushing toward the Haunted Mansion or other park hot spots, this window has a lot to offer: waffles with heavenly toppings (fresh fruit, chocolate hazelnut spread, whipped cream, etc.), ice cream cookie sandwiches, funnel cakes (dusted with powdered sugar and cinnamon or strawberries and cream), specialty coffees, and more. Sleepy Hollow is near the Liberty Square bridge. Eat on the patio and get a stunning view of Cinderella Castle at no extra charge. S · $ · ❤

Main Street
TABLE SERVICE

THE CRYSTAL PALACE: What's the big draw here? Winnie the Pooh and his pals host meals all day. One of the Magic Kingdom's cherished landmarks, this spot takes its architectural cues from a similar structure that once stood in New York, and from San Francisco's Conservatory of Flowers, which still graces that city's Golden Gate Park. The place is spacious, with tables scattered amid a Victorian-style indoor garden, complete with flowers and hanging greenery. Tables in the front look out on flower beds, while those at the east end have views of a courtyard. The restaurant is on a path at the end of Main Street, U.S.A.

Offerings vary according to season and available produce. The all-you-can-eat buffet features a variety of breakfast items every morning; for lunch and dinner there's spit-roasted carved meat, chicken, pastas, fish, sides, and dessert offerings. The salad bar, with its peel-and-eat shrimp, cold pasta salads, and variety of greens and grains, is most satisfying. The cost for breakfast is about $32 for adults and $19 for kids ages 3 through 9; lunch and dinner run about $45 for adults and $27 for children. Reservations are a must. BLD·$$–$$$·❤

PLAZA RESTAURANT: This windowed establishment, next to the Plaza Ice Cream Parlor, is done up in mirrors with sinuous Art Nouveau frames. The menu has salads, burgers, and hot and cold sandwiches—plus ice cream, shakes, floats, and sundaes. Mickey's Kitchen Sink is served in a sink shaped like Mickey's pants and big enough for two. It may be possible to make reservations for early in the day, but this eatery operates mostly on a walk-up basis. Arrive early—there is usually a wait. LD·$$·❤

TONY'S TOWN SQUARE: Tony's decor was inspired by Walt Disney's feature *Lady and the Tramp* (which can be viewed in the waiting area). The terrazzo-style patio offers a fine view of Town Square (though tables there are in limited supply). The menu offers a variety of Italian specialties, including calamari, cannelloni, and artisanal pizza. Other staples include salad with chicken, steak, and pasta. Entrées include pasta primavera, chicken Parmesan, and shrimp scampi. If you require gluten-free pasta, just ask—Tony is happy to accommodate. Top it off with an Italian sweet (gelato, tiramisú, or chocolate cake with hazelnut filling) or foamy cappuccino. If you time it right, you can fold your napkin, settle the bill, and wander onto Main Street to enjoy the fireworks from one of the best vantage points in the park. Or consider a Wishes Dining Package, which pairs a fixed-price lunch with a spot in a reserved viewing area for Wishes. For details, call 407-W-DINE or visit *www.disneyworld.com*. Reservations are highly recommended. LD·$$$·❤

HOT TIP!

Tomorrowland Terrace's dessert party offers unlimited snacks and a viewing of Wishes, the Magic Kingdom's fireworks show. Prices vary, but expect to pay about $59 per adult and $35 per child. For details and reservations up to 180 days in advance, call 407-WDW-DINE (939-3463). The dessert buffet is presented in the waterside dining area at Tomorrowland Terrace, while Wishes viewing is offered from the Dessert Party's reserved viewing area on Main Street, U.S.A.

Magic Kingdom Resorts

Is the Magic Kingdom open late when you plan to visit? If so, consider heading over to the Contemporary, Polynesian, Grand Floridian, or Wilderness Lodge to have an early dinner, and then return to finish the day at the park. Each of the aforementioned resorts is reachable by monorail and/or water taxi. Remember to keep sporting that MagicBand bracelet if you used it for admission or keep your ticket handy for re-entry into the Magic Kingdom. Transportation generally runs for one hour after the park's posted closing time for the day (this does not include Extra Magic Hours). Note that, as with most WDW eateries, reservations are necessary at resort restaurants. Don't forget to book that table!

FAST FOOD & SNACKS

CASEY'S CORNER: Casey's is a grand slam for baseball fans—and those who just happen to love the food associated with "America's pastime," big old hot dogs and salty fries. This old-fashioned stop is on the west side of Main Street (near the Crystal Palace). Tables line the sidewalk, where a ragtime pianist often tickles the ivories. There's a back room with indoor seating. The fare retains the mood—hot dogs, chili cheese dogs, barbecue slaw dogs, corn dog nuggets, fries, brownies, cotton candy, Cracker Jack, and soft drinks. Hot dogs come in regular and foot-long sizes. Note that it is possible to order items à la carte. Casey's is a popular spot and a true Magic Kingdom classic. LDS·$·❤

MAIN STREET BAKERY: After an extensive refurbishment, this Main Street classic reopened as a turn-of-the-twentieth-century bakery and coffee shop. If the sight of this old-fashioned storefront doesn't lure you in, the aroma most certainly will. The Main Street Bakery is a nice choice for a light breakfast, coffee break, or midafternoon rest stop. The vast array of tea and coffee concoctions comes courtesy of Starbucks. Assorted pastries, fresh-baked cookies, fresh fruit and veggies, and other snacks are also served. BLDS·$·❤

PLAZA ICE CREAM PARLOR: This happy place for ice cream lovers boasts the Kingdom's largest variety of hand-scooped ice cream flavors. It's perfect for a before-the-parade or an on-the-way-out-of-the-park nosh. Children enjoy the Mickey Mouse kids' cone. To keep things moving, choose flavors and desired number of scoops before jumping in line. They have floats and sundaes—including those served in a waffle bowl and the Mickey's Kitchen Sink for two (which is actually a sink-like version of the Mouse's red drawers). The parlor is busiest before and after Magic Kingdom parades and fireworks presentations. **S · $ · 🐭**

Tomorrowland
FAST FOOD & SNACKS

AUNTIE GRAVITY'S GALACTIC GOODIES: Ice cream may not seem futuristic, but chances are it'll be around at least another billion years, give or take. Located across from the Tomorrowland Speedway, Auntie G's offers up chilly smoothies made from non-fat yogurt (strawberry-banana, orange, and raspberry), soft-serve ice cream, sundaes, and floats (made with soda or coffee). Soft drinks are available, too. There's virtually no atmosphere in this corner of the galaxy, but we still gravitate toward the goodies. **S · $ · 🐭**

COSMIC RAY'S STARLIGHT CAFE: Ray's seems like several quick-service counters in one. There are separate stations, with a slightly different menu offered at each. Choose Bay 1 for rotisserie chicken, barbecue pork sandwiches, grilled chicken sandwiches, and chicken breast nuggets; Bay 2 and Bay 3 for cheeseburgers, chicken sandwiches, veggie burgers, hot dogs, chicken nuggets, and Greek salad. Sides include french fries and green beans. A kosher selection is available. An Audio-Animatronics lounge lizard known as Sonny Eclipse entertains in the dining area throughout the day. **L D S · $–$$ · 🐭**

LUNCHING PAD AT ROCKETTOWER PLAZA: If it's a snack or simple meal you're after, stop at the base of the Astro Orbiter located smack-dab in the center of Tomorrowland's concrete plaza. This window dispenses hot dogs on oversize buns, ham-and-cheese-stuffed pretzels, cream-cheese-stuffed-pretzels, Mickey pretzels, chips, soda slushies, milk (regular and soy), and soft drinks. **L D S · $ · 🐭**

TOMORROWLAND TERRACE: This stark spot serves simple fare such as cheeseburgers, chicken breast nuggets, and salads. Some tables on the lower terrace afford views of Cinderella Castle. It operates seasonally, so it may not be open during your visit to the park. **L D S · $ · 🐭**

Baby Needs

Babies. They're a needy lot. Fortunately, most of the requisite supplies can be found somewhere at Disney World—if you know where to look. Formula and jarred food can be purchased at the Baby Care Center in each of the theme parks and at every WDW resort. Most restaurants have kids' menus with toddler-friendly food (mac and cheese, chicken nuggets, and the like).

If your baby is partial to a specific formula or brand of food, consider shipping a box of it to your hotel before you leave home. Keep in mind that there are several grocery stores near Walt Disney World. If you have a car, it is worth the trip (a Guest Relations clerk can help with directions). The selections are more varied, as are the prices. Stash perishables in an in-room refrigerator—they are standard in all Disney-owned-and-operated resorts. Some other points of interest regarding baby diners at Walt Disney World:

- Most eateries have high chairs and booster seats. Request one when you make your restaurant reservation.

- Stroller use inside restaurants is discouraged due to fire codes. Park it outside.

- WDW restaurants are often chilly. Be sure to pack a sweater or blanket.

- Be it a fast-food or table-service restaurant, bring toys to keep little ones busy.

- The following resorts have 24-hour snack bars: Grand Floridian, Dolphin, Polynesian Village, Wyndham, and Buena Vista Palace (on Hotel Plaza Boulevard). The middle-of-the-night pickings may be slim, but milk and cereal are served around the clock.

- If you'd like a spot to nurse an infant, head to a Baby Care Center in any of the theme parks. They all have rooms with rocking chairs.

- If you're headed for a long day in a theme or water park, pack simple, healthy snacks for hungry toddlers. And look for the Mickey check symbol on menus (see page 246 for details).

- To make your dining experience less harried, consider feeding your baby before you get to the restaurant.

- If you prefer organic milk (and more) for your children, consider ordering from *gardengrocer.com* or swinging by a local grocery store (for details, see Baby Food on page 47).

In Epcot

The eclectic, international lineup of fare offered here threatens to overshadow the attractions themselves. With no fewer than 11 different countries represented in the World Showcase section of the park, Epcot provides guests with the opportunity to eat their way around the world without leaving Central Florida. Less ambitious diners will likely have their taste needs met, too—there's a bountiful food court in Epcot's Future World, as well as a smattering of simple yet satiating snack spots and quick-service locations. Reservations are an important factor in the Epcot dining equation; call 407-WDW-DINE (939-3463) up to 180 days in advance.

DID YOU KNOW?

More than 30 tons of fruits and vegetables have been grown at The Land pavilion in Epcot and served to guests dining in Walt Disney World restaurants.

Future World

TABLE SERVICE

CORAL REEF (The Seas with Nemo and Friends): This water-themed restaurant is all about nibbling on creatively prepared fish under the watchful eyes of their brethren. The place is decorated in cool greens and blues to complement its surroundings, and every table has a panoramic view of a living coral reef; some are right up against the glass. (Don't worry: You are not actually eating Epcot residents—most of Disney's catches come fresh from fishing boats each day.) Menu items run the gamut from a bounty of fresh

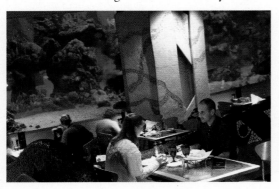

fish and shellfish, including shrimp, mahi mahi, and salmon—prepared in a number of ways—to grilled New York strip steak and oven-roasted chicken breast for those who are satisfied by simply spying on the fish. The menu tends to vary seasonally. Reservations are recommended. **L D · $$$ · ❤**

GARDEN GRILL (The Land): Guests are often so distracted by the sights and the jovial hosts (Chip, Dale, and friends) that they don't realize the restaurant is actually moving. As the eatery revolves, and it does so quite slowly, it moves past scenery featured in the Living with the Land boat ride. The view was designed with diners in mind, and provides them with a peek into a farmhouse window that's out of viewing range of the waterborne passengers.

Breakfast includes sticky buns, fruits, eggs, potato barrels, biscuits and gravy, and waffles. For lunch, the Grill serves salad, beef filet, turkey breast, sausage with peppers and onions, etc. The dinner menu features rotisserie meats, sustainable fish of the day, fresh vegetables (some of which are grown inside The Land Pavilion), and a small selection of desserts. Cost for breakfast is about $32 for adults, $19 for kids; lunch runs about $41 for adults, $25 for kids; dinner is about $45 for adults, $27 for kids. (Prices may be a bit higher during peak times of year.) Beverages and dessert are included. Meals are served family style (communal platters for the table). Reservations are recommended.

The restaurant moves in a circle. It's imperceptible to most, but if you are highly sensitive to motion, it may be best to dine in a more stationary environment. **B L D · $$–$$$ · ❤**

FAST FOOD & SNACKS

ELECTRIC UMBRELLA (Innoventions Plaza): This large establishment is a good bet when the weather is temperate enough to allow dining at the tables on the terrace outside—or when bound for the World Showcase with finicky eaters in tow. (There are indoor tables, too.) Offerings include chicken Caesar salad, flatbread (topped with tomato, basil, mushroom, feta, and arugula), French Dip burger, sausage & pepper sandwich, fries, and soft drinks. Dessert options include strawberry cheesecake, cupcakes, and no-sugar-added brownies. It's possible to get yogurt or an orange instead of fries with some menu selections. **L D S · $–$$ · ❤**

FOUNTAIN VIEW (Innoventions Plaza): Set beside that drama queen of a water fountain known as Fountain of Nations, this new Epcot destination is actually a futuristically themed Starbucks. As such, it is an ideal spot for a satisfying java jolt, a light meal, or a sweet snack. Sandwiches, pastries, cookies, and crunchy veggies are available—as are teas, Frappuccino drinks, and more. **B L D S · $ ·** 🐭

SUNSHINE SEASONS (The Land): It's the closest thing to a mall food court you'll find in a WDW park, but a bit more upscale. Located near the entrance to Soarin' Around the World on the pavilion's lower level, Sunshine Seasons is an ideal destination for parties who can't quite agree on any one type of fare—there's bound to be something for everyone. Tables are scattered in several seating areas, beneath colorful hot-air balloons. Snagging a table can be a challenge during peak mealtimes. (There can be a bit of pedestrian congestion, too, thanks to the enormous popularity of the Soarin' attraction.) **Sandwich Shop** is home of the oak-grilled vegetable flatbread, fish tacos, and more. The **Soup and Salad Shop**'s creative salads include Power Salad (with oak-fired chicken, quinoa, almonds, and honey vinagrette) and seared tuna with sesame rice wine dressing. Soups are made fresh daily. **The Grill Shop** features rotisserie chicken and slow-roasted pork. Sustainable catch of the day is also offered. **Wok Shop** serves Mongolian beef with fried rice, sweet and sour chicken, and shrimp stir-fry. The **Bakery** offers freshly made desserts. In addition to the seasonally inspired rotating desserts—expect to

find brownies, ice cream bars, and other sweet treats. There is a grab-and-go area with items such as sushi, fruit and cheese plates, fresh vegetables, hard-cooked eggs, salads, ice cream, and other snacks.

A word of advice: It's often a good idea to split up your party and stand in several lines at the same time. That'll increase your chances of actually eating together. Before doing so, select a table. That way, everyone in the group will know where to meet after they forage for their meals. It's also a nice spot to take a load off your feet while waiting for your Soarin' Fastpass+ window to kick in. **B L D S · $ – $ $ ·** 🐭

World Showcase
TABLE SERVICE

AKERSHUS ROYAL BANQUET HALL
(Norway): The Norwegian castle of Akershus dominates Oslo's harbor and is considered the most impressive of all Norway's medieval fortresses. It is actually half fortress and half palace, and many of its grand halls continue to be used for elaborate state banquets. At Epcot's castle-like Akershus, guests are treated to authentic royal Norwegian cuisine. They also get to dine with royalty—as Disney princesses interact with guests during all meals.

An all-inclusive price entitles hungry Epcot guests to enjoy dishes that don't often leave Scandinavia. Included in the family-style sampling of the Norwegian *koldbord* is smoked salmon and seafood, Norwegian cheese, and

PHOTO BY JILL SAFRO

Let 'em Eat Cake!

What could possibly make celebrating a special occasion at Walt Disney World even more special? How about a custom-made, personalized cake? You can have one delivered to just about any table-service eatery on Disney property. Simply call the Cake Hotline (407-827-2253) at least 72 hours in advance to place an order.

If you miss the ordering deadline, don't despair—no one has to go cake-less at Disney World (perish the thought!). Spontaneous cake delivery is possible, provided you request one at the podium when you check in at a restaurant. At meal's end, you will receive a 6-inch non-personalized cake. It will add about $23, plus tax (and a few more calories), to the total.

chilled salads. Norwegian-inspired entrées include seafood, beef, and poultry selections. A kids' menu is available. Dessert and soft drinks are included.

For breakfast, guests enjoy the all-you-care-to-eat fare (bacon, eggs, potatoes, and sausage are brought to your table) as Disney characters mingle with diners. Belle, Ariel, Jasmine, Snow White, Sleeping Beauty, and even Mary Poppins have made appearances. The character appearance schedule varies. Reservations are necessary. Cancellations must be made at least 24 hours in advance to avoid paying the $10-per-person surcharge. Breakfast costs about $47 for adults (ages 10 and up) and $29 for kids (ages 3–9); lunch is about $49 (adults) and $30 (kids); dinner costs about $58 (adults) and $34 (kids). Prices may be higher during peak seasons. BLD·$$–$$$·❤

BIERGARTEN (Germany): Located in the back of the St. Georgsplatz in the Germany pavilion, this huge, tiered eatery is a jolly stop on the Epcot world tour. This is partly because of the long tables that encourage togetherness among guests. But equal credit for the *gemütlich* (pleasant) atmosphere goes to the spot's lively entertainment.

There are scheduled appearances by Bavarian musicians—each clad in lederhosen or dirndl—who play accordions, cowbells, a musical saw, and a harp-like stringed instrument known as the "wooden laughter." The entertaining shows take place at scheduled times in the dining room. The schedule is usually posted at the door. Diners are usually invited to join the fun on the dance floor.

The food is hearty and presented as an all-you-can-eat buffet, featuring all sorts of sausages (such as bratwurst, Regensburger, and knackwurst), frankfurters, rotisserie chicken, spaetzle, assorted cold dishes, potato salad, cucumber salad, and many more German specialties. Because entertainment is intermittent, there's plenty of time to enjoy the pleasant setting. Reservations are highly recommended, particularly during peak seasons (book as early as possible). LD·$$–$$$·❤

CHEFS DE FRANCE (France): "Bright lights, big dining room" describes this airy Parisian brasserie. With some of France's best chefs responsible for this kitchen, the results are usually rewarding. The menu features fresh ingredients readily available from Florida purveyors, though the restaurant imports as many key ingredients from France as possible.

The offerings are in the nouvelle French cuisine style, which involves lighter sauces using less cream and butter than in classic French cooking. Menu items include broiled salmon, beef short ribs, and roasted chicken. Soups and appetizers such as onion soup, lobster bisque, and escargot are all-day staples. Chocolate tarts and crème brûlée are dessert specialties of note.

Chefs de France is one of the most popular World Showcase eateries, year in and year out. Reservations are recommended (book as early as possible). LD·$$$–$$$$·❤

LE CELLIER STEAKHOUSE (Canada): This wine-cellar-like spot is a favorite place for a memorable meal. The restaurant has low ceilings, stone walls, and candlelight, all of which contribute to the atmosphere.

There's a full menu of tempting items, starting with a (complimentary) bread basket that includes fresh-baked pretzel roll, plus sourdough, and whole-grain creations. Considered a "Signature" restaurant for both lunch and dinner (translation: It costs more to eat here than at most other WDW places and requires two Dining Plan credits per meal), the steakhouse specializes in high-quality beef. The filet mignon with white truffle-butter sauce is a real crowd-pleaser. Many choose to start with a longtime favorite cheddar cheese soup made with Moosehead beer, but the *poutine* (fries with cheddar, truffle salt, and a red wine reduction) are a popular starter, too. Canadian beers and wines make for memorable pairings. Reservations are a must—this is an extremely popular and relatively tiny restaurant. LD·$$–$$$·❤

LA HACIENDA DE SAN ANGEL (Mexico): Open for dinner (starting at 4 P.M.), this festive facility fits nicely on the shore of World Showcase Lagoon. The menu features starters such as *queso fundido* (warm cheese with poblano pepper and chorizo); *agua chile de camaron* (shrimp ceviche), and *crema de elote* (creamy corn soup). Entrées include a mixed grill for two, short ribs with salsa de chile, and grilled tilapia. We are particularly fond of the *parrillada del mar* (seafood platter for two). For dessert, there's chocolate mousse, corn ice cream, and fruit empanadas.

If you book a table for about 8:30 P.M., you may be treated to prime seats for IllumiNations (Epcot's nightly pyrotechnic extravaganza). While windowside tables cannot be guaranteed, there's always standing room. As an added bonus, the show's soundtrack is pumped into the eatery. It's quite impressive. **D · $ $ $ · ❦**

MONSIEUR PAUL (France): One flight above Chefs de France, this eatery is filled with mementos of Chef Paul Bocuse's extraordinary culinary honors. It is an elegant bistro, but a bit less formal than its predecessor, Bistro de Paris.

The menu was crafted by Chef Francesco Santin, who worked with Chef Bocuse in his restaurant in Lyon, France, for 15 years. It features starters such as a ravioli d'escargots appetizer and mussel soup with saffron and light fennel cream. Main course selections include grilled beef tenderloin with mushroom crust, roasted free-range chicken, and seared scallops with vegetables. The wine list is *très* French. You might want to stroll around the World Showcase

promenade to walk off your meal—and your warm Grand Marnier dessert soufflé. Note that this can be one of the most expensive Disney World restaurants, and it's a Disney Dining Plan Signature eatery. The dress code is "resort casual" —no tank tops or tattered clothing, please. Reservations are recommended. **D · $ $ $ $ · ❦**

NINE DRAGONS (China): This stop on Epcot's varied international restaurant tour transports guests to modern China when in the palatial dining room. À la carte selections allow guests to sample provincial cuisines. The menu includes starters such as walnut shrimp toast, dumplings, and pot stickers. Entrée selections range from sweet-and-sour pork to Kung Pao chicken, veggie stir-fry, five-spiced fish, and Chinese barbecue. (No MSG is used in any dish.)

A selection of Chinese teas, beers, and wines is available. Desserts include banana cheesecake egg roll, strawberry red bean ice cream, caramel-ginger ice cream, and ginger cake. Reservations are recommended. **L D · $ $ – $ $ $ · ❦**

RESTAURANT MARRAKESH (Morocco): It's not every day that you can slip into an exquisitely tiled Moroccan palace and be entertained by belly dancers and musicians as you polish off a plate of Moroccan cuisine. Want to know how authentic this place is? The king of Morocco sent craftspeople to Epcot to make sure they were creating a real Moroccan atmosphere. (Unfortunately, he didn't send his chef—the fare isn't apt to dazzle aficionados of Moroccan cuisine.) The menu includes roast lamb, chicken brochette, beef shish kebab, and couscous. Sampler platters are available. Reservations are recommended, but it is often possible to get in without too much of a wait. **L D · $ $ $ · ❦**

ROSE & CROWN PUB AND DINING ROOM (United Kingdom): Don't let the word "pub" throw you. While this place serves up some of the best brews on Disney property, its dining area is also known for such crowd-pleasing dishes as traditional fish and chips, steak, fish, shepherd's pie, and bangers and mash (sausages with mashed potatoes). Appetizer-wise, we recommend the Rose & Crown cheese plate. One of the side dishes that makes us happy? Mushy peas! (Sort of a lumpy-but-flavorful pea porridge.) For dessert, there are Jaffa tarts, sticky toffee pudding, and Banoffee tarts. Bass Ale from England, Harp lager and Guinness stout from Ireland, and more are on tap. (They're served cold, not at room temperature, as some British guests may prefer.)

Special Requests

All WDW table-service eateries that accept reservations strive to accommodate food allergies and intolerances such as gluten, salt, wheat, shellfish, lactose, peanuts, etc., if requested at least 72 hours in advance. Kosher meals may be pre-ordered up to a day ahead at many table-service eateries. Note that 48 hours' notice is needed for eateries at the Swan and Dolphin, Yak & Yeti restaurant, and Rainforest Cafe. (Kosher meals are not available at Garden View Afternoon Tea [Grand Floridian] and Epcot's Teppan Edo and Tokyo Dining.) Make your request when booking your table by calling 407-WDW-DINE (939-3463). Note that kosher requests require a credit card guarantee and must be canceled within 24 hours of the reservation to avoid a penalty.

The decor is pretty—mainly polished woods, etched glass, and brass accents. In fine weather, it's nice to lunch under a canopy on the terrace outside and watch the FriendShip water taxis cruising across World Showcase Lagoon.

As for the pub's architecture, it incorporates three distinct styles. The wall facing the World Showcase promenade is reminiscent of urban establishments popular in Britain since the 1890s, while that on the south side evokes London's seventeenth-century Ye Olde Cheshire Cheese pub, with its brick-walled flagstone terrace, slate roof, and half-timbered exterior. The canal facade, with its stone wall and clay-tile roof, reminds visitors of the charming pubs so common in the English countryside.

The pub section of the Rose & Crown serves such snacks as fish and chips—along with all the brews noted earlier and traditional British mixed drinks, such as shandies (Bass Ale and Sprite),

Food & Wine Festival

Once a year, Epcot's hopping dining scene expands exponentially in what's known as the International Food & Wine Festival. The event, which usually runs from mid-September through early November, is a celebration of the flavors of dozens of nations. Those countries without permanent stations at World Show-case set up temporary displays from which authentic samples of food, wine, and other spirits are sold. The samples range in price from about $3 to $8. It's possible to eat and drink your way around the world for about the same price as some table-service restaurants.

The festival also features demonstrations from top chefs, as well as wine and cooking seminars. For details, call 407-824-4321, or visit *www.disneyworld.com*. Make reservations as early as you can—this is one popular festival.

and black and tans (Bass Ale and Guinness stout). The pub is quite popular, so it's often necessary to queue up at the door. Note that the pub section also spills out onto the World Showcase promenade—where the first-come, first-served waterside tables make for a nice spot to sip a drink and, possibly, enjoy some fish and chips from a nearby snack stand. Reservations are not available in the pub areas, but recommended for the adjacent dining room.

If you're lucky, you'll catch a performance by the pub's artist-in-residence. Feel free to sing along as she bangs out familiar tunes on her modest upright piano. She is quite a crowd-pleaser, so expect lots of company at the bar as you sip your pint. **L D S · $ $ $ · ❤**

SAN ANGEL INN (Mexico): The food at this establishment located to the rear of the plaza inside the Mexico pyramid (a corporate cousin of the famous Mexico City restaurant of the same name) may come as a surprise to most visitors. Although the tacos and tortillas and other specialties that usually fall under the broad umbrella of Mexican food are available, the menu also offers a wide variety of more subtly flavored fish, poultry, and meat dishes.

To start, there's *tostadas de tinga* (pulled chicken on fried corn tortillas with black refried beans, green tomatillo sauce, queso fresco, and sour cream) and beef tacos; plus much more. Entrées include *carne asada* (New York strip steak served with cheese enchilada), *peto an salsa poblana* (grilled wahoo fish served over roasted potatoes with vegetables and poblano sauce), and grilled fish tacos. The dinner menu is a bit more elaborate than at lunch. Mexican desserts are largely unfamiliar to many diners, with the possible exception of the *mousse de chocolate*, but are well worth trying. *Bebidas* (drinks) such as Dos Equis, Sol, and Tecate beer, and margaritas make good accompaniments. Note that some of the dishes here have a bit of a kick. Oddly enough, this eatery does not offer hot sauce as a condiment. (Though they can whip you up a batch, should you have a hankerin' for heat.) Reservations are recommended. L D · $ $ $ · ✿

SPICE ROAD TABLE (Morocco): Built on the shores of World Showcase Lagoon, this eatery's style was inspired by outdoor cafes along the shores of the Mediterranean. Popular for its stunning views of IllumiNations and its freshly prepared, palate-pleasing fare, Spice Road Table has made its way onto Epcot diners' must-do list. The eatery's whitewashed facade is accented in icy shades of blue from the famous "Blue City of Chefchaouen" in Morocco's Rif Mountains.

The menu features Mediterranean small plates: zesty harissa chicken rolls; lamb sliders; salted cod croquettes; mussels with preserved lemons and tomato sauce baked in an earthenware tagine pot; Moroccan merguez sausage with a fresh tomato salad; garlicky jumbo shrimp in a spicy chile pepper sauce; fried calamari, and more. Mediterranean specialty entrées include coriander-crusted rack of lamb and the mix grill skewers. Dessert selections include a chocolate pyramid with almond ice cream, saffron and lemon custard, and almond and rosewater cake. Soft drinks, beer, wine, and organic sangria are served. Reservations are recommended. L D S · $ $ – $ $ $ · ✿

TEPPAN EDO (Japan): Tokyo Dining's lively neighbor, Teppan Edo offers a dinner-as-show experience. Guests sit around a large teppan grill and watch as a nimble chef demonstrates just how quickly enough chicken, beef, seafood, and vegetables can be chopped, seasoned, and stir-fried. Teppan Edo entrées are sizzling and satisfying. Soups, salads, sushi, desserts, and cocktails (including Japanese beer and sake) are also on the menu. Don't wear your finest attire: There's always the potential for a little splattering. Reservations are recommended. L D · $ $ – $ $ $ · ✿

HOT TIP!

Thanks, in part, to the Disney Dining Plan and "Epcot After 4" (an admission pass for locals), World Showcase tends to be exceptionally busy in the evening hours year-round. Reservations for table-service eateries are an absolute must.

HOT TIP!

That gift card burning a hole in your pocket? Disney Gift Cards may be redeemed at all Disney-owned-and-operated dining, shopping, and recreation locations where credit cards are accepted. If you lose track of what's left on your card, simply call the number on the back to find out.

TOKYO DINING (Japan): A nice escape for lunch or dinner, this restaurant features freshly prepared sushi, sashimi, edamame, tempura, grilled items, bento boxes, and prix-fixe lunch specials. Other choices: garden salad, ika salad, miso soup, grilled chicken, grilled salmon, and grilled steak/shrimp tempura combo. Finish with something sweet, such as chocolate ginger cake, green tea cheesecake, or soft-serve ice cream. Beer, wine, and a full sake list are available. There are a few windowside tables that offer a great view of IllumiNations—Reflections of Earth. If you get there early, you may get lucky and snag one! Reservations are recommended. L D · $ $ – $ $ $ · ✿

TUTTO GUSTO (Italy): A welcome retreat for grown-ups, Tutto Gusto is a wine bar that transports guests to an ancient Italian wine cellar. Tutto Italia's next-door neighbor offers more than 200 wines, including grappa; Italian beers and specialty drinks; coffee concoctions; and a marvelous small-plate menu. Nibble on imported Italian cheeses, Sicilian eggplant salad, marinated olives, seafood salad, white asparagus, cured sliced meats, paninis (pressed sandwiches on ciabatta baguette), pastas, and more. For dessert, consider strawberries with mascarpone cream, cannoli, or mocha tiramisu. Reservations are not accepted—come in the afternoon for the smallest crowds. *Salute!* L D S · $ $ – $ $ $

TUTTO ITALIA (Italy): There's an impressive menu at one of the most popular (and expensive) World Showcase destinations, and the addition of outdoor tables makes it one of the more appealing spots for an Epcot meal. Traditional starters such as fried calamari, fresh mozzarella with tomatoes and basil, and Caesar salad can actually make a meal in and of themselves. Entrées extend toward fresh pastas—spaghetti, ravioli, fettuccine, and lasagna. The menu includes fish, steak, and chicken. Paninis are offered at lunch. For dessert, choose from items such as gelato, sorbet, cannoli, tiramisu, and

One-Stop Sweet Shop

A yummy destination on the World Showcase landscape, the Germany pavilion's Karamell-Küche is sure to satisfy your sweet tooth—provided that you're a fan of fresh, gooey caramel draped or drizzled over chocolate, cookies, crunchy apples, and much more.

cheesecake. Wine, beer, and specialty teas, coffees, and cocktails are served. Reservations are recommended. **LD·$$$–$$$$·**❤

VIA NAPOLI (Italy): It was a long time coming (roughly 30 years!), but Epcot's Italy finally has a pizza place. Tucked into the back of the pavilion, this welcome addition has a casual atmosphere and seating for 300. How serious are they about the pizza? They import the flour from Italy and select water so the crust tastes as authentically Neapolitan as possible. In addition to pizza, specialties include pastas, salads, sandwiches, soft drinks, and Italian wine. The Aqua Fresca is quite refreshing (signature seasonal fruit cooler). Dessert offerings include *zeppole di catarina* (ricotta cheese fritters), gelato, sorbet, and tiramasu. Reservations are recommended. **LD·$$·**❤

FAST FOOD & SNACKS

BLOCK & HANS (American Adventure): Mickey-shaped pretzels, anyone? You can get them here, along with cheese-y dipping sauce. Cream-cheese and jalapeño-and-cheese-stuffed pretzels are served, too. Wash them down with a soft drink, craft beer, or black cherry hard cider or (hard) root beer. **S·$·**❤

LES HALLES BOULANGERIE PATISSERIE (France): The pastry shop in the France pavilion is not hard to find: Just follow the wonderful aroma, then watch the crowds lining up to consume the fresh baguettes (standard and mini), croissants, quiches, cheese plates, ham and cheese or turkey sandwiches, cheese tartines, soups, salads, éclairs, fruit tarts, chocolate mousse, and more. Beer, wine, lemonade, smoothies, coffee, and other soft drinks are served. Hint for those who hate to wait: This is a favorite snack spot among Epcot veterans; your best bet is to head here as soon as World Showcase opens or while other guests are watching IllumiNations. *Note that this shop, located toward the back of the pavilion, opens at 9 A.M.* **BLDS·$–$$·**❤

LA CANTINA DE SAN ANGEL (Mexico): Located just outside the entrance to Mexico's pyramid, this eatery serves grilled chicken with cascabel sauce over rice; beef tacos (on fresh corn tortillas); Mexican salads; nachos topped with cheese, ground beef, black beans, jalapeños, tomatoes, and sour cream; cheese empanadas; fresh, housemade guacamole with corn tortilla chips; and *churros con cajeta* (churros with caramel) and *paletas* (fruit ice pops). Beer, margaritas (frozen and on the rocks), and soft drinks (including Mexican apple soda) are available. Kids' picks include cheese empanadas and chicken tenders, both served with tortilla chips and fruit. **LDS·$–$$·**❤

LA CAVA DEL TEQUILA (Mexico): Mexico's national drink is the star of this show—there are more than 200 varieties to choose from. Also on the cocktail menu are sangria, mezcal, beer, wine, and specialty drinks. Snack on *queso blanco* (warm, white nacho cheese with pico de gallo sauce and tortilla chips), or chips with guacamole or salsa—or go chip-crazy and order them with all three! Doors open at noon. It's tiny, so expect a wait to get in. **S·$–$$**

Check, Please!

Paying for a meal at Disney World is a piece of cake—especially if you have a MagicBand or Disney resort ID (and load it with your Disney Dining Plan or back it up with a credit card). Both are accepted by most restaurants on Walt Disney World property. Notable exceptions: eateries at the Swan and Dolphin resorts, Four Seasons, and the resorts on Hotel Plaza Boulevard, and some snack carts. Simply scan your MagicBand bracelet or resort ID when the bill arrives (don't forget to add a tip where appropriate), and the charge will appear on your hotel statement when you check out. (If you are not staying at a WDW-owned-and-operated resort, visit *www.disneyworld.com* for details on how you can get the most from the MagicBand service.)

Of course, there are many alternative ways to pay the piper. In addition to United States currency, traveler's checks and most major credit cards are accepted in most locations. Foreign currency is a no-no. Disney currency (aka Disney Dollars) works like cash in all Disney-owned-and-operated venues. Disney Gift Cards are accepted at most of the aforementioned locations, too. (If you plan to pay with a gift card, tell your server when you place your order.)

REFRESHMENT COOL POST (between China and Germany): This is a nice spot for a cold drink (soft drinks and beer are served) and a snack. Frozen beverages (including a mango smoothie) with African rum, ice cream, hot dogs, and cookies are all on the menu. S·$·🐭

FIFE & DRUM TAVERN (The American Adventure): Located in front of the Liberty Inn, this small brick edifice proffers American favorites. Among the options: turkey legs, popcorn, ice cream, slushes, soft drinks, wine, beer, and hard root beer. L D S·$–$$·🐭

KABUKI CAFE (Japan): Step up to cool down at this quick-service kiosk, where the specialty of the house is Kakigori, aka shaved ice. Flavors include cherry, tangerine, sweet strawberry, and more. Other chilly treats include green tea or ginger ice cream and strawberry smoothies (be sure to ask about the smoothie flavor of the day). Kabuki also offers edamame, sushi (California rolls and "box-style" salmon, shrimp, and tuna), Japanese beer (including frozen Kirin), plum wine, sake (hot and cold), and soft drinks. L D S·$–$$·🐭

KATSURA GRILL (Japan): Located to the left of the plaza, the exterior of the restaurant was inspired by the historic sixteenth-century Katsura Imperial Villa near Kyoto, Japan.

Among the fare here is Japanese chicken cutlet curry (a peppery sauce over rice with a panko-breaded chicken breast). That, along with teriyaki chicken, salmon, or beef (basted with soy sauce and sesame oil as it broils), sushi, miso soup, udon noodles, and edamame typify the offerings. Drink choices include hot and cold sake, plum wine, green tea, beer, and soft drinks. The garden serves as a respite for those who want a break from the hustle and bustle of a busy Epcot day. Kids dig the koi pond—the fish are enormous! L D S·$–$$·🐭

KRINGLA BAKERI OG KAFE (Norway): Tucked between the Norway pavilion's wooden church and a cluster of shops, this popular eating spot serves kringlas, sweet pretzels reserved for special occasions in Norway; Troll horns (flaky pastry filled with cream and tart cloudberries); smørbrøds, sandwiches such as open-faced smoked salmon and eggs, ham and apple, Norwegian club, or roast beef; traditional Kjøttke (Norwegian meatballs), lefse (potato flatbread rolled with sweet cinnamon butter), and vegetable tortes. There are salads, berry cream puffs, Norwegian school bread, fruit cups, sweet pretzels with chocolate, rice pudding, and no-sugar-added trifle. Soft drinks, wine, beer and coffee cocktails are served. L D S·$–$$·🐭

L'ARTISAN DES GLACES (France): An artisanal ice cream and sorbet shop, this spot fills cones and cups with 10 heavenly flavors of ice cream and 6 sorbets—all crafted in-house. The ingredients are all simple and fresh: milk, sugar, cream, eggs, and fruit. How cool is that?! There are usually more than a dozen flavors from which to choose. Adults over age 21 may top their order off with a liqueur. S·$·🐭

LIBERTY INN (The American Adventure): To many visitors from other countries, American food means hot dogs, burgers, chicken nuggets, apples, and fries—and these are the staples at the Liberty Inn, located to the left of The American Adventure show on the far side of the lagoon. Also available here: clam chowder; fried shrimp served with Old Bay seasoning; New York strip steak with fries and steamed broccoli; red, white, and blue salad; grilled chicken BLT sandwich; and Southwest chicken salad. Cobbler, brownies, cookies, and fruit cups round out the selections. For those in search of a meat-free meal, the vegetarian plate will do. L D S·$–$$·🐭

LOTUS BLOSSOM CAFE (China): The counter-service cafe is adjacent to the House of Good Fortune shopping gallery in the China pavilion. It offers orange chicken with steamed rice, beef noodle soup, Hong Kong–style vegetable curry (with or without chicken), shrimp fried rice, and sesame chicken salad, plus pot stickers, pork and vegetable rolls, and kid-friendly selections. Unlike most traditional Chinese cooking, the food here is prepared on a flat grill, as opposed to stir-fried. There is a small, covered seating area. L D S · $ – $ $ · ❤

REFRESHMENT PORT (Canada): Another good spot for a thirst quencher or a quick snack —croissant doughnuts, ice cream in waffle cones, chicken nuggets, and drinks. It's on the World Showcase promenade, near Canada. S · $ · ❤

SOMMERFEST (Germany): Bratwurst or frankfurter on a roll with sauerkraut, curry-wurst, Nudel Gratin (baked macaroni with cheese custard—a fan favorite), cold potato salad with eggs, hand-twisted pretzels, Black Forest cake, apple strudel with vanilla sauce, soft drinks, shots of Jägermeister and Berentzen Apfel, steins of seasonal German beer, and red and white wines are offered at this small, covered spot located toward the rear of the pavilion; additional outdoor seating is nearby. L D S · $ – $ $ · ❤

TANGIERINE CAFE (Morocco): Named for the Moroccan city of Tangier, this casual spot serves lentil salad, hummus, tangierine couscous salad, marinated olives, and tabbouleh, as well as lamb, chicken and falafel wraps, rotisserie chicken, beef, and lamb combination platters, and veggie platters. For dessert, there are pastries such as baklava. Specialty coffees, frozen drinks, and beer are available, too. L D S · $ – $ $ · ❤

YORKSHIRE COUNTY FISH SHOP (United Kingdom): A perfect choice for a simple meal, this stand offers classic fish and chips. (Don't forget the malt vinegar.) Soda, iced tea, light lemonade, Bass ale, and Harp lager are also available on draft. For dessert, there's Victoria sponge cake filled with jam and buttercream, and whole, seasonal fruit. L D S · $ – $ $ · ❤

Epcot Mealtime Tips

- The international restaurants of World Showcase offer some of the best dining on the property. Since many of them are very popular, it's a good idea to arrange advance reservations for all table-service restaurants by calling 407-WDW-DINE (939-3463) long before arriving. However, it's important to note that some tables may be available for same-day seating. To make arrangements, head to Guest Relations first thing in the morning, visit *mydisneyexperience.com*, or call the aforementioned number. Meals *may* be booked at some individual restaurants, but don't count on it.

- Don't dismiss the idea of an early seating if you can get it: A 5 P.M. dinner may not only be welcome, but may provide an opportunity to spend time enjoying the pleasant, more temperate evening hours at Epcot's World Showcase.

- Lunch provides guests with another chance to enjoy the most popular Epcot restaurants. It also has an additional appeal: With reservations for 1 P.M., it's possible to spend some of the busiest hours in the park consuming a pleasant meal while less fortunate visitors are waiting in some of the longest lines of the day.

- If you aren't able to secure reservations for a meal, don't despair. There are satisfying alternatives to a traditional sit-down restaurant. Tutto Gusto (Italian wine bar) and Spice Road Table (in Morocco) both offer small plates and full service. Japan has Katsura Grill, good for sushi and chicken curry. Sample Mexican lunch specialties at La Cantina. Try the smoked salmon sandwiches at Kringla Bakeri og Kafe in Norway, the fish and chips in the United Kingdom, or Germany's bratwurst sandwiches and soft pretzels.

- Cravings for conventional fast foods will be satisfied at the Electric Umbrella in Innoventions and at the Liberty Inn in The American Adventure. Sunshine Seasons, in The Land pavilion, offers a bit of everything. However, it can get extremely congested at mealtime rush hours.

- The most unadventurous eaters can still find something pleasing—even in the more exotic restaurants of World Showcase. If you're undecided, ask at Guest Relations to see a booklet describing the menus. Keep in mind that most restaurants have menus for kids.

In Disney's Hollywood Studios

Lights, camera, lunch! This theme park, which was designed to resemble a working Hollywood backlot circa the 1940s, tackles the role of feeding guests with style and whimsy. Here you can sit in a classic car and enjoy a meal at a drive-in, rub elbows with the beautiful people at a reproduction of the Hollywood Brown Derby, and play the part of sitcom kid as you're served by "Mom" or "Dad" at the 50's Prime Time Cafe (no elbows on the table, please!). While the attention to theming is obvious, it doesn't upstage the fare. The eateries at Disney's Hollywood Studios are a breed apart. Some feature decor that returns guests to a bygone era; others recapture memorable moments from the big or small screen. All reprise a beloved part of Hollywood's star-studded heritage. The Studios has five full-service restaurants, whose atmospheres and menus are so distinct they satisfy altogether different moods and whims. Reservations are necessary; call 407-WDW-DINE (939-3463). Now grab a napkin, and get ready for your close-up.

TABLE SERVICE

50'S PRIME TIME CAFE: This retreat is an amusing amalgam of comfort food, kitschy 1950s-style kitchen nooks, and attentive servers of the "No talking with your mouth full" ilk. Nostalgia abounds, meant to bring guests back to the childhood of yesteryear; and TVs broadcast black-and-white clips from favorite fifties comedies (all related to food). Guests are waited on by "Mom" (and other family members) with considerable enthusiasm: They encourage everyone to keep their elbows off the table, eat their vegetables, and clean their plates (or no dessert!). Misbehave and you may have to stand in the corner (the 1950s version of the "time-out").

Adding to the appeal is the menu, which is packed with comfort foods. For openers, there is a choice of housemade chicken noodle soup or onion rings. Specialties of the house include meatloaf, served with mashed potatoes and vegetables; fried chicken; and old-fashioned pot roast. There are wedge salads and chicken pot pies, too. Milk shakes, ice cream sodas, and root beer floats are filling accompaniments. And when you've finished everything on your plate, you may order dessert. Standouts include s'mores—graham crackers topped with chocolate and toasted marshmallows—sundaes, apple crisp, and no-sugar-added cheesecake topped with whipped cream and strawberry sauce. A full bar is available. Guests of all ages love this place. Reservations are recommended. **L D · $$–$$$ · 🅜**

HOLLYWOOD & VINE: The distinctive Art Deco facade ushers guests into a contemporary version of a 1950s diner—all stainless steel with pink accents. An elaborate 42-by-8-foot wall mural depicts notable Hollywood landmarks, including the Disney Studios, Columbia Ranch, and Warner Brothers (back when they were the only film studios in the San Fernando Valley). At the center of the mural is the Carthay Circle Theatre, where *Snow White and the Seven Dwarfs* premiered in 1937.

The buffet breakfast and lunch, known as Disney Junior Play 'N Dine, are character affairs featuring Sofia the First, Doc McStuffins, Jake the Never Land pirate, and Handy Manny (characters are subject to change). The morning meal includes Mickey waffles, frittatas, fruit, pastries, and a create-your-own omelet station. Lunch may offer items such sustainable fish of the day, salads, and lobster mac and cheese.

Minnie Mouse hosts the evening meal, along with Mickey, Daisy, Donald, and Goofy. The new "Minnie's Seasonal Dine" buffet offers carved meats, pasta dishes, strip steak, chicken parmesan, and "seafood offerings such as cioppino, peel-and-eat shrimp, and mussels. The impressive dessert section boasts a chocolate fountain (among other treats). Soft drinks are included. Beer and wine are served at an extra cost.

GOOD MEALS, GREAT TIMES

Dinner starts at about $50 for adults and $30 for kids; lunch runs about $40 (adults) and $24 (kids); breakfast is about $32 for adults and $19 for kids. Prices are higher during peak times. Reservations are necessary. **B L D · $ $ – $ $ $ · 🖤**

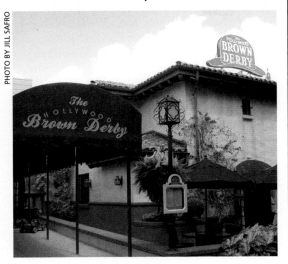

HOLLYWOOD BROWN DERBY: The home of the famous Cobb salad is alive and well. This re-creation of the former Vine Street mainstay is quite faithful, right down to the caricatures (reproduced from the original Derby collection) that cover the walls. Gossip queen rivals Louella Parsons and Hedda Hopper (portrayed by actresses) may still be spotted dining here, just as they did in the heyday of the real Brown Derby. The place is decorated predominantly in teak and mahogany, and the elegant chandeliers and perimeter lamps (shaped like miniature derbies) are reminiscent of those in the original eatery.

The menu features the famed Cobb salad, created by owner Bob Cobb in the 1930s. It's a mixture of ever-so-finely chopped fresh salad greens, tomato, bacon, turkey, egg, blue cheese, and avocado, served with French dressing.

Desserts are tempting—particularly double vanilla crème brûlée and the legendary grapefruit cake, a Brown Derby institution. Some of the selections are a bit highbrow (and high-priced) for the theme park crowd, but if you're up for a splurge, this spot will likely rise to the occasion. We recommend the seafood cioppino; the filet mignon gets good marks, too.

The slightly formal atmosphere is not likely to enchant most children, but youngster-friendly fare is available. The New World wine list is excellent. Reservations are recommended. Should you find yourself without reservations, consider dining at the Hollywood Brown Derby Lounge (see above, right). **L D · $ $ $ · 🖤**

HOLLYWOOD BROWN DERBY LOUNGE: An alfresco oasis, the Brown Derby Lounge serves cocktails, wines by the glass, and tapas-style plates. Signature drinks are named for the park's very own Citizens of Hollywood performers Shelby Mayer, Honey Darling, Jack Diamond, etc. Small plates can come filled with savory treats: Derby sliders, andouille crusted shrimp, artisanal cheeses and charcuterie, Cobb salad, Florida tomato soup, and more. There is a tempting lineup of sweets, too—including warm blueberry cobbler, banana toffee cake on cocoa crunch and strawberry-banana pearls, Brown Derby original mini grapefruit cake, and dessert trios. Seating is limited and reservations are not accepted, so there may be a wait for a table. Drinks may be made to go. The Hollywood Brown Derby Lounge usually opens at about noon and closes an hour or so before the rest of the park does. **L D · $ $**

MAMA MELROSE'S RISTORANTE ITALIANO: This pleasant Italian restaurant (with a California twist) is located in a warehouse that has been converted into a large dining room. Flatbreads are prepared in a wood-burning oven. The menu also features housemade pasta, grilled fish, and vegetarian options. Favorite dishes have included seafood arrabbiata, charred strip steak, and oven-baked chicken parmesan. They have penne alla vodka, too (served plain or with shrimp or chicken). Reservations are recommended. **L D · $ $ – $ $ $ · 🖤**

SCI-FI DINE-IN THEATER: A convincing re-creation of a drive-in theater, the atmosphere here is completely absorbing. The tables are actually flashy, 1950s-era cars, complete with fins and whitewalls. Stars twinkle overhead in the "night sky," and drive-in theater speakers are

Water Park Dining

Disney's duo of water parks, Typhoon Lagoon and Blizzard Beach, provides plenty of chances to defy Mom's plea to wait an hour to splash after you nosh. The fare is limited to the quick-service kind (who wants a sit-down meal in a soggy swimsuit?), and the quality of the offerings has been stepped up a bit of late. Typhoon Lagoon offers hot Italian sandwiches, fresh fruit bowls, meatball subs, and more.

At Blizzard Beach, you can order mozzarella sandwiches and hot dogs wrapped in a soft pretzel. Snacks are sold at spots with names like Typhoon Tilly's (🐭), Leaning Palms (🐭), and Avalunch (🐭). Frozen drink specialties flow at Let's Go Slurpin' (Typhoon Lagoon) and at Blizzard Beach's Polar Bear Pool Bar.

Some folks prefer to pack a picnic lunch. Coolers may be brought into both of Disney's water parks, but alcoholic beverages and glass containers may not.

mounted beside each car. Most seats are within cars, with most featuring front- and backseat counters facing front. Not terribly conducive to meaningful table talk, but ideal for viewing the large movie screen, where a 45-minute compilation of the best (and worst) science-fiction trailers and cartoons plays in a continuous loop. There are a couple of traditional tables within oversize cars—if this is your preference, make that known when you book the table and expect to wait a bit when you arrive.

Selections include Reuben sandwiches, pork ribs, burgers, and shrimp pasta. Kids enjoy the mac and cheese. Desserts include cheesecake, milk shakes, and ice cream sundaes. Reservations are recommended. *Warning: Some of the movie trailers feature monsters and may frighten your little ones.* L D · $$–$$$ · 🐭

FAST FOOD & SNACKS

ABC COMMISSARY: Located near the Chinese Theater, this spot recently featured fish and chips, chicken club sandwiches, salads, New York strip steak, and cheeseburgers. Desserts included chocolate mousse, no-sugar-added strawberry parfait, and chocolate peanut butter cupcakes. The restaurant is huge and does indeed resemble an actual studio commissary. We could do without the ads for ABC shows, which play on a continuous loop from TVs scattered throughout the dining area. Enough already! L D S · $ · 🐭

BACKLOT EXPRESS: Designed to resemble the crafts shops on an old studio backlot, this eatery is near the Star Tours—The Adventures Continue attraction. The indoor seating areas carry out the prop-shop theme, with paint-speckled floors, car engines, and various other spare prop parts. Typical menu offerings include cheeseburgers, hot dogs, salads, and chicken nuggets. For dessert, there's chocolate mousse and no-sugar-added strawberry parfait. Soft drinks, beer, and wine are available. L D S · $ · 🐭

DINOSAUR GERTIE'S ICE CREAM OF EXTINCTION: Soft-serve ice cream is Gertie's go-to treat—vanilla, chocolate, or swirl, in a cup or cone. Mickey-shaped ice cream bars, cookies and cream sandwiches, trail mixes, and fruit are served, too. Gertie's operates seasonally. S · $ · 🐭

HOLLYWOOD HILLS AMPHITHEATER: If your stomach starts growling while waiting for Fantasmic! to begin, you can keep it quiet with a visit to this snack shack. Savory items include nachos with cheese, hot dogs, popcorn, and more. Sweet treats such as ice cream bars, frozen bananas, fresh fruit, caramel corn, churros, and glazed almonds are also sold. Wash it all down with a soft drink, beer, or wine. S · $–$$ · 🐭

ICE COLD: Need to cool off on a hot day? Swing by this stand near the park entrance. It sells ice cream, iced coffee, cool juices, and fizzy drinks. Other snack items include whole fruit, trail mix, pastries, and chips. S · $ · 🐭

MIN AND BILL'S DOCKSIDE DINER: This waterside window offers smoked sausage and franks in pretzel rolls, foot-long chili cheese dogs, chips, frozen lemonade, soft drinks, and beer. *Note that Min and Bill's may not be operating during all of 2017.* S · $ · 🐭

PHOTO BY JILL SAFRO

OASIS CANTEEN: A tiny tin shack that sits beside the Indiana Jones Epic Stunt Spectacular, the Oasis Canteen dispenses funnel cakes topped with strawberries, vanilla ice cream, powdered sugar, or cinnamon; soft-serve ice cream in waffle cones or cups (chocolate, vanilla, or swirl); bottled water; and domestic draft beer. **S·$·**

PIZZERIZZO: Occupying the space once filled by Toy Story Pizza Planet, this new Muppet-themed eatery continues the pizza tradition with family-friendly fare and soft drinks. You'll find it directly across the courtyard from the Muppet★Vision 3-D attraction. **LDS·$·**

STARRING ROLLS CAFE: In a hurry? Head here to get the day off to a quick start, or take a nice break. Pastries, muffins, croissants, and no-sugar-added desserts are sold at this sweet-smelling shop. For lunch, there are sandwiches, soups, salads, and sushi. Soft drinks are served, too. Get there early if you really want sushi—they are always sold out by the time we arrive. This spot usually closes by 4 P.M. and may not be operating in all of 2017. **BLS·$–$$·**

PHOTO BY JILL SAFRO

SUNSET RANCH MARKET: A celebration of California's outdoor lifestyle, this cluster of snack stands has something for just about everyone. Rosie's All-American Cafe specializes in cheeseburgers, chicken nuggets, fried green tomato sandwiches, and strawberry shortcake. Catalina Eddie's offers plain and pepperoni pizzas, chicken Caesar salads, and desserts. Fruit and vegetables, juice, and soft drinks are sold at Anaheim Produce. The nearby Toluca Legs Turkey Co. offers turkey legs. Hollywood Scoops has a selection of creamy treats (including one of the no-sugar-added variety). And look no farther than Fairfax Fare for smoked specialties, including ribs and chicken, foot-long chili dogs, barbecue pork sandwiches, plus salads and dessert items. Umbrellas dot the outdoor seating area. Soft drinks are available at most locations, as is beer (with proper ID). **LDS·$·**

THE TROLLEY CAR CAFE: Step into this trolley station/Starbucks for coffee-based beverages, sweet treats, savory snacks, and more. The cheery red building is at the corner of Hollywood and Sunset boulevards. **BLDS·$·**

Studios Mealtime Tips

- To avoid traffic jams at fast-food spots, consider eating at one of the restaurants that offer advance reservations—Hollywood Brown Derby, 50's Prime Time Cafe, Sci-Fi Dine-In Theater, Hollywood & Vine, or Mama Melrose's Ristorante Italiano.

- To arrange for reservations in advance, call 407-WDW-DINE (939-3463). Same-day seating is impossible for table-service restaurants at Disney's Hollywood Studios.

- The many indoor and outdoor nooks within the Backlot Express seating area are nicely removed from the beaten path; relative quiet can frequently be enjoyed there.

- The Fantasmic! "dinner and a show" package offers diners guaranteed seating for the nighttime spectacular. For details, see the Hot Tip at left.

GOOD MEALS, GREAT TIMES

In Animal Kingdom

You'll have no trouble finding something to sink your teeth into at one of Animal Kingdom's eateries. Disney's nature-oriented theme park has four table service restaurants and takes "quick service" quite seriously—there are plenty of places to keep stomachs from growling like the beasts at the Kilimanjaro Safaris attraction.

TABLE SERVICE

RAINFOREST CAFE: Like the Oasis, the region it borders, this cafe is a lush, soothing tropical jungle. Unlike the Oasis, any quiet moment here is merely a calm before the storm—as brief thunder storms occur throughout the day inside the eatery. Gushing waterfalls, twisting tree trunks, and colorful fish add to the ambience. The environmentally conscious cuisine includes Planet Earth Pasta and the portobello mushroom wrap. There is no net-caught fish, nor beef from countries that destroy rainforest land to raise cattle. Reservations are recommended. B L D S · $$–$$$

TIFFINS: Tiffins' exotic menu features cuisine from the many areas that inspired the creation of Disney's Animal Kingdom. Guests may eat indoors or in outdoor dining areas with waterfront views. The all-day menu has included black-eyed pea fritters, fried mussels, roasted beet salad, Berbere-spiced lamb chop, Wagyu strip loin and braised short rib, chermoula-rubbed chicken, hoisin-glazed halibut, and whole-fried sustainable fish. For dessert there's lime cheesecake, chocolate ganache with carmelized banana, sorbet tasting, and more. This Discovery Island destination is a Disney Dining Plan Signature restaurant (it requires two table-service credits). Reservations are recommended. L D · $$$$ · 🐭

TUSKER HOUSE: Harambe village sets the stage for a dining adventure at this buffet restaurant. All meals are hosted by favorite Disney characters. At press time, the characters scheduled to attend were Donald, Daisy, Mickey, and Goofy (the latter 3 are subject to change). Reservations are recommended for all meals. Book as far in advance as possible. Tusker House opens at 8 A.M. B L D · $$$ · 🐭

YAK & YETI: This place opens daily at 11 A.M. (though it doesn't serve breakfast). It specializes in Asian fusion cuisine. Menu items include chicken tikka masala, crispy mahi mahi, baby back ribs, lo mein, and seared miso salmon. Among the tempting dessert options are fried (sweet) wontons and mango pie. You'll find Yak & Yeti in Asia, near Kali River Rapids. African beers and cocktails are available, too. L D S · $–$$$ · 🐭

FAST FOOD & SNACKS

ANANDAPUR ICE CREAM TRUCK: Cool off with a soft-serve from Asia's local ice cream truck. The refreshing snack is available by the waffle cone, cup, or in a soda float. Bottled water and a variety of soft drinks (including root beer and light lemonade) are also served. S · $ · 🐭

CREATURE COMFORTS: A shop known as Creature Comforts has been converted into a home fit for a mermaid. Yep, the sippers' sanctum known as Starbucks is open for business on Discovery Island. It currently comforts creatures with all manner of coffee concoctions, pastries, and snacks. B L D S · $ · 🐭

DINO-BITE SNACKS: Restaurantosaurus's neighbor, this snack shack proffers soft drinks and sweet treats. Order items such as hand-scooped ice cream, ice-cream cookie sandwiches, churros, and fresh-baked cookies. S · $ · 🐭

FLAME TREE BARBECUE: If you can't find this eatery, just follow your nose. It serves a fragrant selection of BBQ sandwiches and platters, all wood roasted. Sample the mild, tomato-based Carolina-style sauce with your chicken, pulled pork, or hickory-smoked St. Louis ribs. Smoked turkey breast sandwiches, smoked chicken salads, turkey legs, fries, onion rings, and chocolate or lime mousse are also options. Platters come with beans and/or cornbread. Fries and onion rings are offered. Beer, wine, and soft drinks are served. There's (new) indoor seating along the river. It's on Discovery Island, near DinoLand, U.S.A. L D S · $–$$ · 🐭

HARAMBE FRUIT MARKET: Sometimes a crunchy apple is just what the doctor—or theme park guest—ordered. Apples, among other healthy snacks, are available at this stand near the entrance to Kilimanjaro Safaris. Stop here for fruit, veggies, water, and more. S · $ · 🐭

HARAMBE MARKET: Enshrined in an old train station, the Harambe Market features four proprietors offering African takes on American favorites: spice-rubbed ribs, sausages, grilled chicken skewers, beef gyro flatbreads, and more. Diners may enjoy the Harambe-style street fare in the open-air courtyard near the Mombasa Marketplace shop. L D S · $ – $ $ · 🐭

KUSAFIRI COFFEE SHOP & BAKERY: The bakery at Tusker House sells fresh-baked treats, fruit, cookies, brownies, cupcakes, and other desserts, plus cereal, yogurt, soft drinks, low-fat milk, and specialty coffees. The walk-up window has no seating, but there are tables at the nearby Dawa Bar. B S · $ · 🐭

PIZZAFARI: This big, colorful dining area has no-nonsense fare that tends to please young palates. Plain, pepperoni, and veggie pizzas; meatball subs; pasta dishes; and salads are on the menu. Little ones enjoy the bread sticks topped with cheese, served with marinara sauce. Animal murals decorate the walls of this restaurant, located on Discovery Island. B L D S · $ – $ $ · 🐭

ROYAL ANANDAPUR TEA COMPANY: After hiking through Africa to get to Asia, park guests can build up quite a thirst. That's where this exotic tea stand comes in handy. Located near the Yak & Yeti in the village of Serka Zong, this hut dispenses a variety of iced and hot teas, specialty coffees, and sweet treats. S · $ · 🐭

RESTAURANTOSAURUS: Located in the heart of DinoLand U.S.A., this spot is a fishing lodge turned commissary for student paleontologists. It offers bacon cheeseburgers, chili cheese hot dogs, grilled chicken sandwiches, chicken nuggets, black bean burgers, roasted chicken with mixed greens—plus chili cheese fries, clam chowder, warm chocolate brownies and cheesecake topped with strawberries. The place is filled with fossils, dinosaur bones, and such; class notes line the walls. L D S · $ – $ $ · 🐭

TAMU TAMU REFRESHMENTS: Stop by this spot in Africa's Harambe for a sweet treat. Here you can choose a double chocolate chip cookie ice cream sandwich or a chocolate waffle with ice cream. The big draw, though, is the frozen pineapple treat known as the Dole Whip (with or without rum). This spot usually opens around 10:30 A.M. L D S · $ · 🐭

TERRA TREATS: Just across the river from Harambe, this kiosk specializes in gluten-free and organic snacks. Folks with food sensitivities, take note: Servers can steer you toward nibbles that will suit you to a tee. S · $ · 🐭

TRILO-BITES: In DinoLand U.S.A., just inside the land's entrance (not far from the dinosaur skeleton bridge), this kiosk dispenses buffalo chicken waffle sliders, waffle sundaes, floats, kids' meals, chocolate mousse, light beer, and soft drinks. L D S · $ · 🐭

YAK & YETI LOCAL FOOD CAFES: Next to Yak & Yeti, the cafes specialize in items with pan-Asian influences. Entrées include Korean-style stir-fry BBQ chicken, teriyaki beef bowl, roasted veggie couscous wrap, chicken fried rice, and ginger chicken salad. Egg rolls are also served. There is ample outdoor seating nearby. L D S · $ – $ $ · 🐭

Animal Kingdom Mealtime Tips

- Tusker House and Rainforest Cafe are the only table-service places to offer breakfast; a few spots, including Creature Comforts, and Kusafiri Coffee Shop & Bakery, have light breakfast options.

- At press time, the restaurants that accepted reservations for all meals were Tusker House and Rainforest Cafe. Yak & Yeti and Tiffins accept lunch and dinner reservations. To arrange for reservations in advance, available up to 180 days ahead for all meals, call 407-WDW-DINE (939-3463). To obtain same-day seating, go straight to the restaurant. We recommend making reservations. Rainforest Cafe may keep longer hours than the Animal Kingdom park.

- The many seating pavilions along the river near Flame Tree Barbecue provide waterside dining that's nicely removed from the hubbub of Discovery Island; it may be relatively calm here, even during prime mealtimes. Please resist the urge to feed any birds that come begging.

- A great place to meet Donald and pals such as Mickey, Daisy, and Goofy is at Tusker House at the daily character meals (three meals a day). The characters appearing here are subject to change—though Donald is always in attendance. Make reservations well in advance.

In Disney Springs

Disney Springs encompasses the Marketplace, the West Side, Town Center, and the Landing (formerly known as Pleasure Island). Restaurants usually operate from about 11 A.M. to midnight; most snack spots are open from 11 A.M. to late into the night. For the details, call 407-939-4636.

AMC DINE-IN THEATRES (West Side): Popcorn and soda are upstaged by selections such as chicken Alfredo and mango margaritas in this in-theater dining experience known as Fork and Screen. Seat-side, table-top service (with a personal call button for the server) allows movie-goers to enjoy dinner and a movie simultaneously. The menu includes appetizers, entrées, desserts, cocktails, and soft drinks—plus classic movie munchies. Seating is reserved (and assigned when you purchase your movie ticket). Guests under age 18 must be accompanied by an adult (over the age of 18). LDS·$–$$·♥

BLAZE FAST FIRE'D PIZZA (Town Square): Pizza fans will be happy to know that Blaze Pizza has made its way to Disney Springs. The 5,000-square-foot eatery fires made-to-order pizzas in just three minutes with the help of super-hot pizza ovens. Guests may customize their 11-inch pies with a staggering array of toppings (included in the price), as well as pick their own cheese and sauce. Gluten-free crusts are an option. The menu also includes nearly a dozen signature pizzas, plus salads, and desserts. LDS·$$–$$$·♥

THE BOATHOUSE (The Landing): An upscale waterfront destination, The Boathouse serves delicacies from land and sea for lunch and dinner. Raw bar highlights include oysters on the half shell, caviar corn blinis, and heavenly crab cakes (large enough to share, though you won't want to). Entrée selections have included coriander-seared tuna, Beach and Sea Lobster

Bake for Two, and baked crab-stuffed lobster. Chicken, pasta, and a large lineup of steak dishes tempt, too. A kids' menu is available. Guests may enjoy drinks and appetizers at any of the three nautically themed bars. Doors close at 2 A.M. Reservations are recommended for tables, but bar stools are designated for walk-ins. LDS·$$$$

BONGOS CUBAN CAFE (West Side): Bongos' slate of traditional and nouvelle Cuban dishes includes plantains, steak topped with onions, and flan. Indoors, the elaborate mosaic mural and palm-leaf railings set the scene; the patio for outdoor seating wraps around a two-story pineapple. Diners are often treated to live music. Reservations are recommended for this Signature restaurant. LDS·$$–$$$ ♥

COOKE'S OF DUBLIN (Marketplace): Raglan Road's quick-service neighbor, this is the place to go for some of the most succulent fish and chips in the World. And don't ask for the recipe—it's a Cooke family secret! Other choices include battered sausages, salads, beef and lamb pie, chicken and mushroom pie, and hog in a box (slow-roasted pork shoulder with roasted potatoes). Save room for a fried candy bar dessert. LDS·$$–$$$·♥

EARL OF SANDWICH (Marketplace): This counter-service spot is brimming with sweet and savory possibilities. Among the fare are hot and cold sandwiches (on warm bread), wraps, tossed salads, and desserts. More exotic selections such as Hawaiian BBQ (ham with fresh pineapple and Swiss cheese), The Original 1762 (warm roast beef sandwich with horseradish sauce and cheddar cheese), and Caribbean Jerk Chicken are served, too. The Veggie sandwich is also an option. Breakfast items include warm sandwiches and baked goods. There are grab-and-go selections, too. Dessert can be cupcakes, muffin crowns, or English trifle. Beer, wine, and Kona coffee are offered. Seating is available inside and out. The Earl welcomes visitors daily from 8:30 A.M. until 11 P.M. To save on your purchase, use the coupon at the back of this book. BLDS·$–$$·♥

FOOD TRUCKS (West Side): Four fancy food trucks—each themed to the "essence" of a Disney theme park—have parked at Disney Springs, West Side. Fantasy Fare serves favorites from Magic Kingdoms around the world. Look

GOOD MEALS, GREAT TIMES

for items such as sticky chicken and waffles from the WDW's Magic Kingdom and corn dogs from Disneyland. Namaste Café spices things up with dishes such as butter chicken, lamb kefta, and tandoori shrimp. Superstar Catering shines the spotlight on favorites from the Studios park: flatbreads, pot roast sandwiches, and more. The World Showcase of Flavors features favorites from Epcot's International Food & Wine Festival. Possibilities include grass-fed beef sliders and grilled chicken gyros. **LDS·$$–$$$·**🐭

GHIRARDELLI ICE CREAM & CHOCOLATE SHOP (Marketplace):

What is it about an old-fashioned ice cream parlor that makes just about everybody giddy? Oh, yes, the ice cream. This spot does it one better and throws in its world-famous chocolate, to boot. Stop in for a chocolaty treat, root beer float, or a malt. We often duck in here for a quick cup of coffee and a chocolate chaser. And there is always a possibility of a free candy sample. How sweet is that?! **S·$–$$**

HOMECOMING: FLORIDA KITCHEN AND SOUTHERN SHINE (Town Center):

"Florida heritage meets New Southern cuisine" at this gustatory homage to the Sunshine State. Created by celebrity chef Art Smith, the menu focuses on Southern favorites such as homemade pimento cheese, Church Lady deviled eggs, Low Country shrimp and grits, and grilled blackstrap pork chop with sawmill gravy. Specialty desserts such as Mockingbird Cake make for a sweet finish.

The family-friendly destination has a design inspired by Florida architecture of the late 1800s, and it supports the "Fresh from Florida" campaign, with the majority of ingredients coming from local farms, ranches, and fisheries. Reservations are recommended. **LDS·$$$**🐭

HOUSE OF BLUES (West Side):

Thanks to the combination of its diverse menu and rustic, folk-art-studded design, House of Blues doesn't disappoint. Menu favorites include flatbreads (grilled, then finished in the pizza oven), lobster mac and cheese, tacos, cornbread, and jambalaya. H.O.B. is a good choice for a meal or a late-night bite. Live music is presented in the eatery and on the front porch on select days. There is a gospel brunch every Sunday. Reservations are recommended. To reserve a table at the House of Blues, call 407-934-BLUE (934-2583). **LDS·$$–$$$**🐭

HOUSE OF BLUES SMOKEHOUSE (West Side):

This quick-service window at H.O.B. offers a variety of BBQ selections (e.g., pulled pork or chicken sandwiches, nachos, smoked turkey legs, ribs, and baked beans), soft drinks, spirits, and more. **LDS·$–$$**🐭

MORIMOTO ASIA (The Landing):

Brought to you by Chef Masaharu Morimoto, TV's original Iron Chef, this eatery features dishes from across Asia. The sophisticated two-story venue offers Pan-Asian cuisine prepared in show-kitchens: dim sum, sushi and other seafood, plus much more. For additional details and menu specifics, visit *www.disneyworld.com*. Reservations are recommended. Note that this is a Disney Dining Plan Signature restaurant for dinner. **LDS· $$$$**🐭

MORIMOTO ASIA—STREET FOOD

(The Landing): This quick-service window, located on Morimoto Asia's patio, serves sushi, rice bowls, bao (flatbread) tacos, sticky ribs, curry rice croquettes, pork egg rolls, beer, and soft drinks. **LDS·$**

PADDLEFISH (Marketplace):

Originally known as the Empress Lilly (after Walt Disney's wife, Lillian Disney), and most recently called Fulton's Crab House, this restaurant has undergone an extensive refurbishment and gotten a new name. Though it looks as if it might set sail at any moment, the sleek replica of a boat that houses the seafood-centric eatery is permanently docked at the edge of Lake Buena Vista. The classic WDW space now features modern interior, an inviting rooftop lounge, and an outdoor waterfront bar.

Paddlefish boasts an elaborate selection of appetizers and entrées featuring the day's arrivals. It's not unusual for lobster risotto, redfish, Alaskan king crab, and lobster corn dogs to appear on the menu. There's plenty for landlubbers, too. Reservations are recommended. Paddlefish is a Signature restaurant for the Disney Dining Plan and requires two table-service credits. **Brunch LD·$$$–$$$$**🐭

PARADISO 37 (The Landing):

A lively, waterfront restaurant and bar (with indoor and outdoor seating, plus a live-performance stage), Paradiso 37 specializes in "swirl margaritas," stocks more than 100 different kinds of tequila, and offers the "coldest beer in the world." They serve food, too!

The menu focuses on "the taste" of the Americas. Starters include fire-roasted corn on the cob with a mild pepper sauce and cheese, salmon cakes, and P37 nachos. Entrées range from Argentinian skirt steak with chimichurri sauce to Chilean-style salmon. **L D S · $ $ – $ $ $**

PLANET HOLLYWOOD OBSERVATORY

(West Side): Planet Hollywood has had a major makeover. The globe is gone and in its place stands a 1900s-style observatory. In addition to a brick exterior, this eatery has added outdoor seating and a bar called Stargazers, featuring live entertainment. Hollywood is still celebrated in the form of Tinseltown memorabilia, but now the "planet" part of the restaurant's moniker gets its due: the ceiling is a planetarium. The menu has salads, sandwiches, pasta, burgers, and desserts. Reservations are recommended. **L D S · $ $ – $ $ $ · ❦**

PORTOBELLO (The Landing): This Italian trattoria is drenched in warm colors that match the rustic Italian cuisine. The menu includes mix-and-match antipasti, handcrafted sausage, pastas, and fish.

At lunchtime, the menu includes sandwiches (meatball, vegetarian, or Italian sub), pizza, and pasta. For dinner, try the Ravioli Gigante (filled with ricotta and spinach) with tomato, basil, and toasted garlic. The full-service bar offers a solid wine list of Italian favorites, specialty cocktails, and beer. For dessert it is tough to resist the housemade tiramisu. **L D S · $ $ $**

RAGLAN ROAD (The Landing): As authentically Irish as you can get on this side of the Atlantic, this warm and lively establishment blends fresh ingredients to create traditional Irish fare with a modern flair. The menu comes courtesy of Kevin Dundon, one of Ireland's best-known chefs. His selections are perfectly complemented by the welcoming atmosphere, complete with antiques and bric-a-brac, free-flowing spirits, and energetic live entertainment. Reservations are accepted for lunch and dinner. The shop stocks Raglan Road–branded merchandise, Irish shirts, CDs, and accessories, Celtic jewelry, cookbooks, family crests, mugs, and more. **L D S · $ $ – $ $ $ · ❦**

RAINFOREST CAFE (Marketplace): The Amazon-emulating eatery transports diners to a makeshift rainforest, complete with banyan trees, tropical fish, waterfalls, and parrots.

Special effects envelop guests in tropical storms, complete with lightning and thunder. Menu items include Planet Earth Pasta, Mojo Bones, and Rumble in the Jungle Turkey Wrap. A shop stocks logo clothing. Reservations may be made by calling 407-827-8500. Without them, expect quite a wait. **B L D S · $ $ – $ $ $ ❦**

SPLITSVILLE (West Side): Some go expecting just to enjoy a little bowling, not realizing that Splitsville's two kitchens turn out impressive casual fare such as freshly rolled sushi, three-pepper calamari, seared ahi tuna, and sliders. They've also got pizzas, cheeseburgers, sandwiches, and salads. Many menu items are gluten free. Huge desserts include sundaes, brownie à la mode, and chocolate cake. There is a full bar and a "mix-your-own" Coca-Cola machine. Food is served lane-side or at "non-bowling" tables. Visit *www.splitsvillelanes.com* for additional details. **L D S · $ $ – $ $ $ ❦**

STARBUCKS (West Side and Marketplace): The Disney Springs links of the famous coffee chain serve up all the usual Starbucks specialties: fresh-brewed coffee (hot or iced), Frappuccino blended drinks, teas, and kids' drinks, plus sweet and savory snack items. **B L D S · $ · ❦**

STK–ORLANDO (The Landing): Two words: *rooftop dining*. Steak is the obvious star, but this lavish restaurant has a lot more to offer. Specializing in American cuisine, most palates can be pleased

The Edison

A lavish "Industrial Gothic"–style venue, The Edison (modeled after the original Los Angeles version) is a 1920s-themed restaurant, bar, and nighttime destination. Designed to resemble a power plant, it recalls a robust era of invention and imagination. The menu features classic American cuisine, craft cocktails, and live music. Reservations are recommended. **D · $ $ $ – $ $ $ $**

here. This modern steakhouse-meets-sleek-lounge opened in 2016 and has been sizzling ever since. Guests may dine on the aforementioned rooftop or in the modern and spacious main dining area. The eatery stands in the space formerly occupied by Pleasure Island's Comedy Warehouse. Reservations are recommended. For updates and menu specifics, visit *www.disneyworld.com*. **L D S · $ $ $ $**

FRONTERA COCINA (Town Center): The brainchild of six-time James Beard Foundation winner Chef Rick Bayless, this spot showcases his gourmet Mexican cuisine. Select from items such as hand-crafted tortas, tacos, salads, fresh-made guacamole, and braised meats—all prepared with locally sourced ingredients. Pair your Mexican meal with a marvelous margarita (the selection is most impressive). Beer, wine, cocktails, and soft drinks are also served. Reservations are recommended. **L D S · $ $ $** ❤

TEA TRADERS CAFE (The Landing): Across the street from the Amphicar launch-site, Tea Traders offers a pleasant respite from the hustle and bustle of The Landing. The counter-service spot (with 6 stools) serves tea in a myriad of ways: loose-leaf, iced, frozen, etc. Scones, cookies, and donuts are also at the ready. The shop sells cast-iron teapots, tea sets, and more tea-based paraphernalia. **L D S · $ – $ $**

PHOTO BY JILL SAFRO

T-REX CAFE: A PREHISTORIC FAMILY ADVENTURE (Marketplace): Dinosaurs throw one heck of a dinner party. See for yourself at this eye-popping dino-themed, interactive feasting facility. When you enter, you'll be greeted by hosts we were all led to believe were extinct. Okay, they're life-size mechanical dinosaurs, but they're still pretty cool. As are the waterfalls, bubbling geysers, and fossil dig site. It's all so distracting, you may forget why you came here in the first place. When your stomach starts growling, appease

it with anything from Jurassic Salad to Mammoth Mushroom Ravioli. With soup, sandwiches, pasta, seafood, and steaks, this place aims to please. Reservations are recommended: 407-828-8739. You'll find it near the LEGO shop. Doors open at 11 A.M. daily and close at 11 P.M. Sunday through Thursday and at midnight on Friday and Saturday evenings. **L D · $ $ – $ $ $ ·** ❤

VIVOLI IL GELATO (The Landing): Also known as Vivoli Gelateria, this family-run establishment comes to you straight from Florence, Italy. Creamy gelato is offered in 24 flavors: hazelnut, coffee, banana, peanut butter, brandied cherry, rice pudding, salted caramel, and much more. Order yours in a cup, cone, float, or waffle boat sundae. There's also a selection of sweet and savory baked treats. Look for biscotti and tortini (sandwiches made of Italian cheeses and meats). There are no seats in this sweet spot across from The Boathouse. **L D S · $ – $ $**

WETZEL'S PRETZELS (Marketplace): Whether you prefer pretzels on the salty or sweet side, this kiosk has something to satisfy. Also served: hot dogs wrapped in a soft pretzel, frozen lemonade, and ice cream (cones, cups, and sundaes). **S · $**

WOLFGANG PUCK CAFE (West Side): Among Wolfgang's specialties are gourmet pizzas, ricotta ravioli, and pesto rotisserie chicken. The menu is equal parts sophisticated and straightforward. There's also a sushi bar. Colorful mosaics decorate his restaurants. Reservations are recommended. **L D S · $ $ $ ·** ❤

WOLFGANG PUCK CAFE—THE DINING ROOM (West Side): Don't be confused by the name. The Dining Room refers to a separate restaurant that just happens to be under the same roof as Wolfgang Puck Café and Express. The formal upstairs Dining Room serves cuisine such as wild mushroom fettuccine, crispy pork schnitzel, and organic chicken. For dessert, there's chocolate lava cake, carrot cake, and more. Reservations are recommended. **D · $ $ $ – $ $ $ $ ·** ❤

WOLFGANG PUCK EXPRESS (Marketplace and West Side): Chef Wolfgang Puck's quick-service spots offer wood-fired pizzas, rotisserie chicken, soups, sandwiches, and fresh salads—among them, BBQ chicken salad. The organic coffee here gets a big thumbs-up. (The West Side location is inside the Wolfgang Puck Café building; the Marketplace spot is near the Disney Days of Christmas shop.) **L D S · $ – $ $ ·** ❤

In WDW Resorts

Each of the nearly 30 resorts at Walt Disney World offers its own set of specially themed eateries. There are clambakes at the Beach Club, luaus at the Polynesian Village, wild game at the Wilderness Lodge, and beignets at Port Orleans French Quarter. Meals may be served buffet, family, or traditional table-service or fast-food style. Disney characters are often on hand (especially for breakfast), and some snack spots stay open 'round the clock. In fact, the resort dining scene has expanded and been upgraded so much of late that the (occasionally arduous) task of resort-hopping is a more worthwhile experience than ever before.

Reservations are an important part of the full-service dining circuit (call 407-WDW-DINE [939-3463]).

All-Star Resorts

Each of these resorts features a colorful, themed central food court. All-Star Sports has the End Zone food court in Stadium Hall. The Intermission food court is in Melody Hall at the All-Star Music resort. And All-Star Movies has the World Premiere food court in Cinema Hall. The food courts offer similar food stands, with Music and Sports having undergone recent refurbishments. The selections include pasta, pizza, burgers, hot dogs, sandwiches, salads, ice cream, a variety of breakfast and baked goods, plus grab-and-go selections. Expect to find kid-pleasers, such as chicken nuggets and mac and cheese, too. **B L D S · $ – $ $ · ♥**

Animal Kingdom Lodge

BOMA—FLAVORS OF AFRICA: Designed to resemble an African marketplace, Boma offers an impressively diverse selection—the fare served represents the continent of Africa. It's one big buffet with multiple stations, and the food is as good as what you'd expect in a fine dining place.

The all-you-care-to-eat affair provides an excellent bang for your Disney dining buck. Breakfast features omelets, cereals, brioche, fresh fruit, sausage, biscuits, ham, corned beef, and more. At dinner, expect to fill your plate with items such as salads (including watermelon rind salad and Tunisian couscous salad), authentic African breads, soups, and stews; grilled seafood, roasted meats, and a nice array of vegetarian selections. For dessert, do sample the decadent

Fill 'er Up—RapidFill Mugs

Buy one cup and get unlimited refills for your entire WDW vacation? It sounds too good to be true. Yet, any guest staying at a WDW-owned-and-operated resort may purchase a plastic mug—for about $9 to $18, depending on how many days the cup is activated for—and refill it with soft drinks for the length of their stay.* At press time, the following resorts offered the popular "RapidFill" refillable mug program (filling stations can be found at the spots noted in parentheses):

All-Star resorts (food courts); Animal Kingdom Lodge (The Mara, Johari Treasures, and Maji pool bar); BoardWalk (Leaping Horse Libations, Boardwalk Joe's, the Pizza Window, and BoardWalk Bakery); Caribbean Beach (food court); Contemporary (Contempo Cafe and Cove Bar); Coronado Springs (Pepper Market and Siesta pool bar); Fort Wilderness (Trail's End restaurant and by the Meadow pool); Grand Floridian (Gasparilla Grill and Beaches Pool Bar); Old Key West (Good's Food To Go and Turtle Shack); Polynesian (Capt. Cook's); Pop Century (food court); Port Orleans (food courts); Saratoga Springs (Artist's Palette and On the Rocks pool bar); Wilderness Lodge (Roaring Fork snack bar); Art of Animation (Landscape of Flavors); and Yacht & Beach Club (Beaches & Cream Soda Shop, Hurricane Hanna's Grill, and Compass Lounge [morning coffee only]).

* Refills may be made at any Disney-owned-and-operated resort, but not at any park.

zebra domes—you'll regret it if you don't. It's tempting to overeat at a bounteous feast such as this, so consider taking tiny portions of everything. You can go back for seconds of your favorites. The wine list includes selections from various African vineyards. Even if you're not staying at the lodge, it's worth the trip. Reservations are required. **B D · $ $ · ♥**

JIKO—THE COOKING PLACE: Jiko offers one of the more unusual Walt Disney World dining experiences. Its cuisine is inspired by the tastes of Africa, with influences from around the globe. Start with one of the paper-thin flatbreads (like roasted chicken with lime chakalaka, lamb chopper cheese, and pickled sweet bell peppers), grilled wild boar tenderloin, artisanal cheeses, or seasonal salads. You may find curry-rubbed lamb

B breakfast   **L** lunch   **D** dinner   **S** snacks   /   **$** under $15   **$$** $15–$36   **$$$** $36–$60   **$$$$** $60 and up

loin, braised beef short ribs, maize-crusted grouper, vegetable and tofu sambusas, and oak-grilled filet mignon on the menu, too. End your meal with a fabulous cheese course and/or sweets such as avocado custard cake, no-sugar-added pistachio and cherry trifle, or seasonal crème brûlée. The wine list is exclusively South African, one of the most extensive collections in the U.S. This is an excellent choice for a grown-up splurge. Though it's hardly a kid favorite—the international, sometimes exotic, cuisine may not appeal to timid palates—there are child-friendly options on the kids' menu. Reservations are recommended. Incidentally, the word *jiko* is Swahili for "the cooking place." The small lounge area offers the full menu, too. D · $$$–$$$$ · 🐭

THE MARA: An impressive quick-service restaurant that has something for everyone—including a small grab-and-go section for those in a hurry. There are a couple of stations at which (excellent) hot entreés are freshly prepared. Among the pre-packaged options are sandwiches, salads, fruit, yogurt, and baked goods. FYI: The eatery is named for a river that flows through Kenya and Tanzania. B L D S · $–$$ · 🐭

SANAA: Pronounced *sa-NAH*, the name of this eatery means "artwork" in Swahili. The Kidani Village spot has a family-friendly menu featuring Disney's take on African-Indian cuisine. The Indian-style bread service, good for sharing and served with a choice of 3 accompaniments, is a nice way to start the meal. Signature dishes include chicken or shrimp curry and slow-cooked beef short ribs. For lunch, try the salad sampler. Even the burgers have an Indian touch, served on soft, warm naan bread. Desserts introduce many tastes, from mango berry tapioca pudding to Tanzanian chocolate mousse. The quality of the fare here is nothing short of outstanding. Reservations are recommended. L D · $$–$$$ · 🐭

PHOTO BY MIKE CARROLL

Art of Animation

LANDSCAPE OF FLAVORS: "Better for you" options is the theme of this vividly adorned food court, where everything is made fresh once it is ordered. Breakfast offerings include egg white frittata, challah French toast, and vegetarian breakfast sandwiches on naan bread, as well as more traditional selections. Four mini shops offer soups, salads, pizza, sandwiches, burgers, pasta, shrimp, chicken, beef stir-fry, grilled fish, and tandoori acorn squash. There is a selection of grab-and-go items, too. Made-to-order beverage options include smoothies and specialty coffees. Also available are organic teas, beers (including a gluten-free selection), wine, coffee, and juices. There is a gelato station, too. Yum. B L D S · $–$$ · 🐭

BoardWalk

AMPLE HILLS CREAMERY: The hand-crafted ice cream—lovingly made with hormone-free milk from grass-fed cows and organic cane sugar—has been garnering raves since it opened in 2016. Flavor offerings may differ from day to day, providing a great reason to come back! You'll find it next to BoardWalk's ESPN Club. S · $ · 🐭

BELLE VUE LOUNGE: This cozy cocktail spot, located on the resort's second floor, offers continental breakfast each morning. Expect to find items such as bagels, cereal, yogurt, whole fruit, muffins, and croissants, plus juice, milk, coffee, and tea. B · $ · 🐭

BIG RIVER GRILLE & BREWING WORKS: Guests may observe (and sample) as the brew-master creates flagship ales and two seasonal brews at this working brew pub. The straightfor-ward-but-satisfying menu generally includes burgers, steaks, and salads. Sandwiches are a cut above. Other menu favorites: flame-grilled meatloaf and Atlantic salmon. The interior has a nice, pubby feel—but we prefer to sit at outdoor tables on the boardwalk (especially in the cool evening hours). Seating is available on a first-come, first-served basis. L D S · $$–$$$ · 🐭

BOARDWALK BAKERY: Trattoria al Forno's next-door neighbor offers baked goods, sand-wiches, soups, salads, and beverages. Sandwiches include roast beef with horseradish mayo and provolone, and smoked turkey on seven-grain bread. Sweet treats (the specialty of this house) run from eclairs and crumb cake to apple tarts and cupcakes. This is also the place for guests to buy and fill their refillable resort mugs. **B S · $ · 🐭**

BOARDWALK PIZZA WINDOW: Nestled into Trattoria al Forno is an opportunity to enjoy freshly prepared plain and pepperoni pizza, served by the pie or the slice. Salads, chips, cookies, beer, wine, and soft drinks are dispensed here, too. The quick-service "window" is usually open from noon until about midnight. **L D S · $ · 🐭**

CRESCENT SOLARIUM: The afternoon tea service offers artisanal cheeses and seasonal accompaniments, tiny sandwiches and canapés on homemade bread, and scones served with clotted cream, lemon curd, and jam; plus pastries, cookies and, of course loose leaf teas. The kids' option, known as Short Sands Beach Tea, features Mickey-shaped sandwiches, a scone, cookies, and chocolate milk. Reservations are recommended. **L S · $$ – $$$ · 🐭**

ESPN CLUB: For sports fans, this joint is pure heaven. The friendly, occasionally frenzied bar/family restaurant is a hard-core sports club. If there's a game being played, chances are it's on one of the million (okay, hundred) TVs. If not, a simple request may result in a channel change.

The standard, reliable fare includes wings, burgers, sandwiches, grilled fish, and salads. Both

PHOTO BY JILL SAFRO

the dining room and the bar area serve cocktails and the full menu. Reservations are not usually accepted, so arrive early. We make an effort to get there at least an hour ahead to get a table or a spot at the bar on days when big games are scheduled. That said, there is an option called "VIP Seating" available during certain popular events. Call 407-WDW-DINE to reserve a banquette-style seat—with prime viewing of the theater-sized screen—on the second tier of the dining room, aka "Sports Central." Note that there is a minimum for each guest in VIP seating. Reservations are required. **L D S · $$ – $$$ · 🐭**

FLYING FISH: The decor elevates the appeal of this upscale dining destination—which recently underwent a thorough and dramatic refurbishment. Be sure to look up—the flying fish chandelier is quite a sight to behold. As always, this restaurant gives most fine, big-city spots a run for their money. (The tab rivals said hotspots, too.)

The menu changes often, but the stars of the show are Chef Tim Majoras' creatively prepared sustainable seafood dishes. You'll always find the signature potato-wrapped snapper with a rich leek fondue and red wine and butter sauce, the crisp crab cakes, plus a char-crusted New York strip steak. We are routinely impressed by the service and find the menu worthy of the price tag. Reservations are recommended. As far as the Disney Dining Plan goes, F.F. is designated as a "Signature" restaurant. **D · $$$ – $$$$ · 🐭**

TRATTORIA AL FORNO: Taste buds take a tour of Italy with Trattoria's tempting array of regional specialties and crowd-pleasing classics. Signature standouts include wood-fired pizzas and pastas prepared *al forno* (baked in an oven). The family-friendly eatery celebrates the diversity of Italian cuisine with housemade mozzarella atop Neapolitan-style pizzas, hand-rolled pastas, seasonal seafood, and vegetables. The exclusively Italian wine list features more than 60 offerings by the bottle and 25 by the glass. Draft and

Dinner at Sea

For Walt Disney World's ultimate dinner-and-a-show splurge, consider reserving the elegant *Grand 1* yacht. You and up to 17 lucky invitees can enjoy a private tour of the lakes near the Magic Kingdom capped off with a viewing of Wishes, the park's fireworks show—all the while devouring delightful delicacies prepared by chefs at the Grand Floridian resort. The possibilities range from an intimate cruise for two, complete with dinner and champagne, to a swinging cocktail party for up to 18, with a boatload of shrimp, chips, wings, beer, wine, and soft drinks.

It costs about $520 (plus tax) per hour to rent the 5-room floating fantasyland. Driver and deckhand are included; refreshments are not. To book, call 407-WDW-PLAY at least 24 hours and up to 90 days ahead. The *Grand 1* docks at the Grand Floridian but can pick up passengers at the Contemporary, Polynesian Village, and Wilderness Lodge.

bottle beers, grapa, cocktails, and soft drinks round out the drink menu. For dessert, choose from selections such as tiramisú, and bombolini (doughnut-like pastry) with dark chocolate and vanilla gelato. Breakfast selections include frittatas, steel-cut oatmeal, waffles, and caramel apple crumb pancakes. **B D · $$–$$$ ·**

Caribbean Beach

OLD PORT ROYALE: The food court in Old Port Royale has a large dining area and the following fast-food counters: Grab N Go Market serves croissants, pastries, ice cream, and other snacks. Italian specialties are the order at the Royale Pizza and Pasta Shop. Soups, salads, and sandwiches are served at Montego's Deli. Burgers and chicken nuggets are among the offerings at Old Port Royale Hamburger Shop, while Bridgetown Broiler Shop serves omelets for breakfast and items such as turkey and beef strip loin for dinner. This food court is convenient, but the fare is just fair. Some kids' meals come in a sand bucket—which makes little diners very happy. **B L D S · $–$$ ·**

SHUTTERS AT OLD PORT ROYALE: The dining room here is as kid-friendly as a table-service eatery can be. Menu selections include chorizo-black bean soup, fish with yucca dumplings and curry-lemon butter sauce, and New York strip with plantain and potato gratin. The eatery is in the Old Port Royale building, across from the food court. In addition to soft drinks, beer, wine, and cocktails are served. Reservations are recommended. **D · $$–$$$ ·**

Contemporary

CALIFORNIA GRILL: Delighting diners for decades, the World-famous California Grill still graces most guests' must-do lists. The West Coast theme shines through in dishes prepared with the freshest seasonal and local produce available.

> ## HOT TIP!
> Would you like to watch Wishes, the Magic Kingdom's fireworks display, from the private perch at California Grill? You'll need to dine in the eatery—but it doesn't have to be during the show itself. If you finish your meal pre-Wishes, return to the second-floor check-in desk later the same day, present the receipt for your meal, and you'll be escorted to the eatery via private elevator.

"Brunch at the Top" features sweet potato pancakes, poached lobster Benedict, shrimp and grits, Chef's frittata, and other creatively prepared dishes. The pre-fixe brunch costs about $80 for adults, $48 for kids (ages 3 to 11).

Dinner standouts include pork two ways with grilled tenderloin, goat cheese polenta, mushrooms, and applesauce; oak-fired filet of beef with heirloom tomato risotto, basil, and tomato butter; and bison tenderloin with olive oil potatoes and Brussels sprouts. Sushi classics include dragon roll with spicy tataki tuna, shrimp tempura, bell pepper, avocado, and chili-soy glaze; and spicy kazan roll (crab, shrimps, and scallops in a spicy fireball sauce).

The wine list—which includes 250 selections, 80 of which are available by the glass—is a nice mix of greatest hits and good finds. There are ten varieties of saki and a selection of (predominantly Californian) craft beers. Housemade desserts provide the finishing touches, and there are sweeping views of the Magic Kingdom and the Seven Seas Lagoon (from select seats).

The restaurant is consistently crowded and the fare is first-rate. Reservations are necessary and must be booked with a credit card. Changes or cancellations must be made at least 24 hours ahead to avoid the $10-per-person fee. This is a Disney Dining Plan "Signature" restaurant (so it requires two table-service credits per diner).

An outdoor perch (exclusively available to California Grill patrons) affords bird's-eye views of the Magic Kingdom and its fireworks presentations (complete with the show's music). Guests (including those planning to visit the lounge) check in on the hotel's second floor and are escorted to the restaurant's express elevator. Dinner starts at 5 P.M. **Brunch D · $$$–$$$$ ·**

PHOTO BY MIKE CARROLL

CHEF MICKEY'S: Chef Mickey and his pals host this buffet-style feast, with dramatic views of the monorail passing above. The eatery serves family-friendly buffet breakfast, brunch, and dinner. The changing menu takes advantage of seasonal offerings; a sundae bar provides a sweet finish. At some point during the meal, Chef Mickey will stop by your table, as will several of his friends. Be prepared to drop your fork and twirl your napkin at a moment's notice. This is a very popular eatery with a loyal following. Kids simply adore the experience. It's a festive spot to celebrate a child's birthday. Reservations are an absolute must. **B•Brunch•D•$$–$$$•**

CONTEMPO CAFE: The Contemporary resort snack bar can be found on the fourth floor, beside Chef Mickey's. This spot serves impressive made-to-order fare. The grab-and-go section offers drinks (including beer and wine), wraps, yogurt, fresh fruit, sushi, desserts, and more. **BLDS•$–$$•**

PHOTO BY MIKE CARROLL

THE WAVE . . . OF AMERICAN FLAVORS: A stellar full-service eatery, this modern establishment features healthy, creative American fusion cuisine. Think "bold cooking inspired by locally sourced ingredients." Starters of note: Wave Appetizer for Two (lump crab, Florida rock shrimp cakes, and fish tacos) and a seasonal salad. Main courses include grilled beef tenderloin, seasonal vegetable stew with wild rice, and a sustainable fish of the day. Tempting desserts come in trios (a sweet sampling of three different selections). And the New World wine list is out of this world. It's possible to try several via flight samplers. The Wave is on the resort's first floor. We would eat breakfast, lunch, and dinner here without a moment's hesitation. The adjacent lounge is a perfect place for an aperitif or after-dinner drink. Reservations are recommended. **BLD•$$–$$$•**

Coronado Springs

CAFE RIX: Stop here for bagels and croissants, salads (Cobb, Greek, and house), chicken Caesar wraps, pastries, gelato, sorbet, beer, wine, soft drinks, and specialty coffee drinks. Additional

Tables in Wonderland

Annual Pass-bearers and Florida residents are eligible for the Tables in Wonderland (T.I.W.) discount dining program. It affords members up to 20 percent savings off food and beverages at many WDW table-service eateries. The discount is good for you and up to 9 members of your party. Present a valid photo ID and your T.I.W. card when you place an order with a server. To net the discount for the rest of the party, the check must be paid by the T.I.W. member. Membership is valid for one year and costs $150 for Annual Passholders and $175 for Florida residents (note that the price went up substantially in 2016). For details, call 407-566-5858. For a list of participating locations, go to: *http://disneyworld.disney.go.com/passholder-program/dining-discounts/.*

snacks include fruit cups, veggies and hummus, side salads, yogurt parfait, and chocolate or Key lime mousse. **BLDS•$–$$•**

LAS VENTANAS: An unpretentious locale for breakfast, lunch, and dinner, Las Ventanas serves up simple-yet-satisfying American cuisine. Breakfast runs from "ancient grain" pancakes to steak and eggs. Mahi mahi sandwiches, signature crab cakes, herb-marinated chicken breast, and chipotle BBQ pork are lunch and dinnertime possibilities. Cap off the meal with sorbet, Key lime pie, or Chambord mascarpone. There are kid-friendly choices (grilled cheese and chicken sandwiches), but the atmosphere is unlikely to enchant wee ones. Reservations are recommended. **BLDS•$–$$•**

MAYA GRILL: Guests here dine inside a Mayan pyramid, beside a volcano (dormant, of course). The menu has a bit of everything: seafood, meat, and poultry, with a touch of Latino spices added to some of the creations. Entrées range from sirloin fajitas to Cornish hens or pan-seared snapper. Desserts include coconut flan and panna cotta. Dinner is usually served from 5 P.M. to 10 P.M. Reservations are recommended. **BD•$$$•**

PEPPER MARKET: This busy, recently refurbished food court has a large seating area and a variety of food stations. Choose from BBQ ribs, Yucatán chicken, paninis, pizza, pasta, salads, empanadas and other Mexican fare— all prepared fresh from scratch. For breakfast, there are eggs, Mickey waffles, breakfast burritos, Southwestern omelets, and more. Anything may be ordered to go. Given this resort's popularity with the convention set, expect a proliferation of hungry humans during traditional weekday breakfast and lunch times. BLDS·$–$$·❤

Disney's Old Key West

GOOD'S FOOD TO GO: A walk-up window with a simple-yet-satisfying menu: Hamburgers, cheeseburgers, deli sandwiches, salads, ice cream, snacks, and breakfast items are among the many offerings at Good's. BLDS·$·❤

OLIVIA'S CAFE: We thoroughly enjoy the Key West manner with which Olivia's approaches its theme. The laid-back setting and menu convey the spirit of the leisure-centric locale. Breakfast includes standards, but also interesting combos like poached eggs served over sweet potato hash, topped with Key West hollandaise. The lunch/dinner menu offers salads, conch chowder, crab cakes, seared scallops, burgers, and sandwiches. End with a Key lime tart, chocolate cake, or a banana bread pudding sundae. The menu changes seasonally. Wine, beer, and specialty cocktails are served. Reservations are recommended for all meals. BLD·$$–$$$$·❤

Fort Wilderness

Many people choose to cook their own meals here. Some supplies are available at the Meadow and Settlement Trading Posts (open from 8 A.M. to 10 P.M. in winter; to 11 P.M. in summer), others may be delivered by a nearby grocery store (see page 227 for details). There is one restaurant.

TRAIL'S END RESTAURANT: True, it's a bit out of the way for anyone but Fort Wilderness guests (and even for some of them!), but for many, this rustic spot is well worth the trip.

The informal log-walled restaurant offers a hearty buffet breakfast. The fare is basic but bountiful. Breakfast selections include grits, biscuits and gravy, and breakfast pizza. Brunch is offered on weekends ($23 for adults; $13 for kids). Lunch is served à la carte and features fried chicken and waffles, sandwiches, salads; sautéed catfish, and fried green tomatoes. For dinner, expect the buffet to have smoked pork ribs, peel-and-eat shrimp, fried chicken, carved meats, a salad bar, plus a variety of side dishes and desserts. Pizza is served nightly from 4 P.M. until 10 P.M. daily. Beer and wine are served by the glass (or mason jar). Reservations are recommended. Breakfast costs about $19 for adults, $11 for kids; lunch is

à la carte; dinner is about $28 for adults, $16 for kids. After the meal, you can relax in a rocking chair on the front porch. It just doesn't get any better than that. (If you plan to eat here, allow extra travel time, just in case.) BLDS·$–$$·❤

Grand Floridian

CÍTRICOS: From the aromas wafting from the open kitchen, it's clear that the chef has vowed to wow you with cuisine from the Americas and the Mediterranean, herb by fragrant herb. The fare varies seasonally but may include such items as sautéed shrimp with tomato, lemon, and feta cheese; or beef short rib. Adventurous palates are most at home here. The menu's not extensive, but the wine list certainly is. Restaurant sommeliers are on hand to recommend wine pairings.

A private dining room is available for parties of up to 12. The lounge is ideal for solo diners or those without a reservation (ask the bartender for a menu). Reservations are necessary for the restaurant. D·$$$–$$$$·❤

GASPARILLA ISLAND GRILL: Breakfast items along the lines of scrambled eggs, waffles, bagels, and cereal are served daily until 11 A.M. After that, made-to-order selections such as sandwiches, burgers, pizza, and salads are available. Grab-and-go options such as salad, sushi, yogurt, fresh fruit, and snacks are on hand 24/7 in this quick-service spot near the marina (note that the middle-of-the-night pickin's may be slim). There is indoor and outdoor seating. If you purchase a refillable mug, this is the place to fill it up. BLDS·$–$$·❤

GRAND FLORIDIAN CAFE: A pleasant spot, the cafe is a relatively reasonably priced, low-key way to check out WDW's poshest resort.

The à la carte breakfast extends a wee bit beyond the usual fare. Lunch and dinner menus

Tea for Two (or Ten)

Teatime with all the trimmings—scones, finger sandwiches, strawberries and cream, etc.—is from 2 P.M. until 5 P.M. in the Garden View Tea Room at the Grand Floridian resort. This elegant lounge overlooks the lovingly tended gardens surrounding the resort's main swimming pool.

The menu includes custom-blended teas from around the world. Guests may also sip coffees and spirited drinks such as port or sparkling wine. Note that guests must be at least 21 years of age (with valid photo ID) to consume alcohol.

The Grand Floridian offers tea parties for kids, too. For information on these special events, turn to page 230.

For details or to make (necessary) reservations, call 407-WDW-DINE (939-3463).

vary seasonally but have traditional American dishes: onion soup, burgers, and the signature Grand Floridian sandwich. The wine selection is excellent. Reservations are recommended, but it may be possible to get a table without one if you're willing to wait. **B L D · $$$ · ❦**

NARCOOSSEE'S: Named for a nearby Central Florida town, Narcoossee's specializes in fresh sustainable seafood—with the occasional land-based entrée making surf-and-turf combinations a decadent possibility. Narcoossee's has upscale selections (and prices), but the atmosphere is rather relaxed. The display kitchen presents dinner dishes such as steamed mussels, grilled steak, and Maine lobster. The international wine selection is quite good—you might even enjoy a pre-dinner glass on the veranda. The view of the Seven Seas Lagoon and Cinderella Castle (in the distance) completes the experience. Brunch offers housemade pastries, shrimp and grits, brioche French toast, lobster eggs Benedict, chicken and waffles, steak and eggs, and pan-fried salmon. Reservations are recommended. The lounge here offers a full menu (and does not require a reservation) as well as a full bar and an abundance of wines offered by the bottle or the glass. The dress code is business casual. The pre-fixe brunch costs about $69 for adults, $41 for kids (ages 3 to 11). **Brunch D · $$$–$$$$ · ❦**

1900 PARK FARE: The atmosphere is reminiscent of an old-time amusement park, but the sophisticated buffet menu and subtle decor make this one of the most elegant character restaurants on the property. Mary Poppins and her friends mingle with guests during the bountiful daily breakfast. Cinderella and members of her royal family visit the dining room during the dinner hours. Keep in mind that the lineup of characters does change from time to time.

Dinner features seafood, salads, pastas, veggies, breads, carved meats, and housemade desserts. The offerings change seasonally. A salad bar and dessert bar stand nearby. There's a kids' buffet, too. It offers pizza, pasta, and vegetables. The restaurant's focal point is Big Bertha, a band organ built in Paris nearly a century ago. She sits in a proscenium and rises 15 feet above the floor. Reservations are recommended. Brunch may be offered seasonally. **B Brunch D · $$$ · ❦**

VICTORIA & ALBERT'S: The dining room in the only AAA 5-Diamond restaurant in Central Florida seats just 60 guests (all of whom must have already celebrated their 10th birthday). It is indulgent without being too haute to handle (although the steep prices may curb some folks' enthusiasm) and is considered by many to be the grand dame of the Disney dining scene.

The 7-course "Chef's Tasting Menu" changes frequently, always offering a selection of farm-fresh fish, poultry, and beef as main courses. But the beauty of this high-end experience is all the little tastes as you make your way through the $185-per-person (plus tax and gratuity) adventure. You might start with lobster or quail, then move on to seared wild turbot or pork tenderloin. The cheese course is worth every calorie. And, even with seven courses, you must reserve room for the indulgent desserts: a flurry of soufflés, chocolate, and more. Perfect portions keep it all surprisingly manageable. The strains of a harp or violin provide a romantic backdrop. The wine list is encyclopedic. Wine pairings are available for an additional $65 per person (do let your server know about any personal wine preferences).

The main dining room also serves a 10-course "Chef's Degustation Menu"—a series of small courses inspired by chef Scott Hunnel's travels to Asia, Spain, Italy, and France. The cost is $235 per person ($340 with wine pairing).

For an extra-special (and extraordinarily splurgy) experience, book the Chef's Table (for up to 10 guests; $250 per person, plus tax and gratuity) or the Queen Victoria Room ($225 per diner, plus tax and tip). With just four tables, the latter provides the restaurant's most exclusive, luxurious setting.

At the end of the meal, all guests are given a souvenir menu to commemorate the occasion. In sum, though the experience is an extremely expensive one, for many it is also quite special. Jackets are required for men. Guests must be at least 10 years old to dine here. Reservations are an absolute must; call 407-939-3862. Restaurant information and sample menus are available at *www.victoria-alberts.com*. D·$$$$

Polynesian Village

CAPT. COOK'S: The captain dispenses snacks and light fare 24 hours a day. It's a good spot for made-to-order breakfast items such as eggs, Mickey waffles, or the ever-popular fried, banana-stuffed Tonga toast. Lunch and dinner bring burgers, (delicious) fish tacos, pulled pork nachos, Thai coconut meatballs, hot dogs, flatbreads (plain, pepperoni, and Hawaiian [marinara, pineapple, onions, ham, mozzarella, and Parmesan]), Caesar salad with chicken, sandwiches and grab-and-go items such as sushi, yogurt, fruit, pastries, and snacks. Milk (plain and chocolate), beer, wine, and soft drinks are also available. Come here to buy and fill the Poly's refillable mug with soft drinks. BLDS·$–$$·❤

KONA CAFE: Warm colors, soft lighting, and South Seas decor render the crisp, fluid design of this open dining space rather cozy and casual. The menu tends toward the exotic side as far as Disney restaurants go, but there's a nice variety of choices. Lunch and dinner menus feature Asian-influenced entrées. Possibilities include teriyaki beef, grilled Kona-coffee-rubbed pork chop, (sumptuous) sushi, and market-fresh sustainable fish. The morning meal offers Tonga toast (banana-stuffed, fried sourdough bread coated with cinnamon sugar), plus traditional breakfast items. There is a solid wine list, and islands-inspired cocktails are served. The pressed-pot coffee is a fan favorite. You'll find Kona Cafe on the second floor of the Great Ceremonial House, just around the corner from 'Ohana. Reservations are recommended for all meals. BLDS·$$–$$$·❤

KONA ISLAND: A coffee bar until noon, this is a super spot for a quick sip on your way to the monorail. Light breakfast items are offered, too.

When five o'clock rolls around, so does the sushi. Roll selections include Volcano (spicy tuna, shrimp salad, and tempura crunch), California Luau (fresh jumbo lump crab, pineapple, and avocado), Tuna Poke (traditional Hawaiian ahi tuna salad), and a cucumber roll (for vegetarians).

Sashimi fans will enjoy the salmon and tuna, as well as the chef's selection of the day. Seating

is limited, but it's possible to get some of the selections to go. Beer, wine, sake, and other cocktails are served. BDS·$–$$·❤

'OHANA: On the second floor of the Great Ceremonial House, this restaurant is a meticulously themed, family-friendly eatery, complete with entertainment. An interesting twist of note: 'Ohana's family-style dinner experience—a South Pacific feast prepared in the restaurant's open-fire cooking pit—does not come with a menu, so no decisions have to be made. The oak-grilled skewers of pork and beef just keep coming. Spicy peel-and-eat shrimp, green salad, pineapple-coconut bread, pan-Asian noodles tossed in teriyaki sauce, and stir-fried veggies are among the accompaniments, and dessert is bread pudding served à la mode with warm caramel sauce. Soft drinks are included. Beer, wine, and cocktails are extra.

'Ohana's setting, which features wood carvings under a vast thatched roof, is rather festive. So much so that there are periodic, boisterous hula hoop, limbo, and coconut-rolling contests for the little ones. Polynesian singers croon from time to time.

Breakfast is also a family affair—make that extended family, as Lilo, Stitch, and their good friends Mickey and Pluto host the morning meal. Breakfast fare is basic and presented family style. Keep in mind that the character lineup does change from time to time. Reservations are strongly recommended. BD·$$$–$$$$·❤

OASIS GRILL: The laid-back Oasis Grill is situated next to the Polynesian's new Oasis pool. It serves up items such as cheeseburgers, fish tacos, chicken avocado wraps, and more. The O.G. is adjacent to the Oasis Bar. LDS·$–$$·❤

PINEAPPLE LANAI: This sweet stop offers WDW's classic Dole Whip frozen pineapple dessert and other tropical treats. It's located on the ground level. **S·$·❤**

TRADER SAM'S GROG GROTTO: It's hard to be grouchy at this spot—Trader Sam will see to that. With a theme inspired by the Jungle Cruise and Enchanted Tiki Room attractions, Trader Sam's features drinks (tropical and otherwise) and small plates such as pan-fried dumplings, chicken lettuce wraps, and sushi rolls. Patio seating is relatively easy to snag, but securing indoor seats often requires time, patience, and a pager. Doors open at 4 P.M. and close promptly at midnight. Note that folks start lining up for the inside seats at about 3:30 P.M. **S·$–$$**

Pop Century

EVERYTHING POP!: The selection at this colorful food court in Classic Hall has included "design your own" pasta, burger, or omelet; pizza; rotisserie chicken and roast turkey; nachos; Asian dishes; seafood; hot dogs; sandwiches (tuna, meatball, turkey, or veggie); salads; breakfast items; and baked goods (tie-dyed cheesecake!). Feel free to join the jolly cast members as they dance the Twist at 8 A.M. and the Hustle at 6 P.M. **BLDS·$–$$·❤**

Port Orleans French Quarter

SASSAGOULA FLOATWORKS & FOOD FACTORY: A food court with a Mardi Gras theme, this spot offers pizza, pasta, burgers, sandwiches, soups, salads, spit-roasted chicken,

HOT TIP!

Guests staying at Port Orleans French Quarter and Riverside may have pizza delivered to their rooms between 4 P.M. and midnight. Call Sassagoula Pizza Express from your resort room telephone to order whole pies, drinks, and sweet snacks. There is a $15 minimum per order and the Disney Dining Plan is accepted. Guests using the Disney Dining Plan should note that pizza delivery requires two D.D.P. entitlements per order. Each order provides enough to satisfy two grown-up appetites (in most cases).

barbecued ribs, ice cream, and bakery products. The Big Easy is well represented here: New Orleans–inspired menu items include classic gumbo, Creole burgers, muffalettas, and jambalaya. **BLDS·$–$$·❤**

Port Orleans Riverside

BOATWRIGHT'S DINING HALL: Southern specialties and American comfort food are the big draw here—think prime rib and jambalaya. Beer, wine, and cocktails are available, as are soft drinks. The restaurant is quite popular, as it's the resort's only table-service eatery, so reservations are encouraged. Walk-up requests are typically admitted when the restaurant opens at 5 P.M. **D·$$–$$$·❤**

RIVERSIDE MILL: This high-ceilinged food court styled in the image of a cotton mill (complete with working waterwheel) offers a half dozen food counters. Collectively, the stands serve pizza; pasta; fried, grilled, and roast chicken; cheeseburgers; salads; sandwiches (including New Orleans–style muffalettas); ice cream; and fresh baked goods. They're big on "create your own" here, too. (You can customize an omelet, salad, and/or pasta dish.) There's ample seating, so it's usually possible to get a table. All items may be packaged "to go." **BLDS·$–$$·❤**

Saratoga Springs

THE ARTIST'S PALETTE: Set in a converted artist's loft within Walt Disney World's sprawling resort, this spot offers breakfast, lunch, and dinner. Among the selections are fresh tossed salads, made-to-order sandwiches, pizza, baked goods, and more. There are some grocery items, as well as a variety of grab-and-go selections. **BLDS·$–$$·❤**

THE PADDOCK GRILL: Head to this quick-service window for freshly prepared sandwiches (grilled chicken, spice-crusted fish, roasted veggie, etc.), chicken chopped salad, bacon cheeseburgers, and housemade potato chips (which were actually invented in Saratoga). **BLDS·$–$$·❤**

THE TURF CLUB BAR & GRILL: A restaurant with an old-fashioned horse racing theme (and a pool table), this low-frills eatery serves pasta, prime rib, grilled meats, sustainable fish, salads, crab cakes, steamed mussels, grilled salmon, steak, roasted chicken breast, spice-rubbed pork tenderloin, and more. **D·$–$$·❤**

B breakfast **L** lunch **D** dinner **S** snacks / **$** under $15 **$$** $15–$36 **$$$** $36–$60 **$$$$** $60 and up

Swan & Dolphin

CABANA BAR & BEACH CLUB: An elegant poolside eatery, the Dolphin's Cabana serves a sophisticated selection of starters, salads, and entrées. Appetizer options include fish tacos and chicken wings. The main bites menu offers Cuban sandwiches, cheesesteaks, grilled chicken BLT, blackened salmon, buttermilk-battered chicken crisps, schnitzel, and burgers made from farm-raised, grass-fed, organic beef. Among the many signature cocktails are the Dolphin Mai Tai, Montego Punch, and the Dark and Stormy. For kids, Cabana serves pizza, burgers, hot dogs, chicken fingers, and more. **L D S · $ – $ $**

THE FOUNTAIN: A soda fountain with some grown-up appeal, this is an ideal spot for a sweet snack or a satisfying meal. Homemade soft-serve ice cream is the house specialty. Be it served in a simple cone or in an elaborate sundae (the caramel apple sundae is a standout), the chilly treat is sure to please. Among the entrées from which to choose are cheeseburgers, Southern pulled pork sandwiches, and Chicago-style hot dogs. Soups and salads can augment the meal, as can fries, onion rings, soft pretzels served with cheese and mustard, or chips and salsa. Drinks-wise, this place has everything from freshly brewed iced tea and specialty coffees to impressively inventive shakes (including the PB&J, coco loco, and peppermint concoctions), plus beer and wine. The Fountain is located at the Dolphin. An adjacent walk-up window, known as Sweet Treats, offers ice cream and heavenly milk shakes for hungry folks on the go. **L D S · $ – $ $**

FRESH MEDITERRANEAN MARKET: The Dolphin's airy eatery offers salads, sandwiches, and soups. The morning menu includes pastries, yogurt, fresh granola, hot cereals, eggs, pancakes, and more. It's also possible to have a light lunch here, provided that you are a salad fan. Fresh offers many wines by the glass, plus sangria, Bloody Marys, beer, and soft drinks. Reservations are recommended. **B L · $ $ – $ $ $**

GARDEN GROVE: This Swan eatery means to transport guests to the peaceful gardens of New York's Central Park—and the 25-foot oak tree is a most realistic touch. The restaurant offers a full breakfast menu (with Disney characters in the house on Saturday and Sunday mornings), and salads, sandwiches, and more for lunch. What's the dinner "special"? It comes with a side of Disney characters. Different nights also bring different fare. At press time, Sunday through Thursday featured a traditional menu of salads, soups, and entrées; Friday and Saturday offered a seafood buffet. Disney characters are on hand for dinner every night and for breakfast on Saturday and Sunday. Reservations are recommended. Visit *www.swandolphin.com* for more information. **B L D · $ $ – $ $ $**

IL MULINO NEW YORK TRATTORIA: A swank Swan destination, Il Mulino offers upscale Italian cuisine in a relaxed yet vibrant trattoria-like setting. Specializing in *Piatti per il Tavolo*, or family-style dining, the spot is ideal for groups. The seasonal menu is characterized by blends of fresh ingredients drawn from the Abruzzi region of Italy. Signature items include *gamberi al Mulino* (jumbo shrimp with spicy cocktail sauce), *gnocchi bolognese* (potato dumplings with meat sauce), *pollo fra diavolo* (chicken in a spicy red sauce with sausage), and *salmone* (sautéed salmon in garlic and olive oil with wild mushrooms and broccoli rabe). *Mangia!*

Dinners begin with an antipasti tasting, on the house (quite the treat!). Enjoy it while perusing the wine list's 250 or so varietals. The children's menu has pizza, pasta, and chicken parmigiana. For reservations, call 407-939-3463 or 407-934-1199, or visit *swandolphin.com*. **D · $ $ $ – $ $ $ $**

KIMONOS: In the mood for sushi with a side of karaoke? You've come to the right place! This Swan lounge is an honest-to-goodness karaoke bar (the only one at Walt Disney World). Some guests come to sing, while others are drawn to the sushi, sashimi, and tempura. It's also possible to order miso soup, salad, edamame, tempura udon, gyoza, and Wagyu beef satay, among other selections. There's a full bar featuring such specialty cocktails as the Sake Sangria and the Mt. Fuji Rain. This spot opens around dinnertime, serving Japanese food and drinks. The singing gets started at about 9 P.M. A good time (and meal) is generally had by all. If you'd like to get some sustenance to go, place your order with the bartender. **D S · $ – $ $**

PHOTO BY JILL SAFRO

Resort to Resort

If you're staying in one resort and dining in another, you need to plan ahead—even if the resorts are linked by monorail or water taxi. Why? The transportation may be operating before dinner, but if you're out late enough you'll have to get yourself home another way.

The good news is you will never be stranded. Bus transportation runs until about 1 A.M.—but it's not direct. If the theme parks are closed, you'll have to take a bus to Disney Springs and transfer to a bus to your hotel. If the theme parks are open, you can take a bus to any park and transfer to one that's headed to your resort. Keep in mind that the trip can take up to 90 minutes in either direction. If that thought is unpleasant, do what we sometimes do: splurge on a cab. Authorized taxis should run between $10 and $30, depending on the destination and traffic. If you have more than three people in your party, request a van (the rate is the same). Ask about calling a cab at the resort's bell services desk.

PICABU: This Dolphin cafeteria is a bit above the norm. Much of the food is usually freshly prepared—with excellent sandwiches and salads, plus a customize-your-own taco and burrito station. The convenience store offers snacks and sundries. The house coffee is Starbucks (free refills during your meal). Note that this spot is a tad pricier than the average Disney World quick-service eatery, but the quality is appreciated by most. And some of the portions are big enough to share. The eatery (and store) is open 24/7. **B L D S · $ – $ $**

SHULA'S: Like the original Shula's in Miami, this Dolphin spot specializes in generous portions of certified Angus beef, plus soups, salads, chicken and fresh fish dishes. For dessert, there's apple crisp, vanilla cheesecake, molten chocolate lava cake, and more. The upscale eatery pays tribute to the 1972 Miami Dolphins—the year coach Don Shula led his team to a perfect NFL season. The prices are steep, but the steaks are first-rate and lovingly prepared. Though the interior celebrates the game of football, this is not a casual sports bar. The dress code is business or resort casual. Reservations are recommended. There is a kids' menu, too. FYI: Shula's is a frequent winner of *Wine Spectator*'s Award of Excellence. **D · $ $ $ $**

SPLASH TERRACE: Just steps from the Swan lap pool, Splash serves sandwiches, pizza, and salads. Made-to-order sandwiches include The Original (smoked Virginia ham, turkey, and provolone on Italian bread) and The Orient Express (sliced flat iron steak with chili mayo on ciabatta bread). Organic and gluten-free snacks are sold. Cocktails and soft drinks are also served. **L S · $**

TODD ENGLISH'S BLUEZOO: A sophisticated member of the Disney dining scene, the menu at this sleek Dolphin spot features coastal cuisine, incorporating an innovative selection of fresh seafood with both international and New American culinary influences. The raw bar's stocked with oysters and middleneck clams. If you prefer your seafood cooked, try the chilled poached jumbo shrimp or chilled Maine lobster tail. A popular starter is the brothy clam chowder with salt-cured bacon and oyster crackers. All of the entrées are tempting: from miso-glazed mero to bluezoo's signature dancing fish (whole fish roasted on a rotating spit).

Not in the mood for a selection from the sea? Consider dry-aged beef or pan-roasted chicken breast. The dessert menu tempts with treats such as warm chocolate cake with a liquid ganache center. Reservations are recommended. It's possible to get food service at the bar, a plus for small groups or solo diners. Closing time at the bar tends to vary nightly (depending on just how crowded the place is). **D S · $ $ $ – $ $ $ $**

Wilderness Lodge

ARTIST POINT: The Pacific Northwest theme of this eatery is announced in landscape murals, while tall red-framed windows look out to Bay Lake. The cavernous dining room is by no means intimate, but it's not without charm.

Artist Point's hallmark is its knack for translating fresh, seasonal ingredients from the Pacific Northwest into flavorful creations. One is the freshly flown-in-salmon served on a smoking cedar plank. The menu may also include beef, pork,

B breakfast   **L** lunch   **D** dinner   **S** snacks   /   **$** under $15   **$$** $15–$36   **$$$** $36–$60   **$$$$** $60 and up

venison, and chicken selections. The wine list includes pinot noirs and syrahs from Oregon and Washington State. If it's offered, we recommend starting your meal with the heirloom tomato salad.

For dessert, loyal visitors swear by the berry cobbler, which is made with seasonal berries and is far from traditional. Ask your server for a description. Reservations are recommended. The dress code is resort casual. Artist Point is a Disney Dining Plan Signature eatery. D · $ $ $ – $ $ $ $ · 🐭

ROARING FORK: Set in a stone-walled area (a bit dungeon like, but in a cool way), this snack bar serves salads, burgers, fries, pizza, sandwiches, chili, and snacks. Breakfast items such as cereal, yogurt, oatmeal, eggs, and waffles are available. Soft drinks, beer, and wine are also offered. This is the spot to top off refillable resort mugs. (Purchase the mug and refill it for free for the length of your stay here or at any Disney-owned-and-operated resort.) B L D S · $ · 🐭

WHISPERING CANYON CAFE: The name is ironic, as there is nothing quiet about this place. A family favorite, Whispering Canyon is one of the most boisterous Disney restaurants. All meals are offered à la carte and "all you can eat" style. The latter means heaping plates keep coming to the table until you say "when."

In the morning, the air is filled with aromas of bacon and potatoes and other breakfast fare (omelets, waffles, etc.). Lunch offers pulled pork sandwiches, fish and chips, salads, and more. For supper, expect such items as baked chicken and smoked pork ribs. The smoothies, milk shakes, and homemade desserts are quite popular. Reservations are recommended. B L D · $ $ $ · 🐭

Yacht & Beach Club

BEACH CLUB MARKETPLACE: The beachy setting extends to this snack bar/convenience store. There are baked goods, grocery items, made-to-order sandwiches, and packaged grab-and-go items—small salads, hard-cooked eggs, fruit cups, and more. There is limited seating. If you purchase a refillable resort mug, head here to fill 'er up. B L D S · $ – $ $ · 🐭

BEACHES & CREAM SODA SHOP: This classic soda fountain is poolside at Beach Club. It offers sundaes, cones, floats, shakes, and sodas. Cheeseburgers, chicken sandwiches, hot dogs, and fries are served, too. Reservations are recommended (this pocket-sized place is very popular). B L D S · $ – $ $ · 🐭

CAPE MAY CAFE: Minnie and her friends greet Beach Club visitors each morning at this whimsical dining area. The breakfast buffet includes all the standards, plus a few specialties. Breakfast doesn't disappoint, but dinner is the big event here. Dinner is an all-you-can-eat New England–style clambake buffet, and it's one of WDW's most popular meals and better values (though it does not include character appearances). The lineup includes crab legs, mussels, steamed clams, carved meat, salads, pastas, corn on the cob, potatoes, and desserts. Soft drinks are included, but cocktails cost extra. Reservations are recommended. B D · $ $ $ · 🐭

CAPTAIN'S GRILLE: This American grill serves steak, seafood, and more. Breakfast features a buffet and an à la carte menu; lunch and dinner are à la carte. The hand-cut salt and vinegar fries pair nicely with the lump crab cake with fire-roasted corn succotash. The house-made potato cheese gnocchi, brined pork tenderloin, and New England–style lobster rolls are all crowd-pleasers. The dessert menu features hazelnut gianduja chocolate cake with salted caramel sauce and gluten-free angel food cake with berry compote. Reservations are recommended. B L D · $ $ – $ $ $ · 🐭

HURRICANE HANNA'S WATERSIDE BAR & GRILL: Hanna's serves burgers and cheeseburgers, lobster and shrimp rolls, chopped field green salad, grilled chicken breast sandwiches, and vegetarian offerings—plus cocktails and frozen concoctions. The kids' menu includes grilled chicken sandwiches, chicken nuggets, and burgers. This is also a refillable WDW resort mug station. L S · $ · 🐭

YACHTSMAN STEAKHOUSE: You know you're in for a serious steak experience the moment you walk through the door. There's an actual butcher shop here. Yes, this Yacht Club eatery delivers an experience to rival those of revered New York City steak houses.

Meals begin with freshly prepared pull-apart onion rolls and may continue with an appetizer such as lobster bisque. There's no skimping on the expertly prepared entrées, so good luck finding room for crème brûlée. In addition to beef, the menu includes lamb, chicken, and seafood entrées. It's possible to feast on side dishes alone, with sautéed mushroom caps, creamed spinach, and truffle mac and cheese all vying for attention. Reservations are recommended. D · $ $ $ – $ $ $ $ · 🐭

WALT DISNEY WORLD

Name & Location	Meals	Style*	Price**	Characters	Theme
Akershus Norway Pavilion, Epcot (page 252)	Breakfast Lunch Dinner	Family style	B: $39/24 L: $38/23 D: $43/24	Belle, Jasmine, Snow White, and Aurora	Fourteenth-century Norwegian castle
Cape May Cafe Beach Club resort (page 281)	Breakfast	Buffet	B: $35/20	Goofy, Minnie, and Donald Duck	Seaside picnic
Chef Mickey's Contemporary resort (page 273)	Breakfast Brunch Dinner	Buffet	Breakfast $40/25 Brunch: $40/21 Dinner: $50/30	Mickey, Minnie, Donald, Goofy, and Pluto	A family celebration
Cinderella's Royal Table Magic Kingdom (page 245)	Breakfast Lunch Dinner	B/L: Family style D: À la carte	B: $63/38 L: $60/36 D: $75/44	B, L, D: Princesses B, L, D: Cinderella greets guests in the Castle lobby	Medieval banquet
The Crystal Palace Magic Kingdom (page 248)	Breakfast Lunch Dinner	Buffet	B: $32/19 L: $45/27 D: $45/27	Pooh, Eeyore, Tigger, and Piglet	Sunlit conservatory
Garden Grill Epcot (page 251)	Breakfast Lunch Dinner	Family style	B: $32/19 L: $41/25 D: $45/27	Mickey, Pluto, Chip, and Dale	Home-style country cooking

* Family-style and buffet meals are all-you-can-eat dining experiences. Family-style features a set menu and table service; buffet-style meals usually present more dining options and are self-serve.

** Adult prices are followed by children's prices (diners ages 3 through 9). Prices may be higher during select "peak" times of year.

CHARACTER DINING

Featured Items	For Dessert	Tip	Wins for . . .
B: Scrambled eggs, potato casseroles, French toast sticks, bacon, sausage, fruit L/D: Norwegian fare and kid-friendly selections	Chocolate mousse cake, lingonberry cheesecake	The eatery is about a half-mile from Epcot's front entrance—plan your travel time accordingly.	It's not Cinderella's Castle, but it's still pretty cool. (It's much easier to score reservations here, too.)
Eggs, breakfast pizza, Mickey waffles, sausage, fruit, cereal, grits	Donuts, muffins, Danish, fresh fruit	For guests staying in the Epcot area, Cape May is one of the best breakfast options.	Best Chance of Getting a Table Without Reservations (But make the arrangements, anyway—there's usually a wait to get in.)
B: Eggs, fruit, pancakes, Mickey waffles, cereal Brunch: BBQ ribs, salmon, mac and cheese, and more D: Carved meats, pasta, seafood, veggies, pizza, salads	Make-your-own sundaes, cheesecake, cookies, and other fresh housemade desserts	A celebration happens every 45 minutes. Be sure to stick around for at least one little napkin-swinging party.	Best All-Around Character Meal (It has a fun and festive setting and a kid-pleasing menu.)
B: Frittata, lobster and crab crepes, eggs, French toast, bacon, pastries L/D: Catch of the day, pork shank, beef short ribs, and beef tenderloin	Seasonal cheesecake, flourless chocolate cake, and dessert trio	Payment in full is required at time of booking for all meals.	Best Setting (The restaurant is inside Cinderella Castle!)
B: French toast, eggs, cereal, frittatas, fruit L/D: Shrimp, carved meats, pasta, veggies, pizza, salad	B: Sticky buns L/D: Cakes, pies, make-your-own sundaes, cookies	Don't be put off by this restaurant's size—the characters make the rounds surprisingly quickly.	Best Theme Park Buffet (Scores points for its lovely setting, convenient location, and appetizing menu.)
B: Sticky buns, scrambled eggs, fruit, waffles L/D: Beef, turkey, fish, veggies, potatoes (mac and cheese for kids)	Freshly made desserts	The room rotates very slowly throughout the meal. It's hardly noticeable to most, but may be disorienting to those highly sensitive to motion.	Best for Vegetarians (Be sure to ask for the vegetarian meal—it's usually a tasty seasonal selection.)

All characters, menu items, and prices are subject to change. Prices are rounded to the nearest dollar. Call 407-WDW-DINE (939-3463) for details or to make reservations. This listing is not comprehensive. Character meals are also presented at the Hilton (Sunday breakfast at Covington Mill) and Buena Vista Palace (Sunday breakfast at Watercress Cafe). See pages 108 and 110 for details.

Name & Location	Meals	Style*	Price**	Characters	Theme
Garden Grove Swan resort (page 279)	Breakfast (weekends) Dinner (daily)	Breakfast: Buffet Dinner: À la carte	B: $21/13 D: $30/18 (plated)	B: Goofy & Pluto (Sat.); Goofy, Pluto, Chip, & Dale (Sun.) D: Goofy & Pluto (Sat.–Thurs.); Goofy, Pluto, Chip, & Dale (Fri.)	Picnic in the park
Hollywood & Vine Disney's Hollywood Studios (page 260)	Breakfast Lunch Dinner (seasonal)	Family style	B: $32/19 L: $40/24 D: $50/30	Breakfast and Lunch: Doc McStuffins, Sofia the First, Handy Manny, and Jake Dinner: Minnie and friends (Visit www.disneyworld.com for details.)	A salute to Playhouse Disney or a seasonal celebration
Wonderland Tea Party Grand Floridian resort (page 230)	Lunch	Tea-party style	$49 (per child, ages 4–12)	Alice and the Mad Hatter	Pint-size, interactive tea party
Mickey's Backyard Barbecue Dinner show at Fort Wilderness (page 300)	Dinner	Buffet	$62/37	Mickey and friends such as Goofy, Minnie, Chip, and Dale	Backyard barbecue/ hoedown
'Ohana Polynesian Village resort (page 277)	Breakfast	Family style	$32/19	Lilo, Stitch, and others, such as Pluto and Mickey	Tropical feast
1900 Park Fare Grand Floridian resort (page 276)	Breakfast Brunch (seasonal) Dinner	Buffet	B: $32/19 D: $45/27	B: Stars like Mary Poppins and Alice D: Cinderella and friends	Turn-of-the-century circus
Tusker House Donald's Dining Safari at Animal Kingdom (page 264)	Breakfast Lunch Dinner	Buffet	B: $32/19 L: $40/25 D: $45/27	Donald, Daisy, Goofy, and Mickey	Safari feast

* Family-style and buffet meals are all-you-can-eat dining experiences. Family-style features a set menu and table service; buffet-style meals usually present more dining options and are self-serve.

** Adult prices are followed by children's prices (diners ages 3 through 9). Prices will be higher during select "peak" times of year.

Featured Items	For Dessert	Tip	Wins for ...
B: Omelets, eggs, bacon, fruit D: Prime rib, roast chicken, cedar plank salmon	Fresh pastries	Dinner, Sunday–Monday offers a choice of entrée with unlimited soup, salad, and dessert buffet; Friday and Saturday features Seafood Sensations Buffet ($36 for adults; $17 for kids).	**Best-kept Secret** (Garden Grove allows for a classic Disney character dining experience without major pre-planning. A true bonus at WDW!)
B: Mickey waffles, scrambled eggs, yogurt L: Salads, pasta dishes, fish, and chicken D: Offerings vary seasonally	Pineapple upside-down cake, Key lime tart	Request Play 'N Dine when you reserve lunch and Minnie's Seasonal Dine when booking dinner.	**Tot-Pleasing** (Little ones love to dine along with Doc McStuffins, who appears at breakfast and lunch.)
PB&J sandwiches, chicken nuggets, fruit, and kid-friendly "tea" (apple juice)	Cupcakes, crispy treats	Parents can stick around for the party, but kids are well supervised. Many adults choose to snooze by the pool or relax in a Grand Floridian lounge.	**Most Fun with Food** (What's cooler to a kid than eating a cupcake? Decorating it first!)
Chicken, ribs, hot dogs, corn on the cob, baked beans	Watermelon, marble cake, and warm fruit cobbler	The dinner show is presented on Tuesday and Thursday evenings from March through December.	**Country Music Fans** (There is a live country band and line dancing.)
Mickey waffles, eggs, biscuits, fruit, bacon	Sweet baked goods	Don't forget your autograph book and camera. The characters spend a good amount of quality time at each table.	**Speediest Service** (Servers keep those family-style platters coming fast and frequently.)
B: Pancakes, eggs, waffles D: Prime rib, pasta, seafood	B: Sticky buns, muffins, Danish D: Key lime pie, cheesecake, bread pudding	Breakfast here is a nice way to start a Magic Kingdom day. The park is just one monorail stop away.	**Fanciest Foods** (The quality is superior to many buffets, and there's plenty to please the kids.)
B: Mickey waffles, quiche, eggs, fruit L/D: Spit-roasted chicken and beef, roasted pork loin, vegetarian offerings, salmon, salads, bread	B: Danish, muffins L and D: Warm cinnamon bread, pudding with vanilla sauce, chocolate cake	This spot is just steps from Kilimanjaro Safaris, making it an ideal location for a pre-safari breakfast or post-safari lunch.	**Best Place to Dine with Donald Duck** (The Duck and his pals greet guests at breakfast, lunch, and dinner.)

All characters, menu items, and prices are subject to change. Prices are rounded to the nearest dollar. Call 407-WDW-DINE (939-3463), or visit *www.disneyworld.com/dining/* for updates or to make reservations. This listing is not comprehensive.

BIRNBAUM'S ★BEST★ RESTAURANT ROUNDUP

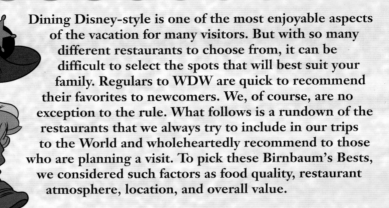

Dining Disney-style is one of the most enjoyable aspects of the vacation for many visitors. But with so many different restaurants to choose from, it can be difficult to select the spots that will best suit your family. Regulars to WDW are quick to recommend their favorites to newcomers. We, of course, are no exception to the rule. What follows is a rundown of the restaurants that we always try to include in our trips to the World and wholeheartedly recommend to those who are planning a visit. To pick these Birnbaum's Bests, we considered such factors as food quality, restaurant atmosphere, location, and overall value.

TOP WDW RESTAURANTS FOR FAMILIES WITH KIDS

TABLE SERVICE

Boma—Flavors of Africa .... Animal Kingdom Lodge resort (p. 270)
Cape May Cafe .... Beach Club resort (p. 281)
Chef Mickey's .... Contemporary resort (p. 273)
Cinderella's Royal Table .... Magic Kingdom (p. 245)
Crystal Palace .... Magic Kingdom (p. 248)
50's Prime Time Cafe....................................... Disney's Hollywood Studios (p. 260)
Garden Grill .... Epcot (p. 251)
1900 Park Fare .... Grand Floridian resort (p. 276)
Rainforest Cafe .... Animal Kingdom and Disney Springs (pp. 264, 268)
Sci-Fi Dine-In Theater .... Disney's Hollywood Studios (p. 261)
T-Rex Cafe ....Disney Springs (p. 269)
Tusker House .... Animal Kingdom (p. 264)
Via Napoli... Epcot (p. 257)
The Wave . . . of American Flavors .... Contemporary resort (p. 274)

QUICK SERVICE

Columbia Harbour House .... Magic Kingdom (p. 248)
Cooke's of Dublin .... Disney Springs (p. 266)
Earl of Sandwich .... Disney Springs (p. 266)
Everything Pop! .... Pop Century resort (p. 278)
Flame Tree Barbecue ....Animal Kingdom (p. 264)
Liberty Inn .... Epcot (p. 258)
The Mara .... Disney's Animal Kingdom Lodge (p. 271)
Pinocchio Village Haus .... Magic Kingdom (p. 246)
Sunset Ranch Market .... Disney's Hollywood Studios (p. 263)
Sunshine Seasons .... Epcot (p. 252)

BEST KIDS' MEAL PRESENTATION

Old Port Royale .... Caribbean Beach resort (p. 273)
(The meal comes in a sand bucket with a shovel.)

BEST PLACE TO CELEBRATE A CHILD'S BIRTHDAY

Chef Mickey's .... Contemporary resort (p. 273)

RUNNER-UP

Mickey's Backyard Barbecue .... Fort Wilderness (p. 300)

BEST FIREWORKS VIEW

California Grill .... Contemporary resort (p. 273)

BEST VEGETARIAN MEALS

Jiko—The Cooking Place
Animal Kingdom Lodge resort (p. 270)

BEST SPLURGE FOR GROWN-UPS

Victoria & Albert's .... Grand Floridian resort (p. 276)

RUNNERS-UP

The Boathouse .... Disney Springs, The Landing (p. 266)
California Grill .... Contemporary resort (p. 273)
Cítricos .... Grand Floridian resort (p. 275)
Flying Fish .... BoardWalk resort (p. 272)
Il Mulino New York Trattoria .... Swan resort (p. 279)
Jiko—The Cooking Place .... Animal Kingdom Lodge resort (p. 270)
Monsieur Paul .... Epcot (p. 254)
Yachtsman Steakhouse .... Yacht Club resort (p. 281)

BEST DINNER SHOW

Hoop-Dee-Doo Musical Revue: This crowd-pleasing saloon hall show has been going like gangbusters since 1974. Enjoy the music and silly humor while feasting on buckets of ribs, fried chicken, mashed potatoes, corn, and strawberry shortcake. Presented at Fort Wilderness (p. 300).

RUNNER-UP

Mickey's Backyard Barbecue: It's more of a big, informal party than a show, complete with a kickin' country band, games for the kids, and line dancing with Disney characters. The self-serve, all-you-can-eat barbecue fare is plentiful. Presented at Fort Wilderness (p. 300).

BEST PIZZA FOR GROWN-UPS

Blaze Fast Fire'd Pizza................................. Disney Springs (p. 266)
Via Napoli .... Epcot (p. 257)

BEST PIZZA FOR KIDS

Pinocchio Village Haus.................................Magic Kingdom (p. 246)
Pizzafari .... Animal Kingdom (p. 265)

BEST FIXIN'S BAR

Cosmic Ray's Starlight Cafe
Magic Kingdom (p. 250)

BEST ROOM SERVICE

Swan and Dolphin resorts
(pages 87 and 281)

BEST BUYS

Trail's End Restaurant ....Pioneer Hall, Fort Wilderness (p. 275)
Boma—Flavors of Africa .... Animal Kingdom Lodge (p. 270)

BEST ITALIAN FARE

Via Napoli .... Epcot (p. 257)

RUNNERS-UP

Il Mulino New York Trattoria .... Swan resort (p. 279)
Portobello .... Disney Springs, The Landing (p. 268)
Trattoria al Forno.. BoardWalk resort (p. 272)

BEST THEME

50's Prime Time Cafe ....Disney's Hollywood Studios (p. 260)

RUNNERS-UP

Sci-Fi Dine-In Theater .... Disney's Hollywood Studios (p. 261)
T-Rex Cafe .... Disney Springs, Marketplace (p. 269)

BEST OUTDOOR DINING

The Boathouse ....Disney Springs, The Landing (p. 266)

RUNNER-UP

STK-Orlando .... Disney Springs, The Landing (p. 268)

288

BEST SEAFOOD

The Boathouse .... Disney Springs, The Landing (p. 266)

RUNNERS-UP

Flying Fish .... BoardWalk resort (p. 272)
California Grill .... Contemporary resort (p. 273)
Narcoossee's .... Grand Floridian resort (p. 276)

BEST CRAB CAKES

The Boathouse .... Disney Springs, The Landing (p. 266)

RUNNERS-UP

Shula's .... Dolphin resort (p. 280)
The Wave . . . of American Flavors .... Contemporary resort (p. 274)

BEST PIÑA COLADA

Tambu Lounge .... Polynesian Village resort (p. 307)

BEST ALL-AROUND WDW RESTAURANT

The Wave . . . of American Flavors .... Contemporary resort (p. 274)

BEST STEAK

Yachtsman Steakhouse .... Yacht Club resort (p. 281)

RUNNERS-UP

Le Cellier Steakhouse .... Epcot (p. 253)
Shula's .... Dolphin resort (p. 280)

BEST SUSHI

Kimonos .... Swan resort (p. 279)

RUNNERS-UP

California Grill .... Contemporary resort (p. 273)
Kona Cafe.................................... Polynesian Village resort (p. 277)

BEST ICE CREAM

Ample Hills Creamery .... BoardWalk resort (p. 271)
Beaches & Cream Soda Shop .... Beach Club resort (p. 281)
L'Artisan des Glaces .... Epcot (p. 258)

BEST SPORTS BAR

ESPN Club
BoardWalk resort (p. 272)

BEST COFFEE

California Grill .... Contemporary resort (p. 273)

RUNNERS-UP

Kona Cafe .... Polynesian Village resort (p. 277)
Boma—Flavors of Africa .... Animal Kingdom Lodge resort (p. 270)
Starbucks... (multiple locations; see Index)
Ghirardelli Ice Cream & Chocolate Shop .... Disney Springs, Marketplace (p. 267)

BEST MILK SHAKE

Ample Hills Creamery .... BoardWalk resort (p. 271)

RUNNERS-UP

Sweet Treats .... Dolphin resort (p. 279)
Beaches & Cream Soda Shop .... Beach Club resort (p. 281)

BEST CHARACTER MEAL

Cinderella's Royal Table .... Magic Kingdom (p. 245)
Hollywood & Vine (dinner) .... Disney's Hollywood Studios (p. 260)

RUNNERS-UP

Akershus Royal Banquet Hall .... Epcot (p. 252)
Tusker House .... Disney's Animal Kingdom (p. 264)
Garden Grill .... Epcot (p. 251)
1900 Park Fare .... Grand Floridian resort (p. 276)

BEST RESORT SNACK BAR

Picabu .... Dolphin resort (p. 280)

RUNNERS-UP

Capt. Cook's .... Polynesian Village resort (p. 277)
Contempo Cafe............................. Contemporary resort (p. 274)

Where to Find ...

From french fries to filet mignon, fried chicken to seared scallops with black truffle spaghettini, Disney dishes truly run the gamut. To help you zero in on the eateries that best fit your needs, we've created a handy index of specialized lists:

PHOTO BY JILL SAFRO

BAKERIES/PASTRY SHOPS
Beach Club Marketplace (Beach Club resort)
BoardWalk Bakery (BoardWalk resort)
Kringla Bakeri og Kafe (Epcot, World Showcase)
Goofy's Candy Co. (Disney Springs, Marketplace)
Kusafiri Coffee Shop & Bakery (Animal Kingdom, Harambe)
Les Halles Boulangerie Patisserie (Epcot, World Showcase)
Main Street Bakery (Magic Kingdom, Main Street, U.S.A.)
Starring Rolls Cafe (Disney's Hollywood Studios)
Sunshine Seasons (Epcot, The Land)

BARBECUE
Flame Tree Barbecue (Animal Kingdom, Discovery Island)
House of Blues Smokehouse (Disney Springs, West Side)
Mickey's Backyard Barbecue (see Dinner Shows, page 300)

BEST BANG FOR THE BUFFET BUCK
(all-you-can-eat)
Biergarten (Epcot, World Showcase)
Boma—Flavors of Africa (Animal Kingdom Lodge)
Cape May Cafe (Beach Club resort)

Chef Mickey's (Contemporary resort)
Hollywood & Vine (Disney's Hollywood Studios)
1900 Park Fare (Grand Floridian resort)
Trail's End Restaurant (Fort Wilderness resort)
Tusker House (Animal Kingdom, Harambe)

BEST WITH BABIES (table service)
Akershus Royal Banquet Hall (Epcot, World Showcase)
Biergarten (Epcot, World Showcase)
Chef Mickey's (Contemporary resort)
Crystal Palace, The (Magic Kingdom, Main Street, U.S.A.)
Donald's Safari Breakfast at Tusker House (Animal Kingdom, Harambe)
Garden Grill (Epcot, Future World)
Hollywood & Vine (Disney's Hollywood Studios)
'Ohana (Polynesian Village resort)
Olivia's Cafe (Disney's Old Key West resort)
Rainforest Cafe (Animal Kingdom and Disney Springs)
Shutters at Old Port Royale (Caribbean Beach resort)
Tony's Town Square (Magic Kingdom, Main Street, U.S.A.)
Trail's End Restaurant (Fort Wilderness resort)

BRUNCH
California Grill (Contemporary resort)
Chef Mickey's (Contemporary resort)
House of Blues (Disney Springs, West Side)
Narcoossee's (Grand Floridian resort)

BUFFET (all-you-can-eat)
Akershus Royal Banquet Hall (Epcot, World Showcase—*appetizers only*)
Biergarten (Epcot, World Showcase)
Boma—Flavors of Africa (Animal Kingdom Lodge)
Cape May Cafe (Beach Club resort)
Captain's Grille (breakfast; Yacht Club resort)
Chef Mickey's (Contemporary resort)
Crystal Palace, The (Magic Kingdom, Main Street, U.S.A.)

Garden Grove (Swan resort)

Hollywood & Vine (Disney's Hollywood Studios)

1900 Park Fare (Grand Floridian resort)

Trail's End Restaurant (breakfast and dinner; Fort Wilderness)

Tusker House (Animal Kingdom, Harambe)

Wave . . . of American Flavors, The (Contemporary resort, breakfast only)

BURGERS

Backlot Express (Disney's Hollywood Studios)

Cabana Bar & Beach Club (Dolphin resort)

Capt. Cook's (Polynesian Village resort)

Cosmic Ray's Starlight Cafe (Magic Kingdom, Tomorrowland)

PHOTO BY JILL SAFRO

Electric Umbrella (Epcot, Future World)

ESPN Club (BoardWalk resort)

Everything Pop! (Pop Century resort)

Food Courts (All-Star resorts)

Fountain, The (Dolphin resort)

Liberty Inn (Epcot, World Showcase)

Old Port Royale (Caribbean Beach resort)

Tortuga Tavern (Magic Kingdom, Frontierland)

Restaurantosaurus (Animal Kingdom, DinoLand)

Riverside Mill (Port Orleans Riverside resort)

Sassagoula Floatworks & Food Factory (Port Orleans French Quarter resort)

Sunset Ranch Market (Disney's Hollywood Studios)

CHEAP EATS—FAST FOOD

Backlot Express (Disney's Hollywood Studios)

Columbia Harbour House (Magic Kingdom, Liberty Square)

Everything Pop! (Pop Century resort)

Flame Tree Barbecue (Animal Kingdom, Discovery Island)

Harambe Market (Animal Kingdom, Harambe)

Katsura Grill (Epcot, World Showcase)

Landscape of Flavors (Disney's Art of Animation resort)

Pinocchio Village Haus (Magic Kingdom, Fantasyland)

Pizzafari (Animal Kingdom, Discovery Island)

Restaurantosaurus (Animal Kingdom, DinoLand)

Sommerfest (Epcot, World Showcase)

Starring Rolls Cafe (Disney's Hollywood Studios)

Sunshine Seasons (Epcot, Future World)

Wolfgang Puck Express (Disney Springs, Marketplace and West Side)

Yorkshire County Fish Shop (Epcot, World Showcase)

CHEAP EATS (relatively speaking)

Table Service

Beaches & Cream Soda Shop (Beach Club resort)

Cape May Cafe (Beach Club resort)

ESPN Club (BoardWalk resort)

Kimonos (Swan resort)

Olivia's Cafe (Disney's Old Key West resort)

Planet Hollywood (Disney Springs, West Side)

Plaza Restaurant (Magic Kingdom, Main Street, U.S.A.)

Rainforest Cafe (Animal Kingdom and Disney Springs, Marketplace)

Spice Road Table (Epcot, World Showcase)

Trail's End Restaurant (Fort Wilderness resort)

T-Rex Cafe: A Prehistoric Family Adventure (Disney Springs, Marketplace)

Tusker House (Animal Kingdom, Harambe)

Via Napoli (Epcot, World Showcase)

DISNEY CHARACTERS (dining with)

(see pages 282–285)

ETHNIC EATERIES

African

Boma—Flavors of Africa (Animal Kingdom Lodge)

Harambe Market (Animal Kingdom, Harambe)

Jiko—The Cooking Place (Animal Kingdom Lodge)

Restaurant Marrakesh (Epcot, World Showcase)

Sanaa (Animal Kingdom Lodge, Kidani Village)

Spice Road Table (Epcot, World Showcase)

Tangierine Cafe (Epcot, World Showcase)

Tiffins (also serves Indian cuisine; Animal Kingdom, Discovery Island)

Tusker House (Animal Kingdom, Harambe)

American

Artist Point (Wilderness Lodge)
Big River Grille & Brewing Works
(BoardWalk resort)
The Boathouse (Disney Springs, The Landing)
Boatwright's Dining Hall (Port Orleans
Riverside resort)
California Grill (Contemporary resort)
ESPN Club (BoardWalk resort)
50's Prime Time Cafe (Disney's Hollywood Studios)
Flying Fish (BoardWalk resort)
Garden Grill (Epcot, Future World)
Grand Floridian Cafe (Grand Floridian resort)
Hollywood Brown Derby (Disney's Hollywood
Studios)
House of Blues (Disney Springs, West Side)
Liberty Inn (Epcot, World Showcase)
Liberty Tree Tavern (Magic Kingdom,
Liberty Square)
Narcoossee's (Grand Floridian resort)

PHOTO BY JILL SAFRO

1900 Park Fare (Grand Floridian resort)
Olivia's Cafe (Old Key West resort)
Sci-Fi Dine-In Theater (Disney's Hollywood
Studios)
Trail's End Restaurant (Fort Wilderness resort)
Wave . . . of American Flavors, The
(Contemporary resort)

British

Earl of Sandwich (Disney Springs, Marketplace)
Rose & Crown Pub & Dining Room (Epcot,
World Showcase)
Yorkshire County Fish Shop (Epcot,
World Showcase)

Canadian

Le Cellier Steakhouse (Epcot, World
Showcase)

Chinese and Southeast Asian

Yak & Yeti (Animal Kingdom, Asia)
Jungle Navigation Co. Ltd. Skipper Canteen
(Magic Kingdom, Adventureland)
Lotus Blossom Cafe (Epcot, World Showcase)
Nine Dragons (Epcot, World Showcase)
Yak & Yeti (Animal Kingdom, Asia)

French

Be Our Guest Restaurant (Magic Kingdom,
Fantasyland)
Chefs de France (Epcot, World Showcase)
Les Halles Boulangerie Patisserie (Epcot,
World Showcase)
Monsieur Paul (Epcot, World Showcase)

German

Biergarten (Epcot, World Showcase)
Sommerfest (Epcot, World Showcase)

Italian/Mediterranean

Blaze Fast Fire'd Pizza (Disney Springs)
Il Mulino New York Trattoria (Swan resort)
Mama Melrose's Ristorante Italiano (Disney's
Hollywood Studios)
Portobello (Disney Springs, The Landing)
Spice Road Table (Epcot, World Showcase)
Tony's Town Square (Magic Kingdom, Main
Street, U.S.A.)
Trattoria al Forno (Disney's BoardWalk)
Tutto Gusto (Epcot, World Showcase)
Via Napoli (Epcot, World Showcase)

Japanese

Kabuki Cafe (Epcot, World Showcase)
Katsura Grill (Epcot, World Showcase)
Kimonos (Swan resort)
Morimoto Asia (Disney Springs,
The Landing)
Teppan Edo (Epcot, World Showcase)
Tokyo Dining (Epcot, World Showcase)

Mexican/Latin American

La Cantina de San Angel (Epcot, World Showcase)
La Hacienda de San Angel (Epcot,
World Showcase)
Maya Grill (Coronado Springs resort)
Paradiso 37 (Disney Springs,
The Landing)
Pecos Bill Tall Tale Inn (Magic Kingdom,
Frontierland)
San Angel Inn (Epcot, World Showcase)

Norwegian
Akershus Royal Banquet Hall (Epcot, World Showcase)
Kringla Bakeri og Kafe (Epcot, World Showcase)

FAMILY-STYLE (all-you-can-eat)
Akershus Royal Banquet Hall (Epcot, World Showcase)
Cape May Cafe (Beach Club resort)
Garden Grill (Epcot, Future World)
Garden Grove (Swan resort)
Hoop-Dee-Doo Musical Revue (see page 300)
Liberty Tree Tavern (Magic Kingdom, Liberty Square)
Mickey's Backyard Barbecue (see page 300)
'Ohana (Polynesian Village resort)
Spirit of Aloha (see page 300)
Whispering Canyon Cafe (Wilderness Lodge)

FRUIT
Aloha Isle (Magic Kingdom, Adventureland)
Harambe Fruit Market (Animal Kingdom, Harambe)
Liberty Square Market (Magic Kingdom, Liberty Square)
Prince Eric's Village Market (Magic Kingdom, Fantasyland)
Sunset Ranch Market (Disney's Hollywood Studios)
Sunshine Seasons (Epcot, Future World)

GOOD FOR GROUPS
The Boathouse (Disney Springs, The Landing)
Boma—Flavors of Africa (Animal Kingdom Lodge)
California Grill (Contemporary resort)
Cape May Cafe (Beach Club resort)
Captain's Grille (Yacht Club resort)
Crystal Palace, The (Magic Kingdom, Main Street, U.S.A.)
Flame Tree Barbecue (Animal Kingdom, Discovery Island)
Flying Fish (BoardWalk resort)
Hollywood & Vine (Disney's Hollywood Studios)
House of Blues (Disney Springs, West Side)
Mickey's Backyard Barbecue (see page 300)
'Ohana (Polynesian Village resort)
Raglan Road (Disney Springs, The Landing)
Sunshine Seasons (Epcot, Future World)
Teppan Edo (Epcot, World Showcase)

Todd English's bluezoo (Dolphin resort)
Tusker House (Animal Kingdom, Harambe)
Via Napoli (Epcot, World Showcase)
Wave . . . of American Flavors, The (Contemporary resort)

HOT DOGS
Backlot Express (Disney's Hollywood Studios)
Casey's Corner (Magic Kingdom, Main Street, U.S.A.)
Liberty Inn (Epcot, World Showcase)
Lunching Pad, The (Magic Kingdom, Tomorrowland)
Min and Bill's Dockside Diner (Disney's Hollywood Studios)
Restaurantosaurus (Animal Kingdom, Dinoland)
Sunset Ranch Market (Disney's Hollywood Studios)
Wetzel's Pretzels (Disney Springs, Marketplace)

ICE CREAM AND FROZEN TREATS
Aloha Isle (Magic Kingdom, Adventureland)
Ample Hills Creamery (BoardWalk resort)
Anandapur Ice Cream Truck (Animal Kingdom, Asia)
Beaches & Cream Soda Shop (Beach Club resort)
Cheshire Cafe (Magic Kingdom, Fantasyland)
Cool Post (Epcot, World Showcase)
Dino-Bite Snacks (Animal Kingdom, DinoLand)
The Fountain (Dolphin resort)
Fountain View (Epcot, Future World)

PHOTO BY JILL SAFRO

Gaston's Tavern (Magic Kingdom, Fantasyland)
Ghirardelli Ice Cream & Chocolate Shop (Disney Springs, Marketplace)
Hollywood Scoops (Disney's Hollywood Studios)

Plaza Ice Cream Parlor (Magic Kingdom, Main Street, U.S.A.)

Plaza Restaurant (Magic Kingdom, Main Street, U.S.A.)

Storybook Treats (Magic Kingdom, Fantasyland)

Sunshine Tree Terrace (Magic Kingdom, Adventureland)

Tamu Tamu Refreshments (Animal Kingdom, Harambe)

KIDS' FAVORITES

Akershus Royal Banquet Hall (Epcot, World Showcase)

Cape May Cafe breakfast (Beach Club resort)

Casey's Corner (Magic Kingdom, Main Street)

Chef Mickey's (Contemporary resort)

Cinderella's Royal Table (Magic Kingdom, Fantasyland)

Cosmic Ray's Starlight Cafe (Magic Kingdom, Tomorrowland)

Crystal Palace, The (Magic Kingdom, Main Street)

50's Prime Time Cafe (Disney's Hollywood Studios)

Garden Grill (Epcot, Future World)

Hoop-Dee-Doo Musical Revue (see page 300)

Liberty Inn (Epcot, World Showcase)

1900 Park Fare (Grand Floridian resort)

'Ohana (Polynesian Village resort)

Pinocchio Village Haus (Magic Kingdom, Fantasyland)

Pizzafari (Animal Kingdom, Discovery Island)

PizzeRizzo (Disney's Hollywood Studios)

Rainforest Cafe (Animal Kingdom and Disney Springs, Marketplace)

Sunset Ranch Market (Disney's Hollywood Studios)

Sunshine Seasons (Epcot, Future World)

T-Rex Cafe: A Prehistoric Family Adventure (Disney Springs, Marketplace)

Tusker House (Animal Kingdom, Harambe)

Whispering Canyon Cafe (Wilderness Lodge)

KNOCKOUT VIEWS

Big River Grille & Brewing Works (outdoor seating; BoardWalk)

The Boathouse (Disney Springs, The Landing)

California Grill (Contemporary resort)

Coral Reef (Epcot, Future World)

Jock Lindsey's Hangar Bar (Disney Springs, The Landing)

La Hacienda de San Angel (Epcot, World Showcase)

Rose & Crown Pub & Dining Room (Epcot, World Showcase)

Sanaa (Animal Kingdom Lodge)

KOSHER (fast-food selections)

ABC Commissary (Disney's Hollywood Studios)

Artist's Palette, The (Saratoga Springs resort)

Cosmic Ray's Starlight Cafe (Magic Kingdom, Tomorrowland)

Electric Umbrella (Epcot, Future World)

Everything Pop! (Pop Century resort)

Food Courts (All-Star and Port Orleans Riverside resorts)

Gasparilla Island Grill (Grand Floridian resort)

Landscape of Flavors (Art of Animation resort)

Liberty Inn (Epcot, World Showcase)

Mara, The (Animal Kingdom Lodge)

Old Port Royale (Caribbean Beach resort)

Pizzafari (Animal Kingdom, Discovery Island)

Roaring Fork (Wilderness Lodge)

LOUNGES AND BARS (with food)

The Boathouse (Disney Springs, The Landing)

Big River Grille & Brewing Works (BoardWalk resort)

Cabana Bar & Beach Club (Dolphin resort)

California Grill Lounge (Contemporary resort)

Cítricos Lounge (Grand Floridian resort)

Crew's Cup (Yacht Club resort)

Crockett's Tavern (Fort Wilderness resort)

The Edison (Disney Springs, The Landing)

ESPN Club (BoardWalk resort)

Hurricane Hanna's (Yacht & Beach Club resorts)

Il Mulino New York Trattoria Lounge (Swan resort)

Jock Lindsey's Hangar Bar (Disney Springs, The Landing)

Kimonos (Swan resort)

La Cava del Tequila (Epcot, World Showcase)
Leaping Horse Libations (BoardWalk resort)
Mardi Grogs (Port Orleans French Quarter resort)
Martha's Vineyard (Beach Club resort)
Mizner's (Grand Floridian resort)
Muddy Rivers (Port Orleans Riverside resort)
Narcoossee's (Grand Floridian resort)
Nomad Lounge (Animal Kingdom, Discovery Island)
Outer Rim (Contemporary resort)
Paradiso 37 (Disney Springs, The Landing)
Portobello (Disney Springs, The Landing)
Raglan Road (Disney Springs, The Landing)
Rainforest Cafe (Magic Mushroom bar; Animal Kingdom and Disney Springs, Marketplace)
River Roost (Port Orleans Riverside resort)
Rix Lounge (Coronado Springs resort)
Rose & Crown Pub (Epcot, World Showcase)
Sanaa lounge (Animal Kingdom Lodge)
Sand Bar (Contemporary resort)
Shark Bar at T-Rex Cafe (Disney Springs, Marketplace)

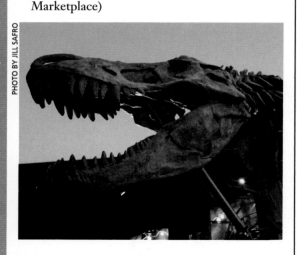

PHOTO BY JILL SAFRO

Siestas Cantina (Coronado Springs resort)
Sommerfest (inside Germany; Epcot, World Showcase)
Splash Terrace (Swan resort)
Tambu Lounge (Polynesian Village resort)
Territory Lounge (Wilderness Lodge)
Trader Sam's Grog Grotto (Polynesian resort)
Tune-In Lounge (Disney's Hollywood Studios)
Turf Club Bar & Grill, The (Saratoga Springs Resort & Spa)
Turtle Shack (Disney's Old Key West resort)
Tutto Gusto (Epcot, World Showcase)
Uzima Springs (Animal Kingdom Lodge)
Yak & Yeti Lounge (Animal Kingdom, Asia)

OPEN 24 HOURS
Capt. Cook's (Polynesian Village resort)
Gasparilla Island Grill (Grand Floridian resort)
Picabu (Dolphin resort)
Sundial Cafe 24-7 (Wyndham hotel)

PIZZA
Blaze Fast Fire'd Pizza (Disney Springs, Town Square)
Capt. Cook's (Polynesian Village resort)
Everything Pop! (Pop Century resort)
Food Courts (All-Star resorts)
Gasparilla Island Grill (Grand Floridian resort)
Mama Melrose's Ristorante Italiano (Disney's Hollywood Studios)
Pinocchio Village Haus (Magic Kingdom, Fantasyland)
Pizzafari (Animal Kingdom, Discovery Island)
PizzeRizzo (Disney's Hollywood Studios)
Riverside Mill (Port Orleans Riverside resort)
Roaring Fork (Wilderness Lodge)
Royale Pizza Shop (Caribbean Beach resort)
Sassagoula Floatworks & Food Factory (Port Orleans French Quarter resort)
Sunset Ranch Market (Disney's Hollywood Studios)
Trail's End Restaurant (Fort Wilderness resort)
Via Napoli (Epcot, World Showcase)
Wolfgang Puck Café (Disney Springs, West Side)
Wolfgang Puck Express (Disney Springs, Marketplace and West Side)

SALADS
Artist's Palette, The (Saratoga Springs resort)
Big River Grille & Brewing Works (BoardWalk)
The Boathouse (Disney Springs, The Landing)
Boma—Flavors of Africa (Animal Kingdom Lodge)
Cape May Cafe (Beach Club resort)
Columbia Harbour House (Magic Kingdom, Liberty Square)
Earl of Sandwich (Disney Springs, Marketplace)
Flame Tree Barbecue (Animal Kingdom, Discovery Island)
Gasparilla Island Grill (Grand Floridian resort)
Hollywood Brown Derby (Disney's Hollywood Studios)
Il Mulino New York Trattoria (Swan resort)
Pecos Bill Tall Tale Inn & Cafe (Magic Kingdom, Frontierland)
Pepper Market (Coronado Springs resort)
Picabu (Dolphin resort)
Pinocchio Village Haus (Magic Kingdom, Fantasyland)

Plaza Restaurant (Magic Kingdom, Main Street, U.S.A.)

Rainforest Cafe (Animal Kingdom and Disney Springs, Marketplace)

Sunshine Seasons (Epcot, Future World)

Wave . . . of American Flavors, The (Contemporary resort)

Wolfgang Puck Café (Disney Springs, West Side)

SEAFOOD

Artist Point (Wilderness Lodge)

The Boathouse (Disney Springs, The Landing)

California Grill (Contemporary resort)

Cape May Cafe (Beach Club resort)

Columbia Harbour House (Magic Kingdom, Liberty Square)

Coral Reef (Epcot, Future World)

Flying Fish (BoardWalk resort)

Kimonos (Swan resort)

Kona Cafe (Polynesian Village resort)

Narcoossee's (Grand Floridian resort)

Paddlefish (Disney Springs, (Marketplace)

Todd English's bluezoo (Dolphin resort)

Wave . . . of American Flavors, The (Contemporary resort)

SNACK BARS (at the resorts)

Beach Club Marketplace (Beach Club resort)

Cabana Bar & Beach Club (Dolphin resort)

PHOTO BY JILL SAFRO

Capt. Cook's (Polynesian Village resort)

Contempo Café (Contemporary resort)

Gasparilla Island Grill (Grand Floridian resort)

Mara, The (Animal Kingdom Lodge)

Picabu (Dolphin resort)

Roaring Fork (Wilderness Lodge)

SOLO DINERS

The Boathouse (Disney Springs, The Landing)

California Grill (Contemporary resort)

Cítricos lounge (Grand Floridian resort)

Crew's Cup (lounge, Yacht Club resort)

ESPN Club (BoardWalk resort)

Flying Fish (BoardWalk resort)

Il Mulino New York Trattoria (Swan resort)

Jiko—The Cooking Place Lounge (Animal Kingdom Lodge)

Narcoossee's Lounge (Grand Floridian resort)

Tune-In Lounge (Disney's Hollywood Studios)

Wave . . . of American Flavors Lounge (Contemporary resort)

Wolfgang Puck Café Bar (Disney Springs, West Side)

STEAK

Be Our Guest Restaurant (Magic Kingdom, Fantasyland)

La Hacienda de San Angel (Epcot, World Showcase)

Le Cellier Steakhouse (Epcot, World Showcase)

Shula's Steak House (Dolphin resort)

STK–Orlando (Disney Springs, The Landing)

Wave . . . of American Flavors, The (Contemporary resort)

Yachtsman Steakhouse (Yacht Club resort)

SUPER SPLURGES (for grown-ups)

Artist Point (Wilderness Lodge)

The Boathouse (Disney Springs, The Landing)

California Grill (Contemporary resort)

Chefs de France (Epcot, World Showcase)

Flying Fish (BoardWalk resort)

Hollywood Brown Derby (Disney's Hollywood Studios)

Il Mulino (Swan resort)

Jiko—The Cooking Place (Animal Kingdom Lodge)

Le Cellier Steakhouse (Epcot, World Showcase)

Monsieur Paul (Epcot, World Showcase)

Morimoto Asia (Disney Springs, The Landing)

Narcoossee's (Grand Floridian resort)

Sanaa (Animal Kingdom Lodge)

STK–Orlando (Disney Springs, The Landing)

Tiffins (Animal Kingdom, Discovery Island)

Victoria & Albert's (Grand Floridian resort)

Yachtsman Steakhouse (Yacht Club resort)

SUSHI

California Grill (Contemporary resort)

Capt. Cook's (Polynesian Village resort)

Kabuki Cafe (Epcot, World Showcase)

Katsura Grill (Epcot, World Showcase)

Kimonos (lounge; Swan resort)

Kona Cafe (Polynesian Village resort)

Kona Island (after 5 P.M.; Polynesian Village resort)

Morimoto Asia (Disney Springs, The Landing)

Splitsville (Disney Springs, West Side)
Tokyo Dining (Epcot, World Showcase)
Wolfgang Puck Café (Disney Springs, West Side)

TERRIFIC THEMING
Akershus Royal Banquet Hall (Epcot, World Showcase)
Be Our Guest Restaurant (Magic Kingdom, Fantasyland)
Biergarten (Epcot, World Showcase)

PHOTO BY MIKE CARROLL

The Boathouse (Disney Springs, The Landing)
Cinderella's Royal Table (Magic Kingdom, Fantasyland)
50's Prime Time Cafe (Disney's Hollywood Studios)
Jungle Navigation Co. Ltd. Skipper Canteen (Magic Kingdom, Adventureland)
Liberty Tree Tavern (Magic Kingdom, Liberty Square)
'Ohana (Polynesian Village resort)
Rainforest Cafe (Animal Kingdom and Disney Springs, Marketplace)
Sanaa (Animal Kingdom Lodge)
Sci-Fi Dine-In Theater (Disney's Hollywood Studios)
T-Rex Cafe: A Prehistoric Family Adventure (Disney Springs, Marketplace)
Tusker House (Discovery Island, Animal Kingdom)

VEGETARIAN SELECTIONS
Boma—Flavors of Africa (Animal Kingdom Lodge)
Columbia Harbour House (Magic Kingdom, Liberty Square)
Cosmic Ray's Starlight Cafe (Magic Kingdom, Tomorrowland)
Everything Pop! (Pop Century resort)
Food Courts (All-Star resorts)
Jiko—The Cooking Place (Animal Kingdom Lodge)
Mama Melrose's Ristorante Italiano (Disney's Hollywood Studios)
Pinocchio Village Haus (Magic Kingdom, Fantasyland)

Pizzafari (Animal Kingdom, Discovery Island)
PizzeRizzo (Disney's Hollywood Studios)
Rainforest Cafe (Animal Kingdom and Disney Springs, Marketplace)
Sanaa (Animal Kingdom Lodge)
Sunset Ranch Market (Disney's Hollywood Studios)
Sunshine Seasons (Epcot, Future World)
Tony's Town Square (Magic Kingdom, Main Street, U.S.A.)
Tusker House (Animal Kingdom, Harambe)
Via Napoli (Epcot, World Showcase)

PHOTO BY JILL SAFRO

Wolfgang Puck Express (Disney Springs, West Side and Marketplace)

WINE AND DINE (great wine lists)
Artist Point (Wilderness Lodge)
Be Our Guest Restaurant ([dinner] Magic Kingdom, Fantasyland)
The Boathouse (Disney Springs, The Landing)
Boma—Flavors of Africa (Animal Kingdom Lodge)
California Grill (Contemporary resort)
Chefs de France (Epcot, World Showcase)
Cítricos (Grand Floridian resort)
Flying Fish (BoardWalk resort)
Hollywood Brown Derby (Disney's Hollywood Studios)
Il Mulino New York Trattoria (Swan resort)
Jiko—The Cooking Place (Animal Kingdom Lodge)
Monsieur Paul (Epcot, World Showcase)
Morimoto Asia (Disney Springs, The Landing)
Narcoossee's (Grand Floridian resort)
Portobello (Disney Springs, The Landing)
Sanaa (Animal Kingdom Lodge)
Shula's Steak House (Dolphin resort)
STK–Orlando (Disney Springs, The Landing)
Tiffins (Animal Kingdom, Discovery Island)
Victoria & Albert's (Grand Floridian resort)
Wave . . . of American Flavors, The (Contemporary resort)
Yachtsman Steakhouse (Yacht Club resort)

Reservations Explained

Disney's reservation system, formerly known as "priority seating," covers most full-service restaurants on WDW property. The name may have changed, but the procedure is the same. It was designed to provide the assurance of a reservation without delays caused by no-shows and latecomers. Here's how it works: You call ahead to request a seating time; you arrive five minutes before the assigned time and check in at the podium; you receive the next available table that can accommodate your party.

It is virtually impossible to walk into a table service eatery without a reservation—secure yours as far in advance as possible. Seating times can be reserved up to 180 days ahead (see box below) for most Walt Disney World eateries by calling 407-WDW-DINE (939-3463), or by visiting *www.disneyworld.com/dine*. The hotline is open daily from 7 A.M. to 10 P.M. The number of tables available in advance varies. If you are unable to book ahead of time, try to make same-day arrangements. *Note that a fee of $10 per person will be charged to guests who do not show up or cancel a reservation less than one day in advance.*

Most Walt Disney World resorts have at least one phone in the main lobby that provides direct contact with the Dine Line. Simply touch 55—the call is free. From other locations, dial 407-WDW-DINE (939-3463). Once at the theme parks, dining reservations can be made at the eatery itself; at City Hall in the Magic Kingdom; in Epcot at Guest Relations by Spaceship Earth; by Hollywood Junction in Disney's Hollywood Studios; and at Guest Relations in Animal Kingdom. Bookings can also be made at Guest

For Disney Resort Guests Only

Do you have a confirmed reservation at a Disney-owned-and-operated resort? If so, you are entitled to a special perk: Call 180 days prior to the first day of your hotel reservation and you can make dining reservations for up to 10 days of your stay. That's like getting a 1- to 10-day jump on everyone else! (Stays longer than 10 days will require a second call. Inquire when you make your first set of dining reservations.) Have your confirmation number handy when you call 407-WDW-DINE.

Advance Planning

While some WDW restaurants always seem to have an open table (like Marrakesh in Epcot's World Showcase), most are booked far in advance. The restaurants for which careful planning is essential include Be Our Guest and Cinderella's Royal Table in the Magic Kingdom (call 180 days ahead and keep your fingers crossed!); Le Cellier Steakhouse and Chefs de France in Epcot; Tusker House breakfast and lunch in Disney's Animal Kingdom; and California Grill in the Contemporary resort.

Relations in the Disney Springs Marketplace and at the West Side.

While the Walt Disney World reservation system is often successful, there are times when the wait for a table can be unexpectedly long. This is most likely to occur during peak mealtimes at restaurants that offer buffets or family-style meals, where patrons will often opt for seconds (or thirds). For this reason, be sure to check in at the restaurant particularly early for all character-hosted meals.

HOT TIP!

At most WDW restaurants, reservations are scheduled in five- or ten-minute intervals. If they don't have a 6 P.M. availability, ask about a 6:05 P.M.

Reservations are necessary for all dinner shows—the Hoop-Dee-Doo Musical Revue, Mickey's Backyard BBQ, and the Polynesian Village resort's Spirit of Aloha; they can be made by calling 407-WDW-DINE (939-3463). Reservations can be booked up to 180 days in advance. If you can't get a table for an early performance, consider a later one (they are usually less heavily booked).

Keep in mind that, with the exception of dinner shows, a WDW seating time does vary from a traditional reservation—you may have to wait a bit when you arrive at your assigned time. Your party will be given the first table that opens up.

Note: Because the dining scene at Walt Disney World is ever-evolving, we advise calling 407-WDW-DINE (939-3463) to confirm current reservation policies.

Dinner Shows

The fact that Disney is expert in family entertainment is nowhere more readily apparent than amid the whooping and hollering troupe of singers and dancers who race toward the stage at Fort Wilderness resort's Pioneer Hall. As guests plow through filling barbecue fare (ribs, fried chicken, strawberry shortcake, beer, wine, and soft drinks), these enthusiastic performers sing, dance, and joke up a storm.

The gags are groaners, but the audience eats 'em up. It's all in the course of an evening at the *Hoop-Dee-Doo Musical Revue*, presented nightly at 4 P.M., 6:15 P.M., and 8:30 P.M. Cost is about $64 per adult and $38 for children (ages 3 through 9) for Category 3 seating; about $67 for adults, $39 for kids in Category 2; and about $72 and $43 for Category 1. (The best views are in Category 1—seating is on the main floor.)

Note that the dining room in Pioneer Hall can be chilly year-round. Bring a sweater to combat the sometimes intense air-conditioning.

HOT TIP!

The Hoop-Dee-Doo Musical Revue is a very popular show. Make your reservations as far in advance as possible.

Also presented at Fort Wilderness is *Mickey's Backyard BBQ*. A country band gets guests out on the floor to kick up their heels, and Disney characters join in the fun.

Dinner consists of plenty of basic picnic favorites: barbecued ribs and chicken, corn on the cob, and baked beans. The seasonal dinner show costs about $62 per adult and $37 for kids. Tickets are required, so book ahead.

Disney's Polynesian luau show is called *Spirit of Aloha*. Set in the beachfront backyard of a Hawaiian house (at the Polynesian Village resort), the show invites guests to join in a musical celebration.

The luau experience combines traditional music as well as more contemporary ditties from the animated Disney film *Lilo & Stitch*. The performers' dancing is some of the most authentic this side of Hawaii. The Spirit of Aloha is presented in an open-air dining theater in Luau Cove, adjacent to the Seven Seas Lagoon.

The all-you-can-eat feast is influenced by the

flavors of Polynesia and includes draft beer, wine, soft drinks, and dessert. Menu items include roasted chicken, barbecued pork ribs, fresh pineapple, Polynesian-style rice, and vegetables. The kids' menu features PB&J sandwiches, mac and cheese, chicken nuggets, and hot dogs. The cost is about $64 for adults and $38 for kids in Category 3; about $72 and $43 for Category 2; and about $76 and $45 for Category 1 (again, the best views are from Category 1 seats).

Plan to arrive at least 30 minutes before showtime, and allow extra time for transportation and parking. (Note that all prices are subject to change.) The show may be canceled due to inclement weather (though tables are sheltered).

Reservations: Arrangements for dinner shows may be made up to 180 days in advance by calling 407-WDW-DINE (939-3463). Groups of eight or more should call 407-939-7707. *Prices include tax and gratuity and may be higher during peak seasons.*

A credit card number is required for all dinner show reservations. Full payment is required upon booking. It's also possible to redeem Disney Dining Plan credits for dinner shows. At press time, all Disney dinner shows were participating in the dining plan. They are considered "Signature" meals and cost two table-service meals per person. *Note that cancellations for dinner shows must be made at least 48 hours prior to showtime to avoid paying full price.*

Bars & Lounges of WDW

What distinguishes Walt Disney World pubs and lounges from many bars in the real world? Well, in addition to over-the-top theming, you can almost always get a savory nibble to accompany that cocktail. Most Disney lounges serve food, be it from their own menu or from that of a neighboring restaurant.

Hours vary, but theme park watering holes (at Epcot, Disney's Hollywood Studios, and Animal Kingdom) shut their doors at park closing time. Pool bars at the resorts keep daytime pool hours. Last call at resort lounges can be anywhere from about 10 P.M. to midnight. Disney Springs Market-place spots stay open till the shops close, usually 11 P.M. Other lounges may keep things going until about 1 A.M.

All-Star Movies, All-Star Music & All-Star Sports

POOL BARS: There are small poolside oases in All-Star Movies, All-Star Music, and All-Star Sports: Silver Screen Spirits, Singing Spirits, and Grandstand Spirits, respectively. Each serves a selection of beer, wine, traditional cocktails, and specialty drinks.

Animal Kingdom

DAWA BAR: A shady spot in a busy neighbor-hood, Dawa is a pleasant place to take a load off weary feet and sip Safari Amber beer and other cocktails. It's next to Tusker House, on Kivulini Terrace. There is occasional live music, too.

NOMAD: Adventurers can take a load off and relish in a savory snack and/or frosty beverage at this exotic new Animal Kingdom destination. The lounge proffers libations from the world over. The freshly prepared cuisine at Nomad Lounge includes vegetarian summer rolls, Indian butter chicken wings, seared Wagyu beef skewers, and honey-glazed, coriander-spiced pork ribs. Festive banners post questions about world travel and the thrill of discovery. Jot your answers on a decorative (and free) tag and cast members will post them to a tag chandelier for all the world to see.

THIRSTY RIVER BAR & TREK SNACKS: In the shadows of Expedition Everest, this casual outdoor oasis offers many spirited selections, including specialty drinks known as the Himalayan Ghost, Durbar Margarita, and Khumbu Icefall. Savory snacks are available too. The menu has featured crudité and hummus, edamame, Asian noodle salads, smoked turkey sandwiches, Bahn Mi (roasted pork topped with pickled vegetables, cilantro, and sriracha dressing), Som Tam (Thai shrimp, green papaya salad, crushed peanuts, and chilis), and sushi.

RAINFOREST CAFE: The colorful Magic Mushroom bar serves, among other things, fruit blends and specialty drinks. Bar stools resemble animal legs (hooves and all). The bar is inside the Rainforest Cafe. Admission to Animal Kingdom is not necessary to enter. It's possible to order off the restaurant's menu from here, too.

YAK & YETI LOUNGE: A small-but-escapist space inside one of the restaurant's themed dining areas, the Yak & Yeti lounge has a fully stocked bar and seating for six. (There's standing room, too.) House specialties include the Yak Attack, Bonsai Blast, Big Bamboo, and Everest Avalanche. Beer, wine, and sake are also served.

Animal Kingdom Lodge

CAPE TOWN LOUNGE AND WINE BAR: Sip African wines at this intimate spot adjacent to Jiko—The Cooking Place. In addition to a full menu, it has the largest selection of African wines in the United States.

MAJI: A poolside bar (*maji* means "water" in Swahili) serves beverages when the Samawati Springs pool is open (in Kidani Village).

SANAA: Located in the resort's Kidani Village, this lounge is within the restaurant of the same name. South African beers and wines are served.

UZIMA SPRINGS: The bar near the main pool serves beer, wine, and specialty drinks during pool hours. The (liquor-free) Espresso Freeze—espresso blended with frozen cappuccino and ice cream—is a nice way to counter the Florida heat.

VICTORIA FALLS: On the mezzanine level overlooking Boma—Flavors of Africa, this lounge offers coffee and spirits, plus the soothing sounds of the falls. (The actual Victoria Falls are located in Africa, between Zambia and Zimbabwe, and are nearly a mile wide.)

Art of Animation

DROP OFF BAR: Open from noon until midnight, this poolside location offers a variety of cocktails (with and without alcohol), soft drinks, and smoothies—plus sushi, sandwiches, fruit, and other snack items.

BoardWalk

ABRACADABAR: A "curious cocktail lounge," adjoining Flying Fish, AbracadaBAR merges the Golden Age of Magic with the magic of the Mouse. The sophisticated social club, once frequented by famous magicians and boardwalk illusionists, is back in the spotlight and open to all. ❤

ATLANTIC DANCE: This club has music, videos, and a deejay. The design is Art Deco, but the tunes are from the '80s through today. It's open Tuesday–Saturday nights, and guests must be at least 21 (with government-issued photo ID) to enter.

Got I.D.?

The legal drinking age in the state of Florida is 21. However, just being 21 isn't enough to get served—you have to prove it. To do so, present a government-issued photo ID. If your driver's license doesn't have a photo, bring it and an official photo ID (a passport is ideal). Otherwise, you'll have to stick to soft drinks.

BELLE VUE LOUNGE: A full bar accompanies old-time tunes from antique radios in this casual space. Continental breakfast is offered (from 6 A.M. until 11 A.M.). Board games are usually available for on-site use (free of charge). There's limited seating at the bar, but there are plenty of tables and comfy couches to lounge on. The lounge starts serving cocktails at about 5 P.M. ❤

BIG RIVER GRILLE & BREWING WORKS: Big River patrons may order appetizers at the bar and sample the brewmaster's flagship ales and specialty beers. They may even get to watch as a new batch is brewed. In addition to the fresh-brewed beer, beverage selections include fresh-squeezed lemonade, strawberry lemonade, pomegranate lemonade, and more. Note that Big River does not accept reservations, so the bar can get crowded during mealtimes (and right after Epcot closes at night). ❤

ESPN CLUB: The sports bar provides live radio and TV broadcasts along with a full menu. With nearly 100 screens, chances are you'll find the game you seek. The place fills up quickly on big game days—arrive at least an hour early on such occasions. Note that on NFL Sundays, the match-ups scheduled for screening are often noted right on the TVs. If not, ask the bartender or inquire at the podium near the front entrance. ❤

JELLYROLLS: Dueling pianos and lively sing-alongs are the draw at this club, serving beer, wine, and other drinks. There is a cover charge in the neighborhood of $12, and guests must be at least 21 years old to enter. (Government-issued photo ID is required.) Requests are encouraged. And don't forget to tip the piano players before you leave. Note that it can be exceptionally cool here: Bring a sweater.

PHOTO BY JILL SAFRO

LEAPING HORSE LIBATIONS: The pool bar—designed to resemble a carousel (hence, the leaping horses)—offers cocktails, sandwiches, soft drinks, and simple snacks during pool hours.

Caribbean Beach

BANANA CABANA: Refreshing drinks and snack items are served at this poolside bar near Old Port Royale.

Contemporary

CALIFORNIA GRILL LOUNGE: Perched atop the Contemporary resort, this revitalized space tops many a "must-visit" list. Tucked within the acclaimed restaurant, the lounge offers the full menu and shares access to California Grill's exquisite wine list that boasts about 250 vintages (about 80 offered by the glass), featuring California's finest. If you need help navigating the wine list, fear not: One of the Grill's 20 sommeliers will be happy to help you make a selection.

In addition to wine, the lounge features sake, craft beers and ciders, mixed drinks, alcohol-free signature drinks, and more. Guests of the lounge may order anything off the restaurant menu (including the spectacular sushi). Just as with the restaurant itself, all guests hoping to visit the California Grill Lounge must check in at the desk on the Contemporary's second floor. From there they are escorted to an express elevator. The lounge does not accept reservations and opens at about 4:30 P.M. daily. ❤

COVE BAR: Set beside the pool in the resort's Bay Lake Tower, Cove Bar serves sweets (apple slices with caramel dipping sauce, fruit, and frozen desserts) and lunch items (shrimp cocktail, turkey BLT wrap, nachos with cheese, veggie wrap, hot dog, and sushi). Wash it all down with one of their specialty drinks, such as the Banana Cabana or Poolside Plunge. ❤

OUTER RIM: Located on the resort's fourth floor across from Contempo Cafe, this modern lounge has about seven bar stools and an abundance of tables with cocktail service. The main draw here is not the view of the large-screen TV, but rather the sweeping views of Bay Lake and Fort Wilderness (on the lake's far shore). Parts of this lounge may host guests

HOT TIP!

At some Walt Disney World lounges, you may order food from a neighboring or nearby restaurant's menu. Just ask.

waiting for a table at the ever-popular Chef Mickey's restaurant, so it can be a tad congested here at mealtimes. Beer, wine, sangria, specialty drinks, and alcohol-free kiddie cocktails are served from about 11:30 A.M. till 10 P.M.

SAND BAR: A full bar is offered poolside, weather permitting. Quick-service food, salads, and sandwiches are available at the adjacent counter area. ❤

THE WAVE . . . OF AMERICAN FLAVORS LOUNGE: On the first floor of the resort, this spacious bar boasts a wine list that is mostly screw cap (yes, that's a good thing)—a quaffable selection of quality vintages. About 50 are available by the glass; tasting flights are a great choice for those who wish to sample several selections. Also poured: organic beers, ports, and specialty drinks. Guests may order from The Wave's outstanding menu, too. Our humble opinion? The Wave is one of the very best Disney World lounges. It's also an excellent place for groups to gather.

PHOTO BY MIKE CARROLL

Coronado Springs

RIX LOUNGE: Located in the resort's main building, this upscale, eye- and palate-pleasing lounge serves specialty drinks, beer, wine, soft drinks, and tapas-style appetizers. Cappuccino is an option. The 300-seat venue features house music and a Mediterranean-inspired atmosphere.

SIESTAS CANTINA: Swimmers can take time out for burgers, sandwiches, tacos, and cocktails at this spot near the pool in the Dig Site area. ❤

Disney's Hollywood Studios

THE HOLLYWOOD BROWN DERBY LOUNGE: An inviting alfresco enclave, the Derby Lounge serves as an extension of the elegant eatery to which it is attached. The all-day menu touts specialty cocktails (including the Grapefruit Cake Martini) and small plates. Choose from items such as andouille-crusted shrimp, Waygu beef sliders, and Florida tomato soup. For a sweet treat, consider the warm blueberry cobbler or banana toffee cake.

PHOTO BY MIKE CARROLL

TUNE-IN LOUNGE: A sitcom living-room setting, with comfy stools and couches, characterizes this lounge next to the 50's Prime Time Cafe. Old TV sets play scenes from beloved sitcoms (all of which feature food). Appetizers, cocktails, beer, and wine are served.

Disney's Old Key West

GURGLING SUITCASE: This pocket-size lounge on the Turtle Krawl boardwalk serves an assortment of Key West specialties along with traditional cocktails, beer, and wine.

TURTLE SHACK: Refreshments at this poolside spot include cocktails and a small selection of fast-food items.

Disney Springs

BONGOS: Mojitos are the specialty of the house, but martinis and other mixed drinks, wine, sangria, and beer are also served. This is a pleasant spot, but we prefer to relax in the big pineapple. Bongos' two-story pineapple bar has indoor and outdoor seating and offers a full bar, plus appetizers. This is one of the more atmospheric spots at Disney Springs, West Side.

DOCKSIDE MARGARITAS: Get "a taste of the Sunshine State" at this new waterside bar at the Marketplace. In addition to creatively blended margaritas, this breezy spot serves rum runners, mojitos, locally brewed craft beers, and Tropical Florida wines such as Key Limen and Mango Mama. Live entertainment is provided most evenings.

HOLE IN THE WALL: Blink and you miss it, this tiny establishment is bookended (and dwarfed) by Raglan Road on the left and Cooke's of Dublin on the right. A full bar is available, but the Irish stout stands out. In addition to the outstanding nibbles (whipped up over at Raglan Road), this diminutive spot boasts something that is beyond rare at Walt Disney World: Happy Hour specials (from 3 to 7 P.M.).

PHOTO BY MIKE CARROLL

HOUSE OF BLUES: Set in the back of the eatery section of H.O.B., this bar serves drinks that are as cool as the atmosphere. It's also possible to have drinks in the enclosed Voodoo Garden (table-service only). Guests may order from the restaurant menu.

JOCK LINDSEY'S HANGAR BAR: An aviation-themed, waterside lounge, Jock Lindsey's seats 150 adventurous guests at a time. Visitors may sip cocktails or specialty drinks and nibble on small-plate treats such as Rolling Boulder Meatballs, Brody's Brats (grilled bratwurst with mustard and pickled cabbage), and Air Pirates Everything Pretzels (with housemade mustard and beer cheese fondue). There's indoor and outdoor seating. The lounge is situated on The Landing, between Paradiso 37 and The Boathouse. FYI: Jock Lindsey is Indiana Jones' frequent pilot and the proud owner of a pet snake named Reggie.

MAGIC MUSHROOM BAR: When the Rainforest Cafe restaurant is mobbed, we recommend taking in the thunderstorms and waterfalls from this central, mushroom-capped bar. Simply saddle a stool (all of which are shaped like animal legs) and enjoy the festive "natural" ambience. You can sip a cocktail and order a snack from the restaurant's menu. There is another Magic Mushroom Bar inside the Rainforest Cafe at Disney's Animal Kingdom. (See page 264.)

PARADISO 37: The bar at Paradiso 37 features an international wine list, an extensive selection of tequilas, frozen margaritas, and the "coldest beer in the world." It is possible to order items from the restaurant's menu, too.

PLANET HOLLYWOOD OBSERVATORY: The redesigned Planet Hollywood lounge space includes an inviting outdoor terrace—perfect for sipping cocktails under the stars.

PORTOBELLO: In the heart of Portobello Country Italian Trattoria, the bountiful bar has an alluring atmosphere and ample seating. An oenophile's dream come true, the international wine list has something for just about everyone. Italy is well represented, and other offerings come from Sonoma, South Africa, Colombia, New York, and other locales. Many wines are available by the glass, bottle, and half bottle. The cordial menu boasts brandy, cognac, port, sherry, grappa, and dessert wines. There's a full bar and a selection of locally brewed, organic beers.

RAGLAN ROAD: Top o' the evening to you! This jovial joint is an authentic Irish pub and simply oozes Irish charm. The polished interior is a meticulously decorated Emerald Isle oasis—complete with freshly prepared Irish cuisine and live entertainment (the latter starting at about 9 P.M.). Oh, and of course, pints of stout and other spirited beverages. This place is popular and can get quite crowded on weekend evenings—get there early if you can.

PHOTO BY MIKE CARROLL

SHARK BAR: This space, inside the T-Rex Cafe, puts the water in watering hole. Anchored under the belly of a Technicolor squid, the aqueous area serves all kinds of cocktails, plus items from the restaurant's menu. (One of our favorite things to order here is the tomato soup.) Guests must be at least 21 to sit at the bar.

Epcot

All eateries, including some fast-food spots, serve alcoholic beverages. A few other Epcot locales specialize in liquid refreshments.

LA CAVA DEL TEQUILA: A warm glow envelopes guests who visit this little lounge in the big pyramid at the Mexico pavilion—and that's before they sample any of the 70-plus tequilas on the menu. In addition to blended margaritas (many made with fresh fruit and spices), guests may sip Mexican beer, wine, cocktails, and soft drinks. Snack selections include fresh guacamole and chips and salsa. This 30-seat escape is open from about noon until Epcot closing time.

PHOTO BY MIKE CARROLL

ROSE & CROWN PUB: This classic pub—a veritable symphony of polished woods, brass, and etched glass—adjoins the Rose & Crown Dining

HOT TIP!

At Epcot's Rose & Crown Pub (located in the United Kingdom pavilion at World Showcase), a specially designed ale warmer can heat your Guinness to 55 degrees—the temperature favored by some patrons at authentic British pubs.

Room in the United Kingdom pavilion. English, Scottish, and Irish beers are available, along with a score of specialty drinks and appetizing snacks imported from the other side of the Atlantic. If you're lucky, there will be live (and lively) piano music during your visit. Feel free to sing along. (Showtimes are listed in the Times Guide, available at park entrances, Guest Relations, and in many shops—just ask.) Seating indoors and out is limited and available on a first-come, first-served basis. ❤

SOMMERFEST: Just outside the Biergarten in Germany, there's a window serving soft pretzels, bratwurst, frankfurters, apple strudel, and other treats. Wash 'em with a stein of cold German beer. They also serve German wines (red and white), Jägermeister, Goldschlager, and soft drinks. There are tables nearby. ❤

TUTTO GUSTO: A happy addition to the Italy pavilion, Tutto Gusto offers 200 different wines (including grappa), beers imported from Italy, Italian specialty drinks, coffee drinks, and a small plate menu. The best time to visit is in the afternoon (that's when crowds are usually lightest). Reservations are not available.

Fort Wilderness

CROCKETT'S TAVERN: You needn't brandish a coonskin cap to belly up to the bar in this rustic saloon, merely a government-issued photo ID to prove you're not a young'un (all guests must be at least 21 years of age to drink spirits of any kind). Tucked into a corner of the Trail's End restaurant, this spot is small but cozy, and the barkeeps are as amiable as they come. Last we visited, there were a couple of domestic beers on tap, plus a full bar. Pizza, chicken wings, and nachos are served, too. The TV is usually tuned to the big game of the moment. ❤

Grand Floridian

CÍTRICOS LOUNGE: As inviting as any lounge on Disney property, this place has one stellar wine list. Old World, New World, red, white, sparkling . . . you name it, they got it. Also on tap are beer, port, sherry, specialty coffees, and creative cocktails (think along the lines of a Citropolitan or Pomegranate Splash).

Soup, salad, and appetizers may be ordered until about 10 P.M. (If it's busy, the bar may continue to serve drinks until the crowd dwindles.) Menu selections have included sautéed shrimp, spiced and slow-cooked beef and pork in crisp phyllo with tamarind sauce, seared tofu, and the exquisitely crispy arancini risotto (fried balls of rice with cremini mushrooms, Asiago cheese, and white truffle aioli). There are a handful of seats at the bar and roughly ten tables in the lounge. If you sit at a table, be sure to place your order with the bartender before grabbing a seat at a table.

MIZNER'S: Named after the eccentric architect who defined much of the flavor of Florida's Gold Coast, this handsome retreat serves beer, wine, cocktails, ports, brandies, and appetizers. Cigars may be purchased here, too (although they must be puffed elsewhere, as this, like most WDW bars, is a nonsmoking venue).

If you're in the mood for a nibble, consider the veal bolognese, PEI mussels (pan-seared with garlic and olive oil), artisanal cheese plate, or sautéed shrimp. Sweet temptations include lemon cheesecake, chocolate banana torte, and seasonal berry gratin. Food is served usually from about 5:30 P.M. until about 10 P.M., while the spirits usually flow until about midnight.

NARCOOSSEE'S LOUNGE: This upscale bar-within-a-restaurant offers a little bit of everything: appetizers, entrées, desserts, and cocktails (including dessert drinks). There is an

HOT TIP!

Grand Floridian visitors take note: The resort's grand lobby is a divine setting in which to savor a fine wine or a frosty brew. While there's no in-lobby service, guests may buy a drink at Mizner's (see above) and sip it while relaxing on an overstuffed lobby chair or comfy couch. If you time it right, you'll be serenaded by the lobby pianist or a live band.

❤ Disney Dining Plan participant at press time

extensive list of international wines, 40 of which are available by the glass. How serious are they about wine here? Our last bartender was a certified sommelier. A large selection of bottled craft beers is available, too. Note that the dress code for this lounge is "business casual." 🐭

POOL BAR: This Grand Floridian pool/beach bar stands by with beer, wine, frozen specialty drinks, soft drinks, and snacks.

Polynesian Village

BAREFOOT BAR: An oasis adjacent to the Lava pool, this bar serves beer, wine, frozen tropical drinks (with and without alcohol), and soft drinks. Items of note: frozen strawberry daiquiri and piña colada. (We like them mixed together, aka The Lava Flow.)

TAMBU: Adjoining 'Ohana, this small tiki bar offers appetizers, cocktails, and specialty drinks in a tropical setting. There is seating at the bar and at tables. Note that the table section serves as the waiting area for guests dining at 'Ohana, so it tends to get very busy at mealtimes.

TRADER SAM'S GROG GROTTO: There's so much to see in this festive first-floor lounge that guests may not notice there is a world beyond Sam's walls. A welcome addition to the Disney bar scene, offering tropical drinks and small plates in a richly themed locale (Jungle Cruise meets the Enchanted Tiki Room), this boisterous grog grotto is a real crowd-pleaser. Drink favorites include the Krakatoa Punch, the Nautilus, and Dark and Stormy. Bottoms up! Sam's doors open at 4 P.M. Guests under 21 are not admitted after 8 P.M. Arrive early if you hope to get a highly coveted, inside seat. Patio seating, aka Sam's Tiki Terrace, is much easier to come by.

Pop Century

PETALS: This poolside watering hole serves beer, wine, and cocktails.

Port Orleans French Quarter

MARDI GROGS: Beer, specialty drinks, and snacks are among the offerings at this pool spot.

SCAT CAT'S CLUB: Next to the Sassagoula Floatworks & Food Factory, this large, informal lounge pays tribute to the uniquely American

music that is jazz. In fact, live jazz music is presented four nights a week (Wednesday through Saturday, from 8 P.M. till about 12 A.M.). In addition to the usual brews and blends, this spot specializes in Southern drinks—including Hurricanes. There is an appetizer menu, too.

Port Orleans Riverside

MUDDY RIVERS: The poolside bar serves beer, specialty concoctions, and snack items.

RIVER ROOST: Situated in a room designed as a cotton exchange, this spacious lounge features specialty drinks, as well as light hors d'oeuvres. Sink into a comfy chair, beside the glow of the fireplace, and sip cocktails with a Southern flair. There are stools at the bar and tables, too. Live entertainment is presented on select evenings (usually Wednesday through Saturday, from 8 P.M. until about midnight).

Saratoga Springs

THE TURF CLUB: This frill-free corner of the resort serves all manner of spirits (from a walk-up window). There's a pool table, too.

Swan & Dolphin

CABANA BAR & BEACH CLUB: Come for the food, stay for drinks. This Dolphin spot's sophisticated air and edgy design is a definite draw for the grown-up set, yet the place doesn't take itself so seriously that it fails to please little ones (think pizza, fruit bars, and lemonade). Grown-up pleasers include the Cuban sandwich and the grilled chicken BLT.

Classic cocktails such as the Mai Tai, Rum Runner, and Caipirinha share the stage with creative, original concoctions. Frozen libations abound, as do beer (micro- and macrobrews), rum, and tequila. Wine, scotch, cognac, cigars and soft drinks are offered, too.

IL MULINO NEW YORK TRATTORIA

LOUNGE: A lovely spot (at the Swan) to sip wines and cocktails and/or enjoy the bar menu, this lounge features live music on Friday and Saturday evenings. There are lots of seats at the bar, plus tables and comfy couches. It's usually open for business starting in the late afternoon.

KIMONOS: This Swan lounge, attractively decorated in Japanese style, has a full bar, as well as sushi and other culinary treats. It opens in late afternoon/early evening, and last call is usually between 10:30 P.M. and 1 A.M. The karaoke starts cranking at about 9:30 P.M.

LOBBY LOUNGE: The Dolphin lobby bar serves beer, wine, cocktails, and soft drinks, sometimes accompanied by live piano music. Lobby Lounge hours are generally 3 P.M. until about 11 P.M.

SHULA'S LOUNGE: This small, austere Dolphin saloon within Shula's Steak House features rich wood tones and plush seating—the perfect place to sip a cocktail while playing armchair quarterback.

SPLASH TERRACE: A poolside oasis near the Swan, Splash offers custom-made sandwiches, pizza, ice cream, snacks, soft drinks, beer, wine, cocktails, and specialty drinks. Open seasonally.

PHOTO BY MIKE CARROLL

TODD ENGLISH'S BLUEZOO BAR:

The underwater mojo of Todd's bluezoo restaurant extends to the sizable bar/lounge area (booths and tables augment the bar seating, easily accommodating large parties). In addition to the liquid refreshments, this is a genuine raw bar—many guests order a cocktail with a side of something fishy.

Last call varies, depending on how crowded the place is at any given moment. Figure on getting the boot between 9 P.M. and 11 P.M.

Wilderness Lodge

TERRITORY LOUNGE: Located between Artist Point and Whispering Canyon Cafe, this rustic homage to the explorers of the Great West is a nice spot for a pre-dinner treat. Appetizers, soft drinks, beer, wine, and cocktails are served. The Pomegranate Sparkler is a no-alcohol treat.

TROUT PASS: This poolside bar serves beer, wine, and frozen drinks.

Yacht & Beach Club

ALE AND COMPASS: The nautically themed Yacht Club lobby lounge offers a full drink menu with premium spirits and light appetizers. Coffee (sans liquor) and light breakfast items are served each morning. The lounge is usually open until about midnight. ♥

PHOTO BY MIKE CARROLL

CREW'S CUP: Styled after a traditional New England waterfront pub, this casual lounge has a seafaring feel to it. It's next door to the Yachtsman Steakhouse and has well over 25 beers. There is also a tempting menu. This is one of our favorite places to relax after a long day in the parks. Nibbles are generally served from about noon until midnight.

HURRICANE HANNA'S WATERSIDE BAR & GRILL: This poolside oasis is a sophisticated yet casual place to sip a beverage and enjoy a savory snack. The menu includes items such as sea salt fries, pulled pork sliders, seared tuna, Hanna's one-third-of-a-pound bacon cheeseburger, and more. Kids' meals come in a small sand bucket, complete with attached shovel. ♥

MARTHA'S VINEYARD: While a full bar is available, a small but satisfying selection of wines from Martha's Vineyard (and other areas) is this Beach Club bar's specialty. Light appetizers are served, too.

Disney Cruise Line

W alt Disney World, which boasts one of the largest fleets of pleasure craft on the planet, has an inimitable nautical neighbor: Disney Cruise Line. And all of its majestic ocean liners—the award-winning *Magic*, *Wonder*, *Dream*, and *Fantasy*—set sail from Central Florida's Port Canaveral. That's a mere 50 miles from Walt Disney World, making the prospect of pairing a visit to WDW with a Disney Cruise a convenient temptation for many a World traveler.

A voyage with Disney Cruise Line, however, is atypical in a number of ways. First, there's the simultaneous catering to families with kids and grown-ups *sans* offspring. In fact, each ship has programming designed to draw young and old, and those in between, to entirely different recreational areas. Then there's the innovative "rotational dining system," a lineup of lavish musical productions, deck-shaking dance parties, and, of course, the possibility of a unique grand finale: a full day at Castaway Cay—Disney's private, tropical island.

Like swaying in a hammock in the aforementioned paradise, the process of selecting a cruise package and combining it with a stay at Walt Disney World should be as carefree as possible. Within this Birnbaum bonus chapter, you'll find detailed information meant to ensure that planning a "land and sea" holiday is smooth sailing. Bon voyage!

Land & Sea Vacations
Pairing a Disney Cruise with a Walt Disney World Vacation

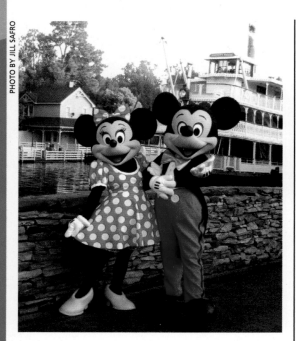

It's the ultimate surf-and-turf experience for Disney fans—a Walt Disney World vacation that's paired with a Disney Cruise. (What better way to chase the Pirates of the Caribbean attraction than by visiting the Caribbean?! Minus real pirates, of course.) And, with the addition of the *Dream* and the *Fantasy* to the fleet, "land and sea" opportunities are limitless. The pages that follow describe how Land and Sea vacations work and give a brief overview of the Disney Cruise Line fleet.

If you've been to Disney's world before (or read the first 300 or so pages of this book), you know that it is not a small one. In fact, it covers 40 square miles—and with about as many attractions, restaurants, and places to stay as one might expect from an area that size. There are four theme parks, two water parks, two dozen hotels, a dining, shopping, and entertainment district, championship golf courses, boating, fishing, tennis, and more. Add a cruise to the mix, and even seasoned Disney veterans run the risk of becoming overwhelmed.

The good news is that a customized vacation package can include just about everything you'd ever want. That frees you up to focus on a very important goal: having fun.

HOT TIP!

Disney Cruise Vacations offers a day-before option at a non-Disney resort with some packages. For information, contact a travel agent or call 800-951-3532.

Surf & Turf

Though "Land and Sea" packages are occasionally offered via *www.disneycruise.com*, most guests build their own vacations (with a little help from DCL or a travel agent). In addition to settling on a travel budget, there are certain decisions to be made: 1. Do you want to cruise before or after you visit WDW? 2. How long do you wish to play on land and on sea? 3. Where do you want to stay on Land? 4. Which Disney Cruise Line itinerary is best for you? (See page 312 for a selection of popular itineraries that depart from Central Florida's Port Canaveral.)

Disney Cruise Line Air Program

If you plan to fly to the port, consider allowing the Disney Cruise Vacations Air Program to help you make the arrangements. In addition to lining up round-trip airfare for your whole party, they will secure motor coach ground transportation and baggage transfers. The service is available in more than 150 cities in the United States, United Kingdom, and Canada. At press time, this service was not included in the price of any Disney Cruise Line vacation packages. For details and pricing, call 877-566-0967.

HOT TIP!

While many folks enjoy "Sea and Land" vacations (starting with a cruise), we prefer to begin with a visit to Walt Disney World. That way we are already in the vicinity of the port on sail-away day, thus alleviating any anxiety about flight delays or late arrivals.

To pair a visit to Walt Disney World with a Disney cruise, contact a travel agent or call 800-951-3532. (That's the number to call if you'd like help finding a hotel near Disney Cruise Line's other home ports, too.)

PHOTO BY JILL SAFRO

Combination Vacation

Walt Disney World/Disney Cruise Line combination vacations can include accommodations on land (at a WDW resort) and a stateroom on a Disney ship. In addition to accommodations, shipboard meals, snacks, soft drinks, and entertainment are included with all Disney Cruise Line packages.

What's not included in a "Land and Sea" combination vacation? Meals and beverages at Walt Disney World (unless the WDW Dining Plan is purchased in advance), transfers to Port Canaveral (these may also be purchased in advance), airfare, excursions, meals ashore in ports of call—with the exception of Castaway Cay, where food and soft drinks are included (see page 343), extra gratuities, laundry or valet services, parking at the port, or any other items not specifically included.

What can be added? Just about everything. Options include tickets to Disney World theme and water parks, dinner shows, and more. For details, visit *www.disneycruise.com*, or call 800-951-3532.

Walt Disney World Resort Options

The following is a comprehensive list of Walt Disney World-owned-and-operated resort hotels. For details on these resorts, turn to our *Transportation & Accommodations* chapter. The information was correct at press time but is subject to change. In addition to Walt Disney World, it's possible to book vacations that pair a cruise with a hotel stay in Miami and other port cities. For additional information, visit *www.disneycruise.com*, or call 800-951-3532.

DELUXE:

Animal Kingdom Lodge (see page 99)

BoardWalk (see page 91)

Contemporary Resort (see page 76)

Dolphin (see page 89)

Grand Floridian Resort & Spa (see page 80)

Old Key West Resort (see page 97)

Polynesian Village Resort (see page 78)

Saratoga Springs Resort & Spa (see page 96)

Swan (see page 89)

Wilderness Lodge (see page 82)

Yacht & Beach Club (see page 86)

MODERATE:

Cabins at Fort Wilderness resort (see page 84)

Caribbean Beach Resort (see page 85)

Coronado Springs Resort (see page 101)

Port Orleans French Quarter (see page 94)

Port Orleans Riverside (see page 95)

VALUE:

All-Star Movies (see page 98)

All-Star Music (see page 98)

All-Star Sports (see page 98)

Art of Animation (see page 103)

Campsites at Fort Wilderness resort (see page 83)

Pop Century (see page 102)

Sample Itineraries

All four Disney ships—the *Magic, Wonder, Dream,* and *Fantasy*—are scheduled to cruise out of Port Canaveral, Florida, in 2017. (Though some visit other home ports, there's usually at least two ships to choose from at all times.) What follows is a sampling of the itineraries offered from Port Canaveral, the port closest to Walt Disney World— and most logically paired with a WDW vacation. Note that most include a stop at Disney's private island, Castaway Cay (see page 343). For a complete list of ports and itineraries, visit *www.disneycruise.com*.

3-Night Bahamian Cruise — *Disney Wonder*
Itinerary A

DAY	ITINERARY
DAY 1	Check in at Port Canaveral Terminal. Aboard by 4 P.M.
DAY 2	Ashore at Nassau at 9:30 A.M. Aboard by 5:15 P.M.
DAY 3	Ashore at Castaway Cay at 8:30 A.M. Aboard by 4:45 P.M.
DAY 4	Ship at Port Canaveral beginning at 7:30 A.M.

4-Night Bahamian Cruise — *Disney Dream*
Itinerary A

DAY	ITINERARY
DAY 1	Check in at Port Canaveral Terminal. Aboard by 3:45 P.M.
DAY 2	Ashore at Nassau at 9:30 A.M. Aboard by 5:15 P.M.
DAY 3	Ashore at Castaway Cay at 8:30 A.M. Aboard by 4:45 P.M.
DAY 4	Full day at sea.
DAY 5	Ship at Port Canaveral beginning at 7:30 A.M.

4-Night Bahamian Cruise — *Disney Wonder*
Itinerary B

DAY	ITINERARY
DAY 1	Check in at Port Canaveral Terminal. Aboard by 4 P.M.
DAY 2	Ashore at Nassau at 9:30 A.M. Aboard by 5:15 P.M.
DAY 3	Ashore at Castaway Cay at 8:30 A.M. Aboard by 4:45 P.M.
DAY 4	Full day at sea.
DAY 5	Ship at Port Canaveral beginning at 7:30 A.M.

7-Night Eastern Caribbean Cruise — *Disney Fantasy*
Itinerary A

DAY	ITINERARY
DAY 1	Check in at Port Canaveral Terminal. Aboard by 3:45 P.M.
DAY 2	Full day at sea.
DAY 3	Full day at sea.
DAY 4	Ashore at Tortola at 7:30 A.M. Aboard by 5:45 P.M.
DAY 5	Ashore at St. Thomas/St. John, U.S. Virgin Islands, at 7:45 A.M. Aboard by 4 P.M.
DAY 6	Full day at sea.
DAY 7	Ashore at Castaway Cay at 9:30 A.M. Aboard by 4:45 P.M.
DAY 8	Ship at Port Canaveral beginning at 7:30 A.M.

7-Night Western Caribbean Cruise — *Disney Fantasy*
Itinerary C

DAY	ITINERARY
DAY 1	Check in at Port Canaveral Terminal. Aboard by 3:45 P.M.
DAY 2	Full day at sea.
DAY 3	Ashore at Cozumel, Mexico, at 8:30 A.M. Aboard by 4:30 P.M.
DAY 4	Ashore at Grand Cayman, Cayman Islands, at 10:30 A.M. Aboard by 5:30 P.M. (This port requires tendering.)
DAY 5	Ashore at Falmouth, Jamaica, at 7:30 A.M. Aboard by 4:45 P.M.
DAY 6	Full day at sea.
DAY 7	Ashore at Castaway Cay at 8:30 A.M. Aboard by 4:45 P.M.
DAY 8	Ship at Port Canaveral beginning at 7:30 A.M.

Before You Sail

What to do, what to do. There are many factors to consider when pairing a cruise package with a stay at Walt Disney World. Among the most important are destination, budget, time available, stateroom needs, and preferred itinerary.

If you want to take the most inexpensive cruise possible, then a shorter cruise in a standard inside stateroom is probably a good choice. If money is no object, consider a 7-night adventure in the super-deluxe Walter E. Disney suite. Of course, there are plenty of things in between.

Check Your Calendar

Determining the length of your cruise depends on several things—the first, how much time do you have in your busy schedule to devote to leisure? If your answer is only four days, don't despair: Disney has short cruises to the Bahamas (most of which include a stop at Disney's own private island, Castaway Cay). If you have at least a week to sail, you may choose a 7-night-or-longer cruise to the Caribbean. For details, call 800-910-3659 or visit *www.disneycruise.com*.

www.disneycruise.com

We've done our best to provide accurate, current information regarding all things Disney Cruise Line. That said, rates, itineraries, excursions, and other specifics are subject to change. For additional information or to book a cruise, shore excursion, and more, visit the interactive website: *www.disneycruise.com*. It's one of the most user-friendly websites we have ever seen.

Check Your Checkbook

The cost of your cruise is the next issue on the planning board. Budget constraints can be eased in several ways: by taking one of the shorter cruises, choosing a less-expensive stateroom class, and by limiting the number of land tours and excursions you take at the various ports of call. (We often forgo pricey excursions because the ships themselves have so much to offer.) Plan to eat aboard the ship, too—meals and snacks are included in the vacation package, as are many extras, including stage shows, movies, tours, lectures, games, bands, deck parties with Disney characters, and more.

Selecting a Stateroom

Sure, you'd like the largest suite on the ship. No question, you want the biggest verandah. And, of course, you absolutely must have a great view. But if these don't fit your budget, there are other appealing options. Consider this: Every stateroom boasts nautical decor, has ample closet space, a television, and a small safe. Inside staterooms can be a bit less expensive and not much smaller than their outside counterparts; on the *Dream* and the *Fantasy* they have virtual portholes (aka "magical" portholes, these high-tech wonders have HD digital screens). On the other hand, should you decide to splurge, know that there are concierge rooms and larger suites with private verandahs where you can savor a refreshing beverage and read the newest page-turner, periodically taking a moment to gaze out at the sea.

Of course, there are other factors to think about when selecting a stateroom. How many people are in your party? Are you traveling with young children? Perhaps a Deluxe Stateroom would suit your family's needs. These accommodations have queen-size beds, bunk beds for the kids, and a split bath (one room with a sink and a toilet and another with a sink and a shower/tub). A curtained divider provides a bit of privacy.

Of course, there's always the Walter E. Disney Suite and the Roy O. Disney Suite—so if money is no object, treat your crew to one of these thousand-plus-square-foot homes away from home. No matter what your requirements, chances are good that Disney Cruise Line can meet them.

What's Not Included with a Cruise?

Rest assured that all of your basic vacation needs are covered by the "all-inclusive" price of the cruise. However, there are always "extras" for which you may want to ante up a little cash. Here's a list of items and services that carry an extra charge while aboard Disney ships:

- Child care for tots ages 6 months to 3 years (see pages 319 and 340)
- Port Adventures (aka shore excursions)
- Expenses incurred while on land in ports of call (with the exception of food and most soft drinks at Castaway Cay)
- Alcoholic beverages and Royal Court Tea
- Palo and Remy (These optional, reservations-necessary, adults-only restaurants carry an extra charge: about $30 per person for dinner and brunch at Palo; about $55 per person for champagne brunch and $85 for dinner at Remy.)
- Vanellope's Sweets & Treats (on the *Dream*)

- Refreshments at Cove Cafe, Vibe, and any bar
- Spa and Bibbidi Bobbidi Boutique services
- Merchandise purchased onboard
- Arcade games and sports simulators
- Photos snapped by the ship's photographers
- Internet usage (see page 321)
- Cell phone usage (see page 322)
- Ship-to-shore telephone calls (There is a sizable fee for all calls, incoming and outgoing. Calls within the ship are free.)

With the exception of non-Disney ports of call, all "incidental" charges will be billed to your stateroom, provided that you leave a credit card number upon check-in. It's a good idea to have some cash on hand (we bring about $300, just in case), but there are few chances to use it. Except for tips, cash isn't accepted on the ships. Same goes for Castaway Cay, with the exception of the post office—stamps must be purchased with cash. Most of the non-Disney port shops accept major credit cards, and most accept U.S. currency.

How to Book a Cruise

In addition to using *www.disneycruise.com* or calling Disney Cruise Line (800-910-3659), many guests book through travel agents.

PAYMENT METHODS: Cruise packages, as well as incidentals, gratuities, hotel bills, and deposits, may be paid by major credit card (Visa, MasterCard, JCB Card, American Express, Diners Club, etc.), Disney gift cards, Disney Rewards Redemption cards, traveler's check, cashier's check, money order, or personal check. Personal checks must bear the guest's name and address, be drawn on a U.S. bank, and be accompanied by proper identification (a valid driver's license with photo or government-issued photo ID). The reservation number must be written on the face of the check. Checks will not be accepted within 21 days prior to vacation commencement date. The final payment for a cruise package must be made between 75 and 150 days prior to the cruise, depending on the itinerary and category. Final payment due date varies for special itineraries.

Payments sent via mail should be addressed to: Disney Cruise Line, P.O. Box 277763, Atlanta, GA 30384-7763.

Payments sent via courier service (e.g., FedEx or UPS) should be sent to: Disney Cruise Line, Bank of America, Lockbox Services, Lockbox 277763, 6000 Feldwood Road, College Park, GA 30349 (407-566-3500).

DEPOSIT REQUIREMENTS: When you book a cruise, you'll get a "due date" for a deposit. The deposit is 20 percent of the total fare. Reservations will be canceled if a deposit is not received by the deadline. (Packages that are booked within the final payment due date or in categories IGT, OGT, and VGT get special instructions.)

CANCELLATION POLICY: Cancellations may be made by phone or mail (we prefer the phone). To avoid the sad fate of paying for a canceled cruise, we recommend insuring your trip.

Fees paid for canceling depend on when that call is made. For cruises of less than 10 days

Ground Transfers

Disney Cruise Line provides reliable, friendly service aboard its motor coaches (aka: buses). Getting to the buses is easy. Upon arrival at Orlando International Airport, take a shuttle to the Main Terminal. Once there, proceed to Disney's Magical Express Welcome Center. It's on Level One, Side B. The real bonus here is the baggage handling: For flights before 10 P.M., Disney reps will pull your tagged luggage and make sure it gets delivered to your room. (Guests arriving after 10 P.M. may collect their luggage and proceed to the Magical Express Welcome Center.) From the airport, a bus will take you to Port Canaveral or a WDW hotel. (For guests with transfers included in their package, your bus departure location and information is included in your cruise documentation.) What if you're staying at a resort that's not designated as a departure location or at an off-property hotel? You'll have to get yourself to one of the WDW departure spots to catch a bus to the ship. Here's the pricing for Orlando ground transfers:

TRANSFER TRIP	PRICE*
Airport to select WDW resort (one-way)	Free**
Select WDW resort to Port Canaveral	$35
Round-trip from Orlando International Airport (MCO) to Port Canaveral	$70
Land and Sea vacation (Orlando airport to select WDW resort; WDW resort to Port Canaveral; Port Canaveral to airport)	$70

*Prices are per person, were correct at press time, and are subject to change.
**Disney's Magical Express transportation is a free service for WDW resort guests. For pricing details about transfers to and from other locations, call 800-951-3532.

where embark or debark is a U.S. port, cancellation fees are as follows:
- For all suites and concierge rooms, the deposit is nonrefundable regardless of when the reservation is canceled.
- For each non-suite/concierge stateroom guest, canceling 74 to 45 days before sailing costs the whole deposit.
- For all rooms, a cancellation within 44 to 30 days costs 50 percent of the vacation price.
- For all staterooms, a cancellation within 29 to 15 days costs 75 percent per guest.
- Should a cruise be canceled less than 14 days ahead, you'll pay for the whole package.

HOT TIP!

Guests who plan to arrive at Port Canaveral the night before setting sail might consider staying at one of these resorts on nearby Astronaut Boulevard:

Country Inns & Suites by Carlson. Rates range from about $89–$129, and there is a shuttle to the cruise terminal; 321-784-8500 or 888-201-1746.

Residence Inn by Marriott. Rates range from about $169–$220; 321-323-1100 or 800-331-3131.

For cruises 10 days or more or less than 10 days where embark and debark is a non-U.S. port, the fees are as follows (this does not apply to cruises out of Port Canaveral, Florida):

- For all suites and concierge rooms, the deposit is non-refundable regardless of when the reservation was canceled.
- For all non-suite/concierge staterooms, canceling within 119 to 56 days before the sailing costs the deposit per guest.
- Canceling within 55 to 30 days costs 50 percent of the vacation cost per guest.
- Canceling within 29 to 15 days costs 75 percent of the vacation package per guest.
- Canceling less than 14 days ahead means you will pay for the whole package.

What to Pack

"Cruise Casual" is the operative phrase with Disney. Shorts, T-shirts, sundresses, and the like are fine daytime wear. At dinnertime, casual takes on a more formal meaning: Set aside flip-flops and plan on nice slacks (jeans are okay, as long as they're in good condition) and a collared shirt for men, with real shoes, as opposed to the tennis kind. The same goes for women, while dresses are fine, too. There is an optional dress-up night, too.

Identification Papers

Unlike a visit to Disney's Epcot, where it only feels as if you're leaving the country, in the case of a Disney Cruise Line vacation, you usually do. Given that, you'll need a passport to provide proper proof of citizenship when passing through Customs for most cruises. (There are some itineraries for which U.S. citizens may use other forms of proof of citizenship such as a state-issued birth certificate.) U.S. government regulations related to passport requirements are subject to change. Therefore, all guests are advised to have a valid passport for all cruises. Visit *http://travel.state.gov*, or call 877-487-2778 for current requirements. Non-U.S. citizens are required to travel with valid government-issued passports at all times.

On 7-night-or-longer cruises, there is a semi-formal and a formal night. While some folks don black tie and sequins, it's fine to sport a less formal look. The *Personal Navigator* (see page 330) will tip you off as to the appropriate attire. Many guests pack pirate garb, too, in anticipation of "Pirates IN the Caribbean" party night—don't forget to pack your puffy shirt and eye patch. (The Pirate party takes place on most sailings.)

Bathing suits are a must, as are beach shoes, wraps, sunscreen, sunglasses, and hats. Some sundries, such as shampoo and body lotion, are provided. Others are available for purchase, but the prices are steep, and the shops aren't always open (U.S. Customs limits the operating hours).

PACK A DAY BAG: Guests may check in at the port and board the ship as early as 1 P.M., but your checked luggage may not arrive until 6 P.M. (though usually earlier). Keep in mind that you will have access to your stateroom beginning at 1:30 P.M., along with most shipboard amenities, including all pools, so pack your swimsuit in a day bag. This should serve as, or fit in, a carry-on, as checked bags will be out of your hands once you surrender them. (Day bags can't be larger than 9

HOT TIP!

You must show your "Key to the World" card (Disney-issued stateroom key and ID) when disembarking or boarding the ship. Adults also need a government-issued photo ID (a passport is ideal). Note that your WDW MagicBand or hotel key won't work on the ship.

What's in a Name?

A whole lot, when it comes to Disney Cruise Line accommodations. Here's a listing of the types of rooms available on each of the ships. Note that it is possible to request side-by-side staterooms, but it can't be guaranteed. For specifics on staterooms, see page 328.

- Standard Inside Stateroom
- Deluxe Inside Stateroom
- Deluxe Ocean-view Stateroom
- Deluxe Family Ocean-view Stateroom (*Dream* and *Fantasy*)
- Deluxe Ocean-view Stateroom with Navigator's Verandah (*Magic* and *Wonder*)
- Deluxe Ocean-view Stateroom with Verandah
- Deluxe Family Ocean-view Stateroom with Verandah
- Concierge Family Ocean-view Stateroom with Verandah (*Dream* and *Fantasy*)
- Concierge 1-Bedroom Suite with Verandah
- Concierge 2-Bedroom Suite with Verandah (*Magic* and *Wonder*)
- Concierge Royal Suite with Verandah

inches by 14 inches by 22 inches and do not count as part of the two-bags-per-passenger quota.) The bag should also include your passports, valuables, breakable items, and anything else you might need during those first hours on board. Note that most airlines require that carried-on liquids be in 3.4-ounce-or-smaller containers and fit into one quart-size, clear, plastic zip-top bag.

Booking Shore Excursions

Shore Excursions, aka Port Adventures, book early. To reserve yours, visit *www.disneycruise.com*. To make last-minute arrangements, visit your ship's Port Adventures desk. Note that Port Adventures are not operated by the Walt Disney Company—not even those on Castaway Cay (see page 343).

For descriptions of all excursions offered in more than 70 worldwide destinations, including Castaway Cay, visit *www.disneycruise.com*. (We considered including all of them here, but that would have added about 600 pages to this book!)

Cancellations or changes to reservations must be made up to 3 days before a cruise starts to get a refund. After that, you pay whether you play or not.

How to Get to Port Canaveral

BY PLANE: Fly to Orlando International Airport. We prefer to arrive the night before or take a flight that is scheduled to arrive in the early morning hours. (That helps avoid potential travel delays.) If you get there on the early side, you can make a day of it. And, if your flight is delayed, you'll still have a shot at making it to the port before the ship sails. (When you book your cruise, ask about the check-in cut-off time. Don't be late!)

FROM THE AIRPORT: As you get off the shuttle and enter the main terminal, proceed directly to the Disney Magical Express Welcome Center. It's on Level 1, Side B of the terminal. After your party has checked in, a Disney rep will direct you toward a motor coach. Don't worry about checked luggage. For guests with transfers, all bags bearing appropriate tags will be claimed by Disney and delivered to your stateroom. (If you are driving to the ship, see information to the right.)

The following details apply specifically to cruises departing from Port Canaveral, Florida. For details for other departure ports (such as Miami, Vancouver, or Barcelona), call 800-910-3659 or visit *www.disneycruise.com*.

DISNEY MOTOR COACH: The bus trip from Orlando International Airport or a Disney World resort to Port Canaveral takes about 90 minutes (without traffic). While on board, you can fill out paperwork (though it is best to do this ahead of time). There's a restroom onboard. Motor coach transportation may be purchased with a cruise package.

CAR SERVICE: Noris Limousine and Florida Towncar offer friendly, reliable service between Orlando International Airport (MCO) and Port Canaveral. For rates, information, or to make a reservation with Noris Limousine, call 407-240-4533, or visit *www.norislimousine.com*. For Florida Towncar, go to *www.floridatowncar.com*, or call 800-525-7246 or 407-277-5466. Reservations are necessary, and cancellations must be made at least 24 to 48 hours in advance. Disney Cruise Line's reservations department can take your car service request, too.

AUTOMOBILE: Disney Cruise Line's Port Canaveral Terminal is located at Cruise Terminal 8 (CT8); 9155 Charles M. Rowland Drive, Port Canaveral, Florida, 32920. It's about a 90-minute drive from Orlando International Airport and from Disney World. The parking facility, which is operated by the Canaveral Port Authority, accepts cash (U.S. currency), Visa, MasterCard, and traveler's checks only. Personal checks are not accepted. Parking costs about $15 per day. Rates are subject to change. Guests may also make a reservation for a parking space prior to arrival. To do so, have a credit card handy and visit *http://portcanaveral.com/cruising/parking.php*.

From Orlando International Airport, take State Road (S.R.) 528 East (Beachline Expressway). Continue over the Indian River and the Banana

River. Turn right onto S.R. 401, which will loop and head north over the channel locks. Stay in the right-hand lane and follow signs to the "A" Cruise Terminals. S.R. 528 is a toll road.

If you are driving from Walt Disney World, take State Road 536 East to 417 (the GreeneWay). Follow 417 to S.R. 528 East (Beachline Expressway). At the fork in the road, veer right to stay on S.R. 528. Continue over the Indian and Banana rivers. Turn right onto S.R. 401. Stay in the right lane and follow signs leading to the "A" Cruise Terminals. Note that 417 and 528 are toll roads.

Guests who are driving from North Florida should take I-95 South exit #205 for S.R. 528 East (Beachline Expressway). Continue over the Indian and Banana rivers. Turn right onto S.R. 401. Stay in the right lane and follow signs to "A" Cruise Terminals.

Drivers originating in South Florida should take I-95 North. Exit at #205 for S.R. 528 East (The Beachline). Take S.R. 528 to S.R. 401. Keep to the right and follow the signs to "A" Cruise Terminals.

GETTING TO PORT CANAVERAL FROM WALT DISNEY WORLD WITHOUT A CAR:

Disney Cruise Line has buses to take guests directly from many WDW resorts. One-way transfers cost $35 per person, while $70 will cover the round-trip. Guests with transfers will get a letter in their resort room with departure details. Bell services will automatically pick up luggage when transfers have been prearranged. (Car services make the trip to and from Port Canaveral, too. See page 318 for details.)

Customized Travel Tips

TRAVELING WITH BABIES

Cribs: If you are traveling with a baby, it is possible to have a playpen-like, foldaway crib sent to your stateroom. (The cribs are 39.8 inches long, 28.25 inches wide, and 31.25 inches high.) Request one when you make a reservation, and confirm it before leaving home. Supplies are limited. Bring a blanket, as the cribs come with fitted sheets only.

Diaper Service: It is possible to have a disposable diaper system sent to your stateroom. You can request it when you make a reservation, or speak with your Stateroom Host or Hostess upon arrival.

Food: Staterooms on all Disney ships have small refrigerators, perfectly safe for storing formula and food. Note that homemade baby food is not permitted on board any Disney ship.

Tag Your Bags

Flying to Orlando International Airport for a cruise out of Port Canaveral? After you book your cruise and purchase ground transfers, you'll get a personalized info packet in the mail. Included in this valuable envelope will be colorful luggage tags. We cannot overemphasize the importance of affixing these tags to all checked luggage. Why? Once you say good-bye to your bags at the airport, you won't see them again until they arrive at your stateroom. Disney reps collect bags and deliver them to your stateroom by 6 P.M.

If you arrive by car or bus, drop your bags with porters at the terminal. They will be delivered to your stateroom for you. Guests who arrive from Walt Disney World via Disney motor coach need to tag their bags, too. (Tags come with cruise documents.) The driver will see to it that tagged bags are removed from the bus and loaded on the ship.

If you'd rather not haul your bags off the ship, expect to use a similar color-coding/character method at the end of your cruise (this applies to all cruises). A set of tags will be left in your stateroom. Slap them on your bags, make a note of the color/character and place them in the hall on the last night of the cruise. (Be sure to keep items such as pajamas, sundries, and clothes for the morning in a day bag.) Look for them in the designated section of the terminal once you debark. Guests participating in onboard airline check-in don't have to claim their bags until their plane lands at their home airport. Restrictions apply. Note that it is not mandatory that guests surrender their bags on the last night of a cruise—but guests are responsible for removing all of their luggage from the ship in the morning.

At least one shop on board sells diapers, formula, and a limited selection of baby food. (The shop isn't always open, as U.S. Customs limits its hours.) If you'd like to save money, pack as many baby rations as possible.

Babysitting: Onboard babysitting is available for tots ages 6 months to 3 years. The cost is $9 an hour for the first child, with a one-hour minimum stay. Each additional child (who must be the first child's sibling) is $8 per hour. The service is offered in the ship's It's a Small World nursery. Reservations for the nursery can be made at *www.disneycruise.com* or on board (based on availability). In-room babysitting is not offered on any ship.

Cold and Flu Advisory

Disney Cruise Line follows extraordinary sanitation efforts to ensure the safety and comfort of guests. Even so, people can get sick. If you or a member of your party experiences any symptom of illness (cold, flu, etc.) within 72 hours of sailing, you may be evaluated by a medical team. (If necessary, Cruise Line representatives will direct you to someone to help your party make alternate plans.) Fees apply at the Health Center.

Once on board, all guests are asked to wash their hands frequently and thoroughly, as this is a highly effective barrier to spreading germs. If you or someone in your party does become ill during your trip, please contact the Health Center. You'll be taken care of there, and immediate treatment will help limit the potential impact to others.

HOT TIP!

If you will be using an ECV (Electronic Conveyance Vehicle) during your cruise, be sure to book an accessible stateroom (other rooms can't accommodate ECVs). No ECV parking is allowed in stateroom corridors or on elevator landings. There are ECV charging stations on Deck 6 midship on the *Magic* and *Wonder*, and on Deck 2 midship, outside Enchanted Garden, on the *Dream* and *Fantasy*.

Other Supplies: Diapers, pacifiers, pool toys, and more can be purchased on board. The ships' shops aren't always open, so take inventory and plan ahead to avoid being caught short. If it's an emergency, inquire at Guest Services. They can help with just about any onboard crisis.

Bottle sterilizers and warmers are available at the Guest Services desk.

TRAVELERS WITH DISABILITIES:

Measures have been taken to make your stay as comfortable and effortless as possible. Disney Cruise Line offers special equipment and facilities for guests with disabilities. Each ship has staterooms that are equipped for guests using wheelchairs. They have ramped bathroom thresholds, open bed frames, bathroom and shower grab bars, fold-down shower seats, handheld showerheads, and lowered towel and closet bars. Captioning is available for stateroom televisions, and for some onboard video monitors and movies. Stateroom communication kits may be reserved upon request. They include door-knock and phone alerts, bed shaker notification, and a strobe light smoke detector; a text type-writer (aka TTY) may also be requested. There is no charge for the kit, but supplies are limited. Make your needs known when you make your reservation and confirm them prior to sailing. Wheelchair-accessible restrooms are available in several common areas on board. There are pool lifts on the *Magic*, *Wonder*, *Dream*, and *Fantasy*. A small number of sand wheelchairs are available on Castaway Cay. American Sign Language interpretation is available for live performances on various cruise dates. (The service is not available on every cruise, so be sure to start planning your trip as far in advance as possible.) For additional information or to make special requests, ask your reservationist. For more information via TTY (text typewriter), please call 407-566-7455.

TRAVELERS WITHOUT CHILDREN: This being a Disney cruise, one could argue that you—the footloose, fancy-free folks—are on their turf. And, as such, you might expect to have youngsters underfoot at all times. This is simply not the case. The Disney ships were designed with three specific types of vacationers in mind: families, kids, and grown-ups without kids. On board, there is an adults-only deck area, complete with its own pool (not to mention music and games). There's a gourmet restaurant (two on the *Dream* and *Fantasy*) and a cozy coffee bar. It goes without saying that those spots, as well as several lounges, are strictly for the grown-up set (as in adults with legal proof of age). Plus, there are countless other ways to enjoy a grown-up getaway in the various ports of call. With that in mind, Castaway Cay (Disney's private island) guarantees you and your ilk a piece of prime beachfront real estate where you can bask in the sun or read a novel in the shade without the fear of sand being kicked in your face. You can even have a massage in a cabana overlooking the ocean. Can you manage to spend days on end without encountering the wee ones of our species? No way. But who'd want to?

MEDICAL MATTERS: The Health Center, located forward on Deck 1, is open daily to provide non-emergency medical care throughout each cruise. All Disney Cruise Line ships have a physician and nurse on call 24 hours a day (even while in port) for conditions that require immediate attention. Health services are provided by a company independent of Disney Cruise Line, and standard prevailing fees will be charged for all medical services. Fees will be charged to your stateroom account.

In extreme cases, Disney Cruise Line will arrange to have a passenger taken to the nearest port to receive medical care. The cost of this varies with the location of the ship and the nearest port. Because all health care provided qualifies as "care outside the United States,"

New Ships on the Horizon!

Ahoy! Disney Cruise Line's family is growing— two new ships, currently being built in Germany, are expected join the fleet as they are completed in 2021 and 2023. The new vessels will be slightly larger than the *Disney Dream* and *Disney Fantasy*, each weighing approximately 135,000 gross tons and housing about 125,000 staterooms. At press time, the ships had not been named. What do *you* think they'll be called? It's fun to speculate.

you will be responsible for paying any charges that are incurred while on board prior to debarkation and submitting the request for coverage to your insurance carrier (all paperwork will be provided).

If you get sick while on shore, your guide should direct you to your ship's tour director at the dock, who will help you get back to the ship.

Regarding younger passengers, know that any child exhibiting symptoms of illness will not be allowed to participate in the youth activities or be cared for in the ship's nursery. No exceptions.

Fingertip Reference Guide

BUSINESS SERVICES: Wait a minute, aren't you here to relax? For those of you who must get a little work done while at sea, there are some business services available for an additional charge. Among them are fax transmission, copies, and AV equipment. Wireless Internet service is available throughout the ships (including staterooms) for a fee. Guests access the Web via cell phone and various personal computing devices. Computer devices are available for rental (at the ships' Connect@Sea desk). Note that the Wi-Fi service at sea can best be described as "low speed." As you sail, you may experience buffering and dropped connections. Internet connectivity can be intermittent based on satellite connectivity. All staterooms have phones (ship-to-shore rates apply), and electrical outlets are laptop friendly. Note that the ships' computers don't accept uploads and do not run any Microsoft Office applications (so any attachments from associated e-mail accounts cannot be opened). There is, however, a handy printer at the ready. Are you planning on holding meetings during your cruise? For details on business services, visit *www.disneymeetings.com.*

CAMERA NEEDS: By all means, bring a camera. Memory cards and accessories are sold on board. There are also roving photographers capturing moments throughout the day. You'll find shots taken at "static locations" (e.g., character sets in the lobby) are available for viewing at photo kiosks at Shutters (the photo store on all Disney ships). These photos may be viewed and purchased during the cruise. (Some photo packages may be purchased in advance, with special promotions.) Pictures taken by roaming

Getting Around It

Travelers with disabilities already know that travel requires a lot of advance planning. Disney has equipped all of its ships with a variety of amenities geared toward those guests with special needs.

Wheelchair-accessible staterooms are equipped with ramp entrances to bathrooms, fold-down shower seats, handheld shower-heads, lowered towel and closet racks, and emergency call buttons.

There is a limited number of sand wheel-chairs available on Disney's private island, Castaway Cay (first come, first served). **Note:** If you will need a wheelchair through-out the cruise, you are encouraged to bring your own.

Throughout the ship, there are wheelchair-accessible restrooms.

Pool lifts are available on the *Magic*, *Wonder*, *Dream*, and *Fantasy*.

Guests with hearing disabilities need not miss any of the fun on board. In-stateroom TVs can be equipped with captioning, and assistive-listening devices may be rented from Guest Services and may be used at most theaters and show rooms. Also available are communication kits equipped with alarm clock, door-knock, and telephone alerts with bed shaker notification. Make your needs known when you book your cruise.

photographers (e.g., in the dining rooms, by the pool, on Castaway Cay, etc.) may be viewed, printed, and purchased at Shutters on all four ships. Photos can be purchased on a single media storage device (CD or USB)—one-stop shop-ping. The photographs are very high in quality (and in price).

DRINKING LAWS: The drinking age on Disney's ships is 21 and is strictly enforced. Valid government-issued photo ID is required. Disney Cruise Line reserves the right to refuse alcohol sales to anyone. On cruises departing from European countries where the legal age is lower than 21, a legal guardian who is sailing with a passenger between the ages of 18 and 20 may sign a waiver allowing their charge to imbibe.

MAIL: Letters and postcards may be mailed from the post office at Disney's private tropical island, Castaway Cay. Stamps are the only things available for purchase here (cash only). It is also possible to mail items from other ports—it's just less convenient. If you plan to buy stamps from the Castaway Cay post office, do so early. The office is operated by Bahamian authorities and may not be open late in the day. Even if it's closed, you can still mail letters from the post office, and items will be delivered with a Castaway Cay postmark. Note that postcards and stamps may be purchased on the ship.

MONEY MATTERS: There is no need for cash on the ship. You can apply a credit card to your account during the check-in process. (Most major credit cards, including MasterCard, JCB, Visa, and American Express, are accepted.) From then on, all you'll need to do is sign for extras you want (including excursions booked on the ship), and these amounts will be charged to that card.

Cash or credit cards will be necessary for meals, taxis, and other purchases made in all ports but Castaway Cay (where a stateroom key is accepted in all cases except for stamps, which must be bought with cash). A few hundred dollars should suffice. Standard gratuities are automatically attached to your cruise folio. Extra gratuities may be charged to a stateroom or paid in cash. Special envelopes will be delivered to your stateroom. They may be used to present extra gratuities and/or receipts for prepaid tips.

Automated teller machines may be available in ports of call, but there are none on the ship. Be sure the machine dispenses U.S. currency before you use it. It's a good idea to alert your bank and credit card company to the fact that you'll be using cards while travelling.

HOT TIP!

If you plan to use your cell phone during your cruise, be sure to check with your wireless provider before leaving home. Ask if you will be able to get service through them while on board and how much voice, data, and text service costs—including roaming rates.

SMOKING: All Disney ships are, for the most part, smoke-free zones. Smoking (including e-cigarettes) is prohibited in all staterooms and verandahs. (Guests who violate this policy are subject to a $250 deep-cleaning fee.) There are designated smoking areas on each ship.

TELEPHONE CALLS: All staterooms have phones with ship-to-shore capability. Rates range from about $7 to $9.50 per minute (rates are subject to change). Toll-free and collect calls can't be placed from ship phones. Wireless service is available in staterooms (fees apply). Be sure to check with your mobile carrier (before you leave home) for talk and text rates and roaming fees. Note that text rates are usually lower than talk rates. Some ports have pay phones (you will need an international calling card to use them).

TIPPING: Some servers, such as bartenders, get an automatic 15 percent gratuity each time you call upon their services, while spa services have an automatic 18 percent tip. That said, folks such as your dining room servers and stateroom host or hostess rely on guests to tip them appropriately. Suggested gratuity amounts will be posted to your account during the cruise (it's okay to leave more if you deem the service to be outstanding). If you prefer to pay in cash, inform Guest Services at the beginning of the cruise. For those guests dining at Palo and Remy, the gratuity amount is at your discretion.

WEDDINGS: Whether you are saying your "I do's" for the first time, committing yourselves to each other, or renewing your vows, Disney Cruise Line has the means to make the occasion exceptionally memorable. Ceremonies may be performed on the ship or at Castaway Cay. Some happy couples invite family members along for the trip, while others prefer to have this time to themselves. For details, call 321-939-4610, or contact your travel agent. Call as far in advance as possible and before you book your cruise.

All Good Things

How time flies when you're having fun. You blink and it's time to go home! Here are a few tips about the debarkation process.

The day before your return to the debarkation terminal, you'll receive an information packet that includes a set of colored/character luggage tags. The color coding designates the area of the terminal in which you can pick them up. Be sure to remove the original tags from the inbound trip before you put new tags on all bags. (Guest Services has extra tags.) You'll also get a U.S. Customs form when applicable. Hand this form in as you leave the terminal (one form per household).

On the night before debarkation, you'll place luggage outside your stateroom. (Bags will be collected and delivered to a color/character-coded area in the terminal.) Keep valuables, clothing for debarkation, medications, tickets, passports, and other key documents with you. (You have the option of "express walk off" if you're able to take your own bags off the ship in the morning.) Your waitstaff will tell you about last-morning breakfast options. After breakfast, it's time to leave the ship, taking all your happy memories and, quite possibly, the promise to return again soon. Of course, guests participating in onboard airline check-in don't have to claim bags until their plane lands at their home airport. Certain restrictions apply.

About to begin the "land" part of your vacation? Fetch your bags in the terminal and make a beeline for the bus depot. Flash your Key to the World card (to show you purchased the transfer) and climb aboard. You're going to Disney World!

All Aboard!

The moment you cross the gangway, you'll realize this vessel is no ordinary home away from home. Step into the grand, multi-story atrium, and, amidst the happy hubbub, your presence is made known in dramatic fashion—with a heart-felt announcement for all to hear. And so begins your high-seas adventure.

The *Disney Magic*, *Wonder*, *Dream*, and *Fantasy* rank among the world's finest ocean-going vessels. The ships are casually elegant and designed to capture the majesty of early ocean liners. They're equipped to satisfy most cruisers, with a mix of traditional seafaring diversions and classic Disney touches. Though some theming and entertainment vary from ship to ship, the accommodations and amenities are similar. As is the service, which is expertly provided by a cast of thousands (representing dozens of countries). All staterooms aboard the quartet of ships are a cut above normal cruising quarters—with an average of 25 percent more space than industry standard. The ships were designed to lure families and grown-ups without offspring to entirely different recreational areas. So, cast aside any preconceived notions you may have about cruising, and expect the unexpected.

Checking In

No matter where it is they call home—be it Bangkok or Boca—all Disney Cruise Line guests begin their respective journeys by checking in at a port terminal. Most Bahamas- and Caribbean-bound guests leaving from Port Canaveral check in at Cruise Terminal 8 (CT8). Guests may choose from several different queues at check-in:

Concierge, Castaway Club (for repeat guests), and general check-in. For details on other ports the ships may visit throughout 2017, call 800-910-3659 or go to *www.disneycruise.com*.

Though no one may board the ship until 1 P.M., guests are welcome to arrive earlier—and guests who check in online choose assigned times in advance. (All guests must board the ship by 3:45 P.M.) The terminal has restrooms and ample seating to relax in while waiting to board. (At Port Canaveral, Florida, there's also a nifty model of the ship to give you a preview of the real thing.) And, if little ones get antsy, there's lots of room for them to roam around, plus a TV that runs a loop of Disney cartoons. Mickey Mouse and his friends occasionally greet guests in the terminal, too.

Okay, we may have gotten ahead of ourselves. Before you can enter the main part of the terminal, all members of your party must go through a security checkpoint. It's a lot like airport security, so save the holey socks for the second day of your trip (you may be asked to remove your shoes, along with jackets, glasses, belts, etc.). Since kids must go through the security check, too, we recommend having snacks and games to entertain them while you wait (in case the line is more than a few minutes long). Once you've cleared security, your whole party needs to go to the check-in counter so ID photos may be taken.

At the counter, you will be asked to present a valid passport for yourself and each member of your party (see page 317). This is also where you'll be asked for all of your completed cruise paperwork (which can also be completed via the

Internet at *www.disneycruise.com* under the "My Online Check-in" section; be sure to select your port arrival time, print and sign the forms, and remember to bring them with you) and a major credit card. This card will be the one to which all of your extra cruise expenses are charged. If you'd like to split expenses with another guest staying in your room, it is possible to register two credit cards. Once the cruise begins, you'll use your stateroom key—aka Key to the World card—to make purchases and to open your stateroom door. The card also serves as ID for debarking and reboarding purposes (though all ports of call also require a photo ID such as a driver's license for guests over age 18). If you'd prefer that any member of your party not have charging privileges, advise a representative at check-in (or indicate your preference when you check in online).

Once the check-in process is complete, take a peek at your watch. Is it before 1 P.M.? If so, sit back, relax, and wait for the boarding process to begin. You could also use the extra time to register kids for shipboard youth activities. If it's after 1 P.M., wait for your boarding number to be called (every party receives one when they check in). When your number's called, grab the kids and your day bags and head for the gangway. All aboard!

The Boarding Experience

After you slip through the entry portal, you'll enter a subdued hallway. This is where you may have your "pre-cruise" photo taken by a Cruise Line photographer. Try to look as stressed out as possible. That'll make the post-boarding shots that much more enjoyable. (You can view/buy the photo on the ship later that day or soon after. Just stop by Shutters, the ship's photo shop.)

On the far side of the photo-op area, there's a door leading to a gangway. Cross it and you'll be deposited in the ship's grand lobby—a dramatic backdrop for a dramatic entrance.

Depending on the time (staterooms are usually ready by 1:30 P.M.) and your level of starvation, you may want to make a quick stop, change, and head out for lunch or a snack. Ships' pools are usually open all afternoon. After that, it's safety drill time! The mandatory safety drill takes place at 4 P.M. on all Disney ships. Once the safety drill is complete, you may head back to your room to prepare for the

sailaway deck celebration known as Adventures Away (*Magic* and *Wonder*) and Sailing Away (*Dream* and *Fantasy*). If you've got an early dinner seating, this is the ideal time to change into your evening attire.

Finally, we simply cannot overemphasize the importance of making reservations for spa treatments and for Palo and Remy (adults-only eateries) as early as possible. (It's best to book before the trip begins, via *www.disneycruise.com*.) Make last-minute spa appointments at the spa itself. For Palo, which begins accepting reservations at about 1 P.M. on day one of the cruise, head for Fathoms (*Magic*), Wavebands (*Wonder*), or D Lounge (*Dream* and *Fantasy*). Reservations for Remy (upscale dining for grown-ups on the *Dream* and *Fantasy*) may be made here, too. Plan to register children for youth activities in the terminal or soon after boarding.

The Disney Ships

The Disney ships are equipped to satisfy even the most savvy of cruisers, with a mix of traditional seafaring diversions and Disney touches. The ships' classic exteriors recall the majesty of early ocean liners. Guests enter a three-story atrium, where traditional definitions of elegance expand to include bronze character statues and subtle cutout character silhouettes along a grand staircase. Recreation areas are designed to draw families and kid-free adults to different parts of the ship. By day, fun in the sun alternates with touring, lunch, indoor distractions, and perhaps even a little bingo action.

Evenings give way to sunset sail-away celebrations, themed dining experiences, and theatrical extravaganzas.

Decked Out

Here's the deck-by-deck rundown, from top to bottom (the first section of this deck-specific data refers to the *Magic* and *Wonder*; the section that follows covers the *Dream* and *Fantasy*). Note that as this book went to press, the *Wonder* was scheduled to undergo refurbishment, so some details may change. For updates, visit *www.disneycruise.com*.

MAGIC AND WONDER

DECK 11: On the *Magic* and *Wonder*, you'll find the teen club Vibe (though access to the club is on Deck 10). This venue is exclusively available to teenage guests (see page 340).

DECK 10: Known as the Wide World of Sports Deck (*Magic* and *Wonder*), we find it a perfect late-night place to watch the moon and stars. There's also a basketball court. And this is one of the best places to be during the sail-away party. Palo is here, too (see page 333). For adults only, this dining spot offers fine cuisine and panoramic views. The *Disney Wonder* has the Outlook Café, too.

DECK 9: Pampering, Disney style, can be enjoyed in the Senses Spa & Salon. At the soothing spa, guests may experience treatments in the villas, as well as a little Rest & Relaxation on the outdoor verandah. Fitness-minded folk can get a one-on-one fitness consultation. There's lots of exercise equipment, saunas, a steam room, and spa treatments. Personal training is offered too. (For details, see page 343.)

Deck 9 is where you'll find the ships' pools: Quiet Cove pool (for adults) and Goofy's family pool, plus a kids' slide and a splash zone for little ones. The *Magic* also has the AquaDunk water slide. This deck is also home to Cove Cafe (a coffee bar/lounge for guests over the age of 18),

Pinocchio's Pizzeria, Cabanas, Daisy's De-Lites, Pete's Boiler Bites, plus Frozone Treats, and Eye Scream (*Magic* only). This is also the location of Edge, the tween-only hangout for 11- to 14-year-olds. The interactive play area has a lab with child-friendly computers, video game consoles, arts and crafts tables, TVs, and comfy couches. Kids can also sing karaoke, take part in scavenger hunts, and more.

DECK 5: Kids have the run of more than half of this deck. It's one of the largest dedicated areas of children's space afloat, with comprehensive, interest-specific activities.

The Buena Vista Theatre is also located here on all ships. A full-screen cinema with Dolby Sound and 3-D technology, it offers films every day, featuring Disney classics and first-run releases. It hosts guest speakers on occasion.

DECK 4: Here you'll find the Walt Disney Theatre, Shutters (photo shop), and Animator's Palate (restaurant). D Lounge (family games and entertainment) can be found on both ships. This is also a lovely deck on which to enjoy a leisurely stroll, a jog, or a nice nap.

The Walt Disney Theatre is a grand venue that features one of the most sophisticated show settings at sea or on land. The formal theater boasts extraordinary lighting and technical facilities and showcases up to three distinct Broadway-style musical productions (each with a decidedly Disney touch) during each cruise.

Animator's Palate is a cheerful restaurant that offers creatively prepared cuisine in a room that features a colorful masterpiece of synchronized light and sound. Deck 4 on the *Magic* and *Wonder* is also the place where you can find Vista art gallery and a duo of shops selling Disney Cruise Line–themed clothing for the family, character merchandise, collectibles, specialty items, jewelry, and sundries (see page 341 for more details).

DECK 3: This is the place for dining and dancing on the *Magic* and *Wonder*; After Hours is an adult-oriented evening entertainment district that offers themed clubs. Both ships feature nightclubs that often have themed parties—and don't forget one of the ship's biggest attractions . . . bingo! There is a sports bar on the *Magic* (O'Gills Pub) and an English pub on the *Wonder*; Radar Trap (*Wonder*) and Sea Treasures (*Magic*) are shops; Keys (on the *Magic*) and a recently spiffed-up Cadillac Lounge (on the *Wonder*) are casual yet sophisticated places to relax and listen to live piano music; and Promenade Lounge is a place to enjoy a drink and hear music (on the *Magic* and *Wonder*). Also here are Tiana's Place (*Wonder*), a new restaurant inspired by Disney's animated feature *The Princess and the Frog*; Carioca's (*Magic*), an eatery inspired by Rio de Janeiro; and Lumière's, serving continental cuisine (on the *Magic*). Lumière's has a French flair and a beautiful mural of Disney's *Beauty and the Beast*. Its counterpart on the *Wonder*, Triton's, has an underwater-like setting of blues, greens, and purples. Guest Services is also on this deck and is open 24 hours a day. The Port Adventures (aka shore excursions) Desk is nearby.

DECK 2: All four Disney ships have staterooms on this deck.

DECK 1: This is where you will find the ship's Health Center. There are some staterooms located here, too.

DECKS 1, 2, 5, 6, 7, AND 8: Shipboard accommodations are spread over these decks.

DREAM AND *FANTASY*

DECK 14: The pinnacle of these sister ships, Deck 14 is the site of Outlook, a lounge that offers sweeping ocean vistas in addition to a variety of adult beverages.

DECK 13: Here you'll find Edge (tweens hangout), Currents (open-air bar), and Goofy's Sports Deck. This is also where concierge guests may enjoy a private sundeck. Deck 13 is the site of Satellite Falls—a waterfall-endowed wading pool for all guests age 18 and older.

DECK 12: This is the home of Meridian (lounge), Palo, and Remy (both are upscale eateries for grown-ups; Remy is très indulgent). Grown-up guests may sip spirits and soft drinks at Waves Bar (*Dream*). Deck 12 is also the site of AquaLab (*Fantasy*) and mini-golf and the AquaDuck water coaster (*Dream* and *Fantasy*).

DECK 11: On the *Dream* and *Fantasy*, this a destination deck for hungry guests: Cove Cafe (coffee bar for adults); Cabanas (buffet); and Flo's Cafe, a quick-service eatery composed of three stations (Luigi's Pizza, Tow Mater's Grill, and Fillmore's Favorites). Also on this deck are Eye Scream, Frozone Treats, and Vanellope's Sweets and Treats. Deck 11 is home to Mickey's Pool, Quiet Cove Pool, Donald's Pool, Nemo's Reef (splash zone), Arr-cade (*Fantasy*), and the Senses Spa & Salon (which extends to Deck 12).

DECKS 10, 9, 8, 7, 6, AND 2: These decks are devoted primarily to staterooms.

DECK 5: Deck 5 is kid-central—and they wouldn't want it any other way! In addition to the It's a Small World Nursery (see page 340), this is the site of the kids' programming areas known as Disney's Oceaneer Club and Lab (page 340), as well as Vibe (teen club). It's also the site of the Buena Vista (movie) Theatre's balcony. Bibbidi Bobbidi Boutique and Pirate's League (princess and pirate makeovers) are here, too. This deck houses the Port Adventures Desk.

DECK 4: Here you'll find the Buena Vista Theatre (movies), Vista Gallery (art), Shutters (photo shop), Connect@Sea Internet area, and Port Shopping Desk. The Walt Disney Theatre is a grand venue that showcases Broadway-style productions (with a distinct Disney flair) during each cruise. This venue extends to Deck 3.

Also found on Deck 4 of the *Dream* and *Fantasy*: D Lounge (family lounge and nightclub) and the ships' respective adults-only entertainment zones. Among the offerings in The District on the *Dream*: Skyline (lounge with panoramic views of various city skylines), District Lounge, Evolution (dance club), a sports bar called Pub 687, and Pink: Wine and Champagne Bar. On the *Fantasy*, expect to find these spots in the Europa entertainment district: La Piazza (a lounge that celebrates Italian plazas), Skyline (bar with panoramic views of famous cities), O'Gills Pub (sports bar), Ooh La La (an elegant champagne bar inspired by a French boudoir), and The Tube (a dance club with a London Underground motif).

DECK 3: This deck is home to the ship's lobby, the Walt Disney Theatre (stage shows), a bar, shops, and restaurants. Bon Voyage lounge is on the port side of the grand lobby. Beyond this imbibing zone are the ship's shops: Mickey's Mainsail, White Caps, and Sea Treasures.

Animator's Palate is a cheerful restaurant that offers creatively prepared cuisine in an impeccably designed dining room (for additional information on the restaurant, see page 331).

Other Deck 3 dining options include Royal Palace (*Dream*) and Royal Court (*Fantasy*).

Guest Services, which is open around the clock, is also located on Deck 3.

DECK 2: The Enchanted Garden eatery is located here.

DECKS 2 AND 5–12: Shipboard accommodations are spread over these decks.

DECK 1: The Health Center is on Deck 1.

Staterooms

The accommodations on Disney's ships range from standard inside rooms to suites with verandahs. All staterooms are a cut above the standard cruising cabin. On average, Disney's staterooms offer more space; most have a split bath (one room with a sink and toilet and another with a sink and a shower/tub), and the majority of them are outside rooms with ocean vistas—many with verandahs.

Staterooms are decorated in a nautical theme with natural woods and imported tiles. Universal amenities include a TV, Wave phones that allow you to call or text another member of your party while on board (two phones are included per stateroom—extras may be rented), telephone with voice mail (and ship-to-shore capability), an in-room safe, a room service menu (in the Directory of Services book), and lots of drawer space. All staterooms also come equipped with small refrigerators. After that, different types of accommodations—which are labeled by category—offer different amenities (verandahs are included in the square footage):

MAGIC AND *WONDER*

CATEGORIES 11A–11C: Standard inside staterooms. They have a queen bed, a single convertible sofa, a privacy divider, and a bath. Each room measures 184 square feet and sleeps up to 3 or 4.

CATEGORIES 10A–10C: Deluxe inside staterooms. These accommodations are similar to those found in categories 11A–11C but have 214 square feet of space and a split bath.

CATEGORIES 9A–9D: Deluxe ocean-view staterooms. These come with a queen bed, a single convertible sofa, a privacy divider, and split bath. Rooms on Deck 1 have two small windows, while those on Deck 2 and above feature one large window. Each room is 214 square feet. It sleeps up to 3 or 4 guests.

CATEGORIES 5A–5C, 6A, AND 7A: Deluxe ocean-view staterooms with verandahs. Each has one queen bed, a single convertible sofa, a privacy divider, split bath, and a verandah. These

Laundry Facilities

Laundry and dry cleaning services are available for a fee. Items will be picked up and delivered to your stateroom. If you'd rather go the self-service laundry route, you can do so in one of several Guest Laundry Rooms. Here you'll find washers, dryers, and ironing equipment. (Due to safety concerns, the laundry room is the only place in which iron use is permitted.) There is no fee to use an iron. Machines run about two bucks a load. Laundry detergent may be purchased here, too. At press time, a small box cost about $1. Simply wave your Key to the World card and charge it to your stateroom account.

Guest Services Desk

If you have any questions or concerns while on board, head to the Guest Services Desk (Deck 3, midship). This is also the spot to go to secure copies of the *Personal Navigator*, color-coded luggage tags (for use on the last day of the cruise), and postage stamps. Should you have any type of problem while on board, bring it to their attention. More often than not, they will resolve the issue in a matter of minutes.

rooms are 268 square feet (including the verandah) and sleep 3 or 4. Category 7A has an enclosed "Navigator's Verandah," a private balcony with nautical touches. Verandahs in 5A–5C are open, while those in 6A feature a solid whitewall verandah. Accommodations are otherwise the same.

CATEGORIES 4A, 4B, AND 4E: Deluxe ocean-view family staterooms with verandah. This room type has a queen bed, a single convertible sofa, and a bed that pulls down from the wall. There is a privacy divider, split bath, and open verandah (verandahs in the aft area are not open). It covers 304 square feet (including verandah) and sleeps up to 5.

CATEGORY 00T: Concierge one-bedroom suites with verandah. These have a queen bed, an area with a double convertible sofa, and a pull-down bed, two full baths, walk-in closet, wet bar, DVD player, open verandah (except for the aft-area staterooms), and concierge service. The suite is 614 square feet (including the verandah) and sleeps up to 4 or 5 guests.

CATEGORY 00S: Concierge two-bedroom suites with verandahs. These suites come with a queen bed, a sleeper-sofa, and a pull-down bed. There are 2.5 baths, a whirlpool tub, walk-in closets, a DVD player, unstocked wet bar, verandah, and concierge service. The suite measures 945 square feet (including the verandah) and sleeps up to 7 guests.

HOT TIP!

The midship elevators are the most crowded throughout the day—especially at mealtimes. Try to use the forward and aft elevators whenever possible.

CATEGORY 00R: Concierge royal suite with verandah. Comes with a queen bed in one bedroom, two twin beds in a second bedroom, and two ceiling pull-down upper berths. There are 2.5 baths, a whirlpool tub in the master bedroom, a living room, media library (with a pull-down bed), dining salon, pantry, unstocked wet bar, walk-in closets, DVD player, private verandah, and concierge service. The suite measures 1,029 square feet (including the verandah) and sleeps up to 7.

DREAM AND FANTASY

CATEGORIES 11A–11C: Standard inside staterooms. They have a queen, a single convertible sofa, upper berth pull-down bed (in some), and a bath with a tub and shower. Each room measures 169 square feet and sleeps up to 3 (category 11C) or 4 (categories 11A and 11B). They also have "magical portholes" (see Category 10A).

CATEGORY 10A: Deluxe inside staterooms. These accommodations are similar to those found in categories 11A–11C, but have 204 square feet and sleep up to 3 to 4 guests. They also have split baths, plus a bit of technological and artistic wizardry known as "magical portholes." These beauties have a real-time digital view that could be seen from a real porthole at any given time of day, and they feature visits from animated Disney characters. Most folks say they forget they are in an inside stateroom—the effect is that convincing.

CATEGORIES 9A–9D: Deluxe ocean-view staterooms. These come with a queen bed, a single convertible sofa, upper berth pull-down bed (in some), split bath, and porthole. Each room is 204 square feet and sleeps up to 3 or 4 guests.

CATEGORIES 8A–8D: Deluxe family ocean-view staterooms. These come with a queen bed, a single convertible sofa, wall pull-down bed (in most) or upper berth pull-down bed, and a split bath with a round tub (in most). Each stateroom features a large porthole window with built-in seating, measures 241 square feet, and sleeps up to 3 or 5. The 8A stateroom has two large porthole windows but does not have a split bath.

CATEGORIES 5A–5E, 6A–6B, 7A: Deluxe ocean-view staterooms with verandahs. Each has one queen bed, a single convertible sofa, pull-down bed if sleeping 4, a split bath, and a

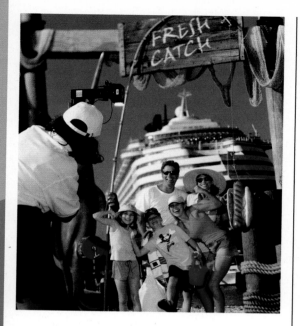

verandah. These rooms are 246 square feet (including the verandah) and sleep up to 3 or 4. The verandahs in 5A and the aft rooms of 6A and 6B feature whitewall verandahs. 7A rooms either have a smaller verandah or an obstructed view. 5E staterooms have larger verandahs and are all aft. Accommodations are otherwise the same.

CATEGORIES 4A–4E: Deluxe ocean-view family staterooms with verandah. This room type has a queen bed, a single convertible sofa, upper berth pull-down bed (in most), a split bath with a round tub (in most) and a shower, and a verandah. Each stateroom is 299 square feet (including verandah) and sleeps up to 5. The verandahs in 4E rooms are twice the size of the verandahs in other Category 4 staterooms.

CATEGORY 00V: Concierge Deluxe family ocean-view staterooms with verandah. This room type has a queen bed, a double convertible sofa, upper berth pull-down bed, full bath (with a vanity, sink, round tub, and shower), half bath (vanity, sink, and toilet), a verandah, and concierge service. Each stateroom covers 306 square feet (including verandah) and sleeps up to 5.

CATEGORY 00T: Concierge one-bedroom suites with verandah. The suites have a bedroom with a queen bed, a living area with a double convertible sofa and a single pull-down bed, a walk-in closet, two full bathrooms (with a whirlpool in the master bath), verandah, and concierge service. The suite is 622 square feet (including verandah) and sleeps up to 5.

CATEGORY 00R: Concierge royal suite with verandah. Comes with a queen bed in the master bedroom, plus a wall pull-down double bed and a wall pull-down single bed in the living room. There are 2 full bathrooms, including a master bath with double sinks, rain shower, and whirlpool tub (there is also a whirlpool tub on the verandah), plus living room, media library, open dining salon, pantry, wet bar, walk-in closet, verandah, and concierge service. The suite measures 1,781 square feet and sleeps up to 5.

The Personal Navigator

An in-house publication called the *Personal Navigator* will help you make the most of every day. Updated daily and delivered to all staterooms (also available via the DCL Navigator App), the publication is a comprehensive listing of a day's onboard activities, events, and entertainment.

The *Personal Navigator* is an indispensable tool. When you get your hands on it (the first one should be waiting for you in your stateroom), read it cover to cover. In addition to listing the lineup of activities scheduled for the rest of the day, it'll provide handy bits of information such as the suggested evening attire for that day. It changes from day to day, so be sure to take note. The *Personal Navigator* also gives the time and location of character appearances, any points of interest the ship may have scheduled, and a notification of any time zone changes, as well as any special offers or promotions for merchandise, events, or services aboard the ship.

Dining

A Disney cruise is not the place to count calories—although most special dietary needs can be accommodated upon request. There's no shortage of rations on these ships. If your tastes

Disney Cruise Line Gifts

Whether you'll be celebrating a special occasion or simply consider a cruise special occasion unto itself, you may want to have a gift delivered to your stateroom. Among the items that can be pre-ordered by calling 800-601-8455 or visiting disneycruise.com are floral arrangements, food and beverage packages, wine packages, cakes, and Disney Cruise Line merchandise. Specialty cakes must be ordered at least 7 days in advance. Other orders must be placed at least 72 business hours before sail date.

are simple (say, a hot dog poolside) or sublime (how does a juicy filet mignon, prepared at Palo, sound?), rest assured you'll never be hungry. Or understimulated, for that matter, as many of the restaurants are downright entertaining. And, thanks to a system called "rotational dining," you will get to experience three restaurants, all the while being made to feel like a VIP by your serving staff. That means you'll eat at a different one of the three main restaurants each evening, often with the same table guests, and enjoy the services of the same waitstaff. Your serving team gets to know you, as well as your likes and dislikes, very well. The system, which is unique to Disney Cruise Line, tends to get the thumbs-up from cruise veterans and newcomers alike. The only exceptions are Palo and Remy, the adults-only, reservations-necessary restaurants.

How do you know where to go on which night? Easy. A ticket with details will be placed in your stateroom. Check the *Personal Navigator* to note the style of attire for the evening.

TABLE SERVICE

ANIMATOR'S PALATE: The pièce de résistance—as far as Disney creativity goes—is without a doubt Animator's Palate, a place where diners not only have to decide what to eat, but also what to watch! Simple surprises abound at each stage of the evening meal. There is an Animator's Palate eatery on each of the four ships, but the dining experience varies depending on which ship you are sailing. The Animator's Palate experience on the *Magic* is a culinary journey—from black-and-white to full color: Upon entering the monochromatic room, note the soft background music and the black-and-white sketches along the wall. While you're doing so, drinks and appetizers will be served. If you ignore this distraction and keep your gaze fixed on the walls, you may notice a bit of color creeping into that sketch of Cinderella. By the

HOT TIP!

Fancy a cocktail with your meal? For an extra charge, guests may enjoy bar drinks at all table-service restaurants aboard Disney Cruise Line ships.

time the entrées make their entrance, the room is ablaze in living color.

If you are sailing on the *Dream* or *Fantasy*, your Animator's Palate experience will be a bit different. Like its siblings on the *Magic* and *Wonder*, the decor was inspired by the magic of Disney and Pixar animation. It's teeming with everything you'd expect to find in an animator's studio: character sketches, paintbrushes, colored pencils, computer workstations, and other tools of the animation trade. Scenes and characters from Disney films adorn the walls, and that totally awesome, animated turtle called Crush actually interacts with diners on the *Dream* and *Fantasy*.

The *Magic*, *Wonder*, and *Fantasy* also feature a show called Animation Magic. Hosted by Sorcerer Mickey, the experience encourages guests to express themselves with a drawing—and over the course of dinner, they'll witness their drawings being brought to life through the magic of Disney animation. The show is a hit with artists of all ages.

Dining rooms details vary, but the menu is the same on all four ships. It's featured starters such as smoked salmon tartare, sliced serrano ham with Manchego cheese and olive bread, and black truffle pasta purseittes. Entrées have included grilled herb crusted pork chop with wine sauce, lemon-thyme marinated all-natural chicken breast, black bean chipotle cakes, and ginger-teriyaki and dusted beef tenderloin. If they're available, we recommend starting with the butternut squash soup and ending with a slice of white chocolate fudge cheesecake or the crunchy walnut cake.

ENCHANTED GARDEN: This picturesque spot, which is located on the *Dream* and *Fantasy*, seems to be truly enchanted, as the immersive, outdoorsy environment transforms from day to night over the course of your dinner.

Breakfast, served buffet style, is offered on select days of each cruise. Ditto for lunch. The daily dinner is a four-course affair of seasonal selections. For an extra charge (plus gratuity), guests may enjoy bar drinks, bottled water, and specialty coffee. Soft drinks (coffee, soda, fruit juice, milk, and tea) carry no charge.

LUMIÈRE'S: Located on the *Magic* only, this elegant spot provides fine dining in a setting inspired by Disney's *Beauty and the Beast*. The sprawling dining room is elegant and softly lit, though a bit more raucous than its cosmopolitan contemporaries. Note that the later seating is usually a bit more sedate (fewer small kids).

Menu selections at dinner have included crispy roasted duck breast with braised napa cabbage, and aged Angus beef tenderloin. Vegetarians can opt for the mushroom-stuffed pasta in a vegetable broth. And vegetarians won't feel at all cheated by the grilled marinated tofu. For dessert, consider crème brûlée or a soufflé.

TRITON'S: Passengers aboard the *Wonder* may dine in the elegant Triton's, where the specialty of the house is seafood. The ocean theme is enhanced by subtly changing lighting with every course, the room getting more under-the-sea-like as the meal progresses. The menu has featured French onion soup; Conchiglie pasta with buttered lobster in a tomato, shrimp, and tarragon brandy sauce; oven-baked salmon royale crowned with king smoked salmon; and roasted rack of lamb. For dessert, there's chocolate mousse, Grand Marnier soufflé, sundaes, and more.

TIANA'S PLACE: A festive homage to New Orleans' dining and entertainment, Tiana's Place takes its inspiration from Disney's animated feature *The Princess and the Frog*. The *Wonder* exclusive transports guests to an era of southern charm, spirited jazz, and street party celebrations. The walls are lined with Princess Tiana's family

photos and culinary awards. Chefs cook up all of her favorite recipes, drawing inspiration from the flavors of the Louisiana bayou. The cuisine is complemented with live music. Performed on the main stage, rhythmic notes of jazz, swing, and blues set the tone for a lively, Big Easy–style supper club.

CARIOCA'S: A vibrant restaurant (on the *Magic*), Carioca's is a tribute to the city of Rio de Janeiro (the second-largest city in Brazil). The name of the eatery, however, honors José Carioca—one of the stars of *The Three Caballeros*. The menu has featured items with Latin-infused flavors such as adobo-rubbed rack of lamb; lobster *croquetas* with banana and lentil salad; and lobster, shrimp, and salmon kebabs with black bean rice and *pico de gallo*. Finish the meal with cream cheese flan with caramel bananas.

ROYAL PALACE/ROYAL COURT: This regal restaurant (Royal Palace on the *Dream* and Royal Court on the *Fantasy*) got its inspiration from classic Disney animated features such as *Sleeping Beauty*, *Cinderella*, and *Beauty and the Beast*. You will find the eatery on Deck 3, midship.

French-inspired, continental cuisine is offered for breakfast, lunch, and dinner. Breakfast is offered on select mornings of each cruise, as is a full-service lunch. A four-course dinner takes place nightly. One of the favorite appetizers at dinner is the *escargots gratinés* (herb-marinated snails). Grilled beef tenderloin and shrimp is a featured entrée. Vegetarian selections such as mushroom-filled pasta are served, too. And do save room for the "sweet temptations" dessert offering: a trio of raspberry mousse slice, mango cheesecake, and a Tahitian vanilla crème brûlée. Yum!

Seating Times and Situations: There are normally two seating sessions for dinner; however, the times vary depending on what itinerary the ship is sailing at the time. The most common times are 5:45 P.M. and 8:15 P.M. If you have a preference, tell your travel agent or reservationist the moment you book your cruise. Requests for any seating cannot be guaranteed. If you get closed out of a preferred seating time, check with Guest Services after boarding. Seating times may open up after boarding. Most seating at table-service restaurants is communal, except at Palo and Remy. If you are traveling as a family with children, expect to be seated with similar travelers. Adults without children will be seated together if possible.

Parents of young children, listen up! There is a dining convenience designed especially for you. Dine and Play lets parents with late dinner seatings check their kids (ages 3 to 11) into the Youth Activities programs starting about 45 minutes after dinner seating has begun. In other words, after the youngsters have downed kid-friendly fare, they can go play while you finish your meal in a leisurely manner. Neat, huh? If you wish to partake of the complimentary Dine and Play service, simply inform your servers upon arrival in the dining room. They will make sure kids get their meals quickly, while serving the grown-ups at a more relaxed pace.

Youth activities counselors arrive in the restaurant 45 minutes after the seating begins, and assign children to groups right there in the dining room. No need for parents to escort Junior to Deck 5. (Though they will eventually have to pick the kids up!) Remember, this service is for guests with late dinner seatings only.

PALO: For adults only (age 18 and up), Palo is an ideal spot for special celebrations or just a quiet, romantic evening. Offering brunch and dinner, Palo is worth the per-person surcharge (at press time, prices were $30 for brunch and dinner) to indulge in a five-star dining experience that includes an ocean view.

True to its roots (*palo* means "pole" in Italian), the restaurant has echoes of Venice, Italy—and the menu reflects some of the best

HOT TIP!

Palo and Remy reservations will not appear on your *Personal Navigator*. (It's not that personal.) Make sure you don't miss it—there's a per-person charge for all meals. Call 800-910-3659 for specifics.

continental fare you'll find on either side of the Atlantic. Dinner appetizers include *fritto di calamari e gamba* and soft potato gnocchi tossed in a piennolo tomato sauce. The entrée menu tempts with selections such as roasted rack of lamb with carrots, caponata, and olive potatoes and *parpadelle con aragosta*.

A warning: Save room for dessert or you will never forgive yourself. The chocolate soufflé (with hot chocolate and vanilla sauces) is beyond amazing. (The sweet soufflé must be ordered in advance.) Of coure, just about every one of Palo's homemade treats yield raves, too.

Brunch at Palo is a special event. (It's only offered on select cruises, making it even more special!) The buffet is so vast that it requires a guided tour. Expect fruit, salads, seafood, heavenly flatbreads, pastries, made-to-order omelets, fish, and chicken entrées, and more.

Palo is for diners ages 18 years and older. Make reservations at *www.disneycruise.com*; at Fathoms (*Magic*), WaveBands (*Wonder*), Royal Court (*Fantasy*), or Royal Palace (*Dream*); or at the restaurant itself starting at approximately 1 P.M. on the first day of the cruise.

REMY: For adults (guests age 18 and older) on the *Dream* and *Fantasy*, Remy is a ritzy, palate-pleasing delight. Considered the most upscale dining experience available on the ship, Remy serves fine French-inspired cuisine for dinner (on all cruises) and brunch (select cruises). The luxurious dining room has Art Nouveau touches and a rich color scheme.

A Tender Subject

Some ports require a process called "tendering." This means, rather than pulling right up to a dock, the ship will pull close to port and drop anchor. Ferries take guests back and forth to shore. It's an efficient system, but it could knock you for a loop if you're not expecting it—especially if you've got an early excursion booked. In this case, you may have to leave a bit earlier than you originally anticipated. That is accounted for in the "meet time" for all excursions.

Tables are set with Frette linens, Riedel glassware, Christofle silverware, and custom-created Bernardaud china.

Once the meal is booked and guests are aboard the ship, they can meet with a sommelier in Remy's wine room to pick out wines for their pending feast (for an additional price).

The evening meal begins with a champagne cocktail and continues with 8 to 9 small (and delectable) courses. There's nothing more thrilling than a table-side visit from the trolley of international cheeses—except, perhaps, for the wine decanting stations and after-dinner coffee service.

The private Chef's Table experience takes place in a special 8-seat dining room and features *Ratatouille*-inspired decor.

Oenophiles appreciate the lovely Wine Room, which accommodates up to 8 guests. Here, guests dine in a glass-walled room with marble flooring amid 900 bottles of wine.

Reservations are required to dine at Remy, and meals come with a $85-per-person surcharge for dinner (an additional $50 for the decadent Dessert Experience) and $55 per person for brunch. Reservations may be made online (75 days ahead for first-time cruisers, 90 for Silver Castaway Club members, 105 days ahead for Gold members, and 120 days in advance for concierge guests and Platinum members).

Like its neighbor, Palo, Remy also has a dress code. Dinner is more formal here than at Palo: jackets, dress pants, and dress shoes for men (ties are optional); dresses, suits, blouses, and dress pants for women. Leave the jeans, shorts, tank tops, yoga pants, sandals, flip-flops, and sneakers in your room. Jackets are optional for brunch.

What to Wear for Dinner: Generally speaking, "cruise casual" is the way to go in all spots except

for Palo and Remy: collared shirts, blouses, cotton pants, jeans (in good condition, without holes), and sundresses are generally acceptable for evenings in all other restaurants—swimsuits, T-shirts, hats, flip-flops, tennis shoes, and tank tops are not. On select nights, there will be a theme: pirate attire, semi-formal, etc. On such days, the desired style of dress will be noted in the *Personal Navigator*. (While parents are the best judges of what attire is appropriate for their children, most guests over the age of 13 are usually comfortable wearing attire that is similar to what is recommended for all passengers.) Note that Palo and Remy, grown-ups-only destinations, are considered more formal and guests are asked to dress accordingly: long pants and shirt are required for men (jacket optional at Palo, required for Remy), and a dress or pants and shirt combo for women. No ripped jeans, shorts, flip-flops, or sneakers, please. Likewise, the indoor area of Meridian Bar, located between Palo and Remy, has the same formal dress code as Palo. However, the outdoor patio of Meridian Bar has a slightly more relaxed vibe (think business casual).

Wine and Dine: Most of the table-service restaurants offer many vintages by the glass or by the bottle. If you order a bottle and fail to finish it by meal's end, ask your server to store it for you. (You'll get it with the next evening's meal.) Disney offers two wine packages (premium and classic selections).

Special Dietary Needs: Certain special dietary needs may be met aboard Disney cruise ships. All requests should be made well in advance, preferably at the time of booking the cruise package. It's always a good idea to confirm the request prior to setting sail.

SELF-SERVE, FAST FOOD, AND SNACKS

VIBE: This teens-only spot—which can be found on all ships—serves up fruit smoothies and other soft drinks. There are lots of games and magazines, and some refreshments are free of charge. This area is hopping all day—and often past midnight. FYI: The teen spots on the *Magic* and *Wonder* used to be known as Aloft and The Stack, respectively.

BEVERAGE STATION: There is a self-serve station on every ship. On the *Magic* and *Wonder*, you'll find it on Deck 9, aft (port side). On the *Dream* and *Fantasy*, look for the beverage station on Deck 11, midship (there is a station on each side of the Mickey pool). Help yourself to water, juice, soda, iced tea, lemonade, coffee, hot chocolate, and hot tea. There is an ice machine, too. The station is open 24/7, though not all selections are available at all times. Soft drinks are free here and with meals, but not at bars or through room service.

CABANAS: Located on all four ships, this casual indoor eatery serves three meals a day. This spot recalls a breezy boardwalk along the coast, with a dash of Disney (e.g., colorful *Finding Nemo*–themed mosaics). Made-to-order breakfast and lunch selections are offered "on the board-walk" on most days (check your *Personal Navigator* for times and specifics). In other words, a variety of food stations proffer freshly prepared edibles. Dinner is a table-service affair. Cocktails may be ordered from the Clam Bar. Cabanas is located on Deck 11, aft on the *Dream* and *Fantasy*; Deck 9 aft on the *Magic*.

COVE CAFE: A cozy, adults-only lounge, Cove Cafe can be found on all ships. It features espresso and specialty coffees and a full bar (fees apply). Complimentary snacks are available. Books and magazines are on hand for on-site perusing, as is a TV (often showing a big game or the news). Board games may be borrowed, too. Guests must be at least 18 years old to visit Cove Cafe, located near the Quiet Cove pool.

DAISY'S DE-LITES: *Magic* and *Wonder*: Visit Daisy's for bagels, fresh fruit, salads, wraps, sandwiches, cookies, and more. Hours are usually from 11 A.M. till 7 P.M. daily.

EYE SCREAM AND FROZONE TREATS: *Magic*, *Dream*, and *Fantasy*: Guests craving a chilly treat can find satisfaction at adjoining snack stations. Eye Scream (with theming inspired by famous eyeball Mike Wazowski) doles out soft-serve ice cream. Mike's neighbor, a snack spot that pays tribute to Frozone from

The Incredibles, serves made-to-order mixed fruit smoothies and cocktails (for a fee).

FLO'S CAFE: *Dream* and *Fantasy*: Flo's Cafe, located on Deck 11 near the Donald pool, is actually a trio of side-by-side walk-up windows, all themed to characters from the animated feature *Cars*. Here you'll find Luigi's Pizza, Tow Mater's Grill, and Fillmore's Favorites. Menu options at these filling stations include pizza (often featuring a special pizza of the day), chicken tenders, salads, sandwich wraps, fruit, burgers, and more. Luigi's tends to stay open the latest of the three.

PETE'S BOILER BITES: *Magic* and *Wonder*: Looking for a tasty treat without the formality of a table-service eatery? Or perhaps a nibble between meals? Head here! Pete proudly serves chicken tenders, burgers, hot dogs, veggie burgers, and tacos.

PINOCCHIO'S PIZZERIA: *Magic* and *Wonder*: This counter-service spot serves spirits and soft drinks (for a fee), and cheese and pepperoni pizzas (no charge for food). There is often a special pizza of the day. Be sure to ask.

ROOM SERVICE

Stateroom dining service delivers 24 hours a day (except on the final night of a cruise, when service stops promptly at 1:30 A.M.)—handy if you're traveling with kids or if you have a snack craving in between meals. Most menu items are included with your cruise package. At press time, selections included soups, salads, sandwiches, burgers, pizza, cookies, and selections for kids. There is a charge for some beverages and snack selections (such as candy, popcorn, wine, beer, soda, and bottled water). Note that a gratuity is not always included.

SPECIAL DINING EXPERIENCES

PIRATES IN THE CARIBBEAN PARTY: If there's one thing Disney really knows how to do right, it's throw a party. On one night during most cruises, guests enjoy a buccaneering soirée. If you own any pirate attire or regalia, wear it to the big event. (You may purchase some from a ship shop, too.) It takes place on the upper decks, where pirate villains set their sights on taking over the ship. An epic battle ensues as the good guys take on the villains. The greatest spectacle of all is the show's grand finale—fireworks (offered on most itineraries). A feast fit for a pirate king is served post pyrotechnics (usually served in Cabanas).

CHARACTER BREAKFAST: An up-close-and-personal morning starring favorite characters is a very Disney way to start the day. (It's offered on select itineraries, usually the 7-night-or-longer cruises.) Everyone may attend one character-hosted breakfast per cruise. Check your Dining Ticket for assigned morning and location (characters vary). Disney characters have even been known to dance with guests. Don't forget to bring your camera.

Many of the character breakfast selections remain staples—eggs, bacon, cereal, fruit, yogurt, and French toast, for example.

CAPTAIN'S GALA DINNER: Even on this, one of the planet's most casual of cruises, there is a chance to don your finery and join the sparkle and glitter of this black-tie (optional) affair. If you'd rather not get completely decked out, go with a business casual look (but not too casual). The French-continental menu is offered in each of the main dining rooms on all ships. A menu favorite is the baked lobster tail served in the shell with lemon pesto mash with asparagus. The Captain's Gala is offered on most cruises of 7 nights or longer.

FAREWELL DINNER: Presented on the final evening of cruises 7 nights or longer, this evening meal is a chance to enjoy favorite dishes, celebrate new friends, and perhaps start planning (or at least dreaming about) your next cruise.

Bars and Lounges

From elegant spots with live piano music to rousing sports bars, Disney ships have a bounty of bars and lounges in which to wet your whistle—many of them located in the ships' grown-ups only entertainment zones (Europa on the *Fantasy*, The District on the *Dream*, and After Hours on the *Magic* and *Wonder*).

BON VOYAGE: A casual lounge located on Deck 3, midship (*Dream* and *Fantasy*). Beverages are available all day.

CADILLAC LOUNGE: Unique to the After Hours zone aboard the *Disney Wonder*), this sophisticated spot celebrates classic cars with soothing music, wine, martinis, and other drinks.

COVE CAFE: This cozy adults-only lounge can be found aboard all of the ships in Disney's fleet. It offers specialty coffees and a full bar (charges apply). Complimentary snacks are available, too. Magazines and books are on hand for on-site perusing, as is a TV. Board games may be borrowed for on-site use.

CURRENTS: A breezy spot with stellar ocean views, Currents is on Deck 13, forward (*Dream* and *Fantasy*).

DISTRICT LOUNGE: This intimate bar is located in the *Dream*'s grown-ups-only District entertainment zone.

DANCE CLUB: A butterfly-themed hot spot, Evolution celebrates all styles of music on the *Dream*. On the *Fantasy*, it's The Tube, a dance spot that pays tribute to the city of London. The venues feature various activities and dance parties. (Guests must be at least 18 years old to come here at night, 21 to imbibe.)

HOT TIP!

If your mobile phone, laptop, or tablet is equipped for wireless Internet access, bring it along. Most areas on the Disney ships offer Wi-Fi service known as Connect@Sea. Rates may vary, but expect to pay 25 cents per megabyte (mb) of data or buy a package of 100 mb for $19, 300 minutes for $39, or 1,000 mb for $89. Prices are per stateroom, and packages may be shared. For additional information, visit *www.disneycruise.com*. Prices are subject to change.

FATHOMS: This After Hours joint (*Magic*) fancies itself a celebration of the sea. It uses special effects, lighting, and sound to create different festive atmospheres. There's a dance floor, plus tables and bar seating. Themed parties are thrown on select evenings.

KEYS: The *Magic*'s version of an intimate piano bar, this lounge serves cocktails and wines by the glass. Keys provides a refined retreat.

LA PIAZZA: The *Fantasy*'s celebration of Italian cities features a festive carousel bar. Venetian masks and glasswork add to the fun.

MERIDIAN BAR: Found on the *Dream* and *Fantasy*, Meridian is located on Deck 12, aft, and has indoor and outdoor seating. The dress code for the indoor area: Dress pants and shirt are required for men and a dress or dress pants for women. On the outside deck, the dress code is cruise casual (jeans and shorts are okay, swimsuits and tank tops are not).

OOH LA LA: A *Fantasy* champagne bar, this space was inspired by a French boudoir.

OUTLOOK CAFÉ: Overlooking the Quiet Cove Pool on the *Wonder* (above Cove Cafe), this lounge serves cocktails and coffee drinks.

PINK: WINE AND CHAMPAGNE BAR: An elegant nightspot designed to look like the inside of a champagne bottle, this lounge is in the *Dream*'s District entertainment zone. Pink definitely gets an A+ for atmosphere.

PROMENADE LOUNGE: This lounge serves cocktails and soft drinks on the *Magic* and *Wonder*. At night, it offers live music.

SIGNALS: On Deck 9 of the *Magic* and *Wonder*, this poolside spot serves cocktails and soft drinks.

SKYLINE: The *Dream*'s District area and the *Fantasy*'s Europa boast Skyline, a cosmopolitan bar with majestic views of famous cities from around the world. The cityscapes change over the course of the evening.

SPORTS BAR: A sports fan's dream, this lounge has a big screen (often featuring a big game), plus suds, wings, hot dogs, or other munchies. It's Pub 687 on the *Dream*, and O'Gills Pub on the *Fantasy* and *Magic*.

THE TUBE: Housed in the *Fantasy*'s Europa district, The Tube is a metropolitan dance club themed to the London Underground (aka the tube).

VISTA CAFÉ: *Dream* and *Fantasy* guests in need of a java jolt can head to this cheery destination on Deck 4, midship. Snacks and cocktails are served, too.

WAVES: An open-air bar on the *Fantasy* and *Dream*, this spot serves beverages all day.

WAVEBANDS: Vintage radios and album covers line the walls and set the stage for a lively dance club. A deejay keeps the place grooving till the wee hours. All manner of drinks are available at this After Hours venue on the *Wonder*.

Entertainment

For some, a deck chair, a good book, and a steady stream of sunshine are all the entertainment required. Others may delight in an evening of dancing or a bingo-filled afternoon. And some are satisfied with nothing short of a Broadway-style stage show. Fortunately, Disney Cruise Line has it all, plus guest lecturers, tours, and more. Note that all shows are not presented every day or on every cruise. The lineup is tweaked from time to time, so details may differ during your cruise.

THE GOLDEN MICKEYS—A TIMELESS TRIBUTE: A dynamic production that pays tribute to the musical legacy of Walt Disney Studios. It's got all the glitz and glamour of a Hollywood celebration, paying homage to the comedy, romance, and heroes (plus a few key villains) of classic Disney animated films. This theatrical event is presented on the *Wonder* and *Dream*. It's a classic crowd-pleaser worthy of a Golden Mickey.

WELCOME ABOARD SHOW: This sweet presentation is a nice way to "meet" your ship's crew. The captain, cruise director, and many of their comrades introduce themselves and welcome guests aboard. Musical numbers and vaudeville-like variety acts round out the bill. This show is presented on most cruises of 7 nights and longer.

FROZEN MUSICAL STAGE SHOW: At press time, a new *Frozen*-inspired musical show was in the works for Disney Cruise Line. The production will transport guests to the icy, beautiful land of Arendelle and feature favorite characters from the beloved film: Anna, Elsa, Kristoff, Olaf, and Hans (okay, Hans may not be a favorite, but he *was* in the film!). For updates, visit *www.disneycruise.com*.

DISNEY'S ALADDIN—A MUSICAL SPEC-TACULAR: A comic musical, this production showcases a variety of classic (and new) tunes and characters from Disney's animated feature *Aladdin* and regales guests with theatrical treats. The action often spills out into the audience, such as when a magic carpet soars overhead or the evil Jafar turns into a gigantic snake (warn timid tots). Rest assured, it all ends happily! Disney's Aladdin—A Musical Spectacular is a *Fantasy* exclusive.

DISNEY'S BELIEVE: Who doesn't believe in the power of pixie dust? A little girl named Sophia certainly does. But her serious-minded father, Mr. Greenaway, is a much tougher sell. Follow his journey from skeptic to believer in this rousing musical stage show. In addition to classic Disney tunes, this crowd-pleaser features the lovely original song "What Makes a Garden Grow." It is presented on the *Dream* and *Fantasy*.

DISNEY DREAMS—AN ENCHANTED CLASSIC: This bedtime story features a galaxy of familiar Disney stars, including the Blue Fairy, Peter Pan, Belle, Beast, Aladdin, Cinderella, and Ariel. Together and through the power of song and dance, the characters teach a skeptical girl about the power of dreams. It takes place on the *Magic* and *Wonder*.

TWICE CHARMED—AN ORIGINAL TWIST ON THE CINDERELLA STORY: A Broadway-style extravaganza (presented on the *Magic* only), this musical production begins with the wedding of Cinderella and Prince Charming. Things take a sudden turn when the wicked Fairy Godfather makes his presence known and, after granting a wish to one evil stepmother, sends the family back in time, where—*gasp*—the glass slipper gets broken! Does this turn of events destroy Cinderella's chances of living happily ever after? You'll just have to catch the show to find out.

DISNEY'S WISHES: As high school kids face graduation day, they discover that the secret to becoming a grown-up is to stay connected to your inner child. And what's a wonderful way to do that? By making a wish and spending a fun-filled, musical—and magical—day at Disneyland. It's a *Fantasy* exclusive.

REMEMBER THE MAGIC—FAREWELL SHOW: This show wraps up the trip as performers celebrate a week of shipboard activities and island-hopping. (This production is presented on the *Magic* and *Wonder* on select cruises.) The *Fantasy* and *Dream* have a good-bye show known as An Unforgettable Journey.

TANGLED—THE MUSICAL: A Disney Cruise Line original, this show follows the story of Rapunzel, from her escape from the tower and the clutches of the evil Gothel to her unlikely friendship with the crown-stealing bandit, Flynn Rider. With a mix of familiar and new songs (all written by Alan Menken and Glen Slater), Tangled is fun for all ages. This one-hour show is presented exclusively on the *Magic*.

DECK PARTIES

When it comes to on-deck celebrations, the area by the family pool is party central. Starting with a Sailing Away Celebration and continuing with daily dancefests with Disney characters, live bands, and fireworks (except on Alaska cruises), it seems like there is always a reason to party. *Frozen*-themed deck parties are offered on select sailings on the *Magic* and *Wonder*.

FAMILY ENTERTAINMENT

D LOUNGE: This family-friendly lounge and nightclub is on all ships (Deck 4, midship). Head here for dance parties, character greetings, games, and more. Mickey Mania lets you put your knowledge of Disney trivia to the test, while Karaoke Night encourages families to take the stage and sing together. Finally, the Family Dance Party gives everyone a chance to kick up their heels (or sneakers) and enjoy a party for guests of all ages. Keep in mind that the entertainment lineup, though always dynamic, is subject to change from time to time.

CHARACTER BREAKFAST: On most cruises that are 7 nights or longer, a bountiful breakfast is hosted by familiar Disney friends. Tickets (no cost) are required.

FOR GROWN-UPS ONLY

The 18-and-over set on the *Magic* and *Wonder* can attend demonstrations (e.g., Disney's Art of Entertaining), lectures and conversations with guest speakers, tours, and specially tailored nighttime events (such as Match Your Mate, a game show in which you and your mate will find out how much you know about each other), as well as theme nights, cabaret shows, and much more.

On the *Dream* and *Fantasy*, adults have the chance to participate in interactive cooking demonstrations as part of the Anyone Can Cook! series; learn the secrets of Disney animation in the Illusion of Life series; and attend a presentation about the making of the ship.

JUST FOR KIDS

The wildly popular kids' programs and activities tend to elicit raves from participants and parents alike. For starters, adults who leave their kids at supervised facilities can be assured that the watchword here is safety. There are plenty of counselors on hand, and the secured programming ensures that they know where every child is at any given time. Kids are checked in with Youth Activities when entering and signed out when exiting with an authorized guardian. Upon check-in, each child is given an electronic wristband, aka Oceaneer band. (It assists with the check-in and check-out process and adds an additional level of security to youth venues.) Records of a child's allergies or other particular needs are entered into their file.

Parents have Wave Phones (which can be found in all staterooms) and can be contacted immediately if their child has a problem or just wants to see them. (Though it has been our experience that youngsters rarely, if ever, want to leave the kids' programming areas.)

Cleanliness is a priority, too. In fact, kids entering the Oceaneer Club and Lab are promptly asked to wash their hands. Play areas are cleaned three times a day, with a deep-down cleansing done at the end of each day.

Kids' programs are concentrated on Deck 5, and kids registered into secured programming always remain in either the Lab or Club. The specially tailored programming is open to kids age 3 and older who are completely potty-trained, able to interact comfortably within the counselor-to-child ratio groups, and able to mix well with peers. (Non-potty-trained tykes may go to a colorfully-themed nursery. Fees apply.)

Kids between ages 3 and 12 can choose to play in the Oceaneer Club or Oceaneer Lab based on whatever interests them. Siblings and friends between the ages of 3 and 12 can play together regardless, as kids are not segregated by age group. And don't worry about little ones ever being dominated by bigger kids—participants are closely monitored at all times.

Kids who exhibit any symptoms of illness—even if it's just a runny nose—will not be allowed to participate. If a child becomes disruptive, he or she will be asked to play with a parent or guardian during open house hours.

Except for the nursery, there is no fee for youth activities on any Disney ship. The following descriptions of the youth activities were accurate at press time, but specifics are subject to change from time to time.

OCEANEER CLUB: A wonderfully detailed adventure zone, this club has several distinctly themed areas on every ship. In addition to computer games, costumes, and other games, there are many organized activities. It's open to all kids age 3 to 12 (potty-trained) on all ships (provided the kids show no sign of illness).

At the Oceaneer Club, kids find a combination of free play and structured activities featuring interactive, playful experiences with some of their favorite Disney characters. These may include reading a story with Belle, learning how to be a pirate from Captain Hook, and even playing games with Mickey Mouse. Lunch and dinner are served (at no extra charge). It's usually open daily from 9 A.M. till midnight.

OCEANEER LAB: The Oceaneer Lab is open to (potty-trained) kids ages 3 to 12 on all Disney ships. It is located on Deck 5, midship. The entertaining space is filled with wacky inventions and opportunities for exploration. There are games, books, toys, child-friendly computers, video games, drawing materials, and more. As with the Oceaneer Club, there are also several imaginative organized activities. It is usually open from 9 A.M. till midnight.

Programs here allow young guests to be very hands-on while learning the skills of Disney animators,

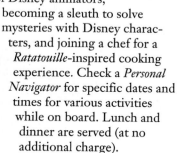

becoming a sleuth to solve mysteries with Disney characters, and joining a chef for a *Ratatouille*-inspired cooking experience. Check a *Personal Navigator* for specific dates and times for various activities while on board. Lunch and dinner are served (at no additional charge).

Reminder: Kids ages 8 to 12 may check themselves in and out of the Oceaneer Lab and Oceaneer Club with their parents' permission.

EDGE: There are video games, arts and crafts, and movie screenings in this tween hangout. There are evening activities such as scavenger hunts and karaoke, too. Edge can be found on Deck 9 on the *Magic* and *Wonder*.

Also a tween space on the *Dream* and *Fantasy*, Edge is located on Deck 13 inside the forward funnel. Its high-tech features include an

> **HOT TIP!**
> Children's menus are available in all shipboard restaurants (with the obvious exceptions of Palo and Remy). Buffets all stock kid-friendly vittles such as mac and cheese and chicken tenders. Note that the "Dine and Play" service is offered during the later dinner seating. It whisks young'uns off to youth activity areas after about 45 minutes.

illuminated dance floor, a video wall, and game-playing.

IT'S A SMALL WORLD NURSERY: Open to kids ages 6 months through 3 years, these colorful spaces are the ships' babysitting centers. For an hourly fee, the nursery offers activities and a quiet area, complete with cribs.

Food is available at the nursery, but if parents provide prepared bottles or jarred food that is clearly labeled with a child's name, staffers will happily feed their hungry tyke. Space is limited and gets booked early. In fact, advance reservations are accepted via *www.disneycruise.com* and on embarkation day on a first-come, first-served basis. Due to the high demand, multiple requests might not be honored —so don't count on securing several sessions, though it can't hurt to try. The fee for the baby-sitting service is $9 per hour for the first child, $8 per each additional child with a one-hour minimum (only siblings net the discount). Nurseries are generally open from 9 A.M. until 11 P.M. Stateroom babysitting is not available on any Disney ship.

TEENS ONLY

Teenaged guests may enjoy their own special hangout and activities while aboard all Disney ships. Vibe is their exclusive place to hang out. (If you are old enough to vote, KEEP OUT!) It's got popular music, games, dance parties, big-screen TVs, and more. Other programs may include karaoke, organized sports activities, a pool party (*Dream* and *Fantasy*), and a whole lot more. Specialty soft drinks, including smoothies, are available for a fee. Vibe is generally open from 11 A.M. till 2 A.M.

FUN AND GAMES

ARCADE: Exclusive to the *Fantasy*, the pirate-themed—and appropriately named—Arr-cade is on Deck 11. You will have to purchase credits to play in the ships' arcade.

BINGO: Perhaps it's something in the ocean air, but nothing brings out the bingo fanatic in you like a few days at sea. The closest thing to gambling that you'll find on a Disney vessel, the bingo sessions are extremely popular. You have to be at least 18 to play, but kids can watch over a grown-up's shoulder and cheer them on.

GAMES: Ping-pong, foosball, shuffleboard, basketball . . . they're all here. Equipment can usually be found by the tables or courts. (Don't monopolize it—it's for everyone to share.) Kooky competitions are sometimes held poolside. The *Dream* and *Fantasy* offer mini-golf and sports simulators (there is a charge to use the simulators). See a *Personal Navigator* for details.

MOVIES: The Buena Vista Theatre shows new film releases—some in 3-D (courtesy of Disney's patented technology). This is the perfect place to head when the weather is less than ideal. Get there early, as the seats fill up quickly.

If you prefer your flicks alfresco, make a beeline for the Goofy or Donald pool. A jumbo screen (on the forward funnel and known as Funnel Vision) broadcasts Disney features, sports, and more throughout the cruise.

Shopping

While on board Disney's cruise ships, you can enjoy tax-free (on all items) and duty-free (select items) shopping.

The shops have limited hours due to U.S. Customs regulations and can't operate during any time when the ship is in port. Use your stateroom key (Key to the World) to buy items in the ship's shops and on Castaway Cay. Purchases will be charged to your stateroom account. (Note that the Castaway Cay post office does not honor Key to the World cards. It accepts cash only.) Shops in all other ports of call generally accept major credit cards, and many accept cash.

ONBOARD SHOPS

PRELUDES (All ships): There is a snack bar/concessions window on either side of the Walt Disney Theatre. Among the items for sale are cookies, candies, nuts, and drinks (spirits and soft drinks are served for a fee, too).

MICKEY'S MAINSAIL (all ships): Mickey stocks Disney and Disney Cruise Line merchandise, including souvenirs, clothing, beach towels, swimwear, mugs, costumes, postcards, snack items, and plush toys. The shop is located on Deck 3 (*Dream* and *Fantasy*) and Deck 4, forward (*Magic* and *Wonder*).

QUACKS (*Magic*, *Dream*, and *Fantasy*): Quacks sells swimming essentials (including the all-important sunscreen), plus merchandise celebrating the ship's waterslide, the AquaDunk. It's on Deck 9, midship, on the *Magic* and 11 on the *Dream* and *Fantasy*.

SEA TREASURES (all ships): Located on Deck 3, forward, the treasures here may include jewelry, loose gemstones, and limited-edition Disney collectibles. There's a selection of clothing, including shirts, sweatshirts, purses, fragrances, hats, jackets, and other Disney Cruise Line logo items. The store also stocks batteries, postcards, disposable cameras, books, magazines, sun-care products, and a limited selection of sundries (including aspirin and Dramamine). Be sure to check out the nightly promotions.

WHITE CAPS (all ships): This is the place for duty-free items such as perfume, watches, jewelry, liquor, and tobacco products. Note that any liquor purchased here may not be consumed while on board. It will be delivered to your room on the last evening of your cruise.

WHOZITS & WHATZITS (*Dream* and *Fantasy*): A tiny shop located on Deck 11, midship, near the Donald pool, Whozits & Whatzits sells deckwear, magazines, sunscreen, towels, and other poolside necessities.

SPORTS AND RECREATION

FITNESS CENTER: The fitness center is located within the Senses Spa & Salon on all ships. There is no fee to use the equipment, which includes treadmills, bikes, stair-climbing machines, free weights, and more. (Some of the machines sport TVs—bring headphones or borrow a pair at the front desk.) Fitness consultations are offered. The fitness center is generally open from about 6 A.M. to 10 P.M., while spa hours run from 8 A.M. to 8 P.M.

WIDE WORLD OF SPORTS DECK (*Magic* and *Wonder*): Deck 10 is home to the Wide World of Sports deck. Though open to everyone, it's a huge kid and teen magnet. The basketball hoops are hopping day and night. Basketballs and other equipment are on-site (no charge). This deck is also popular with casual strollers, though jogging on the *Magic* and *Wonder* is relegated to Deck 4 (where one lap is about one-third of a mile). Deck 4 is where you'll find the shuffleboard court, too.

GOOFY'S SPORTS DECK (*Dream* and *Fantasy*): Located on Deck 13, aft, the always bustling Goofy's Sports Deck is an all-ages, open-air activity center. The basketball court can easily be converted to a volleyball court or a small soccer arena. The zone also has a sports simulator (soccer, golf, tennis, and basketball; fees apply) and an honest-to-goodness (or is that Goof-ness?) mini golf course.

SWIMMING (*Magic* and *Wonder*): There are three guest swimming areas on board, all located on Deck 9: Dory's Splash Zone (*Wonder*), Nephews' Splash Zone (*Magic*), Twist 'n' Spout water slide (*Magic* and *Wonder*), and AquaLab (*Magic* and *Wonder*) are located toward the back, or aft; Goofy's Family Pool is midship; and the Quiet Cove Adult Pool is on Deck 9, forward. Though the names are self-explanatory, we'll state the obvious: the splash zones are for the wee young'uns and their friends. The Quiet Cove pool

is earmarked for splashers age 18 and up. Don't let the name fool you; Quiet Cove may be for grown-ups, but it isn't always the picture of serenity. Organized games engage giddy adults from time to time. Finally, Goofy's pool is for everyone, but kids under age 10 must be accompanied by an adult, and swimmers must be potty-trained. Goofy's pool and Quiet Cove have two whirlpools each.

SWIMMING (*Dream* and *Fantasy*): Deck 11 is pool central on these ships. Donald's Pool is the family pool and can be found midship. Mickey's Pool is strictly for kids and their guardians, and the Quiet Cove pool is a grown-ups-only splash zone. Nemo's Reef is a spray zone for the toddler set (swim diapers are required at all times).

AQUADUCK (*Dream* and *Fantasy*): Tired of all that poolside relaxation? Head for Deck 12 and the ship's ultimate adrenaline inducer: the AquaDuck. This 765-foot-long "water coaster" propels guests through a clear tube on a journey that includes a trip over the ocean and through the forward funnel, and a 4-deck drop. Check a *Personal Navigator* for operating hours. Guests must be at least 42 inches tall to ride the AquaDuck and 54 inches tall to ride alone. Kids under age 7 must be accompanied by someone 14 years of age or older. It's a hoot—and not as scary as it looks.

AQUADUNK (*Magic*): Step into the 3-story, translucent tube, the trapdoor opens and . . . *kerplunk!* The ride is quick and splashy. Guests must be at least 48 inches tall to take the plunge.

AQUALAB (*Magic, Wonder,* and *Fantasy*): Found on Deck 12, aft, on the *Fantasy* and Deck 9, aft, on the *Magic* and *Wonder*, Aqualab is a family splash zone. This interactive playground is open to guests age 3 and up. Families may frolic among pop jets, bubblers, and geysers, and slip along the "Twist 'n' Spout" waterslide. (Guests must be at least 38 inches tall to ride.)

DORY'S SPLASH ZONE (*Wonder*): Deck 9, aft, is home to the *Wonder*'s new watery fun zone. It's a great spot for tots to cool off.

NEPHEWS' SPLASH ZONE (*Magic*): Deck 9, aft, is home to the *Magic*'s "splashtacular" zone. Designed for guests age 3 and under, the 500-square-foot play area features geysers and bubble jets and a soft deck surface.

SATELLITE FALLS (*Dream* and *Fantasy*): A watery haven for grown-ups, this Deck 13, forward, spot has a circular splash pool with benches and a cascading curtain of water.

SPA & SALON (All ships): Pampering, Disney style, can be enjoyed at the ships' ocean-view spas and salons—known as Senses on all Disney ships. Here, fitness-minded folk can work with a trainer, take a class, or work out solo. As for the pampering, well, that can come by way of any number of treatments.

Book appointments ahead of time by visiting *www.disneycruise.com*, or go to the spa when you board the ship. The spa and salon are open to guests age 18 and older.

The spa is open from 8 A.M. to 8 P.M. every day, except on days when the ship is docked at its home port. Prices are posted in the spa. If you miss a reserved treatment, your stateroom will be charged. Note that Cabana Massages (located at Serenity Bay on Castaway Cay) and the Vista Spa Villas (indoor-outdoor treatment villas for one or two at Vista Spa) may be booked here, too.

Spa amenities include sandals and robes for use during treatments, steam room, sauna, locker room, showers, and more. A selection of beauty products is available for purchase.

CHILL SPA (all ships): A spa within a spa, Chill is a place reserved exclusively for teen guests. It offers a variety of spa services and treatments, including facials, massages, and manicures.

Reservations for Chill Spa may be made by phone or on-site any time after 1 P.M. on the first day of your cruise. Appointments book fast—book as soon as you board.

Castaway Cay

If you've ever dreamed of getting away to a private, tropical island, the folks at Disney Cruise Line have made it easy to fulfill that fantasy. Almost every Disney Cruise Line trip that departs from Port Canaveral or Miami, Florida, wraps up with a visit to Castaway Cay (pronounced *key*), a tiny island in the Abacos, one in the string of Bahamian isles. This little patch of paradise was secured for the sole use of passengers cruising on Disney ships. It's small—only 3.1 miles long by 2.2 miles wide—and most of it was intentionally left undeveloped so that nature lovers may enjoy the still-unspoiled terrain.

Here you can take a ride in a glass-bottom boat, go back to nature on a kayak adventure, try your wings at parasailing, or go snorkeling offshore—and then return to a barbecue feast. Of course if you'd prefer to loll about in a palm-tree-shaded, beach-side hammock, refreshing beverage in hand, well, that can be arranged.

Other island amenities include biking, beach games, organized activities for kids and teens; a shaded pavilion complete with billiards, ping-pong, basketball, shuffleboard, and more; Disney character greetings; plus a secluded grown-ups-only beach.

Returning guests (they always come back!) will be pleased to see that this happy place has gotten even happier—recent additions include an expansion of the family beach, two water play areas known as Pelican Plunge and Spring-a-Leak, and nearly two dozen furnished beach cabanas.

For details or to book Castaway Cay port adventures, visit *www.disneycruise.com*.

WE'RE GOING TO DISNEY WORLD!

DAY 1

_____
DATE

FLIGHT INFORMATION

RESORT & CONFIRMATION NO.

PARK WE PLAN TO VISIT TODAY

FASTPASS+ ASSIGNMENTS:

1. Attraction: _____
   Time: _____

2. Attraction: _____
   Time: _____

3. Attraction: _____
   Time: _____

DINING RESERVATIONS

NOTES

DAY 2

_____
DATE

PARK WE PLAN TO VISIT
in the morning

PARK WE PLAN TO VISIT
in the afternoon/evening

FASTPASS+ ASSIGNMENTS:

1. Attraction: _____
   Time: _____

2. Attraction: _____
   Time: _____

3. Attraction: _____
   Time: _____

DINING RESERVATIONS

NOTES

A DAY-BY-DAY TRIP TRACKER

DAY 3

_____
DATE

PARK WE PLAN TO VISIT
in the morning

PARK WE PLAN TO VISIT
in the afternoon/evening

FASTPASS+ ASSIGNMENTS:

1. **Attraction:** _____
   Time: _____

2. **Attraction:** _____
   Time: _____

3. **Attraction:** _____
   Time: _____

DINING RESERVATIONS

NOTES

DAY 4

_____
DATE

PARK WE PLAN TO VISIT
in the morning

PARK WE PLAN TO VISIT
in the afternoon/evening

FASTPASS+ ASSIGNMENTS:

1. **Attraction:** _____
   Time: _____

2. **Attraction:** _____
   Time: _____

3. **Attraction:** _____
   Time: _____

DINING RESERVATIONS

NOTES

WE'RE GOING TO DISNEY WORLD!

DAY 5

_____

DATE

PARK WE PLAN TO VISIT
in the morning

PARK WE PLAN TO VISIT
in the afternoon/evening

FASTPASS+ ASSIGNMENTS:

1. Attraction: _____
   Time: _____

2. Attraction: _____
   Time: _____

3. Attraction: _____
   Time: _____

DINING RESERVATIONS

NOTES

DAY 6

_____

DATE

PARK WE PLAN TO VISIT
in the morning

PARK WE PLAN TO VISIT
in the afternoon/evening

FASTPASS+ ASSIGNMENTS:

1. Attraction: _____
   Time: _____

2. Attraction: _____
   Time: _____

3. Attraction: _____
   Time: _____

DINING RESERVATIONS

NOTES

A DAY-BY-DAY TRIP TRACKER

DAY 7

_____
DATE

PARK WE PLAN TO VISIT
in the morning

PARK WE PLAN TO VISIT
in the afternoon/evening

FASTPASS+ ASSIGNMENTS:

1. Attraction: _____
   Time: _____

2. Attraction: _____
   Time: _____

3. Attraction: _____
   Time: _____

DINING RESERVATIONS

NOTES

Last Day

_____
DATE

CHECK-OUT TIME

FLIGHT INFORMATION

NOTES

Index

Where in the World?
(photo locations)

Magic Kingdom:
1. Jungle Cruise, Adventureland
2. Town Square Exposition Hall
3. Walt Disney World Railroad,
   park entrance
4. Cinderella Castle, during Wishes
5. Festival of Fantasy parade
6. Splash Mountain, Adventureland

Epcot:
1. Test Track, Future World
2. Morocco Pavilion (from World
   Showcase Lagoon)
3. Imagination! pavilion, Future World
4. Mexico pavilion (right side)
5. World Showcase Lagoon during
   IllumiNations (from Japan)
6. The Seas with Nemo & Friends
   pavilion, Future World

Disney's Hollywood Studios:
1. Olaf meet-and-greet location
2. The Great Movie Ride
3. Rock 'n' Roller Coaster facade
4. Twilight Zone™ Tower of Terror,
   inside the lobby
5. Sci-Fi Dine-In Theater
6. Mickey at "Mickey and Minnie
   Starring in Red Carpet Dreams"

Animal Kingdom:
1. Flik in It's Tough to be a Bug!,
   Discovery Island
2. Adventurers Outpost,
   Discovery Island
3. Harambe Market
4. Entrance to Dinosaur,
   DinoLand U.S.A.
5. Maharajah Jungle Trek, Asia
6. The Tree of Life (as it "awakens")

Coupons

10% OFF
ENTIRE PURCHASE

Offering authentic Disney collectibles,
exquisite crystal mementos,
and sparkling hand-blown glass gifts.

Subject to terms and conditions on reverse side.

FREE TRAIN OR CAROUSEL RIDE
with the purchase of one ride

Little ones and the young at heart can enjoy an
old-fashioned carousel or train ride on the Marketplace
Carousel or the Marketplace Train Express.

Subject to terms and conditions on reverse side.

FREE
CHOCOLATE BAR
with purchase of
a specialty sundae

Subject to terms and conditions on reverse side.

ENJOY 10% OFF
YOUR DINING EXPERIENCE

Subject to terms and conditions on reverse side.

20% OFF
food and beverages

(Excludes alcohol)
Experience a world of magical flavors
at Joffrey's Coffee and Tea Co. kiosks
throughout *Walt Disney World*® Parks and Resorts.

Subject to terms and conditions on reverse side.

10% OFF
ENTIRE PURCHASE

Renowned for unique, beautiful, and exclusive
fashion jewelry and accessory collections.

Subject to terms and conditions on reverse side.

7 47599 10470 1

Coupons

20% OFF LUNCH
or 10% OFF DINNER

for up to 8 guests in the HOB Restaurant
(discount on food and non-alcoholic beverages only)

Enjoy distinctive Southern-inspired cuisine in an enjoyable atmosphere filled with creative folk art. Opens daily at 11:30 A.M. For reservations, call 407-934-2623.

Subject to terms and conditions on reverse side.

Receive $15 Off
with your purchase of $75 or more

Valid at 7 conveniently located
Orlando Harley-Davidson stores

Subject to terms and conditions on reverse side.

50% OFF

any accessory with the purchase of any regular-priced headphone, earbud, or wireless speaker

Subject to terms and conditions on reverse side.

10% OFF
food only at lunch and dinner

Subject to terms and conditions on reverse side.

15% OFF
one item of your choice

Featuring a colorful array of bags and lifestyle accessories designed to lighten your day.

Subject to terms and conditions on reverse side.

10% OFF
ENTIRE PURCHASE

Experience Art that Pops!
Embellish your life with whimsical and unique art, toys, and jewelry.

Subject to terms and conditions on reverse side.

Coupons

10% OFF
Nine Dragons Restaurant, Lotus Blossom Café, and merchandise

(offer good for lunch and dinner; excludes alcohol)

Subject to terms and conditions on reverse side.

MEDITERRANEAN SMALL PLATES

10% OFF
Food, beverages, and merchandise

(offer good for lunch and dinner; excludes alcohol)

Subject to terms and conditions on reverse side.

10% OFF
Food and beverages for up to 4 Guests

(offer good for lunch and dinner; excludes alcohol)

Subject to terms and conditions on reverse side.

10% OFF
Food, beverages, and merchandise

(offer good for lunch and dinner; excludes alcohol)

Subject to terms and conditions on reverse side.

Disney's
HILTON HEAD ISLAND
RESORT

A Disney Vacation Club Resort

Save on Accommodations
on select dates in 2017

For offer details and to check availability call 407-939-7652 and ask about the Birnbaum Offer.

Subject to terms and conditions on reverse side.

Disney's
VERO BEACH
RESORT

A Disney Vacation Club Resort

Save on Accommodations
on select dates in 2017

For offer details and to check availability call 407-939-7652 and ask about the Birnbaum Offer.

Subject to terms and conditions on reverse side.

TERMS AND CONDITIONS

Located at Epcot®

Park admission is required.

Coupon cannot be combined with any other offers.

Coupon cannot be redeemed for cash
in whole or in part.

Reproduction of coupon not accepted.

Offer subject to change without notice.

Expires 12/31/17

TERMS AND CONDITIONS

Located at Epcot®

Park admission is required.

Coupon cannot be combined with any other offers.

Coupon cannot be redeemed for cash
in whole or in part.

Reproduction of coupon not accepted.

Offer subject to change without notice.

Expires 12/31/17

TERMS AND CONDITIONS

Located at Epcot®

Park admission is required.

Coupon cannot be combined with any other offer.

Reproductions of coupon not accepted
in whole or in part.

Offer subject to change without notice.

www.moroccopavilion.com

Expires 12/31/17

TERMS AND CONDITIONS

Located at Epcot®

Park admission is required.

Coupon cannot be combined with any other offers.

Coupon valid for lunch and dinner.

Coupon cannot be redeemed for cash
in whole or in part.

Reproduction of coupon not accepted.

Offer subject to change without notice.

Expires 12/31/17

TERMS AND CONDITIONS

The number of rooms allocated for this offer is very
limited. Length of stay requirements may apply.
Reservations cannot be made more than
11 months prior to check-in date.

Excludes 3-bedroom Beach Cottages
at Disney's Vero Beach Resort.

Cannot be combined with any other discount or
promotion. Advance reservations required.

For information about Disney's Vero Beach Resort,
visit *https://beachresorts.disney.go.com*

Offer expires 12/31/17

© Disney

TERMS AND CONDITIONS

The number of rooms allocated for this offer is very
limited. Length-of-stay requirements may apply.
Reservations cannot be made more than
11 months prior to check-in date.

Excludes 3-bedroom Grand Villas
at Disney's Hilton Head Island Resort.

Cannot be combined with any other discount or
promotion. Advance reservations required.

For information about Disney's Hilton Head Island
Resort, visit *https://beachresorts.disney.go.com*

Offer expires 12/31/17

© Disney

Coupons

10% OFF
ADMISSION
for up to 4 guests

Immerse yourself in a fascinating and educational dolphin encounter open to all guests ages 13 and up.

Call 407-WDW-TOUR (407-939-8687) for reservations.

Subject to terms and conditions on reverse side.

15% OFF
admission to the Behind the Seeds Tour at The Land for up to 10 guests

Bring the entire family backstage for a one-hour, interactive tour of the greenhouses and fish farm at The Land. For same-day reservations, present coupon at the Tour Desk next to the entrance of Soarin'. Or call ahead to 407-WDW-TOUR (407-939-8687) and mention the Birnbaum offer. Admission to Epcot® is required.

Subject to terms and conditions on reverse side.

10% OFF
Epcot® Dive Quest admission

Dive into a scuba diving adventure open to all certified scuba divers ages 10 and up.

Call 407-WDW-TOUR (407-939-8687) for reservations.

Subject to terms and conditions on reverse side.

10% OFF
ADMISSION

This amazing aqua adventure takes you on a tour of the aquarium and into the water to explore The Seas with Nemo & Friends marine environment using a Scuba Assisted Snorkel unit.

Call 407-WDW-TOUR (407-939-8687) for reservations.

Subject to terms and conditions on reverse side.

20% OFF
2-Hour WALT DISNEY WORLD® Guided Fishing Excursion for you and up to 4 guests.

To make your reservation, call 407-WDW-BASS (407-939-2277) and mention the coupon to be added in the Additional Comments section. This coupon must be presented upon arrival.

Subject to terms and conditions on reverse side.

FREE SAME-DAY REPLAY
WITH PURCHASE OF A TEE TIME

Subject to terms and conditions on reverse side

Book your tee time now by calling 407-WDW-GOLF or go online at www.golfwdw.com

TERMS AND CONDITIONS

Admission to Epcot® theme park is required.

Reproductions of coupons will not be accepted.

Coupon may not be redeemed for cash
in whole or in part.

Offer subject to change without notice.

All tours and experiences are subject to availability.

© Disney

Expires 12/30/17

TERMS AND CONDITIONS

Epcot admission is not required or included.

Reservations recommended and are subject to
availability. Ages 13 years and above.

No jewelry allowed in the aquarium; no cameras
allowed in backstage areas. Forfeit entire price of
the tour if you fail to show or cancel within 2 days
of your reservation.

Reproductions of coupon not accepted.
Coupon may not be redeemed for cash in whole
or in part. Offer subject to change without notice.

All minors must be accompanied by a paying adult.

© Disney

Expires 12/31/17

TERMS AND CONDITIONS

Epcot admission is not required or included.

Reservations recommended and are subject to
availability. Ages 8 years and above.

No jewelry allowed in the aquarium; no cameras
allowed in backstage areas. Forfeit entire price of
the tour if you fail to show or cancel within
2 days of your reservation.

Reproductions of coupon not accepted.
Coupon may not be redeemed for cash in whole or in part.
Offer subject to change without notice.

All minors must be accompanied by a paying adult.

© Disney

Expires 12/31/17

TERMS AND CONDITIONS

SCUBA certification is required for this program.

Epcot admission is not required or included.

Reservations recommended and are subject to
availability. Ages 10 and above.

No jewelry allowed in the aquarium; no cameras
allowed in backstage areas. Forfeit entire price of
the tour if you fail to show or cancel within 2 days
of your reservations.

Reproductions of coupon not accepted.
Coupon may not be redeemed for cash in whole or in part.
Offer subject to change without notice.

All minors must be accompanied by a paying adult.

© Disney

Expires 12/31/17

TERMS AND CONDITIONS

Offer good on Disney's Palm, Disney's Magnolia, and
Disney's Lake Buena Vista Golf Courses. Must present
coupon at check-in to receive this offer. Photocopies or
other replications will not be accepted. Offer only valid
with non-discounted Day Guest and Resort Guest rates.
Complimentary replay round is on a same-day, space-
available basis, and must be played on the same day as the
original round. This may not be combined with any other
offer and is not valid for twilight, super twilight, or other
discount offers. Offer not valid for tournament, group,
league, or any other organized group play. May not be
redeemed for cash. Offer subject to change without notice.

© Disney

Expires 12/31/17

TERMS AND CONDITIONS

All excursions are subject to availability.

Prices and terms are subject to change without notice.

Offer not valid with any other discounted rate.

This coupon may not be redeemed for cash in whole
or in part, and may not be reproduced.

© Disney

Expires 12/31/17

Coupons

FREE UPGRADE

Book at *www.alamo.com*
or call 1-800-462-5266.

Reference Coupon Code **AU526WSD9**
at the time of reservation.

Subject to terms and conditions on reverse side.

LOCATED AT DISNEY'S CONTEMPORARY RESORT

15% OFF ALL SAMMY DUVALL'S WATERSPORTS CENTRE ACTIVITIES

• PARASAILING
• WATERSKIING, WAKEBOARDING, AND FAMILY TUBING
• PERSONAL WATERCRAFT
RESERVATIONS ARE SUGGESTED.

Subject to terms and conditions on reverse side.

Kid's Nite Out
RECREATION & RESORT MANAGEMENT, INC.

$5 OFF
child care services

AND/OR $5 OFF ANY BABY EQUIPMENT RENTAL
OF 4 DAYS OR MORE

Subject to terms and conditions on reverse side.

CHARACTERS IN FLIGHT

$10 FLIGHTS
8:30 A.M.–10 A.M.

20% OFF all tickets
after 10 A.M.

Take flight and experience
360-degree views of Disney
Springs and areas of the
Walt Disney World® Resort in a giant tethered helium
balloon (weather permitting).

Subject to terms and conditions on reverse side.

10% OFF
One single or double stroller rental

To make a reservation, go to
www.magicstrollers.com

Subject to terms and conditions on reverse side.

20% OFF
ONE-TIME MEMBERSHIP FEE

To sign up for "the purple place to store
your vacation stuff," go to
www.ownerslocker.com/Birnbaum

Subject to terms and conditions on reverse side.

TERMS AND CONDITIONS

Must present coupon at check-in to receive discount. Discount does not apply to merchandise. Call for activity restrictions. All activities are subject to availability. Sammy Duvall's reserves the right to cancel due to inclement weather.

Terms and conditions subject to change without notice. Coupon not valid with any other discount. Coupon cannot be copied or reproduced. Coupon cannot be redeemed for cash.

Please book online at *www.sammyduvall.com* and use coupon code Birnbaum. For more information, visit *www.sammyduvall.com* or call (407) 939-0754.

Expires 12/31/17

Rent a compact through midsize vehicle, now through December 31, 2017, and get a free upgrade. One coupon per Alamo rental and void once redeemed. Offer is subject to standard rental conditions. Blackout dates may apply. 24-hour advance reservation required. Not valid with any other discount or promotional rate. Availability is limited. Subject to availability and valid only at these participating Orlando, Florida, Alamo locations: **Buena Vista Place Hotel, Orlando Walt Disney Car Care Center, Orlando International Airport, Shades of Green, and Walt Disney World Dolphin**.

Taxes, other governmentally-authorized or imposed surcharges (including GST/VAT), license and concession recoupment fees, airport and airport facility fees, fuel, one-way rental charge, and optional items (such as CDW up to U.S. $30 per day) are extra.

In the U.S. check your insurance and/or credit card for rental vehicle coverage. Renter and additional driver(s) must meet standard age, driver and credit requirements. Subject to change without notice. Void where prohibited. Coupon VOID if bought, bartered or sold for cash. © 2016 Alamo Rent A Car. All rights reserved. In the U.S., offer valid for a one-car-class upgrade applied at the time of reservation. Must present original coupon at time of rental.

TERMS AND CONDITIONS

Located at Disney Springs® West Side.

Coupon cannot be combined with any other offer.

Reproductions of coupon not accepted in whole or in part.

Minors must be accompanied by a paying adult.

Offer subject to change without notice.

For more information, call (407) 938-9433.

Expires 12/31/17

TERMS AND CONDITIONS

Coupon cannot be combined with any other offer.

Reproductions of coupon not accepted in whole or in part.

Offer subject to change without notice.

For more information, visit *www.kidsniteout.com*, or call 1-800-696-8105

Expires 12/31/17

TERMS AND CONDITIONS

Limit one Owner's Locker Membership per unique coupon code. Owner's Locker reserves the right to require that this coupon be presented when the locker is picked up. Sign-up must be made online at: *www.OwnersLocker.com/Birnbaum*

The coupon code below must be entered to sign up. The unique coupon code can only be used once. Not valid with any other promotion.

Subject to change without notice

Coupon code:

936815717

Expires 12/31/17

TERMS AND CONDITIONS

Limit one stroller reservation per unique coupon code. Reservation must be made online at *www.magicstrollers.com*

The coupon code below must be entered to make the reservation. The unique coupon code can only be used once. This coupon must be returned with the stroller at the end of the rental to receive the discount. Not valid with any other promotion. Subject to change without notice.

Coupon code:

849725817

Expires 12/31/17

Coupons

B BASIN
15% OFF Merchandise

Subject to terms and conditions on reverse side.

Wetzel's Pretzels

FREE PRETZEL

**When you purchase 2 pretzels
of equal or greater value**

Subject to terms and conditions on reverse side.

SOMETHING SILVER

www.somethingsilver.com

10% OFF
ENTIRE PURCHASE

OFFERING STYLISH, HIGH QUALITY
JEWELRY FROM TOP NATIONAL AND
INTERNATIONAL DESIGNER COLLECTIONS

Subject to terms and conditions on reverse side.

Located at DISNEY SPRINGS® West Side

curl®
by sammyduvall

10% OFF
all Curl® merchandise

**Nixon • Roxy • Tom's • Billabong
Reef • Oakley • Maui Jim**

Subject to terms and conditions on reverse side.

DUNCAN®

The Original. World's #1.™

20% OFF
ENTIRE PURCHASE

Famous yo-yos and skill toys, Est. 1929

Subject to terms and conditions on reverse side.

Sprinkles

FREE ICE CREAM TOPPING

With each ice cream purchase

"The Original Cupcake Bakery"

Subject to terms and conditions on reverse side.

TERMS AND CONDITIONS

Valid only at Disney Springs™ West Side
and Marketplace locations.

Coupon not valid with any other offers or discounts.

Limit one per coupon.

Coupon must be surrendered at time of purchase.

Reproductions of coupon not accepted.

Not redeemable for cash in whole or part.

Offer subject to change without notice.

www.wetzels.com

Expires 12/31/17

TERMS AND CONDITIONS

Offer good at Walt Disney World Basin locations.

Coupon cannot be combined with any offer.

Reproductions of coupon not accepted.

Coupon may not be redeemed for cash in
whole or in part.

Offer subject to change without notice.

Expires 12/31/17

1-888-77-BASIN | BASIN.COM

TERMS AND CONDITIONS

Must present coupon to receive discount.

Discount does not apply to sale items or electronics.

Terms and conditions subject to change
without notice.

Coupon not valid with any other discount.

Coupon cannot be copied or reproduced.

Coupon cannot be redeemed for cash.

For more information, visit
www.curlsurf.com, or call (407) 842-1302.

Expires 12/31/17

TERMS AND CONDITIONS

Located at Disney Springs.

Must present coupon to receive discount.

Coupon cannot be combined with
other offers or discounts.

Reproductions of coupon not accepted.

Coupon not redeemable for cash.

Offer subject to change without notice.

Expires 12/31/17

TERMS AND CONDITIONS

Valid only at the Disney Springs™ Town Center location.

One free topping for each ice cream item purchased.

Coupon cannot be combined with
any other offers or discounts.

Coupon not redeemable for cash in whole or part.

Coupon must be surrendered at time of purchase.

Reproductions of coupon not accepted.

Offer subject to change without notice.

www.sprinkles.com

Expires 12/31/17

TERMS AND CONDITIONS

Valid only at Duncan Toys in Disney Springs, Walt
Disney World. Valid on any product in the store.
Not valid on prior purchased. Coupons may not be
combined and cannot by bought, sold, or exchanged
for cash or coupons. Not valid with any other offer.
Local and state taxes, as applicable, are payable by
bearer. Must present original coupon at time of
purchase. Photocopies prohibited. Valid for coupon
recipient only. Limit one coupon per person, per visit.
Nontransferable. Offer good while supplies last. Void
where prohibited or restricted. Where required, cash
value of 1/100 of 1 cent. Not valid at yo-yo.com

www.Yo-Yo.com

Expires 12/31/17

PERMANENT
PEACE

How To Stop
Terrorism and War
— Now and Forever

ALSO BY THIS AUTHOR

PERMANENT
PEACE

How To Stop
Terrorism and War
— Now and Forever

•

BY ROBERT M. OATES

INSTITUTE

of

SCIENCE, TECHNOLOGY AND PUBLIC POLICY

JOHN HAGELIN, PH.D., DIRECTOR

This book is a revised version of *Creating Heaven on Earth* (1988) by the same author, with amendations and additions.

Published by the Institute of Science, Technology and Public Policy
Henn Mansion
1000 North Fourth Street
Fairfield, Iowa 52557

ISBN 0-615-12070-9

Printed in the U.S.A.

Design by Shepley Hansen
Copyediting, formatting, and indexing
by Martha Bright
Typeface: Janson

CONTENTS

THE CORE IDEA:

How to Stop Terrorism and War — Permanently

Terrorism CAN be stopped. The civilized world is not defenseless against sociopaths armed with box cutters and contaminated envelopes.

We can draw these encouraging conclusions from a sustained research effort that has lasted more than a quarter century. Terrorist attacks have been devastating, but they have also served to highlight a profound scientific discovery — a discovery thoroughly documented in published scientific research, yet previously ignored by government and the media — the discovery of a technology of peace.

Terrorism amounts to unknown people attacking unknown targets with unknown weapons at unknown times. Against such stealth warfare, as America has learned, even the strongest nations are defenseless, and their citizens helpless. But the new technology of peace promises to eradicate this weakness. Repeated research has shown that any nation can now create an invincible defense against both terrorism and conventional attack. And if governments won't act, a relative handful of their citizens can do it for them — taking peace into their own hands.

Knowledge is power. This book has been written to empower people everywhere, in and out of government, with the knowledge that can generate a permanent state of world peace. To that end, every reader is invited to go through this book with a single question in mind: "In light of what I've read, how strongly should I support the use of this new approach to peace?"

THE LIMITS OF VIOLENCE

The tragedy of September 11, 2001, was a terrifying way to realize the need for a totally new defense technology. As Americans learned that day to their horror — when suddenly malevolent airliners sliced into the World Trade Towers — no traditional means can stop resolute and cunning terrorists willing to sacrifice their lives.

In those awful hours, and in the months of anthrax after, it became clear that the world needs a completely new approach to defense — a preventive technology — one that can stop an attack before it has even been conceived. Whether the source of terrorism is foreign governments, independent terrorists, or indigenous psychotics, the American people (and all other people) need a systematic technology that will stop them all.

Ignorant of such a technology, the U.S. in the fall of 2001 fought back against terrorism in the only way it knew. Wave after wave of unopposed aircraft dropped countless bombs on what was, for all the hostility and brutality of its recent rulers, a poor and defenseless nation. If these attacks promised to stop terrorism, they might have made more sense. But decades of experience in the Middle East have shown that killing terrorists (and, inevitably, innocent civilians) only creates more terrorists. For years into the future, as the United States government well knows, Islamic fundamentalists will be recruiting young men to a life of terrorism against America with tales of a heartless, faceless, seemingly endless bombing of an entire Islamic nation.

Moreover, the certain terrorist reprisals for this bombing will only embody a central principle of every religion: *As you sow, so shall you reap.* In the language of physics: Every action has an equal and opposite reaction. Once the vicious cycle of terrorism has begun — heartless attacks and vengeful retaliations — killers on all sides will be killed, bombers will be bombed, destroyers will be destroyed. It is understandable that Americans and their government, shocked and outraged by the terrorist atrocities, struck back with overwhelming violence. But in a fight against terrorists who can kill millions with a crop duster, and who have demonstrated the patience to wait years for revenge, such attacks are doomed to eventual self-destruction.

A REVOLUTIONARY APPROACH

Fortunately, a long-term research effort has now defined an alternative approach. The studies have shown that it is possible, through deliberate intervention, to end the cycle of attack and revenge — through completely peaceful means. They have defined a technology of *peace* — a systematic procedure that makes it possible to switch on peace as straightforwardly as we switch on the lights.

But taking advantage of this discovery requires a revolution in thinking. Until now, national defense has been based on objective, physical science — on weaponry made largely of metal, using chemical, electronic, and nuclear technologies. But defense based on such a purely objective approach has reached its failing point: We can attack anyone, but we cannot defend ourselves.

Fortunately, this new technology has been documented nearly fifty times and confirmed in nineteen published scientific studies. Instead of objective, physical techniques, this approach uses methods that are subjective and consciousness-based — including meditation technologies known and preserved for thousands of years in the timeless Vedic tradition of India.

The Vedic (VAY-dik) explanation, in two parts, can be stated quickly — though it may take the entire book to demonstrate the underlying concepts convincingly:

1. The cause. In the Vedic understanding, all types of social violence and warfare have an underlying origin, namely social stress and tension, the fear and hostility between factions, nations, religions, and even competing civilizations. It is this societal stress and disorder — the chaos in the collective consciousness of any given nation, and in the world as a whole — that breaks out as violent crime, warfare, and terrorism.

2. The solution. For many years, based on hundreds of research studies, the medical community has accepted that meditation by an individual can calm down stress, tension, and hostility in that individual. More recently, the new studies have shown that large groups of meditators, gathered together with the intent to benefit the society around them, create the same calming effect in the wider community. Repeated tests have shown that assemblies of experts in the much-researched Transcendental Meditation® program calm down stress, tension, and hostility in the collective consciousness of the surrounding society — as measured by reduced crime, warfare, and terrorism.

The evidence indicates, in other words, that the peace technology is "wireless" — like radio and cell phones — broadcasting a coherent influence through an invisible field. In place of a broadcasting station, this subjective technology makes use of the most richly complex technological device ever created: the human brain. Just as radio stations radiate music through the underlying electromagnetic field, so research indicates that the minds of people who are expert in meditation, when gathered together to meditate in one location, radiate harmony and peacefulness through an underlying field of consciousness.

THE EVIDENCE

It's obvious that such a radically new theory needs strong scientific support. In this case, as we will see in Chapter Two, the research is plentiful. Repeated studies show that whenever a large assembly of meditation experts gathers at a single location:

- As the attendance numbers at the assembly *increase*,
- Violent crime, warfare, and terrorism all *decrease*.

If the number of participants at such an assembly goes up and down, the statistics on violence go up and down with strong (inverse) correlation. The most remarkable study, based on Rand Corporation statistics, shows that during the three largest Transcendental Meditation assemblies ever held in the West — near or exceeding 7,000 people at each assembly — terrorism declined worldwide by 72% (see Chapter Two).

"This is exciting research," says a foreign relations scholar, Professor Ved Nanda, director of the International Legal Studies Program at the University of Denver. "It is a non-traditional conception, but the straightforward evidence gives the theory credence in my eyes."

Says Raymond Russ, professor of psychology at the University of Maine and editor of the *Journal of Mind and Behavior*, "The hypothesis definitely raised some eyebrows among our reviewers. But the statistical work is sound. The numbers are there."

THE SOURCE

As with many scientific discoveries, the credit for this one goes largely to a single individual, a man now widely known in the West. Nearly fifty years ago, Maharishi Mahesh Yogi left India to demonstrate to a scientific world that meditation is a scientific reality, with provable benefits for the individual. By 1980, with hundreds of studies on his Transcendental Meditation technique published in academic journals, meditation had made it to the medical mainstream. Millions of dollars in research funds from the National Institutes of Health now support further studies on the Transcendental Meditation program.

In the last twenty years, moreover, Maharishi has expanded his focus from individual meditation and individual benefits to large-group meditations and society-wide benefits. In 1960, few people thought meditation a practical tool for healthy and successful life, but the research transformed our medical understanding. In a parallel way, since 1980 few people have thought that large groups of meditation experts can directly create a more peaceful world — but the research is in the journals, and the terrorists are inside our borders. There will never be a better time to catch up with the evidence.

THE CONTENTS

To that end, we will explore this new approach to peace, both theory and practice. The basic plan of the book is to compare key aspects of the timeless Vedic wisdom with scientific evidence as well as the latest scientific theories.

In **Chapter One**, we will lay out the hypothesis in detail.

In **Chapter Two**, we will review the research evidence that supports the hypothesis. Time and again, first-class scientists have devised ingenious scientific studies that have survived highly skeptical, even hostile, reviewers, and achieved publication in mainstream academic journals. The drama of these stories brings to life the rigor of the studies.

In **Chapters Three, Four,** and **Five** we will seek to answer the question, How can a group of people sit in one room, meditating with eyes closed, and transform the society around them? Only a radically new paradigm could possibly answer that question convincingly. In chapters that form the heart of this book, we will delve into such a new paradigm — the Vedic theories as revived in a scientific age by Maharishi. These theories combine the timeless Vedic understanding of consciousness, on the one hand, with the latest theories of quantum physics, on the other. From the standpoint of modern society, the result is a completely new understanding of life and the world — a new paradigm that combines human intelligence with nature's intelligence. To make sense of this new approach to peace, in other words, we must understand the most profound secret of human life — the most precious knowledge of seers and sages in every age — how the human mind can gain direct access to, and harness, the limitless power of the intelligence of nature. This is, on the one

THE CORE IDEA · 7

hand, a practical book, focused on how to stop terrorism and war. Paradoxically, however, our urgent need to stop such gross destruction drives us to understand the most subtle essence of consciousness and life.

In **Chapter Six**, Maharishi explains the implications of all that has gone before, outlining both the theory and procedures in his own words, and drawing conclusions about what he terms the unlimited possibilities of human life — the possibilities that unfold when the individual grows to full *enlightenment*, when individual human intelligence attains alliance with, and gains the support of, the intelligence displayed everywhere in the natural world.

Finally, in **Action Steps**, readers will find practical steps they can take immediately to help bring permanent peace to our world. It is no longer necessary for peace-loving people to wring their hands and hope for the best — or to wait for governments, peace agencies, or the United Nations to act. Even one such person, or a few, or a few thousand, can make it possible for this technology of peace to be used on a massive scale, and permanently, to transform the future of the world.

Doubtless these new ideas challenge our preconceptions. But the subject admits of both scientific investigation and systematic intellectual analysis. In a body of thought he calls Vedic Science[SM], Maharishi has revived ancient understandings in a systematic manner that opens them to objective testing. The upshot, in an era of worldwide terrorism, could not be more practical. As Maharishi says, "Now we have it in our power to eliminate terrorism at its basis. It is simply ignorance to believe that by killing a few terrorists, we can put an end to terrorism. What is needed is to remove the root cause of terrorism by creating an indomitable influence of coherence and harmony in the collective consciousness of the entire world."[1]

Anthrax is here. Nuclear warheads are missing. Chemical weapons are rife. Future terrorist attacks could easily be much more devastating — and the United States government, with its vast military power, can no longer protect its own citizens. In such a crisis — as it seems to this author — no responsible leader of society, nor any responsible citizen, can afford to ignore a possibility so thoroughly verified scientifically.

The only responsible course is to look carefully into this newly validated approach to permanent world peace, to ask the hard questions, and to come to an informed conclusion. We need the courage to think new thoughts, and to evaluate them thoroughly. Since terrorism is now a global scourge, and since no other approach stops terrorism — as experience in the Middle East has shown for decades — it is not overly dramatic to say that the future of the world hangs in the balance.

1

PERMANENT PEACE:
Context and Hypothesis

For forty young men, the introduction to the ease and power of this new technology of peace began with a midnight plane ride from London to Africa.

As we ducked into the 707, the first news was good — there were only five or six other people on the plane, and sleeping across empty seats would be possible for all. The low passenger count wasn't really a surprise. This was Zambian Airways. The next stop was the capital city: Lusaka.

We were late onto the plane, which backed out as we buckled up, and we plowed steeply upward into the night sky before a stir passed through the delegation of forty. Someone had picked up a newspaper from the seat beside him. Soon other papers had come from the flight attendants. There weren't enough for everybody, and I had to wait several minutes until the man in front of me passed his copy back. It was the *Lusaka Times*, the official paper printed in Zambia's capital, dated that same day, Monday, November 4, 1978. A banner headline across the top of the front page declared, "Lusaka Bombed Again."

As our plane hummed through the blackness, each of us huddling under a cone of light, the newspapers told us why we were heading for Zambia. Neighboring Rhodesia (now Zimbabwe) was entrapped in a bitter civil war, blacks against whites, a bloody conflict that had been escalating for years and showed no sign of easing. The whites had the government and the army, the blacks the numbers and the will. Zambia, a black republic landlocked inside Rhodesia in the southeastern quadrant of Africa, had been dragged in as a staging ground for two different guerrilla factions. Rhodesia had lately taken to repeated bombing raids of its neighbor, partly to harass the guerrillas and partly to convince Zambia not to host them. Bombing had been frequent the past month. The newspaper didn't say so, but now we knew: We were going there to stop it.

The forty of us on that plane could accurately be called a delegation of meditation experts. Each of us had been practicing the Transcendental Meditation technique for many years and the advanced TM-Sidhi® program for at least a year. Most of us had put in a year or more on long meditation courses, devoting time and attention to more profound personal experience during meditation and, as scientific research has by now made clear, to the refinement of the operation of the brain and nervous system. But it was only recently, in the past couple of years, that it had begun to appear we were doing something else as well. We were preparing to create peace in the world.

The first research had appeared in 1974. In eleven American cities where at least one percent of the population had learned the basic Transcendental Meditation technique, the crime rate fell. Since then, hundreds of cities around the world had gone over the one percent mark, and the trend had held good. Not only did the crime rate go down, but hospital admissions declined and traffic accidents decreased. Then, in just the past summer, in August 1978, as many TM-Sidhi-trained experts as possible gathered in a single state or province of 108 nations.

With the advanced TM-Sidhi program, especially when practiced in groups, the radiating effect seemed much stronger.

For forty of us, the next step was a plane ride to Zambia.

If our mission seemed dramatic — to end the fighting in that
war-torn nation — our lifestyle was staid. Once we arrived in
Lusaka, we took up residence at the Andrews Motel, the finest
travelers' facility in Lusaka, and essentially never left the grounds
for the next six weeks. We did make an early trip to tell local government officials of our aims in Zambia, but we never met a soul
who had anything to do with the fighting, and, in fact, we hardly met anyone at all. Our day consisted of long stretches of group
meditation, punctuated by meals and three daily meetings. There
was no intent, in other words, to affect Zambia's situation through
discussion or persuasion. Our focus was simply to stay together,
meditate, and radiate the abstract influence of harmony and
peacefulness which experience had shown to be effective.

And it certainly appeared to be effective once again. As far as
we could tell from reading the newspaper and listening to the
radio, peace returned to Zambia overnight. Bombing stopped
on the day after our arrival, and there were no serious incidents
of either domestic or international violence reported in Zambia during the six weeks of our stay. Probably the strongest
indication of the success of the project came a month after we
arrived. We had intended to leave at that time, but two government officials came on separate visits to the Andrews Motel to
ask us to stay. Both the Provincial Secretary for Lusaka Province
(a rank equivalent to governor) and the Provincial Minister
(comparable to a Senator) told us that the month prior to our
arrival had been the worst since Zambia's independence and that
the change since that time was both obvious and welcome. Now
national elections were scheduled, the first in years, and as in
most third-world countries, Zambia had a tradition of unrest on
election day. The newspaper had recently featured prominent
stories on the violence expected. The Provincial Secretary and

the Minister asked us to stay at least two more weeks, until the elections were over.

We did stay. The elections were held in an atmosphere of peace and calm throughout the nation.

Two days after the election, we packed up and caught the daily flight back to London at nine in the morning. That afternoon Lusaka was bombed.

FROM ANECDOTES TO HARD EVIDENCE

To those of us on that trip, the results were striking. But if you tell a story like that to a social scientist, prepare yourself for a tolerant smile and a polite dismissal of merely anecdotal evidence. An anecdote is a story, and the word often means joke. Anecdotes are not treated seriously by scientists. Researchers want objective evidence, repeated and statistically significant.

In the more than twenty years since that Zambian adventure, that is just what they have received. The basic idea is simple to state: Like ripples on a pond radiating outward from a pebble's splash, ripples of orderliness and harmony radiate outward from concentrated groups of meditation experts. And the evidence for this idea has been, precisely, repeated and statistically significant. Not only do signs of social disorder go down — such as violent crime, fires, traffic accidents, warfare, and terrorism — but signs of coherence and progress go up. Patent applications, for example, stock market levels, and economic indicators have all been shown to rise. Taken together, the evidence shows that during fifty demonstrations, the majority of them covered in nineteen studies accepted for publication in academic journals, society has become more peaceful, more coherent, and more progressive — in every statistical sense that has been tested to date.

Such groups of meditation experts have been called Super Radiance assemblies. The name comes from the superradiant effect in optical physics, in which a small proportion of coherent photons in a beam of light influence all other photons to join with them in the powerfully coherent stream that we call laser light. Just as the small number of coherent photons makes the whole beam coherent, so the research indicates that even a small number of people creating internal coherence through group meditation radiate that coherence throughout society. The beneficial society-wide effect generated by these Super Radiance assemblies has been named (in the scientific tradition of the Doppler Effect and the Meissner Effect) the Maharishi Effect, in recognition of the Maharishi Mahesh Yogi, the scientist of consciousness who first predicted the effect and who provided the meditation techniques that make it possible.

THE OBVIOUS QUESTIONS

In a society that has emphasized objective science and life based on the paradigm of materialism, these ideas can seem surprising. For someone new to the possibility, therefore, any number of questions naturally come up. Such questions might break down into three general types:

1. Does the research really prove the existence of the Maharishi Effect? Aren't the results just coincidence — affected by the weather, the time of year, or other factors going on in the society?

2. Who are the people involved in Super Radiance? For people unfamiliar with the concept of a *technology* of peace, it can help to know who supports that technology. You can tell an idea by the friends it has. Also, such people would most likely want to know the nature of Maharishi's qualifications as a scientist and educator.

3. Beyond the simple statement that Super Radiance groups "radiate" an influence of harmony and peace, what plausible theory could possibly account for this effect? How can people sit meditating with eyes closed in one place and influence criminals and soldiers in the surrounding environment — even, with a group large enough, halfway around the world?

Such questions are obviously sensible, and brief answers are in order here — as an introduction to the more detailed discussions in the chapters that follow.

As for the first set of questions, the statistical evidence for the Maharishi Effect will be covered in detail in Chapter Two. One point worth noting now, however, is that in keeping with good scientific procedure, the experimental studies have been replicated many times. Since the fall of 1978, the TM® organization has held many large Super Radiance assemblies. Each assembly can be seen as a definable experiment, with meditation experts first gathering, then dispersing. Often specific predictions about the positive effects have been made to scientists and the media before the assemblies have gathered. The result: Each assembly has coincided with statistically significant changes in the surrounding society. Elaborate statistical precautions have ruled out the possibility that weather, holidays, or other extraneous factors interfered with the experiments. Even if the theory is not understood, objective evidence strongly supports the existence of the Maharishi Effect.

Second, it is certainly important to know what kind of person is involved in Super Radiance. One good way to find out is to visit Maharishi University of Management. On its campus in Fairfield, Iowa, the university has long been the site of the largest collection of people practicing Maharishi's Transcendental Meditation program in the West — attracting faculty, staff, and students from across America and from more than sixty nations around the world. Thus, visitors who wish to gauge the character of people who take part in Super Radiance can do so by meeting at the university and in town a cross-section of the world's meditating population.

The quality of these people is indicated in part by expert appraisals. For example, as one sign of scholarly acceptance of Maharishi University of Management, as well as its faculty and staff, the university is accredited by the nation's oldest and largest accrediting organization.* After its most recent three-day site visit by six academics from around the nation, the North Central Association again granted accreditation for ten years, the longest period allowable. As another indication of expert support, the National Institutes of Health, after a thorough ten-day site visit to the university, have awarded nearly $20 million in research grants to investigate the benefits for the individual of the Transcendental Meditation technique.

Academic experts also speak highly of the students they meet. After an early site visit, James T. Townsend, who was at that time professor of mathematical and experimental psychology at Purdue University, reported that, "The student interest in matters intellectual and the general enthusiasm, creativity, and energy was striking, much higher than I am accustomed to seeing in the typical undergraduates at other universities."

"I've been to 200 campuses all over the country," said Jack Burnham, then chairman of the art department at Northwestern University. "The students I've encountered at M.U.M. are better motivated, more like a family. They seem to be more wide awake, more lively in terms of their thinking."

As for Maharishi himself, nearly fifty years of his teaching activity around the world have made him a familiar figure. He is the latest significant teacher in the long history of the Vedic tradition in India, a tradition which has maintained unbroken for thousands of years a richly detailed understanding of subjective knowledge — knowledge about consciousness, technologies of consciousness, and the use of those technologies to produce evolution to higher states of human functioning. Although he appears uniformly blissful and content, Maharishi is clearly a man on a mission. He takes no vacations and often works twenty-two hours a day, wearing out a three-shift relay of secretaries

---

*The university is accredited by The Higher Learning Commission and a member of the North Central Association, www.ncahigherlearningcommission.org, 312-263-0456.

and assistants. He enjoys having a worldwide organization, he once said, because it means that someone is always awake, somewhere in the world, with whom he can carry on his ceaseless activity by telephone. Trying to condense Maharishi's achievements into a short list, to give some idea of his knowledge and intentions, one might include:

1. In the ancient annals of the Vedic tradition, he is the first teacher of meditation to have his techniques taught to six million people worldwide, more by far than any such teacher in recorded history. In this regard, moreover, he may be best understood by his goals. While for thousands of years only a few people were deemed worthy of learning true Vedic meditation, and society as a whole was left to fend for itself, Maharishi's repeatedly stated goals are to bring enlightenment to every single individual on Earth, and to establish a permanent state of world peace.

2. He is the first teacher of meditation in many centuries to revive the Vedic truth that meditation is not based on individual effort, on arduous concentration, but rather takes place spontaneously and naturally once the mind is given the correct start. It is this transformation in understanding, embodied in his Transcendental Meditation technique, which has opened the benefits of daily meditation to all people everywhere.

3. He is the first Vedic representative to demonstrate such mastery of the mechanics of the meditation process that he could train tens of thousands of other people to teach the Transcendental Meditation technique. The success of these teachers has been demonstrated by 600 research studies on the benefits of the Transcendental Meditation program, which has been shown to be significantly more effective than other meditation or relaxation techniques tested to date (see pages 176–185).

4. Before turning his attention to the Vedic knowledge of consciousness, Maharishi received his university degree in physics. This combined expertise from modern science and ancient wis-

dom has meant that Maharishi is uniquely qualified as a scientist of consciousness — in position to bring about a synthesis of objective, materialist science with the subjective science of pure, abstract consciousness.

5. Finally — and most relevant to a world on the brink of a war between civilizations — after a lapse of uncounted centuries he has revived the knowledge of *rashtriya kavach* (national armor), the invincible power of peace radiated by large group meditations.

A FIELD THEORY OF CONSCIOUSNESS

As for the third set of questions: Is there a sound explanation for this society-wide, even worldwide, effect — the Maharishi Effect? Can science produce a theory for what at first sounds impossible?

The short answer to this is, yes. There is a solidly documented theory enunciated by Maharishi, a theory consonant with the latest scientific thought in other fields. In Maharishi's Vedic understanding, the reason that orderliness and harmony can ripple throughout society is that consciousness itself is at basis an omnipresent, underlying field. Like the gravitational field and the electromagnetic field, consciousness is an infinite, unbounded, nonmaterial reality through which waves can radiate over even astronomical distances.

Radio provides an analogy. Radio waves work the same way and, one hundred years ago, the concept was just as hard to believe. Marconi invented the first radio in the late nineteenth century. He gathered his friends to tell them he could use a small box to transmit his voice many miles through thin air. There was no longer any need for intervening wires, he assured them. His voice could travel invisibly through the atmosphere. At that time, however, the electromagnetic field was imperfectly understood and the natural result was that no one believed Marconi's protestations. When he gave demonstrations, people thought he had hidden wires. Finally, he had to send assistants in a boat far out to sea and transmit messages back and forth, with witnesses at both ends, to establish the veracity of his claims.

A century later we are familiar with the radio, however, as well as with broadcast television, radar, and other examples of the phenomena physicists call *fields* and *field effects*. The electromagnetic field, for example, exists everywhere in the universe. This field is nonmaterial, unbounded and all-pervading, as though all the universe were submerged in an invisible, untouchable ocean. Radio, television, X-rays, radar (and the Sun, among other sources of light) all work by sending waves through this electromagnetic field. These waves can't be seen, but they have their effects. When you turn on your television, you gain the benefit of an electromagnetic field effect — the picture has come to your home as waves traveling through the electromagnetic field from a broadcasting station or satellite (unless, of course, you have cable). The gravitational field works the same way, as do the two other *force fields* of nature, as well as the *particle fields*, whose propagating waves we call *subatomic particles*. As the basic mechanism of nature, therefore, accounting for every aspect of the apparently physical universe, invisible, nonmaterial waves move through invisible, nonmaterial fields. Although Marconi's contemporaries thought that impossible, even insane, we have grown used to the notion by now.

To understand the Maharishi Effect, therefore, it is only necessary to posit that consciousness operates like every other aspect of nature. In this view consciousness is also an infinite, invisible field — with waves that radiate throughout society.

THE NATURE OF CONSCIOUSNESS

This is not our normal understanding of consciousness, of course. In fact, in modern society, the concept of consciousness is not often considered at all. We know we are conscious, we know we are awake. But what is wakeful*ness*, what is conscious*ness*? We vaguely picture our mind inside our head, closed up in our skull, as though the brain and the mind were one and the same. But Maharishi's understanding indicates that consciousness, like other aspects of nature, is a field, an unbounded, all-pervasive ocean everywhere available. From this standpoint, the human brain is an intricate broadcasting and receiving station for the waves that travel the field of consciousness.

Though the field nature of consciousness is a new idea in an age of objective science, in fact it is an idea thousands of years old. While it is true that scientists have validated the central points of the theory in just the past decade, the theory itself was first laid down in the dawn of recorded history. The civilization which gave rise to these ideas — the Vedic civilization which flourished in India millennia into the past — took human consciousness as its chief point of focus. The great "scientists" of that civilization investigated subjective truths rather than objective truths — mind rather than matter. They did their investigations sitting with eyes closed, using mental technologies to probe the depths of human awareness.

In exhaustive records still available, these pioneers of consciousness meticulously catalogued three aspects of their subject: (1) the various inward levels of the mind — the deep, foundational levels of consciousness which uphold the surface level of mental activity experienced every day; (2) the relationship between mind and matter — between the laws of consciousness and the laws of the material world; and (3) the hidden potentials of consciousness — detailed descriptions of higher states of consciousness.

The central tenet of the ancient Vedic wisdom, as brought to light in a scientific age by Maharishi, is that human life can be lived on a much higher plane than the mature, well-adjusted adulthood commonly held to be the highest goal in modern societies. In fact, as Maharishi points out, the whole of the ancient Vedic literature is filled with precise descriptions of enlightenment — of higher states of consciousness — and in these higher states, theoretically, a person becomes much more awake. Perception is said to refine and knowledge to deepen. Just as the fuzzy vision of a nearsighted man can be turned to clarity with the right type of glasses, so the relative dullness of ordinary states of consciousness can be sharpened in these more evolved states.

It is through the experience of these higher states of consciousness, Maharishi indicates, that the ancient *Rishis*, the seers, cognized the deepest realities of humanity and nature. They gained the knowledge directly, subjectively, through immediate awareness of creation's mechanics.

THE TECHNOLOGY OF PEACE:
THE HYPOTHESIS

Until recently these Vedic descriptions, when considered at all, have been thought mystical — even imaginary. But two things have happened in recent years to change that perception. First, after long centuries of neglect and repression associated with foreign conquests of the Indian subcontinent, Maharishi has revived the ancient Vedic teachings in a holistic and systematic manner. Second, in just the past few years it seems that modern science has begun to catch up with ancient wisdom. Going more deeply into their respective fields, physicists have glimpsed an ancient understanding of nature, and physiologists an ancient understanding of human nature. The two together, in the light of Vedic wisdom, reveal a profound reality: Nature and human nature are, in fact, united at their source. As the five fingers appear independent, but are, in fact, united as one hand, so the all-pervading force and matter fields of the material world appear separate, but are in fact integrated in one fundamental unified field of consciousness.

To put the hypothesis compactly: The human mind can bring peace to the world because the human mind is *one* with the world, at the most basic level.

From the standpoint of modern science, the most useful aspect of these understandings is that they can be tested rigorously. Ancient, subjective knowledge can now be checked through modern, objective means. Ideas usually deemed metaphysical or mystical can resolve to objective fact. It is this objectively verifiable nature of the central Vedic teachings that has led Maharishi to term his teaching Vedic Science.

One particular principle of his Vedic Science is central. The Vedic literature prescribes a technology whereby even a small percentage of any given population can create the invincible defense shield of *rashtriya kavach*. Rather than focusing on weapons, military preparedness, and other aspects of a strategy based on the outer, objective level of life, the Vedic strategy was to focus inwards, through a technology for enlivening the inner, subjective strength of consciousness. In Maharishi's explanations, even a few experts specializing in this subjective defense technology radiate an influence so coherent and powerful that no enemy would dare to attack — and, more significantly, an influence so harmonious and positive that no enemy would even be born. Thousands of years ago the Vedic seer Patanjali encapsulated this idea in a single phrase: *Tat sannidhau vairatyagah*, which means, "In the vicinity of the settled mind, hostile tendencies fall away."

This understanding can be summed up in an analogy. Imagine a time thousands of years into the future when intrepid archaeologists dig down and find the remains of a large television broadcasting station. The machinery has been perfectly preserved, all the wiring and gauges and switches still intact. There is a handbook for operating the broadcasting machinery, written in a language the archaeologists understand. They take the handbook, read the directions, and throw the switches to turn on the equipment. Nothing happens. They pore over the machinery, re-read the manual, and still cannot get the machinery to respond. They are about to give up when one of their number notices a long cord extending from the machinery. It ends in a three-pronged plug. It is lying on the floor. The archaeologist picks up the plug, sticks it into a wall socket nearby, throws the switches again, and the broadcasting station hums to life.

In the understandings Maharishi brings to light in his Vedic Science, we today are archaeologists of consciousness, just now beginning to dig down and unearth the capabilities latent in the human brain. The brain is a magnificent piece of electronic equipment, more complexly wired than the largest computer. There are billions of neurons, each neuron with thousands of filaments — thousands of connectors that reach out for other neurons — and the number of possible connections is astronomically large. But until recently, if the Vedic understanding is accurate, we have forgotten how to take this magnificent piece of equipment and connect it to its source.

In his Vedic Science, Maharishi indicates that there is at the basis of nature a field of all possibilities, an infinite field of pure consciousness — and that the human mind can enliven its dormant capabilities by directly contacting ("plugging into") this field. Once the mind settles down to attune itself with this field of infinite potential, then, like the broadcasting station, the mind and brain can begin to work with the splendor of their full potential and radiate into their environment a powerful influence of peace and positivity.

ONE HYPOTHESIS IN FOUR PARTS

It is possible to emphasize four postulates of this understanding from Vedic Science, four concepts which can be taken by a scientific age as predictions or hypotheses ready to be tested. Each one of these conceptions has already been the subject of some of this century's most revealing scientific investigation. Each will be a major subject in the succeeding chapters in this book. These four hypotheses:

1. One unified field. Vedic Science maintains that there exists one basic field of existence — not many different fields of nature but one unified field that is infinite, timeless, and transcendental — a field which underlies and supports all other fields, all the mechanics of nature's functioning. As the same ocean gives rise to all waves, so the same unbounded, omnipresent field is said to give rise to all the laws of nature that structure our universe.

2. The human connection. Human beings bond with this unified field through a fourth major state of consciousness. In Maharishi's explanations of the Vedic wisdom, the human mind can settle down deep within its own nature and directly contact this underlying unified field — by experiencing a unique fourth state of consciousness. This fourth state of consciousness is precisely described and is said to be completely different from the common three states of waking, sleeping, and dreaming. As a farmer can drop a well to an underground reservoir, so the human mind can settle down deep within its own nature and directly experience the unified field.

3. Evolution of human nature. Human nature, in the Vedic understanding, evolves toward higher states of consciousness. The Vedic texts maintain that, once the human mind begins to attune itself with the deepest level of creation, human nature leaves behind its apparently fixed status and begins to evolve rapidly. Life starts to become more successful — more coherent, progressive, and harmonious. Mistakes decrease, suffering falls away, and this qualitative improvement builds up over time as the mind begins to experience higher states of consciousness.

4. A technology of peace. In his Vedic Science, Maharishi explains that Super Radiance assemblies create invincible defense spontaneously — through a harmonious, coherent, and positive state of consciousness generated throughout an entire nation. In the lore of the hunter, a man with no fear will not be attacked by wild animals. In the understandings of Vedic Science, a nation with no stress, anxiety, or internal incoherence will not be attacked by its enemies. And Maharishi emphasizes that even a small fraction of the population can radiate this field effect, this harmonizing, positive influence, throughout the collective consciousness of the entire nation. Those few minds, as they become fully attuned to nature's laws at their source, purify stress, tension, and fear from their environment. They create an impenetrable harmony and unity in the collective consciousness of the nation that disallows invasion by an enemy. Even a single lamp can light an entire room; even one group of highly trained minds can enlighten an entire society — and thereby create the invincible defense of *rashtriya kavach*.

As recently as ten or fifteen years ago, such notions could have been dismissed as mystical dreaming, seemingly absurd and surely unscientific. But objective research has progressed rapidly. Recent investigations in physics, physiology, and sociology bear directly on these four Vedic principles. In every case, the latest evidence indicates that the traditional understandings are accurate.

1. Physicists have defined one unified field of all the laws of nature. Confirming the Vedic explanation, the deepest penetrations of quantum physics have revealed that all the different force and particle fields of nature find their common source in one superfield, one unified field of all the laws of nature. Reminiscent of the ocean that gives rise to all waves, this field can be mathematically defined as an infinite, eternal, transcendental reality at the basis of nature's functioning, a home of all the laws of nature, which spontaneously gives rise to all the natural forces and subatomic particles that structure our universe (Chapters Three and Four).

2. Physiologists have defined a fourth major state of human consciousness. Encouraged by Vedic definitions, inventive and well-controlled experiments by neurophysiologists at UCLA, Harvard, the French National Institute of Medical Research, and other research centers have defined a fourth major state of consciousness. Identified in people practicing the Transcendental Meditation technique and the advanced TM-Sidhi program, this fourth state is markedly different from the three common states of consciousness. It is identified by increased orderliness in brain wave functioning, a profound level of physical rest, and many other physiological changes (Chapter Five).

3. Hundreds of research studies have demonstrated rapid growth toward higher states of human functioning. Hundreds of published research studies, carried out at major universities and research centers throughout America and around the world, have shown that regular experience of this fourth state of consciousness leads to progressive improvement in both body and mind. These studies documenting the benefits of the Transcendental Meditation and TM-Sidhi programs show that human nature need no longer be fixed, that it is possible to measurably and markedly unfold potentials latent within both mind and body (Chapter Five).

4. Open, public statistics have shown measurable improvement in whole societies which coincide with large Super Radiance assemblies. As we will see in a detailed discussion of the research in Chapter Two, the data are repeated and impressive.

To understand Super Radiance, we must delve deeply into these four basic principles of Vedic Science. The Unified Field, the fourth state of consciousness, rapid evolution of human nature, and the production of peace through *rashtriya kavach* — are now well-documented elements in a long-lost understanding of human life. The central chapters of this book will demonstrate in detail how these essential Vedic understandings enunciated by Maharishi have been validated point for point by objective experiment and by the most profound insights of modern, objective science — the quantum mechanical discoveries that explain the subatomic functioning of our apparently physical world.

THE NATURE OF SCIENCE

In a scientific age these ideas undoubtedly come as a surprise. Yet throughout the history of science, leading scientists have pulled ideas once thought mystical or metaphysical into the realm of objective research. Yesterday's myth is today's hard fact. People once thought the shape of the Earth a metaphysical question, a matter of personal belief, of subjective preference, beyond any objective test. Even one hundred years ago, physicists considered the inside of the atom utterly unknowable, as much a matter of pure speculation as the angel population on the head of a pin. But the progress of analytic thought and the improvement of measuring instruments eventually included the shape of the world and the contents of the atom within the range of science.

Science is not determined by subject matter, in other words. Science is determined by evidence. The history of science is a history of old ideas confronted by new data — and if the data has been carefully gathered, the old ideas give way. It's often wrenching for people to change the conceptions they acquired growing up. For example, when Galileo proclaimed that the Sun, rather than the Earth, is the center of the universe, the authorities of his day locked him up for the last eight years of his life.

By now it is clear, however, that any theory is scientific if it can be treated scientifically. A theory is accepted because its logic is sound, because its reach is broader than competing theories, because it explains phenomena otherwise inexplicable (or, to put this another way, it predicts things otherwise unpredictable), and because, at those points where it can be experimentally verified, the results are consistently positive.

It is now possible to see that major tenets of the ancient Vedic literature, measured by these criteria, belong within the realm of science. Their structure is consistent, their reach is broad, their explanatory or predictive value is great, and at all the points where they are open to objective investigation, the findings are consistently positive.

Maharishi comments upon the objective validation of Vedic wisdom in these terms:

> Now we have this knowledge from three sources. We have it from the ancient tradition of the Vedic literature. We have it from personal experience through Transcendental Meditation and the TM-Sidhi program. And we have it from the objective investigations of modern science. Now we can use the term Vedic Science. And this Vedic Science is so very profound, it harnesses the total potential of nature's organizing power, which is located in the unified field of all the laws of nature. It allows the human mind to align itself with all the laws of nature at their source, on the basis of the intimate relationship between consciousness and matter. This is the glory of Vedic Science.

KNOWLEDGE FOR ACTION

When former United States President Ronald Reagan first put forward his controversial Star Wars anti-missile proposal, the Strategic Defense Initiative, his stated motives could be universally admired. "I call upon the scientific community in our country," he said, "those who gave us nuclear weapons, to turn their great talents now to the cause of mankind and world peace: to give us the means of rendering these nuclear weapons impotent and obsolete." President Reagan's specific proposal was often questioned — as are its recent incarnations in the administration of George W. Bush — but Reagan's intent was unarguable. There has been an urgent need for a totally new technology, a systematic procedure which could put the threat of war behind us. Since warfare has morphed to worldwide terrorism, moreover, a type of war utterly resistant to traditional, objective means of defense, the need has become only the greater.

Certainly nothing we have attempted in the past has given any hope of success. Nations have sometimes tried to avoid conventional war by a massive build-up of weapons — but the stockpiling of weapons has never led to anything but more warfare. As psychologist Abraham Maslow said, in a far different context, your capacities are your needs. In the context of material weaponry, if you *can* fight a war, you will. America has by far the most weaponry in the world, and it has in recent years gone to war repeatedly — in Kuwait, Kosovo, and Afghanistan, with more wars threatened by the U.S. government. Building weapons to attain peace is like dousing a fire with gasoline.

Peace talks and cease fires, however, have been no more effective. Researchers have located roughly 8,000 peace treaties concluded in the three millennia of recorded history, and their average life span has been approximately nine years. In recent times, the United Nations was founded to preserve peace through continuous discussions and negotiations, and since it was founded there have been more than 150 wars in the world.

Moreover, terrorist warfare resists weaponry and negotiations even more tenaciously than conventional warfare. As we have seen, attacks against terrorists only create more terrorists. Perversely, however, ignoring terrorists has the same effect as attacking them: It gives them reason to attack again. Most discouraging of all, peace talks serve only to inflame terrorists, who fear that treaties will bargain away their absolutist claims — and their frenzied attacks work to destroy any budding peace process. By now these self-aggravating dynamics of terrorism have stimulated terrorists to a level of ferocity and destructiveness that was previously unimaginable, threatening a global conflict that could last for decades.

Whether talking of conventional or terrorist warfare, therefore, neither weapons nor negotiations have ever produced a lasting peace. In fact, the whole history of the world amounts to a scientific experiment decisively disproving these two traditional attempts at peace creation.

But now a new technology of peace has become available. Rather than tinkering with weapons and treaties, hoping thereby to create a peaceful atmosphere in the world, Maharishi's approach is to create a peaceful atmosphere directly — through a sophisticated mechanics of consciousness, a technology of peace. This subjective approach is not aimed at the *means* of war, but the *cause* of war — at the tension, fear, and anger felt by people everywhere.

It is admittedly a totally new approach — but as has never been more obvious, only a new seed can yield a new crop.

THE WORLD PEACE ENDOWMENT FUND

Maharishi's response is a plan to deploy a permanent Super Radiance group numbering 40,000. Research mentioned previously has shown that temporary groups of approximately 7,000 have, three times, reduced terrorism worldwide by an average 72%. For three years, from 1988 to 1990, moreover, a single philanthropist supported a group of 8,000 meditation experts in India. Over those years, world events became almost unimaginably positive. Not only did the war of the Soviet Union on Afghanistan come to an end, as well as the long, bitter war between Iran and Iraq, but the Berlin Wall fell, the Soviet Union dissolved and the Cold War simply melted away.

In Maharishi's view, a Super Radiance group five times larger than that assembly of 8,000 will create an indomitable influence of harmony and peace that will purify the collective consciousness of the entire world — and create a permanent state of world peace. This group will also be gathered in India, where Maharishi has already trained more than 175,000 people in the Vedic technologies of consciousness (including, in addition to group meditation, special Vedic performances that also reduce negativity in the world). In addition, he recommends that each nation gather its own Super Radiance group, to create an invincible defense for its citizens.

In 1990, that single philanthropist had to cease his support of the Indian group of 8,000. As a result, the assembly had to disband and, discouragingly, the world has spiraled downward toward a new world war. The lack of financial support has thus hindered the widespread use of Super Radiance. As Maharishi has often said, "World peace is now only a matter of money."

One source of such money in every nation is the government, which has both the responsibility and the resources to establish large Super Radiance groups. In case governments are slow to act, however, a World Peace Endowment Fund has been established. This takes the creation of world peace out of the hands of politicians and gives the opportunity instead to peace-loving people in every nation. Because costs in India are so low, a Super Radiance group of 40,000 can be maintained for approximately $125 per person per month — $60 million per year, less than the cost of a single sophisticated fighter plane. More than $100 million has already been raised, and to ensure that the needed support will be available in perpetuity, the goal for the endowment fund is one billion dollars in total, with the group to be supported by interest on the principal. With such a fund in place, providing permanent support for a powerful Super Radiance group, Maharishi is confident not only that terrorism will cease, but that the world will enjoy a state of permanent peace and progress. As he states,

> The wise retaliation against terrorism will be to take a step which will completely root out terrorism forever — and this will be by creating a very strong influence of positivity and harmony in world consciousness so that any kind of negative trends do not arise.

To examine this approach, it can help to investigate in detail the four principles of Vedic Science — the four ancient "predictions" now open to scientific investigation. And the place to begin is with the research evidence on the technology of peace itself.

For anyone looking into the use of Super Radiance to end terrorism and war, the first question is obvious: Is the Maharishi Effect an objective reality?

2

PERMANENT PEACE:
The Evidence

The temperature was ten below zero on the thermometer, with a slicing wind chill at forty below. It was after midnight, but bundled workers were still up there, hanging off the girders in the drifting snow, picked out in the glare of temporary stadium lighting.

They were working on a 60,000 square foot metal building that was going from design to finished structure in exactly three weeks — shattering previous construction records by a factor of three. On the far end of campus another large crew was smashing down through frozen ground, in the most bitter December in memory, laying pipe and wires for 200 mobile homes then trucking across three states for instant installation.

In the three weeks from Thanksgiving to mid-December, 1983, many such logistical miracles took place. The staff, faculty, and students of Maharishi University of Management in Fairfield, Iowa, were preparing to house and feed more than 7,000 people overall, an increase of 6,000 from their usual numbers. For the first time, under conditions of extreme time urgency, enough meditation experts would gather in one spot to affect, in theory, the level of stress all around the world.

The experience of previous assemblies had indicated that the number of experts required would be, in relative terms, exceedingly small — the square root of one per cent of the population to be affected. For example, the United States population was then 255,000,000, which required a meditation assembly of the square root of one per cent of that number, or 1,600 people. The previous experiments had demonstrated that the square root of one per cent seemed to be a threshold level — under that level not much happened, while over that level a measurable effect suddenly appeared in the society. Similar threshold levels are common in physics, producing sudden *phase transitions*. As water decreases in temperature, for instance, when the temperature reaches 32 degrees Fahrenheit, the water undergoes a relatively quick phase transition to ice.

To reach the experimentally demonstrated phase transition threshold for a global effect, with a worldwide population then at 4.8 billion, 7,000 people was predicted to be the necessary number. To reach that number, experts in Maharishi's Transcendental Meditation program, and the advanced TM-Sidhi program, would need to arrive from all over the world.

The result on campus was three weeks of organized pandemonium. While the new "Grand Assembly Hall" sprouted from the ground, the food services took over the student union and the gymnasium, preparing to feed six times more people than usual. Thousands of beds were pulled out of storage, thousands more purchased and installed in every conceivable nook and cranny. The mobile homes arrived in a two-day caravan, and round-the-clock crews dug them in and hooked them up — each home to house six people.

As the assembly-opening day approached, December 17, the enthusiasm on campus was summed up in the name given to the assembly: A Taste of Utopia. The conference was intended as a

global sociological experiment to find out whether it was possible to radiate a "taste of more problem-free life" to every part
of the planet. At a succession of press conferences, Maharishi
University of Management Professors David Orme-Johnson,
Charles Alexander, and Michael Dillbeck made predictions
about the effects they expected, and they also lodged these predictions with a committee of independent scientists around the
United States. Many of the predictions concerned public statistics: a worldwide decrease in crime, accidents, and illness,
along with a rise in stock markets and patent applications. Other
predictions included a decrease in international tension and
conflict and an increase in positivity and success by heads of state.
In sum, the prediction was simple: The entire world should experience measurable improvement in any area of life for which data
could be obtained during one specific three-week period.

With workers still driving rivets and connecting wiring, the
Taste of Utopia began as scheduled on December 17, 1983.
Attendance at the daily Super Radiance assembly increased in a
couple of days from the usual average of 1,600 to more than 4,000.
Over the next week thousands more people arrived, streaming
in from every part of the globe, until the human flood at last rose
to the required level. On the day that attendance in the group
meditations finally reached 7,000, people in the brand new Grand
Assembly Hall stood and cheered for five minutes.

WORLDWIDE STATISTICAL IMPROVEMENTS

What everyone wanted to know, of course, was whether there
was good statistical reason for the cheering.

As the data became available, the answer became clear. First,
American statistics came in. Traffic fatalities over the year-end
holidays dropped to an all-time low despite the fact that miles
driven were at an all-time high. The fatalities were 41.6% fewer
per mile driven than the mean for the prior 16 years (control-
ling for both miles driven and the effect of the 55 mph speed
limit). Infectious diseases dropped 15% compared to the weeks

just before and just after the assembly and 32% compared to the mean of the five previous years during the same three weeks. Patent applications, which are ordinarily within one or two percent of the official predictions made by the United States Patent Office, suddenly increased 15% over these predictions during the weeks of the assembly, then dropped back toward normal values immediately after the assembly (the Patent Office predictions take into account any seasonal increases that might ordinarily be expected).

For international data, the research design adopted was to seek data from Australia, South Africa, and England, countries widely dispersed around the globe that keep good statistical records. Patent applications were available for all three countries; applications went up sharply in all three. When combined with the United States figures, mathematical analysis showed the *p value* (probability of mere coincidence) at $p<.04$ — less than four chances in one hundred. Traffic fatalities were not available on the needed weekly basis from England, but they declined markedly in both Australia and South Africa — despite, in South Africa, a usual tendency to increase at that time of year ($p<.0001$ — less than one chance of coincidence in ten thousand). Only Australia could supply disease data weekly; compared with a strong upward trend before and after the assembly, infectious disease declined there nearly 15% as compared to the mean of the five previous years, the same as in the United States.

The predictions about international affairs were also upheld by systematic *media analysis*, or *content analysis* — a widely accepted procedure for determining the content of media reporting each day. In a typical program of content analysis, the analyst might count on a daily basis the number of newspaper stories on a given topic, for example, or the number of reported events of a specific type. In this case, the media analysis focused on the number of positive events in international affairs — defined as peace talks, cease fires, harmonious statements by heads of state, etc. For the three weeks before the assembly, the percentage of positive events worldwide, as compared to the total number of international events of all types, was 18.7%. During the assembly this percentage increased by 60% to 31.5%, and after the assembly it declined again to 13.5%.

Finally, the World Index of stocks reported daily in the *Wall Street Journal* showed a remarkable upward move during the three weeks of the assembly. Under certain circumstances, stock prices can be a clear objective measure of the overall mood in any given society. If people who trade in the stock market feel optimistic and confident, they buy stocks; if they feel fearful and depressed, they sell stocks. Unless an overriding economic factor comes into play (as, for instance, a marked change in interest rates), an upsurge in optimism and good feeling throughout society ought to be accompanied by an upsurge in stock prices. This is just what happened during the Taste of Utopia assembly.

A dramatic worldwide experiment had provided strong evidence that Super Radiance can provide a worldwide influence of harmony and progress. The question still remained, however, why Maharishi had felt such urgency about the precise timing of the Taste of Utopia course. It was only ten years later that light was shed on this issue. In the early 1990s, with the Berlin Wall down, former government officials of the Soviet Union brought out records of high governmental discussions. Those records related to a Soviet fighter plane which, earlier in the fall of 1983, had shot down an American airliner that strayed over Communist territory in Korea. What the records indicated was that the Soviet military could not believe that America would not retaliate massively. For that reason, by the holiday season — at exactly the time the Taste of Utopia course convened — the records showed that Soviet planners were closer than at any time before or since to launching a pre-emptive nuclear strike. The first time a Super Radiance group was large enough to generate a statistically measurable influence of harmony and peace throughout the entire word, it occurred at the most dangerous moment of the Cold War. No statistical analysis can estimate the chance of that happening by mere coincidence.

IN SEARCH OF PUBLICATION

Despite the dramatic nature of the Taste of Utopia course, and the strong statistical significance of the results, the course was arguably more significant to the participants (who knew of all the previous experiments) than it would have been to independent scientists. To a scientist looking at that single study, even the many statistical changes around the world, though impressively consistent, happened just the one time — and were therefore vulnerable to arguments of coincidence. With a paradigm-shattering phenomenon like Super Radiance, no one-time study could be completely convincing to independent and highly skeptical scholars.

To gain scientific acceptance and publication in mainstream academic journals, therefore, it was necessary to produce studies with many replications, and with tight statistical controls, studies that would be difficult to argue away. Across the decade of the 1980s, researchers at Maharishi University of Management took up that challenge. Using ever more rigorous experimental design and statistical analysis, these researchers persevered until, as this book goes to press, nineteen studies on Super Radiance have attained academic publication.

For those unfamiliar with research procedures, the fact that a particular study is published means more than that it has simply been printed and distributed. Most research journals are *refereed*; that is, distinguished experts in the field (the referees, or peer reviewers) read and judge every study that is submitted. These referees are concerned with the logic and consistency of the theory being tested, as well as with the research methodology — the scientific and statistical procedures that have been used in any particular study. When the theory being tested in a

THE EVIDENCE • 37

study is new or particularly controversial, the referees tend to read such a study even more critically than usual and judge it against the strictest requirements.

Such heightened defenses, designed to protect the academic world from an onslaught of the faulty and the ill-considered, faced the researchers from M.U.M. For years the journal referees asked, in ways rigorously methodological, the many common sense questions that any sensible person would want to ask about Super Radiance: Does it work every time it is tried? Do the changes always begin after the gathering of a group of meditators? Do the changes ordinarily cease when the gathering breaks up? How do we know the changes weren't going to occur anyway? Do such changes ordinarily happen at the same time of year? What other factors might explain the same results? Just generally, in such a complex system as human society, how can one ever be sure of the effect caused by any one particular agent?

KNOWLEDGEABLE OR BIASED?

The M.U.M. researchers knew from the beginning that they would have to deal with such questions — as well as with skepticism about their motives. After all, they all worked at Maharishi University of Management, and they all took part in Super Radiance assemblies themselves. It can be argued that this familiarity made them particularly knowledgeable on the topic, but it can also be argued that it made them biased. This issue was addressed directly in an academic exchange over a research paper on Super Radiance that was eventually published by the *Journal of Conflict Resolution* (see discussion below). One of the reviewers assigned to the study said he would accept research on Super Radiance only if it were done by "an independent, scientific body such as the National Academy of Sciences." But as the editor of the journal, Bruce Russett, responded, "This is a bit of a catch-22. It is almost impossible to imagine a body like the National Academy of Sciences being willing to fund such a research effort without some prior appearance of evidence for the hypothesis. . . . Most research — at least the presentation of new findings — is performed by scholars who begin with the belief that their hypotheses are plausible. Who else would spend the effort?"

It can be said in defense of M.U.M.'s researchers, moreover, that their research methodologies have been not only rigorous but transparent and easily verifiable. Whereas the data in many social science research studies is gathered privately by the researchers — through, for example, questionnaires they devise themselves — the evidence in Super Radiance studies has come almost exclusively from open public statistics (war deaths, crime rate, traffic accidents), data gathered by governments and other independent organizations and available to anyone who wants to see it.

From one perspective, this data is plentiful. The technology of peace is supposed to affect the entire society; therefore, statistics which measure any aspect of society should demonstrate the effect. But there are challenges to data collection. It is true, for example, that many of the statistics that are available measure only the negative aspects of society (including crime, fires, infectious disease rate, drugs, divorce rate, etc.) while many of the most important statistics from a human point of view, such as number of smiles passed between mother and child, or number of poems written per capita per day, are not available. Moreover, it is sometimes true that relevant statistics are not available in relevant ways — daily or weekly numbers may be needed and only monthly or yearly figures obtainable. These limitations, however, are usually challenges rather than insurmountable obstacles. Super Radiance research can ordinarily be carried on simply by collecting public data and analyzing it intelligently. Any researcher can do it. The Maharishi Effect data fits one of the most important scientific requirements: Replication of the results by other researchers is easily performed.

THE CONCEPT OF
COLLECTIVE CONSCIOUSNESS

Whatever the source of the evidence, the theory is certainly a challenge to those steeped only in objective, materialist science. It is a theory that depends in part on a sociological concept — that of *collective consciousness*. In the words of Dr. David Orme-Johnson, who was for two decades the chairman of M.U.M.'s department of psychology, "What the Super Radiance studies show is that a few individuals, when they experience more coherence within their own consciousness, radiate increased coherence into the collective consciousness of the entire society."

In this usage, collective consciousness means roughly what news magazines mean by *national mood*, stock brokers mean by the *investor climate*, and historians mean by the German word *Zeitgeist* (spirit of the times). There is an overall tone or flavor characteristic of any particular population in any particular period, a reality well-known to the traveler who rapidly moves from, say, England to Italy to Egypt. There is a national character indigenous to each country and usually it is easily perceived. It is this overall quality which Orme-Johnson defines in the following way:

> Collective consciousness we see as the sum total of the influences of all the individual consciousnesses within a society. An analogy is provided by a series of small magnets. If they are put all together with their poles aligned, they create an overall field which then, in turn, affects all the individual magnets. Collective consciousness arises in the same way, from the individual members of a society, and then it has a reciprocal influence on those same individuals, modifying their thought and behavior. Incoherent individuals create an incoherent collective consciousness, which increases the probability of crime, sickness, accidents, etc. We hypothesize that a Super Radiance group of sufficient size creates an influence of coherence which increases the coherence in the collective consciousness of the entire

nation, and that this overall improvement helps produce increased coherence within the individuals of that society.

If the individuals in a society are thought of as smokestacks, each one puffing a certain amount of stress and anxiety into the atmosphere, then the collective consciousness is the overall result. If the collective consciousness is polluted by the individuals, then the whole atmosphere is filled with excessive stress and negativity, which in turn affects the individuals. In Maharishi's understanding,

> All occurrences of violence, negativity, conflicts, crises, or problems in any society are just the expression of growth of stress in collective consciousness. When the level of stress becomes sufficiently great, it bursts out into external violence and war, or internal crime, accidents, and disorder.

In Maharishi's Vedic understanding, therefore, a single underlying cause stimulates all types of violence — including crime, conventional warfare, and terrorism.

THE SIGNIFICANCE OF THIS RESEARCH

The research studies that validate this theory are often repeated, impressively structured, and convincingly consistent — as independent scholars have attested. Such independent academic experts have encountered the Super Radiance studies as journal referees, or as discussants at annual academic meetings, and their views offer confidence that a detailed review of this research will be fruitful. We have seen comments from two such scholars in the first pages of this book. In addition, David Edwards, professor of government at the University of Texas (Austin), has given an especially close reading to several of the Maharishi Effect studies. Says Dr. Edwards,

> The claim can be plausibly made that the potential impact of this research exceeds that of any other ongoing social or psychological research program. The research has survived a broader array of statistical tests than most research in the field of con-

flict resolution. I think this work, and the theory that informs it, deserve the most serious consideration by academics and policy makers alike.

Ted Robert Gurr, emeritus professor of government and politics at the University of Maryland, has been considered for decades one of America's two or three leading experts in the field of peace studies and conflict resolution. His view of the research:

> In the studies that I have examined on the impact of the Maharishi Effect on conflict, I can find no methodological flaws, and the findings have been consistent across a large number of replications in many different geographical and conflictual situations. As unlikely as the premise may sound, I think we have to take these studies seriously.

The purpose of this chapter is to give every reader the chance to understand why specialists such as these have found the Super Radiance research compelling. This research effort, which has lasted more than two decades, amounts to an intriguing voyage of discovery — as M.U.M. researchers have sought to answer one searching question after another. Since the ability to create permanent world peace is at issue, moreover, no research effort could be more worthy of extended study.

FIELD EFFECTS ON THE INDIVIDUAL

Before looking at the studies showing that Super Radiance assemblies create statistical changes in the society around them, it will be useful to look briefly at three studies indicating that individual brains can indeed both broadcast influences and receive them.

1. Receiving influences. During the first large Super Radiance assembly in North America, 3,500 experts in the Transcendental Meditation and TM-Sidhi programs gathered in Amherst, Massachusetts, in 1979. On six separate days, researchers measured the brain wave patterns of people who were 1,200 miles away from that Super Radiance assembly. At exactly the time that the large group began to meditate, the brain wave patterns of the people 1,200 miles away became significantly more orderly and coherent. As we will see in Chapter Five, the practice of the Transcendental Meditation technique results in increased brain wave coherence. This study indicates that the increased coherence enjoyed by people in a large group can be radiated to, and experienced by, others at a significant distance.*

2. Sending and receiving. An expert in the Transcendental Meditation program sat in one room and meditated while a person who had not yet learned to meditate sat in the next room running a computer program that tests how quickly a person can calculate. The person at the computer was hooked to electroencephalographic machinery to test his brain wave patterns. At the point when the meditator in one room began meditating, the non-meditator in the other room showed (1) a marked increase in brain wave coherence, and (2) improved performance on the computer test. Since the non-meditating person was not told of the meditator, nor any other relevant aspects of the test, the results strongly indicate that the increased coherence characteristic of meditation was radiated by the meditator to the non-meditator.†

3. Physiological indication of enhanced brain functioning. During a sixty-day period, the numbers of people attending a large group meditation at Maharishi University of Management in Fairfield, Iowa, varied greatly (due to special courses that temporarily attracted meditation experts from out of town). For those sixty days, forty non-meditating people who lived in Fairfield were tested on a daily basis for the production of serotonin. Serotonin is a powerful neurotransmitter which research has shown to produce a feeling of happiness and contentment and, in one study, even euphoria. Many other studies have shown that low levels of serotonin correlate not only with poor emotional moods but with increased aggressiveness and violence. The study showed that on days when attendance was high at the Super Radiance assembly on campus, the non-meditators showed a marked increase in serotonin production — 400% higher than on the days of lowest attendance — offering a plausible neurophysiological mechanism to explain reduced hostility and aggression in society at large.*

These studies demonstrate physiological effects associated with Super Radiance, effects which can help account for the statistical changes that occur in crime, war, terrorism, and other social indicators. If during Super Radiance assemblies, the brains of people in the society as a whole become more orderly and coherent and the brain chemistry better balanced, then it is more understandable why people in that society would become more orderly and coherent in their thoughts and behavior and less aggressive in their actions.

Regardless of these possible mechanisms, however, the central question is whether the Maharishi Effect actually does appear in the society as a whole. This is the bottom line question: Can a measurable, society-wide influence of harmony and peace be radiated by groups of meditation experts? The vast majority of the research on Super Radiance goes to answer exactly this question.

REVERSING THE CRIME WAVE

The first researcher to succeed in gaining academic publication for a study examining this new approach was Dr. Michael Dillbeck. A psychologist who earned his Ph.D. at Purdue University, Dr. Dillbeck has the good-humored patience and clear eye for detail that mark the best statistical researchers. His research papers, like the paintings of Persian miniaturists, are filled with precise and daunting detail, the perfect style to break

*Journal of Social Behavior and Personality, in press.

a paradigm-shattering idea into the well protected fortification of academic publication.

This first study was on crime. The topic was especially significant because crime — in any society where open warfare or terrorism is not present — is the most disorderly and violent disturbance of the peace. If the Transcendental Meditation program is a methodology for the direct creation of peace in the world — capable of dissolving even the extreme social violence represented by warfare and terrorism — it must surely be able to reduce crime.

For his first paper, Dr. Dillbeck went back to the original Super Radiance discovery. In 1974, researchers Garland Landrith III and Candace Borland had found eleven cities in which more than one percent of the population had begun the basic Transcendental Meditation technique. In those cities — in an era of constantly rising crime — the crime rate fell suddenly and markedly. This study did not involve the advanced TM-Sidhi program, nor the gathering of meditators into groups. In lieu of group practice, people practiced the basic Transcendental Meditation technique privately in their own homes for twenty minutes twice a day. This approach required a much larger percentage of the population than does Super Radiance — one percent rather than the square root of one percent.

That original study, however, left a number of questions unanswered. In the first place, though it took several years to get all the police data, twenty-four cities had actually crossed the one percent threshold in 1972, rather than eleven, and they all needed to be included in the study. In the second place, there are many social factors that affect crime, such as income levels, unemployment, and age, and these had not been taken into account. To be demonstrated as the cause, Super Radiance would need to stand alone, unencumbered by these other factors.

To tighten this study into statistically convincing shape, Dr. Dillbeck's first step was to carefully match each of the twenty-four cities which reached the one-percent threshold in 1972 with other cities that were statistically similar in all the factors which affect crime. To have these cities chosen objectively, he enlisted the aid of an independent consultant from Bowling Green State University. Once he received the choices for the twenty-four matching cities, Dr. Dillbeck ran a statistical check to see if the two groups of cities were actually a good fit. Eight demographic variables were most important, eight variables which have often been shown to correlate strongly with average crime rate: (1) city population, (2) population density per square mile, (3) unemployment rate, (4) income, (5) median years of education, (6) percentage change in residence each year, (7) percentage of families below the poverty level, and (8) percentage of persons in the age range of fifteen to twenty-nine (the range with the highest probability for involvement in crime).

No one city, however carefully chosen, could ever be an exact match for any other city on all these variables. If the control cities were well-chosen, however, then the averages for the twenty-four one-percent cities should have been quite close to the averages for the twenty-four control cities. The figures showed that the independent consultant had done his job well. Seven of the variables matched almost exactly. The only significant difference: The one-percent cities had a higher median for years of education. Higher levels of education have sometimes correlated with lower crime rate.

To deal with this single statistical imbalance, Dr. Dillbeck took recourse to a statistical tool known as ANCOVA (analysis of covariance) to control for the inequality in education. If a statistician were measuring people's height and wanted to control for the fact that one person was standing on a box, he would subtract the height of the box from that person's overall measurement to find his real height. Dr. Dillbeck used standard ANCOVA procedures to find and subtract the effect that higher education could have given to the one-percent cities.

CRIME GOES DOWN IN TWENTY-FOUR CITIES

Only this one ANCOVA adjustment was needed to produce statistical parity between the two groups of cities. Against this statistically neutral background, then, the crime rate figures stood out sharply. In 1973, the year after the one percent threshold was reached in the initial twenty-four cities, there was a marked average decrease in crime in those cities. In the control cities, on the other hand, as in the nation at large, the average crime rate continued to climb. The difference between the two was, by standard statistical checks, significant at the $p<.002$ level, less than two chances in 1,000 that such a strong result could have happened by chance. Researchers will usually call a particular finding *significant* if it reaches $p<.05$, less than 5 chances in 100 (1 in 20) of mere coincidence. Most social science journals will publish research significant at the $p<.05$ level. If the level reaches $p<.01$, (1 in 100) it is called *highly significant*, and $p<.001$ (1 in 1,000) is called *very highly significant*. By these criteria, Dr. Dillbeck's first finding ($p<.002$) was highly significant and missed being very highly significant by only one chance in 1,000.

To add to the strength of the study, Dr. Dillbeck followed the crime rate in all forty-eight cities over the next five years. Through that whole period, the rate of increase in crime in the one percent cities was significantly lower than in the control cities ($p<.02$). Crime thus dropped significantly in the first year, and continued to grow more slowly over the next five. Dr. Dillbeck did a bivariate analysis for both the changes (the probability that they could have both occurred by chance) and the result was very highly significant ($p<.001$.). Dr. Dillbeck's careful work paid off. He had accounted for every factor usually thought to affect crime, and still the result was statistically strong. In 1981 his study was published in the *Journal of Crime and Justice.**

---

*Journal of Crime and Justice, 4, 25–45.

FROM *TM* TO THE *TM-SIDHI* PROGRAM

Even before this study appeared, however, several unpublished experiments had already shown that there was a more powerful way to transform the social environment. To the basic Transcendental Meditation technique this approach added two more factors: (1) the use of the advanced TM-Sidhi program, including Yogic Flying; and (2) assembly of the meditation experts into large groups that practiced the techniques all together.

The Transcendental Meditation technique by itself allows the mind to settle down deep within itself to experience a state of perfect silence, a state of least excitation. In this state, when the mind is experiencing the deepest level of its own intelligence, Maharishi indicates that the mind is also experiencing the deepest level of intelligence in the natural world (see discussion in the next chapter).

By contrast, the advanced TM-Sidhi program allows the mind not only to *experience* this basic level of nature's intelligence but, as it were, to *stir* that intelligence, to give it a direction, to cause it to move within itself. Finally, in the TM-Sidhi technique known as Yogic Flying, a purely consciousness-based technique leads to spontaneous activity in the body, which lifts up and hops forward (although the meditator is typically sitting crosslegged on the floor). The body can go through a long sequence of hops that might appear strenuous, yet the mind remains deeply settled within. In Maharishi's analysis, the result is to profoundly enliven nature's intelligence, creating waves which, as indicated by the research discussed in this chapter, radiate throughout the entire society.

Whatever the explanation, the research quickly demonstrated that large assemblies of experts in both Transcendental Meditation and TM-Sidhi programs were much more powerful in their effects. The effectiveness of these Super Radiance groups proved important to M.U.M.'s researchers. To create societal changes with only the basic TM technique, practiced by indi-

viduals on their own, required that one percent of the population learn to meditate. But by adding the TM-Sidhi program and
gathering the meditators into Super Radiance assemblies, the
statistical effects began to appear when attendance reached a
level exponentially smaller — the square root of one percent. In
the United States this Super Radiance number was, in the early
1980s, about 1,600. For England it was 400. For the world as a
whole it was 7,000. These were manageable numbers, attendance
figures that could be deliberately produced in different spots on
the globe and thus statistically investigated in many different
times and places.

Dr. Dillbeck set out to capture the statistical reality of what
was then called the extended Maharishi Effect (the effect as
produced by Super Radiance groups). To produce powerful statistical effects, his strategy this time was to write one research
paper that reported on four separate experiments. "Regardless
of how strong any one experiment is," Dr. Dillbeck said, "It can
still seem easy to dismiss as mere coincidence. When you report
on four experiments at once, however, you make coincidence a
very difficult argument to sustain."

As the main focus of his study, Dr. Dillbeck once again emphasized crime rate as the best available indicator of social incoherence, of stress in the collective consciousness. As experiments he picked four of the largest Super Radiance assemblies
held between 1978 and 1984, assemblies held where crime rate
data was available for evaluation. The first was a summer-long
project in the state of Rhode Island in 1978, part of the worldwide Ideal Society campaign, in which more than 300 experts
in the TM-Sidhi program gathered in the smallest state in the
union. The second assembly involved 3,500 such experts who
visited New Delhi, India, in the fall of 1980 for a course on
Maharishi's Vedic Science. The third assembly took place in
Puerto Rico with 200 meditators gathered for a long course that
lasted more than six months. Finally, a gathering of 1,200 med-

itators took place in Manila, the Philippines, in the late summer and fall of 1984.

In every case, crime rate dropped markedly in the local area for the duration of the Super Radiance assembly. After the assembly, crime climbed back to pre-assembly levels. In every case, the results were statistically significant and, as Dr. Dillbeck had predicted, the joint statistical probability that crime had dropped all four places merely by chance was vanishingly small. The joint p value was less than one in one million.

THE SECOND ACCEPTANCE BY AN ACADEMIC JOURNAL

After completing his study, Dr. Dillbeck sent it to the *Journal of Mind and Behavior*. The editor of this journal, Dr. Raymond Russ, professor of psychology at the University of Maine, was immediately intrigued by what he saw. "On the one hand, the paper was based on an extremely unconventional idea," Dr. Russ said. "On the other hand, this idea was backed up by rigorous statistical analysis, a level of mathematical sophistication rarely seen in psychological or sociological studies."

To deal with this unusual challenge, Dr. Russ took an unusual step. Not only did he submit the paper to experts in psychology, who were asked to judge the clarity, consistency, and completeness of the theory being proposed. He also submitted it to an expert in statistical analysis, a non-psychologist, who was asked to judge whether the appropriate statistical tools had been applied and if they had been applied correctly. When the referees were finished with their analysis, Dr. Russ received word from the psychologists that the theory sections were internally logical and consistent, and from the statistician that the mathematical methods were correct and competently applied. Said Dr. Russ:

> I decided to publish. The theory being proposed was a complete departure from the norm in either psychology or sociology, but this study was well-done. The statistical evidence was persuasive. What I had to consider is that judging new ideas in any

scientific field is an extremely delicate task. On the one hand, you never want to propound errors. On the other hand, you need to keep the field open for innovation and progress. In this case, Michael Dillbeck had written a strong paper with solid evidence. I didn't see how I could deny that paper publication.

For the second time, Dr. Dillbeck's systematic statistical approach had won academic acceptance. This time, moreover, because the numbers of people involved in the Super Radiance assemblies were so small, the evidence more clearly pointed toward a mechanism based on an underlying field. Said Dr. Dillbeck,

> These findings give credence to a field theory of consciousness. The proportion of participants in the TM-Sidhi program was extremely small in each experiment, and because the participants were often involved in residential courses of limited duration in which they did not interact with the general population, it seems impossible that they could have affected society by any direct personal interaction. Thus, it appears that some kind of field effect is implied by these results, by virtue of which an influence is spread throughout a social system.*

AN EXPERIMENT WITH OPEN WAR

While Michael Dillbeck was polishing his multiple-city crime rate studies, two other M.U.M. psychologists were planning one isolated, dramatic experiment to demonstrate that Super Radiance can neutralize open warfare. The aim of the experiment was to significantly reduce the nearly nonstop fighting in war-torn Lebanon.

Dr. David Orme-Johnson, then head of the psychology department at M.U.M., is a graduate of Columbia University with his Ph.D. from the University of Maryland. While teaching at the University of Texas in the early 1970s, Dr. Orme-Johnson produced one of the earliest and most influential studies on

---

*Journal of Mind and Behavior, 8, 67–194.

the Transcendental Meditation technique, a study showing that regular practice of TM allows the autonomic nervous system to become more settled and stable. Since then Dr. Orme-Johnson has published more than eighty scientific papers on the Transcendental Meditation technique.

Dr. Charles Alexander, then associate professor of psychology at M.U.M., earned both his B.A. and Ph.D. from Harvard University. One of the most significant published studies by Dr. Alexander showed that TM extended the life span of elderly people. Among a number of widely respected books he produced, Dr. Alexander was co-editor of a book from Oxford University Press, *Higher Stages of Adult Development* — a book enthusiastically received by experts in the field.

It was Dr. Alexander who conceived the Lebanon experiment originally. He explained,

> Previously, all experiments on Super Radiance had been what researchers call naturalistic experiments. Super Radiance assemblies had gathered for various reasons, and researchers had decided after the fact to gather statistics and see what the effect had been. The statistical evidence had been strong, but many researchers prefer an experiment that has been deliberately created by the experimenters, with predictions made in advance. That was what we wanted to do in Lebanon.

Known as the International Peace Project, this study was funded in part through a grant honoring William Ellinghaus, President of American Telephone and Telegraph, and supplied by the Fund for Higher Education in New York.

The project was designed to bring together in Jerusalem 200 experts in Maharishi's Vedic Science, people who practiced both TM and the advanced TM-Sidhi program. Jerusalem was chosen, rather than a city in Lebanon, because Israel already had 30,000 people trained in the basic Transcendental Meditation technique and several hundred more in the advanced TM-Sidhi program. As Dr. Dillbeck's one percent research had shown, the

30,000 TM meditators should have been enough to produce the Maharishi Effect for a population half the size of Israel and Lebanon together. Thus, in theory, the Super Radiance assembly would have to attract enough additional people to take care of the other half of the population. This Super Radiance number was 197.

In several ways this study was more revealing than the research previously discussed.

1. Prospective study: In the first place, as Dr. Alexander indicated, the International Peace Project was what scientists call a prospective study rather than a retrospective study. Precise predictions of the results were made in advance. Drs. Orme-Johnson and Alexander took the unusual precaution of lodging these predictions with leading independent scientists in both the United States and Israel. The clear-cut predictions, made months before the study took place, made clear that statistics were not being chosen after the fact simply because they happened to work.

2. Multivariate study: In the second place, the experiment was designed as a multivariate study. Most earlier studies on Super Radiance had focused on only one benefit at a time — on the reduction of warfare, for instance, or decreases in crime or traffic accidents. But Super Radiance is defined as a holistic influence that affects the entire society at once. Given this holistic definition, it should be possible to measure many different variables in a society and demonstrate improvement in them all simultaneously. That was one goal of this study. The researchers predicted, among other things, that as numbers at the Super Radiance assembly rose, automobile accidents and fires in Jerusalem should decrease, the Israeli stock market and the national mood (as measured by content analysis of the local newspapers) should improve, and, most important, the continuing warfare in neighboring Lebanon should decrease, as measured both by reported war deaths and by content analysis of media sources. If Super Radiance affected all of these variable simultaneously, the results would be much more convincing.

3. Internal replication: In the third place, the International Peace Project provided, quite inadvertently, an experiment that replicated itself a number of times within two months. The goal of the program was to gather 200 experts and keep them together throughout August and September of 1983, but practical considerations made this impossible. Suitable hotel space was only irregularly available, most students had to leave at the end of August to return to school, and many employed people found it difficult to get long leaves of absence. As a result the number of meditation experts slowly built up for the first two weeks of August, attained high levels for the second two weeks, and then rose and fell irregularly throughout September. Though unplanned, this up-and-down pattern produced a compelling experiment. The statistics on crime, fires, the war, etc., would now have to move repeatedly, in correlation with the attendance numbers at the Super Radiance assembly, rather than only once.

4. Time series analysis: Finally, Drs. Orme-Johnson and Alexander chose to use a powerful method of statistical analysis, known as *impact assessment analysis*, or *time series analysis* (or, for the most technical term, *Box-Jenkins autoregressive integrated moving averages*). This statistical tool gives a mathematical answer to the question, "In such a complicated system as human society, how do you know that such a result wasn't going to happen anyway, even without the Super Radiance group?" This is especially important in a societal study, since societies are replete with an infinite number of internal influences, any one of which might theoretically confound the study. Time series analysis, however, takes into account whatever influences have already been present in a society (even if they are unknown), then analyzes the impact (if any) of some new factor in the continuing situation.

Using such time series analysis, researchers can, for instance, look at the daily history of automobile accidents for several months up until the day a Super Radiance group first gets together. Time series analysis allows them to construct a mathematical formula which accounts for all the systematic ups and downs those automobile accidents were already showing, day by day. That formula (or statistical model) therefore automatically takes into account all the different factors that have already been affecting automobile accidents significantly, because those factors are reflected in the changing pattern of the statistics — *even if these causative factors involved aren't known to the researchers.*

Such a powerful tool can radically simplifiy the apparent complexity in human society. With time series analysis, the infinite number of social influences, most of them small, tend to cancel one another out. Only those significant influences capable of causing measurable changes remain. In a crime study, for instance, specific types of crime may be found to increase every Friday and Saturday, which is explained by what researchers call a *weekend effect* (that is, more colloquially, by people with time on their hands and liquor or other drugs in their systems). The same crime study may find strong increases every summer, and closer analysis may explain this by a correlation of violent crime with higher temperatures. However, it is not necessary to understand the mechanism that causes every significant pattern in the data. If, in the automobile accident example, accidents move up and down in a monthly cycle, but the reason for this is not known, the monthly cycle is still reflected in the statistical model. This model can then be used to generate predictions about the immediate future of automobile accidents — if only the current causative factors (known and unknown) are in play. If automobile accidents suddenly drop much lower than the prediction, for example, this is strong evidence that a new influence has suddenly appeared.

CRIME, FIRES, ACCIDENTS, AND WAR DEATHS
ALL AFFECTED AT ONCE

With the study so tightly designed and the mathematical tool so powerful, if the Maharishi Effect were an objective reality, this new factor should certainly appear. That is just what happened — in great detail. Every one of the predictions was confirmed, and the results on all of them were statistically significant. The most heartening single statistic showed that when attendance at the Super Radiance assembly was high (in the highest quartile, the 25% of days with highest attendance), as compared with days when attendance in the lowest quartile, war deaths in neighboring Lebanon dropped an average of 76%. When Super Radiance numbers went up, moreover, the Lebanon war intensity (as measured by content analysis of daily newspapers) decreased ($p<.01$), automobile accidents decreased ($p<.0005$), fires decreased ($p<.0001$), and the Israeli stock market went up ($p<.025$).

Four other features of the study were intriguing.

1. Two weeks of strongest results. Events in the two weeks when the Super Radiance attendance was continually high were dramatically more positive than during the other six weeks of the study. War deaths in Lebanon averaged only 1.5 per day during that two-week high-attendance period and more than 20 per day the rest of the time. Automobile accidents were 15% lower during that two-week period than during the other six weeks, fires 26% lower, and the stock market 27 points higher (averaging 457 as opposed to 431). These marked changes during the two weeks of continuously high attendance provided additional evidence that an increase in meditation experts can provide an increase in the Maharishi Effect.

2. Effect stronger when closest to the source. The effect of the Super Radiance assembly appeared to be stronger closer to the source. Even when the attendance at the assembly was relatively low, local statistics in Jerusalem were positively affected. As the numbers rose, statistics in Israel as a whole began to change, and only when the numbers were high (in the highest quartile, the highest 25%), did warfare in Lebanon drop significantly. This is consistent with the theory of the Maharishi Effect — to influence a larger area with a larger population, a larger Super Radiance number is required.

3. Effect stronger when all variables combined. When all the variables were combined mathematically into a single index, the correlation between the numbers of people meditating together and this sum of all the variables was even more striking. Statistical evidence always becomes more powerful when many different ways of looking at the data are employed simultaneously. If the various approaches cancel each other out, then no real underlying effect is indicated. If the various approaches reinforce each other, the underlying effect is more strongly defined.

When the standardized Z score combining fires, traffic accidents, crime, the war, the stock market, and newspaper content analysis (known collectively as the Quality of Life Index) was plotted over the Super Radiance attendance, the two lines tracked each other's up-and-down movements very closely over the entire 60-day period (see chart opposite). The connection is easily seen — the two lines moved up and down with unmistakable correlation. As a visual image of the Maharishi Effect, this one chart could serve admirably — one picture indicating that dramatically different aspects of a society, from stocks to war deaths to traffic accidents, all correlate highly with the number of people practicing the technology of peace.

Such a visual image has an analytical role as well. Reviewers of research occasionally argue that the mathematical analysis used on a given experiment is so complex, with so many factors decided upon by researchers, that any correlations found may actually be created by the analysis. In this case, however, such an argument is not sustainable. The correlation is so strong it can be seen by the naked eye — before any mathematical analysis is begun.

Reduced Conflict in Lebanon and
Improved Quality of Life in Israel

----- TM-Sidhi Program Participants
——— Composite Index of Quality of Life

p = .018

Increasing numbers of participants in Maharishi's Transcendental Meditation and TM-Sidhi programs led to improved quality of life in Israel. The chart shows the strong correspondence between the numbers of the TM-Sidhi participants and a composite quality of life index comprising many variables, including war intensity and war deaths in Lebanon, Israeli national stock market prices and national mood, and auto accident rates, number of fires, and crime rates in Jerusalem and Israel.

4. Increased social coherence. Finally, as the Super Radiance numbers increased, various statistics which usually have no relationship with each other suddenly began to move in step. Many different social measures ordinarily do not relate to one another at all. No one would try to predict stock prices, for instance, by looking at statistics on automobile accidents, or fires, or crime. Most such measures have nothing to do with one another, that is, they have no causal effect on each other (in technical terminology, they are *orthogonal* to one another). This was exactly the situation during weeks on the International Peace Project when the meditating numbers were low — the different measures moved independently of each other (in statistical terms, there was high *variability* among the measures). When the Super Radiance numbers increased, however, there was a strong tendency for all the different measures to begin moving together and to move in the predicted direction.

This tendency to coherence was so marked that its *p* value was less than one in ten thousand. Thus, when the Super Radiance group became large enough, factors in society that are normally uncorrelated (random or incoherent), suddenly became correlated (orderly or coherent). This sudden decrease in variability, or increase in coherence, strongly suggests that some new factor, a factor not previously evident, had begun to affect all the statistics simultaneously. Says Dr. Orme-Johnson,

> The question posed by the data is why does the group practice of Transcendental Meditation and the TM-Sidhi program lead to wide-spectrum changes in the society? The answer we suggest is that these Super Radiance assemblies produce a marked increase in the coherence of the collective consciousness in the society. From physics we know that an incoherent system is one with destructive interference: the various wave patterns interfere with each other in such a way as to annihilate each other. A coherent system, on the other hand, shows constructive interference: the waves reinforce each other, rather than canceling each other out. This is what the statistics show in a society affected by a

Super Radiance group. The different elements in the society decrease in destructive interference. Crime is one aspect of society destructively interfering with another, and crime decreases. Automobile accidents are a clear example of destructive interference, and automobile accidents decrease. In every sphere of action, there is an increase in orderliness and cooperativeness. The interests of the society tend to be supported more by each member. The collective consciousness has been purified of negativity and stress, and the results can be measured in many different ways.

OLD IDEAS AND NEW FACTS

The International Peace Project had been dramatically conceived. The statistical results were strongly significant, and supportive of the theory in many detailed ways. Now Drs. Orme-Johnson and Alexander decided to aim high: They submitted their results to the journal usually deemed the leading publication in the field of peace studies, the *Journal of Conflict Resolution* edited at Yale University. The ensuing struggle for publication took more than three years — a struggle that made for an instructive case study on the evolution of scientific thought.

As mentioned in the first chapter, the history of science is a history of repeated collisions between old understandings and new evidence. Any such confrontation between old ideas and new facts can take on a poignant human reality. Long-accepted notions about the world are usually deep-seated and emotionally difficult to relinquish. This emotional commitment is frequently reinforced because many erroneous understandings of nature are based on what seem to be reasonable, common sense observations.

In Galileo's case, for instance, every sighted human being can see with his own eyes that the Sun revolves around the Earth. It happens every day. This perception makes people feel important because it makes the earth seem the center of creation. When Galileo spoke up for scientific evidence showing that, in fact, the Sun was the center of the solar system and that the Earth revolved around the Sun, he thus ran headlong into both common sense perceptions and deep emotional attachments. People simply could not accept the new idea. They locked him up.

A similar collision between preconceptions and scientific evidence occurred in the 19th century. The famous Michelson-Morley experiment attempted to measure changes in the apparent speed of light as the experimental apparatus was moved either toward or away from the source of light. If a football player runs toward his quarterback to catch a pass, the ball hits his hands at a higher rate of speed than it does if he runs away from the quarterback. Relative velocity depends on the motion of both the source and the receiver. But the Michaelson-Morley experiment, done to the highest tolerances possible in the nineteenth century, showed that the speed of light never changed, regardless of motion by the source or the receiver. This was such a radical experimental finding, it so deeply violated every known law of physics, that no scientist was able to do anything with it for a generation. Then Albert Einstein took hold of the idea. Clinging firmly to the experimental finding, he let go of all preconceptions. The result was his theory of relativity, in which the speed of light was held invariant, and the other basic building blocks of the physics of his time, the measurements of distance and time, lost their absolute status.

These collisions between old ideas and new facts are usually personally shocking to most researchers. Thomas Kuhn, who first developed the idea of the *paradigm shift*, the radical changes that periodically occur in scientific thought, noted that such a shift usually takes about thirty years after the experimental evidence is in. What that means, basically, is that an entire generation of experts, nurtured on the old ideas, has to grow old and retire before the new understandings become widely accepted.

As the struggle at the *Journal of Conflict Resolution* illustrates, the statistical evidence supporting the Maharishi Effect causes the kind of confrontations and internal conflicts common to all collisions between old beliefs and new evidence. In the case of the International Peace Project, the concept of the Maharishi Effect flouted all accepted scientific understanding, yet the experiment was conducted in a particularly rigorous form. The study was prospective and multivariate, with seven internal replications, and analyzed with the rigorous and illuminating tool of time series analysis. The results were significant for all of the variables, the results were stronger closer to the source, the correlation to Super Radiance could be seen with the naked eye when all variables were combined, and normally uncorrelated statistics became highly coherent. Moreover, alternate explanations such as weather, holidays, etc., were statistically ruled out. In such a case, the evidence strongly supported a causal interpretation.

THE JOURNAL'S FIRST REACTION

Dr. Bruce Russett, professor of political science at Yale, was then editor of the *Journal of Conflict Resolution*. Confronted with what was doubtless the most unconventional study he had ever received, Dr. Russett decided to send it out to four different referees, two more than he usually used. The responses he received were widely various. One granted that the study was "logically and methodologically coherent," but strongly recommended against publication because "the hypothesis, to be frank, I regard as absurd." Although this view would doubtless have been shared by many of that reviewer's colleagues, yet it is also a clear example of "don't confuse me with the facts." Dr. Russett to his credit did not consider it a final word. Taking a different view of the same situation, another reviewer said, "The fundamental assumptions of a 'unified field' and a 'collective consciousness' are not within the paradigm under which most of us operate. Yet if one will, for the sake of argument, accept these premises as plausible, then the research conforms quite well to scientific standards."

One referee, Dr. Robert Duval, professor of political science at West Virginia University, withheld his recommendation because he had spotted what seemed to him a possible flaw in the statistical design. "One may conjecture," Dr. Duval said, "that instead of TM-Sidhi techniques influencing conflict in Lebanon, the level of conflict led the participants to hurry down to the hotel and meditate at the first sign of violence across the border." His hypothesis was that the warfare in Lebanon tended to be episodic. If a flare-up led meditators to race down to the assembly, the flare-up would then pass of its own accord, making it look like Super Radiance had caused the decline.

The M.U.M. researchers replied that this seemed extremely unlikely. In the first place, the number of daily drop-ins at the assembly was very small. Most participants came from places outside Jerusalem, and they usually came for a week or more at a time. In the second place, assuming that assembly participants did react to news of the war, that still couldn't account for the changes in crime, traffic accidents, fires, and the stock market. If the war were causing the attendance changes, then there should be no correlation between those same attendance changes and the other variables. Dr. Duval, however, had suggested a stringent statistical test — the use of *transfer function analysis* (also known as *lead-lag analysis*) to produce *cross-correlations*, a statistical tool which would indicate whether changes in warfare lagged behind changes in the Super Radiance attendance, or changes in attendance lagged behind changes in the warfare. Obviously, the cause must come first. Dr. Duval felt confident that his conjecture was correct and he reported that he "suggested the addition of transfer functions to identify the direction of causation — smug in the belief that a negative lag in the cross-correlations would reveal that the number of participants was the result, not the cause, of the activity."

SUPER RADIANCE IS THE CAUSE

Transfer function analysis, a branch of time series analysis, is a particularly laborious and time-consuming process. Drs. Orme-Johnson and Alexander hadn't thought it necessary, given the strong correlation of the Super Radiance attendance with so many different variables at once. But this type of give and take is common before journal acceptance. They therefore put months into careful transfer function analysis of every individual variable, from war deaths to the stock market, then did the same for composite indices that combined the variables in different ways.

The results strongly supported the Super Radiance hypothesis. Approximately half the time, the Super Radiance attendance changed first and the warfare and the other variables second (most commonly one day later). The other half the time, the two changes occurred on the same day. Most significantly, there was never any indication that warfare or the other variables led the Super Radiance attendance.

Confronted with this evidence, Dr. Duval gracefully relented. Even when the attendance and the war changed on the same day, Dr. Duval commented, that indicated the assembly attendance was the causative agent. Although such simultaneous changes seem to be, in Dr. Duval's words, "a toss-up," with "simultaneous causation," yet, "In this case, with daily measures of the dependent variables, the TM proponents win the toss-up. News travels fast, but not, I would think, that fast." Even he, in other words, did not imagine that (1) fighting could have broken out, (2) causing meditators to run down to the assembly, after which (3) fighting would calm down of its own accord — all in one day. If the attendance increased and the fighting decreased on the same day, the only logical presumption was that the attendance increase caused the warfare decrease. As for those times when the changes in Super Radiance *preceded* the changes in the dependent variables, the interpretation was obvious. As a result, "The direction of causation," in Dr. Duval's phrase, moved unambiguously from the Super Radiance assembly toward the declines in war deaths, crime, traffic accidents, and the other variables.

The journal's editor, Dr. Russett, now faced with conflicting recommendations, had to make his own choice. He felt ambivalent himself, but could not side with the reviewer who had simply dismissed the Super Radiance hypothesis. Mentioning the example of Galileo's travail, Dr. Russett said, "The practice of censorship in science, as in more overtly political realms, can be very unedifying."

After extensive thought, Dr. Russett decided in favor of publication. In an unusual "Editor's Comment" which he printed with the research paper (along with a commentary by Dr. Duval), Dr. Russett said, "The following article presents and tests a hypothesis that will strike most readers (myself included) as, to say the least, unorthodox. . . . Yet the hypothesis seems logically derived from the initial premises, and the empirical testing seems competently executed. These are the standards to which manuscripts submitted for publication in this journal are normally subjected."

It was a decision deliberately made in favor of the scientific process, a decision to pay attention to statistical evidence rather than theoretical preconceptions or unexamined "common sense."

CORRELATION AND CAUSATION

The attentive reader might still feel that, even though the study was published, it has a major flaw. The International Peace Project study and, in fact, all other Super Radiance studies, are based not on direct causative evidence (billiard ball to billiard ball), but rather on statistical correlations. In a correlated study, two types of data *covary* (move with obvious, if not perfect, synchrony), but without a provable mechanism connecting them. It is a scientific commonplace, of course, that "correlation does not imply causation." A robin may arrive the day before spring weather begins, but that does not mean the robin brought the weather with him. It is an unalterable limit of the scientific process that even high correlations cannot be said to *prove* a causative influence of one factor upon another.

In fact, however, it is a limitation of the scientific process in general that no amount of evidence of *any* type can affirmatively prove that a theory is true. Scientific investigation depends upon inductive logic — upon the piling up of individual facts until a scientist finally makes an inductive leap. If scientists drop a ball five times and it drops to earth five times, they have a preliminary indication; ten times, and they have a trend; after fifty, or one hundred, or five hundred times (how many is a subjective judgment that depends on the individual researcher), scientists feel justified in saying that "It is consistent with repeated evidence that a dropped ball falls to earth." But they cannot say that the theory is finally proved. As with all inductive logic, the next trial could conceivably result in the ball rocketing upward to the moon. No pile of facts, however high, can prevent the next fact from disproving the thesis.

All of this is also true of evidence based on correlations. But in addition to the standard inductive issues, studies based on correlations are also open to the type of *reverse causation* suggested by Dr. Duval, as well as to *third-factor causation* (see below). Nevertheless, researchers routinely make informed conclusions from their statistical correlations. If studies show a high correlation between one aspirin a day and reduced heart disease, no scientist puts forward the "reverse causation" notion that a healthier heart makes you want to take one aspirin per day.

Moreover, analysis based on correlations can be carefully constrained, if the data is clear enough, so that a reasonable person is driven by strong logic to a single conclusion. In the International Peace Project, for example, the correlations between Super Radiance and social coherence were far too strong to convincingly argue coincidence. With coincidence untenable, researchers were left with three possible explanations to choose among:

Causal interpretation — the changes in Super Radiance attendance caused the changes in society,

Reverse causation — the changes in society caused the changes in Super Radiance attendance, or

Third-factor causation — some unknown third factor caused both the Super Radiance attendance and the changes in society to covary in close correlation.

As we have seen, statistical analysis ruled the second choice out; reverse causation was impossible because the Super Radiance changes happened first. As for the third possibility — that day after day for sixty straight days, some unknown factor caused normally uncorrelated variables such as war deaths, traffic accidents, and fires to go up and down together, while also causing Super Radiance attendance to go up and down in close correlation — this strains credulity untenably. No reviewer of this research has even suggested such a notion, and for good reason.

In such a situation, the only logical conclusion from such strongly correlated data is the first one — that Super Radiance caused the changes. Drs. Orme-Johnson and Alexander had been successful. One powerfully conceived and executed experiment had provided a breadth and depth of evidence nearly unarguable — and there were many more studies to come.*

TERRORISM AND GLOBAL SUPER RADIANCE

Now that the technology of peace had been convincingly shown to reduce warfare as well as crime, the next question was, would it also reduce terrorism? A terrorism study, however, could only be worldwide. No single nation suffers from sufficient daily or weekly acts of terrorism to provide a meaningful study. Taking the world as a whole, however, it is unfortunately true that attacks have been frequent enough to convincingly show whether Super Radiance is effective against terrorism, as well.

After the Taste of Utopia course took place, two strong statistical studies were done to test whether the Maharishi Effect

*_Journal of Conflict Resolution_, 32, 776–812.

could be demonstrated worldwide. Both of these studies focused directly on warfare and terrorism.

One of the studies analyzed data on the three largest Super Radiance assemblies that have yet been held in the West — the Taste of Utopia Assembly in Iowa (7,000), a World Peace Assembly held in Washington, D.C. (5,600), and a second World Peace Assembly held in the Netherlands (6,000). Though the last two of these assemblies were not large enough, in theory, to affect the whole world, yet their size was sufficient to affect at least major portions of the world's population — enough to generate effects that should be statistically measurable.

To test whether these groups could generate a global Maharishi Effect, Dr. Orme-Johnson went in search of an unambiguous statistic that would measure disorderliness in the collective consciousness of the whole world. The most dramatic statistic he could think of was worldwide terrorism — a choice that has taken on great significance nearly two decades later. At the time, however, the chief question was, who kept such a statistic? The Department of Defense said it didn't. The United Nations said it didn't. Finally, one of Dr. Orme-Johnson's calls directed him to the right source. Daily terrorism data had been collected for a number of years by America's best-known think tank, the Rand Corporation.

With those statistics in hand, the research paper was simple to complete. The three large assemblies had all taken place within two years of each other. Dr. Orme-Johnson computed the average casualties caused by terrorism in all the weeks of those two years when assemblies were not in session, then the average for the weeks when the assemblies were in session. The result was, during the Super Radiance assemblies, a 72% average reduction in terrorism.

Dr. Orme-Johnson also did a systematic analysis of media sources and found that all forms of international conflict had dropped by one-third during the assemblies. During the same weeks, the World Index of stocks had also increased significantly. Three separate types of measurement, applied to three different assemblies, added up to two significant conclusions. First, large Super Radiance assemblies are accompanied by a worldwide influence of statistically measurable positivity. Second, terrorism all around the world can be controlled from a single spot — a finding that has taken on much increased significance now that American vulnerability to terrorist attack has been made so tragically clear. This study, more than any other, explains Maharishi's decision to create a super-group of 40,000 meditation experts in one place.*

AFFECTING WAR FROM A WORLD AWAY

While Dr. Orme-Johnson worked on this study, Dr. Charles Alexander collaborated with an M.U.M. Ph.D. student in psychology, John Davies, to devise another global study. The idea was to focus once again on the fighting in Lebanon, but to see if this fighting could be affected not just once, from nearby, but repeatedly, and from greater distances. Lebanon, unfortunately, could be the basis for an excellent experiment. Fighting there was almost continuous — had been, indeed, almost continuous for a decade — and the international media had easy access to this endless warfare, providing daily records of both the battles and the casualties. In addition, this long-running Lebanese war consisted of conventional warfare, largely practiced by the Israelis, as well as guerrilla-style and terroristic warfare by several different groups, so that a single experiment would test the ability of Super Radiance to calm down all types of fighting.

This time, however, rather than focusing on the single Super Radiance assembly in Israel known as the International Peace Project, the two researchers chose to measure the effects of six additional Super Radiance assemblies as well — every group that had ever been large enough, in principle, to affect the fight-

---

*Journal of Offender Rehabilitation, in press.

ing. One of these assemblies, a tiny gathering of roughly one hundred, had been held in Beirut, in Lebanon itself. Another had
gathered in Yugoslavia, north and west of Lebanon around the
corner of the Mediterranean — theoretically the 2,000 attendance
at this course was large enough, by the square root of one percent formula, to radiate its effect as far as Lebanon. The largest
and most distant assembly tested was the Taste of Utopia course,
with 7,000 people gathered nearly half a world away in Iowa.

This time, moreover, because the entire study would be based
on media content analysis, the two researchers wanted to remove
any question people might have about the way in which the statistical data was gathered. One of the strongest aspects of Super
Radiance research, as mentioned above, is that the statistical evidence is ordinarily open, public data, collected by governments
and other agencies, and available to any reviewer who wishes to
double-check the numbers. In this case, however, the data would
be gathered privately, just for this experiment. For this reason,
Dr. Alexander and Davies wanted to take an extra step to remove
any doubts about the objectivity of the data. To do this, they contacted the Center for International Development and Conflict
Management (CIDCM) at the University of Maryland, which
is often considered America's leading institution in the field of
peace studies. They were looking for a recommendation for an
independent expert in the field of media content analysis. Once
CIDCM made its recommendation, the analyst was assigned ten
separate media sources and told to monitor them on a daily basis
for the two-and-one-quarter-year period that included the seven
Super Radiance assemblies. He was given no other information
about the study's theory or methodology, and was not told which
dates were experimentally significant.

The structure of this study made it one of the most powerful
in the history of the social sciences. The study produced daily
data on war deaths and injuries and on the overall level of fighting for 841 consecutive days. Time series analysis will work

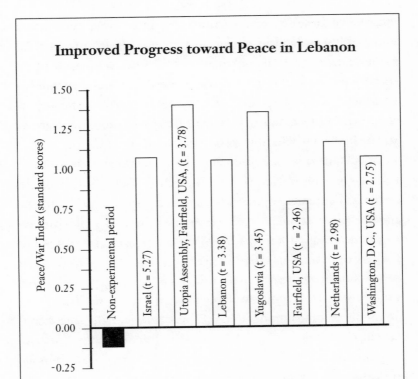

Improved Progress toward Peace in Lebanon

Peace/War Index (standard scores)

1.50

1.25

1.00

0.75

0.50

0.25

0.00

-0.25

Non-experimental period

Israel (t = 5.27)

Utopia Assembly, Fairfield, USA, (t = 3.78)

Lebanon (t = 3.38)

Yugoslavia (t = 3.45)

Fairfield, USA (t = 2.46)

Netherlands (t = 2.98)

Washington, D.C., USA (t = 2.75)

Seven large assemblies of participants in the Transcendental Meditation and TM-Sidhi programs in various parts of the world had an extremely significant positive influence on the Lebanese conflict, as indicated by a 66% increase in cooperation among antagonists, a 48% reduction in the level of conflict, a 71% reduction in war-related fatalities, and a 68% reduction in war-related injuries.

beginning with only 40 data points; more than 800 such points makes the statistical analysis extremely powerful. Moreover, 93 of those days, more than a tenth, were days on which one of the seven separate assemblies was meeting. With this large number of data points to work with, if the effect shown on the days of the meditation assembly were large, the statistical significance would be overwhelming.

And as it happened, the results were spectacular — even by the strongly significant standards that the Maharishi University of Management researchers had come to expect. In the first place, analysis showed that on the days of the assemblies, as compared to all the other days, war deaths in Lebanon dropped an average of 71%. This was consistent with the 76% decline in war deaths found by the International Peace Project, but with much greater statistical significance.

As in the International Peace Project, however, the most convincing evidence came from a combined analysis of all the factors measured: (1) war deaths, (2) war injuries, (3) war intensity (battles and other fighting as measured by content analysis), and (4) progress toward peace (troop withdrawals, peace negotiations, and other peaceful steps as measured by content analysis). The independent daily content analysis showed that on the 748 days with no Super Radiance assembly, the average result was a small worsening in violence and other news about the war. On the 93 days of the Super Radiance assemblies, on the other hand, the average result was a strong improvement in peacefulness — averaging more than one standard deviation in the positive direction (see chart opposite).

Because of the large number of days in the study, and the exceptionally strong results, the mathematical analysis of the probability of coincidence yielded a number almost inconceivable, $p<.0000000000000000001$ — less than one chance of coincidence in ten million trillion. It is of some interest that, partially on the strength of this study, Dr. John Davies was hired by the University of Maryland's Center for International Development and Conflict Management (CIDCM), where he now oversees the research.*

THE MAHARISHI EFFECT IN LONG-TERM STUDIES

As these studies have shown, a large amount of evidence demonstrates a powerful short-term statistical effect from temporary Super Radiance assemblies, both locally and globally. According to the theory, however, this Maharishi Effect should also last as long as any particular assembly stays together. The collective consciousness should continue to be purified and the thoughts and behaviors of people in the society should continue to be more harmonious and progressive. But by the mid-1980s, this type of research, a longitudinal study of a long-running Super Radiance assembly, had never been attempted.

The possibility first occurred to Dr. Orme-Johnson and another of his co-workers, Dr. Paul Gelderloos, an assistant professor of psychology who had come to Maharishi University of Management from the Netherlands. In the mid-1980s they began discussing the M.U.M. Super Radiance group. Approximately 1,600 meditation experts had stayed together much of the time since the middle of 1982 at the university. This was then the square root of one percent of America's population. Given the predictions of Maharishi's Vedic Science, and all the experience with Super Radiance up to that point, 1982 should have marked a clear-cut change in social indicators throughout the United States. Not just one type of statistic here or there should have improved, but a broad range of measures should all have shown improvement simultaneously.

To test the hypothesis, M.U.M. researchers compiled a list of twelve indicators, which they termed the Quality of Life Index, and designed a study that covered the most recent twenty-five years in American history, from 1960 through 1984. The choice

*Journal of Social Behavior and Personality, in press.

of indicators was carefully made. It was intended to cover a broad range of society — crime, justice, health, economic welfare, creativity, education, marital stability, and safety — while utilizing only the most holistic and central indicator in each field.

The idea was to cover each area of society, but in the smallest total of indicators possible, in order to generate a statistically parsimonious picture. In economics, for instance, only one statistic was used: gross national product (GNP), adjusted on a per capita basis and allowing for inflation. That one figure is generally thought to give a clearer indication of the economic health of the nation than any other. It was not necessary to add in unemployment figures, for instance, because when GNP goes up, unemployment ordinarily goes down, and the unemployment statistic is therefore largely redundant. For this Quality of Life Index, it was also necessary to choose statistics that were available uniformly throughout the twenty-five years of the study. Although drug abuse dropped for the first time in years in 1982, for instance, and Scholastic Aptitude Test scores increased in that year for the first time since they were first publicly reported in 1967, neither statistic was used in the Quality of Life index because neither was available through most of the 1960s.

The twelve indicators finally chosen covered a cross-section of American society:

1. **Crime rate:** A basic measure of orderliness in a society.

2. **Percentage of civil cases reaching trial:** A measure of underlying harmony; if cases go to trial, all other means of agreement have failed.

3. **Infectious disease rate:** An obvious measure of health in society.

4. **Infant mortality:** A widely used measure of the overall level of development in a nation.

5. **Suicide rate:** The only mental health variable available continuously from 1960 through 1984.

6. Cigarette consumption per capita: One measure of the health-consciousness in a society.

7. Alcohol consumption per capita: Another measure of health habits, also important because of the widespread incidence of alcoholism (a societal health problem which is statistically far greater than drug abuse).

8. GNP per capita: An encompassing measure of the economic vitality of the nation.

9. Patent applications: One of the few ways to measure creative activity in the nation.

10. Number of educational degrees conferred: The best indicator of the desire a society's citizens have to enhance their knowledge and skills and to improve the quality of their lives.

11. Divorce rate: The single statistic that best portrays the stability of the family structure.

12. Traffic fatalities: A significant cause of mortality in America and also a simple measure of the alertness and orderliness of people in one of their most common activities.

Choosing such a wide range of variables helps the design of the study act as its own check for reliability, as it did in the International Peace Project. While individual indicators might conceivably change for individual reasons (crime, for instance, could decline for completely different reasons than infectious disease), if all the indicators taken together move strongly downward, it is hard to argue that many different reasons for many different indicators all happened to coincide by accident. To put it the other way, if the various indicators all tend to act at once, it is a strong argument for a single underlying cause.

AMERICAN LIFE IMPROVES

Once the statistics had been chosen and gathered and statistical analysis began, the results of the study were as predicted. From the beginning of the study in 1960, the trend of the Quality of Life Index was steadily downward, worsening rapidly after 1967, until 1975. In that year the bottom was reached, followed by a slight improvement over the next six years until 1982, when the rate of improvement suddenly jumped upward sharply. For the first fifteen years of the study, as the Index steadily declined, an average of six of the statistical measures improved in any given year while the other six declined (with the declines being of greater magnitude). In one year crime might ease a bit, for instance, but infectious disease worsen, while in the next year the two indicators might exchange roles. After the bottom was reached in 1975, however, there was a slight shift — for the next six years an average of seven indicators improved while five declined. Then, in 1982 the pattern suddenly changed to ten positive and only two negative (and only one of them unambiguously negative), and the average of all the indicators moved upward sharply.

The study produced several interesting insights. First, in the years 1975 and 1976, there had been a very large increase in the number of people learning the basic TM technique, due to nationwide television coverage. More than a quarter of a million Americans learned in 1975 alone. It might be expected that such a sudden large increase in the numbers of people practicing TM would be noticeable in the social statistics, and the fifteen-year downward trend did bottom out in those years. Although the upward trend was not at first strong, the Quality of Life Index did not decline after that year.

This was also the year that Maharishi, to the surprise of even those closest to him, chose to publicly declare the "dawn of the Age of Enlightenment." He was responding to the first crime rate study. If science could prove that a small handful of people could change the trends of a whole city, he said, then the technology for creating a better world was clearly at hand. At the time, with the American political system still recovering from the presidential impeachment proceedings and the entire Western world afflicted with both inflation and recession, talk of a dawning Age of Enlightenment seemed to most of the world unimaginable. To skeptical questions, Maharishi laughed, saying, "If we are going to be first to proclaim the dawn, then we must do so while it is still dark."

By 1982, the TM-Sidhi program was available, and the Super Radiance attendance at Maharishi University of Management first exceeded 1,600 people, a level it maintained — with occasional larger assemblies — through the mid-1980s. In 1982, the Quality of Life Index moved sharply upward and continued upward the next two years, when the study was completed. Using regression analysis, one of the best established statistical techniques and the tool of choice in such a study, this sudden increase is significant at the $p<.0001$ level.

Did Super Radiance cause the dramatic improvement in the statistical measures? Perhaps an improved quality of life encourages more people to learn meditation, rather than the other way around. This question of causality was addressed statistically through cross correlation analysis. As in the International Peace Project, the analysis showed that the Super Radiance attendance frequently led the statistical changes in time, while the reverse was never the case. Statisticians sometimes express this by saying that the number of meditators could predict the increase in quality of life, while an increase in quality of life could not predict an increase in the number of meditators. This statistically significant finding argues for the statistical existence of the Maharishi Effect as a long-term causal factor in the creation of a more ideal society.

Here is a summary of the statistical findings through 1983 (the results in 1984 were, on average, slightly better yet):

1. Crime rate: In 1976 and 1977, after the rapid rise of numbers of practitioners of the Transcendental Meditation technique, crime fell for two consecutive years — the first time this had ever happened. Then, from 1981 to 1983, crime fell for three consecutive years, decreasing 0.78% in 1981, 4.3% in 1982, and 7.6% in 1983 (both the 1982 and 1983 crime rate totals were lower than in any other year since the beginning of the study). This meant there were 1,300,000 fewer crimes in 1982 and 1983 than there would have been if previous trends had continued. It was sometimes suggested that crime had fallen because of a reduction of the percentage of American citizens in the high-crime age group of 15–29, but the size of this group declined only one or two percent per year and could not account for the larger percentage drops.

2. Percentage of civil cases reaching trial: This percentage dropped 7.58% in 1982 and 11.48% in 1983 to reach an all-time low of 5.4% of all civil cases going to trial.

3. Infectious disease rate: Dropped 4.23% in 1982 and 7.02% in 1983 (the largest drop in 16 years).

4. Infant mortality rate: Decreased 5.88% in 1982 and 2.68% in 1983, continuing a long-standing trend.

5. Suicide rate: The only negative variable to increase in both years, 1.08% in 1982 and 2.3% in 1983.

6. Cigarette consumption per capita: Decreased 1.90% in 1982 and 6.26% in 1983 (the largest decline in the 25 years).

7. Alcohol consumption per capita: Decreased 3.52% in 1982 and 2.64% in 1983, the second and third largest decreases in the 25 years.

8. GNP per capita: Declined 2.81% in 1982 in the third year of a major recession; however, that recession turned around in the middle of that year (the stock market started a year-long upswing in August) and by the end of the year one of the strongest economic recoveries on record was under way. GNP per capita rose 2.25% in 1983.

9. Patent application rate: Increased 2.51% in 1982, but then had an anomalous drop of 11.26% in 1983 (the largest decrease by far throughout the period) when the application fee was increased late in 1982. The compensation came in 1984, when patent applications rose more than 12%, the largest rise in the years of the study.

10. Degrees conferred: Rose slightly (0.31% and 0.98%) after declining for the previous five years.

11. Divorce rate: Declined 4.46% in 1982 (a decrease three times larger than the previous record set twenty-one years earlier) and then again 0.18% in 1983 (the only time divorce rate declined in two consecutive years).

12. Traffic fatality rate: Declined 10.95% in 1982 (the largest decrease of any year except 1974, when the 55-mile-an-hour speed limit went into effect) and then again 4.60% in 1983 (the third largest drop in the years of the study). This decrease in traffic fatalities received a good deal of media attention. A common explanation for the drop is that drivers were drinking less and buckling up more. But this would not contradict the Super Radiance theory, which postulates precisely the sort of increase in social coherence that would lead people to do what they have long known they should.*

THE LONG TERM IN FINE FOCUS

Such a long-run study that uses yearly statistics can give a broad indication of statistical changes, but the same type of statistics going week-by-week or month-by-month can produce more detailed information. In such tight-focus studies, short-run fluctuations in the Super Radiance attendance can be matched against short-run fluctuations in the social statistics, allowing time series analysis to be used to increase the accuracy of analysis. If the attendance and the social statistics correlate strongly over weeks and months and years of continual fluctuation, the statistical significance can be much stronger.

---

*Social Science Perspectives Journal, 2(4), 127–146.

In recent years, three such fine-grain longitudinal studies have been made of the M.U.M. Super Radiance group. The first of these was carried out by Dr. Michael Dillbeck. He compared M.U.M.'s Super Radiance attendance for four consecutive years, 1982–85, with the three clearest indicators of violence and disorder in the society — homicides, suicides, and traffic fatalities. He compared weeks when M.U.M.'s group exceeded the Super Radiance number (the square root of one percent) in the United States with weeks when it did not, and he used a rigorous form of time series analysis to control for any seasonal or long-term cycles or trends in the data that might have accounted for the changes.

With such extraneous factors controlled, there was a strong, statistically significant correlation between fluctuations in the Super Radiance attendance and fluctuations in the statistics on violence — when attendance went up, violence went down. The Super Radiance changes frequently preceded the changes in violence; the reverse was never the case. Because Dr. Dillbeck had more than 200 weeks of data in his study and because of the meticulous structure of his mathematical analysis, he gained publication for this study in *Social Indicators Research*, usually cited as the leading journal dealing with social quality of life, with a daunting reputation for analytical rigor. Such a detailed, week-by-week analysis adds strength to the statistical likelihood of the Maharishi Effect. In the words of Dr. Dillbeck,

> It establishes a causal connection between group practice of Maharishi's Transcendental Meditation program and decreased deaths by violence in a way that is difficult to do with monthly or yearly data. It is highly unlikely, for example, that other possible causes of decreased traffic fatalities would coincidentally covary with weekly fluctuations in the number of participants in the [Super Radiance group].*

Social Indicators Research, 22, 399–418.

IMPROVING THE ECONOMY LONG-TERM

A second longitudinal study used the same Super Radiance attendance figures to show their effect on a completely different aspect of society. In 1982, the first year that M.U.M.'s group meditation attendance began to regularly exceed the Super Radiance number for the United States, the American economy began a steady climb that lasted nearly a decade, then the longest peacetime economic expansion in the nation's history. In that time, the stock market crashed spectacularly, with no effect on the steady economic growth, and the Federal Reserve Board engineered its first ever "soft-landing" for the economy, raising interest rates to rein in inflation without slowing the expansion down into recession. The theory of the Maharishi Effect, of course, is consistent with just such a recession-resistant economy. As we have seen, the statistical evidence shows that Super Radiance groups not only decrease the violence and disorder in a society, but also increase the creativity (patent applications), confidence (stock markets), and economic vitality (GNP) throughout that society. This evidence indicates that as the collective consciousness of a society becomes more orderly and coherent, it also becomes more creative and progressive. The Maharishi Effect seems to work as an engine for economic growth.

To subject this implication to a closely detailed, longitudinal study, M.U.M. economist Dr. Kenneth Cavanaugh examined the relationship between M.U.M.'s Super Radiance attendance on the one hand and a dread two-part economic indicator known as the *misery index* — a combination of the inflation rate and the unemployment rate — on the other. The misery index was first tracked in the late 1970s after a decade of *stagflation*, when the economy lagged in the doldrums but inflation raced upward anyway. A high *misery index* indicates the worst of both worlds for any economy — sluggish performance and a runaway currency.

Dr. Cavanaugh is another of M.U.M.'s statistical experts. He earned his Ph.D. at the University of Washington with a time series analysis of the stock markets, and he has been studying and contributing to time series methodologies since their inception as a statistical tool. For this study he tracked Super Radiance attendance at the university since the group first formed in 1979, several years before it began to regularly reach the square root of one percent of America's population. He extended the study for nearly nine years, through 1987. He compared this attendance data with the government's monthly reports on unemployment and inflation. Using time series procedures to control for other influences on the economic data, Dr. Cavanaugh showed a strong and statistically significant inverse correlation between the attendance and the misery index. Once again, increases in the Super Radiance attendance led in time the decreases in the misery index.

Here was clear statistical evidence that the United States economy had not only experienced an eight-year boom coincident with the M.U.M. Super Radiance assembly, but that month-by-month changes in the nation's economic performance had been influenced by month-by-month changes in the size of the Super Radiance group. Another way of looking at the same data shows that in periods of higher attendance the misery index dropped more than it did in periods of lower attendance (see chart on next page). This type of evidence is extremely difficult to explain away and, even in the conservative field of economics, this study was accepted and published in the *Proceedings of the American Statistical Association* for 1987.

Discussing these findings, Dr. Cavanaugh refers to one aspect of the theory of collective consciousness unfolded by Maharishi in his Vedic Science. Economic performance is often affected by governmental decisions. Decisions by the government, in turn, are strongly influenced by the collective consciousness of the nation. In fact, Maharishi states that any government is just the "innocent mirror of the nation's collective consciousness." Maharishi considers this relationship between collective con-

Decreased Inflation and Unemployment—
Improvement in the "Misery Index"

From April 1979 to January 1987, the "misery index"—the sum of the monthly inflation and unemployment rates—decreased in the U.S. and Canada during and following months when more than 1,500 people (approximately the square root of 1% of the U.S. population) participated daily in the group practice of Maharishi's Transcendental Meditation and TM-Sidhi program at Maharishi International University in Iowa. Smaller declines were found for both countries when the group size averaged 1,100–1,500.

sciousness and government vital for the rapid progress of any society, and he has frequently discussed it at length:

> If the people in the country are disorderly, only the fruit of dis-orderly action will come to the nation. If the people create chaos in society, then this can only result in chaos in government. Every experienced member of a government knows this from his own experience. A new man in government may have a great desire for accomplishment. The same man, full of enthusiasm and ambitious for his community, when he comes to the legislature and sits there — he finds his whole thinking changes. So many legislators are beautiful people — when you have them to your home for din-ner they are so intelligent and full of good will — but when they sit in the legislature, what they do is so different. This has always embarrassed the leaders of governments everywhere. They are not able to think in the halls of government what they are able to think at home. It's because their thinking gets tossed about by the effects produced by all the people in the nation, by the disorder in the collective consciousness of that nation.

In a democracy, governmental leaders do their best to stay in touch with the collective consciousness of the nation, with what is called "the will of the people," if for no other reason than to get re-elected. But Maharishi describes a mechanics subtler than any deliberate attempt by a governmental official to mod-ify his behavior to suit his constituents. Maharishi describes an automatic process, an innocent process. According to this the-ory, collective consciousness drives government decisions direct-ly; if the nation's collective consciousness is gripped by war fever, then the government goes to war.

At one point in his misery index study, Dr. Cavanaugh touched on this relationship between government and collective con-sciousness. Governmental actions do affect the economy, but those governmental actions themselves can be understood as reflections of the collective consciousness. Why did the Feder-al Reserve Board finally engineer a soft landing for the economy? Why, for the first time, did it raise interest rates early enough to slow inflation before the economy overheated, then lower the rates again before the economy slipped down into recession? In the theory of collective consciousness, such effective governmental action (or, in this case, quasi-governmental action) is possible only when the collective consciousness of the nation is clear and orderly enough to support such intelligent actions. In Dr. Cavanaugh's words,

> In Maharishi's Vedic Science, improved governmental effectiveness is a predicted effect of the purification of national consciousness. Every action of the national government is seen as the expression of national consciousness, just as every action of an individual is seen as an expression of that individual's consciousness. Shortsighted or misguided governmental policies are seen as resulting from the growth of stress, disharmony, and disorder in the collective consciousness of the nation. If the government is suddenly found to be more effective and successful in its undertakings, in other words, one should look to see what has caused an improvement in the quality of the collective consciousness.

CREATING INTERNATIONAL HARMONY

This collective consciousness theory of governmental success is both provocative and of great potential importance. It deserves a more thorough study on its own, and it has received one from M.U.M. psychologist Dr. Paul Gelderloos, working in collaboration with Dr. Cavanaugh. Drs. Gelderloos and Cavanaugh studied the effect of M.U.M.'s Super Radiance attendance in yet a third and totally new area — not on violent deaths, not on economics, but rather in the crucial arena of international relations.

In the late 1980s, the world underwent a dramatic transformation toward peace and freedom. One man, the president of the Soviet Union, Mikhail Gorbachev, conventionally received a great deal of the credit. For his contributions, he was named *Time* magazine's Man of the Decade. The theory of collective consciousness expounded in Maharishi's Vedic Science, however, would propose a deeper explanation. In this theory, it would be argued that the many Super Radiance assemblies, and especially the permanent group maintained at M.U.M. for over a decade, purified the collective consciousness of the world. With stress and disorder receding in the collective consciousness, governments were left to make more orderly and useful decisions.

To test this hypothesis, the study emphasized the relationship between the two superpowers of that time, the United States and the Soviet Union. There had then been no large TM group in the Soviet Union, but it was possible that the long-term effects of the many Super Radiance assemblies all around the world had had a cumulative impact in the Soviet Union. Moreover, Maharishi had often suggested that increases in coherence in America could lead directly to increases in coherence in the Soviet Union. Since these two superpowers had been primary rivals for so long, with a great deal of attention on and influence over one another, changes in one nation's collective consciousness could have a direct effect on the thoughts and actions of leaders in the other.

To investigate such questions, Dr. Gelderloos found an ideal source of monthly data. In Switzerland, the Zurich Project on East-West Relations maintained a continuous content analysis of many news sources to monitor the relationship between the superpowers. The Zurich Project kept track of both the statements made by heads of state and other key governmental leaders and the overt actions taken by each government toward the other. The statements and actions were both termed events, and the Zurich Project scored these events as hostile, neutral, or friendly, and kept a running record of the percentages in each category month by month.

Such a data bank was ideal for research on the Maharishi Effect. It was extensive and detailed, and it had been compiled by an independent organization with no preconceptions about the possibilities of Super Radiance assemblies. Drs. Gelderloos and Cavanaugh tracked this data every month from 1979 to 1986, comparing it with monthly fluctuations in M.U.M.'s Super Radiance attendance.

The results of this analysis showed, first, that contrary to the usual portrayal in the public press, positive statements and actions ordinarily came from the American side first and were then taken up by the Soviet Union (the most famous example was the "Zero Option," the suggestion to remove all intermediate-range missiles from Europe, first proposed by President Reagan in 1982, then revived by President Gorbachev in 1986 and put into treaty form in December 1987).

The second finding was that positive American statements and actions were highly correlated with increases in Super Radiance attendance at M.U.M. As in every similar experiment to date, attendance increases preceded the positive moves by the American government. The third finding (consistent with one of the findings of the International Peace Project) was that small increases in attendance would predict positive actions by American leaders, while large increases in attendance would also predict positive actions by Soviet leaders. There was nothing tentative about these correlations; the chance of mere coincidence was less than one in ten thousand.

This was the first statistical definition of *rashtriya kavach* — the armor of the nation. When the Super Radiance influence became large enough, when the collective consciousness of America had been sufficiently purified of stress and fear, then the statistics showed that the enemy of the nation began to act in a more friendly manner. On a surface inspection of daily events of those years, it might seem that President Mikhail Gorbachev of the Soviet Union had single-handedly produced a more harmonious and peaceful atmosphere in the world. But a close analysis of the actual changes that took place month by month tells a quite different story. The data suggest that credit should not go so much to the Soviet Union as to America, and in Amer-

ica, credit should go to governmental leaders, but more fundamentally to those who had taken part in Super Radiance for so
long.*

THE WASHINGTON, D.C.,
DEMONSTRATION PROJECT

In 1993, one last, large experiment on the technology of
peace was conducted. By then, in the view of the scientists
involved, enough research had been conducted and published.
Those studies, they felt, should have been sufficient to convince
any open-minded scholar or government official that, given the
repeated failure of all other approaches to peace, this new one
should definitely be tried. But still, as a way of drawing attention to the phenomenon, one final demonstration was planned
for Washington, D.C.

For this study, the lead researcher was Dr. John Hagelin, a
quantum physicist trained at Harvard who had worked at both
the European Center for Nuclear Research (CERN) and the
Stanford Linear Accelerator (SLAC). By 1993, Dr. Hagelin had
published seventy-five research articles on unified quantum
field theories (see next chapter) and had become the Director
of the Institute of Science, Technology and Public Policy.

For the Demonstration Project in Washington, Dr. Hagelin
recruited a twenty-seven-member Review Board of scientists and
public leaders to oversee the study, and he lodged predictions
in advance with this Board and with the D.C. police. In his discussions with the police, moreover, Dr. Hagelin asked how
much reduction of violent crime would be necessary — in the
hot-weather months of June and July when violent crime usually climbs to its peak — for the police to be impressed. The
answer came back: twenty percent. The police spokesman went
on to say that the only way to get such a large reduction was to
have a blizzard in July.

*Proceedings of the American Statistical Association, Alexandria, Va., 1990.

In the first week of June, 1,000 meditation experts gathered in Washington. Two weeks later the attendance increased to 2,500 and the first week in July it topped out at 4,000 where it stayed until the group broke up late in the month. Because this was a test of the ability of Super Radiance to calm violence, the study focused on the three types of crime that involve outright violence of one person upon another — homicide, rape, and assault.

Although the D.C. police were extremely slow reporting their final data, and the published study did not appear for several years, once the data was in hand the Super Radiance effect was once again easy to see. In the previous five years, as temperatures rose and then fell again from April through October in a smooth, hill-like curve, violent crime rose and fell in close correlation. This is not surprising. It is no secret that some people become edgy and hostile in the heat, and it has long been known to police forces that increased personal violence is directly related to increased temperatures.

In 1993, during the Demonstration Project, temperatures rose in June as usual, then jumped to near-record temperatures in July. But as temperatures peaked, violent crime suddenly plummeted, dropping far below average levels. With crime plotted against temperature, and the Demonstration Project in 1993 compared with the average of the five previous years, the dramatic drop in crime in 1993 is especially apparent (see charts opposite). Again, no mathematical analysis is necessary to see the Maharishi Effect clearly. By comparison with time series predictions based largely on temperature, the reduction exceeded 23%. Careful investigation and statistical controls indicated that this sharp drop could not be attributed to other possible causes, including lower temperatures, increased precipitation, weekend effects, or changes in police and community anti-crime activities.

The Washington Demonstration Project was another of the studies done as a prospective study, with predictions lodged in

Five Years Prior to Demonstration Project

Average Temperature and HRA Crime, 1988–1992

1993 Demonstration Project

Temperature and HRA Crime, 1993

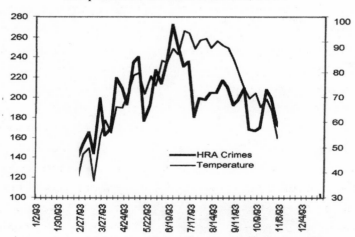

For the five years prior to the Washington, DC, crime Reduction Project (top chart) violent crime tracked closedly with temperature from spring to fall. During the 1993 project (bottom), violent crime suddenly plummeted despite near-record heat.

advance. The overall decline in violent crime was impressive —
and it is especially significant that the D.C. police representative who had provided the crime data, appearch as a co-author
on the published paper.*

PERMANENT PEACE AS AN OBJECTIVE REALITY

Taken overall, this cascade of statistical evidence suggests
that governments — or groups of responsible citizens — can take
control of the destiny of their own nations. First, it appears they
can use this newly validated technology of peace to provide a true
national defense — by producing a peaceful influence in the collective consciousness of the whole world. Second, it appears they
can use that same technology to transform their own societies
within — by systematically reducing crime, traffic accidents, and
fires, while also giving their economy a powerful boost by
decreasing unemployment and inflation and increasing the creativity, confidence, and productivity of their people.

The research supports, in fact, a suggestion which Maharishi
has often made: Governments everywhere would do well to
establish a separate department to handle the collective consciousness of the nation. The government already has departments to handle problems of education, labor, economics, and
many other specific aspects of national life. Now the results of
published studies suggest that any government could establish
one department which would help to handle the problems in
every other department.

Those people who have already been involved in this activity, the meditation experts who went to Zambia and Rhodesia,
to Israel and Lebanon, to the Philippines, the Taste of Utopia,
and Washington, D.C., can tell anyone interested how deeply
satisfying it is to be involved in such a project, how thrilling it
is to gather together and watch once again as the society
improves in unmistakably measurable ways.

Social Indicators Research, 47, 153–201.

A world filled with such Super Radiance groups — anchored by the 40,000 group in India — is a vision of possibilities often discussed by Maharishi, the man who has made possible this scientific approach to peace.

> A very, very beautiful time is coming for the world. Now we have it in our power, through the collective performance of TM and the TM-Sidhi program, to create a glorious new atmosphere in the world, to bring a new sunshine to human existence. When we create the Maharishi Effect on a permanent basis, we will see economies everywhere more successful, politics everywhere more successful, religions everywhere more successful. International relations will be more loving. Negativity in the family of nations will simply disappear. The trends of time are now completely in the hands of every nation.

To accept this possibility, however, and to have the confidence to act on it, we must investigate the mechanics through which Super Radiance occurs. It is hard to accept a new idea until we can visualize how it works. And the requisite idea in this case is not incremental. To the extent research has validated the Maharishi Effect, in fact, to that extent we must seek a wholly new understanding of both human life and the natural world. In the currently dominant paradigm of objective science — based on a purely materialist worldview — it is simply not possible to explain how an influence of permanent world peace can radiate from an assembly of meditation experts.

For this reason, to explain this technology of peace, M.U.M. researchers refer to a radically new concept — to the theoretical field nature of consciousness. They argue that like the electromagnetic field, through which TV pictures radiate, consciousness must also have a field nature through which the statistically measurable influence of peace radiates.

To understand such a postulated field theory of consciousness, especially in the Vedic-based explications of Maharishi, it is necessary to delve into two profound, underlying principles, two of the four basic hypotheses listed in Chapter One. In Maharishi's understanding:

1. The unified field. The field of consciousness is understood to be, in fact, the most basic level of nature's functioning, one fundamental and completely unified field.

2. The fourth state. The human mind can directly experience this unified field in a *fourth major state of consciousness.*

To understand Super Radiance, in other words, we must first understand subtle and profound aspects of both the natural world and human consciousness. Put another way, we must now understand how modern scientific theory and experiment have caught up with the timeless Vedic wisdom of consciousness.

The place to start is at the deepest levels of nature's functioning. Physics in the twentieth century has plumbed the depths of material creation and exposed the delicate inner workings of the apparently physical world.

What can these profound scientific explorations tell us about a single unified field of all the laws of nature?

3

THE UNIFIED FIELD:
Home of All the Laws of Nature

In his Vedic Science, Maharishi explains that nature's basis is one unbounded field of infinite potential — a field that is unmanifest and transcendental. In this understanding, stars and planets, trees and people all have a common source in one invisible, unmanifest essence of existence. It is through this field, Maharishi maintains, that the influence of large group meditations radiates. For this reason, the fundamental Vedic explanation of Super Radiance begins with this one principle.

The topic explored in this chapter: How the investigations of modern physics have been able to uncover and precisely define such a hidden, unified basis of the universe.

Such a view of nature does not seem to square with our common sense experience of the world, of course. When we open our eyes and look around, we see specific objects everywhere and a "transcendental field" nowhere. Yet the Vedic literature repeatedly maintains that the surface appearance of nature hides the deeper reality, that deep beneath the ever-changing surface of creation lies *parame vyoman*, the "imperishable transcendental field."

In the Upanishads, a Sanskrit compilation said to contain the essence of the four central Vedas, there is a well-known story that graphically describes this unmanifest field of pure potentiality. The story is cast as a conversation between father and son about the seed of the banyan tree, a seed which happens to be hollow. It begins with a command by the father.

> "Bring me a fruit of the banyan tree."
> "Here is one, sir."
> "Break it."
> "It is broken, sir."
> "What do you see there?"
> "Some seeds, sir, exceedingly small."
> "Break one of these."
> "It is broken, sir."
> "What do you see there?"
> "Nothing at all."
>
> The father said, "My son, that subtle essence, which you do not perceive there — in that very essence stands the being of the huge banyan tree. In that which is the subtle essence all that exists has its self. That is the True, That is the Self, and thou, Svetaketu, art That."

To people raised in a society based on science and a materialist worldview, this understanding of an unmanifest essence of existence may seem surprising — but we can find it in every tradition and every culture. In China, Lao-Tsu spoke of the Tao, "Born before heaven and earth/In silence and the void,/Standing alone and unchanging." In Rome, Plotinus spoke of the One, "the source of life, the source of intelligence, the origin of being. . . . All these entities emanate from the One without any lessening, for it is not a material mass." In the modern European tradition, theologian Meister Eckhart based his metaphysics on the "nothingness that is beyond existence," an "eternal silent undifferentiated one-ness," and William Wordsworth can serve as an example of many poets and artists:

And I have felt a sense sublime of something far more deeply
    interfused,
Whose dwelling is the light of setting suns,
And the round ocean and the living air,
And the blue sky, and the mind of man;
A motion and a spirit, that impels
All thinking things, all objects of all thought,
And rolls through all things.

It is the Vedic tradition, however, which defines this view most
precisely and which systematically builds the full development
of human life on its foundation. Certainly Maharishi has used
this concept as the basis of his teaching, and he has taken great
care to be detailed and exact in his definition. It is not a poetic
feeling he is speaking of, nor a mystical abstraction. Even before
modern physics began to glimpse the unified field as a mathematically definable reality, Maharishi spoke of it in a systematic way. Writing in the 1960s, and using the phrase "the absolute
field" as the label, he said,

> The absolute field lies at the root of everything. It is the
> omnipresent, essential constituent of creation, beyond all rela-
> tive existence, beyond the realm of time, space, and causation,
> the boundaries of the ever-changing, phenomenal states of life.
> It enjoys the status which knows no change, the status of eter-
> nal existence. The different aspects of creation, of relative exis-
> tence, of all the forms and phenomena in the ever-changing
> states of life in the world are as ripples and waves, having their
> basis in this vast, transcendent ocean. But in itself it is unlimit-
> ed, unbounded, unmanifest, unchanging, eternal. It is the
> absolute state of existence.

If, despite the surface appearance of nature, the world is constructed with such an absolute field at its basis, it should be possible to recognize it. "Beyond the realm of time, space, and causation," "the status which knows no change," "unlimited, unbounded, unmanifest" — these phrases are not ambiguous. While they

may once have seemed to be pure metaphysics, they have been defined in the past few decades with mathematical precision.

Let us retrace the path that modern physics has blazed, moving from the surface level of the world deep into the heart of creation's mechanics — and then remain awhile at that source and explore its mechanics thoroughly. Several books have been devoted to the mysteries of modern physics and their apparent parallels with what is loosely called Eastern thought. None, however, has focused on the simple, central themes emphasized by Maharishi in his Vedic Science: (1) Nature is structured in layers, from the gross, surface level we see around us to the finest inner level, the unified field, and (2) all of the more superficial, manifest levels of nature emerge from, and depend upon, that single, unmanifest unified field.

In the past seventy-five years, these two points have been elucidated in detail by the discoveries of modern physics. Because Maharishi has explained the timeless Vedic teachings in a systematic, structured format, and because quantum physics has progressed so deeply in its understanding of the natural world, for the first time the subtle teachings of saints and enlightened masters in every generation have been paralleled by objective, scientific investigation.

Specifically, discoveries during the twentieth century have revealed that nature does exist in layers, and that these levels descend hierarchically inward, from outer, surface aspects of the everyday objects we live with, through the successively finer inward levels represented by molecules and then atoms and then subatomic particles — penultimately to the abstract level of pure quantum fields — and finally to a single unified field of all the laws of nature. The secrets which physics has uncovered on this inward journey to the heart of physical reality present us with a profound new understanding of nature's possibilities — an understanding worth detailed attention. Let's take that journey, step by step, and understand the hidden world that physics has discovered — a transcendental realm that helps explain not only Super Radiance and permanent peace, but also the highest possibilities of human life in enlightenment.

THE JOURNEY TO THE CENTER

Why is it that physics, this one particular discipline, has uncovered such important knowledge about the structure of the world? It is simply due to the nature of physics as a discipline, to the project which physicists assign to themselves. In the words of E.C.G. Sudarshan, a physicist from the University of Texas who first helped define the weak force, one of nature's four fundamental forces,

> Physics is the uncompromising search for the truth of the world's structure. Unlike other branches of science, it won't stop with partial answers, answers true at only the molecular level — like chemistry, for instance — or even at the atomic level. Physics is searching for the deepest answers. For this reason it seems far more than coincidental that when physics discovers the basis of physical reality, it parallels in every respect the ancient teaching about an eternal, all-pervasive field of infinite potential. It seems likely that we are witnessing a convergence of investigative paths upon a single truth.

The ancient Greek Archimedes, speaking of the invention of the lever, said, "Give me a place to stand and I will move the world." We are, in a sense, looking for that standpoint, looking for that transcendent location from where all the universe could theoretically be moved. And physics has glimpsed such a level. At the heart of nature is an unbounded, unmanifest field of infinite possibilities, a standpoint for the application of infinite leverage — or, to change the image, a master switchboard for all the laws of nature.

THE DISAPPEARANCE OF MATTER

Through most of the past several centuries, scientists thought of the universe as a huge machine, a clockworks cloned infinitely in every direction. The workings of reality at every level, from the surface appearance of this world outward to the extremes of the universe and inward to the mechanics of the atom, were thought to be just the workings of solid material parts interacting with minute precision.

In the 1600s, Sir Isaac Newton brought these ideas to an ordered and intricate summation. The laws he formulated dominated scientific thinking for the next three hundred years, and at the core of his thinking was the understandable, common-sense conjecture that the world around him was constructed of solid matter. He envisioned nature's ultimate reality as tiny, hard pellets of indestructible material.

> It seems probable to me that God in the beginning formed matter in solid, massy, hard, impenetrable, movable particles, of such sizes and figures, and with such properties, and in such proportions to space, as most conduced to the end for which he formed them; and that these primitive particles being solids, are incomparably harder than any porous bodies compounded of them; even so very hard, as never to wear or break in pieces; no ordinary power being able to divide what God himself made one in the first creation.

For a few brief years at the beginning of this century, three hundred years after Newton, physicists thought they had finally found these basic building blocks of nature. The atomic model of nature began to gain general acceptance among physicists at that time, and in the original form of this theory the atom was conceived as a tiny solar system — with the part of the Sun played by protons and neutrons coalesced in the nucleus, and planets played by tiny whirling electrons. It was possible to envision these protons, neutrons, and electrons as Newton's "solid, massy, hard, impenetrable, moveable particles."

The size of the particles, however, was much smaller than had been previously imagined, and the space between them much greater. The ensuing feelings of perplexed wonder on the part of physicists was well-captured by Sir Arthur Eddington. The man whose stellar measurements during an eclipse of the Sun first provided verification of Albert Einstein's theories of relativity, Eddington wrote an influential textbook entitled *The Nature of the Physical World*, published in 1928. In the introduction to that work he describes everyday reality in these words:

> I have settled down to the task of writing these lectures and have drawn up my chairs to my two tables. Two tables? Yes; . . . One of them has been familiar to me from earliest years. It is a commonplace object of that environment which I call the world. How shall I describe it? It has extension; it is comparatively permanent; it is colored; above all it is substantial. . . . It is a thing. . . .
>
> Table No. 2 is my scientific table. It is a more recent acquaintance and I do not feel so familiar with it. It does not belong to the world previously mentioned — that world which spontaneously appears around me when I open my eyes. . . . My scientific table is mostly emptiness. Sparsely scattered in the emptiness are numerous electric charges rushing about with great speed, but their combined bulk amounts to less than a billionth of the bulk of the table itself. . . . It makes all the difference in the world whether the paper before me is poised as it were on a swarm of flies and sustained shuttlecock fashion by a series of tiny blows from the swarm underneath, or whether it is supported because there is substance below it; . . . all the difference in conception at least, but no difference to my practical task of writing on the paper.

Even this picture of solid matter as minute and particulate chaos was not to last. The tiny subatomic "particles" soon began to disappear altogether in the by now well-chronicled development of the theory of quantum mechanics.

One of the first steps was taken by Werner Heisenberg, a physicist with the intellectual daring to accept experimental imprecision as an unwavering postulate of the new physics. Appearing at the same time as Eddington's book, Heisenberg's *uncertainty principle* accepts as a definite, unalterable fact the following experimental impasse: When physicists try to pin down one of the subatomic particles — such as an electron, for instance — they find they cannot, ever, with any certainty. As Heisenberg first realized, when a physicist tries to measure an electron, for example, he can either determine its position, but then have no clear ideas of its motion. Or he can measure the momentum, but then have no precise knowledge of the position. Or he can get a statistical approximation of both position and momentum, but not know either one precisely.

When physicists tried to lay hold of one of Newton's small, massy particles, in other words, they found it evaporating in their grasp. If a subatomic quantum were such a massy particle, it would of necessity have both a position and momentum at every given instant, but as Heisenberg made clear, it simply does not. As the physicists pressed forward with their search, penetrating ever deeper layers of nature's functioning through the newly developing theories of quantum mechanics, they found the reason for this evasiveness of the smallest particles. Such small particles, as particles, simply have no real existence.

Though their speciality is still frequently, and anomalously, called *particle physics*, experts in subatomic physics no longer picture solid particles floating in empty space. Indeed, they don't think in terms of empty space at all. Instead their investigations have led them to the idea that space is filled completely by pulsating fields. What we think of as material particles moving through empty space turn out on closer inspection to be nothing but the omnipresent field itself, fluctuating and vibrating. Fritjov Capra, a physicist at the University of California, has written in the *Tao of Physics*,

> The quantum field is seen as a fundamental, physical entity; a continuous medium which is present everywhere in space. Particles are merely local condensations of the field; concentrations of energy which come and go, thereby losing their individual character and dissolving into the underlying field.

A wave on the ocean appears to have its own reality; it can be measured, it can be seen to move, it can slap up against the side of your boat. And yet such a wave is nothing different from the water around it, nothing but a local fluctuation or excitation in the unbounded ocean.

In just that way, quantum mechanics now describes particles as waves, as localized fluctuations or excitations in the underlying field. In fact, the equations used by quantum scientists are termed *wave mechanics*, and the mathematical formalism that describes the attributes and actions of any particular quantum is known as the *wave function*. Moreover, a quantum field has no physical or material reality. The ocean is made of water, which moves as waves, but a quantum field is made of "no-thing" — it has no substance.

In such a theory, the conception of solid matter disappears altogether. Einstein put this plainly: "We may therefore regard matter as being constituted by the regions of space in which the field is extremely intense. . . . [T]here is no place in this new kind of physics both for the field and matter, for the field is the only reality."

As of the 1930s, then, physics had clearly discovered that nature is built in layers. It had also discovered something even more important: The laws of nature are completely different at different layers. On the outer, surface level of life, solid matter does obviously have a real existence; if you are holding a book in your hand, you can be sure that it will continue to exist there, solid and sure, and not dematerialize mid-sentence. At an inner, subtle level, however, where the physicists sought the ultimate reality of solid matter, what they found instead was fields and waves and "no thing" specific.

Which of these realities is true? The simple answer: They both are. The reality depends on which level is taken as the standpoint. Pictures in a news magazine show politicians, entertainers, athletes, and the other celebrity personalities of the day.

But if you look at any one of those pictures closely, under a lens, you see only colored dots on white paper. The president of the United States or tiny color blotches? It depends on which level is being viewed. Solid matter or nonmaterial fields? It depends on which level of nature is being investigated.

THE APPEARANCE OF THE TRANSCENDENT

In the fifty years since Heisenberg's discovery, the journey of physics toward the center of creation has passed further milestones. As the fields were discovered and defined, for instance, the fields themselves were found to have a basic level, a most fundamental aspect called the *state of least excitation*, or the *vacuum state*. With this discovery the unmanifest, transcendental basis of nature first began to make its appearance in scientific thought.

The discovery of this most basic level of a particular field was first made in quantum electrodynamics, the subatomic theory that defines the electromagnetic field. Quantum electrodynamics explains light, electricity, X-rays, and magnetism, among many other natural phenomena. It is such a complete and precise theory that experts have called it the most accurate and successful physical theory ever devised.

The vacuum state of this electromagnetic field, as of every field, begins where subatomic particles come to an end. Its existence can be explained in terms of excitation. An electron, to take an example, exists in different states of excitation; it can be thought of as vibrations or fluctuations or excitations of the underlying electron field. Research has shown that any one electron can exist in many different, discrete levels, or states, of excitation. It can be very active or relatively sedate. And there is an absolute lower limit to the different states of excitation an electron can experience. When it relaxes below a certain point, it simply drops out of existence altogether.

When a tuning fork has almost stopped vibrating, its musical note ceases to exist. When an electron has almost stopped vibrating, it itself ceases to exist. In that situation, an electron is not fluctuating enough to have the effect of a particle at all. It relapses into the state of least excitation of the field — also called the vacuum state because it is devoid of all real particles.

On the one hand, therefore, this vacuum state, as its name suggests, contains nothing; even the subatomic particles which structure the universe have not yet begun to have what the physicists now call a real existence. But the vacuum state is said to be not only completely empty; it is also said to be infinitely full. Although it has nothing within it, it is the source of all subatomic particles, the beginning point for the building blocks of nature. The vacuum state is a field of infinite potential. This paradoxical reality has been commented on by E.C.G. Sudarshan. "Physics is considered to be simply the distillation of common sense," he says. "But instead its findings strain our abilities of comprehension. In no case is this more evident than with the vacuum state. The source of 'real' things has no 'real' things within it."

Although the vacuum state has no excitations or vibrations large enough or strong enough to appear in the real world, it has been found to contain what the physicists call virtual particles (or fluctuations). In the words of John Lewis, professor of planetary science at the University of Arizona, "The vacuum state is an unmanifest level containing all possible states of matter and energy in virtual form. These unmanifest states exist as virtual fluctuations in the vacuum field." Moreover, although these virtual particles, or virtual fluctuations, do not embody sufficient energy to appear as "real" particles, yet since there are an infinite number of such virtual particles, even the slight amount of energy associated with each one adds up to infinite energy overall. The vacuum state is, paradoxically, filled with infinite potential.

The fluctuations within the vacuum state aren't really there; they are virtually there, almost there. Given the right conditions, these virtual particles pop out into the real world like popcorn out of a pan. Says the University of California's Capra,

The distinction between matter and empty space finally had to be abandoned when it became evident that virtual particles can come into being spontaneously out of the void, and vanish into the void. . . . The Vacuum is far from empty. On the contrary it contains an unlimited number of particles which come into being and vanish without end.

Here, therefore, with the vacuum state, the state of least excitation of the field, the parallel with Vedic understanding first becomes compelling. The hollow banyan seed is echoed in the vacuum state. The "subtle essence" of existence, the empty "source" of all creation, seems here to have gained objective definition. When physicists analyze the nature of the vacuum in detail, moreover, the parallels with the ancient Vedic predictions become marked. Says the physicist Sudarshan,

> The vacuum state is transcendental and unmanifest, yet it is the source of all manifestation. It is omnipresent and all-pervasive, since it underlies all of the various excited (or active) states of the universe. Further, it is non-spatial, non-temporal, immutable, and absolute. According to the quantum field theory, the vacuum state represents perfection — it is the level where orderliness is perfect and entropy [randomness and disorderliness] is zero. In addition, the vacuum state is a field of silence and non-action which is totally unaffected by any level of activity. Though energy and matter propagate from the vacuum state, it itself always remains undiminished — it is a source of infinitely varied manifestation.

This profound level of definition, based on the mathematical formalisms which describe the vacuum state, can also be understood in relatively simple terms. The vacuum state is **transcendental** (in the sense of *beyond*, or *outside of*) because it is beyond even the subtlest fluctuations of the real world; it is **unmanifest** because its fluctuations are not excited enough to become manifest in the real world; it is **omnipresent** because it is a continuous, all-pervasive background for all the more excited states of existence; it is **non-spatial** because, as Einstein showed, space has meaning only as a measure of the distance between objects or events, and there are no objects or events in the vacuum state (it is, to use other words, empty of anything which could give it boundaries or limitations — it is unbounded); it is **non-temporal** because time is a measure of change, but there is nothing in the vacuum state to change (it is therefore eternal in the most meaningful sense — not that it exists for a long, long time, but rather that it simply has no connection to time); and it is **absolute** since there is nothing within it to establish relationships — it is prior to all relationships, to all relativity.

At this level of nature, then, the Vedic and scientific views are parallel. Maharishi's description of the absolute field — "beyond the realm of time, space and causation," "the status which knows no change," "unlimited, unbounded, unmanifest" — has now been paralleled by objective understandings. According to the physicists, moreover, the vacuum state (of the electromagnetic field, or any other field) exists not only in its own untouchable realm, but it also forms the substance of the solid world we see around us. At the finest levels, each aspect of nature is made up of such a field of all possibilities. In other words, when subatomic particles go from the virtual to the real world, they do not actually leave the vacuum level. In their real-world form, they are still but fluctuations or vibrations in, or of, the vacuum state. If every wave on the surface of the ocean is but a part of the ocean's water, every photon of light in the universe is but a wave of the vacuum state of the electromagnetic field. Every particle in the world, and in us, is structured of an unmanifest field of unbounded potential. We are, literally, made of infinite possibility.

TOWARD THE UNIFIED FIELD

One more step remains to be taken. The vacuum state was first defined at the mid-point of the twentieth century in the theory of quantum electrodynamics — the fundamental theory of electromagnetism. At that time, however, there were no theories available that gave one unified picture of the functioning of the whole of nature, no theories that could provide a unified understanding of all the forces or fields that make up the apparently physical world. In the 1950s there seemed to be a large number of infinite, unbounded fields — one for electrons, one for protons, one for the strong nuclear force, etc. — each field with its own vacuum state. Within a decade, physics had reduced this plethora of fields down to four fundamental force fields, as well as four fundamental particle fields, but this still meant eight separate departments in nature, some of them not yet well understood.

Such a situation was not satisfying to physicists. For the smooth functioning of natural law, from the galactic to the subatomic levels, it seemed that all of creation must be one integrated whole. In the words of Heinz Pagels, formerly director of the New York Academy of Sciences and author of two of the most popular books on quantum physics, *The Cosmic Code* and *Perfect Symmetry*,

> The dream of Einstein was the search for a master law of the universe. He sought in vain for one unified picture of nature from which all the other physical laws could be deduced — but in recent years many other physicists have taken up his quest. The goal is to construct a theory that begins with one master law and results in only one logically possible universe. Not that everything in that universe would be determined — not that you or I had to come into existence right from the beginning — but that the master law would generate a universe characterized by the laws of nature as we know them. This is the physicist's dream.

Since the late 1960s, physics has made tremendous progress in realizing Einstein's dream. Theoretical physicists have developed models that reveal an underlying unity, in which the four force fields and the four particle fields of nature exist in one fully unified wholeness. Physicists today look to these theories for the deepest understanding of nature.

The argument can be understood by focusing on the side of the force fields. The four forces which physicists sought to unify comprise:

1. Electromagnetism, which not only accounts for television, lightning, and the functioning of the human nervous system, but also provides the connecting mechanism that holds atoms together and connects atoms within molecules;

2. Gravity, an attractive force that operates over long distances, though relatively weakly;

3. The strong force, the force which binds together the nucleus of the atom; and

4. The weak force, a second subatomic force, responsible for radioactivity and instrumental in the fusion reaction within the Sun which provides energy for life on Earth.

In the 1960s, beginning with a paper published by Sheldon Glashow and culminating in work done separately by Steven Weinberg and Abdus Salaam, two of these four forces were theoretically unified. This electro-weak unification showed that electromagnetism and the weak force were, at a more fundamental level, not two separate realities but rather two aspects of the same underlying field. If we imagine a microscope cranked to progressively higher levels of magnification, resulting in the ability to perceive the natural world at progressively finer distance scales, we come eventually to a level fine enough (small enough) to reveal the fundamental unity of phenomena that appear, more superficially, unrelated. As two branches in a tree can be, in fact, two extensions of one underlying limb, so the electromagnetic force and the weak force are, in fact, two aspects of a single underlying field. This theory was so beautifully conceived — so elegant and so powerful, to use two of the words physicists often employ to define a mathematical picture of nature which seems to them compelling — that Glashow, Weinberg, and Salaam received the Nobel Prize for their work even before any experimental evidence proved their theory correct. Such evidence has come in, however — the discovery of three new particles predicted by their theory.

In the 1970s the unification project continued with the creation of so-called Grand Unified Theories by Glashow and others, theories which revealed the underlying unity of the strong force with the weak and electromagnetic forces. With the development of these theories, the three most powerful forces were found to be unified — all but gravity.

For many years, gravity resisted successful unification. This is partially because gravity is so different from the other forces. Though it operates over long distances, it is extremely weak when compared to the other three forces; if held together by gravity instead of electromagnetism, a single atom of hydrogen — one proton circled by one electron — would have a radius larger than that of the known universe.

Finally, however, through the use of a mathematical formalism known as *supersymmetry*, physicists have succeeded in devising completely unified field theories which unite all four of the natural force fields (and all particle fields, as well). All such supersymmetric theories define the existence of what is sometimes called the *superfield* — one *unified field* which contains within it the seeds of all the force and matter fields in nature. This newly defined unified field stands in a parental role to all the fields, all the particles, all the forces. With these theories the understanding of nature has reached a completely unified description.

As with many other aspects of quantum physics, this ultimate reality of nature can be imagined in different ways. Daniel Freedman of MIT and Peter Van Nieuwenhuizen of the State University of New York, two leaders in the development of supersymmetric supergravity theories, have said that the mechanics for the production of real particles from the unified field can also be viewed in terms of a "super particle" with an arrow in an auxiliary space of many dimensions. As the arrow rotates, the particle becomes in turn a graviton, a gravitino, a photon, a quark, and so on. The quanta of all the forces are present in the theory, and they are unified, or derived from a common source.

However this process is imagined, the overall picture is encouraging. With it, every different aspect of nature can be understood as arising from a single, unified field. These super-unified theories, moreover, are supported in the two ways most congenial to the mind of the modern physicist. First is simply the mathematical structure of the theories themselves. As Freedman says,

> To begin with, the equations in the theories have in themselves a high degree of symmetry, and if there is one thing theoretical physics has learned in the twentieth century it is that symmetry is one of the major principles of successful theories. Another aspect is that, using superunified approaches, when you write down a theory from a general set of ideas, you don't wind up with 100 adjustable parameters. This is important because physicists in general have a prejudice that, when God created the laws of the universe, he did not randomly choose, for example, the masses arbitrarily. The assumption is that there is a simple set of equations from which everything can be derived, and the super unified approach seems to be providing that.

In recent years, the most successful unified field theories have been known as *superstring* theories. In these theories, what were once considered to be the subatomic particles are now considered to be string-like rather than point-like. Instead of a superparticle, there is now a superstring, elastic and closed end-to-end like a donut. The various rotations and vibrations of this string give rise to the various force and matter fields of nature.

John Hagelin, the Harvard-trained physicist who has worked at both the European Center for Nuclear Research and the Stanford Linear Accelerator, the two leading centers of unified field research, has been an important contributor to this search for physical unification, and his publications on this topic have been among the most cited papers in the field. His recent formulation of a Grand Unified Theory, sometimes called the *Flipped SU(5)* model, has been called the leading candidate for a successful Grand Unified approach.

Any Grand Unified Theory is the last link in the chain of unification before the superunification in the unified field. Hagelin's Flipped SU(5) theory is important because it is the only Grand Unified Theory that can be connected backward or inward to the superstring in the unified field, and also forward or outward to the force and particle fields that actually make up the universe. In 1984, Hagelin accepted the appointment as chairman of the physics department at Maharishi University of Management, and in addition to his traditional credentials, he is recognized as being the best-informed physicist on the ancient understandings of Vedic Science.

Hagelin frequently makes presentations on the nature and qualities of the unified field at the heart of creation. In his lectures on these superunified theories, Hagelin usually starts with a review of the progress made by twentieth-century physics in understanding the progressively deeper layers of nature's functioning. He begins by reviewing the "dissolution" of solid particles.

The particle concept goes very deep in the history of science. You can call it "billiard ball mechanics." Since Newton at least it has dominated the conceptual framework of science, and it is in a sense a hangover of three centuries of studying billiard balls and their ilk. Even today most physics students begin their study of physics by analyzing the rolling of balls on inclined planes. But this notion of solid, massy particles, so deeply ingrained in our thinking, is simply inadequate at the quantum mechanical level. This concrete, familiar concept, which was supposed to be the basis of nature, slipped through our fingers in the first part of this century. We were left with something much more abstract — waves in an underlying quantum mechanical field.

And as Hagelin says, the shift from particles to fields was not the conclusion of this move from the concrete to the abstract.

> The wave function is a more abstract, more unlocalized, more expanded concept than the particle. Nevertheless we are familiar with waves, we have an image of waves in a field, such as waves on the surface of a lake. But then at the most abstract level of the field — the state of least excitation, or vacuum state, where the lake has, as it were, settled down completely — in that state the quantum field itself has no definable shape. The vacuum state, in fact, is the coexistence of all possible shapes of the field simultaneously. This can't happen with the surface of a lake. There cannot possibly be the simultaneous superposition of all possible shapes of such a classical field. So we find that even the term "field," as we know it, is inappropriate to describe the quantum mechanical reality. The notion of field also dissolves, and we are left with an abstract, unlocalized something that does not even have a definite shape.

DISCOVERY OF THE UNIFIED FIELD

This progression away from the concrete and toward the abstract culminates in the recent definitions of the unified field, which is, in a sense, the simultaneous superposition not just of all possible shapes of one field, but of all possible fields. In his Vedic Science, Maharishi indicates that it is the nature and qualities of this fully unified field at the basis of nature which offer to human beings a life of infinite potential — including the ability to directly create peace in the world. A detailed description can help explain why.

In the first place, as Hagelin points out, the unified field is both extremely abstract and very real.

> As one's attention is brought to the most fundamental level of nature, there is a transition in the structure of natural law. From this most basic standpoint, it is possible to see that the apparent laws of nature at more superficial levels are the result only of an approximate and fragmented viewpoint. At the level

of the unified field, nature is completely abstract but infinitely energetic and dynamic, and within that level of infinite energy all the laws of nature are found united. Out of this most fundamental level of nature's functioning arise all the laws of nature which uphold the functioning of the more superficial and complicated levels. The unified field is thus highly abstract, but very real. From there, all the laws of nature originate.

How can we picture the relationship between the unified field and the surface level of nature? One way to understand it is historically — to consider the origin of the universe. According to the most widely accepted theories, all the laws of nature were lively in a unified state just a billionth of a second after the big bang first began the universe. At that historical moment, cosmologists now theorize, all the mass and energy of the universe was compressed into a radius smaller than the nucleus of an atom. This seed of creation was unimaginably hot, and in this white hot point of essentially infinite energy, the laws of nature existed in one inseparable unity.

The evolution of the universe as we now know it is pictured in terms of the breaking of a perfect symmetry that existed in that seed-point of natural law. Within that unified, unstructured wholeness, symmetry was perfect: Along every possible axis, the structure of the field was identical. From the center of a large globe, the view is identical in every direction. From *anywhere* in a supersymmetric field, the view is identical in every direction.

From this field of undifferentiated, perfectly symmetrical unity, differences and variety came about in the universe when, as the seed-point of matter and energy expanded and cooled, the symmetry that exists at the level of the unified field began to break down. This has been likened by physicists to a crystallization process, a process reminiscent of amorphous fog hitting a cold window and crystallizing into beautiful, highly specific patterns. As the universe cooled, there was a process known by theoretical physicists as *spontaneous, sequential, dynamical symmetry breaking*. One after the other, the four forces of nature crystallized out and began their own independent levels of functioning. Like the petals of a flower opening out one by one from the unity of the bud, the laws of nature opened out one by one from their completely unified state. Heinz Pagels is one of the few physicists who has discussed these latest discoveries in layman's terms. In *Perfect Symmetry*, Pagels imagines the process running backwards, as if a time-lapse film of a budding flower were seen in reverse.

> Here, for the first time, we see a remarkable feature of the modern theory of the origin of the universe: the further back in time we go, the hotter the universe becomes, and broken symmetries are restored. The universe and all its particle interactions are becoming more and more symmetrical as we descend deeper into the big bang. . . . Conversely, were we to progress forward in time, we would see that as the temperature falls, those perfect symmetries are broken. Now the physical differences between the various interactions — strong, weak and electromagnetic — become apparent. The universe today, with its relatively low temperature, is the frozen remnant of the big bang. Like an ice crystal that has frozen out of a uniform water vapor, it has lots of structure — the galaxies, stars and life itself.

SMALLER THAN THE SMALLEST

According to these unified theories, moreover, the unified level of nature is not a historical reality only, not something that existed at only the most remote moment in time and has since ceased to take any part in creation. In the deepest understanding, the perfect symmetry of the unified field exists at every point, omnipresent, deep within the structure of nature. Starting at any given point, you can approach the unified field through a series of steps of unification, each step taking place, in John Hagelin's phrase, at "finer and finer time and distance scales" — that is, in areas and time-frames which are smaller and smaller. If we imagine that our microscope focuses in beyond the atomic level, beyond the level of subatomic particles, and down to the finest possible level of nature, there we would find the closest approximation to a point value of space and time, what is known to physicists as the *Planck scale* of nature's functioning. Beyond this unimaginably minute level, transcendental to every aspect of the apparently physical universe, physicists say that the unified field is fully lively.

The Planck scale is considered by physicists to be the fundamental scale of physics, the smallest size possible in nature. This is true because at the Planck scale the whole notion of size — and not only size, but all concept of space and time — cease to have any meaningful reality. As Hagelin says,

> At the level of the Planck scale, gravity also becomes a quantum reality. This means that the arena of the gravitational field, the four-dimensional manifold of space-time which Einstein first defined, no longer has a definite shape. The four-dimensional geometry of our familiar world assumes the quantum aspect of the simultaneous coexistence of all possible shapes. Thus space and time as concepts to describe nature become inappropriate. If you want to find the distance between two points, you can't find a well-defined answer. If you try to lay down a ruler on the manifold, you find there are an infinite number of manifolds simultaneously. All geometries coexist and there ceases to be any definition of distance.

In other words, it is not possible to move to a smaller time or distance scale than the Planck scale because, at the Planck scale, smaller no longer means anything. The geometry of space-time, the backdrop for the other three forces, or fields, of nature, finally itself dissolves into a shape-shifting, indefinite, ever-changing reality. In fact, in Hagelin's understanding it is not possible even to *think* about the unified field in any reasonable way. This is true because,

At the Planck scale of superunification, space and time have no currently viable definition, and there is no way to determine what comes first and what comes second. And when that happens, even causality becomes suspect. Causality is a fundamental aspect of empirical science. Science is involved with questions of why. We assume you can ask why something happened, what caused it, and have that be a reasonable question. But a cause, to be a cause, must precede the effect. Why is this chalk in two pieces in my hands? Because, at some time in the past, I broke the two pieces apart. Sequence in time is fundamental to causality. If you can't define sequence, you can't define a reasonable causality, and if you can't define causality, the whole project of empirical science and logical exploration comes into question.

Yet this indefinable, even unthinkable, essence of existence, which is found at every point throughout the universe, is by its very nature a source of infinite potential — a vibrantly dynamic field of unbounded possibilities. At that finest level of nature's functioning, the transition of space-time geometry becomes so dynamic that Hagelin calls it a boiling of that geometry into a space-time foam. In the words of Heinz Pagels,

> On large-distance scales such as those we experience every day, space-time looks flat and smooth like the ocean surface seen from on high; but up close at the Planck scale it is churning and foaming like the ocean in a storm. If physicists are to describe the microworld of Planck-scale distances, then little remains of the concept of a space-time continuum upon which the description of nature has so far been based.

What is this foam made of? Each bubble is a universe within itself. Says Hagelin, "As we go from grosser levels of nature down to that finest level of the Planck scale, there appears a continuous effervescence, a continuous bubbling up of entirely separate universes."

Every possible universe, every possible law of nature, every possible combination of particles, forces, and fields — all the possibilities of creation are continually roiling up from the infinitely creative dynamism of the unified field of all the laws of nature. This is the reality at the basis of existence. Eddington's writing table has a solid layer on the surface, but when we take our attention to the finer and finer levels deep within, we come upon, first, a swarm of subatomic particles, and finally a foam of infinite potential — a field of all possibilities.

These latest unified field theories thus give us a penetrating, and apparently paradoxical, insight into the workings of nature. The particular, solid, material objects which we see around us on the surface level of existence, and even the fundamental force and particle fields that lie deep within the functioning of nature, are but varying expressions of one unified field of all the laws of nature. On the one hand, this is a field of infinite creativity, roiling with unbounded possibilities, but on the other hand, it is completely abstract and unmanifest, beyond space and time, beyond, and devoid of, all forces and particles. Although it gives rise to an infinity of universes, it itself is beyond all the hubbub on the surface level of life — a field of infinite silence, of perfect peace.

Summing up his discussion of the progress physics has made in describing the ultimate workings of nature, both microscopically and cosmologically, Heinz Pagels makes his most important point in simple language:

> When historians of science look back on the 1970s and '80s, they will report that for the first time scientists constructed rational mathematical models based on the laws of physics which described the creation of the universe out of nothing. And that will mark the beginning of a new outlook on the creation of existence.

FROM MATTER TO MIND

The tale of the hollow banyan seed thus seems an appropriate analogy for the mainstream ideas of modern physics. In the current theories of physics, the source of all the force and particle fields that make up the universe is beyond any specific manifestations seen in the real universe. It is beyond space, beyond time, beyond forces, beyond particles, transcendental and absolute, a field of silence and peace. Yet that empty, silent field is somehow a field of fullness, a field of infinite potential that can give rise to not just one specific type of creation, but to an infinite foam of universes.

For someone seeking a standpoint for Archimedes' lever, or else a master switchboard — not just for this universe but for all possible universes — quantum physics has thus uncovered an ideal candidate in the unified field. The ancient Vedic wisdom propounded such a basic unified field, and now physics has at least glimpsed its reality.

There is only one difficulty with this discovery as it has been made through objective science. It doesn't seem to be of any practical use. There is no apparent way for a human being to take up a position at this transcendental level, no way to take advantage of the infinite potentiality which is lively there.

In his Vedic Science, however, Maharishi posits a profound possibility. The ancient Vedic tradition of knowledge maintains that the human mind can directly *experience* the unified field. This is not on the basis of surface-level thinking and logical analysis, but rather on the basis of direct immersion in, or conscious identification with, this field. The mind can theoretically settle down deep within itself and, in experiencing its *own* source, experience the source of all creation.

Thinking about a cool swim on a hot day is one thing; diving directly into the water quite another. Direct experience is beyond thought; it is real, tangible — it gets you wet, it cools you off. This has been one of the main emphases in Maharishi's teaching of Vedic Science — the unified field is not a thought, not a concept, but a reality which can be directly experienced. The experience of the unified field, he says, is an experience beyond all thought, beyond even the finest levels of the thinking process.

This is the purpose of meditation — a direct dive into the unified field, experienced as the pure, unbounded, transcendental essence of one's own consciousness, as the simplest state of one's own awareness. And this direct dive is, in theory, the fundamental mechanics of Super Radiance, as well. To radiate peace, in other words, contact the field of infinite peace within.

VEDIC SCIENCE AND MODERN SCIENCE

It will take two more chapters to thoroughly discuss this concept. Before moving on, however, it might be useful to take a quick look back and gauge how thoroughly the Vedic concept of the unified field has been verified. Here again is Maharishi's description of the "absolute field" which he offered more than forty years ago:

> The absolute field lies at the root of everything. It is the omnipresent, essential constituent of creation, beyond all relative existence, beyond the realm of time, space and causation, the boundaries of the ever-changing, phenomenal states of life. It enjoys the status which knows no change, the status of eternal existence. The different aspects of creation, of relative existence, of all the forms and phenomena in the ever-changing states of life in the world are as ripples and waves, having their basis in this vast, transcendent ocean. But it itself is unlimited, unbounded, unmanifest, unchanging, eternal. It is the absolute state of existence.

Certainly we can say that modern science has begun to catch up with ancient wisdom. But can we contact — can we directly experience — this unmanifest, eternal field?

If so — if mind and matter can really be united at their source — then the relationship between nature and human nature, between creation and consciousness, must be considerably different from the way it seems on the surface level of life. In the everyday world, mind seems to be one thing — nonmaterial, insubstantial, never localized in any solid object — and matter something else entirely — physical, substantial, localized.

THE UNIFIED FIELD • 1 1 9

But physics has already shown us that solid matter does not, at its basic level, have a solid existence. The subatomic particles, out of which the entire apparently physical universe is constructed, are in actuality but waves in an underlying field that is itself completely nonmaterial, completely insubstantial, that is unmanifest, transcendental, timeless, and infinite. If mind is nonmaterial, found nowhere fixed as specific substance, physics now tells us that matter, at its basis, is no less.

And physics has even more to say on this topic. To a surprising extent, the explorations of quantum physics have uncovered an indissoluble interfusion of mind and "matter." It will prove fruitful to spend one more chapter with some of this century's greatest physicists, finding out what more they can tell us about the nature of nature — and its relationship with consciousness.

4

CONSCIOUSNESS AND CREATION:
From the Standpoint of Physics

The mysterious intelligence of creation is one essence of childhood awe. The filigreed wonder of snowflakes, the mathematical beauty of coiling seashells, the delicate architecture of spring flowers, all the inherent genius of nature and life seem to speak of a living logic embedded in the world.

Given the orderly, predictable world of nature, it is sometimes difficult to understand how we ever talked ourselves out of the obvious, innocent perception that intelligence is infused in every aspect of creation. It is true that, at a certain stage of the evolution of scientific thinking, many scientists pictured the material aspect of creation as dead and inert, and the constructs of galaxies, planets, and life as simply the chance congregations of material bits piling up randomly. But science has advanced. Distinctions that once seemed obvious, such as that between solid matter and empty space, have dissolved. And as we will see in this chapter, quantum mechanics has brought into question even the ultimate distinction upon which science itself is based — the distinction between the scientist and what he is studying, the distinction between the living mind of the observer and the inert matter being observed.

In the world of quantum physics, as leading physicists have often said, mind and matter have become inextricably intertwined.

THE VEDIC UNDERSTANDING

In the Vedic tradition, this is no surprise. Such a union between consciousness and creation is the central Vedic assertion about the functioning of the world. The unbounded, transcendental field at the basis of nature, now glimpsed by modern physics as the unified field, is seen by Maharishi, in his Vedic Science, as itself *made* of consciousness. Heinz Pagels called this fundamental level "nothing," and it certainly is "no-thing" — without physical substance. But in the Vedic understanding, it *is* consciousness. In this view, mind and matter are closely intertwined because the unified field, the source of matter, is itself a field of mind, of awareness, of pure, unbounded consciousness.

This startling assertion — which underlies the mechanics of Super Radiance, of permanent peace — has been the basis of Maharishi's teaching for nearly fifty years. Maharishi comes from the tradition of teachers in northern India, a line founded ages ago by the illustrious sage Shankara. Perhaps the most respected intellect in India's history, Shankara expresses this view of creation's essence simply. "That reality pervades the universe," he said, "but no one penetrates it. It alone shines. Its nature is pure consciousness."

Commenting on this central understanding in 1963, when even the electro-weak unification was but a gleam in the eyes of physicists and completely unified field theories hardly a dream, Maharishi gave the definition of the absolute field already quoted, and added this point:

> With the rapid pace of development in nuclear physics, the day does not seem far off when some theoretical physicist will succeed in establishing a unified field theory. The discovery of this one basis of material existence will mark the ultimate achieve-

ment in the history of the development of physical science. This will assist in turning the world of physical science toward the science of mental phenomena. And at the extreme limit of this investigation will be found the state of pure consciousness, that field of transcendental nature lying beyond all the relative existence.

By now, the discovery of the unified field has taken place in the most advanced theories of quantum mechanics — and in recent years Maharishi has brought this point up to date.

> Now from the investigations of modern science we have the unified field, the home of all the laws of nature. And from Vedic Science we know this field to be a field of pure awareness, of infinite creativity. It is the field of intelligence pure, of consciousness pure.

In this understanding, the geometrical creativity exhibited by snowflakes, the mathematical intelligence structured into sea shells — all the orderly and precise manifestations of nature — have their source in one limitless reservoir of creativity and intelligence, a pure field of abstract consciousness. The surprise, as we will see, is how completely modern physicists agree with this view. The investigations of physics, apparently objective to exclusion, apparently a dry parsing of the mechanics of inert objects, have unintentionally unveiled a mind-matter symbiosis deep within the structure of nature.

Pondering these quantum discoveries in the first decades of the twentieth century, physicist Max Planck, who first discovered the quantized nature of the subatomic world and for whom the Planck scale is named, put a bold conclusion in stark logical terms: "I regard consciousness as primary. I regard matter as derivative of consciousness." Eugene Wigner, a Nobel Laureate in physics, put one conclusion from this understanding in these words: "The next revolution in physics will occur when the properties of mind will be included in the equations of quantum physics."

THE OBSERVER IS THE OBSERVED

Why are many physicists coming to believe that the study of physics must in some way include the study of consciousness? An entry-level answer is provided by Erwin Schrödinger, one of the most influential quantum mechanical pioneers of the first half of this century. Writing in a late-career book entitled *Mind and Matter*, Schrödinger turned to the crucial question about the relationship between consciousness and scientific truth. In the view he propounded, the problem starts where science begins. The fateful first step of scientific investigation is, in Schrödinger's neologism, to *objectivate* the world. "We exclude the subject of cognizance," he says, "from the domain of nature that we endeavor to understand." Scientists, in other words, are excluded from the realm they are studying which has the effect of objectivating the world. It becomes subject-less by definition — dead, inert, mere matter. This is a central scientific assumption, of course; it is the basis of the concept of objective investigation. The person doing the study is supposed to have no involvement with what is being studied. To put this most simply, mind is supposed to be observing matter.

But this basic assumption leaves us prey, as Schrödinger says, to a "pandemonium of disastrous logical consequences." The inconvenient reality, as Schrödinger takes several chapters to explain, is that much of what is supposedly out there, in the world, is in reality structured in here, in consciousness, all along. To make his point, Schrödinger takes the example of light.

> If you ask a physicist what is his idea of yellow light, he will tell you that it is transversal electromagnetic waves of wavelength in the neighborhood of 590 millimicrons. If you ask him: But where does yellow come in? he will say: In my picture not at all, but these vibrations, when they hit the retina of a healthy eye, give the person whose eye it is the sensation of yellow.

The electrons and protons in a yellow flower petal are not themselves yellow, nor are the photons of light reflecting from the petal somehow splashed with yellow paint. Nor, in the eye, is there a yellow chemical created, any more than in the brain yellow electricity moves about. Yellow is nowhere to be found in the objective world at all, which consists only of vibrating energy, or more exactly, fluctuations of the underlying field. Yellowness, as Schrödinger pointed out, is created only in "the subject of cognizance." Yellow is in the mind of the perceiver, a response wholly within consciousness.

The locus of this creation can be found nowhere in the "objectivated" picture of the world, as Schrödinger explains. He switches his analysis from sight to hearing and seeks for the place where waves, passing through the air, finally register as sound.

> We can follow the pressure changes in the air as they produce vibrations of the ear drum. . . . We may reach an understanding of how [this] sets up an electrical and chemical process of conduction in the nervous fibre with which it is in touch. We may follow this conduction to the cerebral cortex and we may even obtain some knowledge of some of the things that happen there. But nowhere shall we hit on this "registering as sound" which is simply not contained in the scientific picture, but is only in the mind of the person whose ear and brain we are speaking of.

Schrödinger's point is that the world we perceive — *as we perceive it* — is structured in our consciousness. If we imagine ourselves small enough to see them (and if they had a localized physical reality), electrons within a rose would look identical to electrons in the air around the rose. The subatomic reality is monotonously the same, a small handful of different types of particles or wave functions, all of each type interchangeable regardless of the large-scale objects of which they are a part. Every electron is identical to every other electron. On the surface level of nature, on the other hand, there is infinite variety, from grains of sand through scudding clouds to swirling galaxies. Despite the absolute identity of the subatomic components, the surface level manifestations can be large or small, hard or soft, sharp or smooth, colorful or dull. And as Schrödinger's analysis makes clear, at this surface level of nature the mind actually helps create the qualities which it is observing. Whether something is rough or smooth, for example, depends upon the scale being observed. What might seem a bumpy road indeed to an ant can be smooth and sumptuous to the driver of an SUV.

Moreover, this commingling of consciousness and creation is not only true of such everyday sense perceptions as color, shape, texture, and smell, but also of the precise mathematical qualities defined and studied by science. In the words of John Kemeny, a physicist and former president of Dartmouth University, "We tend to say that objects have masses, velocities, energy, etc. Actually these are free creations of the human mind, which have proved useful for the formulation of theories about experience."

Einstein's theory of relativity showed that mass and energy, for example, which we commonly think of as two obviously independent qualities of any object, are actually not separate realities, but rather two different ways of looking at the same thing. Mass was always conceived as lumpish, inert, resistant to change, while energy was considered, well, energetic — ceaselessly in motion, dynamic, the *source* of change. But in the twentieth century we found that matter and energy are one. $E=mc^2$ means more than that mass can be turned into energy; it means, in truth, that mass and energy are interchangeable views of one reality. Physicists who specialize in quantum mechanics, for example, list the mass of subatomic particles in units which measure energy. The separateness and specificity of mass and energy are "free creations of the human mind."

THE THING IN ITSELF

Immanuel Kant made this point a centerpiece in his philosophy. What we know are the categories in our minds, he said. When we see a brick, we know it as a brick because we have a brick category in our mind. If later we need a door stop or a paper weight — if different categories surface in our mind — then we may see the brick totally differently. In Kant's understanding we experience our mental categories, not the reality. Of the *ding-an-sich* (the thing-in-itself), we know nothing. In an era of quantum physics we can understand this thoroughly. We know nothing (through our direct sense perception) of the subatomic reality in a brick; we see only what is created by our consciousness in response to the photons coming from it. We know nothing of the *ding-an-sich*.

Twentieth-century psychologist Abraham Maslow agreed with this eighteenth-century assessment of Kant. Said Maslow, "We do not so much cognize the nature of the world as it actually is, as we do the organization of our own inner world outlook." Physicist Fritjov Capra makes the point in terms of scientific knowledge:

> Physicists have come to see that all of their theories of natural phenomena, including the laws they describe, are creations of the human mind; properties of our conceptual map of reality, rather than of reality itself.

And Eddington, the brilliant British physicist who was unmatched for translating physics into the vernacular with a flair both dramatic and poetic, put it this way:

> [W]e have found that where science has progressed the farthest, the mind has regained from nature that which the mind has put into nature. We have found a strange footprint on the shores of the unknown. We have devised profound theories, one after another, to account for its origin. At last, we have succeeded in reconstructing the creature that made the footprint. And lo! It is our own.

ACCOUNTING FOR THE OBSERVER

Albert Einstein in his theories of relativity established a similar truth, not at the level of our everyday experience, but at the cosmological level, the scale of astronomical distances and extreme speed. As part of his profound reworking of Newton's laws of gravitation, in equations which united, on the one hand, matter with energy and, on the other, space with time, he also showed that the basic elements of physics — the measurements of distance and time — could no longer be absolutely relied upon. Rulers and clocks, which seem so simple and sound, suddenly became suspect.

Through an elegant logic (which Einstein himself best explains for the layman in his book *Relativity*), he proved that knowledge of distance and of time is no longer absolute and invariant, but depends instead upon the motion of the observer. Clocks can speed up or slow down, measuring rods lengthen or shorten, depending on the relative motion of different observers measuring the same phenomenon. The most basic measuring units of physics turn out to be elastic and unreliable unless the exact situation of the physicist himself is known. In the words of John Lewis, professor of planetary science at the University of Arizona,

> Most non-scientists and even many scientists are as yet unaware of the profound new perspectives which relativity theory has developed and how much these perspectives alter our "common sense" notion of reality. Whereas classical physics spoke of objective reality independent of the observer, relativity theory posits that we can never separate the two — the observer has become an integral part of any statement about reality.

FROM MATTER TO MIND

Both the vast cosmological level of nature (as described by Einstein) and the level of everyday human experience (as analyzed by Schrödinger) are thus characterized by a close interconnection between subject and object, between the observer and the observed. And the progress of quantum physics has extended this interconnection down to the subatomic level, the most fundamental level, where, in fact, the confluence of matter and consciousness becomes most complete and compelling.

We should expect this interpenetration of matter and mind from Maharishi's discussions. As mentioned at the start of this chapter, even superficial inspection of our world — a mere noting of snow flakes and seashells — gives us reason to believe that nature is infused with intelligence. Before the discovery of the unified field, Maharishi based his logic on just such simple observations:

It's just at the level of common sense. It is obvious there is something deep within physical values which is the cause of change and progress. We see order in creation. There is some intelligence working at every level of existence, some orderliness at the atomic level, at the molecular level. And there is obvious orderliness in the sequence and progression of life. Everything is growing, and growing in an orderly way: an apple tree produces apples, a banana tree produces bananas; the apple tree doesn't grow guavas. Some order is there, some intelligence is there.

At the quantum level, this intelligence "deep within physical values" becomes insistently clear. To start a subatomic analysis of this idea at the most precise point, we must say that no subatomic particle ever *occupies* a precise point. The mathematical formalism of quantum mechanics (the wave function originally developed by Erwin Schrödinger) does not describe a small fleck of matter sitting at a particular point, or moving on an exact path, or trajectory. Rather, the wave function describes, for each point in space and time, a *probability* that the 'particle' will be at that point, if you looked for it.* Thus, the 'particle'† does not travel a particular and specific path, but exists only as waves of ever-changing probabilities. We have seen earlier that 'particles' are actually waves — now we see that they are waves of probability — nothing specific or definite, but rather just constantly changing odds for where the 'particle' might be.

---

*Speaking more precisely, it is the square of the wave function that yields such probabilities.
†Because the considerations discussed in this section definitely rule out the notion that subatomic 'particles' are, in fact, actual particles, we will use single quotes around the word from here out.

Obviously, this is a radical reconceptualization of "physical reality." A billiard ball, as it rolls across a table, actually *is* somewhere at all times. By contrast, a subatomic 'particle' in motion might be here and might be there — but it *is* nowhere at all.

And there is another step to the logic. A 'particle' is described by probabilities, and probabilities are intellectual constructs only. That is, these intellectual constructs, or patterns of intelligence, have no existence in the four-dimensional world of material objects. As an example, if a certain group of 100 houses each has a 50% probability of a tree in the front yard, none of those houses has half a tree. In the physical world, each house has either a whole tree or none, and the 50% probability is only a mathematical structure, a mental reality. It is a pattern of intelligence you can hold in the mind, but not in your hands.

In the words of Henry Pierce Stapp, a physicist at the Lawrence Berkeley Laboratory and a main contributor to the S-matrix version of quantum mechanics, this probabilistic nature of subatomic 'particles' indicate that they are "idea-like rather than matter-like." As Stapp goes on to say, "Just as in classical mechanics there is no natural place for consciousness, so in quantum mechanics there is no natural place for matter."

Eddington, after a review of quantum mechanical realities, put the same point more compactly: "The stuff of the world is mind-stuff."

THE OBSERVER AFFECTS THE OBSERVED

The quantum world is "idea-like," made of "mind-stuff," and the human mind consists obviously of mind-stuff. This apparent commonality between nature's intelligence and human intelligence opens the possibility that the subatomic intelligence displayed in nature can become inextricably involved with the intelligence of the (apparently independent) observer. We have already seen that the surface level of the world, as we observe it, is created within the consciousness of the observer. Now, at the quantum mechanical level, we find that the world *itself* is, in one precise sense, "created" by the consciousness of the observer.

Left to itself, recall, a 'particle' has no precise position, only probabilities of position. The same is true for other qualities of a 'particle.' Of the property physicists call *spin*, for example, the 'particle' has a 50-50 chance of being either "spin up" or "spin down."* The central point is that, left to itself, and in all such cases, a 'particle' exhibits only probabilities, and no particular position or spin.

But physicists won't leave 'particles' to themselves. They perform experiments to specify particular parameters of a given 'particle.' In quantum experiments, what's more, they can only measure one quality at a time — position, for example, or spin. Assume that a physicist chooses to measure spin. When the 'particle' encounters the measuring device, a specific spin will suddenly be exhibited — either up or down — a spin that registers on the device, and thus manifests in the large-scale classical world.

There is, however, a crucial distinction between such a quantum measurement and measurements in the everyday, classical world. In the classical world, if you measure, say, the length of a box, you get a measurement of that length — a quantity that you clearly know existed before you measured it. In the quantum world, if you measure, say, spin, then you get a measurement of that spin — but that quality did *not* exist before you measured it. Through the act of measurement, amorphous probabilities suddenly resolve to one particular actuality. By choosing to measure spin, the physicist has brought that spin quality into manifest existence. Where there was no actual quality of any

---

*The quantum quality of *spin* does not mean that a real 'particle' is really spinning. Spin is just a word physicists use to describe a quality they can't directly perceive or define. Moreover, "spin up" and "spin down" are terms used to refer to two different aspects of this basic quality which can be mathematically described and experimentally confirmed, though the words up and down have no more real meaning in this context than the word spin itself.

type, only probabilities, there is now a definite spin — either spin up or spin down.

Put most dramatically, physicists choose which aspects of the subatomic reality they wish to transform from probabilities to actualities. If they measure for spin, spin will manifest at the classical level; if they measure for position, position will manifest. The intrinsic nature of subatomic reality is profoundly altered by the manner in which it is observed — infinite probabilities become a single actuality.

In the words of John Wheeler, once a student of Erwin Schrödinger, who first helped formulate the concept of black holes, this intervention through measurement "destroys the concept of the world 'sitting out there' with the observer safely separated from it by a 20 centimeter slab of glass." Objective distance — "objectivation" — has been replaced by subjective involvement. Once an electron's spin has been measured, its situation has forever been altered. As Wheeler says,

> The universe will never afterward be the same. To describe what has happened one has to cross out that old word 'observer' and put in its place the new word 'participator.' In some strange sense, the universe is a participatory universe.

Such considerations have led many physicists to conclude, in this sense as well, that mind and matter, consciousness and creation, are fundamentally interfused. In the words of French physicist Bernard D'Espagnat, "The doctrine that the world is made up of objects whose existence is independent of human consciousness turns out to be in conflict with quantum mechanics and with facts established by experiment." E.C.G. Sudarshan expresses the point succinctly. In quantum mechanical theory, he says, "consciousness is an integral element of the observed physical field."

John Wheeler has extended this understanding to include an entirely new approach to physics. According to Wheeler, we have gone beyond the Era of Motion in physics (that pre-Newtonian stage when Kepler, Galileo, and others first founded modern physics on the billiard ball basis, the measurement of the motion of solid bodies) and also beyond the Era of Laws (the epoch from Newton to, approximately, Heisenberg), and moved on now to an Era of Meaning, where the search by physicists to *explain* creation can be seen as, in actuality, an integral part of the *mechanics* of creation. As Kemeny said, the qualities studied in physics are a free creation of the human mind. In Wheeler's terms, the universe is a participative universe. "Physics, on this view," Wheeler says, "is the child of meaning even as meaning is the child of physics." Consciousness, the generator of meaning, is an integral component of what it itself is studying.

KNOWINGNESS IN NATURE

Yet another link in the chain is significant. The indwelling intelligence at the subatomic level of nature not only interacts with the intelligence of human observers, it also interacts with itself. In the basic mechanisms of quantum mechanics, physicists have found specific examples of an inexplicable knowingness, or awareness, an instantaneous communication of, and reaction to, specific information. Somehow, certain aspects of subatomic reality act as if they know things they shouldn't — as if they have immediate access to information, even at a great distance.

One of the most famous examples first surfaced in Albert Einstein's famous challenge to quantum mechanics in 1935. Originally discussed by Einstein and two other physicists in a paper published in that year, the challenge is known as the Einstein-Podolsky-Rosen (EPR) paradox. Einstein was the first physicist to see that, if Schrödinger's wave function accurately describes the subatomic reality, two 'particles' can communicate instantly — even over arbitrarily vast distances. In the situation Einstein suggested, two 'particles' are allowed to *entangle*, to interact closely, then to separate at high speed. No matter how far apart they get, the wave function indicates that when one of them is measured and suddenly displays a particular quality, say, spin, the other instantly makes a complementary change, also displaying spin. Moreover, if the first 'particle,' when measured, displays spin up, the second is instantaneously spin down. Even if the two 'particles' have traveled intergalactic distances from each other, the wave function (the mathematical description) shows that this instantaneous correlation still occurs — one 'particle' seems to "know" what has happened to the other — a quantum expression of awareness, or knowingness, that can span, in principle, from one edge of the universe to another. Within months Schrödinger published a paper acknowledging this seeming impossibility, calling it the "entanglement relation," and terming it "not *a* but *the* central quality of quantum mechanics."

Einstein, however, called this phenomenon "spooky action-at-a-distance." He simply did not believe it. From Einstein's perspective, in fact, there was no magic in the paradox. The reason why the first 'particle' measured spin up and the second spin down, in his view, was that they were, respectively, spin up and spin down all along. In this understanding, spin up and spin down did not suddenly pop into existence from a fog of probabilities, but rather both 'particles' had the quality of spin from the beginning — and this spin parameter (also known as a *variable*) was simply hidden, unknown to the physicist running the experiment, until the 'particles' were measured. By extension, Einstein aimed to resurrect key aspects of nineteenth-century classical physics. In the view he suggested, quantum 'particles' are actually real particles, with real positions, motion, spin, etc., and quantum mechanics is forced to talk in terms of probabilities simply because it is ignorant (until a measurement takes place) of what these variables are. This view came to be known as the *hidden variable theory*.

It took fifty years, but eventually Einstein's view was put to the test. An ingenious experiment was designed that could distinguish between Einstein's "real particle," hidden variable theory, on the one hand, and the probability approach of conventional quantum mechanics, on the other. In some of the most famous physical findings of the late twentieth century, conventional quantum mechanics won the competition unambiguously. Einstein was wrong, hidden variables did not exist, 'particles' were not physically real.

There was now no doubt: In an EPR-style measurement of once-entangled 'particles,' neither 'particle' has the, say, spin quality until an experiment measures spin on one of them. Then they both have it — instantaneously, at any distance. Einstein thought this impossible, but the evidence proves it so. One 'particle,' even separated from the other by arbitrarily vast distance, "knows" what happens to the other, and acts upon that knowledge.

Another example of this type of "spooky" quantum knowingness is the famed double slit experiment, perhaps the most often performed and deeply discussed experiment in the history of physics. In this experiment, a beam of light is sent through two tiny slits to land on a flat wall. Because of the wave nature of light, the two rays of light that go through the two slits interfere with each other; they spread out after passing through the slits and, where the high points of the two waves meet together, they build up to a wave even higher (constructive interference), while at those points where the high point of one wave hits the low point of another, they cancel each other out (destructive interference). This results in alternating bands of bright light and complete darkness on the wall behind the slits — a phenomenon known as an *interference pattern*.

The experiment becomes most interesting when the original light source is dialed down in intensity so that the beam of light becomes exceedingly faint. Instruments are employed which emit, in fact, only one photon of light at a time. What happens when only one photon goes through the apparatus? Obviously, a single photon should go through only a single slit, so there should be no question of an interference pattern appearing on the back wall. Surprisingly, however, if both slits are open, a photon going through one of them will land only as predicted by the interference pattern — it will never land in those places where the interference pattern is dark. Furthermore, when a large number of photons is put through the apparatus, one by one, the interference pattern forms again. In other words, each of the photons acts individually as if it were aware that both slits are open. On the other hand, if the second slit is closed, individual photons will land with no regard for the interference pattern; when a large number of such photons go through the apparatus, no interference pattern appears. Few experiments have been so deeply pondered, from so many angles, as this one; it has led some physicists to provocative questions. Says H. P. Stapp, of the Lawrence Berkeley Laboratory,

> The central mystery of quantum theory is, How does information get around so quick? How does the particle know that there are two slits? How does the information about what is happening everywhere else get collected to determine what is likely to happen here?

These two examples of inexplicable knowingness are not peripheral to quantum mechanics. Rather, they emerge from theory and experiment considered to be at the heart of the quantum world. We thus have further reason to conclude that, at the subatomic level, the idea of an indwelling intelligence or awareness, expressed by the subatomic 'particles,' is consistent with the most basic quantum mechanical functioning.

THE INTELLIGENCE OF NATURAL LAW

There is yet one final argument for the confluence of matter and mind. It is, in its first guise, a simple one that derives from common sense, inhering within the mathematical basis of physics itself. The main point: Mathematical formulas constructed, or discovered, within the human mind correspond exactly to specific laws of nature at work in the world. The subtle structures of human intelligence codified in mathematical formulas correspond precisely to the subtle structures of intelligence displayed in nature. The structure of intelligence embodied within the formula $E=mc^2$, for example, a formula originally cognized in human consciousness, fits perfectly with the mechanics of nature.

Furthermore, these mathematical structures need not occur to the mind only when it happens to be studying nature's functioning. In a famous example, complex formulas originally discovered in the mid-nineteenth century as pure mathematics by the German mathematician Carl Friedrich Gauss were later found by Einstein to describe exactly certain aspects of nature's gravitational laws. Mathematical patterns seen within the mind were only later found to describe 'physical' reality. What this suggests is that there is an uncanny fit between mind and matter, or in the words of Nobel Laureate Eugene Wigner, an "unreasonable effectiveness of mathematics in the physical sciences."

In quantum mechanics, moreover, this match of mathematics with nature goes beyond simple parallels. Instead, math and nature appear to become one. We have seen that, in conventional quantum mechanics, the 'particle' has no physical existence before measurement. It consists, instead, of probabilities, of abstract intellectual patterns described in the wave function. This means that the wave function does not describe qualities that exist independently in the 'particle.' As the EPR experiments showed, 'particles' *have* no real, independent existence. This implies that the probabilities described in the wave function are, prior to measurement, the only reality of the 'particle' — which would indicate that knowledge *about* the 'particle' *is* the 'particle.' In this sense, it can be argued that reality and our knowledge about reality cease their independent existence. Werner Heisenberg summed this up in these words:

> The laws of nature which we formulate mathematically in quantum theory deal no longer with the particles themselves but

with our knowledge of the elementary particles. . . . The conception of objective reality . . . evaporated into the . . . mathematics that represents no longer the behavior of elementary particles but rather our knowledge of this behavior.

Objective reality has evaporated into mathematics. Objective, physical structures have evaporated into subjective, mental structures. At the quantum level, this is to say, there is no way to distinguish between the laws of nature themselves and the math (the knowledge) that describes those laws of nature — no way to distinguish between the intelligence in nature and the intelligence within the human mind. This provides the most precise context for Einstein's famous aphorism, "One may say that the eternal mystery of the world is its comprehensibility."

THE SOURCE OF NATURE'S INTELLIGENCE: THE UNIFIED FIELD

In modern physics, then, the world can no longer be thought of as "objectivated." It is impossible for an observer to step back from nature and be uninvolved, for mind to be disentangled from matter. We have seen that:

1. Our experience of the everyday world, our experience of such qualities as red and big and smooth, is a free creation of our consciousness.

2. Measurements of such fundamental physical parameters as velocity and distance depend essentially on the motion of the observer.

3. Nature's basic subatomic 'particles' have no real physical existence prior to measurement, existing instead as probabilities, or patterns of intelligence.

4. The intelligence of the observer interacts with the intelligence of nature; by choosing which quality of the 'particles' to measure, the physicist determines which quality will be transformed from abstract probabilities to physical actuality.

5. The intelligence within nature interacts with itself; subatomic 'particles' have instant access to information at even intergalactic distances, and act on that knowledge.

6. Human intelligence, expressed in mathematical formulas, matches precisely with physical laws of nature; at the quantum level, such mathematically codified intelligence is (prior to measurement) all there is to the 'particle.'

We thus have many indications — both common sensical and quantum mechanical — that intelligence, or awareness, or consciousness, is deeply infused in the natural world. But if that is true, where does this intelligence originate? For an answer to this question, we must turn again to the theory of the superfield — the unified field of all the laws of nature. To this point in the chapter, we have been discussing subatomic 'particles' in themselves, rather than as fluctuations of underlying fields. But it is finally the field theoretic viewpoint which is most all-encompassing and illuminating. The single unified field, especially, which gives rise to all other fields, to all forces and 'particles' in nature, is the most basic conception in physics. If nature displays qualities of intelligence, or consciousness, at more superficial levels, then it is logical to assume that the unified field must itself be characterized by intelligence, or consciousness.

To identify qualities of consciousness in the unified field, moreover, no long chain of reasoning is necessary.

1. Not material. To begin with, we remember that the unified field has no material nature. It resides beyond the Planck scale, and the Planck scale is far smaller than any atom — the basic unit of the apparently material world. Beyond the Planck scale, even time and distance have lost their meaning, and the unified field exists in an abstract, unmanifest realm transcendental to the entire physical universe.

2. Inherent intelligence. The unified field, though not physical or material, has internal order, internal structure or pattern,

that can be defined through mathematical formalisms. The field algebra that describes the unified field is a set of formulas describing the structured orderliness, the intelligence, that inheres *within* the unified field. Patterns or structures such as atoms, snowflakes, or galaxies have internal orderliness that can be described by human intelligence with mathematical formulas. So does the unified field. If the unified field displayed no such internal intelligence — if it were instead random, disorderly, and chaotic, like tinker toys disassembled on the floor — it would not be possible to describe it with the formulas of the field algebra. But the unified field *is* characterized by inherent, mathematically describable intelligence — a level of intelligence sufficient to underlie all the forces and 'particles' that structure the intergalactic universe. John Hagelin makes the point in these terms:

> All the laws of nature are intelligent, orderly principles which govern nature at every level. This doesn't necessarily mean that a law of nature can think, but rather that it expresses intelligence in its functioning. Any law of nature can be written out mathematically. It can be tested repeatedly and found to be orderly, systematic, invariant. And this quality of orderliness and intelligence expressed by every law of nature is found in its most concentrated form in the unified field. By this I mean that at the level of the unified field, the laws of nature are the most compactified, the most concentrated, the most complete. And though they are simpler and more compact in their expression, they describe a greater wealth of diverse phenomena at the more superficial levels of nature.

In this sense, then, the unified field is the most concentrated field of intelligence in nature. It contains in seed form all the orderliness, all the logical and mathematically describable relationships which appear eventually as all the more superficial laws of nature that govern the apparently physical world.

3. Inherent creativity. By similar logic, the unified field displays not just intelligence but infinite creativity. The unified field is more fundamental than all the other force and particle fields that structure creation, and through its own self-interactions it gives rise to those fields as fluctuations of its own nature. From within itself, it gives rise not just to this universe, but to a foam of infinite universes. In Hagelin's words, "The unified field is the fountainhead of natural law. From this unified source all the particles and forces of nature are generated through the process of dynamical symmetry breaking." This spectacular creativity is likewise embodied in the field algebra that describes the unified field and its self-interactions.

Thus, the unified field, which has no material nature, is characterized obviously by inherent intelligence and creativity.

DEEPER QUALITIES OF CONSCIOUSNESS IN THE UNIFIED FIELD

In addition to these aspects of consciousness easily seen by anyone, Maharishi has frequently discussed other qualities of consciousness that might readily occur only to a specialist in the field of consciousness itself. A brief discussion of four of these qualities can indicate how thoroughly the unified field — a conception from the field of physics — embodies aspects of pure, abstract consciousness, as described by a master of the Vedic tradition.

1. Self-interaction, self-referral: In Maharishi's descriptions, the primary quality of consciousness is that it interacts only with itself, that it refers only to itself. If consciousness is the most fundamental aspect of creation, then at that basic level it has nothing to refer to *other* than itself. "Consciousness," Maharishi says, "is that which is conscious of itself."

This self-referral quality results because consciousness has the inherent ability to know. This ability of consciousness to know, to be aware, is irrepressible and for that reason, in words Maharishi has often used, consciousness cannot hold itself back from knowing its own nature. Consciousness becomes aware of consciousness itself. Most significantly, in his understanding, this self-referral mechanics *stirs* consciousness within itself. It generates a dynamism within the silence of pure consciousness — fluctuations or vibrations of consciousness which eventually appear as the 'particles' (the wave-like patterns of intelligence) that make up the apparently physical world.

From the standpoint of the unified field, the picture is strikingly similar. As Hagelin has made clear in a paper titled "Is Consciousness the Unified Field?" the quality of self-interaction or self-referral is embodied in the unified field. The unified field interacts with itself. The internal dynamism of this self-interaction appears as all the more superficial fields, all the forces and particles, which give rise to the ever-expanding universe — an internal, transcendental mechanics described by Hagelin as "the infinite (non-perturbative) self-interaction which is necessary for the force and matter fields displayed at the level of Grand Unified Theories."

An automobile engine acts only within itself — the pistons move up and down within the cylinders — yet the result is that the wheels turn and the auto moves down the road. Similarly, the unified field interacts with itself alone; it is perfectly self-sufficient, containing the total potential of natural law, and the infinite dynamism contained within it is expressed only in a self-interacting, or self-referral, way. Yet it is this internal, self-referral activity which, at grosser time and distance scales, appears as the forces and phenomena of nature and generates the entire evolution of the universe.

2. Pure knowledge: Maharishi indicates that the self-referral nature of consciousness amounts to *pure knowledge* — knowledge of consciousness itself, by itself, within itself. In that self-referral state, consciousness has knowledge only of its own nature. This is knowledge that is pure and unmanifest, not yet encompassing the details involved in the manifest universe. Similarly, the unified field contains all the laws of nature — but in a form yet unmanifest. The laws of nature — the information or knowledge that gives rise to more superficial levels of nature's functioning — are completely available in this field, but they are still "pure," unsullied by contact with the ever-changing fluctuations of the quantum fields at more superficial levels. This is information in isolation, knowledge alone — pure knowledge.

3. **Infinite organizing power:** Maharishi often refers to a dictum from information theory (a branch of mathematics that has been applied to quantum mechanics, among many other fields): Knowledge has organizing power. To build a home accurately and efficiently, the contractor needs plans from the architect. In any situation, it is accurate information, useful knowledge, that underlies the organizing power that leads to creation. In Maharishi's explanations, the basic field of pure consciousness, by knowing itself, is the home of *pure* knowledge, abstract but complete knowledge — the knower knowing itself completely. He indicates that such complete knowledge — pure, unsullied, self-referral knowledge — is a field of infinite organizing power, responsible for the entire creation. In the same way, all the laws of nature which inhere within the unmanifest unified field — the compactified knowledge at the basis of nature — give rise to all aspects of the manifest universe, to all the beautifully broken symmetries which make up creation. Being the field of pure knowledge for the entire creation, the unified field exhibits an infinite organizing power which can be seen displayed in atoms, mountains, and galaxies.

4. **Infinite correlation:** In his descriptions of the unified field of pure consciousness at the basis of creation, Maharishi commonly refers to its quality of infinite correlation. As he says, "Tickle it here and it laughs over there." In Maharishi's understanding, this quality of infinite correlation helps explain how Super Radiance groups appear to radiate a statistically measurable influence of harmony and peace into the environment. Increased coherence experienced by the Super Radiance group in one spot is also experienced by others at a distance. Similarly, in quantum mechanics, we have seen that 'particles,' once

entangled, can travel to even astronomical distances in opposite directions and still display an instantaneous (or infinite) correlation. This basic aspect of quantum mechanics is accounted for in the field algebra describing the unified field which, being beyond all space and time, infinitely correlates not just particular 'particles,' but all aspects of its own nature.

In sum, the intelligence displayed at every level of nature must have an origin. The logical choice for this origin is the unified field of all the laws of nature, which is the transcendental source of the entire manifest universe. On even cursory reflection, the unified field is found to display such obvious qualities of consciousness as intelligence and creativity, and even such subtle aspects of consciousness as self-referral, pure knowledge, infinite organizing power, and infinite correlation. We have seen Heinz Pagels' view that "everything comes out of nothing," and there is, of course, nothing physical in the unified field. But a definition of the unified field which better fits the evidence seems the one we have from Shankara: "Its nature is pure consciousness."

FROM MODERN SCIENCE TO VEDIC SCIENCE

In this chapter we have seen that mind, or intelligence, or consciousness is deeply ingrained in the apparently physical world. It is the mathematical and theoretical details of this fusion of matter and mind which are compelling to physicists. After a detailed review of the discoveries from quantum mechanics, for instance, E.C.G. Sudarshan said that if physics were to continue in the direction it now takes, "physical theory would become a theory of consciousness. We are approaching this situation as a limit: consciousness creates everything out of nothing."

The English physicist Sir James Jeans foresaw such a consciousness-based understanding of creation even in the first years of the quantum revolution:

> The stream of knowledge is heading toward a non-mechanical reality. . . . [T]he old dualism of mind and matter . . . seems

likely to disappear, not through matter becoming in any way more shadowy or insubstantial than heretofore, or through mind becoming resolved into a function of the working of matter, but through substantial matter resolving itself into a creation and manifestation of mind.

This means that modern physics is converging on an ancient understanding. Moving in this direction, moreover, we come to the outer boundary of objective science. Even if they are viewed as separate, neither the unified field nor consciousness can be plumbed by objective methods. In the realm of the unified field — beyond the Planck scale of nature — space, time, and causality come to an end. Nothing can be measured because measurement no longer makes any sense. Dimension and position lose their meaning and before and after become indistinguishable. In the realm of consciousness, similarly, direct objective measurement is inconceivable, since conscious experience is by definition subjective, the essence of the subject. No investigative method based on objects can gain access to this nonmaterial essence of mind, or pass judgments on the realities which inhere in its makeup.

In the Vedic view, of course — a view consistent with the opinions of many of this century's leading physicists — these two points are one. Objective means cannot penetrate the unified field because the unified field is itself subjective — a pure field of consciousness, of abstract, concentrated awareness or intelligence. At the Planck scale, in this view, as even the appearance of matter and objective investigation dissolves, what remains is mind.

This understanding, now glimpsed by modern science but long understood in Vedic Science, is logically and esthetically satisfying, in the same way that the unification of the four forces of nature is logically and esthetically satisfying. It simply seems more sensible and more elegant if all the naturally appearing phenomena in nature — and consciousness is certainly such a phenomenon — can be accounted for in one simple and holistic understanding. It would violate the long procession of science toward a single, completely unified understanding of natural phenomena if the intelligence displayed by the human mind and the intelligence displayed in nature were found to be separate and noncongruent — like two incompatible computer systems. It is much more logical and parsimonious to conclude — as so many factors in this chapter indicate — that human intelligence and nature's intelligence are two aspects of a single underlying unity, finding their common source in the unified field.

MECHANICS OF SUPER RADIANCE

This conclusion, furthermore, can help explain the mechanics of permanent peace — by helping to explain how the human mind can gain access to the most fundamental field in creation. As we have seen, the direct creation of peace through large assemblies of meditation experts makes no sense based on the outmoded understandings of nineteenth-century, classical physics. Especially in the notions of "billiard-ball physics," the extreme of physical, materialist science wherein objects have to bounce off each other to interact, there is no way to explain how people can sit in one room, meditating with eyes closed, and affect criminals and soldiers even thousands of miles away.

But human communication exists on a wide continuum. It begins with direct physical contact, continues through speech and semaphore-like signaling, moves on to telephones, faxes, cable TV, and other wire-based technologies, and culminates (so it seems to most people) in broadcast radio and TV, satellite video and cell phones, all of which use radiating impulses that propagate through the underlying electromagnetic field. It is this last jump to field-based communication, as Marconi found out, which challenges common sense most urgently. But it is also field-based communication that offers the ultimate in convenience and communicative power. A single person can now sit in a single spot and — through an interview on CNN, for example — radiate his ideas to every corner of the world.

Against this background, Super Radiance represents simply another step toward abstraction and power. It is defined as a field-based approach, but it does away with hardware technologies such as broadcasting stations and receivers, and substitutes the human nervous system in a dual role, as both sender and receiver. Because it is avowedly a field-based technology, Super Radiance is not limited to billiard-ball mechanics, but can take recourse to either of the two long-distance mechanisms that inhere in any quantum field:

1. Field effects: Long-range propagation of influences through wave-like perturbations of the underlying field (radio, etc.); and

2. Infinite correlation: Long-range correlations that are instantaneous and unmitigated by even astronomical distance (the EPR phenomenon).

If Super Radiance is inconsistent with outmoded nineteenth-century classical physics, in other words, it is completely consistent with modern quantum physics. Quantum fields support long-range influences and correlations as inherent aspects of their nature. If the surface-level appearance of the world, the world as it appears when we open our eyes each morning, encourages us to think in the old-style, classical way, quantum discoveries have freed us from such "common sense" boundaries. Despite contrary evidence from our senses, the Earth revolves around the Sun. Despite superficial, common sense notions, at the quantum level, invisible, long-range propagations and correlations are the norm.

GETTING CONNECTED

But for this view to be persuasive, there must be a mechanics whereby the individual human mind can gain access to the underlying level of quantum fields — and especially to the fundamental unified field. We have seen that the unified field is transcendental and unmanifest, immune to objective contact. But this still allows for the possibility that it can be contacted subjectively. This is exactly the understanding Maharishi puts forward in his Vedic Science. The means is a subjective technology, the technology of consciousness known as the Transcendental Meditation and TM-Sidhi programs. This meditation technology, Maharishi explains, allows the individual human mind to settle down deep within its own nature. By arriving at its *own* most basic level of intelligence, it also arrives at the most basic level of intelligence in *nature* — the unified field of natural law.

Thus, Maharishi has sometimes called his Transcendental Meditation program the Technology of the Unified Field, and in his many talks on the topic he makes the Vedic position clear:

> Modern science has been wise to use the objective approach so far. Through the systematic investigations of the objective approach, the physicists have discovered all the different relative levels of nature, all the specific natural laws. But now a different field has been discovered, the unified field of all the laws of nature. It has certainly been located through objective means, and the physicists have been able to gain some glimpse of its transcendental reality. But no measuring tools which measure centimeters or seconds will ever be adequate to examine the unified field. To gain the full experience of this field, now it is time to start to experience it on its own level, on the level of consciousness. Now it is time to bring the subjective approach, to create a laboratory in the field of consciousness through the Transcendental Meditation and TM-Sidhi program. This beautiful technology allows the individual to directly experience the unified field as the finest, most silent level of his own awareness.

In Maharishi's view, this ability to contact the unified field, to experience the unity of consciousness and creation at their common source, is of far more than theoretical interest. Yes, it would be interesting simply to *know* that modern science and Vedic Science have converged on one theoretical understanding of existence. But this convergence is not just an intellectual curiosity. What makes it practical is that the human mind can gain direct access to nature's essence, to the infinite energy and intelligence that give rise to creation. In Maharishi's words,

> The unified field is that Planck scale level of nature's functioning, from where time is generated, from where space is generated, from where energy is generated, from where all the laws of nature begin to take their specific shapes. When the human mind settles down and becomes identified with that level of infinite orderliness, then it becomes consciously stationed at the basis of the universe. This is how we can gain the support of all the laws of nature for our every thought and action. And this is how we can radiate an influence of peace and coherence throughout our environment. By enlivening that basic field of infinite orderliness and harmony in one place, we enliven it everywhere.

DIRECT EXPERIENCE IN A
FOURTH STATE OF CONSCIOUSNESS

In Maharishi's understanding, then, it is meditation that makes the unified field a practical discovery. Physics may tell us that the unified field is a field of infinite intelligence and creativity. But a reservoir is useful only if a pipeline brings the water to your house. The unified field is useful only if a pipeline can be established for its direct experience.

To understand how the connection between human intelligence and nature's intelligence is possible, it is necessary to study the field of consciousness itself — especially the concept of *states of consciousness*. While it is true that science has found no objective means to measure the inner *content* of consciousness (what thoughts or feelings a person might have, for instance), yet for years neurophysiologists have been able to precisely define overall *states* of consciousness. Every normal person experiences three major states of consciousness every day — sleeping, dreaming and waking. By using indirect measurements — by measuring brain waves, metabolic rate, and other physiological indicators — researchers have defined these three common states of consciousness. They can't tell what you are thinking in the waking state, or imagining in the dream state. But they can tell which state you are in. They know how the neurophysiology operates during each of the three states.

This neurophysiological evidence now becomes crucial. According to the Vedic tradition, the human mind comes into union with the unified field during a highly specific *fourth* state of consciousness. That means that deep in meditation, when the mind contacts its own basis — and the basis of nature — the body should function in a new and unique way. Brain wave patterns and metabolic activity should be measurably different from the styles of functioning they display during sleeping, dreaming, and waking. For this reason, the Vedic description of a fourth state of consciousness, often repeated by Maharishi, can be taken as yet another prediction open to scientific investigation.

To this point in the book, the promise of permanent peace has been confirmed by objective science in three significant ways. First, repeated and rigorous research has documented the existence of Super Radiance and the Maharishi Effect. Second, the latest advances in theoretical physics have identified one unified field at the basis of creation. Third, detailed reflection on the quantum realm by many leading physicists has revealed, at the deepest level of nature's functioning, not solid matter but abstract intelligence, or consciousness.

Thus, the best science is consistent with the Vedic description of a transcendental, fully unified field of consciousness at the basis of both human life and the natural world — a field that could theoretically be used to transform the world.

Now it is time to find whether there is a pipeline to this field of infinite potential.

Is the fourth state of consciousness an objective reality?

5

THE FOURTH
STATE OF
CONSCIOUSNESS:
Pipeline to the Infinite

For centuries into the past, the fourth state of consciousness has seemed as elusive as the unicorn — as much a
myth, as much a merely storied essence of purity and
innocence. Poems have extolled the beauties of this ineffable
state, tales have identified this subtle reality as the key that
unlocks the full potential of life, paintings and statues have
shown wise men with crossed legs and closed eyes enjoying its
fullness in blissful contentment.

Yet what is this fourth state really? In the modern scientific
civilizations, this most basic state of consciousness has been so
elusive as to essentially disappear altogether. In an objective
world the fourth state of consciousness has had no objective status, and thus it has simply dropped out of sight. Until recently
it was rarely spoken of, or even thought of, and life has been lived
as well as it could be through the recurring cycle of the three
common states — waking, sleeping, and dreaming. What the

Vedic tradition defines as the most crucial capability of human consciousness — the faculty of contacting the field of infinite potential at the basis of creation — has been unknown to most and closed to nearly all.

This disappearance of the fourth state of consciousness, however, has set the stage for one of the most intriguing detective stories of modern science. Scientific investigation has been a profound tool for gaining knowledge, a systematic means for inducing nature to yield her deepest mysteries. Its methods and machinery have proved equal to even this most delicate task. Following clues provided by Vedic teachings, biomedical researchers picked up the trail of pure consciousness early in the 1970s. Some of the early tracking was ambiguous, but with the appearance of more sophisticated equipment and more refined experimental design, the descriptions became precise and the identification clear. The elusive, quasimythical pipeline to the infinite had been captured objectively at last.

PERSONAL EXPERIENCE

Because of the importance ascribed to this fourth state of consciousness in Maharishi's Vedic Science — because it is said to be the state that connects the individual mind with a field of unbounded possibility — the idea deserves systematic attention. The plan of this chapter will be first, to listen to descriptions of the fourth state from sources both ancient and modern, and second, to survey the scientific research that quantitatively defines this state.

As with the other ancient descriptions discussed in this book, the Vedic description of the fourth state of consciousness has been recorded in simple, straightforward language. It is known in Sanskrit as *samadhi* (unwavering mind), or simply as *turiya* (the fourth). We can turn to the Upanishads for a definition that places it in the context of the common three states of consciousness, those experienced by every ordinary person every day:

The first is the waking state, the experience of the reality
   open to everyone;
The attention goes outward, enjoying the world in all its
   variety.
The second is dreaming, the experience of subjective, inner,
   imaginative worlds. . . .
The third is deep sleep, when the mind rests and all awareness
   [both inner and outer] is suspended.
The fourth is the pure Self alone. . . .
It is ineffable, beyond thought.
It is indefinable.
It is known only through becoming it.
It is the end of all activity, silent and unchanging.

These definitions suggests a central principle long emphasized by Maharishi: Knowledge is different in different states of consciousness. In the sleeping state of consciousness, for example, the mind is aware of no knowledge at all. The sleep state is a state of total dullness in which "all awareness is suspended," and knowledge of anything whatever, real or imagined, has disappeared altogether. In the dreaming state, on the other hand, there is knowledge available, but it is unreliable. Dreams are self-created, "subjective, inner, imaginative worlds," without direct connection to the real world. The world of dreams evaporates with the morning light.

Only with the waking state do we find knowledge as commonly understood. It is true that the waking state of consciousness is limited in its scope. It yields direct perception of only the outer, surface level of nature — "the attention goes outward, enjoying the world in all its variety" — and the inner, more subtle workings of nature, everything from the molecular level to the unified field, is unavailable, sealed away from the mind's direct perception as if the mind were still asleep. But the mind in the waking state is at least directly aware of nature's surface, and it gains knowledge that is usually both coherent and useful. If, in a dream, the ground may suddenly dissolve into water or dissipate into air, in the waking state the earth is always solid beneath our feet. Knowledge in the waking state may be incomplete, but at least it's practical for day-to-day existence.

Analyzing states of consciousness thus, in terms of the type of knowledge they yield, what could a fourth state of consciousness be? It must be different from lack of awareness (sleep), or awareness of imaginary visions (dream), or awareness of the surface level of nature (waking). Thought about this way, the fourth state of consciousness can first be understood as a self-referral state, a state of self-interaction — as human awareness circling back to become aware of itself — as awareness of awareness alone. In the Vedic understanding of the fourth state, consciousness is said to turn back upon itself and become aware only of its own inner nature — "the pure Self alone."

This is *samadhi* (unwavering mind), an experience Maharishi calls *pure consciousness* or *transcendental consciousness* or the state of *pure knowledge*. Tracing the path the mind takes to this most inward experience, Maharishi says,

> Once we give the mind the correct angle it will settle down automatically to more refined, inner levels. As the mind experiences finer aspects of the thinking process, it experiences more refined levels of awareness. This makes the mind more and more awake. And when our awareness has gained maximum wakefulness, the next step of refinement allows the mind to transcend the field of thinking. We attain a field of pure awareness, of transcendental consciousness, in which the mind is awake within itself, but without a thought. This is the state of pure consciousness, a state of least excitation of consciousness, and in this self-referral state, consciousness is its own observer. It is the observer, the observed, and the process of observation — all three values in one — a quality of awareness we can call pure knowledge.

In this state, rather than no awareness at all, as in the sleep state, there is what Maharishi terms "maximum wakefulness." Yet there are no thoughts in that awareness, neither the imaginary creations of dreaming nor the more common thoughts of the waking state. In a definition of this fourth state published in his translation and commentary on the Bhagavad-Gita in 1967, Maharishi says "there is no trace of sensory activity, no trace of mental activity," and that the awareness in this state of *samadhi* is like "a lamp which does not flicker in a windless place."

If we are watching a movie, the colorful images on the screen might begin to fade away, becoming lighter and lighter, until our vision transcends the particular images altogether and confronts only the pure white screen. The pure screen would be there without the activity of the movie. In a similar way, the mind can settle down deep within its own nature, experiencing finer and finer aspects of the thinking process, until finally it transcends particular thoughts altogether and is left only with pure con-sciousness — the background, or screen, upon which all thoughts and feelings play.

The major limitation to this analogy is that, in a movie, there is duality — the audience is left to watch the white screen — while in the fourth state of consciousness, there is indivisible unity — consciousness is left aware of its *own* pure nature. It is, in Maharishi's phrase, a "self-referral mechanics." In the fourth state of consciousness, the observer and the observed are com-pletely unified.

This self-referral nature of pure consciousness seems to Maharishi an important tie to the quantum mechanical level of creation, and especially to the unified field. As we have seen, the unified field is a completely self-sufficient, self-interacting real-ity. It is the self-interacting mechanics deep within the unman-ifest unified field that give rise to all the laws of nature on the more superficial levels of creation.

For Maharishi, this self-referral nature of the unified field completes the logical connection between consciousness and cre-ation. "The unified field is found by modem physics to be self-referral in its nature," he says, "and this identifies it as a field of consciousness. For only consciousness in its pure state can be fully self-referral."

This self-referral state of consciousness, moreover, is in itself a unified field of consciousness. As Maharishi pointed out above, in the fourth state of consciousness, consciousness itself is the observer and it is also the observed. In fact, as he has often explained, consciousness is the observer, the observed, and also the *process of observation* — all three in one unified wholeness. In the fourth state, therefore, consciousness is in a completely unified state. In this sense, both the fourth state of consciousness and the unified field of natural law are completely unified and self-referral — interacting only within themselves.

Speaking in 1983 at the Taste of Utopia assembly, Maharishi developed the relationship between the fourth state, pure consciousness, and the unified field of physics:

> We know from the ancient Vedic literature that the world must rise to enjoy the full dignity of life. And if that is to be, it can only be on the basis of the fourth state of consciousness, the experience of consciousness in its self-referral state, which is now coming up in scientific language as the unified field of all the laws of nature. The unified field is a lively field of all possibilities at the basis of creation. It is a transcendental reality. And because the unified field is completely self-referral, then knowledge of it can only be completely self-referral. It can only be gained by the mind within itself in its self-referral state, in pure consciousness, transcendental consciousness, where the awareness is open to itself alone. In this state, the mind identifies itself with the self-referral reality of the unified field. That level of consciousness alone is a suitable field for directly cognizing the unified field, for completely identifying with the self-referral nature of the unified field, in a state in which consciousness actually has no difference from the unified field.

In this quotation, the most significant point is the last. In the fourth state of consciousness, "consciousness actually has no difference from the unified field." The mind does not *think* about the unified field. By settling down to its own perfectly united state, the mind *becomes* the unified field, the home of all the laws of nature.

As already indicated, there is no direct objective way to investigate this analysis. Both the unified field and the inner content of consciousness are beyond the reach of objective experiment. For someone who has not had the personal experience of such a state of consciousness, intellectual understanding alone cannot provide complete satisfaction. A strawberry can only be fully known by tasting it; pure consciousness can only be known through a direct dive into that infinite ocean, by immediate personal experience. As Maharishi says,

> The glory of pure consciousness can be experienced directly and recognized as the ultimate reality. The mind can be led systematically to the subtlest limit of relative experience and then, transcending this subtlest experience of the excited states of creation, it can reach the field of the ultimate, absolute, unmanifest state of least excitation — the unified field of all the laws of nature. Matter can be glamorous, but this experience is glorious. Its nature is happiness, wisdom, creativity, and strength. It is self-sufficient, self-referral, invincible in its own right.

THE STATE OF LEAST EXCITATION

If this inner experience of the fourth state of consciousness cannot be directly measured, however, the outer, physical parameters certainly can. A fourth state of consciousness, to be understood as more than myth, must make its appearance in the scientific laboratory.

Although the fourth state of consciousness is not a state most people ordinarily experience, it is said to be a completely natural state, and it is not uncommon for people to recognize in its description memories of one or two special moments in their lives. It is also not difficult to find, in the writings of artists and poets, descriptions of specific experiences which make new sense in this context. Wordsworth, for instance, has described such an experience:

> that serene and blessed mood,
> in which the affections gently lead us on —
> and even the motion of our human blood
> almost suspended, we are laid asleep
> in body, and become a living soul;
> while with an eye made quiet by the power
> of harmony, and the deep power of joy,
> we see into the life of things.

As we will see, this quotation provides some specific clues for scientific research. One of Wordsworth's successors Alfred, Lord Tennyson describes a related experience in one of his letters:

> out of the intensity of the consciousness of individuality, the individuality itself seemed to dissolve and fade away into boundless being; and this not a confused state, but the clearest of the clearest, the surest of the surest . . . . utterly beyond words.

The German philosopher Georg W.F. Hegel, for whom meditation experience was the touchstone of philosophy, described a similar state of deep inner quiet in which a self-referral experience reveals the deepest being of life. He said,

> The condition of ecstasy through which alone that which is true Being comes to be known, is [referred to as] a simplification of the soul, through which it is brought into a state of blissful repose, because its object is itself, simple and at rest.

These and countless other such passages from all cultures and throughout the ages have been largely ignored in recent times. They have been termed mystical, a word which has come to mean vague, imaginary, impractical, and unreal. And given the varied, unsystematic, and imprecisely poetic way in which these descriptions have usually been stated, such confusion is not hard to understand. To reclaim the fourth state of consciousness from this obscurity, it needs to be defined scientifically.

PHYSICAL CLUES TO
STATES OF CONSCIOUSNESS

Fortunately researchers have made rapid progress in this field since the early 1970s. Biomedical experts have constantly improved in their ability to measure the operations of the body and nervous system that underlie the various states of the human mind. The key experimental fact is this: For every major state of consciousness, the human physiology operates in a measurably different way. Two of the most important tests involve the metabolic rate (the amount of oxygen consumed by the body) and the brain wave patterns (the electrical activity of the brain). For more than forty years, researchers have had enough knowledge to measure these two physiological indicators and, in ordinary cases, tell whether a person is awake, asleep, or dreaming. Even if a subject feigns sleep, for instance, his metabolic rate and brain wave activity will give him away.

These scientific definitions of the common states of consciousness provide a background for the elusive state of pure consciousness. If such a fourth state exists, it should stand out clearly against the other three, eliciting, at the least, completely different metabolic rate and brain wave activity. Moreover, these physiological dimensions should not only be different, but they should differ in directions that suggest the fourth state of consciousness as it has been so far defined. In the descriptions that we have seen, for instance, the fourth state of consciousness is said to be "a state of least excitation," "the end of all activity," a state in which "even the motion of our human blood almost suspended, we are laid asleep in body." Speaking of this in terms of metabolic rate, we might therefore expect to find the fourth state of consciousness characterized by a marked decline in metabolic activity — that is, by a deep state of physical rest.

On the other hand, as indicated by the "alertness" in "restful alertness," the fourth state of consciousness is said to be a state of "maximum wakefulness," "clearest of the clearest," in which "we see into the life of things," in which the mind attains a state of such refined awareness that it can "see into" the subtlest level of nature and "identify itself with the unified field." If all this is true — if the mind really does become more wakeful and more capable of subtle experience, even though the body is settling down to a deep state of rest — then brain wave measurements (and other relevant physiological tests) should reflect this different style of functioning.

FINDING THE SUBJECTS

To take measurements of such a state, the state itself must first be available. This has been a major contribution of the TM and TM-Sidhi programs. When Maharishi first started his teaching in the late 1950s, even the concept of a fourth state of consciousness was absent from scientific circles. Science deals with empirical data, and the fourth state of consciousness was at that time not empirically verifiable — because essentially no one was experiencing it. Since that time, however, nearly six million people have taken up the practice of the basic Transcendental Meditation technique, over a million of those in the United States, and tens of thousands have learned the advanced TM-Sidhi program. Twenty years ago experimenters seeking the fourth state of consciousness might have been forced to backpack equipment up a Himalayan peak, but now they can easily find a population of expert meditators in any American city.

The nature of the actual technology also lends itself to research. In the first place, both the Transcendental Meditation technique and the TM-Sidhi program are taught through highly systematic procedures which are followed precisely everywhere in the world that the techniques are taught. This means that experimenters can avail themselves of a subject population meditating according to uniform instructions, even to the finest details. Also, because these techniques are natural procedures for the human mind and physiology, and therefore extremely easy to practice — requiring no effort or concentration — a broad cross-section of the population can be included in the studies. There are no requirements, no necessary level of intelligence or educational attainment. Even children from the age of ten can easily learn the practice. A random sample of meditators in any city includes people of every age and from every socio-economic class, and thus scientific studies need not become biased due to a narrow range of subject types.

THE FIRST STUDIES

When the experimenting began, the search for a physiological fingerprint of the fourth state seemed at first quite straightforward. Even the first study published on the Transcendental Meditation technique, research done by physiologist R. Keith Wallace at UCLA and published first in *Science* magazine in 1970, and then in variant forms in 1970 and 1972 in the *American Journal of Physiology* and in *Scientific American*, showed an extremely deep state of rest for the body and alterations in the usual brain wave activity. Wallace used these and other indications to define what he tentatively labeled "a fourth major state of consciousness," or a "wakeful hypometabolic state."

But the search was not going to be that simple. When other researchers tried to duplicate and enlarge upon these findings, different studies produced contrasting results. It took most of a decade for the reason to become clear. A researcher is only as good as his measuring equipment; much of the equipment being used was not equal to this delicate task.

The first questions concerned metabolic activity. Wallace showed that when people practiced the TM technique, theoretically experiencing the fourth state of consciousness, their metabolic rate (as measured by their oxygen consumption) decreased an average of sixteen percent. This was a significant figure. During a night's sleep, the metabolic rate of an average person will decline only eight percent. Moreover, during sleep the body takes nearly six hours to slow down to its lowest rate of oxygen consumption, while Wallace's tests indicated that during the TM technique it takes only a few minutes to settle down to a level of rest twice as deep. These figures strongly suggested a fourth state of consciousness, since such deep rest is not ordinarily experienced in waking, sleeping, or dreaming.* Refining this early study, however, to generate precise and consistent measurements of the fourth state of consciousness required technological advances.

UPGRADING THE EQUIPMENT

The most prevalent means to measure oxygen intake in the early 1970s, for instance, was to strap the subject into something very like a gas mask, and these masks proved too cumbersome to consistently measure a refined level of metabolic activity. They were, first, simply too heavy and uncomfortable. Their weight tended to pull the head over and down, causing constant interruption of the meditation. In addition, there was an enclosed space before the subject's nose and mouth shaped like a muzzle. For people practicing the TM technique, breathing would decrease to the point where they were not forcing air out of the muzzle. No new air would come in, and this would lead to a temporary increase in the rate of breathing to restore air flow in the mask. This kept people from fainting, but it also destroyed the accuracy of the test.

One of the people who solved this problem was John Farrow, a Ph.D. in neurobiology from Cornell University who held a research position with the University of California for nearly a decade — first with the Irvine campus in the Los Angeles area and then in San Diego. Farrow undertook a detailed study of possible changes during the fourth state of consciousness, a study published in 1982 in the journal *Psychosomatic Medicine*. To be certain of gaining an accurate picture of oxygen consumption during the fourth state, Farrow used three different measuring technologies, all of them quite new. As he explains,

---

Science, 167, 1751–54; *American Journal of Physiology*, 221, 795–99.

The most satisfactory system was then the newest and the most sophisticated. We attached a pair of magnetic coils to the subject's sternum and backbone, to measure chest movement, and another pair to the abdomen and lower back to measure movement of the abdomen. Although this doesn't directly measure air flow or oxygen consumption, studies at Harvard had shown what seems obvious from common sense — the movements of the chest and abdomen are accurately related to the volume of air moving in and out. One of the major advantages of this procedure, since it involved nothing attached at the nose or mouth, was that most of the subjects had no idea we were even looking for oxygen consumption or breath rate with this particular test.

DEEPER LEVELS OF REST

Using this more precise and non-invasive technology, Farrow was able to show that Wallace's original findings were, if anything, conservative. Wallace had reported a sixteen percent average decrease in oxygen consumption during the TM technique. Farrow found, with practiced meditators, much greater decreases than that, averaging in some subjects as much as forty percent over the whole twenty-minute meditation period and reaching the sixty percent level in the last few minutes. Moreover, in some subjects the physical rest attained such a profound level that occasionally the breath rate would be suspended altogether. For periods ranging from twenty seconds to one minute, these people would simply not breathe at all. Farrow comments,

> We were most interested in this breath stoppage phenomenon because we had seen it unexpectedly in earlier research on the TM technique, and we knew that the classic definition of *samadhi* included such a total suspension of normal physiological activity. What we found in this study was that these breath stoppages definitely did exist in many subjects, usually repeatedly in any one meditation. And remarkably, at the end of each breath stoppage, there was no compensatory overbreathing. The breath

would simply stop at the end of an expiration, and then after a period resume again at the same level. This was a strong indication that the breath stoppage was a natural phenomenon and did not involve any oxygen deprivation for the physiology.

Farrow's study was also designed to investigate another aspect of these suspensions in breath rate. Each subject was furnished with a small button placed immediately under one thumb. This button was electrically attached to the same equipment that was measuring the breath rate. When the subject pressed the button, a record was made that could later be correlated with the breath stoppages, and the subjects were told to press this button immediately after any experience they had of complete mental quietness (transcendental consciousness, or pure consciousness). In virtually every case, this button was pressed just after a period of breath suspension. The deep state of mental quietness correlated with the deep state of physical rest. "Laid asleep in body . . . we see into the life of things" — deepest rest and purest awareness seemed to go together.

This was also important because it showed that the fourth state of consciousness, like waking, sleeping, and dreaming, can be experienced in different levels, or stages. When a person is in the waking state, for instance, he can be very sleepy, or fairly alert, or completely wide awake. In the same way, Farrow's study indicated that people who practice the TM technique experience many different levels of awareness, a range of alertness that can become progressively more refined and wakeful and which culminates in a pure state of perfect inner clarity.*

FINE-GRAIN STUDIES ON DEEP REST

Since Farrow's studies were completed, much more work has been done to analyze the precise nature of the resting process during the fourth state of consciousness. Much of this investigation was done by a research team at the University of Cali-

---

*Psychosomatic Medicine, 44(2), 133–53.

fornia (Irvine), under the direction of physiologist Archie Wilson. This one laboratory has published more than forty journal articles, papers, and abstracts on the physiological indications of the fourth state of consciousness during the Transcendental Meditation technique. The result has been to pinpoint many details of the changes that occur during the fourth state. In the words of one of the researchers,

> Our main goal has been to do in-depth studies of tissue metabolism, blood flow, individual cell activity, and other specific aspects of physiological functioning. Our findings are not based on the more superficial level of global reduction of oxygen consumption in the whole body, but rather on the precise responses in individual systems within the body. Global changes have origins which are not precisely defined, but in-depth studies are more discriminating, and because the results are consistent from many different levels of the physiology, the results are much more confirmatory.

Decreased cortisol. One of the first results found by this University of California laboratory was that, during the practice of the TM technique, the levels of cortisol in the blood dropped sharply. Cortisol is known as a "stress hormone," a chemical secreted by the body in response to tense or stressful situations. It tends to excite the system and make it ready for intense activity. A decrease in cortisol is thus a chemical measurement of decreased tension and stress and increased relaxation and rest. Further research showed that, in fact, in many subjects cortisol was essentially not produced at all for the twenty minutes of meditation, a unique finding not ordinarily seen in other forms of relaxation or even in sleep.*

Rest in red blood cells. A companion study isolated red blood cells from the blood stream. Samples were taken not only before and after meditation, but also during the theoretical

*Journal of Biomedicine, 1, 73–88.

experience of the fourth state as well (with a sampling tube set up and taped to the subject's forearm before the meditation began). The results showed a marked decrease in metabolic activity in the red blood cells during the meditation period, a decrease which did not appear in people during other types of relaxation or during sleep.* Dr. Alaric Arenander, a research neurophysiologist then on the faculty at UCLA, has commented on the importance of this study:

> Since red blood cells are not present in the muscle tissue and connected to nerves, but rather float freely in the circulatory system, the decrease in their metabolism cannot be caused simply by less activity in the nervous system. Ordinarily their metabolism does not decrease significantly even in deep sleep. It thus seems likely that the decrease during meditation is chemically induced through hormones released into the blood. The reason such a hormone has not been previously discovered is that most research on hormones has been done by stressing the subject, by scaring him with loud noises, for instance, or causing slight physiological damage, and then seeing what hormones are produced in response. The research has been biased toward excited states of physiological functioning. But now the TM technique has given us a systematic means of de-exciting the system, and we are finding that there is a unique style of physiological functioning produced as a result.

A COHERENT BRAIN

Metabolic studies have yielded significant information, but common sense indicates that another type of study may be even more important. The most direct physical correlate of the mind is the brain. To identify the fourth state of consciousness, a clear picture of the brain's functioning is vital.

In this area as well, the search for the fourth state of consciousness turned into a detective story, with elusive clues, ingen-

---

*Journal of Hormones and Behavior, 10(1), 54–60.

ious deductions, and the utilization of new research method-ologies. Only after fifteen years of work did the identification become solid and well-documented in the scientific journals.

The challenge for the researchers was once again posed by the machinery being used. The basic tool for brain wave research is the electroencephalograph (EEG). Using this equipment, researchers attach electrodes to several points on the surface of a person's head. The wires lead into a machine that translates the incoming electrical information into back-and-forth motions by automatic pens. Paper is unrolled past these pens, and the electrical activity recorded at each point on the subject's scalp is transformed into a continuous wavy line. By examining these lines, a researcher can track the brain's activity.

On the one hand, this EEG technology has made a vital contribution to brain research. The irregular lines of a person asleep, for instance, appear to be quite different from those of a person awake. On the other hand, as a true picture of what is occurring inside the brain, this paper record has serious defects; it is, as one researcher has put it, like trying to find out what is happening inside Grand Central Station by putting one ear to an outside wall.

Many of the problems center on the pen-and-paper apparatus. Though the recording pens are light and mounted on the end of slim and flexible arms, still they cannot accurately record all the rapid and delicate fluctuations in the brain's electrical activity. The researcher is reduced to the amateur eyeball method, making estimates based on the surface appearance of the lines.

These inherent limitations of the basic EEG device slowed down the search for the fourth state of consciousness. Wallace's original study had found some unusual shifts in the electrical patterning, but two later studies reported that people practicing the TM technique often seemed simply drowsy and sometimes fell asleep. The fourth state of consciousness — the subject of rapturous poetry and subtle philosophy for thousands of years — was in danger of being labeled nothing more than a nap.

DECODING THE ELECTROENCEPHALOGRAPHY

The first breakthrough in this impasse was produced by a French physiologist, Dr. Jean-Paul Banquet, who performed his research both at Harvard Medical School and at the French National Institute for Medical Research, and published a half dozen studies in the most respected journals of electroencephalography. Starting his studies, Banquet (pronounced bahn-KAY) did not question that people sometimes fell asleep when meditating. Most people who practice TM report falling asleep occasionally. To Banquet that seemed a logical result of the deep rest and relaxation produced by the TM technique — if people were excessively tired when they started a meditation. But Banquet was puzzled by the finding that people not asleep spent most of their meditation period drowsy. In general, as many previous studies had shown, people don't stay drowsy for fifteen or twenty minutes at a time. They either wake up or fall asleep. Banquet's guess was that the confusion came from the obscure pen-and-ink paper record.

The EEG pattern usually associated with drowsiness is a particularly difficult one to read. When people are relaxed but still awake (usually with eyes closed) their brains often generate an increase in the well-known *alpha waves*. When people are in light sleep or dreaming, on the other hand, their brains will usually give off more *theta waves*. By obvious inference, between these two states of relaxed wakefulness and light sleep is the state of drowsiness, in which the brain generates alpha and theta alternately — a confused scramble of a line known to EEG experts as *mixed low frequencies*.

This fuzzy mixture was the pattern that seemed to appear frequently with meditators, for periods which Banquet found suspiciously long. He adopted two tests to resolve the confusion. First, he designed his study to allow his subjects to practice the

TM technique until the paper record showed the typical pattern of mixed low frequencies. He then had his researchers produce a slight but clearly audible click, a standard test intended to produce what is known as the *orienting reaction*. When a drowsy person hears such a noise, he is startled and wakes up — orienting to the click. His brain wave patterns change to alpha alone, or even to the faster *beta* patterns that commonly indicate focused mental activity. It usually takes a few minutes for the brain wave patterns to settle back toward the sleep configuration.

In Banquet's study, however, when the researchers tried to produce the orienting reaction in the meditating subjects, they found they couldn't. The brain wave patterns did jump momentarily, indicating that the subjects heard the noise, but then they immediately returned to the same unusually persistent mixed low frequencies. Apparently these subjects did not go from drowsiness to waking. Whatever state of consciousness they were experiencing, it seemed unaffected by the interruption, a finding consistent with both the ancient description of the fourth state as *samadhi*, unwavering mind, and with the reports of TM meditators who report that noise does not interfere with their meditations.

This simple test confirmed Banquet's suspicion that he wasn't dealing with subjects drowsy for twenty straight minutes. To analyze the situation further, he adopted a then-new technology. He bypassed the pen-and-ink recording device and ran the electrical brain wave information straight into a computer — a computer programmed to perform a Fourier transform on the incoming information. A Fourier transform is designed to take any complex electronic signal and analyze it into its component parts, reading out, in this case, what percentage of the signal is theta waves, what percentage alpha, and so on.

The result was unusual. Instead of drifting back and forth from alpha waves to theta waves as drowsy people do, Banquet's subjects tended at many points in meditation to produce the two patterns simultaneously and continuously. With more experienced meditators, moreover, a second and deeper period in the meditation was correlated with powerful and continuous *trains* of rhythmic theta waves, totally unlike the flickering, irregular theta usually found in light sleep and dreaming. Occasionally such a solid train of theta waves was accompanied by a continuous, cohesive pattern of beta waves as well. Beta indicates even greater wakefulness than alpha; it usually predominates in normal daily activity and characterizes the active thinking process. Like theta, beta is also ordinarily random and chaotic in its appearance. Yet the beta train that sometimes appeared in what Banquet termed the third and deepest meditative state was rhythmic and consistent, showing up at about twenty cycles per second with, on occasion, a harmonic overtone at forty cycles per second. The subjects in this study, who were also equipped with a button to press after the deepest experiences of pure consciousness, generally pressed it after the appearance of this third stage of EEG activity.*

Taken as a whole, and even without reference to the research on deep physical rest, Banquet's work appeared to define a fourth state of consciousness. As he said,

> The main EEG changes we recorded appeared to individualize the meditative state. . . . These changes during meditation are of special interest inasmuch as they are not produced by other techniques like autosuggestion and hypnosis. It is also noteworthy that the TM subjects displayed the persistence of an alert state of consciousness, being able to answer questions and perform voluntary movement without any noticeable modification of the brain wave pattern of deep meditation.

COHERENCE IN BRAIN FUNCTIONING

Perusing the imprecise paper records produced by his equipment, Banquet thought he detected something remarkable. Not only did traces from one particular region of the brain fre-

---

Electroencephalography and Clinical Neurophysiology, 35, 143–151.

quently appear as a consistent, unvarying train, it also seemed that at those times different traces from differing parts of the brain appeared to become unusually synchronous or coherent with one another.

This hinted at a new finding. The brain usually operates in a highly incoherent and disorderly way. During mental tasks, each part of the brain normally changes rapidly, and different parts of the brain display little or no harmony in their operations. In a word, during active wakefulness, brain wave activity is usually scattered. During relaxed wakefulness, especially with eyes closed, the brain settles down to some degree and there is ordinarily some increase in coherence, but Banquet thought he was seeing an increase far beyond the normal range. Such an apparent increase of brain wave coherence would also be intriguing from the standpoint of the Super Radiance effect. We have seen that increased peace in any society amounts to increasing coherence — increasing orderliness and harmony — among all the components of that society. If *internal* coherence, coherence of the brain, could be found during the fourth state of consciousness, that could help explain how such peace-creating social coherence is generated.

RADAR TECHNOLOGIES APPLIED TO EEG COHERENCE

The breakthrough this time came from an unlikely source. Paul Levine is by training a physicist (his Ph.D. is from Cal Tech), rather than a physiologist. As chief scientist at Megatek Corporation in San Diego, California, he was throughout the 1970s a specialist in problem solving with space-age equipment. As it happened, his outside expertise was just what neurophysiologists needed to decode the complex brain wave patterns in the fourth state of consciousness.

Levine drew on his background in radar technology. The computer programs used in radar are highly specialized instruments for extracting meaningful information from a complex incoming signal — to distinguish, for example, a distant plane from a nearby bird. Levine used the radar approach to programming to sort out the confusing dance of information that comes from the human brain.

The target was brain wave coherence. The means was a program that excluded all coherence unless it were extremely high. Levine programmed the computer to refuse all patterns that were not at least ninety-five percent coherent — ninety-five percent in step with one another. The reason was clarity. Such a high threshold for coherence would, he knew, indiscriminately rule out all low end information. Whatever coherence did remain, however, would be unambiguous. In addition, the program was written so that this high-level coherence would have to appear persistently. The testing period was broken down into two-and-one-half-second segments. If coherence appeared in one of these brief periods but not the next, the computer was set to reject it. This ruled out even ninety-five percent coherence that was isolated and possibly an artifact — the sort of stray finding sometimes mimicked by random muscle movements.

This was a stringent program, but Levine and his co-workers assumed that if the fourth state of consciousness is a significant phenomenon, it should survive even this tight a test.

Levine tested more than fifty subjects altogether, a high number. Published EEG studies not infrequently have as few as five subjects, and fifteen is considered a large sample. In this study, moreover, the subjects included not only the experts in the Transcendental Meditation technique, but also new meditators and non-meditator controls. Tests were taken during waking, sleeping, and dreaming, as well as in the meditation period.

With this innovative and conservatively structured test, the results gave clear definition to Banquet's original surmise. Nearly every TM subject showed, during the meditation period, a marked increase in coherence between widely separated parts of the brain — even subjects who were very new to the practice. During an eyes-closed resting period before the beginning of meditation, some subjects showed an increase in coherence, as expected, but then, with the beginning of the TM practice, the level of coherence would ordinarily rise sharply from this basal level. The coherence would typically begin in the alpha range, and then in many cases spread to the theta and beta bands. In addition, people who had meditated for a greater number of years had, in general, greater coherence in the brain wave patterning. The strongest coherence, dominant in theta, alpha, and beta, was shown by the longest-term meditator, a woman of twenty-six who had been meditating regularly since the age of ten.*

Writing in the paper in which this data was presented, Levine and his co-workers said,

> [From these results] it would seem that the Transcendental Meditation technique produces a higher incidence of strong coherence in the alpha/theta band than is experienced in the normally encountered states of wakefulness and sleep, and that this feature in fact provides a unique EEG "signature" of the physiological state reached during the technique. . . . It now appears that this characteristic activity tends to occur in a highly coherent form among the central and frontal [regions of the brain].

Through state-of-the-art experimental methodology, the fourth state of consciousness had received another clear definition. Since the time of Levine's study in the mid-1970s, furthermore, many replications using variants of his approach have produced similar results, and six papers have been published in reputed journals. Internal coherence during the fourth state, a plausible basis for the coherence radiated outward into the society, is by now a well-documented result.

THE STATE OF MAXIMUM WAKEFULNESS

Another important question can be asked. Does the fourth state of consciousness seem to be, in terms of physiological evidence, a state that matches Maharishi's definition of "maximum wakeful-

---

*Proceedings of the San Diego Biomedical Symposium, 15 (1976).

ness"? Several research findings combine to give a positive answer.

One such indication was presented by Levine's study. Tests of people practicing the TM technique showed an increase of brain wave coherence, while tests of people as they fell asleep showed a progressive disappearance of any coherence already present. The stage of deep sleep was characterized by extremely low coherence throughout the night. This suggested that there is a continuum of coherence, extending from least coherence corresponding to least wakefulness (deep sleep), through somewhat greater coherence during the waking state, to maximum coherence — corresponding, it seems, to "maximum wakefulness" — during the fourth state of consciousness.

The validity of this interpretation is supported in another study by Banquet. While again showing the non-interruptable, rhythmic trains in the brain wave patterns, he also analyzed his data using standard ratios known as the *wakefulness coefficient* and the *activation coefficient*. The wakefulness coefficient is determined by comparing alpha waves (relaxed wakefulness) with delta waves (deep sleep). If the percentage of alpha is higher, the wakefulness coefficient is higher. Similarly, the activation coefficient compares beta waves (thinking and activity) with alpha waves (awake but relaxed). If the percentage of beta is higher, the activation coefficient is higher.

By these measures, Banquet showed that people practicing the TM technique do experience "restful alertness" — both deep rest and heightened inner wakefulness. They display a markedly lower activation coefficient than control subjects do when either resting or asleep, and yet a dramatically higher wakefulness coefficient than controls sitting relaxed with their eyes closed — four times higher. Even in terms of brain functioning, that is, the fourth state of consciousness is associated with quietness, with low levels of activity (low coefficient of activation) but also with increased wakefulness (high coefficient of wakefulness).*

Revue d'Electroencephalographie et de Neurophysiologie Clinique, 4, 445–53.

WAKEFULNESS IN THE PHYSIOLOGY

Two other studies, performed at the University of California have confirmed this understanding in terms of vascular physiology.

Increased blood flow to the brain. One of these has shown that, during the practice of TM, there is a marked redistribution of blood flow in the body. The muscles maintain a roughly normal flow, but there is a sharp decrease of blood flow to the bodily organs and a matching increase in blood flow to the brain. The increase of blood in the brain is, conservatively estimated, twenty percent more than usual, a particularly impressive finding since blood flow to the brain almost never increases to any large degree. Even a one-mile run will ordinarily result in less than a ten percent increase. During the fourth state of consciousness, the brain is exposed to more than the common amount of oxygen and nutrients, which could easily help explain the subjects' report of greater alertness.*

Increased AVP. The second finding may be even more significant. There is in the body a naturally occurring hormone named *arginine vasopressin* (AVP). Studies have associated AVP with, on the one hand, regulation of blood pressure and, on the other, direct improvements in learning ability and memory. This latter effect, the increase of mental clarity, has been so well established that AVP is now used as a prescription medicine to decrease the effects of senility. Ordinarily, AVP does not change significantly in the blood stream through the normal 24-hour cycle. With experienced meditators, however, this natural hormone has been shown to increase a remarkable 500% during the regular period in which people meditate each day. This increase in AVP can also also help account for the experience of "maximum wakefulness."†

American Journal of Physiology, 245(Cell Physiol. 14), C457–C461.
†*American Journal of Physiology*, 235(1), R89–R92.

THE PURE SELF ALONE

Physiological evidence has thus provided objective indicators of the fourth state of consciousness. In the words of researcher John Farrow,

> We have been excited to find indications of quiet, inner mental alertness with a highly quiescent physiological state. Taking the various measurements together, the combination appears clearly unique. It's not surprising that this particular style of physiological functioning should be associated with a unique mental state.

The physiological definition of the fourth state of consciousness is a remarkable parallel for the mental experience of the state as it has long been described. The central indicators of this state:

1. A state of least excitation. During the fourth state of consciousness, the body rests more deeply than in sleep, a quality of rest that produces a previously unknown style of metabolic functioning. At the same time, the brain becomes less random and disorderly, and display a low activation coefficient.

2. A state of heightened wakefulness. During the fourth state of consciousness, increased wakefulness is indicated by the increase in brain wave coherence, the increase in coefficient of wakefulness in brain wave patterns, the increase in blood flow to the brain, and the increase in the hormone AVP.

3. Unwavering mind. Rather than the different parts of the brain functioning in different ways, each part itself constantly changing, there is a marked increase in coherence between different parts of the brain, and each part tends to produce continuous, rhythmic, unchanging patterns, patterns which are responsive to but not interrupted by outside noise.

4. Self-referral and self-sufficient. The metabolic activity of the body becomes more self-sufficient, requiring less oxygen, while the mind becomes even more awake than normal without requiring any outside stimulation to maintain this wakefulness.

For Maharishi, these physiological discoveries have been important examples of the interplay between the understandings of ancient Vedic Science and the investigations of modern science. He says,

> This is why we are fortunate to live in an age of science. The fourth state of consciousness is now no more a fantasy or only a metaphysical reality. Now we have it on the objective basis of modern science. The Transcendental Meditation technique produces its own style of physiology — brain wave patterns are different, the metabolic rate is different — and due to that particular style of activity in the body, the mind experiences a state of least excitation, the fourth state of consciousness. The teachings of Vedic Science have now been verified in the research laboratories of modern science.

BENEFITS OF THE FOURTH STATE

Research evidence, moreover, can provide one more indication of the significance of this state of pure consciousness: It can define the remarkable transformation that occurs in the lives of individual people who experience that fourth state on a regular basis. This is a book about the creation of permanent world peace — about the use of large assemblies of meditation experts to transform the quality of life everywhere on Earth — but a brief review of the benefits enjoyed by individuals reveals the profundity of pure consciousness.

By looking at the physiological profile of the fourth state, one might expect certain benefits to show up in research evidence. The deep rest and relaxation experienced during pure consciousness, to take one instance, might be expected to produce a more relaxed and stress-free style of functioning after the meditation period; since reduced stress has been often correlated with improved health, moreover, improvement in overall health might also be expected. The increased coherence and integration of brain waves, moreover, could plausibly be expected to produce increased mental abilities such as intelligence and creativity, and perhaps even improved psychological functioning.

The same predictions might also be made on a more profound basis. Maharishi explains that when people experience pure consciousness, they directly contact the unified field of all the laws of nature. By so doing, Maharishi indicates, they align themselves with the limitless intelligence of nature or, in other words, they gain the support of all the laws of nature for their every thought and action. Thus, regular experience of the fourth state of consciousness produces, in Maharishi's phrase, "life in accord with natural law." And if the life of the individual does in fact come in tune with the most fundamental level of the intelligence in nature, then the above predictions might also be made on that basis alone. If the physical body comes increasingly in tune with nature's intelligence, for example, it should become increasingly healthy, and if the mind comes increasingly in tune with nature's intelligence, it should become increasingly intelligent and creative.

Once again, the Transcendental Meditation technique allows a detailed scientific definition of such benefits produced by the fourth state. By now, more than 600 studies on the Transcendental Meditation technique have been conducted at more than 200 universities and research institutions in 30 countries. Inspired by these studies on the TM technique, hundreds of other studies have appeared on other meditation and relaxation techniques. The most significant studies, therefore, have been those that have compared the results on the TM technique against the other techniques tested to date.

Such comparisons are important because, among all these techniques, only the Transcendental Meditation technique is avowedly intended to quickly produce the experience of pure consciousness in a simple, natural way. By contrast, the relaxation techniques tested to date are all intended to produce only physical relaxation (sometimes styled the "relaxation response"). Discussion of these techniques by their inventors and promoters usually betrays no interest in, or even knowledge of, the fourth state of consciousness. Even the studies on other meditation techniques (usually Zen meditation or its American version called "mindfulness") rarely discuss the fourth state of consciousness. In the Zen tradition it is thought that people must meditate with great effort and concentration over many years before they can hope to experience pure consciousness (known as *satori* in the Zen vocabulary). Thus, comparisons between the TM technique and the other techniques amount to comparisons between (1) a technique intended to produce rapid and natural experience of the fourth state (an intention thoroughly validated by the research discussed above) and (2) techniques intended to produce the fourth state either very slowly or, much more commonly, not at all.

The scientific comparisons between these approaches have been methodologically powerful — frequently using *meta-analysis* to compare results from many previously conducted studies. The results of such meta-studies, which draw conclusions from very large data sets, are much more convincing than results from single studies standing alone.

These comparative studies have produced, from a large amount of evidence, a revealing insight. Repeatedly it has been shown that the experience of pure consciousness during the Transcendental Meditation technique generates benefits markedly greater than those gained from other techniques — for the body, for the mind, and for psychological maturity.

REDUCED ANXIETY

From the perspective of peace in the world, the key individual benefit would logically be increased inner peace. Those peaceful within themselves could most logically create peace around them. When psychologists aim to measure inner peace, moreover, they usually do so in terms of reduced anxiety — since anxiety is the first psychological/emotional sign of excessive stress. Significantly, the first meta-analysis comparing meditation and relaxation techniques, conducted at Stanford University and published in the *Journal of Clinical Psychology*, focused on reduced anxiety.

When Dr. Kenneth Eppley did a search for such anxiety studies, testing the ability of various techniques to reduce anxiety, he found more than 100, far more than are usual in meta-analysis. These studies tested the effectiveness of every well-known meditation or relaxation technique, including the Transcendental Meditation technique, other types of meditation, the much-researched Progressive Muscle Relaxation technique, the "relaxation response," and many others.

The results of Dr. Eppley's comparative analysis challenged the common perception that all meditation and relaxation techniques are equally effective. Comparing all the studies together, the regular experience of the fourth state of consciousness through the TM technique reduced anxiety more than twice as much as any other approach. The large number of studies made the outcome particularly convincing. Peace-creating people should experience inner peace — and this is just what these results showed.

How strong are the studies? Moreover, Dr. Eppley had so many studies to work with that he was able to answer two other questions often raised about meditation research in general. In any new field of research, it is typical that the first research studies — called pilot studies — are fairly simple tests to see if results are produced and more research is warranted. These first studies are often done quickly and inexpensively, with less-than-rigorous research designs. For instance, they may have such limitations as:

1. **One-time testing** (a *cross-sectional* study), rather than pre-post testing with a time lag in between (a *longitudinal* study).

2. **A small number of subjects** — which makes the results less definitive.

3. No control group — which makes it harder to rule out alternative explanations for the findings.

4. No random assignment to the control group — which means that people can "self-select" into the experimental and control groups, and self-selected subjects bring their own biases and predispositions with them.

5. A large dropout rate among test subjects before the study ends — which can seriously bias the results. For example, if all the most anxious people drop out of the study, leaving only the least anxious people to take the final test, the post-testing would show less anxiety on the average even if the meditation technique itself had no effect.

These issues have often been raised with meditation research. In the late 1970s, many initial studies on all techniques used less-than-rigorous designs. It is possible to argue that positive results from some of the studies might have been due to sloppy design. According to this criticism, researchers who were biased toward a specific meditation or relaxation technique might get the results they wanted because the studies were not rigorous enough.

Choosing only the strongest studies. Dr. Eppley was in a position to answer such questions definitively. First, he analyzed all the results to see which aspects of research design actually made a difference in this body of research. He found four factors most significant — (1) control groups, (2) random assignment to those groups, (3) longitudinal design, and (4) low dropout rate (known as low attrition). From the overall group of more than 100 studies, he then chose only those studies which matched those criteria.

The results of this comparison showed that the more stringent research designs, as suspected, did deflate results for most techniques. In studies with rigorous methodologies, these techniques produced a reduction of anxiety fifty percent less than in all of the studies taken together. In other words, these techniques had seemed to be more effective in the weaker studies than they actually turned out to be when investigated in more rigorous studies. With the Transcendental Meditation technique, however, the results held steady. In the well-designed studies, in fact, the reduction of anxiety by Transcendental Meditation was slightly greater than in all the studies taken together. When Dr. Eppley restricted his analysis to only the best studies, this is to say, the experience of the fourth state of consciousness was shown to reduce anxiety not just twice, but four times as well as the other approaches.

Dealing with research bias. The second question Dr. Eppley was able to answer concerned researcher bias. It is possible to argue that results for the Transcendental Meditation program were the most impressive because the researchers were biased. For this reason, Eppley made a selection of only those studies that (1) were well designed, and (2) had been done by researchers who were either neutral or actively hostile toward Transcendental Meditation (as judged by the written expressions in each study). In other words, he wanted only those studies that were both rigorous and objective. The results indicated conclusively that the stress-reducing effects of Transcendental Meditation are not the result of experimental bias. In fact, in this selection of studies by neutral or hostile researchers, the Transcendental Meditation technique was found to reduce anxiety slightly more effectively than it did in all the studies taken together.* These findings, in the largest comparative study of meditation and relaxation techniques ever undertaken, increase the confidence in other research on the Transcendental Meditation technique.

REDUCING THE STRONGEST STRESS

The Transcendental Meditation technique also has been used to combat the most debilitating type of stress, known as Post

*Journal of Clinical Psychology, 45, 957–974.

Traumatic Stress Disorder. Working with Vietnam veterans, psychiatrist Dr. James Brooks randomly assigned one group of veterans to psychological counseling and a second group to the Transcendental Meditation technique. He did a longitudinal study, with pre- and post-testing over a three-month period. He had no dropouts. As expected, the psychological counseling had little effect; psychologists have been frustrated by this problem for years.

The fourth state of consciousness, however, as experienced during the Transcendental Meditation technique, produced significant reductions in anxiety, depression, alcohol consumption, insomnia, and family problems. This study demonstrated that even the most challenging type of stress is relieved by the fourth state.*

REDUCED USE OF HEALTH INSURANCE

Physicians commonly estimate that eighty percent of all disease is either caused or exacerbated by stress. Thus, the stress reduction produced by the fourth state of consciousness should improve physical health markedly. This has been shown by a five-year study of health insurance statistics published in the journal *Psychosomatic Medicine*. This study tracked 2,000 people all across the country who practiced the Transcendental Meditation program. The data was collected by an insurance company. The statistics from the meditation group were compared to a control group selected by the insurance company to match the Transcendental Meditation group for age, education, profession, and other variables. The overall result was that, compared to the control group, people experiencing the fourth state of consciousness on a regular basis needed major surgery 76 percent less often, and had 55 percent fewer tumors and 87 percent less heart disease.†

Journal of Counseling and Development, 64, 212–215.
†*Psychosomatic Medicine*, 49, 499–507.

Benefits begin when the Transcendental Meditation technique is begun. Another study of insurance statistics utilized data from the Canadian government. Because Canada has national cradle-to-grave health-care coverage, it was possible to trace people's records back years before they learned the Transcendental Meditation technique. This was important because, as a criticism of the first insurance study, it was possible to argue that people who began meditation were extremely healthy even before they started to meditate. The Canadian study made it possible to investigate whether the health benefits began with the onset of meditation.

The study was also significant because it tracked not just health-care utilization, but actual health-care costs as well. Prior to this study, no research project had found a program that could reduce health-care costs long-term. Some programs helped contain costs — helped to keep the upward spiral of prices from increasing so rapidly. But nothing had actually decreased costs on a sustainable basis.

This study, however, found that in the years before they learned the Transcendental Meditation technique, the subjects' health-care costs averaged the same as for all people in their age range. Once they began to meditate, on the other hand, their health-care costs began to decline — an average of 10 percent each year. This marked reversal in costs identified meditation as the causal factor. Among people who had previously shown the highest pattern of health care costs, moreover, the reductions were most dramatic — 18 percent a year and 54 percent in three years. These declines were inflation adjusted. Since health-care costs were rising rapidly each year, furthermore, the actual cost savings were considerably greater. In sum, the health transformation caused by the fourth state of consciousness is a fiscal, not just a physical, reality.*

[*_American Journal of Health Promotion_, in press.

BENEFITS FOR THE MIND

The fourth state of consciousness produces not only rest and relaxation but also, as we have seen, significant enhancements to brain functioning, and such improvements in brain functioning could plausibly lead to improved cognitive abilities. In fact, repeated studies have shown that people who practice the Transcendental Meditation technique enjoy cumulative increases in both intelligence and creativity. As one example, although IQ ordinarily ceases to grow at age eighteen, and students at four control universities actually declined in IQ by two points (probably due to late nights and other lifestyle choices), students at Maharishi University of Management (where everyone meditates twice daily) increased in IQ five points in two years and nine points in four years.*

Improved cognitive abilities. Other studies have shown improved verbal and analytical thinking, consistent with improved functioning in the left hemisphere of the brain** and improved synthetic and holistic thinking, consistent with improved functioning in the right hemisphere of the brain.[†]

Among the most significant cognitive findings is that the fourth state of consciousness improves field independence — the ability to focus on a specific object or task despite a distracting background.[§] People with high field independence have been shown in other research to have strong character — to be able to resist outside influences and make decisions for themselves. Thus the improved brain functioning characteristic of the fourth state of consciousness seems not only to improve mental abilities, but also to enhance psychological development.

Improved psychological maturity. Such psychological development has been conclusively demonstrated in another sig-

---

Personality and Individual Differences, 12, 1105–1116.

**The Journal of Creative Behavior*, 13, 169–180.

[†]*Journal of Clinical Psychology*, 42, 161–164.

[§]*Perceptual and Motor Skills*, 65, 613–614.

nificant meta-analysis. This study investigated the psychological quality of *self-actualization*, which is the closest concept in psychology to the Vedic concept of enlightenment. Originally coined by psychologist Abraham Maslow, self-actualization means that the various hidden potentials within the mind and the psychology have been fully developed (fully realized, fully actualized). A person high in self-actualization is thought to be well developed in every aspect of life, including (1) moral reasoning, (2) self-regard, (3) emotional maturity, (4) capacity for warm interpersonal relationships, and (5) successful response to external challenges. In this study, which compared the results from forty-two previously conducted studies on all types of meditation and relaxation techniques, people who regularly practiced the Transcendental Meditation technique demonstrated growth in self-actualization that was three times greater than did people practicing the other techniques. In addition, long-term practitioners of the Transcendental Meditation technique score among the highest of all groups that have ever taken this test of self-actualization.*

VEDIC PREDICTIONS AND
SCIENTIFIC VALIDATION

The plan of this book has been to take Maharishi's articulation of central tenets of the Vedic tradition and compare them against the relevant science. As we have seen in the last four chapters, the Vedic "predictions" have fared well under such rigorous examination.

1. **Super Radiance.** Repeatedly published scientific evidence has validated the prediction of society-wide changes created by Super Radiance assemblies.

2. **Unified field.** Physics has glimpsed one unified field of all the laws of nature.

Journal of Social Behavior and Personality, 6, 189–247.

3. Mind and matter. Leading physicists have realized that a profound connection exists between consciousness and the apparently physical world — and especially between the unified field of consciousness and the unified field in physics.

4. Fourth state. Physiologists have defined a fourth state of consciousness, the putative pipeline to the unified field, with physiological fingerprints consistent with the ancient descriptions, and profound benefits for individual life.

For people in modern societies, these findings can be a great surprise. None of these understandings was widely known in the modern world until Maharishi began his teaching, and none makes much sense based on simple observation of the surface level of life and the world. But these profound concepts have now received strong support from the objective methods of modern science. Subjective truth and objective truth have converged; Vedic Science and modern science have shaken hands. At no time in recorded history have we had such a solid platform for understanding, and giving credence to, the teachings of sages and seers throughout the ages. As Maharishi states of his own experience,

> In the beginning days, we taught this technology purely on the subjective level of the experience people had when they started meditating. But then, when the scientists became interested, their research was helpful. In a modern world, scientific language has proved to be a good way to communicate. But really, this whole knowledge is nothing new. Nothing useful is new under the sun. We only brushed off the dust deposited on this ancient knowledge and now it is expressed in a more systematic way. Now we know that it is possible for the unified field, the field of all possibilities, to be opened to human contact. This potential of human life, known from past records and hinted at by the scientific discovery of the unified field, is verified by our personal experience.

The most vital contribution of this knowledge for a world still in turmoil is, of course, Super Radiance. Based on the evidence already presented, it is time now to discuss the far-reaching implications of this discovery. It is time to consider the possibility of a world transformed by the power of a technology of peace, a world free from warfare and terrorism, a world free from poverty and ignorance, a world enjoying a permanent state of peace and progress.

Perhaps, in light of the profound and detailed support that Maharishi's explanations have received, the reader will agree: No one can discuss such implications of Super Radiance — and the Vedic understanding of life — more authoritatively than Maharishi himself.

6

A PERMANENT STATE
OF WORLD PEACE:
Maharishi in His Own Words

His Holiness Maharishi Mahesh Yogi has been teaching around the world since the 1950s. He came out from India, one man traveling alone, carrying with him only knowledge. His traveling expenses were paid by students he left behind. He made contacts in each new city by sitting in the airport until someone offered to help. His accommodations were provided by people he met at his lectures. His goal was simple, but compelling: "To end suffering in the world in this generation."

Since those earliest days of his work, millions of people have begun the practice of the Transcendental Meditation technique and tens of thousands the advanced TM-Sidhi program. Hundreds of scientific studies have validated his central assertions. Now the evolution of consciousness enjoyed by many individuals has made possible a mechanism for the rapid transformation of the world as a whole — through the use of large Super Radiance assemblies, the technology of peace.

What this means is that Vedic knowledge is once again available to the world, and available this time in a form that is systematic, scientifically verifiable, and easily usable. Because quantum discoveries have plumbed the depths of the natural world, and because Maharishi has adopted orderly and scientific procedures and vocabulary, the subtlest and most profound understandings of human life and cosmic creation can now be clearly understood and systematically acted upon. Ancient secrets have become practical realities. After his years of one-pointed dedication, Maharishi speaks now in terms of great fulfillment.

"This is a very, very beautiful time for the world," he says. "Now we have the knowledge of that collective performance which creates such a beautiful atmosphere everywhere on earth. New trends, new tendencies of life come up, the whole world consciousness gets purified, when large groups practice TM and the TM-Sidhi program together in one spot. A new sunshine is being created for human existence."

Physics has glimpsed the unified field and physiology the fourth state of consciousness. But these can seem abstract and difficult to understand for some people. For this reason, Maharishi often discusses Super Radiance with a simple analogy.

Maharishi: "How does Super Radiance come about? This 'how' is answered in the performance of a gardener. The gardener waters the root of the tree. Quietly this enlivens the sap, which is the colorless basis of all the brown of the trunk, the green of the leaves, the yellow of the petals. All the leaves and branches and trunk of the tree are just the expression of that colorless sap, and when this sap becomes enlivened deep within, then the whole tree becomes healthier and fresher. It begins to radiate happiness. Radiance outside depends on something that goes on inside. Just like that, when a large number of experts in TM and the TM-Sidhi program function from that self-referral level at the basis of natural law — from that source of all the laws of nature — then this enlivens all the laws of nature. Such a group enlivens natural law by functioning at that level which is the fountainhead of natural law. Then, even without making any effort, this gives nourishment to the whole civilization, to all the tendencies in the world. The performance is inner, the performance is completely self-referral. But the effect is global, it is universal."

After humanity's long history of suffering and strife, it is difficult to believe that human life on earth can drastically change for the better. Maharishi often talks of a coming "Heaven on Earth," and he is very well aware that this is a challenge to credulity.

Maharishi: "The idea of Heaven on Earth must seem an unbelievable thing, like telling a dream to someone. Man has lived with problems and suffering throughout the ages. History does not record a time when man was free from suffering, and so life was declared a struggle. 'Life is a struggle' — it's a very common axiom in English. But now a new time has come for the world, and it is a scientific phenomenon we are witnessing. It's not impractical idealism we are talking about, high-sounding moral values with no basis. This is something that has been verified subjectively by millions of people, something that has been verified objectively by all these hundreds of experiments. It is a technology, like the use of a lever, to do something previously found impossible. As long as it was not known, nothing could be done. But now we have it. We have it on the basis of ancient Vedic Science. We have it on the basis of modern science. And we have it on the basis of personal experience.

"The unified field has been glimpsed today even by the field of physics. Physicists know the unified field to be that total potential of natural law which is responsible for the existence and maintenance of the whole creation. Natural law governs life everywhere, and the total potential of natural law is the unified field, that unmanifest, transcendental level of nature which we experience when consciousness settles down to its self-referral state of functioning. Infinite dynamism and intelligence is there.

When the mind identifies itself with that dynamism and intelligence in the transcendental state of consciousness, then it enlivens all the laws of nature throughout creation. We nourish all the trends and tendencies of life everywhere. It is this that will allow the whole world to live the best that life has to offer. It is this that will allow us to make obsolete the old understanding that life is a struggle and to end suffering for mankind in this generation."

This view of life's possibilities seems most directly challenged by worldwide terrorism, and by the rapidly escalating destruction caused by the retaliatory "war on terrorism." To Maharishi, however, terrorism and the brutal counterattacks against terrorism not only highlight the need for a new approach to defense, but provide an urgent context in which such a new approach will in fact be tried. His logic begins with a dissection of traditional means of defense.

Maharishi: "The old strategy of defense was based on violence. It was based on the willingness to die for one's country. But this is an outmoded concept in today's world. With the weapons available today, if any nation creates an enemy, no amount of dying can save the country. Powerful nations can destroy any other nation, but even they are powerless to defend their own people. Times have changed and old patterns of defense must change. All the mechanical and technical means of destruction, they are capable of destroying, but they have no value of saving. This is why the only possibility for any nation today is to make use of that knowledge which will stop the very birth of an enemy. It is just a matter of using a scientific discovery in favor of man's life here on earth."

To disallow the birth of an enemy, Maharishi indicates, a nation must radiate a nourishing influence of harmony and peacefulness into the international environment, thereby creating what he terms invincible defense.

Maharishi: "Through the Super Radiance program, the collective consciousness of a nation can be purified of stress and fear.

The entire collective consciousness of the nation can become more positive, more evolutionary, more life-supporting. That means the nation will radiate an influence of harmony and positivity that will create only friends. Any nation now, by using this technology, is capable of losing all of its enemies. Any nation now is capable of changing all enmity to friendliness. And when the intensity of orderliness in the collective consciousness becomes strong enough, then cultural integrity is restored in the nation and the nation becomes invincible to damaging influences from outside. Coherence in collective consciousness leads to invincibility for the nation. And this is not a hope. It is supported by all these studies on coherence-creating groups. The ancient Vedic technology of defense has now been validated by objective science."

This is certainly a new approach, but all the old approaches have manifestly failed to stop terrorism and war. When speaking of terrorism, which is a crime against humanity, Maharishi often speaks about crime in general, and the futility of punishing criminals as a way to put an end to crime.

Maharishi: "Crime has been there in every generation. Governments, who are responsible to keep order in their whole territory, have always implemented punishments. 'If you do this wrong, this is the punishment.' They have put the criminals to jail, they have put them to be destroyed. But what we see is that punishment continues generation after generation and crime continues generation after generation. Wrongdoers have been destroyed, but new criminals keep bubbling up in every age. This is why I am very happy to be able to say that we have come to a solution of this long-standing, continuously existing tradition of crime and criminals. To cut the story short, we do this by educating the people to always think and act in the evolutionary direction of Natural Law. We know the universe is an ever-expanding universe. The infinite diversity of creation is being administered in a very systematic manner without any problem, age after age. So we want to take recourse to this higher intelligence of Natural Law which, in this scientific age, has been realized as the most fundamental level of everyone's awareness. This seat of all creativity and all evolutionary processes is within the consciousness of everyone. That is why it is absolutely simple and easy that everyone could be educated to have access to his own evolutionary direction."[2]

In Maharishi's understanding, this emphasis on education rather than punishment and destruction has a more than practical significance. It is not just a question of what will work better, in Maharishi's view, but also what is ethically and morally right.

Maharishi: "If you take care of education then you will not be required to commit a global sin. When you destroy a country, then you are killing, and killing is a sin. Whether you are a Christian or a Hindu or a Moslem, killing is sin. This killing of so many people out of revenge, this destruction of whole countries, this whole thing is very wild and mad and unwanted in the world. And it is not necessary. You kill so many people, but you will not be able to stop the continuity of these terrorists, these mischief mongers. You cannot. So why commit a sin, a national sin, where the whole nation will go to perdition? Our program is to prevent terrorism. We are all for destroying terrorism. But destroy so it cannot come up again. Our advocacy is to finish it once for all and let not forthcoming generations be victims to terrorism again and again."[3]

Ethical discussions about violence and retribution, as all ethical discussions, turn on definitions of right and wrong, good and bad. In Maharishi's discussions of the topic, the definition of good is straightforward.

Maharishi: "Everything good is evolutionary. Everything good is in tune with all the laws of nature, and leads spontaneously to progress and fulfillment."

When people do wrong, moreover, including all those who kill and destroy, he blames their education and their teachers.

Maharishi: "This is just due to lack of guidance, lack of proper guidance. Violation of natural law is a crime against creation but people everywhere are found violating the laws of nature. And when they violate any law of nature, then they suffer. If they eat something wrong, they fall sick. The violation of natural law must always create stress, and stress must project itself in problems and failures. And this arises because of a lack in the field of education."

These points relate not merely to terrorism and war, but to human life as a whole. And they raise the question, how can one live in tune with all the laws of nature? There are innumerable laws of nature operating at different levels of natural functioning. As Maharishi points out, it is not possible to know and master all the laws of nature through intellectual endeavor. However, he indicates, it is possible to live in accord with natural law — spontaneously and innocently.

Maharishi: "Hunting the laws of nature one by one, it would not be possible to fathom the full range of natural law and to know all the laws of nature. We can study the isolated values of different laws of nature through the branches of modern science, but these laws of nature do not become a living reality merely by intellectual comprehension. Now, fortunately, a technology has arisen which allows the human mind to come into tune with the full potential of natural law. The unified field is that collectedness of all the laws of nature. Through TM and the TM-Sidhi program the mind is allowed to settle down deep within and identify itself with that self-sufficient level, that level which is the total potential of natural law. In this way, even without knowing all the laws of nature intellectually, yet man is able to gain the support of all the laws of nature for his every thought and action. The formula for the individual is: Transcend. Open your awareness to the home of all the laws of nature, and then stabilize the home of all the laws of nature in your awareness. In this way you will spontaneously behave in accordance with all the laws of nature. The laws of nature become a reality of daily life. In Vedic Science this totality is so beautifully understood; not only do the natural laws come to be known, but the totality of natural law could become a living reality for every single individual born on earth. This is the gift of Vedic Science."

Although his main focus in the worldwide crisis caused by terrorism and retribution is on the permanent establishment of one large group of 40,000 meditation experts, Maharishi also emphasizes the importance of training every individual to gain the support of natural law through evolution of the nervous system.

Maharishi: "The main effect of TM and the TM-Sidhi program is to culture the individual physiology to act in accord with the laws of nature. We experience the fourth state of consciousness, pure consciousness, and that experience takes the nervous system to a particular style of functioning. As we repeat our meditations, this inspires the nervous system to function in that new style more and more. And this procedure brings a gradual and systematic culturing of the physical nervous system until all thoughts and all actions come out from the unified field of all the laws of nature. The human physiology has that capacity whereby the whole life can be lived according to the laws of nature — spontaneously right, unmistakably right. This is the technology whereby the glories of the unified field could be brought into daily life."

When speaking of individual evolution, Maharishi always emphasizes that the practice of the Transcendental Meditation technique is a completely natural process and, therefore, simple and effortless.

Maharishi: "Having taught Transcendental Meditation to so many millions of people in the world, we know, and those who practice it know, how simple it is. It is very simple for everyone because it is one's own nature. Just as speaking is spontaneous, so the inner creativity which is the nature of the Unified Field is discovered spontaneously within the Transcendental Consciousness of everyone.

As he has always made clear, as well, the Transcendental Meditation technique can be practiced by anyone from any location, religion, or walk of life.

Maharishi: "It's absolutely useful for everyone on earth regardless of his state of mind, regardless of the level of his intelligence, and regardless of his state of awakening — whether fully awakened, waking, dreaming, sleeping states of consciousness — it doesn't matter. In whatever state of consciousness one may be, the reality at the basis of every other state of consciousness is the self-referral state of Transcendental Consciousness. Fortunately, for the last forty or fifty years we have taught Transcendental Meditation throughout the world, and we have a huge record of scientific research that the capable scientists in all fields of knowledge have recorded as the benefits coming from this Transcendental Consciousness. What comes to us a result is an open door to perfection for everyone on earth."[4]

In Maharishi's explanations, the end result of alternating meditation and action is that the nervous system is trained to a new style of functioning — a style that supports enlightenment. In the common three states of consciousness (the sleeping state, the dreaming state, and the waking state), we have different levels of experience — we know different "worlds," in Maharishi's terminology. But even in waking state, we know only the superficial levels of the natural world, missing out entirely on subtler levels and, ultimately, the unified field, where nature's intelligence is most concentrated.

Maharishi: "Everyone experiences that there is a world of waking state, there is a world of dreaming state — these are different worlds. So far, it has been a time of ignorance for life on earth, dark ages where man would only live waking state of consciousness, dreaming state of consciousness and sleep state of consciousness. Waking, dreaming and sleeping. With the grace of the eternal Vedic tradition of knowledge, the great enlightened teachers of the Vedic tradition have preserved the knowledge of Unity Consciousness for all times."[5]

Maharishi describes Unity Consciousness as the highest state of human development, a state of full enlightenment, in which, among other realities, the individual intelligence is fully united with nature's intelligence. Maharishi describes this highest state of consciousness and its benefits in quotations from his book Maharishi Vedic University: Introduction.

Maharishi: "When individual awareness is established in the Home of all the Laws of Nature — the Unified Field of all the Laws of Nature in Transcendental Consciousness — thinking is free from weakness, and action is free from mistakes. In this state of enlightenment the individual meets with no resistance in achieving his goals; problems and failures are foreign to his life — he can know anything, do anything, and accomplish anything."[6]

"The consciousness of the student, flowing in Nature's perfect theme of evolution, naturally evolves into the spontaneous ability to function from the level of Cosmic Intelligence. He spontaneously handles every individual aspect of his daily life on the ground of the fully awake Cosmic Intelligence in his awareness."[7]

"The individual life gains access to Cosmic Intelligence — the evolutionary power of Nature — and evolves to the supreme level of awakening of Cosmic Life in [the Vedic quotation] *Aham Brahmasmi* — 'I am totality.'"[8]

Such individual enlightenment, as Maharishi describes it, is obviously desirable. But if we needed every single person to seek and attain enlightenment before world peace could be established, the time required would be discouragingly long. This is why Maharishi emphasizes Super Radiance as the highest priority today.

Maharishi: "This is our great joy. From one spot in the world we can create that beautiful influence of coherence and harmony which radiates around the world. From one spot we can create invincibility for every nation and when the influence of coherence in world consciousness has become strong enough, then people everywhere will not be able to do wrong. They will not be able to do wrong, either for themselves or for others. This is a very great achievement of our time, that a few knowledgeable people should sit together, operate within that field of pure knowledge at the basis of creation, and radiate an influence which motivates people from within to do only good, to do nothing wrong or negative."

Maharishi suggests that this is possible because the underlying unified field connects all the more superficial aspects of nature.

Maharishi: "When we enliven the unified field in one place, we enliven it everywhere. It is that field of infinite correlation, where everything is connected with everything else. Everywhere the laws of nature become more lively and naturally everyone begins to live more in tune with natural law. This is how we can nourish the minds and hearts of all people around the world. This is how we have placed ourselves in a position to think about the welfare of the whole world. We have that technology whereby we can enliven natural law within the hearts and minds of even those people on the far side of the globe. We can remove the thorny edge from their performance. We can remove the negativity from their performance. We will do it for our own benefit, for our own growth to higher states of consciousness, but we will bring human life everywhere in tune with all the laws of nature. And this is how we know we can restructure our society, how we can administer our society on that universal basis, how we can rebuild our nation on the basis of all possibilities, how all governments can function with that high efficiency with which the unified field governs the universe."

This technology is so powerful, Maharishi indicates, and so useful, that it can be used in any country, with any system of government.

Maharishi: "It is not the system of government that is important. Every system can rise to fulfillment, every system can bring satisfaction to the aspirations of all the people. The situation today is that all governments have such beautiful constitutions. The constitutions are ideal, but the achievements are not up to the dignity of the constitutions in any part of the world. With all the power, with all the national resources, with all the good will of the people, with all the highly intelligent experts assembled to handle every field, yet no government has been able to create an ideal society."

The frustration felt by governmental leaders everywhere, born of their inability to satisfy the nation as a whole, can now be alleviated, Maharishi explains, through Super Radiance.

Maharishi: "Every head of state is like a father — he wants to do everything he can to make his family happy. Now all those age-old aspirations of heads of state will be fulfilled with these large groups who learn to operate on the level of the unified field. Nations have always been administered by man-made law. Now the technology is available to use the skilled hand of nature to administer society. Any government will be perfect when the society is governed by national law and natural law both simultaneously. It has taken us these long years, but today we stand with that formula in our hand which can bring invincibility and ideal society to every nation. Only a handful of people in any country, through their daily Super Radiance program, can enliven the unified field in that nation. This will enliven the unified field in national consciousness and thereby enable the government to govern with the same silent perfection with which the government of nature governs the universe."

The results of such systematic Super Radiance programs, in Maharishi's description, will be almost unimaginably positive.

Maharishi: "It is very easy for anyone with even the slightest intelligence to understand that if the unified field could be accessible to anyone, nothing would be impossible for him. All man could ever want will be there with this support from all the laws of nature. There will be no negativity, no suffering. Life will not have to be a struggle any more. Those days should be forgotten. Children will read in the history books that there was a time when the hospitals were filled, when the jails were filled, when doctors were always worried and lawyers were up late at night unable to rest. They will read this, but it will all be a tale of the past. Now every government can make use of this formula. Here is the secret of successful society. We are very proud to say today that the world is going to be a better world, and a better world is going to be the best world. We can't have any expression greater than to say that heaven will be lived on earth."

If most people in the world had to understand these possibilities and believe them before they could come to pass, it would again be true that Maharishi's proposals would hardly be practical. But Maharishi is convinced that widespread discussions are not necessary.

Maharishi: "Our program is based on reality. It is not based on gossip and goodwill. This Vedic field of consciousness, this Unified Field from physics, this is reality. It's not a matter of acceptance of principle. It's not creating mutual understanding. It is creating the effect. Peace is not on the level of understanding. It is not on the basis of discussions. It is not on the basis of persuasion. Persuasive procedures have always failed. It is on the basis of creating the effect, creating the effect that disharmony will not exist."[9]

And for this, Maharishi emphasizes, a single group of 40,000 is absolutely vital.

Maharishi: "It is on the unseen level, the transcendental level, the level of self-referral consciousness. From there we can mold life in the world as we want it. And for that our effort is to have 40,000 in one place — a very strong center to create coherence and a unified, harmonious value for the whole world consciousness from one centralized place. One and one half hours in the morning and in the evening they will go for their meditation and Yogic Flying, and during the day they will do their Vedic performances, yagya performances. This will be their profession. We can't put them to any other work to earn their financial support. Their daily performance is a very delicate performance. One has to be well rested in order to perform from that rested state of Transcendental Consciousness which is a lively field of Natural Law. It is from there that the practice is done, practice of meditation and yagya. So in order to be effective, one's life has to be given over to that ultimate level of total Natural Law, the Unified Field — one's own Transcendental Consciousness. It's from there that the Laws of Nature govern the universe without problems. And with this program, it will be a happy, affluent world without negativity, without problems. When light is shining in a room, darkness doesn't come. Intense darkness doesn't come, faint darkness doesn't come, any kind of darkness is absent in the presence of light. When these 40,000 people will generate coherence in world consciousness, then coherent world consciousness will not allow any negative thing to sprout."[10]

Any government anywhere could easily support such a group. But Maharishi also addresses his proposal to responsible citizens everywhere — and especially in America, which has been the subject of the most drastic terrorist attacks, and which has responded with the most destructive retaliation.

Maharishi: "My message is for everyone, and if people are leaders in the society, more for them. For anyone who has life and who likes to be a champion of peace and happiness for others — and if not for others, for himself. And especially we should tell the wealthy of America, all the competent, peace-loving people of America, that all the physical sciences have discovered the Unified Field and the Unified Field has also been verified in the Vedic Literature."[11]

Maharishi has often said that world peace is now only a matter of money. With sufficient funding for the 40,000 group, the Maharishi Effect can be created everywhere in the world — and maintained permanently. The world is racked by terrorism and war, but Maharishi is confident that the timeless Vedic wisdom, now verified by modern science, can transform the destiny of the world. And for this, as for every achievement in his life, he gives both credit and gratitude to his own teacher, His Divinity Brahmananda Saraswati, whom Maharishi calls Guru Dev *(enlightened teacher).*

Maharishi: "Now we have that simple formula to change the trends of time. It is such a fulfilling time. I remember the first days of teaching nearly fifty years ago in India. From the Vedic literature and at the feet of my master, Guru Dev, I had learned that life is bliss, that life is infinity, immortality. But when I looked to the world, I found it completely opposite. And I saw that something was lacking between the field of action and the field of knowledge.

"I started to teach and I had that confidence that this is such a simple, natural, effortless technology whereby everyone could fathom one's own inner genius — that infinite creativity, that pure intelligence — and with this I thought it should be possible to eliminate negativity and suffering from the world. That was the aspiration. And now this ancient Vedic knowledge has been verified by modern science. Now we know that every man, born as a man, has it as a natural birthright to enjoy the support of all the laws of nature. And now we know that Super Radiance groups are completely sufficient to influence the far ends of the earth. It is a very, very great joy. That goal which I kept before me all these years, that life should not be a struggle, is now achievable for all mankind. For this we can only say, All glory to Guru Dev. Jai Guru Dev."

ACTION STEPS:

What You Can Do Now
To Create Permanent World Peace

By now, most readers will have made up their minds about the reality and effectiveness of Super Radiance. Those who simply can't believe it have stopped reading. Those who feel confident it works can skip to "Spread the Word" on the next page. For those who now feel that this technology of peace *might* work, two points:

1. Proven failure. Certainly, there is no other approach to permanent peace that works. As we've seen, the whole history of the world amounts to an experiment proving the failure of both weapons and peace talks as means to create lasting peace.

2. Proven success. Super Radiance is supported by the evidence of nineteen academically published studies — evidence that strongly indicates it *does* work. Not only do these studies show that it calms down violence, but also that it stimulates innovation and economic progress.

Given these facts, we can conclude at least this: We have compelling reason to give Super Radiance a try. Most significantly, we have compelling reason to support the creation of a single Super Radiance group of 40,000. The upside is, conservatively speaking, spectacular — a vision of the entire world enjoying a lasting era of harmony and progress. The downside is nonexistent. Even the most hardened skeptic can see that, if this new approach somehow failed now, for the first time, the world would be in no more dismal and dangerous a situation than it is today. The risk/benefit analysis yields 100% scientifically demonstrated benefit, and 0% risk.

Ideally, for all these reasons, governments everywhere will implement Super Radiance rapidly. Certainly, since September 11, 2001, governmental officials have been much more open to in-depth discussion about the possibility.

But if governments won't move quickly enough — and the history of bold governmental innovation is undeniably discouraging — then peace-loving people everywhere can take the future of the world into their own hands.

For those readers now disposed to such action, here are three suggested steps that can bring results immediately.

1. SPREAD THE WORD

The first requirement is to get the facts about Super Radiance to as many people as possible. The Vedic principles explained by Maharishi amount to a completely new paradigm in human understanding. Without that understanding — and without knowledge of the research evidence that supports it — the United States, for example, is left to two discouraging alternatives: (1) bomb more people and hope for the best, or (2) hope for the best. Neither can possibly stop future terrorist attacks. What's needed is to disseminate this new knowledge, knowledge that can systematically produce a peaceful world.

Here are three ways to spread this knowledge quickly.

1. Send the Website: Go to *createpermanentpeace.com*, which includes a brief essay recounting the theory and evidence discussed in this book. A button on this site allows you to e-mail a live link to the site, with a few lines of e-mail message enclosed. Instantly, you can let your whole list choose to learn, with a single click , how permanent peace can be attained.

2. Read and share the free mini-book: On that same Website, another link allows you (and everyone on your list) to download a mini-book, also entitled *Permanent Peace* — absolutely free. There is no charge for this mini-book because this knowledge is too significant to be constrained by money. This mini-book has been edited down from the full book (it amounts to about 35% of its contents). Although it can't be as convincing in detail as the book in its entirety, it downloads, e-mails, and reads much more quickly. For particular people you think will have interest, e-mail the entire mini-book, or its first few pages, or print it out and pass it around as freely as you like.

3. Purchase/donate: A third link on *createpermanentpeace.com* allows you to purchase the soft-cover edition of *Permanent Peace* that you now hold in your hand — at $19.95 per copy — with 80% of the purchase price donated to the Endowment Fund for Permanent World Peace (20% is reserved for printing and marketing). In one stroke, you can both spread knowledge and support peace financially. The goal of this donation feature is to make this book a rapidly self-replicating phenomenon — spread by people of goodwill. For those who can, you are encouraged to buy a few books, or a few hundred, or a few thousand. Give them away to family, friends, local and national business, academic and opinion leaders, wealthy philanthropists and foundations, and governmental and political leaders in your city and state, and in Washington, D.C. Many of these people will buy additional books and add to the self-replicating wave. The goal is clear: The more widely and quickly this idea becomes known, the faster it will be adopted. And virtually your entire investment will be donated — 80% of the purchase price — to help ensure permanent peace directly. To take advantage of this donation feature, please order the book on the Website (*createpermanentpeace.com*). or by phone at 866-85PEACE (although the shipping and handling fee must double for phone orders — to six dollars total for the least expensive shipping). For books purchased through bookstores and other such outlets, the purchase price must be shared, and the donation necessarily reduced.

2. SUPPORT THE WORLD PEACE FUND

The most immediately effective step any person can take (and the most powerful step in the long run) is to donate to the Endowment Fund for Permanent World Peace. As mentioned in Chapter One, the research has shown that even one group of 8,000 experts in Maharishi's Transcendental Meditation technique can reduce terrorism by 72%.

Now the Endowment Fund for World Peace has been established to permanently support a group five times that large — 40,000 people altogether. Since the power of Super Radiance increases as the square of the number of people involved, such a group will generate an influence of peace and harmony twenty-five times more powerful than any group gathered to date. To the extent that previous research is accurate, this one powerful group will be able to radiate an influence that will transform the trends of time everywhere in the world. The goal is to end terrorism and warfare forever — and create a permanent state of world peace.

As we also saw, this group will be gathered in India, where Maharishi already has available more than 175,000 experts trained in the Transcendental Meditation and TM-Sidhi programs, as well as in other Vedic technologies — known as *yagyas* — special Vedic performances that also reduce negativity in the world. Because costs in India are so low, such a group can be maintained for approximately $125 per person per month — or $60 million per year. The cost would be, conservatively, ten times higher in the West. To ensure that such monies will be available in perpetuity, an endowment fund has been started to raise one billion dollars. The principal of this fund will be preserved, and only the interest used to maintain the group.

As this book goes to press, $100 million has already been raised. Currently, this money is intended to set up and support for several years an initial group of 10,000 meditation experts ñ which would itself be the largest Super Radiance group ever assembled. If considerably more is raised quickly, however, this initial $100 million could go to develop housing and other facilities for all 40,000, with the new money available for continuing support.

In any event, to completely end the age-long traditions of violence and warfare of all sorts, the single most vital step is to establish the 40,000 group in perpetuity. There are several ways to raise the money still needed.

1. The entire fund from a single donor, or donation group: Assume the $100 million raised so far goes to set up the infrastructure for the full 40,000 Super Radiance group. To raise the one billion dollar fund which would support the group permanently, there are a significant number of people in the world who could donate that amount by themselves. Many more people could do the same by organizing a small group of friends and colleagues.

Although this would be a magnificent act of philanthropy, it would also be in the donors' self-interest. The wealthy are often the targets of direct terrorist attack, and they would also stand to lose the most from their investments if the world economy were to be severely shaken by consistent, well-thought-out terrorist attack.

Anyone who has attained the financial resources to make such a far-reaching donation is invited to contact the Institute of Science, Technology and Public Policy at 641-472-1200. If you have further questions, people at the fund will be able to set up a meeting to answer them for you. All philanthropists want to feel that their contributions have created greater good in the world — and no good could be greater than the creation of lasting world peace.

(If you don't have such resources yourself, but know such a person personally, you are encouraged to give them a copy of this book, and contact the Institute for help in setting up a meeting.)

2. One million dollars per investor: While larger donations are being sought, every individual and family that can donate one million dollars is being invited to do so. The $100 million raised to date has been done in this way — a minimum of one million dollars per individual or family. Tens of thousands of such people live in the United States alone and only 1,000 are needed to gather one billion dollars. The more quickly such donations come in, the more quickly the full 40,000 experts will gather — giving the world its best chance of ending warfare and violence of all kinds. People who have one million dollars available could hardly find a more fruitful and satisfying way to invest it. If you have such resources, or know someone who has, please act as soon as possible.

3. A grass roots program supported by peace-loving people everywhere: There are many ways this could work, including millions of small donations. But one systematic approach would be for families each to "adopt" a single Vedic peace-creator (or Vedic *pandit*) in India. By donating $125 per month ($1500 per year) these families could each support a single Vedic pandit. If the first families to do so would also spread the word enthusiastically in person and especially through e-mails, the necessary total of families — over and above those who donate in other ways — could be gathered quickly. In this case of widespread support for the Endowment Fund for Permanent World Peace, many more people could enjoy the satisfaction of helping to directly create permanent peace in the world.

3. MAKE YOURSELF A PEACE CREATOR

The most significant personal step you can take is to learn to enjoy the fourth state of consciousness on a regular basis — by learning the Transcendental Meditation technique. This allows you to not only experience inner peace, but to radiate that peace around you. As we have seen, the research shows that if one percent of any given population learns the basic TM technique, crime rate and other negativity in that society declines. People already practicing Transcendental Meditation can then apply to learn the TM-Sidhi program, to increase both their personal benefits and their peace-creating power exponentially.

The Transcendental Meditation technique is simple to learn and easy to practice, but it must be learned in person from a trained teacher — because each student's experience is different, and the teacher must be there to give the correct guidance. To find a teacher or teaching center in your area, you have two choices:

Telephone: In the United States and Canada, you can call 888-LEARNTM (532-7686). You will be automatically connected to a number near you.

Internet: From anywhere in the world, you can access a Website URL with worldwide connectivity: *Maharishi.org/locations/locations.html*. From this Web page, people in the United States and Canada can enter their area code, and be shown a phone number near them. People from other countries can click on a link, "For other locations worldwide," and fill out a brief form. Someone will then contact you.

A FINAL WORD

The world will always need more people expert in meditation. But at this historical moment, the shortcut to global peace is provided by Super Radiance. And this means the highest priority is to fund the largest possible Super Radiance group. World peace *does* now seem just a matter of money — and not much money, at that, given the resources available in the world. To fully invest the Endowment Fund for Permanent World Peace with one billion dollars requires considerably less than, for example, the

United States Department of Defense spends in a single day.

The consequences of not creating this group of 40,000 — in a world of rogue nuclear warheads and designer infections — are too horrible to contemplate.

Rather than fretting and worrying over such horrific possibilities, however, it seems obvious that the time has come to act.

The time has come to choose the only alternative research has presented to us.

The time has come to support Super Radiance — on a scale that can eliminate warfare and terrorism, and directly create an indomitable influence of harmony and peace — both globally and permanently.

ENDNOTES

Most of the quotations from Maharishi Mahesh Yogi are taken from the earlier version of this book, *Creating Heaven on Earth*. Quotations new in this version are footnoted below.

1. From an advertisement published in the Sunday, September 23, 2001 edition of the *New York Times* and *Washington Post*.
2. International press conference, National Press Club, September 28, 2001.
3. Press conference (above).
4. *Enlightenment Magazine*, 2(3), 3.
5. *Enlightenment Magazine*, 12, 30.
6. Maharishi Mahesh Yogi, *Maharishi Vedic University: Introduction*. India: Age of Enlightenment Publications, 1994, p. 146.
7. Maharishi (above), p. 47.
8. Maharishi (above), p. 201.
9. Press conference (above).
10. Press conference (above).
11. Press conference (above).

THE AUTHOR

Robert Oates is the author of a dozen books and has lectured on four continents. After graduating from the University of Southern California *summa cum laude*, number one in his class, Mr. Oates earned an M.A. in American History from the University of California at Los Angeles. While studying for his Master's, he learned the Transcendental Meditation technique and his education turned to the field of consciousness and human enlightenment — including years of study with Maharishi Mahesh Yogi. In the past decade, he has worked for the Institute of Science, Technology and Public Policy, under the direction of Harvard-trained physicist John Hagelin, as a policy fellow focusing on health care, election finance reform, and conflict resolution. Earlier in his career, Mr. Oates played ten years as a semi-pro quarterback and was inducted into the Semi-Professional Football Hall of Fame.

ACKNOWLEDGEMENTS

My first and constant debt of gratitude is to His Holiness Maharishi Mahesh Yogi, without whose brilliance of awareness, systematic and practical intelligence, mastery of the Vedic technologies of consciousness, and astonishing vision, this book could not have been conceived, nor a page of it written. Second, I would like to acknowledge David Orme-Johnson, Michael Dillbeck, Charles Alexander, Kenneth Cavanaugh and the other researchers whose powerful methodological designs and indefatigable perseverence — working on a series of published studies that will live forever, I believe, in the annals of scholarship — made the Maharishi Effect the most thoroughly demonstrated reality in the social sciences. Also, I wish to thank especially John Hagelin, Ph.D., who is Director of the Institute of Science, Technology and Public Policy among his many other responsibilities, not only for supporting this book at every stage, but also for laying open the complexities of quantum field theory and the unified field in a manner accessible to the ordinary mortal. Even more significantly, Dr. Hagelin has also led the worldwide fundraising effort that has already begun to make Maharishi's vision of permanent peace a living reality.

In the writing of this book, I had the great blessing, first, of being born to a great writer — Robert Oates, Sr. — who not only taught me to write these many years ago, but who still on this project saved me from many an extraneous or infelicitous word. I received, as well, careful readings and sage suggestions from my profoundly literate wife, Patricia, and from Barney Sherman, Bob and Carol Markowitz, John Fagan, and (with notable depth) Barbara Dreier. This collection of practical kindnesses was capped by Craig Pearson, Executive Vice-President of Maharishi University of Management, who somehow, from a packed schedule, carved the time for deep reading and a thoughtful, detailed, and even drastic set of suggested revisions, after which I had a book.

For copyediting, formatting, and indexing, I had the benefit of the merry clarity and nonesuch precision of Martha Bright, and for cover and interior design the inevitable grace of the estimable Shepley Hansen.

INDEX